W9-AHG-417

Study Guide

for

Coon and Mitterer's

Introduction to Psychology
Gateways to Mind and Behavior

Eleventh Edition

Thuy Karafa
Ferris State University
Dennis Coon

THOMSON
WADSWORTH

Australia • Brazil • Canada • Mexico • Singapore • Spain • United Kingdom • United States

© 2007 Thomson Wadsworth, a part of The Thomson Corporation. Thomson, the Star logo, and Wadsworth are trademarks used herein under license.

ALL RIGHTS RESERVED. No part of this work covered by the copyright hereon may be reproduced or used in any form or by any means—graphic, electronic, or mechanical, including photocopying, recording, taping, Web distribution, information storage and retrieval systems, or in any other manner—without the written permission of the publisher.

Printed in the United States of America
1 2 3 4 5 6 7 10 09 08 07 06

Printer: Globus Printing

ISBN: 0-495-09734-9

Thomson Higher Education
10 Davis Drive
Belmont, CA 94002-3098
USA

For more information about our products, contact us at:
Thomson Learning Academic Resource Center
1-800-423-0563

For permission to use material from this text or product, submit a request online at
http://www.thomsonrights.com.
Any additional questions about permissions can be submitted by email to **thomsonrights@thomson.com.**

TABLE OF CONTENTS

Introduction to Psychology and Research Methods

Chapter Overview

Psychology is the scientific study of behavior and mental processes. Psychology's goals are to describe, understand, predict, and control behavior. Psychologists answer questions about behavior by applying the scientific method and gathering empirical evidence. Psychologists may research such topics as development, learning, personality, sensation and perception, biopsychology, cognition, gender, social influence, culture, and evolution.

Psychology grew out of philosophy. The first psychological laboratory was established by Wilhelm Wundt, who studied conscious experience. The first school of thought in psychology was structuralism, a kind of "mental chemistry." Structuralism was followed by the rise of functionalism, behaviorism, Gestalt psychology, psychoanalytic psychology, and humanistic psychology. Five main streams of thought in modern psychology are behaviorism, humanism, the psychodynamic approach, biopsychology, and cognitive psychology.

The training of psychologists differs from that of psychiatrists, psychoanalysts, counselors, and social workers. Nearly 30 percent of all psychologists are employed full-time at colleges or universities. Some psychologists conduct basic research while others do applied research. Clinical and counseling psychologists specialize in doing psychotherapy. Other specialties are industrial-organizational, educational, consumer, school, developmental, engineering, medical, environmental, forensic, psychometric, and experimental psychology.

Scientific investigation involves observing, defining a problem, proposing a hypothesis, gathering evidence/testing the hypothesis, publishing results, and forming a theory. Many psychological investigations begin with naturalistic observation, which is informative despite its limitations. In the correlational method, the strength of the relationship between two measures is investigated. Correlations allow predictions, but they do not demonstrate cause-and-effect connections.

Experiments show whether an independent variable has an effect on a dependent variable. This allows cause-and-effect connections to be identified. In an experiment, only participants in the experimental group are exposed to the independent variable. A placebo effect occurs when participants believe they have taken a pill to alter their body's chemistry. This is valuable to doctors and patients since the patients' beliefs can maximize the effects of the medication. However, in formal experiments, to determine the true effect of certain pills, controlling the placebo effect is necessary. Therefore, a single-blind experiment is implemented. To control for experimenter effects, a double-blind experiment is implemented.

The clinical method employs detailed case studies of single individuals such as the four Genain sisters who all became schizophrenic before age 25. In the survey method, people in a representative sample are asked a series of questions. This provides information on the behavior of large groups of people.

A key element of critical thinking is an ability to weigh the evidence bearing on a claim and to evaluate the quality of that evidence through careful comparisons, analyses, critiques, and syntheses. Critical thinking is invaluable when evaluating the accuracy and credibility of pseudo-sciences. Belief in various pseudo-psychologies is based in part on uncritical acceptance, the fallacy of positive instances, and the Barnum effect.

Information in the popular media varies greatly in quality and accuracy. It is wise to approach such information with skepticism regarding the source of information, uncontrolled observation, correlation and causation, inferences, over simplification, single examples, and unrepeatable results.

Learning Objectives

1. Define psychology, explain reasons for studying it, and how psychology can be both a science and a profession.

2. Describe what behavior is and differentiate overt from covert behavior.

3. Explain what empirical evidence is and give an example of it. Explain how this search for empirical evidence set psychology apart from other fields of study and why some topics in psychology are difficult to study.

4. Define the term critical thinking and describe its four basic principles.

5. Write a brief summary of each of the following areas of specialization in psychology.

    a. developmental

    b. learning

    c. personality

    d. sensation and perception

    e. comparative

    f. biopsychology

    g. cognitive

    h. gender

    i. social

    j. cultural

    k. evolutionary

6. Explain why and how animals are used in research and define the term animal model in your discussion. List a way in which psychological research may benefit animals.

7. List and explain the four goals of psychology and its ultimate goal, including why the word *control* has a special meaning for psychologists that is distinct from the everyday meaning of the word.

8. Use the following schools of psychology to answer the five questions below: structuralism, functionalism, behaviorism, Gestalt psychology, psychodynamic school, and humanism.

    a. its founder

    b. reasons it was founded

    c. its goal

    d. its impact on modern psychology

    e. its possible value in psychotherapy

9. Describe the role of women in psychology's early days and contrast it to today.

10. Briefly describe the five major perspectives in modern psychology; the two newest fields of study, cognitive neuroscience and positive psychology; and explain what it means to be eclectic.

11. Explain how understanding human diversity may help us better understand ourselves and the behavior of others. Define the terms cultural relativity and norms.

12. Characterize the differences in training, emphasis and/or expertise among psychologists, psychiatrists, psychoanalysts, counselors, and psychiatric social workers. Describe the roles of clinical and counseling psychologists, the largest areas of specialization among psychologists, and their major sources of employment. Define the term "scientist-practitioner" model and list the three points in the professional code for psychologists established by the APA.

13. Differentiate basic from applied research and explain the problem with using common sense as a source of information. List and define the six steps of the scientific method. Include the concepts of hypothesis, operational definition, and theory formulation. Explain the importance of publication and describe the parts of a research report.

14. Describe the technique of naturalistic observation including its advantages and disadvantages. Include the terms observer effect and observer bias. Explain what the anthropomorphic fallacy is and how it can lead to problems in psychological research. Define the term observation record.

15. Describe what a correlational study is and its advantages and disadvantages. Explain what a correlation coefficient is, what it means, how it is expressed numerically and as a graph, and how it does NOT show causation.

16. List and describe the three variables in the experimental method. Explain the nature and purpose of the control group and the experimental group and why subjects are randomly assigned to the groups.

17. Explain what statistically significant results are, why the replication of results is important, and the value of meta-analysis.

18. Describe the single-blind and double-blind experimental approaches and how they control for the placebo effect and the experimenter effect, respectively. Include the concept of self-fulfilling prophecy.

19. Briefly describe the clinical method of research including when it is used and its advantages and disadvantages.

20. Briefly describe the survey method of investigation including its advantages and disadvantages, a definition of population and sample, and a discussion of courtesy bias, gender bias, and internet surveys.

21. Indicate the foundations and fallacies of each of the following pseudopsychologies and explain why these pseudopsychologies continue to thrive even though they have no scientific basis:

   a. palmistry

   b. phrenology

   c. graphology

   d. astrology

22. List the suggestions that will help you become a more critical reader of psychological information in the popular press.

The following objective is related to the material in the "Psychology in Action" section of your text.

1. List seven suggestions that the author gives to help you become a more critical reader of psychological information in the popular press.

RECITE AND REVIEW

What is psychology? What are its goals?

Psychology—Spotlight on Behavior: Pages 12-17

1. Psychology is both a science and a _____ .

2. Psychology is defined as the scientific study of behavior and _____ processes.

3. Psychologists study overt and covert _____ .

4. Psychologists seek empirical _____ based on scientific observation.

5. Scientific observation is _____ so that it answers questions about the world.

6. _____ beliefs are sound practical beliefs that are based on our everyday experiences without scientific observation.

7. Answering psychological questions requires a valid research _____ .

8. Critical thinking is the ability to _____ , compare, analyze, critique, and synthesize information.

9. Developmental psychologists study the course of human _____ .

10. Learning theorists study how and why _____ occurs.

11. Personality _____ study personality traits and dynamics.

12. Sensation and perception psychologists study the _____ organs and perception.

13. Comparative psychologists study different species, especially _____ .

14. Biopsychologists study the connection between biological processes and _____ .

15. Cognitive psychologists are mainly interested in _____ .

16. Gender psychologists study differences between _____ and _____ .

17. Social psychologists study _____ behavior.

18. Cultural psychologists study the ways that culture affects _____ .

19. Evolutionary psychologists are interested in patterns of behavior that were shaped by _____ .

20. Other species are used as _____ models in psychological research to discover principles that apply to human behavior.

21. Psychology's goals are to describe, _____ , predict, and control behavior.

How did psychology emerge as a field of knowledge?

A Brief History of Psychology—Psychology's Family Album: Pages 17-21

1. Historically, psychology is an outgrowth of philosophy, the study of _____ , reality, and human nature.

2. The first psychological _____ was established in Germany by Wilhelm Wundt.

3. Wundt tried to apply scientific methods to the study of conscious _____ by using introspection or "looking inward."

4. Functionalism was concerned with how the mind helps us _____ to our environments.

5. Behaviorism was launched by John B. _____ .

6. Behaviorists objectively study the relationship between stimuli and _____ .

7. The modern behaviorist B. F. Skinner believed that most behavior is controlled by _____ reinforcers.

8. Cognitive behaviorism combines _____ , reinforcement, and environmental influences to explain behavior.

9. Gestalt psychology emphasizes the study of _____ units, not pieces.

10. According to the Gestalt view, in psychology the whole is often _____ than the sum of its parts.

11. The psychoanalytic approach emphasized the _____ origins of behavior.

12. Psychoanalytic psychology, developed by Austrian physician Sigmund _____ , is an early psychodynamic approach.

13. Humanistic psychology emphasizes free will, subjective experience, human potentials, and personal _____ .

14. Psychologically, humanists believe that self- _____ and self-evaluation are important elements of personal adjustment.

15. Humanists also emphasize a capacity for self-actualization—the full development of personal _____ .

What are the major trends and specialties in psychology?

Psychology Today—Five Views of Behavior: Pages 21-22

1. Much of contemporary psychology is an eclectic _____ of the best features of various viewpoints.

2. Five main streams of thought in modern psychology are behaviorism, _____ , the psychodynamic approach, biopsychology, and cognitive psychology.

3. Cognitive _____ attempts to uncover the relationship between mental events and neural activities in the brain.

4. Positive psychology focuses on topics that relate to _____ human functioning.

Human Diversity—Appreciating Social and Cultural Differences: Pages 22-24

1. To fully understand behavior, psychologists must be aware of human _____ as well as human universals.

2. Our behavior is greatly affected by cultural _____ and by social norms (_____ that define acceptable behavior).

Psychologists—Guaranteed Not to Shrink: Pages 24-28

1. Psychologists who treat emotional problems specialize in _____ or counseling psychology.

2. Psychiatrists typically use both _____ and psychotherapy to treat emotional problems.

3. Freudian psychoanlysis is a specific type of _____ .

4. Both counselors and psychiatric social workers have _____ degrees.

5. Some major _____ in psychology are clinical, counseling, industrial-organizational, educational, consumer, school, developmental, engineering, medical, environmental, forensic, psychometric, and experimental psychology.

6. Scientific research in psychology may be either _____ or applied.

How do psychologists collect information?

Scientific Research—How to Think Like a Psychologist: Pages 28-31

1. Scientific investigation in psychology is based on reliable evidence, accurate description and _____ , precise definition, controlled observation, and repeatable results.

2. Six elements of a scientific method involve observing, defining a _____ , proposing a hypothesis, gathering evidence/testing the hypothesis, publishing _____ , and forming a theory.

3. To be scientifically _____ a hypothesis must be testable.

4. Psychological concepts are given operational _____ so that they can be observed.

5. A _____ is a system of ideas that interrelates facts and concepts.

6. Published research reports usually include the following sections: an _____ , an introduction, a methods section, a _____ section, and a final discussion.

7. The tools of psychological research include naturalistic observation, the correlational method, the experimental method, the _____ method, and the survey method.

Naturalistic Observation—Psychology Steps Out! Pages 31-32

1. Naturalistic observation refers to actively observing behavior in _____ settings.

2. Two problems with naturalistic studies are the effects of the observer on the observed (the observer _____) and _____ bias.

3. The anthropomorphic fallacy is the error of attributing human qualities to _____ .

4. Problems with naturalistic studies can be minimized by keeping careful observational _____ .

Correlational Studies—In Search of the Perfect Relationship: Pages 32-35

1. In the correlational method, the _____ between two traits, responses, or events is measured.

2. Correlation coefficients range from +1.00 to −1.00. A correlation of _____ indicates that there is no relationship between two measures.

3. Correlations of +1.00 and −1.00 reveal that _____ relationships exist between two measures.

4. The closer a correlation coefficient is to plus or _____ 1, the stronger the measured relationship is.

5. A positive correlation shows that _____ in one measure correspond to increases in a second measure.

6. In a negative correlation, _____ in one measure correspond to decreases in a second measure.

7. Correlations allow us to make _____ , but correlation does not demonstrate causation.

8. Graphing a linear relationship between two measures forms a straight line. When curvilinear relationships are graphed, a _____ line results.

How is an experiment performed?

The Psychology Experiment—Where Cause Meets Effect: Pages 35-37

1. _____ -and-effect relationships in psychology are best identified by doing a controlled experiment.

2. In an experiment, conditions that might affect behavior are intentionally _____ . Then, changes in behavior are observed and recorded.

3. In an experiment, a variable is any condition that can _____ , and that might affect the outcome of the experiment (the behavior of subjects).

4. Experimental conditions that are intentionally varied are called _____ variables.

5. _____ variables measure the results of the experiment.

6. Extraneous variables are conditions that a researcher wishes to _____ from affecting the outcome of the experiment.

7. Extraneous variables are controlled by making sure that they are the same for all _____ in an experiment.

8. Subjects exposed to the independent variable are in the experimental _____ . Those not exposed to the independent variable form the control _____ .

9. Extraneous variables that involve personal _____ , such as age or intelligence, can be controlled by randomly assigning subjects to the experimental and control groups.

10. If all extraneous variables are _____ for the experimental group and the control group, any differences in behavior must be caused by differences in the independent variable.

11. The results of an experiment are statistically significant when they would occur very rarely by _____ alone.

12. Meta-analysis is a statistical technique to _____ the results of many studies.

Placebo Effects—Sugar Pills and Saltwater: Pages 37-39

1. Experiments involving drugs must control for the placebo _____ that is always present when drugs are involved in a study.

2. In a single- _____ study, subjects don't know if they are getting a drug or a placebo. In a double- _____ study, neither experimenters nor subjects know who is receiving a real drug.

3. Researchers must minimize the experimenter effect (the tendency for people to do what is _____ of them).

4. In many situations, the experimenter effect leads to self-fulfilling _____ .

What other research methods do psychologists use?

The Clinical Method—Data by the Case: Pages 39-40

1. Clinical psychologists frequently gain information from _____ studies.

2. Case studies of the four Genain sisters who developed schizophrenia by the age of 25 are valuable since they allow scholars to investigate the relationship between mental disorder and _____ .

3. Case studies may be thought of as _____ clinical tests.

Survey Method—Here, Have a Sample: Pages 40-42

1. In the survey method, information about large populations is gained by asking people in a representative _____ a series of carefully worded questions.

2. _____ in research can occur when the race, ethnicity, age, sexual orientation, and gender of researchers and participants are not representative.

3. _____ bias refers to the tendency for women to be under-represented as researchers and as participants in research.

4. The value of surveys is lowered when the sample is biased and when replies to questions are _____ because of _____ (a tendency to give socially desirable answers).

How does psychology differ from false explanations of behavior?

Critical Thinking Revisited—Evaluating Claims and Evidence: Pages 42-43

1. Critical thinking is the ability to _____ , compare, analyze, critique, and synthesize information.

2. Critical thinking involves a willingness to evaluate _____ and _____ .

3. Scientific observations usually provide the highest quality _____ about various claims.

Pseudo-psychologies—Palms, Planets, and Personality: Pages 43-46

1. Palmistry, phrenology, graphology, and astrology are _____ systems or pseudo-psychologies.

2. Belief in pseudo-psychologies is encouraged by uncritical acceptance, the fallacy of positive instances, and the _____ effect, named after a famous showman who had "something for everyone."

How dependable is psychological information in the popular media?

Psychology in Action: Psychology in the News—Separating Fact from Fiction. Pages 46-48

1. _____ and critical thinking are called for when evaluating claims in the popular media.

2. You should be on guard for _____ or biased sources of information in the media.

3. Many claims in the media are based on unscientific observations that lack control _____ .

4. In the popular media, a failure to distinguish between correlation and _____ is common.

5. Inferences and opinions may be reported as if they were _____ observations.

6. Single cases, unusual _____ , and testimonials are frequently reported as if they were valid generalizations.

CONNECTIONS

What is psychology? What are its goals? Pages 12-17

1. _____ biopsychology	a. hidden from view
2. _____ psychology	b. brain waves
3. _____ personality theorist	c. systematic observation
4. _____ covert behavior	d. animal behavior
5. _____ commonsense beliefs	e. detailed record
6. _____ scientific observation	f. human and animal behavior
7. _____ understanding	g. "why" questions
8. _____ EEG	h. brain and behavior
9. _____ empirical evidence	i. direct observation
10. _____ comparative psychology	j. traits, dynamics, individual differences
11. _____ description	k. influencing behavior
12. _____ control	l. proof based on everyday experiences

How did psychology emerge as a field of knowledge? Pages 17-21

1. _____ Wundt	a. father of psychology
2. _____ Titchener	b. natural selection
3. _____ James	c. behaviorism
4. _____ Darwin	d. functionalism
5. _____ Maslow	e. conditioned responses
6. _____ Pavlov	f. Gestalt
7. _____ Skinner	g. color vision
8. _____ Wertheimer	h. introspection
9. _____ Ladd-Franklin	i. psychoanalysis
10. _____ Freud	j. self-actualization

What are the major trends and specialties in psychology? Pages 21-28

1.	_____ social psychologist	a.	self-image
2.	_____ psychodynamic view	b.	information processing
3.	_____ behavioristic view	c.	Ph.D., Psy.D., Ed.D.
4.	_____ humanistic view	d.	M.D.
5.	_____ biopsychology	e.	internal forces
6.	_____ cognitive view	f.	physiological processes
7.	_____ counseling psychologist	g.	environmental forces
8.	_____ psychologist	h.	investigates attitudes and persuasion
9.	_____ positive psychology	i.	marital consultant
10.	_____ psychiatrist	j.	optimal behavior

How do psychologists collect information? Pages 28-35

1.	_____ observer effect	a.	tentative explanation
2.	_____ scientific method	b.	formal log
3.	_____ common sense	c.	specific procedures
4.	_____ hypothesis	d.	related traits, behaviors
5.	_____ operational definition	e.	coefficient error
6.	_____ Clever Hans	f.	head signals
7.	_____ Jane Goodall	g.	controlled observation
8.	_____ observational record	h.	unscientific information
9.	_____ correlational study	i.	behavioral change due to awareness
10.	_____ correlation of +3.5	j.	naturalistic observation

How is an experiment performed? Pages 35-40

1.	_____ single-blind experiment	a.	effect on behavior
2.	_____ identify causes of behavior	b.	experimental method
3.	_____ independent variable	c.	varied by experimenter
4.	_____ dependent variable	d.	excluded by experimenter
5.	_____ extraneous variables	e.	reference for comparison
6.	_____ control group	f.	done by using chance
7.	_____ random assignment to groups	g.	sugar pills
8.	_____ placebos	h.	control placebo effects

What other research methods do psychologists use? Pages 40-42

1. _____ survey methods		a.	Phineas Gage
2. _____ lobotomy		b.	participation is voluntary
3. _____ case studies		c.	clinical method
4. _____ gender bias		d.	representative of population
5. _____ valid sample		e.	inaccurate answers
6. _____ courtesy bias		f.	public polling techniques
7. _____ ethical research		g.	under-representation of women

How does psychology differ from false explanations of behavior? How dependable is psychological information in the popular media? Pages 42-48

1. _____ evaluate media claims		a.	evaluating claims and evidence
2. _____ pseudo-psychology		b.	astrology
3. _____ phrenology		c.	hand writing analysis
4. _____ critical thinking		d.	analysis of the shape of skulls
5. _____ anecdotal evidence		e.	evidence explaining a claim
6. _____ graphology		f.	being skeptical

CHECK YOUR MEMORY

What is psychology? What are its goals? Pages 12-17

1. Psychology can best be described as a profession, not a science.

   TRUE or FALSE

2. Psychology is defined as the scientific study of human behavior.

   TRUE or FALSE

3. Although it is a covert activity, dreaming is a behavior.

   TRUE or FALSE

4. Statements like "The more motivated you are, the better you will do at solving a complex problem" is a commonsense belief that has been shown to be true.

   TRUE or FALSE

5. The term *empirical evidence* refers to the opinion of an acknowledged authority.

   TRUE or FALSE

6. Critical thinking utilizes commonsense beliefs as the foundation for evaluating and judging the quality of evidence obtained.

   TRUE or FALSE

7. The term *data* refers to a systematic procedure for answering scientific questions.

   TRUE or FALSE

8. Cognitive psychologists are interested in researching memory, reasoning, and problem solving.

   TRUE or FALSE

9. Animal models are used to discover principles that can be applied to animals only.

   TRUE or FALSE

10. Naming and classifying are the heart of psychology's second goal, understanding behavior.

    TRUE or FALSE

11. Control refers to a psychologist's ability to alter conditions that affect a participant's behavior.

    TRUE or FALSE

How did psychology emerge as a field of knowledge? Pages 17-21

1. In 1879, Wundt established a lab to study the philosophy of behavior.

   TRUE or FALSE

2. Wundt used introspection to study conscious experiences.

   TRUE or FALSE

3. Edward Titchener is best known for promoting functionalism in America.

   TRUE or FALSE

4. The functionalists were influenced by the ideas of Charles Darwin.

   TRUE or FALSE

5. Behaviorists define psychology as the study of conscious experience.

   TRUE or FALSE

6. Watson used Pavlov's concept of conditioned responses to explain most behavior.

   TRUE or FALSE

7. Believing that human's behaviors are controlled by rewards, B. F. Skinner invented the "Skinner box" to study primarily animals' responses.

   TRUE or FALSE

8. Cognitive behaviorism combines thinking and Gestalt principles to explain human behavior.

   TRUE or FALSE

9. Margaret Washburn was the first woman in America to be awarded a Ph.D. in psychology.

   TRUE or FALSE

10. Mary Calkins was the first woman president of the American Psychological Association in 1905 and did early research on memory.

    TRUE or FALSE

11. Women account for approximately 75 percent of college students who major in psychology today.

    TRUE or FALSE

12. "The whole is greater than the sum of its parts" is a slogan of structuralism.

    TRUE or FALSE

13. Freud's psychodynamic theory of personality focused on the unconscious thoughts, impulses, and desires with the exception of sex and aggression since they describe negative views of human behavior.

    TRUE or FALSE

14. According to Freud, repressed thoughts are held out of awareness, in the unconscious.

    TRUE or FALSE

15. Carl Jung and Erik Erikson were two neo-Freudians who firmly believed in Freud's psychodynamic theory.

    TRUE or FALSE

16. Humanists generally reject the determinism of the behavioristic and psychodynamic approaches.

    TRUE or FALSE

What are the major trends and specialties in psychology? Pages 21-28

1. The five major perspectives in psychology today are behaviorism, humanism, functionalism, biopsychology, and cognitive psychology.

   TRUE or FALSE

2. Cognitive neuroscience studies the relationship between mental events and the environment.

   TRUE or FALSE

3. Humanism offers a positive, philosophical view of human nature.

   TRUE or FALSE

4. Positive psychology focuses on the negative aspects of the self in order to achieve one's happiness and well-being.

   TRUE or FALSE

5. The cognitive view explains behavior in terms of information processing.

   TRUE or FALSE

6. To understand behavior, psychologists must be aware of the cultural relativity of standards for evaluating behavior.

   TRUE or FALSE

7. To reduce inaccurate stereotypical images of psychologists, the Golden Psi Media Award was created to be given to media programs that accurately depict the professions of psychologists.

   TRUE or FALSE

8. Most psychologists work in private practice.

   TRUE or FALSE

9. The differences between clinical and counseling psychology are beginning to fade.

   TRUE or FALSE

10. To enter the profession of psychology today you would need to earn a doctorate degree.

    TRUE or FALSE

11. The Psy.D. degree emphasizes scientific research skills.

    TRUE or FALSE

12. More than half of all psychologists specialize in clinical or counseling psychology.

    TRUE or FALSE

13. Clinical psychologists must be licensed to practice legally.

    TRUE or FALSE

14. Over 40 percent of all psychologists are employed by the military.

    TRUE or FALSE

15. Studying ways to improve the memories of eyewitnesses to crimes would be an example of applied research.

    TRUE or FALSE

How do psychologists collect information? Pages 28-35

1. The scientific method involves testing a proposition by systematic observation.
   TRUE or FALSE

2. An operational definition states the exact hypothesis used to represent a concept.
   TRUE or FALSE

3. Clever Hans couldn't do math problems when his owner left the room.
   TRUE or FALSE

4. Operational definitions link concepts with concrete observations.
   TRUE or FALSE

5. Most research reports begin with an abstract.
   TRUE or FALSE

6. Jane Goodall's study of chimpanzees made use of the clinical method.
   TRUE or FALSE

7. Concealing the observer helps reduce the observer effect.
   TRUE or FALSE

8. Anthropomorphic error refers to attributing animals' behaviors, thoughts, emotions, and motives to humans.
   TRUE or FALSE

9. A correlation coefficient of +.100 indicates a perfect positive relationship.
   TRUE or FALSE

10. Strong relationships produce positive correlation coefficients; weak relationships produce negative correlations.
    TRUE or FALSE

11. Perfect correlations demonstrate that a causal relationship exists.
    TRUE or FALSE

12. The best way to identify cause-and-effect relationships is to perform a case study.
    TRUE or FALSE

How is an experiment performed? Pages 35-40

1. Extraneous variables are those that are varied by the experimenter.
   TRUE or FALSE

2. Independent variables are suspected causes for differences in behavior.
    TRUE or FALSE

3. In an experiment to test whether hunger affects memory, hunger is the dependent variable.
    TRUE or FALSE

4. Independent variables are randomly assigned to the experimental and control groups.
    TRUE or FALSE

5. A person who takes a drug may be influenced by his or her expectations about the drug's effects.
    TRUE or FALSE

6. Neither the single-blind nor the double-blind experiment can control the placebo effect since it is always present when drugs are involved in a study.
    TRUE or FALSE

7. In a single-blind experiment, the experimenter remains blind as to whether she or he is administering a drug.
    TRUE or FALSE

8. Subjects in psychology experiments can be very sensitive to hints about what is expected of them.
    TRUE or FALSE

What other research methods do psychologists use? Pages 40-42

1. Phineas Gage is remembered as the first psychologist to do a case study.
    TRUE or FALSE

2. Case studies may be inconclusive because they lack formal control groups.
    TRUE or FALSE

3. The case study of the four Genain sisters who developed schizophrenia by the age of 25 is an example of environmental (nature) influence.
    TRUE or FALSE

4. Gender bias in research occurs when researchers assume that there are no differences between men and women; therefore results based on men cannot be applied to women.
    TRUE or FALSE

5. Representative samples are often obtained by randomly selecting people to study.
    TRUE or FALSE

6. Representative sampling is an advantage of web-based research.

   TRUE or FALSE

7. A tendency to give socially desirable answers to questions can lower the accuracy of surveys.

   TRUE or FALSE

How does psychology differ from false explanations of behavior? Pages 42-46

1. Critical thinking is the ability to make good use of intuition and mental imagery.

   TRUE or FALSE

2. Critical thinkers actively evaluate claims, ideas, and propositions.

   TRUE or FALSE

3. A key element of critical thinking is evaluating the quality of evidence related to a claim.

   TRUE or FALSE

4. Critical thinkers recognize that the opinions of experts and authorities should be respected without question.

   TRUE or FALSE

5. Pseudo-scientists test their concepts by gathering data.

   TRUE or FALSE

6. Phrenologists believe that lines on the hands reveal personality traits.

   TRUE or FALSE

7. Graphology is only valid if a large enough sample of handwriting is analyzed.

   TRUE or FALSE

8. Astrological charts consisting of positive traits tend to be perceived as "accurate" or true, even if they are not.

   TRUE or FALSE

9. The Barnum effect refers to our tendency to remember things that confirm our expectations.

   TRUE or FALSE

How dependable is psychological information in the popular media? Pages 46-48

1. The existence of dermo-optical perception (sixth sense) was confirmed by recent experiments.
   TRUE or FALSE

2. Psychological courses and services offered for profit may be misrepresented, just as some other products are.
   TRUE or FALSE

3. At least some psychic ability is necessary to perform as a stage mentalist.
   TRUE or FALSE

4. Successful firewalking requires neurolinguistic programming.
   TRUE or FALSE

5. Violent crime rises and falls with lunar cycles.
   TRUE or FALSE

6. If you see a person crying, you must infer that he or she is sad.
   TRUE or FALSE

7. Individual cases and specific examples tell us nothing about what is true in general.
   TRUE or FALSE

8. Information found on the Internet such as "Learn to speak Klingon" is usually accurate, therefore verification is not necessary.
   TRUE or FALSE

FINAL SURVEY AND REVIEW

What is psychology? What are its goals?

Psychology—Spotlight on Behavior: Pages 12-17

1. Psychology is both a _____ and a _____ .

2. Psychology is defined as the scientific study of _____ and _____ .

3. Psychologists study both overt and _____ behavior.

4. _____ beliefs are sound practical beliefs that are based on our everyday experiences without _____ observation.

5. Psychologists seek _____ evidence based on scientific observation. They settle disputes by collecting _____ .

6. _____ observation is structured and systematic.

7. Answering psychological questions requires a valid _____ .

8. Critical thinking is the ability to evaluate, compare, analyze, _____ , and _____ information.

9. _____ psychologists study the course of human development.

10. Learning _____ study how and why learning occurs.

11. _____ theorists study personality traits and dynamics.

12. _____ and perception psychologists study the sense organs and perception.

13. _____ psychologists study different species, especially animals.

14. _____ study biological processes and behavior.

15. _____ psychologists are mainly interested in thinking and mental processes.

16. _____ psychologists study differences between males and females.

17. Social psychologists study _____ .

18. _____ psychologists study the ways that culture affects behavior.

19. _____ psychologists are interested in patterns of behavior that were shaped by natural selection.

20. Other species are used as _____ in psychological research to discover principles that apply to human behavior.

21. Psychology's goals are to describe, understand, _____ , and _____ behavior.

How did psychology emerge as a field of knowledge?

A Brief History of Psychology—Psychology's Family Album: Pages 17-21

1. Historically, psychology is an outgrowth of _____ .

2. The first psychological laboratory was established in Germany by _____ .

3. Wundt's goal was to apply scientific methods to the study of _____ by using _____ or "looking inward."

4. The first school of thought in psychology was _____ , a kind of "mental chemistry."

5. _____ was concerned with how the mind helps us adapt to our environments. William _____ was one of its proponents.

6. _____ was launched by John B. Watson, who wanted to study the relationship between _____ and responses.

7. The modern behaviorist B. F. _____ believed that most behavior is controlled by positive _____ .

8. _____ behaviorism combines thinking and environmental influences to explain behavior.

9. _____ psychology emphasizes the study of whole experiences, not elements or pieces.

10. According to Max _____ and other _____ psychologists, the whole is often greater than the _____ of its parts.

11. The _____ approach emphasizes the unconscious origins of behavior.

12. The Austrian physician, Sigmund _____ , developed a psychodynamic system called _____ .

13. _____ psychology emphasizes free will, subjective experience, human _____ , and personal growth.

14. Psychologically, humanists believe that _____ , self-evaluation, and one's _____ of reference are important elements of personal adjustment.

15. Humanists also emphasize a capacity for _____ —the full development of personal potential.

What are the major trends and specialties in psychology?

Psychology Today—Five Views of Behavior: Pages 21-22

1. Five main streams of thought in modern psychology are _____ , _____ , the psychodynamic approach, _____ , and cognitive psychology.

2. Much of contemporary psychology is an _____ blend of the best features of various viewpoints.

3. Cognitive neuroscience attempts to uncover the relationship between _____ events and _____ activities in the brain.

4. _____ psychology focuses on topics that relate to optimal human functioning.

Human Diversity—Appreciating Social and Cultural Differences: Pages 22-24

1. To fully understand behavior, psychologists must be aware of human _____ , as reflected in personal and _____ differences.

2. Our behavior is greatly affected by _____ values and by social _____ (rules that define acceptable behavior).

Psychologists—Guaranteed Not to Shrink: Pages 24-28

1. Psychologists who treat emotional problems specialize in _____ or _____ psychology.

2. _____ are medical doctors who typically use both drugs and _____ to treat emotional problems.

3. Freudian _____ is a specific type of psychotherapy.

4. Both counselors and _____ workers have Master's degrees.

5. _____ psychologists specialize in the growth of children; _____ psychologists help design machinery; _____ psychologists study classroom dynamics.

6. Scientific research in psychology may be either basic or _____ .

How do psychologists collect information?

Scientific Research—How to Think Like a Psychologist: Pages 28-31

1. Scientific investigation in psychology is based on reliable _____ , accurate description and _____ , precise definition, controlled observation, and repeatable results.

2. Six elements of a scientific method involve observing, defining a problem, proposing a _____ , gathering evidence/testing the hypothesis, publishing results, and forming a _____ .

3. To be _____ valid a hypothesis must be _____ .

4. Psychological concepts are given _____ definitions so that they can be observed. Such definitions state the exact _____ used to represent a concept.

5. A _____ is a system of ideas that interrelates facts and concepts. In general, good _____ summarize existing _____ , explain them, and guide further research.

6. The results of scientific studies are _____ in professional _____ so they will be publicly available.

7. The tools of psychological research include naturalistic observation, the correlational method, the _____ method, the clinical method, and the _____ method.

Naturalistic Observation—Psychology Steps Out! Pages 31-32

1. Naturalistic observation refers to actively observing behavior in _____ , which are the typical _____ in which people and animals live.

2. Two problems with naturalistic observation are the effects of the observer on the _____ and observer _____ .

3. The _____ fallacy is the error of attributing human qualities to animals.

4. Problems with naturalistic observation can be minimized by keeping careful _____ .

Correlational Studies—In Search of the Perfect Relationship: Pages 32-35

1. In the _____ method, the strength of the relationship between two traits, responses, or events is measured.

2. Correlation _____ range from +1.00 to −1.00.

3. A correlation of _____ indicates that there is no relationship between two measures. Correlations of +1.00 and −1.00 reveal that _____ relationships exist between two measures.

4. The _____ a correlation coefficient is to plus or minus 1.00, the stronger the measured relationship is.

5. A _____ correlation or relationship shows that increases in one measure correspond to increases in a second measure.

6. In a negative correlation, _____ in one measure correspond to _____ in a second measure.

7. Correlations allow prediction, but correlation does not demonstrate _____ .

8. Graphing a _____ relationship between two measures forms a straight line. When _____ relationships are graphed, a curved line results.

How is an experiment performed?

The Psychology Experiment—Where Cause Meets Effect: Pages 35-37

1. Cause-and-effect relationships in psychology are best identified by doing a _____ .

2. In an experiment, conditions that might affect behavior are intentionally varied. Then, changes in behavior are _____ and _____ .

3. In an experiment a _____ is any condition that can change, and that might affect the outcome of the experiment.

4. Experimental conditions that are intentionally varied are called _____ variables; they are potential _____ of changes in behavior.

5. _____ variables measure the results of the experiment; they reveal any _____ on behavior.

6. _____ variables are conditions that a researcher wishes to prevent from affecting the _____ of the experiment.

7. Extraneous variables are _____ by making sure that they are the same for all subjects in an experiment.

8. Subjects exposed to the independent variable are in the _____ group. Those not exposed to the independent variable form the _____ group.

9. Extraneous variables that involve _____ characteristics, such as age or intelligence, can be controlled by _____ assigning subjects to the experimental and control groups.

10. If all extraneous variables are identical for the experimental group and the control group, any differences in behavior must be caused by differences in the _____ variable.

11. The results of an experiment are _____ significant when they would occur very rarely by chance alone.

12. _____ is a statistical technique for combining the results of many studies.

Placebo Effects—Sugar Pills and Saltwater: Pages 37-39

1. Experiments involving drugs must control for the _____ effect that is always present when _____ are involved in a study.

2. In a _____ study, subjects don't know if they are getting a drug or a placebo. In a _____ study, neither experimenters nor subjects know who is receiving a real drug.

3. Researchers must also minimize the _____ (the tendency for people to do what is expected of them).

4. In many situations, the experimenter effect leads to _____ prophecies.

What other research methods do psychologists use?

The Clinical Method—Data by the Case: Pages 39-40

1. Clinical psychologists frequently gain information from _____ , which focus on all aspects of a single _____ .

2. _____ of the four Genain sisters who developed schizophrenia by the age of 25 are valuable since they allow scholars to investigate the relationship between mental disorder and _____ .

3. Case studies may be thought of as natural _____ of the effects of brain tumors, accidental poisonings, and other unusual conditions.

Survey Method—Here, Have a Sample: Pages 40-42

1. In the survey method, information about large _____ is gained by asking people in a _____ sample a series of carefully worded questions.

2. _____ in research can occur when the race, ethnicity, age, sexual orientation, and gender of researchers and participants are not _____ .

3. _____ bias refers to the tendency for women to be _____ as researchers and as participants in research.

4. The value of surveys is lowered when the sample is _____ and when replies to _____ are inaccurate or untruthful.

How does psychology differ from false explanations of behavior?

Critical Thinking Revisited—Evaluating Claims and Evidence: Pages 42-43

1. In psychology, critical thinking skills help _____ claims about human behavior.

2. Critical thinking involves evaluating the quality of the _____ used to support various claims.

3. _____ observations usually provide the highest quality evidence about various claims.

Pseudo-psychologies—Palms, Planets, and Personality: Pages 43-46

1. Palmistry, _____ , graphology, and astrology are _____ -psychologies.

2. Belief in false psychologies is encouraged by _____ acceptance, the fallacy of _____ instances, and the _____ effect.

How dependable is psychological information in the popular media?

Psychology in Action: Psychology in the News—Separating Fact from Fiction. Pages 46-48

1. _____ and _____ thinking are called for when evaluating claims in the popular media.

2. You should be on guard for unreliable or _____ sources of information in the media.

3. Many claims in the media are based on unscientific observations that lack _____ groups.

4. _____ does not demonstrate causation. In the popular media, a failure to distinguish between _____ and causation is common.

5. Inferences and opinions may be reported as if they were objective _____ .

6. Single _____ , unusual examples, and testimonials are frequently reported as if they were valid _____ .

MASTERY TEST

1. Data in psychology are typically gathered to answer questions about
   a. clinical problems
   b. human groups
   c. human cognition
   d. overt or covert behavior

2. Who among the following would most likely study the behavior of gorillas?
   a. developmental psychologist
   b. comparative psychologist
   c. environmental psychologist
   d. forensic psychologist

3. An engineering psychologist helps redesign an airplane to make it safer to fly. The psychologist's work reflects which of psychology's goals?
   a. understanding
   b. control
   c. prediction
   d. description

4. Who among the following placed the greatest emphasis on introspection?
   a. Watson
   b. Wertheimer
   c. Washburn
   d. Wundt

5. Which pair of persons had the most similar ideas?
   a. Titchener—Skinner
   b. James—Darwin
   c. Watson—Rogers
   d. Wertheimer—Maslow

6. The behaviorist definition of psychology clearly places great emphasis on
   a. overt behavior
   b. conscious experience
   c. psychodynamic responses
   d. introspective analysis

7. As a profession, psychology is fully open to men and women, a fact that began with the success of
   a. O'Sullivan-Calkins
   b. Tyler-James
   c. Ladd-Franklin
   d. Neal-Collins

8. The idea that threatening thoughts are sometimes repressed would be of most interest to a
   a. structuralist
   b. psychoanalyst
   c. humanist
   d. Gestaltist

9. "A neutral, reductionistic, mechanistic view of human nature." This best describes which viewpoint?
   a. psychodynamic
   b. cognitive
   c. psychoanalytic
   d. biopsychological

10. Which of the following professional titles usually requires a doctorate degree?
    a. psychologist
    b. psychiatric social worker
    c. counselor
    d. all of the preceding

11. Who among the following is most likely to treat the physical causes of psychological problems?
    a. scientist-practitioner
    b. psychoanalyst
    c. forensic psychologist
    d. psychiatrist

12. More than half of all psychologists specialize in what branches of psychology?
    a. counseling and comparative
    b. applied and counseling
    c. psychodynamic and clinical
    d. counseling and clinical

13. When critically evaluating claims about behavior it is important to also evaluate
    a. the source of anecdotal evidence
    b. the credentials of an authority
    c. the quality of the evidence
    d. the strength of one's intuition

14. Which of the following pairs is most different?
    a. pseudo-psychology—critical thinking
    b. graphology—pseudo-psychology
    c. palmistry—phrenology
    d. psychology—empirical evidence

15. The German anatomy teacher Franz Gall popularized
    a. palmistry
    b. phrenology
    c. graphology
    d. astrology

16. A tendency to believe flattering descriptions of oneself is called
    a. the Barnum effect
    b. the astrologer's dilemma
    c. the fallacy of positive instances
    d. uncritical acceptance

17. Descriptions of personality that contain both sides of several personal dimensions tend to create
    a. an illusion of accuracy
    b. disbelief and rejection
    c. the astrologer's dilemma
    d. a system similar to phrenology

18. If an entire population is surveyed, it becomes unnecessary to obtain a
    a. control group
    b. random comparison
    c. random sample
    d. control variable

19. Control groups are most often used in
    a. naturalistic observation
    b. the clinical method
    c. parascience
    d. experiments

20. Concealing the observer can be used to minimize the
    a. observer bias effect
    b. double-blind effect
    c. observer effect
    d. effects of extraneous correlations

21. A psychologist studying lowland gorillas should be careful to avoid the
    a. anthropomorphic error
    b. Gestalt fallacy
    c. psychodynamic fallacy
    d. fallacy of positive instances

22. Testing the hypothesis that frustration encourages aggression would require
    a. a field study
    b. operational definitions
    c. adult subjects
    d. perfect correlations

23. In experiments involving drugs, experimenters remain unaware of who received placebos in a
    _____ arrangement.
    a. zero-blind
    b. single-blind
    c. double-blind
    d. control-blind

24. The idea that Clever Hans's owner might be signaling him was an informal
    a. research hypothesis
    b. self-fulfilling prophecy
    c. operational definition
    d. dependent variable

25. In psychology, the _____ variable is a suspected cause of differences in
    _____.
    a. independent, the control group
    b. dependent, the experimenter effect
    c. independent, behavior
    d. dependent, correlations

26. A person who is observed crying may not be sad. This suggests that it is important to distinguish between
    a. individual cases and generalizations
    b. correlation and causation
    c. control groups and experimental groups
    d. observation and inference

27. In an experiment on the effects of hunger on the reading scores of elementary school children, reading scores are the
    a. control variable
    b. independent variable
    c. dependent variable
    d. reference variable

28. Which of the following correlation coefficients indicates a perfect relationship?
    a. 1.00
    b. 100.0
    c. −1
    d. both A and C

29. Jane Goodall's studies of chimpanzees in Tanzania are good examples of
    a. field experiments
    b. experimental control
    c. correlational studies
    d. naturalistic observation

30. To equalize the intelligence of members of the experimental group and the control group in an experiment, you could use
    a. extraneous control
    b. random assignment
    c. independent control
    d. subject replication

31. Which method would most likely be used to study the effects of tumors in the frontal lobes of the brain?
    a. sampling method
    b. correlational method
    c. clinical method
    d. experimental method

32. Cause is to effect as _____ variable is to _____ variable.
    a. extraneous, dependent
    b. dependent, independent
    c. independent, extraneous
    d. independent, dependent

33. The specific procedures used to gather data are described in which section of a research report?
    a. introduction
    b. abstract
    c. method
    d. discussion

34. Which of the following correlations demonstrates a cause-effect relationship?
    a. .980
    b. 1.00
    c. .50
    d. none of the preceding

35. A graph of a perfect negative relationship would form a
    a. straight line
    b. circle
    c. horizontal line
    d. U-shaped line

36. A researcher statistically combines the results of all of the published results concerning the effects of sugar on hyperactive behavior in children. In order to draw a conclusion about the effects of sugar on hyperactivity, the researcher has used
    a. the double-blind technique
    b. experimental replication
    c. natural clinical trials
    d. meta-analysis

37. Appreciating an orchestra playing Mozart's fifth symphony more than a musician playing a solo on a clarinet reflects _____ psychology.
    a. Gestalt
    b. cognitive
    c. behavioral
    d. biopsychology

38. An in-depth study on the life history of the four Genain sisters is an example of the
    a. survey method
    b. correlational method
    c. scientific method
    d. clinical method

39. The fact that all four identical Genain sisters developed schizophrenia and were in and out of mental hospitals by the age of 25 suggests that their disorder was influenced by
    a. only environmental conditions
    b. nature
    c. heredity
    d. both A and B

40. Carlie believes that blind people have unusually sensitive organs of touch. She based her beliefs on personal experiences and everyday observation. Carlie's sound practical belief is an example of _____.
    a. commonsense
    b. scientific observation
    c. uncritical acceptance
    d. representative sample

41. To combat stereotypical images of psychologists, the Golden Psi Media Award has been given to two episodes of the television program *Law & Order: Special Victims Unit* for
    a. the dramatic display of psychologists who were more disturbed than their patients.
    b. the accurate depiction of psychologists' ethics and scientific training.
    c. alerting the public of potential mind-controlling therapists who victimize or seduce their patients
    d. portraying psychologists as independent wealthy therapists.

42. To control for placebo effects, a _____ study is used.
    a. correlational
    b. single-blind
    c. clinical case
    d. Web based

43. Which term refers to the tendency for women to be under-represented as psychological researchers and as participants in research?
    a. experimenter bias
    b. observer bias
    c. gender bias
    d. male bias

LANGUAGE DEVELOPMENT - Introduction to Psychology and Research Methods

Word roots

Cognitare is the Latin word that means "to think" or "to know." Several words in the field of psychology are derived from this Latin root, and these words all refer in some way to the processes of thinking, reasoning, or knowing. Examples you will find in later chapters include cognitive, cognition, and precognition.

What is psychology? What are its goals?

Preview: Why Study Psychology (p. 12)

> (12) *riddle*: puzzling question
> (12) *brimming*: overflowing

(12) *panorama*: wide-ranging view

Psychology—Spotlight on Behavior (p. 12-17)

(12) *"You can't teach an old dog new tricks"*: it is difficult for people (as well as dogs) to learn new ways of doing things

(13) *blazing hot*: very hot (*blazing* suggests fire)

(13) *frazzled*: tired out; close to losing control and falling apart

(13) *stalled*: stopped, engine won't start

(13) *leaning on the horn*: blowing the horn in an automobile

(13) *lethargic*: drowsy; lacking energy

(14) *Mozart*: Wolfgang Amadeus Mozart (1756-1791), a famous Austrian composer and pianist

(14) *transcend*: to rise above or go beyond the limits of

(14) *guru*: personal religious teacher and spiritual guide

(14) *open-minded*: able to accept new ideas

(14) *gullible*: believe everything you hear

(14) *conception*: the moment when egg and sperm meet and a new being is created

(14) *discern*: understand

(15) *porpoises*: a black, blunt-nosed whale of the North Atlantic and Pacific Ocean

(15) *who you regard as "family"*: close non-related people who you consider as your relatives.

(15) *humankind*: all human beings considered as a whole

(16) *hyperactive*: excessively active; always moving about and cannot sit still

(16) *bystander apathy*: lack of interest or concern among witnesses to an accident or crime

(16) *diffusion of responsibility*: responsibility for action is spread out and lessened; it is not clear who should act

(16*) to pitch in* (…so no one feels required *to pitch in.*): to get involved

(16) *perplexing*: very hard to understand

(16) *forecast*: to predict

(16) *stranded*: left without means to depart or leave

(16) *boil down*: to reduce or narrow

How did psychology emerge as a field of knowledge?

A Brief History of Psychology—Psychology's Family Album (p. 17-21)

(17) *probe*: examine in detail

(17) *heft*: to get the feel of, to lift something up

(18) *Charles Darwin*: the scientist who proposed the theory of evolution

(18) *deduced*: inferred from reason

(18) *glandular activity*: activity results from glands that make up the endocrine system

(18) *radical*: changes of a sweeping or extreme nature

(19) *"designed culture"*: a culture that is created using positive reinforcements to produce wanted behaviors from individuals.

(20) *foremothers*: women who preceded our present time

(20) *Freud believed that mental life is like an iceberg*: the unknown of the unconscious mind is hidden below consciousness like the large part of a submerged iceberg is below the surface of the water

(20) *slips of the tongue*: The tongue speaks before the mind realizes all of the consequences

(20) *Freudian slips*: While the mind is thinking about the obvious, the tongue speaks about hidden, unrevealed thoughts

(21) *undercurrent*: an underlying or hidden attitude; a hint

What are the major trends and specialties in psychology?

Psychology Today—Five Views of Behavior (p. 21-22)

(21) *clashes:* strong disagreements

(23) *Mechanistic* (somewhat *mechanistic* view of human nature): can be explained by mechanical laws; no free will

(23) *reductionistic* (neutral, *reductionistic*, mechanistic view of human nature): reducing to the simplest terms

(24) *trivet*: a short-legged metal or ceramic plate for holding hot dishes at the table

Psychologists—Guaranteed Not to Shrink (p. 24-28)

(24) *About $30 an hour. (And going up.)*: You need to pay $30 more to visit a psychiatrist than if you visit a psychologist

(24) *shrinks*: a slang term for psychiatrists or head doctors

(25) *postgraduate*: training or education beyond the bachelor's degree

(25) *buffoons*: people who look foolish; clowns

(25) *sensational*: intended to produce a thrilling effect

(26) *goatee*: a beard that has been trimmed down to a point on the chin

(27) *keen*: insightful

(27) *Hang out a shingle*: start up a business by hanging up a sign

(27) *rebirther*: a guide who takes you through the birth experience again

(27) *primal feeling facilitator*: a guide who tries to help you understand your most basic feelings

(27) *cosmic aura balancer*: a guide who tries to help you balance unseen forces around the body

(27) *Rolfer*: a person who gives deep massage for therapy

(28) *odds are*: it is likely

How do psychologists collect information?

Scientific Research—How to Think Like a Psychologist (p. 28-31)

(28) *haphazard*: not planned; random

(29) *hunch*: guess

(29) *disconfirm*: prove not true in all cases

(29) *itching* to discover: having a strong desire to discover

(30) *isolated*: not connected to anything else

(30) *Psychologists would drown in a sea of disconnected facts*: they would be very confused

(30) *journals:* periodicals that present research and reviews in a specific subject area

Naturalistic Observation—Psychology Steps Out! (p. 31-32)

(31) *to make out* (I was too far away *to make out* what he was eating): to be able to see; distinguish

(31) *tampered with*: affected by

(32) *a wealth of information*: a large amount of information

Correlational Studies—In Search of the Perfect Relationship (p. 32-35)

(32) *causation*: the act that produces or causes an effect

(33) *confirm*: prove or verify

(33) *TV zombie effect*: watching too much television turns people into passive and uninterested students

(34) *randomly*: by chance; not according to any set plan

(34) *mud to brew*: coffee to make

(34) *on a higher plane*: on a more important level

(34) *educated guesses*: guesses based on the best information available

How is an experiment performed?

The Psychology Experiment—Where Cause Meets Effect (p. 35-37)

(36) ***Heads, and the subject is in the experimental group, tails, it's in the control group***: the person is placed in one group or the other according to which side of a coin lands facing up (in other words, completely according to chance)

(36) ***dunces***: stupid, ignorant people

(36) ***hung over***: feeling sick (headache, stomachache) because of drinking too much alcohol the day before

(37) ***synthesize***: to combine into a single unit

Placebo Effects—Sugar Pills and Saltwater (p. 37-39)

(37) ***inert substances***: substances that have no active properties to affect behavior

(38) ***infusion machine***: a machine that allows doctors to inject saline and other solutions into a vein rather than multiple veins of their patients.

(39) ***simulated***: copied or of similar condition of the original

(39) ***loophole in the statement***: the statement has a misleading logic (sound judgment based on inference)

(39) ***coincidence***: two events happened to occur at the same time by chance

What other research methods do psychologists use?

The Clinical Method—Data by the Case (p. 39-40)

(39) ***foul-mouthed***: using obscene, crude, and socially unacceptable language

(39) ***rampage***: an uncontrollable aggressive act of violence

Survey Method—Here, Have a Sample (p. 40-42)

(40) ***blue-collar workers***: workers in trades, industrial settings, and manual labor; refers to the blue work shirts many such workers wear on the job

(41) ***rich tapestry***: filled with luxurious and abundant diversity of color

(41) ***prejudice***: judgments made before contrary information can be gathered or learned

How does psychology differ from false explanations of behavior?

Critical Thinking Revisited—Evaluating Claims and Evidence (p. 42-43)

(42) ***bouncing off the walls***: acting very excitedly or wildly

(42) ***sugar buzz***: overexcitement and nervous energy caused by eating foods or drinking beverages that contain large amounts of sugar

(42) ***implications***: possible results

(42) *anecdotal evidence*: evidence that could explain a claim

(42) *attest*: to declare truthfully

(42) *high-strung*: nervous; easily excited

(42) *sugar highs*: same as a sugar buzz (see above definition)

(42) *boisterous*: being loud, wild, and disorderly in behavior

(43) *hyper*: excessively active

(43) *pitfalls*: hidden dangers

(43) *anecdotes*: retelling of personal incidents or stories

Psuedo-Psychologies—Palms, Planets, and Personality (p. 43-46)

(43) *skeptical*: critical, not believing that everything you read is true

(44) *zodiac*: an imaginary belt in the nighttime sky that contains the apparent paths of the planets

(44) *vague*: very general, not specific

(44) *ring of truth*: sounds like it could be true

(44) *nitpicking*: unjustified criticism

(44) *hemmed in*: held back from doing something

(45) *nuisance*: something that is annoying or troublesome

(45) *to "buy" outrageous claims*: to believe claims that are too extraordinary to be true

(45) *occult*: beyond the range of ordinary knowledge; mysterious

(45) *Bermuda Triangle*: an area of the ocean where some people claim that ships are mysteriously lost

(45) *UFOs*: Unidentified Flying Objects. Typically refers to alien space craft visiting earth

(45) *provisional*: until more information can be found

(45) *clear-cut*: having a well-defined description

(45) *stringently*: being narrowly and strictly defined

How dependable is psychological information in the popular media?

Psychology in the News—Separating Fact From Fiction (p. 46-48)

(46) *bias*: slanted to include too many members of one group

(46) *National Enquirer*: a weekly tabloid newspaper that publishes wild, sensational stories that are often untrue

(46) *awash*: overflowing

(46) *subliminal*: functioning below the level of awareness

(47) ***ESP***: extra sensory perception; knowledge outside what could be learned through the senses

(47) ***testimonials***: statements recommending a product or treatment

(47) ***mentalists***: type of magician whose tricks involve knowing what people are thinking

(47) ***charlatans***: people who pretend to be experts of a profession

(47) ***callused***: skin that has become thick and hard

(47) ***moon madness***: belief that a full moon causes certain people to commit crimes or act strangely

(48) ***sweep him off to a weekend hideaway***: take him away for a romantic weekend trip

(48) ***corollary***: something that naturally accompanies or follows

Solutions

RECITE AND REVIEW

What is psychology? What are its goals?

1. profession
2. mental
3. behavior
4. evidence
5. planned or structured
6. Commonsense
7. method
8. evaluate
9. development
10. learning
11. theorists
12. sense (or sensory)
13. animals
14. behavior
15. thinking
16. males; females
17. social
18. behavior
19. evolution
20. animal
21. understand

How did psychology emerge as a field of knowledge?

1. knowledge
2. laboratory
3. experience
4. adapt
5. Watson
6. responses
7. positive
8. thinking
9. whole
10. greater
11. unconscious
12. Freud
13. growth
14. image
15. potentials

What are the major trends and specialties in psychology?

1. blend
2. humanism
3. neuroscience
4. optimal

Human Diversity—Appreciating Social and Cultural Differences: Pages 22-24

1. diversity (or differences)
2. values; rules

Psychologists—Guaranteed Not to Shrink: Pages 24-28

1. clinical
2. drugs
3. psychotherapy
4. Master's
5. specialties
6. basic

How do psychologists collect information?

1. measurement
2. problem; results
3. valid (or useful)
4. definitions
5. theory
6. abstract; results
7. clinical

Naturalistic Observation—Psychology Steps Out! Pages 31-32

1. natural
2. effect; observer
3. animals
4. records

Correlational Studies—In Search of the Perfect Relationship: Pages 32-35

1. correlation (or relationship)
2. zero
3. perfect
4. minus
5. increases
6. increases
7. predictions
8. curved

How is an experiment performed?

1. Cause
2. varied
3. change
4. independent
5. Dependent
6. prevent
7. subjects
8. group; group
9. characteristics
10. identical
11. chance
12. combine

Placebo Effects—Sugar Pills and Saltwater: Pages 37-39

1. effect
2. blind; blind
3. expected
4. prophecies

What other research methods do psychologists use?

1. case
2. heredity
3. natural

Survey Method—Here, Have a Sample: Pages 40-42

1. sample
2. Biases
3. Gender
4. untruthful (or inaccurate); courtesy bias

How does psychology differ from false explanations of behavior?

1. evaluate
2. claims; evidence
3. evidence

Pseudo-psychologies—Palms, Planets, and Personality: Pages 43-46

1. false
2. Barnum

How dependable is psychological information in the popular media?

1. Skepticism
2. unreliable (or inaccurate)
3. groups
4. causation
5. valid (or scientific)
6. examples

CONNECTIONS

What is psychology? What are its goals? Pages 12-17

1.	H.	5.	L.	9.	I.
2.	F.	6.	C.	10.	D.
3.	J.	7.	G.	11.	E.
4.	A.	8.	B.	12.	K.

How did psychology emerge as a field of knowledge? Pages 17-21

1.	A.	5.	J.	9.	G.
2.	H.	6.	E.	10.	I.
3.	D.	7.	C.		
4.	B.	8.	F.		

What are the major trends and specialties in psychology? Pages 21-28

1.	H.	5.	F.	9.	J.
2.	E.	6.	B.	10.	D.
3.	G.	7.	I.		
4.	A.	8.	C.		

How do psychologists collect information? Pages 28-35

1.	I.	5.	C.	9.	D.
2.	G.	6.	F.	10.	E.
3.	H.	7.	J.		
4.	A.	8.	B.		

How is an experiment performed? Pages 35-40

1.	H.	4.	A.	7.	F.
2.	B.	5.	D.	8.	G.
3.	C.	6.	E.		

What other research methods do psychologists use? Pages 40-42

1.	F.	4.	G.	7.	B.
2.	A.	5.	D.		
3.	C.	6.	E.		

How does psychology differ from false explanations of behavior? How dependable is psychological information in the popular media? Pages 42-48

1.	F.	2.	B.	3.	D.

4. A.	5. E.	6. C.

CHECK YOUR MEMORY

What is psychology? What are its goals? Pages 12-17

1. F	5. F	9. F
2. F	6. F	10. F
3. T	7. F	11. T
4. F	8. T	

How did psychology emerge as a field of knowledge? Pages 17-21

1. F	7. T	13. F
2. T	8. F	14. T
3. F	9. T	15. F
4. T	10. T	16. T
5. F	11. T	
6. T	12. F	

What are the major trends and specialties in psychology? Pages 21-28

1. F	6. T	11. F
2. F	7. T	12. T
3. T	8. F	13. T
4. F	9. T	14. F
5. T	10. F	15. T

How do psychologists collect information? Pages 28-35

1. T	5. T	9. F
2. F	6. F	10. F
3. F	7. T	11. F
4. T	8. F	12. F

How is an experiment performed? Pages 35-40

1. F	4. F	7. F
2. T	5. T	8. T
3. F	6. F	

What other research methods do psychologists use? Pages 40-42

1. F	3. F	5. T
2. T	4. T	6. F

7. T

How does psychology differ from false explanations of behavior? Pages 42-46

1. F	4. F	7. F
2. T	5. F	8. T
3. T	6. F	9. F

How dependable is psychological information in the popular media? Pages 46-48

1. F	4. F	7. T
2. T	5. F	8. F
3. F	6. F	

FINAL SURVEY AND REVIEW

What is psychology? What are its goals?

1. science; profession
2. behavior; mental processes
3. covert
4. Commonsense; scientific
5. empirical; data
6. Scientific
7. research method
8. critique; synthesize
9. Developmental
10. theorists
11. Personality
12. Sensation
13. Comparative
14. Biopsychologists
15. Cognitive
16. Gender
17. social behavior
18. Cultural
19. Evolutionary
20. animal models
21. predict; control

How did psychology emerge as a field of knowledge?

1. philosophy
2. Wilhelm Wundt
3. conscious experience; introspection
4. structuralism
5. Functionalism; James
6. Behaviorism; stimuli
7. Skinner; reinforcers
8. Cognitive
9. Gestalt
10. Wertheimer; Gestalt; sum
11. Psychoanalytic (or psychodynamic)
12. Freud; psychoanalysis
13. Humanistic; potentials
14. self-image; frame
15. self-actualization

What are the major trends and specialties in psychology?

1. behaviorism; humanism; biopsychology

2.	eclectic	3.	mental; neural	4.	Positive

Human Diversity—Appreciating Social and Cultural Differences: Pages 22-24

1. diversity; cultural
2. cultural; norms

Psychologists—Guaranteed Not to Shrink: Pages 24-28

1. clinical; counseling
2. Psychiatrists; psychotherapy
3. psychoanalysis
4. psychiatric social
5. Developmental; engineering; educational
6. applied

How do psychologists collect information?

1. evidence; measurement
2. hypothesis; theory
3. scientifically; testable
4. operational; procedures
5. theory; theories; observations
6. published; journals
7. experimental; survey

Naturalistic Observation—Psychology Steps Out! Pages 31-32

1. natural settings; environments
2. observed; bias
3. anthropomorphic
4. observational records

Correlational Studies—In Search of the Perfect Relationship: Pages 32-35

1. correlational
2. coefficients
3. zero; perfect
4. closer
5. positive
6. increases; decreases
7. causation
8. linear; curvilinear

How is an experiment performed?

1. controlled experiment
2. observed; recorded
3. variable
4. independent; causes
5. Dependent; effects
6. Extraneous; outcome
7. controlled
8. experimental; control
9. personal; randomly
10. independent
11. statistically
12. Meta-analysis

Placebo Effects—Sugar Pills and Saltwater: Pages 37-39

1. placebo; drugs

2. single-blind; double-blind   3. experimenter effect   4. self-fulfilling

What other research methods do psychologists use?

1. case studies; subject   2. Case studies; heredity   3. clinical tests

Survey Method—Here, Have a Sample: Pages 40-42

1. populations; representative   3. Gender; under-represented
2. Biases; representative   4. biased; questions

How does psychology differ from false explanations of behavior?

1. evaluate   2. evidence   3. Scientific

Pseudo-psychologies—Palms, Planets, and Personality: Pages 43-46

1. phrenology; pseudo   2. uncritical; positive; Barnum

How dependable is psychological information in the popular media?

1. Skepticism; critical   3. control   5. observations
2. biased   4. Correlation; correlation   6. cases; generalizations

MASTERY TEST

How dependable is psychological information in the popular media?

1. D, p. 12	17. A, p. 44	33. C, p. 31
2. B, p. 15	18. C, p. 40	34. D, p. 32
3. B, p. 16	19. D, p. 35	35. A, p. 34
4. D, p. 17	20. C, p. 31	36. D, p. 36
5. B, p. 18	21. A, p. 32	37. A, p. 19
6. A, p. 18	22. B, p. 29	38. D, p. 39
7. C, p. 20	23. C, p. 37	39. C, p. 39
8. B, p. 21	24. A, p. 29	40. A, p. 13
9. D, p. 23	25. C, p. 35	41. B, p. 25
10. A, p. 25	26. D, p. 47	42. B, p. 37
11. D, p. 26	27. C, p. 35	43. C, p. 41
12. D, p. 28	28. D, p. 32	
13. C, p. 42	29. D, p. 31	
14. A, pp. 42-43	30. B, p. 36	
15. B, p. 43	31. C, p. 39	
16. D, p. 44	32. D, p. 35	

Brain and Behavior

Chapter Overview

The brain and nervous system are made up of networks of neurons. Nerve impulses are basically electrical. Communication between neurons is chemical in that neurons release neurotransmitters which affect other neurons. Rather than merely carrying messages, neuropeptides regulate the activity of neurons in the brain.

The nervous system includes the central nervous system (CNS), consisting of the brain and spinal cord, and the peripheral nervous system (PNS). The PNS includes the somatic system and the autonomic system, with its sympathetic and parasympathetic branches.

Conventional brain research relies on dissection, staining, ablation, deep lesioning, electrical recording, electrical stimulation, micro-electrode recording, EEG recording, and clinical studies. Newer methods such as a PET scan and fMRI scan make use of computer-enhanced images of the brain and its activities.

The brain is divided into two cerebral hemispheres; each has different specialized abilities. The left hemisphere processes information sequentially while the right processes information simultaneously and holistically. Each hemisphere contains four lobes. The basic functions of the lobes are as follows: occipital lobes—vision; parietal lobes—bodily sensation; temporal lobes—hearing and language; frontal lobes—motor control, speech, and abstract thought. Association areas of the cortex are related to complex abilities such as language, memory, and problem solving.

The brain is subdivided into the forebrain, midbrain, and hindbrain. The subcortex includes important brain structures at all three levels. These are: the medulla ("vegetative" functions), the pons (a bridge between higher and lower brain areas), the cerebellum (coordination), the reticular formation (sensory and motor messages and arousal), the thalamus (sensory information), and the hypothalamus (basic motives). The limbic system is related to emotion.

The endocrine system is the second type of chemical communication in humans. It is made up of glands that secrete hormones into the bloodstream to regulate internal and external behavior such as growth, sex, anxiety, and sleep. Irregular secretion of the growth hormone can affect a person's development. Too little will result in hypopituitary dwarfism and too much will result in giantism and acromegaly.

Hand dominance ranges from strongly left- to strongly right-handed, with mixed handedness and ambidexterity in between. In general, the left-handed are less strongly lateralized in brain function than are right-handed persons.

Learning Objectives

1. Name the basic unit that makes up the nervous system, state what it is specifically designed to do, and list and describe its four parts.

2. Explain how a nerve impulse (action potential) occurs and how it is an all-or-nothing event. Include the terms *resting potential, threshold, ion channels,* and *negative after-potential.*

3. Describe the difference between the nature of a nerve impulse and the nature of the communication between neurons. Explain how nerve impulses are carried from one neuron to another. Include an explanation of receptor sites; the types of neurotransmitters; and the functions of neuropeptides, enkephalins, and endorphins.

4. Differentiate a nerve from a neuron. Describe the effect of myelin on the speed of the nerve impulse. Describe how neurilemma repairs neurons and explain what determines whether or not a neuron or nerve will regenerate. Include the current research techniques for alleviating brain damage.

5. Chart the various subparts of the human nervous system and explain their functions.

6. Describe the spinal cord and explain the mechanism of the reflex arc, including the types of neurons involved.

7. Describe the following techniques for studying the brain: clinical study, ablation, deep lesioning, electrical brain stimulation, micro-electrode recording, EEG, CT scan, MRI, functional MRI, and PET scan.

8. Describe the main difference between the brains of lower and higher animals and differences between the brains of people who score high on mental tests and those who score low. Include a description of the cerebrum and cerebral cortex and an explanation of corticalization.

9. Describe the two hemispheres of the brain, the corpus callosum, and the problem of spatial neglect; explain how and why the brain is "split" and the resulting effects; and differentiate the functions of right and left hemispheres.

10. Describe the function(s) of each of the following and describe the causes and effects of aphasia, agnosia and facial agnosia and compare the sex differences in the hemispheric responsibility for language:

    a. occipital lobes

    b. parietal lobes (include the somatosensory areas)

    c. temporal lobes

    d. frontal lobes (include the motor cortex)

    e. associative areas (include Broca's and Wernicke's areas)

11. List the three areas of the subcortex and explain the function of each of the following parts of the subcortex:

    a. hindbrain (brainstem): 1) medulla 2) pons 3) cerebellum 4) reticular formation

    b. forebrain: 1) thalamus 2) hypothalamus

12. Name the structures that comprise the limbic system; explain its overall function, the specific functions of the amygdala and the hippocampus, and the significance of "pleasure" and "aversive" areas in the limbic system; and list the six basic functions of the brain.

13. Explain the purpose of the endocrine system; describe the action of hormones in the body; and describe the effects that the following glands have on the body and behavior:

   a. pituitary (include a description of gigantism, dwarfism, and acromegaly)

   b. pineal

   c. thyroid (include a description of hyperthyroidism and hypothyroidism)

   d. adrenal medulla adrenal cortex (include a description of virilism, premature puberty, and the problems of anabolic steroids)

The following objectives are related to the material in the "Psychology in Action" section of your text.

1. Describe brain dominance and handness, including their relationship to speech; whether handedness is inherited; how the dominant hemisphere is determined; and the incidence, advantages, and disadvantages of being right-or left-handed.

2. Describe the element of handedness that appears to be inherited.

RECITE AND REVIEW

How do nerve cells operate and communicate?

Neurons—Building a "Biocomputer": Pages 52-57

1. The _____ and nervous system are made up of linked nerve cells called _____ , which pass information from one to another through synapses.

2. The brain consists of approximately _____ neurons, which form a _____ to produce thought, intelligence, and consciousness.

3. The basic conducting fibers of neurons are _____ , but dendrites (a receiving area), the soma (the cell body and also a receiving area), and _____ terminals (the branching ends of a neuron) are also involved in communication.

4. A _____ refers to an inactive neuron's electrical charge (-60 to -70 millivolts).

5. The firing of an action potential (_____ _____) is basically electrical, whereas communication between neurons is chemical.

6. An action potential occurs when the _____ potential is altered enough to reach the threshold for firing. At that point, sodium _____ flow into the axon, through _____ channels.

7. After each action potential, potassium ions flow out of the _____ , restoring the resting potential.

8. The _____ potential is an all-or-nothing event.

9. Experiencing and reacting to events in the environment lag slightly behind the actual occurrences of the events because _____ takes time.

10. Neurons release neurotransmitters at the synapse. These cross to _____ sites on the receiving cell, causing it to be excited or inhibited. For example, the transmitter chemical acetylcholine activates _____ .

11. Some neurotransmitters act to _____ (move it closer to firing) the next neuron, and some neurotransmitters act to inhibit (make firing less likely) the next neuron.

12. Disturbances of any neurotransmitters found in the brain can have serious consequences, such as too _____ can cause muscle tremors of Parkinson's disease or too _____ can cause schizophrenic symptoms.

13. Chemicals called neuropeptides do not carry messages directly. Instead, they _____ the activity of other neurons.

14. Opiate-like neural regulators called enkephalins and endorphins are released in the brain to relieve _____ and stress.

15. _____ may help explain how some women who suffer from severe premenstrual pain and distress have unusually low endorphin levels.

What are the functions of major parts of the nervous system?

The Nervous System—Wired for Action: Pages 57-60

1. To understand the capability of neural networks, a hybrot was built by combining living _____ with artificial electrical components. A hybrot has the capability to learn to _____ an F-22 fighter jet using a simulation program.

2. Nerves are made of large bundles of _____ and dendrites. Neurons and nerves in the peripheral nervous system can often regenerate; damage in the central nervous system is usually _____ , unless a repair is attempted by grafting or implanting healthy tissue.

3. Axons are coated with a fatty layer called _____ , which helps nerve impulses move faster down the axons. _____ also wraps around axons, but it forms a "tunnel" so damaged fibers can repair themselves.

4. The nervous system can be divided into the _____ nervous system (the _____ and spinal cord) and the peripheral nervous system.

5. The CNS includes the somatic (_____) and autonomic (_____) nervous systems.

6. The autonomic system has two divisions: the sympathetic (emergency, activating) _____ and the parasympathetic (sustaining, conserving) _____ .

7. Thirty-one pairs of spinal _____ leave the spinal cord. Twelve pairs of cranial _____ leave the brain directly. Together, they carry sensory and motor messages between the brain and the body.

8. The simplest _____ is a reflex arc, which involves a sensory neuron, a connector neuron, and a _____ neuron.

How do we know how the brain works?

Research Methods—Charting the Brain's Inner Realms: Pages 60-63

1. Conventional brain research relies on dissection, staining, ablation, deep lesioning, electrical recording, _____ stimulation, micro-electrode recording, EEG recording, and _____ studies.

2. Computer-enhanced techniques are providing three-dimensional _____ of the living human brain and its _____ . Examples of such techniques are CT scans, MRI scans, and PET scans.

3. The _____ scan produces images of the brain by using X-rays, the _____ scan produces images of the brain by using a magnetic field, and the _____ scan produces images

of the brain as well as the activities of the brain by detecting positrons emitted by a weak radioactive glucose in the brain.

How is the brain organized and what do its higher structures do? Why are the brain's association areas important? What happens when they are injured?

The Cerebral Cortex—My, What a Big Brain You Have! Pages 63-71

1. The human _____ is marked by advanced corticalization, or enlargement of the cerebral _____ , which covers the outside surface of the cerebrum.

2. Using a PET scan, Haier and colleagues found that intelligence is related to _____ : A less efficient brain works much harder than a more efficient brain.

3. Neurological _____ signs result from brain abnormalities or injuries and do not include obvious behavioral symptoms but rather they include such behavioral signs as clumsiness, _____ gait, and poor hand-eye coordination.

4. The _____ cerebral hemisphere contains speech or language "centers" in most people. It also specializes in _____ , calculating, judging time and rhythm, and ordering complex movements.

5. The _____ hemisphere is largely nonverbal. It excels at spatial and perceptual skills, visualization, and recognition of _____ , faces, and melodies.

6. "Split brains" have been created by _____ the corpus callosum. The split-brain individual shows a remarkable degree of independence between the right and left _____ .

7. Another way to summarize specialization in the brain is to say that the _____ hemisphere is good at analysis and processing information sequentially; the _____ hemisphere processes information simultaneously and holistically.

8. The most basic functions of the lobes of the cerebral cortex are as follows: occipital lobes— _____ ; parietal lobes—bodily sensation; temporal lobes— _____ and language; frontal lobes—motor control, speech, and abstract thought.

9. Association areas on the cortex are neither _____ nor _____ in function. They combine information from the senses and they are related to more _____ skills such as language, memory, recognition, and problem solving.

10. Damage to either Broca's area or Wernicke's area causes _____ and language problems known as aphasias.

11. Damage to Broca's area causes problems with _____ and pronunciation. Damage to Wernicke's area causes problems with the _____ of words.

12. Damage in other association areas may cause agnosia, the inability to _____ objects by sight. This disability can sometimes impair the ability to recognize _____ , a condition called facial agnosia.

13. Research conducted by Haier and his colleague has shown brain _____ in males and females particularly involving the concentration of gray and white _____ of the brain.

What kinds of behaviors are controlled by the subcortex?

The Subcortex—At the Core of the (Brain) Matter: Pages 71-74

1. All of the brain areas below the _____ are called the subcortex.

2. The medulla contains centers essential for reflex control of _____ _____ , breathing, and other "vegetative" functions.

3. The pons connects the medulla with _____ brain areas and it influences _____ and arousal.

4. The cerebellum maintains _____ , posture, and muscle tone.

5. The _____ lies inside the medulla and the brainstem, influences _____ , and does not mature until _____ . It also directs sensory and motor messages, and part of it, known as the RAS, acts as an _____ system for the cerebral cortex.

6. The thalamus carries _____ information to the cortex. The hypothalamus exerts powerful control over eating, drinking, sleep cycles, body temperature, and other basic _____ and behaviors.

7. The limbic system is strongly related to _____ and motivated behavior. It also contains distinct reward and punishment areas.

8. A part of the limbic system called the amygdala is related to _____ . An area known as the hippocampus is important for forming _____ .

9. PET and fMRI scans show that brains of individuals with spider phobias and aphasias have developed _____ changes as a result of learned experiences.

Does the glandular system affect behavior?

The Endocrine System—Hormones and Behavior: Pages 74-77

1. The endocrine system provides _____ communication in the body through the release of _____ into the bloodstream. Endocrine glands influence moods, behavior, and even personality.

2. Many of the endocrine glands are influenced by the pituitary (the " _____ gland"), which is in turn influenced by the hypothalamus.

3. The pituitary supplies _____ hormone. Too little GH causes _____ ; too much causes giantism or acromegaly.

4. Body rhythms and _____ cycles are influenced by melatonin, secreted by the pineal gland.

5. The thyroid gland regulates _____ . Hyperthyroidism refers to an overactive thyroid gland; hypothyroidism to an underactive thyroid.

6. The adrenal glands supply _____ and norepinephrine to activate the body. They also regulate salt balance, responses to stress, and they are a secondary source of _____ hormones.

7. Most drugs like anabolic steroids are synthetic versions of _____ .

How do right- and left-handed individuals differ?

Psychology in Action: Handedness—If Your Brain Is Right, What's Left? Page 77-80

1. Hand dominance ranges from strongly left- to strongly right-handed, with _____ handedness and ambidexterity in between.

2. Ninety percent of the population is basically _____ , 10 percent _____ .

3. The vast majority of people are right-handed and therefore _____ brain dominant for motor skills. Ninety-seven percent of right-handed persons and 68 percent of the left-handed also produce _____ from the left hemisphere.

4. _____ people in the past were forced to _____ as right-handed people; therefore, there are fewer left-handed older people living than right-handed older people.

5. In general, the _____ are less strongly lateralized in brain function than are _____ persons.

CONNECTIONS

How do nerve cells operate and communicate? Pages 52-57

1. _____ soma
2. _____ neurilemma
3. _____ axon collateral
4. _____ myelin
5. _____ dendrites
6. _____ axon terminals
7. _____ axon

What are the functions of major parts of the nervous system? Pages 57-60

1. _____ spinal cord
2. _____ autonomic system
3. _____ parasympathetic branch
4. _____ peripheral nervous system
5. _____ sympathetic branch
6. _____ brain
7. _____ somatic system

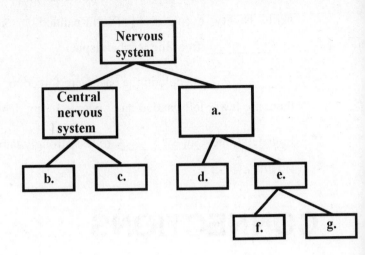

How do we know how the brain works? Pages 60-63

1. _____ CT scan
2. _____ EEG
3. _____ deep lesioning
4. _____ PET scan
5. _____ ablation

a. brain waves
b. radioactive glucose
c. surgery
d. electrode
e. computerized X-rays

How is the brain organized and what do its higher structures do? Why are the brain's association areas important? What happens when they are injured? Pages 63-71

1. _____ Wernicke's area
2. _____ temporal lobe
3. _____ cerebellum
4. _____ Broca's area
5. _____ parietal lobe
6. _____ frontal lobe
7. _____ occipital lobe

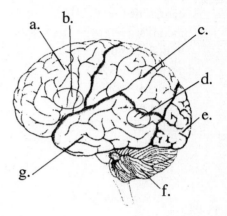

Areas of the Brain

1. _____ Wernicke's Area
2. _____ Broca's area
3. _____ facial agnosia
4. _____ aphasia
5. _____ motor cortex
6. _____ somatosensory area

a. language impairment
b. language production
c. language comprehension
d. receives bodily sensations
e. controls voluntary movements
f. impaired facial recognition

What kinds of behaviors are controlled by the subcortex? Pages 71-74

1. _____ midbrain
2. _____ reticular formation
3. _____ cerebrum
4. _____ medulla
5. _____ hypothalamus
6. _____ corpus callosum
7. _____ pituitary
8. _____ spinal cord
9. _____ thalamus

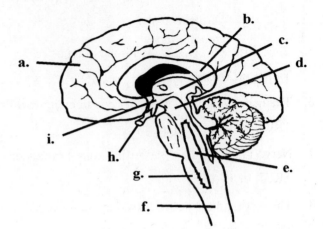

Does the glandular system affect behavior? Pages 74-77

1. _____ hypopituitary dwarfism
2. _____ pituitary
3. _____ anabolic steroids
4. _____ testes
5. _____ pineal gland
6. _____ thyroid gland
7. _____ acromegaly
8. _____ adrenal glands

a. testosterone
b. metabolism
c. growth hormone
d. epinephrine
e. melatonin
f. synthetic of testosterone
g. too much growth hormone
h. too little growth hormone

CHECK YOUR MEMORY

How do nerve cells operate and communicate? Pages 52-57

1. The dendrites receive incoming information from the neurilemma.

   TRUE or FALSE

2. Human axons may be up to a meter long.

   TRUE or FALSE

3. The resting potential is about plus 70 millivolts.

   TRUE or FALSE

4. The interior of the axon becomes positive during an action potential.

   TRUE or FALSE

5. The action potential is an all-or-nothing event.

   TRUE or FALSE

6. The negative after-potential is due to an inward flow of potassium ions.

   TRUE or FALSE

7. Nerve impulses travel faster in axons surrounded by myelin.

   TRUE or FALSE

8. The resting potential is caused by an inward flow of potassium ions.

   TRUE or FALSE

9. Neurotransmitters activate other neurons; neuropeptides activate muscles and glands.

   TRUE or FALSE

10. Enkephalins are neuropeptides.

    TRUE or FALSE

11. Neuropeptides regulate the activity of other neurons.

    TRUE or FALSE

12. Many drugs imitate, duplicate, or block neurotransmitters to excite or inhibit an action potential.

    TRUE or FALSE

What are the functions of major parts of the nervous system? Pages 57-60

1. Built purely from artificial electrical components, a hybrot can learn to fly an F-22 fighter jet plane.

   TRUE or FALSE

2. The neurilemma helps damaged nerve cell fibers regenerate after an injury.

   TRUE or FALSE

3. Neurons in the brain and spinal cord must last a lifetime; damage to them is usually permanent.

   TRUE or FALSE

4. The word *autonomic* means "self-limiting."

   TRUE or FALSE

5. The parsympathetic branch quiets the body and returns it to a lower level of arousal.

TRUE or FALSE

6. Researchers have had some success in stimulating regrowth of cut nerve fibers in the spinal cord.

TRUE or FALSE

7. The sympathetic system generally controls voluntary behavior.

TRUE or FALSE

8. Thirty-one cranial nerves leave the brain directly.

TRUE or FALSE

9. "Fight-or-flight" emergency reactions are produced by the autonomic nervous system.

TRUE or FALSE

10. Activity in the parasympathetic system increases heart rate and respiration.

TRUE or FALSE

11. In a reflex arc, motor neurons carry messages to effector cells.

TRUE or FALSE

How do we know how the brain works? Pages 60-63

1. Deep lesioning in the brain is usually done surgically.

TRUE or FALSE

2. Micro-electrodes are needed in order to record from single neurons.

TRUE or FALSE

3. CT scans form "maps" of brain activity.

TRUE or FALSE

4. Electroencephalography records waves of electrical activity produced by the brain.

TRUE or FALSE

5. Radioactive glucose is used to make PET scans.

TRUE or FALSE

How is the brain organized and what do its higher structures do? Why are the brain's association areas important? What happens when they are injured? Pages 63-71

1. Elephants have brain-body ratios similar to those of humans.

   TRUE or FALSE

2. The corpus callosum connects the right and left brain hemispheres.

   TRUE or FALSE

3. The cerebellum makes up a large part of the cerebral cortex.

   TRUE or FALSE

4. Much of the cerebral cortex is made up of gray matter.

   TRUE or FALSE

5. Damage to the left cerebral hemisphere usually causes spatial neglect.

   TRUE or FALSE

6. In general, smart brains tend to be the hardest working brains.

   TRUE or FALSE

7. The right half of the brain mainly controls left body areas.

   TRUE or FALSE

8. Roger Sperry won a Nobel prize for his work on corticalization.

   TRUE or FALSE

9. According to Richard Haier, a less efficient brain works harder and still accomplishes less than a more efficient brain because a less efficient brain uses less glucose to process information.

   TRUE or FALSE

10. Neurological soft signs include clumsiness, awkward gait, and poor hand-eye coordination.

    TRUE or FALSE

11. Cutting the reticular formation produces a "split brain."

    TRUE or FALSE

12. Information from the right side of vision is sent directly to the right cerebral hemisphere.

    TRUE or FALSE

13. The right hemisphere tends to be good at speaking, writing, and math.

    TRUE or FALSE

14. The left hemisphere is mainly involved with analysis.

    TRUE or FALSE

15. The right hemisphere sees overall patterns and general connections. The left brain focuses on small details.

    TRUE or FALSE

16. An inability to move the right side of the body is the most common neurological soft sign following an injury to the brain.

    TRUE or FALSE

17. Both brain hemispheres are normally active at all times.

    TRUE or FALSE

18. The motor cortex is found on the occipital lobes.

    TRUE or FALSE

19. The somatosensory area is located on the parietal lobes.

    TRUE or FALSE

20. Electrically stimulating the motor cortex causes movement in various parts of the body.

    TRUE or FALSE

21. Large parts of the lobes of the brain are made up of association cortex.

    TRUE or FALSE

22. Damage to either brain hemisphere usually causes an aphasia.

    TRUE or FALSE

23. A person with Broca's aphasia might say "pear" when shown an apple.

    TRUE or FALSE

24. Damage to Wernicke's area causes the condition known as mindblindness.

    TRUE or FALSE

25. Women are much more likely than men to use both cerebral hemispheres for language processing.

    TRUE or FALSE

26. Research has shown women have more white matter and men have more grey matter in their brains.

    TRUE or FALSE

What kinds of behaviors are controlled by the subcortex? Pages 71-74

1. The cerebrum makes up much of the medulla.

    TRUE or FALSE

2. Injury to the medulla may affect breathing.

TRUE or FALSE

3. Injury to the cerebellum affects attention and wakefulness.

TRUE or FALSE

4. The reticular formation is the switching station for sensory messages and is fully developed at birth.

TRUE or FALSE

5. Smell is the only major sense that does not pass through the thalamus.

TRUE or FALSE

6. Stimulating various parts of the limbic system can produce rage, fear, pleasure, or arousal.

TRUE or FALSE

7. The hippocampus is associated with hunger and eating.

TRUE or FALSE

8. PET scans show reduced neurological change among individuals who have experienced spider phobias as a result of having undergone cognitive therapy.

TRUE or FALSE

Does the glandular system affect behavior? Pages 74-77

1. Androgens ("male" hormones) are related to the sex drive in both men and women.

TRUE or FALSE

2. Hormones secreted during times of high emotion tend to increase memory loss.

TRUE or FALSE

3. After watching violent scenes, men had high levels of testosterone in their bloodstream.

TRUE or FALSE

4. "Normal short" children grow faster when given synthetic growth hormone, but their final height is not taller.

TRUE or FALSE

5. Activity of the pituitary is influenced by the hypothalamus.

TRUE or FALSE

6. A person who is slow, sleepy, and overweight could be suffering from hypothyroidism.

TRUE or FALSE

7. Virilism and premature puberty may be caused by problems with the adrenal glands.

TRUE or FALSE

8. Steroid drugs may cause sexual impotence and breast enlargement in males.

   TRUE or FALSE

9. There is much evidence to support that steroids do improve performance, which is why all major sports organizations ban the use of steroids.

   TRUE or FALSE

How do right- and left-handed individuals differ? Pages 77-80

1. Left-handers have an advantage in fencing, boxing, and baseball.

   TRUE or FALSE

2. Most left-handed persons produce speech from their right hemispheres.

   TRUE or FALSE

3. To a degree left or right handedness is influenced by heredity, especially by a gene on the X chromosome.

   TRUE or FALSE

4. On average, left-handed persons die at younger ages than right-handed persons do.

   TRUE or FALSE

FINAL SURVEY AND REVIEW

How do nerve cells operate and communicate?

Neurons—Building a "Biocomputer": Pages 52-57

1. The brain and nervous system are made up of linked nerve cells called _____ , which pass information from one to another through _____ .

2. The brain consists of approximately 100 billion neurons, which form a _____ to produce thought, intelligence, and consciousness.

3. The basic conducting fibers of neurons are axons, but _____ (a receiving area), the _____ (the cell body and also a receiving area), and axon terminals (the branching ends of an axon) are also involved in communication.

4. A resting potential refers to an electrical charge (-60 to -70 millivolts) of an _____ .

5. The firing of an _____ _____ (nerve impulse) is basically electrical, whereas communication between neurons is chemical.

6. An action potential occurs when the resting potential is altered enough to reach the _____ for firing. At that point, _____ ions flow into the axon, through ion channels.

7. After each action potential, _____ ions flow out of the axon, restoring the resting potential.

8. The action potential is an _____ event.

9. Because _____ takes time, our response to events in the environment lags slightly behind the actual occurrence of those events.

10. In chemical synapses, neurons release _____ . These cross to receptor sites on the receiving cell, causing it to be excited or inhibited. For example, the transmitter chemical _____ activates muscles.

11. Some neurotransmitters act to excite the receiving neuron by increasing its ability to _____ an action potential, and some neurotransmitters act to inhibit the receiving neuron by _____ its ability to fire.

12. Disturbances of any neurotransmitters found in the brain can have serious consequences, such as too little dopamine can cause muscle tremors of _____ or too much dopamine can cause _____ .

13. Chemicals called _____ do not carry messages directly. Instead, they regulate the activity of other neurons.

14. Opiate-like neural regulators called enkephalins and _____ are released in the brain to relieve pain and stress.

15. Neural regulators may help explain how some women who suffer from severe premenstrual pain and distress have unusually _____ levels.

What are the functions of major parts of the nervous system?

The Nervous System—Wired for Action: Pages 57-60

1. To understand the capability of neural networks, a _____ was built by combining living neurons with artificial electrical components; it has the capability to learn to _____ an F-22 fighter jet with a simulation program.

2. _____ are made of axons and associated tissues. Neurons and nerves in the _____ nervous system can often regenerate; damage in the _____ nervous system is usually permanent.

3. Axons are coated with a fatty layer called myelin, which helps nerve impulses move _____ down the axons. Neurilemma also wraps around axons, but it forms a "tunnel" so damaged fibers can _____ themselves.

4. The nervous system can be divided into the _____ nervous system (the brain and _____) and the peripheral nervous system.

5. The CNS includes the _____ (bodily) and _____ (involuntary) nervous systems.

6. The autonomic system has two divisions: the _____ (emergency, activating) branch and the _____ (sustaining, conserving) branch.

7. Thirty-one pairs of _____ nerves leave the spinal cord. Twelve pairs of _____ nerves leave the brain directly. Together, these nerves carry sensory and _____ messages between the brain and the body.

8. The simplest behavior is a _____ _____ , which involves a sensory neuron, an _____ neuron, and a _____ neuron.

How do we know how the brain works?

Research Methods—Charting the Brain's Inner Realms: Pages 60-63

1. Conventional brain research relies on _____ (separation into parts), staining, ablation, deep lesioning, electrical recording, electrical _____ , micro-electrode recording, EEG recording, and clinical studies.

2. Computer-enhanced techniques are providing three-dimensional images of the living human brain and its activities. Examples of such techniques are CT scans, _____ scans, and _____ scans, which record brain activity.

3. The CT scan produces images of the brain by using _____ , the MRI scan produces images of the brain by using a _____ , and the PET scan produces images of the brain as well as the activities of the brain by detecting positrons emitted by a weak _____ in the brain.

How is the brain organized and what do its higher structures do? Why are the brain's association areas important? What happens when they are injured?

The Cerebral Cortex—My, What a Big Brain You Have! Pages 63-71

1. The human brain is marked by advanced _____ , or enlargement of the cerebral cortex, which covers the outside surface of the _____ .

2. Using a PET scan, Haier and colleagues found that intelligence is related to brain efficiency: A _____ efficient brain works much harder than a _____ efficient brain.

3. Neurological _____ _____ result from brain abnormalities or injuries and do not include obvious behavioral symptoms but rather they include such behavioral signs as clumsiness, awkward gait, and poor hand-eye coordination.

4. The right cerebral _____ contains speech or language "centers" in most people. It also specializes in writing, calculating, judging time and rhythm, and ordering complex _____ .

5. The left hemisphere is largely nonverbal. It excels at _____ and perceptual skills, visualization, and recognition of patterns, _____ , and melodies.

6. "Split brains" have been created by cutting the _____ . The split-brain individual shows a remarkable degree of independence between the right and left _____ .

7. Another way to summarize specialization in the brain is to say that the left hemisphere is good at _____ and processing information sequentially; the right hemisphere processes information _____ and holistically.

8. The most basic functions of the lobes of the cerebral _____ are as follows: occipital lobes—vision; parietal lobes—bodily _____ ; temporal lobes—hearing and language; frontal lobes—motor control, _____ , and abstract thought.

9. Association areas on the cortex are neither _____ nor _____ in function. They _____ information from the senses, and they are related to more complex skills such as _____ , memory, recognition, and problem solving.

10. Damage to either Broca's area or Wernicke's area causes speech and language problems known as _____ .

11. Damage to _____ area causes problems with speech and pronunciation. Damage to _____ area causes problems with the meaning of words.

12. Damage in other association areas may cause _____ , the inability to identify objects by sight. This disability can sometimes impair the ability to recognize faces, a condition called _____ _____ .

13. Research conducted by Haier and his colleague has shown brain specialization in males and females particularly involving the concentration of _____ and _____ matter of the brain.

What kinds of behaviors are controlled by the subcortex?

The Subcortex—At the Core of the (Brain) Matter: Pages 71-74

1. All of the brain areas below the cortex are called the _____ .

2. The _____ contains centers essential for reflex control of heart rate, breathing, and other "vegetative" functions.

3. The _____ connects the medulla with higher brain areas and it influences sleep and arousal.

4. The _____ maintains coordination, posture, and muscle tone.

5. The _____ lies inside the medulla and the brainstem, influences attention, and does not mature until adolescence. It also directs sensory and motor messages, and part of it, known as the RAS, acts as an activating system for the _____ _____ .

6. The _____ carries sensory information to the cortex. The _____ exerts powerful control over eating, drinking, sleep cycles, body temperature, and other basic motives and behaviors.

7. The _____ system is strongly related to emotion and motivation. It also contains distinct _____ and punishment areas.

8. The part of the limbic system called the _____ is related to fear. An area known as the _____ is important for forming lasting memories.

9. PET and fMRI scans show that brains of individuals with spider phobias and aphasias have developed neurological changes as a result of _____ _____ .

Does the glandular system affect behavior?

The Endocrine System—Hormones and Behavior: Pages 74-77

1. The _____ system provides chemical communication in the body through the release of hormones into the _____ .

2. Many of the endocrine glands are influenced by the _____ (the "master gland"), which is in turn influenced by the _____ .

3. The _____ supplies growth hormone. Too little GH causes dwarfism; too much causes giantism or _____ .

4. Body rhythms and sleep cycles are influenced by _____ , secreted by the _____ gland.

5. The thyroid gland regulates metabolism. Hyperthyroidism refers to an _____ thyroid gland; hypothyroidism refers to an _____ thyroid.

6. The _____ glands supply epinephrine and norepinephrine to activate the body. They also regulate salt balance, responses to _____ , and they are a secondary source of sex hormones.

7. Most drugs like anabolic steroids are _____ versions of testosterone.

How do right- and left-handed individuals differ?

Psychology in Action: Handedness—If Your Brain Is Right, What's Left? Pages 77-80

1. _____ _____ ranges from strongly left- to strongly right-handed, with mixed handedness and _____ in between.

2. _____ percent of the population is basically right-handed, _____ percent left-handed.

3. The vast majority of people are _____ and therefore _____ brain dominant for motor skills. Ninety-seven percent of right-handed persons and 68 percent of the left-handed produce speech from the _____ hemisphere.

4. Left-handed people in the past were forced to _____ as _____ people; therefore, there are fewer left-handed older people living than right-handed older people.

5. In general, the left-handed are less strongly _____ in brain function than are right-handed persons.

MASTERY TEST

1. At times of emergency, anger, or fear, what part of the nervous system becomes more active?
   a. corpus callosum of the forebrain
   b. sympathetic branch of the ANS
   c. parasympathetic branch of the PNS
   d. Broca's area

2. The highest and largest brain area in humans is the
   a. cerebrum
   b. cerebellum
   c. frontal lobes
   d. gray matter of the callosum

3. A tumor in which brain area would most likely cause blind spots in vision?
   a. occipital lobe
   b. temporal lobe
   c. somatosensory area
   d. association cortex

4. Neurotransmitters are found primarily in
   a. the spinal cord
   b. neurilemmas
   c. synapses
   d. motor neurons

5. Enkephalins are an example of
   a. acetylcholine blockers
   b. neuropeptides
   c. receptor sites
   d. adrenal hormones

6. Electrically stimulating a portion of which brain area would produce movements in the body?
    a. occipital lobe
    b. frontal lobe
    c. parietal lobe
    d. temporal lobe

7. When a neuron reaches its threshold, a/an _____ occurs.
    a. volume potential
    b. ion potential
    c. action potential
    d. dendrite potential

8. A person's ability to work as a commercial artist would be most impaired by damage to the
    a. left temporal lobe
    b. right cerebral hemisphere
    c. left cerebral hemisphere
    d. frontal association cortex

9. Electrically stimulating the brain would most likely produce anger if it activated the
    a. association cortex
    b. limbic system
    c. parasympathetic branch
    d. reticular activating system

10. Information in neurons usually flows in what order?
    a. soma, dendrites, axon
    b. dendrites, soma, axon
    c. dendrites, myelin, axon terminals
    d. axon, soma, axon terminals

11. Regulating the activity of other neurons is most characteristic of
    a. neuropeptides
    b. acetylcholine
    c. reflex arcs
    d. resting potentials

12. Nerve impulses occur when _____ rush into the axon.
    a. sodium ions
    b. potassium ions
    c. negative charges
    d. neurotransmitters

13. Experiments involving the grafting of nerve cells have been
    a. unsuccessful at present
    b. successful in animals
    c. successful only in the peripheral nervous system
    d. successful only in the CNS

14. A person who says "bife" for bike and "seep" for sleep probably suffers from
    a. Broca's aphasia
    b. Wernicke's aphasia
    c. functional agnosia
    d. the condition known as "mindblindness"

15. Damage to which part of the limbic system would most likely impair memory?
    a. thalamus
    b. hypothalamus
    c. amygdala
    d. hippocampus

16. Involuntary changes in heart rate, blood pressure, digestion, and sweating are controlled by the
    a. thoracic nerves
    b. parietal lobes
    c. somatic system
    d. autonomic system

17. In which of the following pairs are both structures part of the forebrain?
    a. medulla, hypothalamus
    b. cerebrum, cerebellum
    c. medulla, thalamus
    d. cerebrum, thalamus

18. Which of the following is a specialized type of X-ray?
    a. PET scan
    b. CT scan
    c. MRI scan
    d. EEG scan

19. Which two problems are associated with the pituitary gland?
    a. dwarfism, acromegaly
    b. virilism, acromegaly
    c. mental retardation, dwarfism
    d. giantism, premature puberty

20. The cerebral hemispheres are interconnected by the
    a. reticular system
    b. cerebellum
    c. cerebrum
    d. corpus callosum

21. Damage to which of the following would most likely make it difficult for a person to play catch with a ball?
    a. reticular formation
    b. limbic system
    c. cerebellum
    d. association cortex

22. Speech, language, calculation, and analysis are special skills of the
    a. right cerebral hemisphere
    b. limbic system
    c. left cerebral hemisphere
    d. right somatosensory area

23. The usual flow of information in a reflex arc is
    a. cranial nerve, connector neuron, spinal nerve
    b. sensory neuron, connector neuron, motor neuron
    c. effector cell, interneuron, connector neuron
    d. sensory neuron, connector neuron, reflex neuron

24. A person will "hear" a series of sounds when which area of the cortex is electrically stimulated?
    a. frontal lobe
    b. parietal lobe
    c. occipital lobe
    d. temporal lobe

25. Which of the following pairs contains the "master gland" and its master?
    a. pineal—thalamus
    b. thyroid—RAS
    c. pituitary—hypothalamus
    d. adrenal—cortex

26. Many basic motives and emotions are influenced by the
    a. thalamus
    b. hypothalamus
    c. corpus callosum
    d. cerebellum

27. Both surgical ablation and _____ remove brain tissue.
    a. the MEG technique
    b. tomography
    c. micro-electrode sampling
    d. deep lesioning

28. Which of the following techniques requires access to the interior of the brain?
    a. micro-electrode recording
    b. EEG recordings
    c. PET scanning
    d. functional MRI

29. Which of the following statements about handedness is false?
    a. Like eye color, handedness is inherited from one's parents.
    b. A majority of left-handers produce speech from the left hemisphere.
    c. The left-handed are less lateralized than the right-handed.
    d. Left-handedness is an advantage in boxing and fencing.

30. Negative after-potentials are caused by the outward flow of _____ from the axon.
    a. negative charges
    b. potassium ions
    c. neurotransmitters
    d. sodium ions

31. Scott was challenged to catch a dollar bill as fast as he could with his thumb and index finger as it fell between them. Scott was successful one time out of five trials. Which statement best explains why Scott failed to catch the dollar bill?
    a. Scott's injury to the temporal lobe has caused him to not see when the dollar bill falls.
    b. This simple yet common test signifies that Scott has serious cognitive deficits and must seek a specialist immediately.
    c. From the time Scott processes the information to when his brain tells the muscles to grab the dollar bill, the dollar bill has already slipped by.
    d. none of the above

32. People with Parkinson's disease lack or have very little of the neurotransmitter _____.
    a. endorphins
    b. epinephrine
    c. serotonin
    d. dopamine

33. Which statement correctly reflects the findings of Haier and his colleagues on the relationship between intelligence and brain efficiency?
    a. A less efficient brain works much harder than a more efficient brain.
    b. A more efficient brain works much harder than a less efficient brain.
    c. A less efficient brain uses less glucose when processing information.
    d. A more efficient brain uses more glucose when processing information.

34. Upon receiving electrical stimulation in the neural network, a_____ (created by combining living neurons with artificial components) has the capability to learn to fly a fighter jet by utilizing a simulation program.
    a. robrot
    b. neurobot
    c. hybrot
    d. fighterbot

35. Upon waking up, Natasha experienced such behavioral symptoms as clumsiness and an awkward gait. Natasha is displaying neurological_____.
    a. hard signs
    b. soft signs
    c. external signs
    d. mental signs

36. In regards to brain concentration and specialization, men have been shown to have more _____ matter than women and women have been shown to have more _____ matter than men.
    a. hard; soft
    b. soft; hard
    c. white; grey
    d. grey; white

37. PET scans have revealed that brains with damage to the left hemisphere develop increased neurological activity in the right hemisphere to compensate for the loss as a result of
    a. learned experiences in therapy.
    b. medical treatment.
    c. bed rest.
    d. B and C

LANGUAGE DEVELOPMENT - Brain and Behavior

Word roots

Soma is the Greek word for "body." Several words in the fields of psychology and biology are derived from this Greek word. These words all refer to either the body of a smaller unit like a cell or to the whole physical body in general. Examples: soma, somatic, somesthetic, psychosomatic, somatoform, and somatization. All of these words will appear in the chapters in your textbook.

How do nerve cells operate and communicate?

Preview: Finding Music in Tofu (p. 52)

   (52) *tofu:* soybean curd, often eaten as an alternative to meat

(52) **Bach**: composer of classical music

(52) **in the zone**: peaking in performance in a particular athletic skill

(52) **blob**: a small lump of thick consistency

(52) **realm**: area of interest

Neurons—Building a "Biocomputer" (pp. 52-57)

(52) **spidery**: composed of thin threads like a spider's web

(52) **wired**: refers to how the nervous system is put together and how it works

(52) **fleeting**: passing quickly; not lasting

(52) **riff**: a repeated phrase of music, usually supporting a solo improvisation

(53) **sweeps down the axon**: moves very fast down the axon

(53) **fastball**: a type of pitch thrown very fast by the pitcher at a baseball game

(53) **major league**: referring to the top baseball teams

(53) **zips along**: moves along at a fast speed

(53) **dominoes**: flat, rectangular blocks used as pieces in a game of the same name

(53) **wave of activity**: the advance of a signal

(55) **bullring**: an arena used for fighting bulls

(55) **sensitive**: highly responsive to certain neurotransmitters

(57) **disabling**: to be too painful for functioning

What are the functions of major parts of the nervous system?

The Nervous System—Wired for Action (pp. 57-60)

(57) **wired for action**: set up and ready to go

(57) **playing catch with a Frisbee:** a game in which a round plastic disk (a Frisbee) is thrown back and forth between people

(57) **ablaze with activity:** extremely active

(57) **unmanned**: without a human present to operate a jet

(58) **coax**: to persuade gently

(58) **B.B. King plays the blues**: a famous musician known for his distinctive blues music

(59) **a flash of anger**: a sudden, quick burst of anger

(59) **fight or flight**: a point at which a person or other animal decides to face danger or flee from it

(60) **grandstand catches:** in baseball, to catch the ball so as to impress the fans

How do we know how the brain works?

Research Methods—Charting the Brain's Inner Realms (pp. 60-63)

(61) *euphoria*: a sense of well being; feeling happy and good all over

(61) *atlas*: map of the brain

(61) *sci-fi movies:* science fiction movies

(61) *invading*: taking over and doing harm

(61) *hypnosis:* an altered state of consciousness in which a person responds easily to suggestions

(61) *peek*: look inside something, usually through a small opening

(61) *ongoing symphony*: current activities of all parts of the brain performing together as a unit

(62) *until even brighter beacons are flashed into the shadowy inner world of thought:* until newer and better techniques reveal more about the little-understood world of thought

How is the brain organized and what do its higher structures do? Why are the brain's association areas important? What happens when they are injured?

The Cerebral Cortex—My, What a Big Brain You Have! (pp. 63-71)

(64) *brighter subjects:* more intelligent

(65) *alien:* foreign; belonging elsewhere

(66) *hit like a thunderbolt*: hit very fast and deadly

(66) *telltale*: something that serves to disclose information

(66) *gallantly:* heroically

(66) *overrides:* takes control over

(66) *right hand not knowing what the left hand is doing*!: a confused state where a person or a group seems to hold two view points at once, and both sides are unaware of the other

(67) *irony:* statements in which the intended meaning is the opposite of the usual meaning

(67) *sarcasm*: saying the opposite of one's true feelings for humor or insult

(67) *coherent*: the pieces are in an organized and logical manner

(67) *wide-angle view:* an analogy to photography; the big picture; a broad, encompassing view

(67) *zooms in on*: an analogy to photography; gets closer to a small portion of the picture

(68) *distorted*: twisted and bent out of its original shape

(68) *your temporal lobes would light up*: your temporal lobes would begin to process the music from your MP3 player

(68) *twitch:* move with a sudden motion

(68) *dextrous*: skillful with one's hands

(68) *stuck on mental tasks*: unable to solve problems using thinking

(68) *labored*: with difficulty

(70) *biocomputer*: combination of biology and computing, in this case the brain

What kinds of behaviors are controlled by the subcortex?

The Subcortex—At the Core of the (Brain) Matter (pp. 71-74)

(71) *karate chop:* hitting with the side of the hand

(71) *vigilant*: being alert and on the lookout for trouble

(71) *bombards:* to send without stopping

(72) *gemstones*: mineral or petrified material that can be cut and polished for jewelry

(72) *switching station*: place where railroad cars are changed from one track to another; in this case, the meaning is that the thalamus is the area of the brain where information from the senses is routed to the correct part of the cortex

(72) *crossroads*: a place where two or more paths come together

(72) *tear it up*: destroy

(73) *memory-like or dream-like experiences*: experiences that are not real, but seem to be so

(73) *half-truth*: something that appears to be totally true but is not completely so

Does the glandular system affect behavior?

The Endocrine System—Hormones and Behavior (pp. 74-77)

(75) *pea-sized*: very small; the size of a pea

(75) *remnant*: left-over; remains

(75) *coming to light:* being discovered

(76) *bark*: outer layer

(76) *anabolic steroids*: any of a group of synthetic steroid hormones; sometimes used by athletes to temporarily increase muscle mass

(76) *ebb and flow*: decreasing and increasing

(76) *ripe old age*: living a long time until you are old

How do right- and left-handed individuals differ?

Psychology in Action: Handedness—If Your Brain Is Right, What's Left? (pp. 77-80)

(77) ***what's right is right:*** a stated position, usually moral, for which there is no dispute

(77) ***people with two left feet:*** clumsy, uncoordinated people

(77) ***left out:*** not invited; not included

(77) ***right-hand man*** (or woman): the important person near one's side

(77) ***agility:*** the ability to move quickly and with coordination

(79) ***leap to any conclusions:*** make a decision before looking at all the facts

(79) ***foolproof:*** absolute; true

(79) ***breech birth:*** the delivery of a baby rear end first, rather than head first

(80) ***masquerading:*** wearing a mask to cover and disguise one's face

(80) ***lopsided:*** not symmetrical or balanced in shape

(80) ***ambidextrous:*** able to use either the right or left hand equally well

Solutions

RECITE AND REVIEW

How do nerve cells operate and communicate?

1. brain; neurons
2. 100 billion; communication network
3. axons; axon
4. resting potential
5. nerve; impulse
6. resting; ions; ion
7. axon
8. action
9. neural processing
10. receptor; muscles
11. excite
12. little dopamine; much dopamine
13. regulate
14. pain
15. Neural regulators

What are the functions of major parts of the nervous system?

1. neurons; fly
2. axons; permanent
3. myelin; Neurilemma
4. central; brain
5. bodily; involuntary
6. branch; branch
7. nerves; nerves
8. behavior; motor

How do we know how the brain works?

1. electrical; clinical
2. images; activity
3. CT; MRI; PET

How is the brain organized and what do its higher structures do? Why are the brain's association areas important? What happens when they are injured?

1. brain; cortex
2. brain efficiency
3. soft; awkward
4. left; writing
5. right; patterns
6. cutting; hemispheres
7. left; right
8. vision; hearing
9. sensory; motor; complex
10. speech
11. grammar; meaning
12. identify; faces
13. specialization; matter

What kinds of behaviors are controlled by the subcortex?

1. cortex
2. heart; rate
3. higher; sleep
4. coordination
5. reticular formation; attention; adolescence; activating
6. sensory; motives
7. emotion
8. fear; memories
9. neurological

Does the glandular system affect behavior?

1. chemical; hormones
2. master
3. growth; dwarfism
4. sleep
5. metabolism
6. epinephrine; sex
7. testosterone

How do right- and left-handed individuals differ?

1. mixed
2. right-handed; left-handed
3. left; speech
4. Left-handed; masquerade
5. left-handed; right-handed

CONNECTIONS

How do nerve cells operate and communicate? Pages 52-57

1. G.
2. D.
3. E.
4. C.
5. A.
6. F.
7. B.

What are the functions of major parts of the nervous system? Pages 57-60

1. C or B.
2. E.
3. F. or G.
4. A.
5. F. or G.
6. C. or B.
7. D.

How do we know how the brain works? Pages 60-63

1. E.
2. A.
3. D.
4. B.
5. C.

How is the brain organized and what do its higher structures do? Why are the brain's association areas important? What happens when they are injured? Pages 63-71

1. D.
2. G.
3. F.
4. B.
5. C.
6. A.
7. E.

Areas of the Brain

1. C.
2. B.
3. F.
4. A.
5. E.
6. D.

What kinds of behaviors are controlled by the subcortex? Pages 71-74

1. D.
2. E.
3. A.
4. G.
5. I.
6. B.
7. H.
8. F.
9. C.

Does the glandular system affect behavior? Pages 74-77

1. H.
2. C.
3. F.

4. A.	6. B.	8. D.
5. E.	7. G.	

CHECK YOUR MEMORY

How do nerve cells operate and communicate? Pages 52-57

1. F	5. T	9. F
2. T	6. F	10. T
3. F	7. T	11. T
4. T	8. F	12. T

What are the functions of major parts of the nervous system? Pages 57-60

1. F	5. T	9. T
2. T	6. T	10. F
3. T	7. F	11. T
4. F	8. F	

How do we know how the brain works? Pages 60-63

1. F	3. F	5. T
2. T	4. T	

How is the brain organized and what do its higher structures do? Why are the brain's association areas important? What happens when they are injured? Pages 63-71

1. F	11. F	21. T
2. T	12. F	22. F
3. F	13. F	23. F
4. T	14. T	24. F
5. F	15. T	25. T
6. F	16. F	26. T
7. T	17. T	
8. F	18. F	
9. F	19. T	
10. T	20. T	

What kinds of behaviors are controlled by the subcortex? Pages 71-74

1. F	3. F	5. T
2. T	4. F	6. T

7. F   8. T

Does the glandular system affect behavior? Pages 74-77

1. T   4. T   7. T
2. F   5. T   8. T
3. T   6. T   9. F

How do right- and left-handed individuals differ? Pages 77-80

1. F   3. T
2. F   4. F

FINAL SURVEY AND REVIEW

How do nerve cells operate and communicate?

1. neurons; synapses
2. communication network
3. dendrites; soma
4. inactive neuron
5. action; potential
6. threshold; sodium
7. potassium
8. all-or-nothing
9. neural processing
10. neurotransmitters; acetylcholine
11. fire; reducing
12. Parkinson's disease; schizophrenia
13. neuropeptides
14. endorphins
15. low endorphin

What are the functions of major parts of the nervous system?

1. hybrot; fly
2. Nerves; peripheral; central
3. faster; repair
4. central; spinal cord
5. somatic; autonomic
6. sympathetic; parasympathetic
7. spinal; cranial; motor
8. reflex; arc; connector; motor

How do we know how the brain works?

1. dissection; stimulation
2. MRI; PET
3. X-rays; magnetic field; radioactive glucose

How is the brain organized and what do its higher structures do? Why are the brain's association areas important? What happens when they are injured?

1. corticalization; cerebrum
2. less; more
3. soft; signs
4. hemisphere; movements
5. spatial; faces
6. corpus callosum; hemispheres
7. analysis; simultaneously
8. cortex; sensation; speech
9. sensory; motor; combine; language
10. aphasias
11. Broca's; Wernicke's
12. agnosia; facial; agnosia
13. gray; white

What kinds of behaviors are controlled by the subcortex?

1. subcortex
2. medulla
3. pons
4. cerebellum

5. reticular formation; cerebral; cortex
6. thalamus; hypothalamus
7. limbic; reward

8. amygdala; hippocampus
9. learned; experiences

Does the glandular system affect behavior?

1. endocrine; bloodstream
2. pituitary; hypothalamus
3. pituitary; acromegaly

4. melatonin; pineal
5. overactive; underactive
6. adrenal; stress

7. synthetic

How do right- and left-handed individuals differ?

1. Hand; dominance; ambidexterity
2. Ninety; 10

3. right-handed; left; left
4. masquerade; right-handed

5. lateralized

MASTERY TEST

How do right- and left-handed individuals differ?

1. B, p. 59
2. A, p. 63
3. A, p. 67
4. C, p. 55
5. B, p. 55
6. B, p. 68
7. C, p. 53
8. B, p. 67
9. B, p. 72
10. B, p. 52
11. A, p. 55
12. A, p. 53
13. B, p. 58

14. A, p. 68
15. D, p. 73
16. D, p. 59
17. D, p. 72
18. B, p. 62
19. A, p. 75
20. D, p. 64
21. C, p. 71
22. C, p. 67
23. B, p. 60
24. D, p. 68
25. C, p. 75
26. B, p. 72

27. D, p. 60
28. A, p. 61
29. A, p. 79
30. B, p. 54
31. C, p. 56
32. D, p. 55
33. A, p. 64
34. C, p. 57
35. B, p. 66
36. D, p. 70
37. A, p. 74

Child Development

Chapter Overview

Heredity affects personal characteristics, including temperament, and it organizes the human growth sequence. Environmental influences can have especially lasting effects during sensitive periods in development. Prenatal development is affected by diseases, drugs, radiation, or the mother's diet and health. Early perceptual, intellectual, and emotional deprivation seriously hinders cognitive development and may lead to a risk of mental illness and delinquent behaviors. Deliberate enrichment of the environment has a beneficial effect on early development.

Most psychologists accept that heredity and environment are inseparable and interacting forces. A child's developmental level reflects heredity, environment, and the effects of the child's own behavior.

Human newborns have adaptive reflexes, are capable of learning, and have visual preferences, especially for familiar faces. Maturation underlies the orderly sequence of motor, cognitive, language, and emotional development.

Emotional attachment of infants to their caregivers is a critical event in social development. Three types of emotional attachments include secure, insecure-avoidant, and insecure-ambivalent. A child may experience separation anxiety disorder when they are reluctant to leave home, go to school, or sleep over at a friend's home. For optimal development, emotional attachment between infants and their caregivers must occur during the infant's first year. Attachment is further enhanced through contact comfort such as during breast-feeding when the caregiver tenderly holds and touches the infant.

Caregiving styles affect social, emotional, and intellectual development. Optimal caregiving includes proactive involvement, a good fit between the temperaments of parent and child, and responsiveness to a child's needs and signals. Three major parenting styles are authoritarian, permissive, and authoritative (effective). Effective parental discipline tends to emphasize child management techniques, rather than power assertion or withdrawal of love. Parents who use authoritative parenting techniques encourage resiliency in their children, teach them to monitor their emotions, and use positive coping skills.

Language development is based on a biological predisposition, which is augmented by learning. Language acquisition begins with prelanguage communication between parent and child and progresses to telegraphic speech. To help children learn language, caregivers tend to use parentese which is characterized by an inflection of a higher pitched and exaggerated voice and repetition of short and simple sentences.

Jean Piaget theorized that children go through a series of cognitive stages as they develop intellectually. Learning principles provide an alternate explanation, which does not assume that cognitive development occurs in stages. Lev Vygotsky's sociocultural theory says that cognitive gains occur primarily in a child's zone of proximal development. Adults who engage in the scaffolding of a child's intellectual growth also impart cultural values and beliefs to the child.

Responsibility, mutual respect, consistency, love, encouragement, and clear communication are features of effective parenting. Effective parenting also utilizes I-messages and logical consequences when trying to manage children's behaviors and get them to accept responsibility for their actions.

Learning Objectives

1. Define developmental psychology.

2. Explain the basic mechanisms of heredity, include a description of the following terms:

    a. chromosome

    b. DNA

    c. gene

    d. polygenic

    e. dominant trait (gene)

    f. recessive trait (gene)

3. Define the terms *human growth sequence, senescence, temperament, nurture (environment),* and *sensitive period.* Give examples of the different temperaments and briefly discuss the impact that environment has on development and the importance of sensitive periods.

4. Distinguish between congenital and genetic problems and discuss the effects of environmental influences (including tobacco, alcohol, and other drugs) on an unborn child. Include a definition of teratogen and describe the relationship between the blood supplies of the mother and her developing child.

5. Distinguish between medicated and prepared childbirth.

6. Compare, contrast, and give examples of the effects of enrichment and deprivation on development.

7. Explain what is meant by the nature-nurture controversy. Define the term *developmental level* and list the three factors that combine to determine it.

8. Name and describe four adaptive reflexes displayed by neonates.

9. Describe the intellectual capabilities and the sensory preferences of a neonate.

10. Discuss motor development and the concepts of *maturation, cephalocaudal pattern, proximodistal pattern,* and *readiness* (include how readiness is related to toilet training).

11. Describe (in general) the course of emotional development, according to Bridges and Izard.

12. Explain the importance of self-awareness and social referencing in development.

13. Discuss the similarities and differences between imprinting and emotional attachment (including the concept of separation anxiety).

14. Differentiate between the three types of attachment identified by Mary Ainsworth.

15. Describe Harlow's experiment dealing with contact comfort, and state the results of the experiment. Relate his findings to one of the important aspects of breastfeeding.

16. Discuss the effects of day care on a child's sense of security and attachment and the importance of play to a child's development.

17. Discuss the meaning and importance of infant affectional needs, the range of effects of maternal caregiving styles, and the importance of paternal influences on the child.

18. Describe Baumrind's three major styles of parenting, including characteristics of both parents and children in each style.

19. Explain how culture effects child-rearing customs and give a brief description of each of the following child-rearing techniques and their effects on children and children's self-esteem: power assertion, withdrawal of love, management techniques. Include the concepts of the *pampered child syndrome* and *resilence*.

20. List and briefly describe the five stages of language acquisition. Include the term *psycholinguist* as well as briefly discuss the terrible two's, the language dance, and the role of innate factors and learning in acquiring language. Explain how parents communicate with infants before the infants can talk, including the terms *signals*, *turn-taking*, and *parentese*.

21. With regard to Piaget's theory of cognitive development:

    a. explain how a child's intelligence and thinking differ from an adult's (include the concept of *transformation*).

    b. explain the concepts of *assimilation* and *accommodation*.

    c. list (in order) and briefly describe each stage, listing the specific characteristics of each stage.

    d. explain how parents can best guide their child's intellectual development.

    e. evaluate the usefulness of Piaget's theory, including a review of current research on infant cognition.

22. Briefly discuss Vygotsky's sociocultural theory, including how his theory differs from Piaget's theory. Define the terms *zone of proximal development* and *scaffolding*.

The following objective is related to the material in the "Psychology in Action" section of your text.

1. Regarding effective parenting techniques, briefly discuss:

    a. the two key ingredients in effective parenting.

        i) the effects of physical punishment and withdrawal of love and guidelines for their use.
        ii) Dinkmeyer and McKay's four ingredients to positive parent-child
        iii) interactions.
        iv) the elements of effective communication, according to Haim Ginott.
        v) Thomas Gordon's concepts of I-messages and you-messages.

vi) the use of natural and logical consequences.

RECITE AND REVIEW

How do heredity and environment affect development?

Heredity and Environment—The Nurture of Nature: Pages 84-90

1. Developmental psychology is the study of progressive changes in _____ and abilities, from _____ to _____ .

2. The nature-nurture debate concerns the relative contributions to development of heredity (_____) and environment (_____).

3. Hereditary instructions are carried by _____ (deoxyribonucleic acid) in the form of chromosomes and _____ in each cell of the body.

4. Most characteristics are polygenic (influenced by a combination of _____) and reflect the combined effects of dominant and recessive _____ .

5. Heredity organizes the general human growth sequence—the general pattern of _____ _____ from birth to death.

6. Heredity also influences differences in temperament (the physical core of _____). Most infants fall into one of three temperament categories: easy children, _____ children, and slow-to-warm-up children.

7. Environment refers to all _____ conditions that affect development.

8. A variety of sensitive periods (times of increased _____ to environmental influences) exist in development.

9. Prenatal development is subject to _____ influences in the form of diseases, drugs, radiation, or the mother's diet and health.

10. Prenatal damage to the fetus may cause congenital problems, or _____ _____ . In contrast, genetic problems are inherited from one's parents.

11. Fetal alcohol syndrome (_____) is the result of heavy _____ during pregnancy, which causes the infant to have _____ birth weight, a small head, and _____ malformations.

12. Exposure to any form of teratogens such as radiation, _____ , and pesticides during pregnancy is likely to cause _____ .

13. Compared to an adult brain, newborn babies have neurons with _____ dendrites and _____ . These neurons grow rapidly, making millions of connections as the newborns interact with their environment in the first three years.

14. To promote successful pregnancies, mothers should eat _____ food, avoid teratogens, and _____ .

15. Prepared childbirth tends to reduce pain and shorten _____ .

16. Early perceptual, intellectual, and emotional deprivation seriously retards _____ .

17. Poverty greatly increases the likelihood that children will experience various forms of _____ which may impede cognitive development and _____ achievement and increase the risk for mental illness and _____ behavior.

18. Deliberate enrichment of the _____ in infancy and early childhood has a beneficial effect on development.

19. Ultimately, most psychologists accept that _____ and environment are inseparable and interacting forces.

20. A child's developmental level (current state of development) reflects heredity, environment, and the effects of the child's _____ _____ .

What can newborn babies do? What influence does maturation have on early development?

The Newborn Baby—The Basic Model Comes with Options: Pages 90-95

1. The human _____ (newborn) has a number of _____ reflexes, including the grasping, rooting, sucking, and Moro reflexes.

2. Newborns begin to _____ immediately and they imitate adults.

3. Tests in a looking chamber reveal a number of _____ preferences in the newborn. The neonate is drawn to complex, _____ , curved, and brightly-lighted designs.

4. Infants prefer human face patterns, especially _____ _____ . In later infancy, interest in the unfamiliar emerges.

5. Maturation of the body and nervous system underlies the orderly _____ of motor, cognitive, language, and emotional development.

6. While the rate of maturation varies from child to child, the _____ is nearly universal.

7. The development of _____ control (motor development) is cephalocaudal (from head to toe) and proximodistal (from the _____ of the body to the extremities).

8. Many early _____ are subject to the principle of readiness.

9. Emotional development begins with a capacity for _____ excitement. After that the first pleasant and unpleasant emotions develop.

10. Some psychologists believe that basic emotional expressions are _____ and that some appear as early as 2.5 months of age.

11. By two to three months, babies display a social smile when other _____ are nearby.

Of what significance is a child's emotional bond with parents?

Social Development—Baby, I'm Stuck on You: Pages 95-101

1. _____ development refers to the emergence of self-awareness and forming relationships with parents and others.

2. Self-awareness (consciousness of oneself as a person) and _____ referencing (obtaining guidance from others) are elements of early _____ development.

3. For optimal development in human infants, the development of an emotional attachment to their primary _____ is a critical early event that must occur during the _____ (within the first year) of infancy.

4. Infant attachment is reflected by _____ anxiety (distress when infants are away from parents).

5. The quality of attachment can be classified as _____ , insecure-avoidant, or insecure-ambivalent.

6. Having a secure attachment style tends to promote caring, _____ , and understanding in adulthood while having an avoidant attachment style tends to promote _____ toward intimacy and commitment to others. An ambivalent attachment style tends to promote _____ feelings about love and friendship in adulthood.

7. The relationship between quality of attachment and the type of caregiving that is provided appears to be _____ in all cultures.

8. High-quality day care does not _____ children; high-quality care can, in fact, accelerate some areas of development.

9. Some characteristics of high-quality day care include having a _____ number of children per caregiver, trained caregivers, an overall group size of _____ children, and minimal staff turnover.

10. Babies need contact comfort, a reassuring feeling they get from _____ their mother.

11. A child's _____ development is also affected by playing with other children. For example, cooperative _____ is a major step toward participation in social life outside the family.

12. An infant's affectional _____ are every bit as important as more obvious needs for physical care.

How important are parenting styles?

Maternal and Paternal Influences—Life with Mom and Dad: Pages 101-106

1. Caregiving styles (patterns of parental care) have a substantial impact on emotional and intellectual _____ .

2. Maternal influences (the effects _____ have on their children) tend to center on caregiving.

3. Super mothers are mothers who go out of their way to provide _____ experiences and encourage _____ in their children.

4. Optimal caregiving includes proactive maternal _____ , a good fit between the temperaments of parent and child, and responsiveness to a child's needs and _____ .

5. Paternal influences differ in their impact because _____ tend to function as a playmate for the infant.

6. Authoritarian parents enforce rigid _____ and demand strict obedience to _____ .

7. Overly permissive parents give little _____ and don't hold children accountable for their actions.

8. Authoritative (_____) parents supply firm and consistent guidance, combined with love and affection.

9. Caregiving styles among various ethnic groups tend to reflect each culture's _____ and _____ . For example, fathers in Arab-American families tend to be strong authority figures, demanding absolute obedience.

10. Effective child _____ is based on a consistent framework of guidelines for acceptable behavior.

11. Good discipline tends to emphasize child management techniques (especially communication), rather than _____ assertion or withdrawal of _____ .

12. _____ techniques tend to produce the highest levels of self-esteem in children.

13. According to Maggie Mamen, _____ parents who pamper and place few limits on their children's behavior will increase the likelihood of their children becoming _____ , self-indulgent, bullying other children, and engaging in criminal activity.

14. An _____ (effective) style of parenting encourages children to manage their emotions and use _____ coping skills to be _____ (able to bounce back after bad experiences), capable, and successful adults.

How do children acquire language?

Language Development—Fast-Talking Babies: Pages 106-109

1. Language development proceeds from control of _____ , to cooing, then babbling, the use of single words, and then to telegraphic _____ .

2. The patterns of early speech suggest a _____ predisposition to acquire language.

3. Psycholinguists (psychologists who study _____) believe that innate language predispositions are augmented by _____ .

4. Prelanguage communication between parent and child involves shared rhythms, nonverbal _____ , and turn-taking.

5. Parents help children learn language by using distinctive caretaker _____ or parentese.

How do children learn to think?

Cognitive Development—How Do Children Learn to Think? Pages 109-115

1. The intellects of children are _____ abstract than those of adults. Jean Piaget theorized that _____ growth occurs through a combination of assimilation and accommodation.

2. Piaget also held that children go through a fixed series of cognitive _____ . These are: sensorimotor (0-2), preoperational (2-7), _____ operational (7-11), and formal _____ (11-adult).

3. Object permanence (the ability to understand that _____ continue to _____ when they are out of sight) emerges during the _____ stage while conservation (the ability to understand that mass, weight, and volume remain _____ when the shape of objects changes) emerges during the _____ stage.

4. Unlike the preoperational stage of development, when children exhibit _____ , children in the formal operational stage of development are less egocentric and can think _____ , hypothetically, and theoretically.

5. Learning theorists dispute the idea that cognitive development occurs in _____ . Recent studies suggest infants are capable of levels of thinking beyond that observed by _____ .

6. Young children don't seem to understand that the _____ of other people contain different information, beliefs, and thoughts than theirs do. In other words, they have a very simplified theory of _____ .

7. A one-step-ahead strategy that takes into account the child's level of _____ development helps adapt instruction to a child's needs.

8. According to the sociocultural theory of Russian scholar Lev Vygotsky, a child's interactions with others are most likely to aid _____ development if they take place within the child's _____ of proximal _____ .

9. Adults help children learn how to think by scaffolding, or _____ , their attempts to solve problems or discover principles.

10. During their collaborations with adults, children learn important cultural _____ and values.

How do effective parents discipline their children?

Psychology in Action: Effective Parenting—Raising Healthy Children: Pages 115-118

1. Responsibility, mutual _____ , consistency, love, encouragement, and clear _____ are features of effective parenting.

2. When disciplining children, consistent discipline (maintaining a _____ rule of conduct) fosters security and _____ , whereas inconsistent discipline fosters insecurity and _____ .

3. Much misbehavior can be managed by use of I- _____ and by applying _____ and logical consequences to children's behavior.

4. I-messages focus on the _____ , and you-messages focus on children's _____ .

CONNECTIONS

How do heredity and environment affect development? Pages 84-90

1. _____ gene
2. _____ senescence
3. _____ congenital problems
4. _____ heredity
5. _____ sensitive period
6. _____ environment
7. _____ enrichment
8. _____ prenatal period
9. _____ FAS
10. _____ temperament

a. DNA area
b. old age
c. nature
d. nurture
e. conception to birth
f. prenatal alcohol exposure
g. magnified environmental impact
h. personality characteristics
i. "birth defects"
j. stimulating environment

What can newborn babies do? What influence does maturation have on early development? Pages 90-95

1. _____ grasping reflex
2. _____ rooting reflex
3. _____ Moro reflex
4. _____ neonate
5. _____ readiness
6. _____ motor development
7. _____ familiar faces
8. _____ maturation

a. rapid motor learning
b. palm grip
c. startled embrace
d. food search
e. control of muscles and movement
f. newborn infant
g. physical growth
h. preferred pattern

Of what significance is a child's emotional bond with parents? Pages 95-101

1. _____ secure attachment
2. _____ insecure-avoidant
3. _____ contact comfort
4. _____ affectional needs
5. _____ separation anxiety
6. _____ resilient
7. _____ social referencing
8. _____ imprinting
9. _____ cooperative play
10. _____ high-quality day care

a. love and attention
b. social development
c. anxious emotional bond
d. positive emotional bond
e. emotional distress
f. observing reactions of others
g. trained caregivers
h. bouncing back after hardship
i. occurs during bottle or breast-feeding
j. attachment to the first seen object

How important are parenting styles? Pages 101-106

1. _____ super mother
2. _____ Asian-American families
3. _____ optimal caregiving
4. _____ paternal influence
5. _____ management techniques
6. _____ authoritative style
7. _____ authoritarian style
8. _____ permissive style
9. _____ power assertion
10. _____ resilience

a. proactive educational interactions
b. strict obedience
c. caregiving style
d. firm and consistent guidance
e. little guidance
f. playmates
g. bounce back from hardship
h. interdependence
i. produce high self-esteem
j. show of force

How do children acquire language? Pages 106-109

1. _____ biological predisposition
2. _____ cooing
3. _____ Vygotsky
4. _____ babbling
5. _____ telegraphic speech
6. _____ turn-taking
7. _____ Noam Chomsky
8. _____ parentese

a. vowel sounds
b. vowels and consonants
c. caretaker speech
d. "Mama gone."
e. hereditary readiness for language
f. psycholinguists
g. conversational style of communication
h. sociocultural theory

How do children learn to think? How do effective parents discipline their children? Pages 109-118

1. _____ assimilation
2. _____ accommodation
3. _____ sensorimotor stage
4. _____ preoperational stage
5. _____ concrete operations
6. _____ formal operations
7. _____ hothousing
8. _____ scaffolding
9. _____ I-message
10. _____ Piaget

a. changing existing mental patterns
b. egocentricism
c. applying mental patterns
d. abstract principles
e. "Will you kids please stop yelling or go outside and play"
f. conservation
g. object permanence
h. skilled support for learning
i. forced teaching
j. stage theory of cognitive development

CHECK YOUR MEMORY

How do heredity and environment affect development? Pages 84-90

1. Developmental psychology is the study of progressive changes in behavior and abilities during childhood.

   TRUE or FALSE

2. Each cell in the human body (except sperm cells and ova) contains 23 chromosomes.

   TRUE or FALSE

3. The order of organic bases in DNA acts as a genetic code.

   TRUE or FALSE

4. Two brown-eyed parents cannot have a blue-eyed child.

   TRUE or FALSE

5. Identical twins have identical genes.

   TRUE or FALSE

6. More children have a slow-to-warm up temperament than a difficult temperament.

   TRUE or FALSE

7. The sensitive period during which German measles can damage the fetus occurs near the end of pregnancy.

   TRUE or FALSE

8. Teratogens are substances capable of causing birth defects.

TRUE or FALSE

9. An infant damaged by exposure to X-rays during the prenatal period suffers from a genetic problem.

TRUE or FALSE

10. Many drugs can reach the fetus within the intrauterine environment.

TRUE or FALSE

11. To prevent FAS, the best advice to pregnant women is to get plenty of rest, vitamins, and good nutrition.

TRUE or FALSE

12. Prepared childbirth tends to reduce the need for pain medications during birth.

TRUE or FALSE

13. Poverty is associated with retarded emotional and intellectual development.

TRUE or FALSE

14. In animals, enriched environments can actually increase brain size and weight.

TRUE or FALSE

15. Factors that influence developmental levels are heredity, environment, and parental discipline.

TRUE or FALSE

What can newborn babies do? What influence does maturation have on early development? Pages 90-95

1. The Moro reflex helps infants hold onto objects placed in their hands.

TRUE or FALSE

2. As early as 9 weeks of age, infants can imitate actions a full day after seeing them.

TRUE or FALSE

3. Babies begin to show a preference for looking at their mother's face over a stranger's face just a few hours after they are born.

TRUE or FALSE

4. Three-day-old infants prefer to look at simple colored backgrounds, rather than more complex patterns.

TRUE or FALSE

5. After age 2, familiar faces begin to hold great interest for infants.

TRUE or FALSE

6. Most infants learn to stand alone before they begin crawling.

TRUE or FALSE

7. Motor development follows a top-down, center-outward pattern.

   TRUE or FALSE

8. Toilet training should begin soon after a child is 1 year old.

   TRUE or FALSE

9. Anger and fear are the first two emotions to emerge in infancy.

   TRUE or FALSE

10. An infant's social smile appears within one month after birth.

    TRUE or FALSE

Of what significance is a child's emotional bond with parents? Pages 95-101

1. Most infants have to be 15 weeks old before they can recognize themselves on videotape.

   TRUE or FALSE

2. Securely attached infants turn away from mother when she returns after a period of separation.

   TRUE or FALSE

3. *Separation anxiety disorder* is the medical term for homesickness.

   TRUE or FALSE

4. Contact comfort is greatly beneficial to premature babies.

   TRUE or FALSE

5. A small number of children per caregiver is desirable in day care settings.

   TRUE or FALSE

6. Children who spend too much time in poor quality day care tend to be insecure and aggressive.

   TRUE or FALSE

7. The question of when secure attachment occurs is less important than the question of whether it occurs at all.

   TRUE or FALSE

8. Children typically first begin to engage in cooperative play around age 4 or 5.

   TRUE or FALSE

How important are parenting styles? Pages 101-106

1. Early patterns of competence are well established by the time a child reaches age 3.

   TRUE or FALSE

2. The "zoo-keeper" mother provides poor physical, emotional, and intellectual care for her child.

   TRUE or FALSE

3. The goodness of fit between parents and children refers mainly to how compatible their temperaments are.

   TRUE or FALSE

4. Responsive parents are sensitive to a child's feelings, need, rhythms, and signals.

   TRUE or FALSE

5. Fathers typically spend about half their time in caregiving and half playing with the baby.

   TRUE or FALSE

6. Paternal play tends to be more physically arousing for infants than maternal play is.

   TRUE or FALSE

7. Since mothers spend more time caring for infants, mothers are more important than fathers.

   TRUE or FALSE

8. Authoritarian parents view children as having adult-like responsibilities.

   TRUE or FALSE

9. Permissive parents basically give their children the message "Do it because I say so."

   TRUE or FALSE

10. The children of authoritarian parents tend to be independent, assertive, and inquiring.

    TRUE or FALSE

11. Asian cultures tend to be group-oriented and they emphasize interdependence among individuals.

    TRUE or FALSE

12. As a means of child discipline, power assertion refers to rejecting a child.

    TRUE or FALSE

13. Severely punished children tend to be defiant and aggressive.

    TRUE or FALSE

14. An authoritarian style of parenting is most effective since it focuses on pampering the child's every need.

    TRUE or FALSE

15. An authoritarian style of parenting is necessary since encouraging resiliency in children is challenging and difficult for most parents and children.

    TRUE or FALSE

How do children acquire language? Pages 106-109

1. The single-word stage begins at about 6 months of age.

   TRUE or FALSE

2. "That red ball mine," is an example of telegraphic speech.

   TRUE or FALSE

3. Noam Chomsky believes that basic language patterns are innate.

   TRUE or FALSE

4. The "terrible twos" refers to the two-word stage of language development.

   TRUE or FALSE

5. The "I'm going to get you" game is an example of prelanguage communication.

   TRUE or FALSE

6. Parentese is spoken in higher pitched tones with a musical inflection.

   TRUE or FALSE

7. Parentese language used by mothers and fathers to talk to their infants does more harm than good to their infants' language development.

   TRUE or FALSE

How do children learn to think? Pages 109-115

1. According to Piaget, children first learn to make transformations at about age 3.

   TRUE or FALSE

2. Assimilation refers to modifying existing ideas to fit new situations or demands.

   TRUE or FALSE

3. Cognitive development during the sensorimotor stage is mostly nonverbal.

   TRUE or FALSE

4. Reversibility of thoughts and the concept of conservation both appear during the concrete operational stage.

   TRUE or FALSE

5. Three-year-old children are surprisingly good at understanding what other people are thinking.

    TRUE or FALSE

6. An understanding of hypothetical possibilities develops during the preoperational stage.

    TRUE or FALSE

7. Playing peekaboo is a good way to establish the permanence of objects for children in the sensorimotor stage.

    TRUE or FALSE

8. Contrary to what Piaget observed, infants as young as 3 months of age show signs of object permanence.

    TRUE or FALSE

9. Hothousing or the forced teaching of children to learn reading or math is encouraged to accelerate their intellectual development and to prevent apathy.

    TRUE or FALSE

10. A criticism of Piaget's theory of cognitive development is that he underestimated the impact of cultural influence on children's mental development.

    TRUE or FALSE

11. Vygotsky's key insight was that children's thinking develops through dialogues with more capable persons.

    TRUE or FALSE

12. Learning experiences are most helpful when they take place outside of a child's zone of proximal development.

    TRUE or FALSE

13. Scaffolding is like setting up temporary bridges to help children move into new mental territory.

    TRUE or FALSE

14. Vygotsky empasized that children use adults to learn about their culture and society.

    TRUE or FALSE

How do effective parents discipline their children? Pages 115-118

1. Consistency of child discipline is more important than whether limits on children's behavior are strict or lenient.

    TRUE or FALSE

2. Encouragement means giving recognition for effort and improvement.

    TRUE or FALSE

3. Logical consequences should be stated as you-messages.

   TRUE or FALSE

FINAL SURVEY AND REVIEW

How do heredity and environment affect development?

Heredity and Environment—The Nurture of Nature: Pages 84-90

1. _____ psychology is the study of _____ changes in behavior and abilities, from birth to death.

2. The nature-nurture debate concerns the relative contributions to development of _____ (nature) and _____ (nurture).

3. Hereditary instructions are carried by DNA (_____ acid) in the form of _____ ("colored bodies") and genes in every cell.

4. Most characteristics are _____ (influenced by a combination of genes) and reflect the combined effects of dominant and _____ genes.

5. Heredity organizes the general human _____ _____ —the general pattern of physical development from birth to death.

6. Heredity also influences differences in _____ (the physical foundations of personality). Most infants fall into one of three categories: _____ children, difficult children, and _____ children.

7. _____ refers to all external conditions that affect development.

8. A variety of _____ _____ (times of increased sensitivity to environmental influences) exist in development.

9. During pregnancy, _____ development is subject to environmental influences in the form of diseases, _____ , _____ , or the mother's diet and health.

10. Prenatal damage to the fetus may cause _____ problems, or birth defects. In contrast, _____ problems are inherited from one's parents.

11. _____ (FAS) is the result of heavy drinking during _____ , which causes the infant to have _____ birth weight, a small head, and _____ malformations.

12. Exposure to any form of _____ such as radiation, lead, and pesticides during pregnancy will likely cause _____ .

13. Compared to an adult brain, newborn babies have neurons with fewer _____ and _____ . These neurons grow rapidly, making millions of connections as the newborns interact with their environment in the first three years.

14. To promote successful pregnancies, mothers should eat _____ food, avoid _____ , and exercise.

15. _____ childbirth tends to reduce _____ and shorten labor.

16. Early perceptual and intellectual _____ seriously retards development.

17. _____ greatly increases the likelihood that children will experience various forms of deprivation which may impede _____ development and educational achievement and increase a risk for _____ illness and _____ behavior.

18. Deliberate _____ of the environment in infancy and early childhood has a beneficial effect on development.

19. Ultimately, most psychologists accept that heredity and environment are inseparable and _____ forces.

20. A child's _____ _____ (current state of development) reflects heredity, environment, and the effects of the child's own behavior.

What can newborn babies do? What influence does maturation have on early development?

The Newborn Baby—The Basic Model Comes with Options: Pages 90-95

1. The human neonate (newborn) has a number of adaptive reflexes, including the _____ , rooting, _____ , and _____ reflexes.

2. Newborns begin to learn immediately and they _____ (mimic) adults.

3. Tests in a _____ _____ reveal a number of visual preferences in the newborn. The neonate is drawn to _____ , circular, curved, and brightly-lighted designs.

4. Infants prefer _____ _____ patterns, especially familiar faces. In later infancy, interest in the _____ emerges.

5. _____ of the body and _____ _____ underlies the orderly sequence of motor, cognitive, language, and emotional development.

6. While the _____ of maturation varies from child to child, the order is nearly _____ .

7. The development of muscular control (_____ development) is _____ (from head to toe) and _____ (from the center of the body to the extremities.)

8. Many early skills are subject to the principle of _____ .

9. Emotional development begins with a capacity for general _____ . After that the first _____ and _____ emotions develop.

10. Some psychologists believe that basic _____ expressions are innate and that some appear as early as 2.5 _____ of age.

11. By age 10 months, babies display a _____ smile when other people are nearby.

Of what significance is a child's emotional bond with parents?

Social Development—Baby, I'm Stuck on You: Pages 95-101

1. Social development refers to the emergence of self- _____ and forming _____ with parents and others.

2. _____ (consciousness of oneself as a person) and social _____ (obtaining guidance from others) are elements of early social development.

3. For optimal development in human infants, the development of an emotional attachment to their primary _____ is a critical early event that must occur during the _____ (within the first year) of infancy.

4. Emotional _____ of human infants to their caregivers is a critical early event.

5. Infant attachment is reflected by separation _____ (distress when infants are away from parents).

6. The quality of attachment can be classified as secure, insecure- _____ , or insecure- _____ .

7. Having a _____ attachment style tends to promote caring, supportiveness, and understanding while having an _____ attachment style tends to promote resistance toward intimacy and commitment to others. An _____ attachment style tends to promote mixed feelings about love and friendship.

8. The relationship between quality of attachment and the type of _____ that is provided appears to be _____ in all cultures.

9. _____ day care does not harm children; excellent care can, in fact, _____ some areas of development.

10. Some characteristics of high-quality day care include having a _____ number of children per caregiver, trained caregivers, an overall group size of _____ children, and minimal _____ turnover.

11. Babies need _____ comfort, a reassuring feeling they get from touching their mother.

12. A child's social development is also affected by playing with other children. For example, _____ play is a major step toward participation in social life outside the family.

13. An infant's _____ needs are every bit as important as more obvious needs for physical care.

How important are parenting styles?

Maternal and Paternal Influences—Life with Mom and Dad: Pages 101-106

1. _____ (patterns of parental care) have a substantial impact on emotional and intellectual development.

2. _____ influences (the effects mothers have on their children) tend to center on _____ .

3. _____ are mothers who go out of their way to provide educational experiences and encourage _____ in their children.

4. Optimal caregiving includes _____ maternal involvement, a good fit between the _____ of parent and child, and responsiveness to a child's needs and signals.

5. _____ influences differ in their impact because fathers tend to function as a _____ for the infant.

6. _____ parents enforce rigid rules and demand strict obedience to authority.

7. Overly _____ parents give little guidance and don't hold children accountable for their actions.

8. _____ (effective) parents supply firm and consistent guidance, combined with love and affection.

9. Caregiving styles among various ethnic groups tend to reflect each culture's _____ . For example, fathers in Arab-American families tend to be strong _____ figures, demanding absolute obedience.

10. Effective child discipline is based on consistent parental _____ concerning acceptable behavior.

11. Good discipline tends to emphasize child _____ techniques (especially communication), rather than power _____ or withdrawal of love.

12. Management techniques tend to produce the highest levels of _____ in children.

13. According to Maggie Mamen, permissive parents who _____ and place few limits on their children's behavior will increase the likelihood of their children becoming spoiled, self-indulgent, _____ other children, and engaging in criminal activity.

14. An _____ style of parenting encourages children to manage their emotions and use _____ coping skills to be _____ (able to bounce back after bad experiences), capable, and successful adults.

How do children acquire language?

Language Development—Fast-Talking Babies: Pages 106-109

1. Language development proceeds from control of crying, to _____ , then _____ , the use of single words, and then to _____ speech (two-word sentences).

2. The patterns of early speech suggest a biological _____ to acquire language.

3. _____ (psychologists who study language) believe that innate language predispositions are augmented by learning.

4. _____ communication between parent and child involves shared rhythms, nonverbal signals, and _____ -taking.

5. Parents help children learn language by using distinctive caretaker speech or _____ .

How do children learn to think?

Cognitive Development—How Do Children Learn to Think? Pages 109-115

1. The intellects of children are less _____ than those of adults. Jean Piaget theorized that cognitive growth occurs through a combination of _____ and accommodation.

2. Piaget also held that children go through a fixed series of _____ stages. The stages are: _____ (0-2), _____ (2-7), concrete operational (7-11), and formal operations (11-adult).

3. _____ (the ability to understand that objects continue to exist when they are out of sight) emerges during the _____ stage while _____ (the ability to understand that mass, weight, and volume remain unchanged when the shape of objects changes) emerges during the _____ stage.

4. Unlike the preoperational stage of development, when children exhibit egocentrism, children in the _____ stage of development are less egocentric and can think abstractly, hypothetically, and theoretically.

5. _____ theorists dispute the idea that cognitive development occurs in stages. Recent studies suggest infants are capable of levels of _____ beyond that observed by Piaget.

6. Young children don't seem to understand that the _____ of other people contain different information, beliefs, and thoughts than theirs do. In other words, they have a very simplified _____ of _____ .

7. A _____ strategy that takes into account the child's level of cognitive development helps adapt instruction to a child's needs.

8. According to the _____ theory of Russian scholar Lev _____ , a child's interactions with others are most likely to aid cognitive development if they take place within the child's zone of _____ development.

9. Adults help children learn how to think by _____ , or supporting, their attempts to solve problems or discover principles.

10. During their collaborations with others, children learn important _____ beliefs and values.

How do effective parents discipline their children?

Psychology in Action: Effective Parenting—Raising Healthy Children: Pages 115-118

1. Responsibility, mutual respect, _____ , love, _____ , and clear communication are features of effective parenting.

2. When disciplining children, _____ discipline (maintaining a stable rule of conduct) fosters security and _____ , whereas _____ discipline fosters insecurity and unpredictability.

3. Much misbehavior can be managed by use of I-messages and by applying natural and _____ _____ to children's behavior.

4. _____ -messages focus on the behavior, and _____ -messages focus on children's characteristics.

MASTERY TEST

1. The universal patterns of the human growth sequence can be attributed to
   a. recessive genes
   b. environment
   c. polygenic imprinting
   d. heredity

2. Exaggerated or musical voice inflections are characteristic of
   a. prelanguage turn-taking
   b. parentese
   c. telegraphic speech
   d. prompting and expansion

3. The emotion most clearly expressed by newborn infants is
    a. joy
    b. fear
    c. anger
    d. excitement

4. Explaining things abstractly or symbolically to a child becomes most effective during which stage of cognitive development?
    a. postconventional
    b. formal operations
    c. preoperational
    d. post-intuitive

5. An infant startled by a loud noise will typically display
    a. a Moro reflex
    b. a rooting reflex
    c. a Meltzoff reflex
    d. an imprinting reflex

6. If one identical twin has a Y chromosome, the other must have a
    a. recessive chromosome
    b. sex-linked trait
    c. dominant chromosome
    d. Y chromosome

7. Ideas about Piaget's stages and the cognitive abilities of infants are challenged by infants' reactions to
    a. hypothetical possibilities
    b. impossible events
    c. turn-taking
    d. separation anxiety

8. The type of play that is observed first in most children is called
    a. selective play
    b. secure play
    c. solitary play
    d. social play

9. The largest percentage of children display what type of temperament?
    a. easy
    b. difficult
    c. slow-to-warm-up
    d. generic

10. Which of the following is a congenital problem?
    a. FAS
    b. sickle-cell anemia
    c. hemophilia
    d. muscular dystrophy

11. A child might begin to question the idea that Santa Claus's sack could carry millions of toys when the child has grasped the concept of
    a. assimilation
    b. egocentricism
    c. conservation
    d. reversibility of permanence

12. In most areas of development, heredity and environment are
    a. independent
    b. interacting
    c. conflicting
    d. responsible for temperament

13. Children who grow up in poverty run a high risk of
    a. insecure scaffolding
    b. hospitalism
    c. deprivation
    d. colostrum

14. By definition, a trait that is controlled by a dominant gene cannot be
    a. eugenic
    b. hereditary
    c. carried by DNA
    d. polygenic

15. _____ development proceeds head-down and center-outward.
    a. Cognitive
    b. Motor
    c. Prelanguage
    d. Preoperational

16. You could test for _____ by videotaping a child and then letting the child see the video on television.
    a. social referencing
    b. self-awareness
    c. the quality of attachment
    d. the degree of readiness

17. After age 2, infants become much more interested in
    a. bonding
    b. nonverbal communication
    c. familiar voices
    d. unfamiliar faces

18. According to Piaget, one of the major developments during the sensorimotor stage is emergence of the concept of
    a. assimilation
    b. accommodation
    c. object permanence
    d. transformation

19. Poverty is to deprivation as early childhood stimulation is to
    a. imprinting
    b. enrichment
    c. responsiveness
    d. assimilation

20. Which principle is most relevant to the timing of toilet training?
    a. readiness
    b. sensitive periods
    c. nonverbal signals
    d. assimilation

21. High self-esteem is most often a product of what style of child discipline?
    a. power assertion
    b. child management
    c. withdrawal of love
    d. the natural consequences method

22. Consonants first enter a child's language when the child begins
    a. babbling
    b. cooing
    c. the single word stage
    d. turn-taking

23. Physically arousing play is typically an element of
    a. the zoo-keeper mother's caregiving style
    b. paternal influences
    c. proactive maternal involvement
    d. secure attachment

24. Insecure attachment is revealed by
    a. separation anxiety
    b. seeking to be near the mother after separation
    c. turning away from the mother after separation
    d. social referencing

25. A healthy balance between the rights of parents and their children is characteristic of
    a. authoritarian parenting
    b. permissive parenting
    c. authoritative parenting
    d. consistent parenting

26. Studies of infant imitation
    a. are conducted in a looking chamber
    b. confirm that infants mimic adult facial gestures
    c. show that self-awareness precedes imitation
    d. are used to assess the quality of infant attachment

27. Threatening, accusing, bossing, and lecturing children is most characteristic of
    a. PET
    b. you-messages
    c. applying natural consequences
    d. management techniques

28. Three-year-old Sheila is unable to fully understand what other people think and feel, because at her age she has a very limited
    a. attachment to others
    b. theory of mind
    c. sensorimotor capacity
    d. zone of proximal development

29. According to Vygotsky, children learn important cultural beliefs and values when adults provide _____ to help them gain new ideas and skills.
    a. scaffolding
    b. proactive nurturance
    c. imprinting stimuli
    d. parentese

30. One thing that all forms of effective child discipline have in common is that they
    a. are consistent
    b. make use of punishment
    c. involve temporary withdrawal of love
    d. emphasize you-messages

31. The intellectual development of babies begins as young as _____ when they start to pay more attention to a person who is looking directly at them than someone who is looking away from them.
    a. two to five days old
    b. two to five weeks old
    c. two to five months old
    d. two years old

32. Children who are securely attached to their parents tend to _____ when they interact with others.
    a. be anxious and remote
    b. be resilient and curious
    c. dislike direct physical contact
    d. lack social skills

33. Which statement correctly states the relationship between sensitive caregiving and secure attachment when applied cross-culturally?
    a. There is no relationship between the two variables in any culture.
    b. A minimal relationship can be found only in the United States.
    c. A relationship between the two variables can be found in all cultures.
    d. A relationship between the two variables can be found in all cultures if both biological parents raised the child.

34. To provide optimal care for children, caregivers
    a. must get involved proactively in educating children
    b. must respond to children's feelings and needs
    c. and children's temperaments should match closely to each other
    d. all the preceding

35. Parents who use a(an) _____ form of parenting tend to teach their children to manage and control their emotions and to use positive coping skills.
    a. authoritative
    b. authoritarian
    c. overly permissive
    d. power assertion

36. Which of the following may involve an increased risk for children who live in poverty?
    a. cognitive development
    b. mental illness
    c. delinquent behavior
    d. all the preceding

37. Cindy wishes to empower her children and make them feel special by giving them everything they need and want. Furthermore, she does not impose limits on their behaviors. According to Mamen, if Cindy continues to pamper her children, she may foster _____ in her children.
    a. self-control
    b. self-indulgence
    c. selflessness
    d. both A and C

LANGUAGE DEVELOPMENT - Child Development

Word roots

Ego is the Latin pronoun that means "I." When combined with other word roots, it refers to the self. Freud used this Latin word to refer to one of the three parts of the personality, which he named id, ego, and superego. Other examples of the use of this root word include egocentric, ego ideal; and these uses will be found in later chapters.

How do heredity and environment affect development?

Preview: A Star is Born—Here's Amy! (p. 84)

(84) *pudgy*: short and plump

(84) *stubby*: short, blunt, and thick like a stub

Heredity and Environment—The Nurture of Nature (p. 84-90)

(84) *the womb to the tomb*: from birth to death

(84) *nature-nurture debate*: the influence of heredity versus environment

(84) *room left over to spare*: extra capacity

(84) *expressed*: shown

(84) *universal*: found everywhere, among all cultures

(85) *susceptibility*: inability to resist

(85) *Score one for those who favor heredity*: those people who favor heredity as the most important factor are correct in this case

(85) *distractibility*: ability to have one's attention drawn in different directions

(86) *restrained*: held back from responding

(86) *cave dwellers*: people who live in caves

(86) *gangsta rapper*: someone who performs the type of music known as "gangsta rap"

(86) *Upper Paleolithic*: late Stone Age (30,000 years ago), characterized by use of rough stone tools

(87) *measles*: a contagious viral disease characterized by red circular spots on the skin

(87) *caregiver*: a parent or significant other person who cares for a child

(87) *syphilis*: a contagious disease transmitted by sexual intercourse or other intimate contact

(87) *HIV*: human immunodeficiency virus; precursor to AIDS

(87) *hemophilia*: a condition that characterizes excessive bleeding due to inadequate coagulation of the blood

(87) *albinism*: hereditary condition that causes a lack of pigment (color) in skin, hair, and eyes (eyes are pink)

(87) *go up in smoke*: disappear

(87) *PCBs*: polychlorinated biphenyls, often found in soil and are suspected cancer-causing agents

(88) *anesthetized*: put into a state of sleep or altered consciousness with a drug

(88) *blooming and pruning*: changing the structure of the neural network

(89) *discord*: disagreement or argument between people

(89) *IQs*: a measure of intelligence

(90) *childproof*: removing items that a child might damage or destroy or that might be dangerous to the child

What can newborn babies do? What influence does maturation have on early development?

The Newborn Baby—The Basic Model Comes with Options (pp. 90-95)

(90) *unfolds*: develops

(91) *inert*: does not have the ability to respond

(91) *trapeze artist*: a performer on the "trapeze," a bar suspended in the air by two ropes

(91) *interplay*: to influence one another

(91) *mimics*: people who copy the actions of others

(91) *soak up*: gather in information, similar to how a sponge gathers in water

(93) *wobbly crawl*: unsteady movement on hands and knees

(93) *tune*: adjust behavior according to each learned skill

(94) *milestones*: significant points in development

(94) *wet look*: reference to a style in which the hair appears to be damp; Coon is using the phrase humorously

(94) *hard-wired*: coded into our genes

(94) *baby buggy*: baby carriage

(94) *dazzling speed*: great speed

Of what significance is a child's emotional bond with parents?

Social Development—Baby, I'm Stuck on You (pp. 95-101)

(95) ***Baby I'm Stuck on You***: a song title used by Coon to indicate extreme fondness

(96) ***incubator***: a machine in which eggs (e.g., chickens and ducks) are kept at a controlled temperature to facilitate hatching

(96) ***decoys***: persons or an inanimate objects that have similar characteristics as other live objects that are used to trick live objects into believing the inanimate object is alive and friendly

(96) ***it's not nice to fool Mother Nature***: it doesn't work well to go against natural animal instincts and development

(97) ***cultivate***: to develop or build

(97) ***forlorn***: unhappy and miserable

(97) ***summercamp blues***: slight sadness while away from home

(97) ***home base***: a baseball reference and a place of safety and refuge

(97) ***superglue***: a type of adhesive with extremely tight bonding

(98) ***plight of children***: the crisis condition of children

(98) ***Romanian orphanages***: desperately understaffed orphanages in the country of Romania where the children suffer from too little care and attention

(98) ***new arrival***: the new child in the home

(99) ***body maps***: representation of the body in the brain

(100) ***menagerie***: collection of wild animals kept for exhibition

(100) ***stockade***: a place where prisoners are kept

(100) ***trivial***: of very little importance

(100) ***spoiling***: implying that babies will turn out "bad" because of too much attention

How important are parenting styles?

Maternal and Paternal Influences—Life with Mom and Dad (pp. 101-106)

(101) ***zoo-keeper mother***: mothers who have too many children to look after and have too much to do to be able to interact with each appropriately.

(101) ***optimal***: the best

(101) **peekaboo**: (peek-a-boo) a game to amuse a baby in which the caregiver repeatedly hides his or her face then reveals it again to the baby

(102) **risk-taking**: behaviors that have a potential for harm

(102) **run amok**: behave in a totally wild or undisciplined manner

(103) **interdependence**: when people view themselves as members of their group from which they receive their status and self-worth

(103) **urban areas**: the core or central areas of large cities

(103) **child-rearing**: raising of children

(104) **anti-social**: contrary or hostile to the well-being of society

(104) **model**: the best example of

(105) **at the root of**: the source or origin

(105) **empower**: to give one power or the right to perform or carry out activities

(105) **daunting:** overwhelming, intimidating, or scary

How do children acquire language?

Language Development—Fast-Talking Babies (pp. 106-109)

(106) **and the like**: other similar things

(106) **"This, too, shall pass"**: A Biblical reference meaning "Do not worry, soon this trouble will be over also"

(107) **language dance**: the development of language through the interaction between the child and the caregivers

(107) **What dis?**: What is this?

(107) **getcha**: get you

(107) **gotcha**: got you

(108) **Nein! Nein! Basta! Basta! Not! Dude!**: ways of saying "no" in different languages. The word "Dude" is an American slang expression young people, mostly males, use with each other as a form of greeting or as a reference to each other

(108) **OOOh pobrecito**: Spanish for "Oh, poor baby"

(108) **birdie**: variation of the word bird, often used when talking to children

(108) **wee-wee**: childish expression for needing to urinate

(109) **full flowering of**: full development of

(109) **richer language**: a complex language by which to communicate

How do children learn to think?

Cognitive Development—How Do Children Learn to Think? (pp. 109-115)

(114) *tutors*: people who serve as one-to-one instructors or guides to others

(110) *illustrious*: well known for extraordinary achievement in academia

(110) *panty-girdle*: a woman's elasticized underwear

(111) *exasperatingly selfish*: to be overly selfish

(111) *Santa Clause*: a mythical figure who delivers toys and other presents to children at Christmastime

(112) *inductive reasoning*: to reason from the specific to the general

(112) *deductive reasoning*: to reason from the general to the specific

(112) *drills*: repeatedly instructs and tests a person

(112) *hothousing*: a botanical term meaning to force plants into early blooming, and used here to mean to push children too fast, too early

(112) *Monopoly*: a popular board game in which players attempt to buy and control property and industries

(112) *road map*: a guide for getting from place to place

(114) *tailored*: carefully chosen and fit to certain information

(114) *mental territory*: ways of thinking, reasoning, and problem-solving

(114) *Hockey cards*: cards that show famous hockey players that many children use to trade for the cards they want

(115) *grown-ups*: adults

(115) *decipher*: to translate or break down

How do effective parents discipline their children?

Psychology in Action: Effective Parenting—Raising Healthy Children (pp. 115-118)

(116) *Brussels sprouts*: one of the small edible heads on the stalks of plants closely related to the cabbage

Solutions

RECITE AND REVIEW

How do heredity and environment affect development?

1. behavior; birth; death
2. nature; nurture
3. DNA; genes
4. genes; genes
5. physical; development
6. personality; difficult
7. external
8. sensitivity
9. environmental
10. birth; defects
11. FAS; drinking; low; facial
12. lead; birth defects
13. fewer; synapses
14. nutritious; exercise
15. labor
16. development
17. deprivation; educational; delinquent
18. environment
19. heredity
20. own; behavior

What can newborn babies do? What influence does maturation have on early development?

1. neonate; adaptive
2. learn
3. visual; circular
4. familiar; faces
5. sequence
6. order
7. muscular; center
8. skills
9. general
10. innate
11. people

Of what significance is a child's emotional bond with parents?

1. Social
2. social; social
3. caregivers; sensitive period
4. separation
5. secure
6. supportiveness; resistance; mixed
7. universal
8. harm
9. small; 12 to 15
10. touching
11. social; play
12. needs

How important are parenting styles?

1. development
2. mothers
3. educational; initiative
4. involvement; preferences
5. fathers
6. rules; authority
7. guidance
8. effective
9. customs; beliefs
10. discipline
11. power; love
12. Management
13. permissive; spoiled
14. authoritative; positive; resilient

How do children acquire language?

1. crying; speech
2. biological
3. language; learning
4. signals
5. speech

How do children learn to think?

1. less; intellectual
2. stages; concrete; operations
3. objects; exist; sensorimotor; unchanged ; concrete operational
4. egocentrism; abstractly
5. stages; Piaget
6. minds; mind
7. cognitive
8. cognitive; zone; development
9. supporting
10. beliefs

How do effective parents discipline their children?

1. respect; communication
2. stable; stability; unpredictability
3. messages; natural
4. behavior; characteristics

CONNECTIONS

How do heredity and environment affect development? Pages 84-90

1. A.
2. B.
3. I.
4. C.
5. G.
6. D.
7. J.
8. E.
9. F.
10. H.

What can newborn babies do? What influence does maturation have on early development? Pages 90-95

1. B.
2. D.
3. C.
4. F.
5. A.
6. E.
7. H.
8. G.

Of what significance is a child's emotional bond with parents? Pages 95-101

1. D.
2. C.
3. I.
4. A.
5. E.
6. H.
7. F.
8. J.
9. B.
10. G.

How important are parenting styles? Pages 101-106

1. C.
2. H.
3. A.
4. F.
5. I.
6. D.
7. B.
8. E.
9. J.
10. G.

How do children acquire language? Pages 106-109

1. E.
2. A.
3. H.

4. B.
5. D.

6. G.
7. F.

8. C.

How do children learn to think? How do effective parents discipline their children? Pages 109-118

1. C.
2. A.
3. G.
4. B.

5. F.
6. D.
7. I.
8. H.

9. E.
10. J.

CHECK YOUR MEMORY

How do heredity and environment affect development? Pages 84-90

1. F
2. F
3. T
4. F
5. T

6. T
7. F
8. T
9. F
10. T

11. F
12. T
13. T
14. T
15. F

What can newborn babies do? What influence does maturation have on early development? Pages 90-95

1. F
2. F
3. T
4. F

5. F
6. F
7. T
8. F

9. F
10. F

Of what significance is a child's emotional bond with parents? Pages 95-101

1. F
2. F
3. F

4. T
5. T
6. T

7. T
8. T

How important are parenting styles? Pages 101-106

1. T
2. F
3. T
4. T
5. F

6. T
7. F
8. T
9. F
10. F

11. T
12. F
13. T
14. F
15. F

How do children acquire language? Pages 106-109

1. F	4. F	7. F
2. F	5. T	
3. T	6. T	

How do children learn to think? Pages 109-115

1. F	7. T	13. T
2. F	8. T	14. T
3. T	9. F	
4. T	10. T	
5. F	11. T	
6. F	12. F	

How do effective parents discipline their children? Pages 115-118

1. T	2. T	3. F

FINAL SURVEY AND REVIEW

How do heredity and environment affect development?

1. Developmental; progressive
2. heredity; environment
3. deoxyribonucleic; chromosomes
4. polygenic; recessive
5. growth; sequence
6. temperament; easy; slow-to-warm-up
7. Environment
8. sensitive; periods
9. prenatal; drugs; radiation
10. congenital; genetic
11. Fetal alcohol syndrome; pregnancy; low; facial
12. teratogens; birth defects
13. dendrites; synapses
14. nutritious; teratogens
15. Prepared; pain
16. deprivation
17. Poverty; cognitive; mental; delinquent
18. enrichment
19. interacting
20. developmental; level

What can newborn babies do? What influence does maturation have on early development?

1. grasping; sucking; Moro
2. imitate
3. looking; chamber; complex
4. human; face; unfamiliar
5. Maturation; nervous; system
6. rate; universal
7. motor; cephalocaudal; proximodistal
8. readiness
9. excitement; pleasant; unpleasant
10. emotional; months
11. social

Of what significance is a child's emotional bond with parents?

1. awareness; relationships
2. Self-awareness; referencing
3. caregivers; sensitive period
4. attachment
5. anxiety
6. avoidant; ambivalent

7. secure; avoidant; ambivalent
8. caregiving; universal
9. High-quality; accelerate

10. small; 12 to 15; staff
11. contact
12. cooperative

13. affectional

How important are parenting styles?

1. Caregiving styles
2. Maternal; caregiving
3. Super mothers; initiative
4. proactive; temperaments
5. Paternal; playmate
6. Authoritarian

7. permissive
8. Authoritative
9. beliefs; authority
10. guidance
11. management; assertion
12. self-esteem

13. pamper; bullying
14. authoritative; positive; resilient

How do children acquire language?

1. cooing; babbling; telegraphic
2. predisposition

3. Psycholinguists
4. Prelanguage; turn

5. parentese

How do children learn to think?

1. abstract; assimilation
2. cognitive; sensorimotor; preoperational
3. Object permanence; sensorimotor; conservation; concrete operational

4. formal operational
5. Learning; thinking
6. minds; theory; mind
7. one-step-ahead
8. sociocultural; Vygotsky; proximal

9. scaffolding
10. cultural

How do effective parents discipline their children?

1. consistency; encouragement
2. consistent; stability; inconsistent

3. logical; consequences
4. I; you

MASTERY TEST

How do effective parents discipline their children?

1. D, p. 85
2. B, p. 108
3. D, p. 94
4. B, p. 112
5. A, p. 91
6. D, p. 84
7. B, p. 113
8. C, p. 100
9. A, p. 85

10. A, p. 87
11. C, p. 111
12. B, p. 90
13. C, p. 89
14. D, p. 84
15. B, p. 93
16. B, p. 95
17. D, p. 92
18. C, p. 110

19. B, p. 88
20. A, p. 94
21. B, p. 105
22. A, p. 106
23. B, p. 101
24. C, p. 98
25. C, p. 102
26. B, p. 92
27. B, p. 117

28. B, p. 111
29. A, p. 114
30. A, p. 116
31. A, p. 91

32. B, p. 98
33. C, p. 98
34. D, p. 101
35. A, p. 105

36. D, p. 89
37. B, p. 105

From Birth to Death: Life-Span Development

Chapter Overview

Life-span psychologists study continuity and change in behavior, as well as tasks, challenges, milestones, and problems throughout life. According to Erikson, each life stage provokes a different psychosocial dilemma.

Childhood problems such as sleep disturbances, fear of the dark, sibling rivalry, and clinging to mothers are normal processes of growing up. These problems can provide opportunities for children to learn and develop skills. Some major problems in childhood are toilet training, feeding disturbances, speech disturbances, learning disorders, attention-deficit hyperactivity disorder, and conduct disorder. Childhood autism and child abuse are examples of the more severe problems that can occur. Behavior modification programs can reduce an autistic child's maladaptive behaviors. Parents who are under tremendous stress and believe in physical punishment are likely to abuse their children. Both emotional and physical abuse can leave long-lasting emotional scars on children.

Adolescence is culturally defined; puberty is a biological event. Early maturation is beneficial mostly for boys; its effects are mixed for girls. Adolescent identity formation is accelerated by cognitive development and influenced by parents and peer groups. As adolescents prolong their identity explorations into the college years, their emerging adulthood has been extended into their mid 20s.

Moral development bridges childhood, adolescence, and early adulthood. Lawrence Kohlberg believed that moral development occurs in stages. Some psychologists question whether moral development is based only on a sense of justice. Caring for others also appears to be important.

Adult development is marked by events that range from escaping parental dominance in the late teens to a noticeable acceptance of one's lot in life during the 50s. Some people experience a mid-life crisis, but this is not universal. Adjustment to later middle age is sometimes complicated by menopause and the climacteric. Biological aging begins between 25 and 30, but peak performance in specific pursuits may come at any point in life. Intellectual declines due to aging are limited.

Life expectancy can be increased by carefully monitoring one's activity level, one's emotional state, what one consumes, and having parents who are over the age of 75. Two major theories of successful aging are disengagement and activity. Activity theory appears to apply to more people. It seems seniors who have a positive outlook on aging tend to live seven and a half years longer than seniors who have a negative outlook. Ageism is especially damaging to older people.

Impending death and bereavement both produce a series of typical emotional reactions. Rather than hospitalizing individuals who are terminally ill, hospice care has emerged as an alternative approach to provide humane care to these individuals.

Subjective well-being (happiness) is a combination of general life satisfaction and positive emotions. People with extraverted and optimistic personalities tend to be happy. Making progress toward your goals is associated with happiness, especially if the goals express your personal interests and values.

Learning Objectives

1. List the life stages experienced by all people; define the terms *developmental task, developmental milestones*, and *psychosocial dilemma*; and explain, according to Erikson, how the resolution of the psychosocial dilemmas affects a person's adjustment to life.

2. Describe the psychosocial crisis and the possible outcome for each of Erikson's eight life stages. Give approximate age ranges for each stage.

3. Discuss the role of stress in a child's life, how to distinguish a normal response to stress from a more serious problem; and describe how parents can help children cope with common stresses, such as sibling rivalry, rebellion, and divorce. Include the concept of *overprotection*.

4. Give a brief description of the following serious childhood disorders and their possible causes:

    a. enuresis

    b. encopresis

    c. overeating

    d. anorexia nervosa

    e. pica

    f. delayed speech

    g. stuttering

5. Give a brief description of the following serious childhood disorders, including symptoms, causes, and treatments:

    a. learning disorder and dyslexia

    b. ADHD

    c. conduct disorder

    d. childhood autism.

6. Describe the characteristics of the abusive parent and the abused child, conditions likely to foster abuse, and what can be done to prevent child abuse.

7. Define and differentiate between adolescence and puberty and describe the advantages and disadvantages of early and late maturation for males vs. females.

8. Explain what Elkind means by children being hurried into adulthood and how social markers are related to hurried adolescence.

9. With regard to the adolescent search for identity:

    a. explain what that means

    b. explain how being a member of a minority ethnic group influences the identity search

    c. describe the interactions between an adolescent and his/her parents

    d. discuss the importance of imaginary audiences

    e. describe the influence of peer groups on the search for identity

    f. discuss the concept of *emerging adulthood*

10. Regarding moral development:

    a. list (in order) and briefly describe each of Kohlberg's three levels (six stages) of moral development

    b. describe what proportions of the population appear to function at each of Kohlberg's moral development levels

    c. explain Gilligan's argument against Kohlberg's system, and describe the current status of the argument

    d. describe the impact of culture on morality

11. Describe Gould's seven common patterns for adults, the dominant activities and goals for each, and the reasons that marriages are particularly vulnerable during the early 30's. Include a comparison of Gould's theory of adulthood to Erikson's and Levinson's theories (Table 4.4).

12. Describe what a midlife crisis is; explain how the midlife transition is different for women than for men; discuss physical and emotional changes at mid-life, including menopause, andropause, the climacteric, and the empty-nest sydrome; and list Ryff's six elements of well-being in adulthood.

13. Describe biological aging and peak performance; differentiate the concepts *maximum life span and life expectancy*; and list suggestions for increasing life expectancy.

14. Describe the role of a gerontologist and discuss the mental capabilities of older adults, including fluid and crystallized abilities and ways to stay mentally sharp.

15. Compare and contrast the disengagement and activity theories of aging. Include a description of Baltes' strategy of "selective optimization with compensation" and the keys to successful aging.

16. Define *ageism* and describe some of the stereotypes that exist regarding older adults. Include Neurgarten's research that refutes these myths and the four main psychological characteristics of healthy aging found in Vaillant's study.

17. Regarding our emotional reactions toward death:

    a. explain what people fear about death

    b. define thanatologist

c. list and briefly characterize the five emotional reactions typically experienced by people facing death, according to Kubler-Ross

d. explain why knowledge of the reactions to impending death is important

e. describe the function of a hospice

f. describe the general reactions of people who survive a near-death experience (NDE).

18. Discuss the general characteristics of each stage of the bereavement process. Include positive ways to cope with grief.

The following objective is related to the material in the "Psychology in Action" section of your text.

1. Briefly discuss the concept of *subjective well-being*, including the role of life satisfaction and positive/negative emotions, and explain how eight personal factors are related to happiness. Include McGregor's and Little's findings regarding integrity, goals, and happiness.

RECITE AND REVIEW

What are the typical tasks and dilemmas through the life span?

The Cycle of Life—Rocky Road or Garden Path? Pages 122-125

1. Life-span psychologists study continuity and _____ over the life span.

2. They are also interested in _____ milestones, or prominent landmarks in personal development.

3. According to Erik Erikson, each life stage provokes a specific psychosocial _____ .

4. During childhood these are: trust versus mistrust, autonomy versus _____ and doubt, initiative versus _____ , and industry versus _____ .

5. In _____ , identity versus role confusion is the principal dilemma.

6. In young adulthood we face the dilemma of intimacy versus _____ . Later, generativity versus _____ becomes prominent.

7. Old age is a time when the dilemma of integrity versus _____ must be faced.

8. In addition, each life stage requires successful mastery of certain _____ tasks (personal changes required for optimal development).

What are some of the more serious childhood problems?

Problems of childhood—Why Parents Get Gray Hair: Pages 125-129

1. Few children grow up without experiencing some of the normal problems of childhood, including negativism, clinging, specific fears, sleep _____ , general dissatisfaction, regression, sibling _____ , and rebellion.

2. _____ parents or parents in blended families should give children who are coping with _____ extra attention to reduce the risk of developing problems in school, _____ , and depression.

3. Major areas of difficulty in childhood are _____ (including enuresis and encopresis) and _____ disturbances, such as overeating, anorexia nervosa (self-starvation), and pica (eating nonfood substances).

4. Other problems include _____ disturbances (delayed speech, stuttering); _____ disorders, including dyslexia (an inability to read with understanding); and attention-deficit hyperactivity _____ (ADHD).

5. Children suffering from conduct _____ engage in aggressive, destructive, and antisocial behavior.

6. Childhood _____ is a severe problem involving mutism, sensory disturbances, tantrums, and a lack of responsiveness to other people.

7. Some cases of autism are being treated successfully with _____ modification.

Child Abuse—Cycles of Violence: Pages 129-131

1. Child abuse (physically or emotionally _____ a child) is a major problem. Roughly _____ percent of all abused children become abusive adults. Emotional support and therapy can help break the cycle of abuse.

2. Factors that increase the risk of child abuse include parental _____ and the belief in _____ .

3. Abused children are experts in " _____ radar", which leaves them hypersensitive to normal expressions of anger.

4. Parents who inflict _____ abuse by neglect, humiliation, intimidation, or terror may leave long-lasting _____ scars on their children.

5. It is recommended that if parents feel the urge to _____ their children, they should sit down, close their eyes, and vividly _____ themselves in a _____ place.

Why is adolescent development especially challenging?

Adolescence—The Best of Times, the Worst of Times: Pages 132-135

1. Adolescence is a culturally defined _____ status. Puberty is a _____ event.

2. On average, the peak growth spurt during puberty occurs earlier for _____ than for _____ .

3. Early maturation is beneficial mostly for _____ ; its effects are mixed for _____ .

4. Establishing a clear sense of personal identity is a major task of _____ . One danger of _____ maturation is premature identity formation.

5. Many adolescents become self-conscious and preoccupied with imaginary _____ (imagined viewers).

6. Adolescent identity formation is accelerated by cognitive development and influenced by _____ and peer groups (age mates).

7. For many young people in North America a period of emerging adulthood stretches from the late _____ to the _____ .

8. David Elkind believes that adolescents today do not show traditional signs of _____ (visible signs that indicate a person's social status such as a driver's license) and have become self-conscious and preoccupied with imaginary _____ (imagined viewers).

9. By taking pride in their ethnic heritage, teenagers from different ethnic groups have _____ self-esteem, a better self-image, and a stronger ethnic _____ when compared to teens who do not take pride in their ethnic identity.

10. As more people enroll in colleges and delay starting a family, the period of _____ adulthood for adolescents has been pushed back from the late teens to the _____ .

11. Remaining dependent on their parents for economic support, the _____ are individuals who are trapped between adolescence and _____ . They are recognized in England as "Kippers," in Italy as "Mammone," and in Germany as "Nesthocker."

How do we develop morals and values?

Moral Development—Growing a Conscience: Pages 135-137

1. Lawrence Kohlberg theorized that _____ development passes through a series of stages revealed by _____ reasoning about _____ dilemmas.

2. Kohlberg identified preconventional, conventional, and postconventional levels of moral _____ .

3. Some psychologists have questioned whether measures of moral development should be based only on a morality of _____ . Adults appear to base moral choices on either _____ or caring, depending on the situation.

4. _____ can be described as combining justice and caring (reason and emotion) when making the best moral judgment.

What happens psychologically during adulthood?

Challenges of Adulthood—Charting Life's Ups and Downs: Pages 138-141

1. Certain relatively consistent events mark _____ in our society.

2. In order, these are: _____ from parental dominance, leaving the _____ , building a workable life, a crisis of questions, a crisis of urgency, attaining stability, and mellowing.

3. Contrary to popular belief, people who are in their early adulthood seem to experience more _____ feelings than people who are in their early 40s or older. Older adults are more likely to feel _____ , secure, self-confident, and _____ .

4. A midlife crisis affects many people in the 37-41 age range, but this is by no means _____ .

5. A transition period during midlife can provide individuals with opportunities for personal growth or make " _____ corrections" as it allows individuals to _____ their identities, their goals, and prepare for old age.

6. Adjustment to later middle age is sometimes complicated for _____ by menopause and for _____ by andropause or a climacteric.

7. Some doctors are using hormones to treat _____ , which can reduce levels of _____ in men leading to a decrease in sex drive, alertness, bone density, and strength.

8. Experts have questioned the value of using hormone _____ therapy (HRT) for both men and women for treating symptoms of normal _____ processes.

9. When the last child leaves home, women who define themselves as traditional _____ may become _____ (the empty nest syndrome).

10. Well-being at midlife is related to self-acceptance, positive relationships, autonomy, mastery, a _____ in life, and continued personal _____ .

What are some of the psychological challenges of aging?

Aging—Will You Still Need Me When I'm 64? Pages 141-146

1. The elderly are the _____ growing segment of society in North America.

2. Biological _____ begins between 25 and 30, but peak performance in specific pursuits may come at various points throughout life.

3. The length of human lives is limited by the _____ life span. _____ expectancy (the average number of years people live) is much shorter.

4. Intellectual declines associated with aging are limited, at least through one's _____ . This is especially true of individuals who remain mentally _____ .

5. The greatest losses occur for fluid abilities (which require _____ or rapid learning); crystallized abilities (stored up _____ and skills) show much less decline and may actually improve.

6. Maintaining a low-fat diet, exercising daily, eating fruits and vegetables, and not smoking are ways in which one can _____ one's life expectancy between one to _____ years for each factor.

7. Gerontologists (those who study _____) have proposed the disengagement theory of successful _____ . It holds that withdrawal from society is necessary and desirable in old age.

8. The activity theory states that optimal adjustment to aging is tied to continuing _____ and involvement. The activity theory applies to more people than disengagement does.

9. For individuals who are over 50, having a _____ outlook on aging by believing that they do not lose "pep" as they get older may _____ their life expectancy by seven years.

10. Ageism refers to prejudice, discrimination, and stereotyping on the basis of _____ . It affects people of all ages, but is especially damaging to _____ people.

11. People who work in fields that require speed and skill often reach their _____ performance between the ages of 30 and 50. To maintain _____ levels of _____ as they age, individuals should practice their skills on a regular basis.

How do people typically react to death and bereavement?

Death and Dying—The Curtain Falls: Pages 146-149

1. Older people fear the circumstances of _____ more than the fact that it will occur.

2. Typical emotional reactions to impending death are denial, _____ , bargaining, _____ , and acceptance.

3. Near-death _____ (NDEs) frequently result in significant changes in personality, _____ , and life goals.

4. One approach to death is the hospice movement, which is devoted to providing humane care to persons who are _____ .

5. Bereavement also brings forth a typical series of _____ reactions.

6. Initial shock is followed by pangs of _____ . Later, apathy, dejection, and depression may occur. Eventually, grief moves toward _____ , an acceptance of the loss.

7. Grief _____ helps people adapt to their loss and integrate changes into their lives.

8. It is recommended that bereaved individuals grieve at their own pace and _____ their emotions and _____ thoughts after the death of a loved one.

What factors contribute most to a happy and fulfilling life?

Psychology in Action: Well-Being and Happiness—What Makes a Good Life? Pages 150-152

1. Subjective well-being (_____) occurs when _____ emotions outnumber _____ emotions and a person is satisfied with his or her life.

2. Happiness is only mildly related to _____ , education, marriage, religion, age, sex, and work. However, people who have an extraverted, optimistic _____ do tend to be happier.

3. People who are making progress toward their long-term _____ tend to be happier. This is especially true if the _____ have integrity and personal meaning.

CONNECTIONS

What are the typical tasks and dilemmas through the life span? Pages 122-125

1. _____ Erik Erikson
2. _____ optimal development
3. _____ developmental milestones
4. _____ trust versus mistrust
5. _____ developmental task
6. _____ autonomy versus shame and doubt
7. _____ initiative versus guilt
8. _____ industry versus inferiority

a. received praise versus lacking support
b. self-control versus inadequacy
c. love versus insecurity
d. freedom to choose versus criticism
e. psychosocial dilemmas
f. mastered developmental tasks
g. notable events or marker
h. skills to be attained

What are some of the more serious childhood problems? Pages 125-131

1.	_____ overprotection	a.	hyperactivity
2.	_____ regression	b.	"soiling"
3.	_____ enuresis	c.	reading disorder
4.	_____ encopresis	d.	shaken baby
5.	_____ pica	e.	"smother love"
6.	_____ dyslexia	f.	bed-wetting
7.	_____ echolalia	g.	eating disorder
8.	_____ ADHD	h.	infantile behavior
9.	_____ child abuse	i.	autism symptom
10.	_____ emotional abuse	j.	humiliate and intimidate

Why is adolescent development especially challenging? Pages 132-135

1.	_____ adolescence	a.	status or role clue
2.	_____ puberty	b.	sexual maturation
3.	_____ social marker	c.	extended into the mid 20s
4.	_____ imaginary audiences	d.	cultural status
5.	_____ twixters	e.	imagined viewers
6.	_____ early-maturing boys	f.	teen's task
7.	_____ emerging adulthood	g.	dominant, self-assured, and popular
8.	_____ identity	h.	trapped in the "maturity gap"

How do we develop morals and values? Pages 135-137

1.	_____ Carol Gilligan	a.	moral dilemma of justice
2.	_____ Lawrence Kohlberg	b.	social contract/individual principles
3.	_____ preconventional	c.	good boy or girl/respect for authority
4.	_____ conventional	d.	avoiding punishment or seeking pleasure
5.	_____ postconventional	e.	focused on the ethics of caring

What happens psychologically during adulthood? Pages 138-141

1. _____ "empty nest"
2. _____ transition period
3. _____ menopause
4. _____ andropause
5. _____ midlife crisis
6. _____ Roger Gould

a. life change
b. reduced testosterone levels
c. adult development
d. children leave
e. end of menstruation
f. last chance for achievement

What are some of the psychological challenges of aging? Pages 141-146

1. _____ climacteric
2. _____ fluid abilities
3. _____ crystallized abilities
4. _____ compensation and optimization
5. _____ ageism
6. _____ gerontologist
7. _____ an aging myth
8. _____ increased life expectancy

a. common prejudice
b. significant physical change
c. daily exercise and low-fat diet
d. expert on aging
e. successful aging
f. accumulated knowledge
g. non-learned motor activities
h. old people are often placed in hospitals

How do people typically react to death and bereavement? What factors contribute most to a happy and fulfilling life? Pages 146-152

1. _____ hospice
2. _____ thanatologist
3. _____ Elizabeth Kübler-Ross
4. _____ NDE
5. _____ bargaining
6. _____ subjective well-being
7. _____ grief
8. _____ resolution

a. intense sorrow
b. expert on death
c. clinical death
d. care for the dying
e. acceptance of loss
f. general life satisfaction
g. five stages of impending death
h. reaction to impending death

CHECK YOUR MEMORY

What are the typical tasks and dilemmas through the life span? Pages 122-125

1. Learning to read in childhood and establishing a vocation as an adult are typical life stages.

   TRUE or FALSE

2. Psychosocial dilemmas occur when a person is in conflict with his or her social world.

   TRUE or FALSE

3. Initiative versus guilt is the first psychosocial dilemma a child faces.

   TRUE or FALSE

4. Answering the question "Who am I?" is a primary task during adolescence.

   TRUE or FALSE

5. Generativity is expressed through taking an interest in the next generation.

   TRUE or FALSE

What are some of the more serious childhood problems? Pages 125-131

1. It is best for parents to protect children from all stressful stimulation, as much as possible.

   TRUE or FALSE

2. Research shows that children from families in which parents stayed together in a bad marriage almost always fared better emotionally than children from families in which parents are divorced.

   TRUE or FALSE

3. Clinging is one of the more serious problems of childhood.

   TRUE or FALSE

4. Supportive and affectionate fathers tend to minimize sibling rivalry.

   TRUE or FALSE

5. Toilet training is typically completed by age 3 or earlier.

   TRUE or FALSE

6. A child who eats mud, buttons, or rubber bands suffers from enuresis nervosa.

   TRUE or FALSE

7. Stuttering is more common among girls than boys.

   TRUE or FALSE

8. Autism can be described as "word blindness."

   TRUE or FALSE

9. ADHD affects 5 times as many boys as girls and may be partly hereditary.

   TRUE or FALSE

10. Eating too much sugar is one of the main causes of hyperactivity in children.

    TRUE or FALSE

11. The first signs of autism often appear in infancy, when autistic children may be extremely aloof and withdrawn.

    TRUE or FALSE

12. Ritalin is used primarily to treat delayed speech.

    TRUE or FALSE

13. Abusive mothers tend to believe that their children are intentionally annoying them.

    TRUE or FALSE

14. One third of abused children become abusive adults.

    TRUE or FALSE

15. Children who have been physically abused are extremely good at detecting the slightest hints of anger in the facial expressions of adults.

    TRUE or FALSE

16. Parents Anonymous is an organization for parents who have autistic children.

    TRUE or FALSE

17. Nearly 25 percent of all American parents have spanked their children with an object.

    TRUE or FALSE

18. Although it is illegal for people to hit other adults, prisoners, and even animals, it is not illegal for American parents to spank their children.

    TRUE or FALSE

19. It is illegal for parents to physically punish their children in any country.

    TRUE or FALSE

Why is adolescent development especially challenging? Pages 132-135

1. The length of adolescence varies in different cultures.

   TRUE or FALSE

2. The average onset of puberty is age 12 for boys and age 14 for girls.

   TRUE or FALSE

3. Early maturation tends to enhance self-image for boys.

   TRUE or FALSE

4. Early-maturing girls tend to date sooner and are more likely to get into trouble.

   TRUE or FALSE

5. Because adolescence is such a turbulent stage for teenagers, permissive parenting techniques remain the best approach for parents to use.

   TRUE or FALSE

6. David Elkind believes that today's adolescents should be "hurried into adulthood" to maximize their potentials.

   TRUE or FALSE

7. By taking pride in their ethnic heritage, teenagers from different ethnic groups have reduced self-esteem, a negative self-image, and a weakened ethnic identity.

   TRUE or FALSE

8. The term *imaginary audience* refers to adolescent peer groups and the influence they have on personal identity.

   TRUE or FALSE

9. Being able to think about hypothetical possibilities helps adolescents in their search for identity.

   TRUE or FALSE

10. Increased conflict with parents tends to occur early in adolescence.

    TRUE or FALSE

11. Early maturation can contribute to adopting a foreclosed identity.

    TRUE or FALSE

12. Twixters are not able to make important decisions in their life, such as a career choice, simply because they are stuck in between childhood and adolescence.

    TRUE or FALSE

How do we develop morals and values? Pages 135-137

1. Lawrence Kohlberg used moral dilemmas to assess children's levels of moral development.
   TRUE or FALSE

2. At the preconventional level, moral decisions are guided by the consequences of actions, such as punishment or pleasure.
   TRUE or FALSE

3. The traditional morality of authority defines moral behavior in the preconventional stage.
   TRUE or FALSE

4. Most adults function at the conventional level of moral reasoning.
   TRUE or FALSE

5. All children will achieve Kohlberg's conventional level of moral development, and approximately 80 percent of all adults will achieve the postconventional level of morality.
   TRUE or FALSE

6. Both men and women may use justice or caring as a basis for making moral judgments.
   TRUE or FALSE

What happens psychologically during adulthood? Pages 138-141

1. According to Gould, building a workable life is the predominant activity between ages 16 to 18.
   TRUE or FALSE

2. A crisis of urgency tends to hit people around the age of 30.
   TRUE or FALSE

3. Maintaining good health is a prominent goal among the elderly.
   TRUE or FALSE

4. Levinson places the midlife transition in the 40-55 age range.
   TRUE or FALSE

5. Only a small minority of the men studied by Levinson experienced any instability or urgency at midlife.
   TRUE or FALSE

6. During the mid-life transition, women are less likely than men to define success in terms of a key event.
   TRUE or FALSE

7. Wealth is one of the primary sources of happiness in adulthood.
   TRUE or FALSE

8. Over half of all women have serious emotional problems during menopause.

   TRUE or FALSE

9. After the climacteric has occurred, men become infertile.

   TRUE or FALSE

10. Andropause is a hormone that can increase women's sex drive, alertness, bone density, and strength.

    TRUE or FALSE

11. Having a sense of purpose in life is one element of well-being during adulthood.

    TRUE or FALSE

What are some of the psychological challenges of aging? Pages 141-146

1. By the year 2020, 1 of every 5 North Americans will be over age 65.

   TRUE or FALSE

2. Peak functioning in most physical capacities occurs between ages 25 and 30.

   TRUE or FALSE

3. The maximum human life span is around 120 years.

   TRUE or FALSE

4. Life expectancy has increased dramatically in the last 200 years.

   TRUE or FALSE

5. Being exposed to secondhand smoke, drinking three alcoholic beverages per day, and having little exercise may reduce one's life expectancy from three to nine years.

   TRUE or FALSE

6. Crystallized abilities are the first to decline as a person ages.

   TRUE or FALSE

7. Perceptual speed declines steadily after age 25.

   TRUE or FALSE

8. People older than 50 who have a positive attitude toward aging live an average of 17 years longer than people with negative attitudes toward aging.

   TRUE or FALSE

9. For many people, successful aging requires a combination of activity and disengagement.

   TRUE or FALSE

10. To remain active and happy in old age, people should use the strategy of selective optimization with compensation by finding ways to continue to perform well on certain tasks to reduce age-related losses.

    TRUE or FALSE

11. Research found that for people over 50, having a positive outlook about aging does not increase their life expectancy.

    TRUE or FALSE

12. Ageism refers to prejudice and discrimination toward the elderly.

    TRUE or FALSE

13. Few elderly persons become senile or suffer from mental decay.

    TRUE or FALSE

How do people typically react to death and bereavement? Pages 146-149

1. Most of the deaths portrayed on television are homicides.

   TRUE or FALSE

2. A living will is not legally binding in most states in the U.S.

   TRUE or FALSE

3. The "Why me" reaction to impending death is an expression of anger.

   TRUE or FALSE

4. Trying to be "good" in order to live longer is characteristic of the denial reaction to impending death.

   TRUE or FALSE

5. It is best to go through all the stages of dying described by Kübler-Ross in the correct order.

   TRUE or FALSE

6. To help reduce the feeling of isolation, Kirsti Dyer suggests that family members or friends should try to be respectful, genuine, aware of nonverbal cues, or just be there for the dying person.

   TRUE or FALSE

7. Medical explanations of NDEs attribute them to brain activities caused by oxygen starvation.

   TRUE or FALSE

8. Hospice care can be provided at home as well as in medical centers.

   TRUE or FALSE

9. Hospice programs are designed to avoid the use of painkilling drugs.

   TRUE or FALSE

10. Bereaved persons should work through their grief as quickly as possible.

    TRUE or FALSE

What factors contribute most to a happy and fulfilling life? Pages 150-152

1. Subjective well-being is primarily a matter of having relatively few negative emotions.

   TRUE or FALSE

2. Subjective well-being is affected by many factors such as our goals, choices, emotions, values, and personality.

   TRUE or FALSE

3. A person who agrees that "The conditions of my life are excellent," would probably score high in life satisfaction.

   TRUE or FALSE

4. Wealthier people are generally happier people.

   TRUE or FALSE

5. Life satisfaction and happiness generally decline with increasing age.

   TRUE or FALSE

6. You are likely to be happy if you are making progress on smaller goals that relate to long-term, life goals.

   TRUE or FALSE

7. Usually, a good life is one that is happy and meaningful.

   TRUE or FALSE

8. Hospice care can be provided at home, as well as in medical centers.

   TRUE or FALSE

9. Hospice programs are designed to avoid the use of painkilling drugs.

   TRUE or FALSE

FINAL SURVEY AND REVIEW

What are the typical tasks and dilemmas through the life span?

The Cycle of Life—Rocky Road or Garden Path? Pages 122-125

1. _____ psychologists study _____ and change from birth to death.

2. They are also interested in developmental _____ , or prominent landmarks in personal development.

3. According to Erik _____ , each life stage provokes a specific _____ dilemma.

4. During childhood these are: _____ versus mistrust, _____ versus shame and doubt, initiative versus guilt, and _____ versus inferiority.

5. In adolescence, _____ versus _____ confusion is the principal dilemma.

6. In young adulthood we face the dilemma of _____ versus isolation. Later, _____ versus stagnation becomes prominent.

7. Old age is a time when the dilemma of _____ versus despair must be faced.

8. In addition, each life stage requires successful mastery of certain developmental _____ (personal changes required for optimal development).

What are some of the more serious childhood problems?

Problems of childhood—Why Parents Get Gray Hair: Pages 125-129

1. Few children grow up without experiencing some of the normal problems of childhood, including _____ , _____ , specific _____ , sleep disturbances, general dissatisfaction, regression, sibling rivalry, and rebellion.

2. _____ _____ or parents in blended families should give _____ who are coping with divorce extra attention to reduce the risk of developing problems in school, drugs, and depression.

3. Major areas of difficulty in childhood are toilet training (including _____ and _____) and feeding disturbances, such as overeating, anorexia nervosa (self-starvation), and _____ (eating nonfood substances).

4. Other problems include speech disturbances (delayed speech, _____); learning disorders, including _____ (an inability to read with understanding); and attention-deficit _____ disorder (ADHD).

5. Children suffering from _____ disorder engage in aggressive, destructive, and antisocial behavior.

6. Childhood autism is a severe problem involving _____ (failure to speak), sensory disturbances, tantrums, and a lack of responsiveness to _____ _____ .

7. Some cases of autism are being treated successfully with behavior _____ .

Child Abuse—Cycles of Violence: Pages 129-131

1. _____ (physically or emotionally harming a child) is a major problem. Roughly 30 percent of all abused children become abusive _____ . Emotional support and therapy can help break the cycle of abuse.

2. Factors that increase the risk of child abuse include parental _____ and the belief in _____ .

3. Abused children are experts in " _____ radar", which leaves them hypersensitive to normal expressions of _____ .

4. Parents who inflict _____ by neglect, humiliation, intimidation, or terror may leave long-lasting emotional scars on their children.

5. It is recommended that if parents feel the urge to _____ their children, they should sit down, close their eyes, and vividly imagine themselves in a _____ place.

Why is adolescent development especially challenging?

Adolescence—The Best of Times, the Worst of Times: Pages 132-135

1. _____ is a culturally defined social status. _____ is a biological event.

2. On average, the peak _____ spurt during _____ occurs earlier for girls than for boys.

3. Early _____ is beneficial mostly for boys; its effects are mixed for girls.

4. Establishing a clear sense of personal _____ is a major task of adolescence. One danger of early maturation is premature _____ formation.

5. Many adolescents become self-conscious and preoccupied with _____ audiences.

6. Adolescent identity formation is accelerated by _____ development and influenced by parents and _____ groups (age mates).

7. For many young people in North America a period of _____ stretches from the late teens to the mid-twenties.

8. David Elkind believes that adolescents today do not show traditional signs of _____ (visible signs that indicate a person's social status such as a driver's license) and have become self-conscious and preoccupied with _____ audiences (imagined viewers).

9. By taking pride in their ethnic heritage, teenagers from different ethnic groups have _____ self-esteem, a better self-image, and a stronger ethnic _____ when compared to teens who do not take pride in their ethnic identity

10. As more people enroll in colleges and delay starting a family, the period of _____ _____ for adolescence has been pushed back from the late teens to the mid 20s.

11. Remaining dependent on their parents for _____ support, the twixters are individuals who are trapped between _____ and _____ . They are recognized in England as "Kippers," in Italy as "Mammone," and in Germany as "Nesthocker."

How do we develop morals and values?

Moral Development—Growing a Conscience: Pages 135-137

1. Lawrence Kohlberg theorized that moral development passes through a series of stages revealed by moral _____ about moral _____ .

2. Kohlberg identified _____ , conventional, and postconventional levels of moral reasoning.

3. Some psychologists have questioned whether measures of moral development should be based only on a morality of justice. Adults appear to base moral choices on either justice or _____ , depending on the _____ .

4. Wisdom can be described as combining _____ and _____ (reason and emotion) when making the best moral judgment.

What happens psychologically during adulthood?

Challenges of Adulthood—Charting Life's Ups and Downs: Pages 138-141

1. Certain relatively _____ events mark adult development in our society.

2. In order these are: escape from parental _____ , leaving the family, building a workable life, a crisis of _____ , a crisis of _____ , attaining stability, and mellowing.

3. Contrary to popular belief, people who are in their early adulthood seem to experience more _____ feelings than people who are in their early 40s or older. _____ adults are more likely to feel happy, secure, self-confident, and at peace.

4. A _____ affects many people in the 37-41 age range, but this is by no means universal.

5. A _____ during midlife can provide individuals with opportunities for personal growth or make "midcourse corrections" as it allows individuals to _____ their identities, their goals, and prepare for old age.

6. Adjustment to later middle age is sometimes complicated for women by menopause and for men by _____ or a climacteric.

7. Some doctors are using hormones to treat _____ , which can reduce levels of _____ in men leading to a decrease in sex drive, alertness, bone density, and strength.

8. Experts have questioned the value of using _____ therapy (HRT) for both men and women for treating symptoms of normal aging.

9. When the last child leaves home, women who define themselves as traditional mothers may become depressed (the _____).

10. Well-being at midlife is related to self- _____ , positive relationships, _____ , mastery, a purpose in life, and continued personal growth.

What are some of the psychological challenges of aging?

Aging—Will You Still Need Me When I'm 64? Pages 141-146

1. The _____ are the fastest growing segment of society in North America.

2. Biological aging begins between 25 and 30, but _____ in specific pursuits may come at various points throughout life.

3. The length of human lives is limited by the maximum _____ . Life _____ (the average number of years people live) is much shorter.

4. _____ declines associated with aging are limited, at least through one's 70s. This is especially true of individuals who remain mentally active.

5. The greatest losses occur for _____ abilities (which require speed or rapid learning); _____ abilities (stored up knowledge and skills) show much less decline and may actually improve.

6. Maintaining a low-fat diet, exercising daily, eating fruits and vegetables, and not smoking are ways in which one can increase one's _____ between one to three years for each factor.

7. _____ (those who study aging) have proposed the _____ theory of successful aging. It holds that withdrawal from society is necessary and desirable in old age.

8. The _____ theory states that optimal adjustment to aging is tied to continuing action and involvement. This theory applies to more people than withdrawal from society does.

9. For individuals who are over 50, having a _____ outlook on aging by believing that they do not lose "pep" as they get older may increase their life expectancy by _____ years.

10. _____ refers to prejudice, discrimination, and stereotyping on the basis of age. It affects people of all ages, but is especially damaging to older people.

11. People who work in fields that require speed and skill often reach their peak performance between the ages of 30 and 50. To maintain high levels of _____ as they age, individuals should practice their skills on a regular basis.

How do people typically react to death and bereavement?

Death and Dying—The Curtain Falls: Pages 146-149

1. Older people fear the _____ of death more than the fact that it will occur.

2. Typical emotional reactions to impending death are _____ , anger, _____ , depression, and acceptance.

3. _____ experiences (NDEs) frequently result in significant changes in personality, values, and life goals.

4. One approach to death is the _____ movement, which is devoted to providing humane care to persons who are dying.

5. _____ also brings forth a typical series of grief reactions.

6. Initial _____ is followed by _____ of grief. Later, apathy, dejection, and _____ may occur. Eventually, grief moves toward resolution, an acceptance of the loss.

7. _____ work helps people adapt to their loss and _____ changes into their lives.

8. It is recommended that bereaved individuals grieve at their own pace and _____ their emotions and _____ thoughts after the death of a loved one.

What factors contribute most to a happy and fulfilling life?

Psychology in Action: Well-Being and Happiness—What Makes a Good Life? Pages 150-152

1. _____ (happiness) occurs when positive emotions outnumber negative emotions and a person is satisfied with his or her life.

2. Happiness is only mildly related to wealth, education, marriage, religion, age, sex, and work. However, people with _____ , optimistic personalities do tend to be happier.

3. People who are making progress toward their long-term goals tend to be happier. This is especially true if the goals have _____ and personal _____ .

4. One approach to death is the _____ movement, which is devoted to providing humane care to persons who are dying.

5. A _____ _____ may help a person ensure that his or her life will not be artificially prolonged during a terminal illness.

MASTERY TEST

1. According to Erikson, a conflict between trust and mistrust is characteristic of
   a. infancy
   b. adolescence
   c. marriage
   d. old age

2. Identity formation during adolescence is aided by
   a. cognitive development
   b. attaining the preoperational stage
   c. emotional bargaining
   d. you-messages from parents

3. Which of the following is not a normal, relatively mild childhood problem?
   a. negativism
   b. clinging
   c. sibling rivalry
   d. delayed speech

4. Infancy, childhood, adolescence, and young adulthood are
   a. developmental tasks
   b. life stages
   c. psychosocial dilemmas
   d. biologically defined social statuses

5. Premature identity formation is one of the risks of early
   a. generativity
   b. preoccupation with imaginary audiences
   c. trust-mistrust resolution
   d. puberty

6. The thought, "It's all a mistake" would most likely occur as part of which reaction to impending death?
   a. anger
   b. freezing up
   c. denial
   d. bargaining

7. The choice of whether to use justice or caring to make moral decisions depends on the
   _____ a person faces.
   a. situation
   b. punishment
   c. level of authority
   d. exchange

8. Which of the following is a correct match?
    a. enuresis—eating disorder
    b. anorexia—speech disturbance
    c. dyslexia—learning disorder
    d. pica—autism

9. According to Erikson, the first dilemma a newborn infant must resolve is
    a. independence versus dependence
    b. initiative versus guilt
    c. trust versus mistrust
    d. attachment versus confusion

10. Seeking approval and upholding law, order, and authority are characteristics of what stage of moral development?
    a. preconventional
    b. conventional
    c. postconventional
    d. postformal

11. An inability to read with understanding defines the problem formally known as
    a. ADHD
    b. dyslexia
    c. NDE
    d. echolalia

12. For both boys and girls, a growth spurt corresponds with _____.
    a. adolescence
    b. puberty
    c. cognitive maturation
    d. less prestige with peers

13. Autonomy, environmental mastery, a purpose in life, and continued personal growth help maintain well-being in old age. This observation supports the _____ theory of successful aging.
    a. disengagement
    b. re-engagement
    c. activity
    d. re-activation

14. Research on well being suggests that a good life is one that combines happiness and
    a. financial success
    b. educational achievement
    c. an introverted personality
    d. achieving meaningful goals

15. According to Erikson, developing a sense of integrity is a special challenge in
    a. adolescence
    b. young adulthood
    c. middle adulthood
    d. late adulthood

16. The event for males that is most comparable to menopause in women is the
    a. andropause
    b. midlife crisis
    c. generativity transition
    d. genophase

17. Grief following bereavement typically begins with _____ and ends with _____.
    a. anger, disengagement
    b. dejection, disengagement
    c. isolation, depression
    d. shock, resolution

18. Physicians typically use the stimulant drug Ritalin to control
    a. encopresis
    b. ADHD
    c. echolalia
    d. anorexia nervosa

19. The smallest number of Levinson's subjects experienced midlife as a(an)
    a. last chance
    b. period of serious decline
    c. time to start over
    d. escape from dominance

20. According to Erikson, a dilemma concerning _____ usually follows one that focuses on identity.
    a. trust
    b. industry
    c. initiative
    d. intimacy

21. Which combination would lead to the highest risk of child abuse?
    a. young parent, high income, child over 3 years
    b. stressed parent, abused as a child
    c. older parent, highly religious, child over 3 years
    d. older parent, uses verbal punishment, median income

22. Foreclosed identity formation is a special risk for
    a. late maturing boys
    b. adolescents
    c. the elementary school years
    d. the preoperational stage

23. Oxygen deprivation in the brain best accounts for which element of a NDE?
    a. the tunnel of light
    b. the pangs of grief
    c. the period of depression
    d. the life review and personality changes

24. People who have many positive emotional experiences and relatively few negative experiences usually rate high in
    a. generativity
    b. moral reasoning
    c. subjective well-being
    d. crystallized abilities

25. Overprotective parenting ignores the fact that _____ is a normal part of life.
    a. rebellion
    b. punishment
    c. rejection
    d. stress

26. Ivar Lovaas has successfully used _____ to treat _____.
    a. Ritalin, echolalia
    b. operant shaping, dyslexia
    c. behavior modification, autism
    d. restricted sugar diets, ADHD

27. Skills that rely on fluid abilities could be expected to show declines beginning in
    a. adolescence
    b. young adulthood
    c. middle adulthood
    d. late adulthood

28. Which of the following is a common myth about old age?
    a. Most elderly persons are isolated and neglected.
    b. A large percentage of the elderly suffer from senility.
    c. A majority of the elderly are dissatisfied with their lives.
    d. All of the preceding are myths.

29. Gould's study of adult development found that a crisis of _____ is common between the ages of 35 and 43.
    a. urgency
    b. questions
    c. dominance
    d. stability

30. With respect to aging, it is least possible to modify which of the following?
    a. life expectancy
    b. crystallized abilities
    c. maximum life span
    d. mental abilities

31. Which of the following statements about physical abuse is true?
    a. It is illegal for teachers to spank a child in several states in America.
    b. It is illegal for parents to physically punish their children in 11 countries.
    c. It is legal for parents to spank their children in the United States.
    d. All the above are true

32. A period of _____ has been extended from the late teens to the mid 20s because young people are _____.
    a. emerging adulthood, prolonging their identity exploration
    b. emerging adolescence, actively exploring their love and worldviews
    c. puberty, immature and irresponsible
    d. none of the above

33. Kohlberg believed that moral development typically begins _____ and continues into adulthood with ___ percent of adults achieving postconventional morality.
    a. at the onset of puberty, 50
    b. in childhood, 20
    c. in early adolescence, 40
    d. in late adolescence, 80

34. Hormone replacement therapy has been used to treat
    a. women who experience menopause
    b. men who experience menopause
    c. men who experience andropause
    d. both women and men who experience menopause and andropause

35. A national survey reported that _____ are more likely to say they often feel happy, truly alive, and peaceful than _____.
    a. young adults, older adults
    b. older adults, young adults
    c. adolescents, older adults
    d. adolescents, young adults

36. _____ are experts at detecting early warning signs of anger and are at risk for developing hypersensitivity to normal expressions of anger in adult relationships.
    a. Children from divorced families
    b. Non-abused children
    c. Abused children
    d. Neglected children

37. Hormone replacement therapy has reduced symptoms caused by menopause and andropause; however, some experts have suggested that it might not be a good idea to treat _____ as a medical problem.
    a. psychological processes
    b. behavioral conditions
    c. biological conditions
    d. normal aging

38. To increase one's life expectancy up to nine years, one should do the following
    a. exercise daily
    b. do not smoke
    c. stay in a happy marriage
    d. all the preceding

39. Seniors' attitudes about aging is positively correlated to their life expectancy. This statement suggests that
    a. a positive outlook on life increases life's expectancy
    b. as people age, their attitude on their life's expectancy increases
    c. aging causes life's expectancy to increase
    d. none of the above

LANGUAGE DEVELOPMENT - From Birth to Death: Life Span Development

Word roots

Autos is the Greek word for "self." Many words in the English language, and several in psychology and other sciences, use this Greek root in combination with other word roots. Examples you will find in this book include autonomic, autonomy, and autokinetic.

What are the typical tasks and dilemmas through the life span?

Preview: The Story of a Lifetime (p. 122)

> (122) *Maya Angelou*: author, poet, historian, musician, songwriter, actress, playwright, film director, and civil rights activist; wrote *I Know Why the Caged Bird Sings* and other works

(122) *Jennifer Lopez*: an American singer and actress

(122) *Tiger Woods*: an American professional golfer

(122) *Hillary Clinton*: New York Senator and wife of former American President Bill Clinton

(122) *Bill Gates*: the CEO of Microsoft computer company

(122) *Oprah Winfrey*: an American actress

(122) *John Glenn*: an American astronaut

(122) *J. K. Rowling*: the author of the Harry Potter series

(122) *road map*: a guide to help you live a happier life

(122) *milestones*: significant points in development

The Cycle of Life—Rocky Road or Garden Path? (pp. 122-125)

(122) *rocky road* or *garden path*: a rocky road symbolizes difficulties in life; a garden path means an easy and pleasant life

(123) *Crayolas*: Brand name for colorful "crayons" that children use for drawing

(123) *dizzying speed*: with rapid, rotating speed

(123) *"entrance into life"*: the idea that life begins when the child starts elementary school, around 6 years old

(123) *turbulent time*: a difficult, rough, and troublesome time

(124) *superficial*: lacking depth, commitment

(124) *dreary*: sad and gloomy

(124) *lived richly*: having lived an active and productive life without regrets

(124) *exact map*: a set of rules to follow

(124) *whirlwind*: very rapid

What are some of the more serious childhood problems?

Problems of Childhood—Why Parents Get Gray Hair (pp. 125-129)

(125) *wiggling*: a squirming motion allowing one to maneuver through small spaces

(125) *smother love*: love that is so close and confining that the person being loved cannot "breathe"

(126) *scrapes*: predicaments or difficult or embarrassing situations

(126) *plumbing the depths...gone down the drain* (his adult interest in *plumbing the depths* of the psyche might have *gone down the drain*): Coon is using a humorous metaphor to suggest that his adult interest in examining the psyche might have totally disappeared

(126) *regressions to more infantile behavior*: behaving like a child

(126) *let off steam*: acting out normally unacceptable behavior by expending excess energy

(126) *serial marriages*: a series of two or more marriages

(126) *bleak*: lacking warm or cheerful qualities

(126) *distraught*: being upset and overwhelmed with sadness

(126) *soiling*: having a bowel movement at night in bed or during the day in clothing, rather than using the bathroom as needed

(127) *chronic*: continuously occurring over a long period of time

(128) *word blindness*: being unable to make out words and therefore being unable to read

(128) *maladaptive*: poorly adjusted

(128) *truancy*: purposely missing or "skipping" school

(129) *parrot back*: repeat or echo back

(129) *head banging*: a self-injurious behavior often done by children with autism; the child repeatedly bangs his or her head against a wall or other solid object

(129) *"spin-out"*: a child with autism may have an underreactive vestibular system in which he/she may perform certain behaviors such as spin him/herself around and around in circles to stimulate this system.

(129) *inept*: unable to perform well in certain situations; not competent

(129) *congenital*: existing at birth

(129) *ingenuity*: a person's own ability and resourcefulness toward solving a problem

Child Abuse—Cycles of Violence (p. 129-131)

(129) *marital discord*: tension and disagreement within a marriage

(130) *corporal punishment*: punishment, such as spanking, inflicted on the body, usually of a child

(130) *legal cures*: using the law to solve social problems

(130) *to curb*: to control, prevent

Why is adolescent development especially challenging?

Adolescence—The Best of Times, the Worst of Times (pp. 132-135)

(132) *"the best of times, the worst of times"*: the opening line of the book, *A Tale of Two Cities*, and used here to reflect the ups and downs of adolescence

(132) *towered over*: being much taller than another

(132) *paint too grim a picture*: describing a situation as holding little hope

(132) *weather adolescence*: get through the adolescent period of life

(133) *flash cards*: cards presented one at a time to children to teach them to read, do math, improve spelling, etc.

(133) **X-rated movies**: of such a nature (usually pornographic) that admission is denied to those under a specified age (usually 17)

(133) **aimless schools**: schools that do not seem to have clear goals for its students

(133) **all grown up with no place to go**: a reference to the fact that some young people may be being pushed too quickly through the adolescent stage of development

(134) **mask**: cover up

(134) **crack down**: suddenly becoming very strict in order to control the child's behavior

(134) **on stage**: standing out, being deliberately different from other people

(134) **jock, prep, brain, hacker, surfer, criminal, cowboy, punk, mod, rapper, druggy:** slang words used to characterize types of students in school settings:

- **jock**: athlete
- **prep**: one who dresses or behaves like a student at a preparatory school (neatly and classically)
- **brain**: very intelligent; "A" student
- **hacker**: one who is very interested in computers
- **surfer**: one who dresses and acts like a person who spends time at the beach surfing
- **criminal**: a person who acts in antisocial ways
- **cowboy**: a person who dresses in traditional Western wear, listens to country music
- **punk**: one who dresses or behaves like a punk rocker (for example, with hair dyed purple or has numerous body piercings)
- **mod**: short for modern; one who is bold in dress, style, behavior
- **rapper**: one interested in rap music
- **druggy**: a person who uses drugs and is involved in the drug culture

(134) **warthog, dervish, gargoyle, aardvark**: words that Coon humorously included with his list of names that students were commonly called in high school; these names are legitimate words, but are probably not used to identify types of students

(134) **cliques**: circle or group held together by common interests or views

(135) **posses**: gangs, but not necessarily gangs who act in antisocial ways

(135) **crews**: similar to gangs, but with less connotation of bad behavior

(135) **duress**: forced compliance

(135) **beyond the void**: past the emptiness that exists in one's future

(135) **forging**: creating

How do we develop morals and values?

Moral Development—Growing a Conscience (pp. 135-137)

(135) **terminal illness**: an illness from which there is no hope of recovery

(137) *yardstick*: an index for measurement

(137) *moral compass*: one's sense of right or wrong that guides behavior

What happens psychologically during adulthood?

Challenges of Adulthood—Charting Life's Ups and Downs (pp. 138-141)

(138) *empirical answers*: solutions to problems based on the use of good data and solution strategies

(138) *settling down*: a period of calmness and reflection

(138) *the die is cast*: decisions made cannot now be changed, and one's fate is now set

(138) *mellowing*: being made gentle and accepting by age or experience

(139) *shop steward*: a person who manages a shop

(139) *dead-end job*: a job offering no hopes of promotion or advancement

(139) *break out*: find a way to leave an uncomfortable or unpleasant situation

(140) *taking stock*: assessing one's situation

(140) *wake-up calls*: events that produce an understanding and recognition of the truth and reality of the situation

(140) *impossible dream*: a goal in life that is very unlikely to be attained

(140) *jet lag*: condition characterized by fatigue and irritability that occurs following long flights through several different time zones

(140) *plummets*: drops rapidly

(140) *gauntlet of modern life*: the difficulties one encounters in living in the present time

What are some of the psychological challenges of aging?

Aging—Will You Still Need Me When I'm 64? (pp. 141-146)

(141) *the graying of America*: a large proportion of Americans are reaching middle age, and their hair may be turning gray—a typical sign of aging

(141) *grandparent boom*: a sudden surge in the number of people who are grandparents

(141) *lucid*: having a clear understanding and awareness

(142) *over the hill*: old, past the prime of life

(142) *infirm*: weak due to health problems

(142) *tallied*: added up

(143) *Those who live by their wit die with their wits*: people who are healthy and maintain a stimulating environment throughout their life tend to retain their intellectual abilities in their 60s

(144) *use it or lose it view*: a belief that if one does not continue to do things they have been accustomed to doing, they will lose the ability to do those activities

(144) *to pass the time*: to do something simply because there is nothing else to do

(145) *dismissal*: being ignored and not taken seriously

(145) *dirty old man*: stereotype of an old man pursuing young women or girls for sexual purposes

(145) *meddling old woman*: stereotype of an older woman interfering in the affairs of others

(145) *senile old fool*: stereotype that an older person is forgetful, childlike, and foolish as a result of old age

(145) *the infirm and demented to aerobic-dancing grandmothers*: a comparison of the weak and the insane grandmothers to the healthy and active grandmothers

(146) *obsolescence*: uselessness; reference to being out of date

How do people typically react to death and bereavement?

Death and Dying—The Curtain Falls (pp. 146-149)

(146) *curtain falls*: life is coming to an end

(147) *futility*: uselessness

(147) *come to terms with*: accept

(147) *freeze up*: become unable to express one's thoughts or feelings

(148) *feverishly*: intensely, very fast

(148) *being of light*: when one is surrounded by a very bright light

(148) *engulfed*: swallowed up or wrapped up

(148) *death can be an excellent yardstick for measuring*: death is used as an index to measure what is important

(148) *unleashes tears and bottled-up feelings of despair*: letting go of feelings of hopelessness, often resulting in expressions of grief.

(148) *sharp pangs of grief*: feelings of intense sadness

(149) *nostalgic*: longing to relive the experience

(149) *full circle in the cycle of life*: from birth to death

What factors contribute most to a happy and fulfilling life?

Psychology in Action: Well-Being and Happiness—What Makes a Good Life? (pp. 150-152)

(150) *marred*: damaged

(150) **dodging life's hard knocks**: avoiding life's more difficult and painful experiences

(151) **tied the knot**: to have gotten married

(151) **crotchety**: stubborn, bad-tempered

(151) **welter**: a massive collection

(151) **"to thine own self be true"**: a Biblical phrase meaning to honor oneself and to stay committed to one's set of values

Solutions

RECITE AND REVIEW

What are the typical tasks and dilemmas through the life span?

1. change
2. developmental
3. dilemma
4. shame; guilt; inferiority
5. adolescence
6. isolation; stagnation
7. despair
8. developmental

What are some of the more serious childhood problems?

1. disturbances; rivalry
2. Single; divorce; drugs
3. toilet training; feeding
4. speech; learning; disorder
5. disorder
6. autism
7. behavior

Child Abuse—Cycles of Violence: Pages 129-131

1. harming; 30
2. stress ; physical punishment
3. rage
4. emotional; emotional
5. strike; imagine; pleasant

Why is adolescent development especially challenging?

1. social; biological
2. girls; boys
3. boys; girls
4. adolescence; early
5. audiences
6. parents
7. teens; mid-twenties
8. social markers; audiences
9. higher; identity
10. emerging; mid 20s
11. twixters; adulthood

How do we develop morals and values?

1. moral; moral; moral
2. reasoning
3. justice; justice
4. Wisdom

What happens psychologically during adulthood?

1. adult development
2. escape; family
3. negative; happy; at peace
4. universal
5. midcourse; reevaluate
6. women; men
7. andropause; testosterone
8. replacement; aging
9. mothers; depressed
10. purpose; growth

What are some of the psychological challenges of aging?

1. fastest
2. aging
3. maximum; Life
4. 70s; active
5. speed; knowledge
6. increase; three
7. aging; aging
8. activity
9. positive; increase

10. age; older   11. peak; high; performance

How do people typically react to death and bereavement?

1. death
2. anger; depression
3. experiences; values
4. dying
5. grief
6. grief; resolution
7. work
8. restrict; upsetting

What factors contribute most to a happy and fulfilling life?

1. happiness; positive; negative
2. wealth; personality
3. goals; goals

CONNECTIONS

What are the typical tasks and dilemmas through the life span? Pages 122-125

1. E.
2. F.
3. G.
4. C.
5. H.
6. B.
7. D.
8. A.

What are some of the more serious childhood problems? Pages 125-131

1. E.
2. H.
3. F.
4. B.
5. G.
6. C.
7. I.
8. A.
9. D.
10. J.

Why is adolescent development especially challenging? Pages 132-135

1. D.
2. B.
3. A.
4. E.
5. H.
6. G.
7. C.
8. F.

How do we develop morals and values? Pages 135-137

1. E.
2. A.
3. D.
4. C.
5. B.

What happens psychologically during adulthood? Pages 138-141

1. D.
2. A.
3. E.
4. B.
5. F.
6. C.

What are some of the psychological challenges of aging? Pages 141-146

1. B.
2. G.
3. F.

4. E.   6. D.   8. C.
5. A.   7. H.

How do people typically react to death and bereavement? What factors contribute most to a happy and fulfilling life? Pages 146-152

1. D.   4. C.   7. A.
2. B.   5. H.   8. E.
3. G.   6. F.

CHECK YOUR MEMORY

What are the typical tasks and dilemmas through the life span? Pages 122-125

1. F   3. F   5. T
2. T   4. T

What are some of the more serious childhood problems? Pages 125-131

1. F   8. F   15. T
2. F   9. T   16. F
3. F   10. F   17. T
4. T   11. T   18. T
5. T   12. F   19. F
6. F   13. T
7. F   14. T

Why is adolescent development especially challenging? Pages 132-135

1. T   5. F   9. T
2. F   6. F   10. T
3. T   7. F   11. T
4. T   8. F   12. F

How do we develop morals and values? Pages 135-137

1. T   3. F   5. F
2. T   4. T   6. T

What happens psychologically during adulthood? Pages 138-141

1. F   4. F   7. F
2. F   5. F   8. F
3. T   6. T   9. F

10. F   11. T

What are some of the psychological challenges of aging? Pages 141-146

1. T	6. F	11. F
2. T	7. T	12. F
3. T	8. F	13. T
4. T	9. T	
5. T	10. T	

How do people typically react to death and bereavement? Pages 146-149

1. T	5. F	9. F
2. T	6. T	10. F
3. T	7. T	
4. F	8. T	

What factors contribute most to a happy and fulfilling life? Pages 150-152

1. F	4. F	7. T
2. T	5. F	8. T
3. T	6. T	9. F

FINAL SURVEY AND REVIEW

What are the typical tasks and dilemmas through the life span?

1. Life-span; continuity
2. milestones
3. Erikson; psychosocial
4. trust; autonomy; industry
5. identity; role
6. intimacy; generativity
7. integrity
8. tasks

What are some of the more serious childhood problems?

1. negativism; clinging; fears
2. Single; parents; children
3. enuresis; encopresis; pica
4. stuttering; dyslexia; hyperactivity
5. conduct
6. mutism; other; people
7. modification

Child Abuse—Cycles of Violence: Pages 129-131

1. Child abuse; adults
2. stress; physical punishment
3. rage; anger
4. emotional abuse
5. strike; pleasant

Why is adolescent development especially challenging?

1. Adolescence; Puberty
2. growth; puberty
3. maturation

4. identity; identity
5. imaginary
6. cognitive; peer
7. emerging adulthood
8. social markers; imaginary
9. higher; identity
10. emerging; adulthood
11. economic; adolescence; adulthood

How do we develop morals and values?

1. reasoning; dilemmas
2. preconventional
3. caring; situation
4. justice; caring

What happens psychologically during adulthood?

1. consistent
2. dominance; questions; urgency
3. negative; Older
4. midlife crisis
5. transition period; reevaluate
6. andropause
7. andropause; testosterone
8. hormone replacement
9. empty nest syndrome
10. acceptance; autonomy

What are some of the psychological challenges of aging?

1. elderly
2. peak performance
3. life span; expectancy
4. Intellectual
5. fluid; crystallized
6. life expectancy
7. Gerontologists; disengagement
8. activity
9. positive; 7
10. Ageism
11. performance

How do people typically react to death and bereavement?

1. circumstances
2. denial; bargaining
3. Near-death
4. hospice
5. Bereavement
6. shock; pangs; depression
7. Grief; integrate
8. restrict; upsetting

What factors contribute most to a happy and fulfilling life?

1. Subjective well being
2. extraverted
3. integrity; meaning
4. hospice
5. living; will

MASTERY TEST

What factors contribute most to a happy and fulfilling life?

1. A, p. 123
2. A, p. 133
3. D, p. 127
4. B, p. 122
5. D, p. 133
6. C, p. 147
7. A, p. 137
8. C, p. 128
9. C, p. 123
10. B, p. 136
11. B, p. 128
12. B, p. 132
13. C, p. 144
14. D, p. 151
15. D, p. 124
16. A, p. 140
17. D, p. 149
18. B, p. 128
19. C, p. 139
20. D, p. 124
21. B, p. 129

22. B, p. 135
23. A, p. 148
24. C, p. 151
25. D, p. 125
26. C, p. 129
27. B, p. 142

28. D, p. 146
29. A, p. 138
30. C, p. 143
31. D, p. 131
32. A, p. 135
33. B, p. 136

34. D, p. 140
35. B, p. 138
36. C, p. 130
37. D, p. 140
38. D, p. 143
39. A, p. 144

Sensation and Reality

Chapter Overview

Sensory systems collect, select, transduce, analyze, and code information from the environment and send it to the brain. Psychophysics is the study of the relationship between physical stimuli and psychological sensations. Both absolute and difference thresholds have been identified for various senses. Subliminal perception occurs, but its impact tends to be weak.

Vision and visual problems can be partly understood by viewing the eyes as optical systems. However, the visual system also analyzes light stimuli to identify patterns and basic visual features. Once visual stimuli are processed in the primary visual cortex, they are further processed by two pathways: the ventral and dorsal pathways. Color sensations are explained by the trichromatic theory (in the retina) and the opponent-process theory (for the rest of the visual system). Common vision problems are myopia, hyperopia, presbyopia, and astigmatism.

The inner ear is a sensory mechanism for transducing sound waves in the air into nerve impulses. The frequency and place theories of hearing explain how sound information is coded. Cochlear implants allow people with nerve deafness to hear human voice again. Other types of deafness are conduction deafness and stimulation deafness (e.g., hunter's notch).

Olfaction is based on receptors that respond to gaseous molecules in the air. The lock-and-key theory and the locations of olfactory receptors activated by different scents explain how various odors are coded. Taste is another chemical sense. A lock-and-key match between dissolved molecules and taste receptors also explains many taste sensations.

The somesthetic, or bodily, senses include the skin senses, the kinesthetic senses, and the vestibular senses. Various forms of motion sickness are related to mismatches between sensory information from the vestibular system, kinesthesis, and vision.

Our awareness of sensory information is altered by sensory adaptation, selective attention, and sensory gating. Pain sensations in particular are affected by anxiety, feelings of control, attention, and the interpretation given to aversive stimuli. Counterirritation can be used to reduce or block an agonizing pain by applying a hot-water bottle to the body.

Learning Objectives

1. Describe how our senses act as a data reduction system and biological transducers and explain the concepts of *perceptual features, feature detectors,* phosphenes, *sensory analysis, sensory coding,* and *sensory localization.*

2. Explain the idea behind the statement: Seeing does not take place in the eyes and differentiate the processes of *sensation and perception.*

3. Define the terms *psychophysics, absolute threshold, difference threshold (and JND), perceptual defense,* and *limen*; explain Weber's law; and describe subliminal perception, including research regarding its effectiveness.

4. Describe hue, saturation, and brightness in terms of their representation in the visual spectrum of electromagnetic radiation.

5. Briefly describe the functions of the lens, the photoreceptors, and the retina. Explain how the eye focuses, the process of accommodation, and the following four vision problems:

   a. hyperopia

   b. myopia

   c. astigmatism

   d. presbyopia.

6. Explain how the different structures in the eye help to control light and send messages to the brain; describe the functions of the rods and cones; explain how the visual area of the brain detects features; and describe the types of agnosia that occur when there is damage to the dorsal pathway and ventral pathways.

7. Explain the relationship between the fovea and visual acuity; describe peripheral vision and the structures responsible for it; and discuss tunnel vision and night vision.

8. Compare and contrast the *trichromatic* and *opponent-process* theories of color vision, including a description of afterimages, simultaneous color contrast, color blindness, color weakness, and the Ishihara Test.

9. Briefly describe the process of dark adaptation including the function of rhodopsin in night vision and night blindness.

10. Explain the stimulus for hearing. Include the terms *compression, rarefaction, frequency,* and *amplitude.*

11. Describe the location and function(s) of the following parts of the ear:

    a. pinna

    b. eardrum (tympanic membrane)

    c. auditory ossicles

    d. oval window

    e. cochlea

    f.   hair cells

    g.   stereocilia

    h.   organ of Corti

12. Describe the frequency theory and the place theory of hearing, the three general types of deafness, and methods of artificial hearing. Include the concepts of *temporary threshold shift* and *tinnitus*.

13. Describe the sense of smell including:

    a.   its nature and how it works

    b.   a description of the condition *anosmia*

    c.   a description of the lock and key theory

    d.   how pheromones work and what they do

14. Describe the sense of taste including:

    a.   its nature and how it works

    b.   the five basic taste sensations

    c.   the tastes to which humans are most and least sensitive

    d.   how the vast number of flavors is explained

    e.   the location and function of the taste buds

    f.   how taste is affected by smell, genetics, and age

15. List the three somesthetic senses and be able to describe the function of each.

16. Describe the five different sensations produced by the skin receptors and why certain areas of the body are more sensitive to touch than other areas and discuss the concepts of *visceral pain, referred pain, somatic pain; warning pain system; reminding pain system; and dynamic touch.*

17. Describe motion sickness and explain how the otolith organs and the semicircular canals of the vestibular system are related to it. Include the sensory conflict theory and space sickness.

18. Describe the three reasons why many sensory events never reach conscious awareness. Include a discussion of the causes of the phantom limb pain, the "runner's high," and acupuncture's ability to relieve pain.

The following objective is related to the material in the "Psychology in Action" section of your text.

1. Discuss factors that influence pain and describe four techniques that can be used to reduce the amount of pain perceived in real life situations.

RECITE AND REVIEW

In general, how do sensory systems function?

General Properties of Sensory Systems—What You See Is What You Get: Pages 156-157

1. Sensory organs transduce physical energies into _____ impulses.

2. The senses act as _____ reduction systems that select, _____ , and code sensory information.

3. A good example of sensory analysis is the identification of basic _____ features in a stimulus pattern.

4. In fact, many sensory systems act as feature _____ .

5. Phosphenes and visual pop-out are examples of feature detection and _____ coding in action.

6. Sensory response can be partially understood in terms of _____ localization in the brain. That is, the area of the brain _____ ultimately determines which type of sensory experience we have.

What are the limits of our sensory sensitivity?

Psychophysics—Life at the Limit: Pages 158-160

1. Psychophysics is the study of _____ stimuli and the _____ they evoke.

2. The _____ amount of physical energy necessary to produce a _____ defines the absolute threshold.

3. For the sense of vision, a person can detect a candle flame from approximately _____ miles away on a clear dark night and for the sense of hearing, a person can detect the ticking of a watch from _____ feet away under quiet conditions.

4. A person's sensitivity to pitch ranges from _____ hertz to 20,000 hertz.

5. The amount of _____ necessary to produce a just noticeable difference (or JND) in a stimulus defines a _____ threshold.

6. In general, the amount of change needed to produce a JND is a constant proportion of the original stimulus _____ . This relationship is known as Weber's _____ .

7. Threatening or anxiety-provoking stimuli may _____ the threshold for recognition, an effect called perceptual _____ .

8. Any stimulus _____ the level of conscious awareness is said to be subliminal.

9. There is evidence that subliminal perception occurs, but subliminal advertising is largely _____ .

How is vision accomplished?

Vision—Catching Some Rays: Pages 160-165

1. The _____ spectrum consists of electromagnetic radiation in a narrow range.

2. The electromagnetic spectrum ranges from violet, with a _____ of 400 nanometers, to red, with a _____ of 700 nanometers.

3. Hue refers to a color's name, which corresponds to its _____ . Saturated or "pure" colors come from a _____ band of wavelengths. Brightness corresponds to the amplitude of light waves.

4. The eye is in some ways like a camera. At its back lies an array of photoreceptors, called _____ and _____ , that make up a light-sensitive layer called the retina.

5. Vision is focused by the _____ of the cornea and lens and by changes in the _____ of the lens, called accommodation.

6. Four common visual defects, correctable with glasses, are myopia (_____), hyperopia (farsightedness), presbyopia (loss of _____), and astigmatism (in which portions of vision are out of focus).

7. The amount of light entering the eye is controlled by movements of the iris, which dilates (_____) and constricts (_____) the pupil.

8. In the retina, the _____ specialize in night vision, black and white reception, and motion detection.

9. The _____ , found exclusively in the fovea and otherwise toward the middle of the eye, specialize in _____ vision, acuity (perception of fine detail), and daylight vision.

10. Individual cells in the visual cortex of the brain act as feature _____ to analyze visual information.

11. After the visual stimulus is processed in the primary visual cortex, further processing of the stimulus occurs via the _____ pathway which determines "what" type of object it is and the _____ pathway which determines "where" the object is in the visual field.

12. The _____ supply much of our peripheral vision. Loss of peripheral vision is called tunnel vision.

How do we perceive colors?

Color Vision—There's More To It Than Meets the Eye: Pages 165-167

1. The rods and cones differ in color _____ . Yellow-green is brightest for cones; blue-green for the rods (although they will see it as colorless).

2. In the _____ , color vision is explained by the trichromatic theory. The theory says that three types of _____ exist, each most sensitive to red, green, or blue.

3. Three types of light-sensitive visual pigments are found in the _____ , each pigment is most sensitive to either red, green, or blue light.

4. Trichromatic theory was unable to explain why people experience _____ or visual sensations that persist after a color stimulus is removed.

5. Beyond the retina, the visual system analyzes colors into _____ messages. According to the opponent-process theory, color information can be coded as either red or green, yellow or blue, and _____ messages.

6. Ultimately, color experiences are constructed in the _____ . This is apparent when you look at a stimulus that produces simultaneous contrast.

7. _____ color blindness is rare, but 8 percent of males and 1 percent of females are red-green color blind or color weak.

8. Color blindness is a sex-linked trait carried on the X (_____) chromosome and passed from mother to son.

9. The Ishihara test is used to detect _____ .

Dark Adaptation—Let There Be Light! Pages 167-170

1. Dark adaptation, an _____ in sensitivity to light, is caused by increased concentrations of visual pigments in the _____ and the _____ .

2. In order for individuals to move from a bright room into a dark room without undergoing dark adaptation, which acquires approximately _____ minutes to see clearly, _____ lights must be on since rods are insensitive to them.

3. Most dark adaptation is the result of increased rhodopsin concentrations in the _____ . Vitamin A deficiencies may cause _____ blindness by impairing the production of rhodopsin.

What are the mechanisms of hearing?

Hearing—Good Vibrations: Pages 170-173

1. Sound waves are the stimulus for hearing. Sound travels as waves of compression (_____) and rarefaction (_____) in the air.

2. The _____ of a sound corresponds to the frequency of sound waves. Loudness corresponds to the amplitude (_____) of sound waves.

3. Sound waves are transduced by the _____ , auditory ossicles, oval window, cochlea, and ultimately, the _____ cells in the organ of Corti.

4. The frequency theory says that the _____ of nerve impulses in the auditory nerves matches the _____ of incoming sounds (up to 4000 hertz).

5. Place theory says that _____ tones register near the base of the cochlea and _____ tones near its tip.

6. Three basic types of deafness are _____ deafness, conduction deafness, and stimulation deafness.

7. Conduction deafness can often be overcome with a hearing aid. _____ deafness can sometimes be alleviated by cochlear implants.

8. Stimulation deafness can be prevented by avoiding excessive exposure to _____ sounds. Sounds above 120 decibels pose an immediate danger to hearing. Two warning signs of stimulation deafness are temporary threshold _____ and tinnitus.

How do the chemical senses operate?

Smell and Taste—The Nose Knows When the Tongue Can't Tell: Pages 173-177

1. Olfaction (_____) and gustation (_____) are chemical senses responsive to airborne or liquefied molecules.

2. Research on anosmia (_____ to detect a single odor) suggests there are receptors for specific odors; approximately _____ different types of receptors are available to produce _____ different combinations of odors that an individual can detect.

3. It is suspected that humans are also sensitive to _____ signals called pheromones, although the evidence remains preliminary. Pheromones may be sensed by the vomeronasal _____ .

4. The lock and key theory partially explains smell. In addition, the _____ of the olfactory receptors in the nose helps identify various scents.

5. The top outside edges of the tongue are responsive to sweet, salty, sour, and _____ tastes. It is suspected that a fifth taste quality called umami also exists.

6. Taste also appears to be based in part on lock-and-key _____ of molecule shapes.

7. Chemical senses of _____ and _____ operate together to allow us to experience the flavor of food.

What are the somesthetic senses and why are they important?

The Somesthetic Senses—Flying by the Seat of Your Pants: Pages 177-180

1. The somesthetic senses include the _____ senses, vestibular senses, and kinesthetic senses (receptors that detect muscle and joint positioning).

2. The skin senses include touch, _____ , pain, cold, and warmth. Sensitivity to each is related to the _____ of receptors found in an area of skin.

3. Distinctions can be made among various types of pain, including visceral pain, somatic pain, referred pain, warning system pain, and _____ system pain.

4. Various forms of motion sickness are related to messages received from the vestibular system, which senses gravity and _____ movement.

5. The otolith organs detect the pull of _____ and rapid head movements.

6. The movement of _____ within the semicircular canals, and the movement of the _____ within each ampulla, detects head movement and positioning.

7. According to sensory conflict theory, motion sickness is caused by a _____ of visual, kinesthetic, and vestibular sensations. Motion sickness can be avoided by minimizing sensory conflict.

Why are we more aware of some sensations than others?

Adaptation, Attention, and Gating—Tuning In and Tuning Out: Pages 180-183

1. Incoming sensations are affected by sensory adaptation (a _____ in the number of nerve impulses sent).

2. Because of physiological nystagmus (involuntary tremors of the eye muscles), vision does not undergo sensory _____ . Physiological nystagmus causes thousands of tiny movements of the _____ muscles to ensure detection of images falling on unfatigued rods and cones.

3. Selective attention (selection and diversion of messages in the brain) and sensory _____ (blocking or alteration of messages flowing toward the brain) also alter sensations.

4. Selective gating of pain messages apparently takes place in the _____ _____ . Gate control theory proposes an explanation for many pain phenomena.

5. "Runner's high," the painkilling effects of the Chinese medical art of acupuncture, and other pain phenomena appear to be explained by the release of a _____ -like chemical in the brain, called beta-endorphin.

6. The brain creates a neuromatrix of one's body to process one's sense of _____ self. This neuromatrix does not recognize that an actual part of the body no longer exists and continues to process nearby sensory stimulations as pain coming from the missing limb.

7. Most amputees have phantom _____ sensations long after losing a limb.

How can pain be reduced in everyday situations?

Psychology in Action: Controlling Pain—This Won't Hurt a Bit: Pages 184-186

1. Pain can be reduced by _____ anxiety and redirecting attention to stimuli other than the pain stimulus.

2. Feeling that you have control over a stimulus tends to _____ the amount of pain you experience.

3. The interpretation placed on a _____ affects how painful it is perceived to be.

4. Sending _____ pain messages to the spinal cord can close the gates to more severe pain. This effect is called counterirritation.

5. _____ is used by pain clinics to reduce people's experiences of _____ by introducing an additional, less intense pain signal such as a mild electrical current to the brain through the fast nerve fiber.

CONNECTIONS

In general, how do sensory systems function? Pages 156-157

1. _____ feature detectors
2. _____ transducer
3. _____ sensory coding
4. _____ data transduction system
5. _____ pop-out
6. _____ phosphenes

a. selects, analyzes, and filters information
b. a system converting a source into another
c. "seeing" stars produced by the retina
d. picking up a stimulus pattern
e. converts features into neural messages
f. detecting a slant among vertical lines

What are the limits of our sensory sensitivity? Pages 158-160

1. _____ Weber's Law
2. _____ psychophysics
3. _____ subliminal perception
4. _____ absolute threshold
5. _____ perceptual defense
6. _____ difference threshold

a. physical stimulus and sensation experienced
b. smallest amount detected
c. detectable change between 2 stimuli
d. increased in constant proportion
e. blocking disturbing stimulus
f. perceived below threshold of consciousness

How is vision accomplished? Pages 160-165

1. _____ ciliary muscle
2. _____ iris
3. _____ cornea
4. _____ blind spot
5. _____ lens
6. _____ fovea
7. _____ retinal veins
8. _____ optic nerve
9. _____ aqueous humor
10. _____ pupil
11. _____ retina

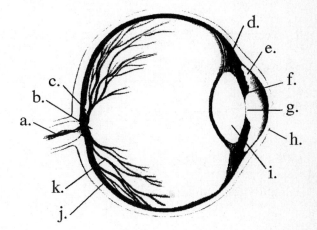

Vision

1. _____ presbyopia
2. _____ cones
3. _____ tunnel vision
4. _____ myopia
5. _____ rods
6. _____ hyperopia
7. _____ visual acuity
8. _____ blind spot

a. sensitive to light
b. sensitive to colors
c. effect of optic nerve
d. nearsightedness
e. farsighted due to aging
f. farsightedness
g. sharpness of images on retina
h. loss of peripheral vision

How do we perceive colors? Pages 165-170

1. _____ afterimages
2. _____ opponent-process theory
3. _____ cause of color-blind
4. _____ visual pigments
5. _____ trichromatic theory
6. _____ ishihara test

a. 3 cones sensitive to red, green, and blue
b. process colors in "either-or" messages
c. image remained after stimulus is gone
d. light-sensitive chemicals in photoreceptors
e. determining color-blindness
f. sex-linked trait on the X chromosome

What are the mechanisms of hearing? Pages 170-173

1. _____ vestibular system
2. _____ cochlea
3. _____ round window
4. _____ auditory canal
5. _____ stapes
6. _____ auditory nerve
7. _____ incus
8. _____ oval window
9. _____ tympanic membrane
10. _____ malleus

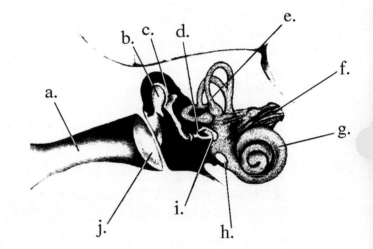

Hearing

1. _____ loudness
2. _____ stereocilia
3. _____ conduction deafness
4. _____ auditory ossicles
5. _____ nerve deafness
6. _____ tympanic membrane
7. _____ place theory
8. _____ pitch
9. _____ frequency theory

a. frequency of wave
b. amplitude of wave
c. eardrum
d. hammer, anvil, stirrup
e. "bristles"
f. process impulse up to 4,000 hertz
g. impulse processed in different places
h. damaged hair cells
i. sound blockage in external and middle ear

How do the chemical senses operate? Pages 173-177

1. _____ lock and key theory
2. _____ taste buds
3. _____ olfaction
4. _____ umami
5. _____ anosmia
6. _____ pheromones
7. _____ gustation

a. sense of smell
b. sense of taste
c. loss of smell
d. similar to chemical molecules' shapes
e. airborne chemical signals
f. receptor for taste
g. "brothy"

What are the somesthetic senses and why are they important? Pages 177-180

1. _____ warning system
2. _____ sensory conflict theory
3. _____ vestibular senses
4. _____ reduced motion sickness
5. _____ kinesthetic senses
6. _____ reminding system

a. sense body damage may be occurring
b. senses body movement
c. semicircular canals and otolith organs
d. sense body damage has occurred
e. reduce sensory conflicts by not moving head
f. sensory mismatch

Why are we more aware of some sensations than others? How can pain be reduced in everyday situations? Pages 180-186

1. _____ selective attention
2. _____ neuromatrix
3. _____ beta-endorphin
4. _____ sensory gating
5. _____ counterirritation
6. _____ acupuncture
7. _____ sensory adaptation

a. habituating to a stimulus
b. focus on a sensory input
c. facilitate or block sensory input
d. insert needles to relieve pain
e. painkilling chemicals
f. ice packs and hot-water bottles
g. produces phantom pain

CHECK YOUR MEMORY

In general, how do sensory systems function? Pages 156-157

1. The electromagnetic spectrum includes ultraviolet light and radio waves.

   TRUE or FALSE

2. Each sensory organ is sensitive to a select range of physical energies.

TRUE or FALSE

3. The artificial vision system described in the text is based on electrodes implanted in the retina.

TRUE or FALSE

4. The retina responds to pressure, as well as light.

TRUE or FALSE

What are the limits of our sensory sensitivity? Pages 158-160

1. It takes only one photon striking the retina to produce a sensation of light.

TRUE or FALSE

2. Humans can hear sounds from 2 to 2,000 hertz.

TRUE or FALSE

3. It is possible to taste 1 teaspoon of sugar dissolved in 2 gallons of water.

TRUE or FALSE

4. Some music fans have been harmed by subliminal backmasking.

TRUE or FALSE

5. The JND for loudness is 1/10.

TRUE or FALSE

6. Weber's law applies mainly to stimuli in the mid-range.

TRUE or FALSE

7. Subliminal self-help tapes and messages flashed on TV for 1/30 of a second have shown to directly influence individuals' behavior.

TRUE or FALSE

How is vision accomplished? Pages 160-165

1. A nanometer is one-millionth of a meter.

TRUE or FALSE

2. The functions of a human eye have often been compared to a camera with the retina as the layer of film.

TRUE or FALSE

3. The lens of the eye is about the size and thickness of a postage stamp.

TRUE or FALSE

4. Farsightedness is corrected with a convex lens.

    TRUE or FALSE

5. The myopic eye is longer than normal.

    TRUE or FALSE

6. There are more rods than cones in the eyes.

    TRUE or FALSE

7. Hubel and Wiesel directly recorded activity in single cells in the visual cortex.

    TRUE or FALSE

8. The blind spot is the point where the optic nerve leaves the eye.

    TRUE or FALSE

9. The fovea contains only retinal arteries and veins.

    TRUE or FALSE

10. If your vision is 20/12 like Gordon Cooper, an American astronaut, you would be able to see 8 feet farther than someone who has 20/20 vision.

    TRUE or FALSE

11. Vision rated at 20/200 is better than average.

    TRUE or FALSE

12. Visual acuity decreases near the edges of the retina.

    TRUE or FALSE

13. If the ventral pathway is damaged, one will not be able to process what the object is in his/her visual field.

    TRUE or FALSE

How do we perceive colors? Pages 165-170

1. Blue emergency lights and taxiway lights are used because at night they are more visible to the cones.

    TRUE or FALSE

2. The trichromatic theory of color vision assumes that black and white sensations are produced by the rods.

    TRUE or FALSE

3. According to the opponent-process theory it is impossible to have a reddish green or yellowish blue.

    TRUE or FALSE

4. The afterimage produced by staring at a red object is green.

    TRUE or FALSE

5. Visual pigments bleach, or breakdown chemically, when struck by light.

    TRUE or FALSE

6. Yellow-blue color weakness is very rare.

    TRUE or FALSE

7. In the U.S. and Canada, stoplights are always on the bottom of traffic signals.

    TRUE or FALSE

8. Complete dark adaptation takes about 12 minutes.

    TRUE or FALSE

9. Dark adaptation can be preserved by working in an area lit with red light.

    TRUE or FALSE

What are the mechanisms of hearing? Pages 170-173

1. Sound cannot travel in a vacuum.

    TRUE or FALSE

2. The visible, external portion of the ear is the malleus.

    TRUE or FALSE

3. The hair cells are part of the organ of Corti.

    TRUE or FALSE

4. Hunter's notch occurs when the auditory ossicles are damaged by the sound of gunfire.

    TRUE or FALSE

5. Cochlear implants stimulate the auditory nerve directly.

    TRUE or FALSE

6. Deaf children can learn spoken language close to a normal rate if they have cochlear implants before the age of 2.

    TRUE or FALSE

7. A 40 decibel sound could be described as quiet.

    TRUE or FALSE

8. A 100 decibel sound can damage hearing in less than 8 hours.

    TRUE or FALSE

9. Every 20 decibels increases sound energy by a factor of 10.

    TRUE or FALSE

How do the chemical senses operate? Pages 173-177

1. At least 1000 different types of olfactory receptors exist.

   TRUE or FALSE

2. Etherish odors smell like garlic.

   TRUE or FALSE

3. Ansomia can be caused by exposure to chemical odors.

   TRUE or FALSE

4. Human pheromones (if they exist) are sensed as a subtle, perfume-like odor.

   TRUE or FALSE

5. Flavors are greatly influenced by odor, as well as taste.

   TRUE or FALSE

6. Taste buds are found throughout the mouth, not just on the tongue.

   TRUE or FALSE

7. Umami is a pleasant "brothy" taste.

   TRUE or FALSE

8. Women are more likely to be supertasters.

   TRUE or FALSE

9. PTC tastes bitter to about 70 percent of those tested.

   TRUE or FALSE

10. The sense of taste tends to be weaker in early childhood than it is later as the body matures.

    TRUE or FALSE

What are the somesthetic senses and why are they important? Pages 177-180

1. Free nerve endings can produce any of the basic skin sensations.

   TRUE or FALSE

2. Vibration is one of the five basic skin sensations.

   TRUE or FALSE

3. Areas of the skin that have high concentrations of pain receptors are no more sensitive to pain than other areas of the body.

   TRUE or FALSE

4. Visceral pain is often felt at a location on the surface of the body.

   TRUE or FALSE

5. Small nerve fibers generally carry warning-system pain messages.

   TRUE or FALSE

6. Pain originating in the heart may be felt all the way down the left arm.

   TRUE or FALSE

7. Most physical skills rely on dynamic touch, which combines touch sensations with kinesthetic information.

   TRUE or FALSE

8. The semicircular canals are especially sensitive to the pull of gravity.

   TRUE or FALSE

9. Motion sickness is believed to be related to the body's reactions to being poisoned.

   TRUE or FALSE

10. A horizontal body position tends to intensify motion sickness.

    TRUE or FALSE

Why are we more aware of some sensations than others? Pages 180-183

1. Unlike other receptor cells, the rods and cones do not undergo sensory adaptation.

   TRUE or FALSE

2. If you wear a ring, you are rarely aware of it because of sensory gating.

   TRUE or FALSE

3. The "seat-of-your pants" phenomenon is related to selective attention.

   TRUE or FALSE

4. Stabilized visual images appear brighter and more intense than normal.

   TRUE or FALSE

5. Mild electrical stimulation of the skin can block reminding system pain.

   TRUE or FALSE

6. Mild electrical stimulation of the skin causes a release of endorphins in free nerve endings.

   TRUE or FALSE

7. The neuromatrix best explains phantom limb pain experienced by many amputees.

   TRUE or FALSE

How can pain be reduced in everyday situations? Pages 184-186

1. High levels of anxiety tend to amplify the amount of pain a person experiences.
   TRUE or FALSE

2. Prepared childbirth training helps women feel in control of the birth process.
   TRUE or FALSE

3. Physical relaxation exercises can be used to lower anxiety in situations involving pain.
   TRUE or FALSE

4. As a means of reducing pain, hot-water bottles are an example of counterirritation.
   TRUE or FALSE

FINAL SURVEY AND REVIEW

In general, how do sensory systems function?

General Properties of Sensory Systems—What You See Is What You Get: Pages 156-157

1. Sensory organs _____ physical energies into nerve impulses.

2. The senses act as data _____ systems that select, analyze, and _____ sensory information.

3. A good example of _____ is the identification of basic perceptual features in a stimulus pattern.

4. In fact, many sensory systems act as _____ detectors.

5. _____ and visual pop-out are examples of feature detection and sensory _____ in action.

6. Sensory response can be partially understood in terms of sensory _____ in the brain. That is, the _____ of the brain activated ultimately determines which type of sensory experience we have.

What are the limits of our sensory sensitivity?

Psychophysics—Life at the Limit: Pages 158-160

1. _____ is the study of physical stimuli and the sensations they evoke.

2. The minimum amount of physical energy necessary to produce a sensation defines the _____ threshold.

3. For the sense of vision, a person can detect a candle flame from approximately _____ miles away on a clear dark night and for the sense of hearing, a person can detect the ticking of a watch from _____ feet away under quiet conditions.

4. A person's sensitivity to pitch ranges from _____ hertz to _____ hertz.

5. The amount of change necessary to produce a _____ difference (or JND) in a stimulus defines a _____ threshold.

6. In general, the amount of change needed to produce a JND is a _____ _____ of the original stimulus intensity. This relationship is known as _____ law.

7. Threatening or anxiety-provoking stimuli may raise the _____ for recognition, an effect called _____ defense.

8. Any stimulus below the level of conscious awareness is said to be _____ .

9. There is evidence that subliminal perception occurs, but subliminal _____ is largely ineffective.

How is vision accomplished?

Vision—Catching Some Rays: Pages 160-165

1. The visible spectrum consists of _____ radiation in a narrow range.

2. The visible spectrum ranges from violet, with a wavelength of _____ , to red with a wavelength of _____ .

3. _____ refers to a color's name, which corresponds to its wavelength. Saturated or "pure" colors come from a narrow band of wavelengths. Brightness corresponds to the _____ of light waves.

4. The eye is in some ways like a camera. At its back lies an array of _____ , called rods and cones, that make up a light-sensitive layer called the _____ .

5. Vision is focused by the shape of the _____ and lens and by changes in the shape of the lens, called _____ .

6. Four common visual defects, correctable with glasses, are _____ (nearsightedness), hyperopia (farsightedness), presbyopia (loss of accommodation), and _____ (in which portions of vision are out of focus).

7. The amount of light entering the eye is controlled by movements of the _____ , which _____ (enlarges) and _____ (narrows) the pupil.

8. In the retina, the rods specialize in night vision, black and white reception, and _____ detection.

9. The cones, found exclusively in the _____ and otherwise toward the middle of the eye, specialize in color vision, _____ (perception of fine detail), and daylight vision.

10. Individual cells in the visual _____ of the brain act as feature detectors to analyze visual information.

11. After the visual stimulus is processed in the primary visual cortex, further processing of the stimulus occurs via the ventral pathway which determines " _____ " type of object it is and the dorsal pathway which determines " _____ " the object is in the visual field.

12. The rods supply much of our _____ vision. Loss of _____ vision is called tunnel vision.

How do we perceive colors?

Color Vision—There's More To It Than Meets the Eye: Pages 165-167

1. The rods and cones differ in color sensitivity. _____ -green is brightest for cones; _____ -green for the rods (although they will see it as colorless).

2. In the retina, color vision is explained by the _____ theory. The theory says that three types of cones exist, each most sensitive to red, green, or blue.

3. Three types of light-sensitive visual _____ are found in the cones, each is most sensitive to either red, green, or blue light.

4. _____ theory was unable to explain why people experience _____ or visual sensations that persist after a color stimulus has been removed.

5. Beyond the retina, the visual system analyzes colors into either-or messages. According to the _____ theory, color information can be coded as either _____ , yellow or blue, and black or white messages.

6. Ultimately, _____ experiences are constructed in the brain. This is apparent when you look at a stimulus that produces simultaneous _____ .

7. Total color blindness is rare, but 8 percent of males and 1 percent of females are _____ color-blind or color weak.

8. Color blindness is a _____ trait carried on the X (female) chromosome and passed from _____ to son.

9. The _____ test is used to detect color blindness.

Dark Adaptation—Let There Be Light! Pages 167-170

1. Dark adaptation, an increase in sensitivity to light, is caused by increased concentrations of _____ in the rods and the cones.

2. In order for individuals to move from a bright room into a dark room without undergoing dark adaptation, which acquires approximately _____ minutes to see clearly, _____ lights must be on since _____ are insensitive to them.

3. Most dark adaptation is the result of increased _____ concentrations in the rods. Vitamin _____ deficiencies may cause night blindness.

What are the mechanisms of hearing?

Hearing—Good Vibrations: Pages 170-173

1. Sound waves are the stimulus for hearing. Sound travels as waves of _____ (peaks) and _____ (valleys) in the air.

2. The pitch of a sound corresponds to the _____ of sound waves. Loudness corresponds to the _____ (height) of sound waves.

3. Sound waves are transduced by the eardrum, auditory _____ , oval window, cochlea, and ultimately, the hair cells in the organ of _____ .

4. The frequency theory says that the frequency of nerve impulses in the _____ matches the frequency of incoming sounds (up to 4000 hertz).

5. Place theory says that high tones register near the _____ of the cochlea and low tones near its _____ .

6. Three basic types of deafness are nerve deafness, conduction deafness, and _____ deafness.

7. Conduction deafness can often be overcome with a hearing aid. Nerve deafness can sometimes be alleviated by _____ implants.

8. Stimulation deafness can be prevented by avoiding excessive exposure to loud sounds. Sounds above _____ pose an immediate danger to hearing. Two warning signs of stimulation deafness are temporary threshold shift and a ringing in the ears, called _____ .

How do the chemical senses operate?

Smell and Taste—The Nose Knows When the Tongue Can't Tell: Pages 173-177

1. _____ (smell) and _____ (taste) are chemical senses responsive to airborne or liquefied molecules.

2. Research on _____ (inability to detect a single odor) suggests there are receptors for specific odors; approximately _____ different types of receptors are available to produce _____ different combination of odors that an individual can detect.

3. It is suspected that humans are also sensitive to chemical signals called _____ , which may be sensed by the _____ organ.

4. The _____ _____ _____ theory partially explains smell. In addition, the location of the olfactory receptors in the nose helps identify various scents.

5. The top outside edges of the tongue are responsive to _____ , _____ , _____ , and bitter tastes. It is suspected that a fifth taste quality called _____ also exists.

6. Taste also appears to be based in part on lock-and-key coding of _____ shapes.

7. Chemical senses of _____ and _____ operate together to allow us to experience the flavor of food.

What are the somesthetic senses and why are they important?

The Somesthetic Sense—Flying by the Seat of Your Pants: Pages 177-180

1. The somesthetic senses include the skin senses, vestibular senses, and _____ senses (receptors that detect muscle and joint positioning).

2. The skin senses include touch, pressure, _____ , cold, and warmth. Sensitivity to each is related to the number of _____ found in an area of skin.

3. Distinctions can be made among various types of pain, including visceral pain, somatic pain, _____ pain, _____ system pain, and reminding system pain.

4. Various forms of motion sickness are related to messages received from the _____ system, which senses gravity and head movement.

5. The _____ organs detect the pull of gravity and rapid head movements.

6. The movement of fluid within the _____ canals, and the movement of the crista within each _____ , detects head movement and positioning.

7. According to _____ theory, motion sickness is caused by a mismatch of visual, kinesthetic, and vestibular sensations. Motion sickness can be avoided by minimizing sensory conflict.

Why are we more aware of some sensations than others?

Adaptation, Attention, and Gating—Tuning In and Tuning Out: Pages 180-183

1. Incoming sensations are affected by sensory _____ (a decrease in the number of nerve impulses sent).

2. Vision does not undergo sensory adaptation due to physiological _____ (involuntary tremors of the eye muscles) which causes thousands of tiny movements of the _____ muscles to ensure detection of images falling on _____ rods and cones.

3. Selective _____ (selection and diversion of messages in the brain) and sensory gating (blocking or alteration of messages flowing toward the brain) also alter sensations.

4. Selective gating of pain messages apparently takes place in the spinal cord. _____ theory proposes an explanation for many pain phenomena.

5. "Runner's high," the painkilling effects of the Chinese medical art of _____ , and other pain phenomena appear to be explained by the release of a morphine-like chemical in the brain, called beta- _____ .

6. The brain creates a _____ of one's body to process one's sense of bodily self. This neuromatrix does not recognize that an actual part of the body no longer exists and continues to process nearby sensory stimulations as _____ coming from the missing limb.

7. Most amputees have _____ limb sensations long after losing a limb.

How can pain be reduced in everyday situations?

Psychology in Action: Controlling Pain—This Won't Hurt a Bit: Pages 184-186

1. Pain can be reduced by lowering anxiety and redirecting _____ to stimuli other than the pain stimulus.

2. Feeling that you have _____ over a stimulus tends to reduce the amount of pain you experience.

3. The _____ or meaning placed on a stimulus affects how painful it is perceived to be.

4. Sending mild pain messages to the spinal cord can close the gates to more severe pain. This effect is called _____ .

5. _____ is used by pain clinics to reduce people's experiences of pain by introducing an additional, _____ intense pain signal such as a mild electrical current to the brain through the fast nerve fiber.

MASTERY TEST

1. A person with tunnel vision has mainly lost the ability to use the _____ and _____ vision.
   a. cones, foveal
   b. photoreceptors, color
   c. iris, retinal
   d. rods, peripheral

2. Sensory conflict theory attributes motion sickness to mismatches between what three systems?
   a. olfaction, kinesthesis, and audition
   b. vision, kinesthesis, and the vestibular system
   c. kinesthesis, audition, and the somesthetic system
   d. vision, gustation, and the skin senses

3. Which of the following types of color blindness is most common?
   a. yellow-blue, male
   b. yellow-blue, female
   c. red-green, female
   d. red-green, male

4. A reasonable conclusion about subliminal perception is that
   a. subliminal stimuli have weak effects
   b. backmasking poses a serious threat to listeners
   c. subliminal tapes are more effective than subliminal advertising
   d. subliminal perception applies to hearing, but not to vision

5. Which of the following does not belong with the others?
   a. Pacinian corpuscle
   b. Merkle's disk
   c. vomeronasal organ
   d. free nerve endings

6. The fact that the eyes are only sensitive to a narrow band of electromagnetic energies shows that vision acts as a(an) _____ system.
   a. opponent-process
   b. gate-control
   c. central biasing
   d. data reduction

7. Which theory of color vision best explains the fact that we do not see yellowish blue?
   a. trichromatic
   b. chromatic gating
   c. Ishihara hypothesis
   d. opponent process

8. A person with inflamed kidneys feels pain in her hips. This is an example of
   a. warning system pain
   b. referred pain
   c. somatic pain
   d. vestibular pain

9. Hubel and Wiesel found that nerve cells in the visual cortex of the brain respond most to specific
   a. phosphenes
   b. perceptual features
   c. areas of the visible spectrum
   d. numbers of photons

10. Which of the following pain control strategies makes use of gate control theory?
    a. counterirritation
    b. distraction and reinterpretation
    c. anxiety reduction
    d. gaining control over pain stimuli

11. New mothers who are depressed take longer than usual to recognize pictures of babies. This is an example of
    a. backmasking
    b. visual accommodation
    c. difference thresholds
    d. perceptual defense

12. According to Weber's law, the _____ is a constant proportion of the original intensity of a stimulus.
    a. absolute threshold
    b. JND
    c. phosphene
    d. sensory limen

13. Dark adaptation is closely related to concentrations of _____ in the _____.
    a. retinal, aqueous humor
    b. photopsin, cones
    c. rhodopsin, rods
    d. photons, optic nerve

14. Sensory analysis tends to extract perceptual _____ from stimulus patterns.
    a. thresholds
    b. features
    c. transducers
    d. amplitudes

15. Which pair of terms is most closely related?
    a. hyperopia—color blindness
    b. astigmatism—presbyopia
    c. myopia—astigmatism
    d. hyperopia—presbyopia

16. The painkilling effects of acupuncture are partly explained by _____ theory and the release of _____.
    a. lock-and-key, pheromones
    b. gate control, pheromones
    c. gate control, endorphins
    d. lock-and-key, endorphins

17. Three photons of light striking the _____ defines the _____ for vision.
    a. retina, absolute threshold
    b. cornea, difference threshold
    c. iris, upper limen
    d. cornea, JND

18. According to the _____ theory of hearing, low tones cause the greatest movement near the _____ of the cochlea.
    a. place, outer tip
    b. frequency, outer tip
    c. place, base
    d. frequency, base

19. Where vision is concerned, physiological nystagmus helps prevent
    a. sensory gating
    b. tunnel vision
    c. sensory adaptation
    d. night blindness

20. Which of the following best represents the concept of a transducer?
    a. Translating English into Spanish.
    b. Copying a computer file from one floppy disk to another.
    c. Speaking into a telephone receiver.
    d. Turning water into ice.

21. Visual pop-out is closely related to which sensory process?
    a. transduction
    b. feature detection
    c. difference thresholds
    d. perception below the limen

22. Rods and cones are to vision as _____ are to hearing.
    a. auditory ossicles
    b. vibrations
    c. pinnas
    d. hair cells

23. You lose the ability to smell floral odors. This is called _____ and it is compatible with the _____ theory of olfaction.
    a. anosmia, lock-and-key
    b. anhedonia, place
    c. tinnitus, gate-control
    d. sensory adaptation, molecular

24. Which two dimensions of color are related to the wavelength of electromagnetic energy?
    a. hue and saturation
    b. saturation and brightness
    c. brightness and hue
    d. brightness and amplitude

25. Temporary threshold shifts are related to
    a. conduction deafness
    b. nerve deafness
    c. stimulation deafness
    d. damage to the ossicles

26. The existence of the blind spot is explained by a lack of
    a. rhodopsin
    b. peripheral vision
    c. photoreceptors
    d. activity in the fovea

27. Which of the following normally has the most effect on the amount of light entering the eye?
    a. fovea
    b. iris
    c. aqueous humor
    d. cornea

28. In vision, a loss of accommodation is most associated with aging of the
    a. iris
    b. fovea
    c. lens
    d. cornea

29. Visual acuity and color vision are provided by the _____ found in large numbers in the _____ of the eye.
    a. cones, fovea
    b. cones, periphery
    c. rods, fovea
    d. rods, periphery

30. Children who are born deaf have a good chance at learning spoken language at an almost normal rate if they receive cochlear implants before they reach the age of:
    a. 2
    b. 9
    c. 12
    d. 16

31. Standing 8 feet farther away than Jacob who has 20/20 vision, Paul is able to identify the furry animal as a mouse. An optometrist might conclude that Paul has a better than average acuity and he has _____ vision.
    a. 20/8
    b. 20/18
    c. 20/12
    d. 20/80

32. S. K. suffered damage to her _____ pathway since she could not identify "what" types of objects were in her visual field, and she did not suffer damage to her _____ pathway since she could still identify "where" the objects were in her visual field.
    a. lateral; ventral
    b. ventral; dorsal
    c. dorsal; lateral
    d. dorsal; ventral

33. Submarine and airplane crewmen are able to move from a well-lit room to a dark room without having to undergo dark adaptation; this is due to the _____ lights in the room.
    a. yellow
    b. green
    c. blue
    d. red

34. Sensory adaptation does not occur with vision because of _____ which produces the involuntary tremors of eye muscles.
    a. anosmia
    b. perceptual defense
    c. physiological nystagmus
    d. feature detectors

LANGUAGE DEVELOPMENT - Sensation and Reality

Word Roots

Photos is the Greek word which means "light." Combining this Greek root with another term forms several words. These words all refer in some way to the action of light. Examples you will find in this or later chapters in the text include photoreceptors and photographic memory.

In general, how do sensory systems function?

Preview: Sensation—A Window on the World (p. 156)

(156) *kaleidoscope*: a constantly changing pattern or scene

(156) *void*: empty space

(156) *drink in*: experience

(156) *gamma rays*: very short wavelength rays emitted by radioactive substances

General Properties of Sensory Systems—What You See Is What You Get (pp. 156-157)

(156) *light years*: the distance light will travel in one year at 186,000 miles per second

(156) *dewdrop*: a very small drop (amount) of moisture found in the early morning resulting from overnight condensation of moisture in the air

(156) *stimulus*: something that causes an activity or response

(156) *attuned*: responsive to

(156) *checkerboard*: a board used for playing the popular games of checkers, chess, and backgammon

(157) *crude*: not sophisticated; simple

What are the limits of our sensory sensitivity?

Psychophysics—Life at the Limit (pp. 158-160)

(158) *tweeter*: loudspeaker for very high-pitched sounds

(158) *it takes a lot of cooks to spoil the broth:* one cook wouldn't spoil the soup, but the changes introduced by a lot of cooks might be enough to spoil it

(158) *subliminal*: below the level of conscious awareness

(159) *subliminal self-help tapes*: audiotapes that are supposed to contain hidden messages that will influence a person subconsciously; played "below" the level of hearing

(159) *faked the whole thing*: made it all up

How is vision accomplished?

Vision—Catching Some Rays (pp. 160-165)

(160) *catching some rays*: slang for sun-tanning; Coon is making a joke because in vision the eye actually does "catch" light rays

(160) *drab*: dull

(160) *sharp*: in focus

(160) *misshapen*: deformed; not in the normal shape

(162) *upshot*: result

(165) *blinders*: flaps on both sides of a horse's eyes to prevent it from seeing objects at its sides

How do we perceive colors?

Color Vision—There's More to It Than Meets the Eye (pp. 165-167)

(165) *there's more to it than meets the eye*: the subject is more complex than it first seems to be

(166) *hoots of laughter*: loud laughter

(166) *clashing*: not matching

(166) *sheepishly*: in an embarrassed or timid manner

Dark Adaptation—Let There Be Light (pp. 167-170)

(168) *embedded*: enclosed in

(169) *artificial lighting*: indoor, rather than outdoor, lighting

What are the mechanisms of hearing?

Hearing—Good Vibrations (pp. 170-173)

(170) *good vibrations*: the title of a well-known pop music song; implies feeling good

(170) *shades*: sunglasses

(170) *tuning fork*: a metal device that gives a fixed musical tone when it is struck with or against another object

(170) *vacuum*: empty space

(170) *collide*: to hit against something

(170) *bristles*: very fine fibers at the top of hair cells

(172) *to break through the wall of silence*: in this case, to hear sounds with the use of a hearing aid

(172) *spurred*: to have increased motivation and interest to start something

(172) *a radio that isn't quite tuned in*: a radio that is not receiving a station clearly

(173) *cobweb*: spider web

(173) *boom box*: large and loud radio; often carried

(173) *hard-of-hearing*: partially or totally deaf

How do the chemical senses operate?

Smell and Taste—The Nose Knows When the Tongue Can't Tell (pp. 173-177)

(173) *wine taster*: a person whose job it is to sample wines in order to judge their quality

(175) *gourmet*: a person very knowledgeable about good food and drink

(174) *camphor*: crystalline substance with a strong odor, generally derived from the wood of the camphor tree

(174) *musky*: having an odor like musk, a substance with a penetrating, long lasting odor obtained from the male musk deer and used in perfume

(174) *ether*: colorless, highly flammable liquid with an aromatic odor

(174) *allergies*: reactions such as sneezing, coughing, and itching caused by sensitivity to substances in the environment such as pollen or dust

(175) *vestigial*: bodily organs such as the appendix that have evolved to the point where they are no longer needed or used

(175) *septum*: partition of tissue that separates the nostrils

(175) *foraged*: searched for

(175) *intricately shaped*: complex and elaborately designed

(176) *breathe fire*: suggestive of being sensitive to spicy food

(176) *cloying*: too rich or too sweet

(177) *coagulated*: thickened into a mass

(177) *a cheese fancier:* a person who likes to eat cheese

What are the somesthetic senses and why are they important?

The Somesthetic Senses—Flying by the Seat of Your Pants (pp. 177-180)

(177) *flying by the seat of your pants*: operating an airplane without the use of instruments; in general, doing a task without really knowing what one is doing

(177) *sobriety test*: a test (such as making a person walk a straight line) to determine if someone has been excessively drinking alcohol

(177) ***rough-and-ready illustration***: quick and easy demonstration

(178) ***carried away***: over-enthusiastic

(179) ***juggler***: a performer who entertains by throwing and keeping a number of objects in the air at the same time

(179) ***embeds***: pushes into

(179) ***gelatin-like***: soft and very pliable substance

(179) ***tug of gravity***: gravity pulling one down

(180) ***motion sickness***: nausea, and sometimes vomiting, caused by the motion of a car, boat, or airplane

(180) ***kinesthesis***: sensory information given by organs located in the muscles, tendons, and joints and stimulated by bodily movement

(180) ***heaving*** (two meanings): moving rapidly up and down; vomiting

(180) ***"green" and miserable with motion sickness***: feeling nauseated; sick to the stomach

(180) ***alien***: foreign; belonging elsewhere

Why are we more aware of some sensations than others?

Adaptation, Attention, and Gating—Tuning In and Tuning Out (pp. 180-183)

(180) ***tuning in and tuning out***: slang for paying attention (*tuning in*) and not paying attention (*tuning out*)

(180) ***sauerkraut***: a salted, fermented cabbage dish from Germany

(180) ***head cheese***: sausage made from the head, feet, and sometimes tongue and heart of a pig

(180) ***pass out at the door*** (you would probably *pass out at the door*): you would faint because of the overpowering bad smell

(182) ***morphine***: an opium-like drug used against pain

(182) ***runner's high***: an adrenaline surge that athletes often report that provides energy to continue competing

(182) ***masochism***: taking pleasure in receiving pain

(182) ***initiation rites***: ritualistic procedures sometimes used to admit people to organizations such as fraternities or sororities

(182) ***addicted***: unable to give up

(182) ***bungee jumping***: a sport requiring a person to jump off a point of great height with his/her legs tied to a strong elastic rope to prevent him/her from hitting the water or ground below as the rope pulls him/her back a few feet

(182) ***jumbled***: mixed up; not organized

(183) ***emanate***: to come from or produce

(183) *queasy*: feeling ill or sick to one's stomach

How can pain be reduced in everyday situations?

Psychology in Action: Controlling Pain—This Won't Hurt a Bit (pp. 184-186)

(184) *tattooing*: making designs on the body by inserting color under the skin or by producing scars {"producing scars" usually termed *scarification*; different from tattooing}

(184) *flood of relief*: the letting go of worry

(184) *"tuned out"*: ignored

(184) *swat*: hit

(185) *epidural block*: anesthesia given to prevent feeling in the lower part of the body

(185) *ice packs*: wraps containing ice to put on injured parts of the body to relieve pain

(185) *hot water bottles*: soft plastic bottles filled with water and put on injured parts of the body to relieve pain

(185) *mustard packs*: wraps containing powdered mustard that are put on injured parts of the body to relieve pain

(185) *take the edge off*: decrease the pain

Solutions

RECITE AND REVIEW

In general, how do sensory systems function?

1. nerve
2. data; analyze
3. perceptual
4. detectors
5. sensory
6. sensory; activated

What are the limits of our sensory sensitivity?

1. physical; sensations
2. minimum; sensation
3. 30; 20
4. 20
5. change; difference
6. intensity; law
7. raise; defense
8. below
9. ineffective

How is vision accomplished?

1. visible
2. wavelength; wavelength
3. wavelength; narrow
4. rods; cones
5. shape; shape
6. nearsightedness; accommodation
7. enlarges; narrows
8. rods
9. cones; color
10. detectors
11. ventral; dorsal
12. rods

How do we perceive colors?

1. sensitivity
2. retina; cones
3. cones
4. afterimages
5. either-or; black or white
6. brain
7. Total
8. female
9. color blindness

Dark Adaptation—Let There Be Light! Pages 167-170

1. increase; rods; cones
2. 30; red
3. rods; night

What are the mechanisms of hearing?

1. peaks; valleys
2. pitch; height
3. eardrum; hair
4. frequency; frequency
5. high; low
6. nerve
7. Nerve
8. loud; shifts

How do the chemical senses operate?

1. smell; taste
2. inability; 400; 10,000
3. chemical; organ
4. location
5. bitter
6. coding
7. smell; taste

What are the somesthetic senses and why are they important?

1. skin
2. pressure; number
3. reminding
4. head
5. gravity
6. fluid; crista
7. mismatch

Why are we more aware of some sensations than others?

1. reduction (or decrease)
2. adaptation; eye
3. gating
4. spinal; cord
5. morphine(or opiate)
6. bodily
7. limb

How can pain be reduced in everyday situations?

1. lowering
2. reduce
3. stimulus
4. mild
5. Counterirritation; pain

CONNECTIONS

In general, how do sensory systems function? Pages 156-157

1. D.
2. B.
3. E.
4. A.
5. F.
6. C

What are the limits of our sensory sensitivity? Pages 158-160

1. D.
2. A.
3. F.
4. B.
5. E.
6. C.

How is vision accomplished? Pages 160-165

1. D.
2. F.
3. H.
4. B.
5. I.
6. C.
7. K.
8. A.
9. E.
10. G.
11. J.

Vision

1. E.
2. B.
3. H.
4. D.
5. A.
6. F.
7. G.
8. C.

How do we perceive colors? Pages 165-170

1. C.
2. B.
3. F.
4. D.
5. A.
6. E.

What are the mechanisms of hearing? Pages 170-173

1. E.	5. D.	9. J.
2. G.	6. F.	10. B.
3. H.	7. C.	
4. A.	8. I.	

Hearing

1. B.	4. D.	7. G.
2. E.	5. H.	8. A.
3. I.	6. C.	9. F.

How do the chemical senses operate? Pages 173-177

1. D.	4. G.	7. B.
2. F.	5. C.	
3. A.	6. E.	

What are the somesthetic senses and why are they important? Pages 177-180

1. A.	3. C.	5. B.
2. F.	4. E.	6. D.

Why are we more aware of some sensations than others? How can pain be reduced in everyday situations? Pages 180-186

1. B.	4. C.	7. A.
2. G.	5. F.	
3. E.	6. D.	

CHECK YOUR MEMORY

In general, how do sensory systems function? Pages 156-157

1. T	3. F
2. T	4. T

What are the limits of our sensory sensitivity? Pages 158-160

1. F	4. F	7. F
2. F	5. T	
3. T	6. T	

How is vision accomplished? Pages 160-165

1. F	6. T	11. F
2. T	7. T	12. T
3. F	8. T	13. T
4. T	9. F	
5. T	10. T	

How do we perceive colors? Pages 165-170

1. F	4. T	7. F
2. T	5. T	8. F
3. T	6. T	9. T

What are the mechanisms of hearing? Pages 170-173

1. T	4. F	7. T
2. F	5. T	8. T
3. T	6. T	9. T

How do the chemical senses operate? Pages 173-177

1. T	5. T	9. T
2. F	6. T	10. F
3. T	7. T	
4. F	8. T	

What are the somesthetic senses and why are they important? Pages 177-180

1. T	5. F	9. T
2. F	6. T	10. F
3. F	7. T	
4. T	8. F	

Why are we more aware of some sensations than others? Pages 180-183

1. F	4. F	7. T
2. F	5. T	
3. T	6. F	

How can pain be reduced in everyday situations? Pages 184-186
1. T

2. T   3. T   4. T

FINAL SURVEY AND REVIEW

In general, how do sensory systems function?

1. transduce
2. reduction; code
3. sensory analysis
4. feature
5. Phosphenes; coding
6. localization; area

What are the limits of our sensory sensitivity?

1. Psychophysics
2. absolute
3. 30; 20
4. 20; 20,000
5. just noticeable; difference
6. constant; proportion; Weber's
7. threshold; perceptual
8. subliminal
9. advertising

How is vision accomplished?

1. electromagnetic
2. 400 nanometers; 700 nanometers
3. Hue; amplitude
4. photoreceptors; retina
5. cornea; accommodation
6. myopia; astigmatism
7. iris; dilates; constricts
8. motion
9. fovea; acuity
10. cortex
11. what; where
12. peripheral; peripheral

How do we perceive colors?

1. Yellow; blue
2. trichromatic
3. pigments
4. Trichromatic; afterimages
5. opponent-process; red or green
6. color; contrast
7. red-green
8. sex-linked; mother
9. Ishihara

Dark Adaptation—Let There Be Light! Pages 167-170

1. visual pigments
2. 30; red; rods
3. rhodopsin; A

What are the mechanisms of hearing?

1. compression; rarefaction
2. frequency; amplitude
3. ossicles; Corti
4. auditory nerves
5. base; tip
6. stimulation
7. cochlear
8. 120 decibels; tinnitus

How do the chemical senses operate?

1. Olfaction; gustation
2. anosmia; 400; 10,000
3. pheromones; vomeronasal
4. lock; and; key
5. sweet; salty; sour; umami
6. molecule
7. smell; taste

What are the somesthetic senses and why are they important?

1. kinesthetic
2. pain; receptors
3. referred; warning

4. vestibular

5. otolith

6. semicircular; ampulla

7. sensory conflict

Why are we more aware of some sensations than others?

1. adaptation

2. nystagmus; eye; unfatigued

3. attention

4. Gate control

5. acupuncture; endorphin

6. neuromatrix; pain

7. phantom

How can pain be reduced in everyday situations?

1. attention

2. control

3. interpretation

4. counterirritation

5. Counterirritation; less

MASTERY TEST

How can pain be reduced in everyday situations?

1. D, p. 165
2. B, p. 180
3. D, p. 167
4. A, p. 159
5. C, p. 178
6. D, p. 156
7. D, p. 165
8. B, p. 178
9. B, p. 162
10. A, p. 185
11. D, p. 159
12. B, p. 158

13. C, pp. 167-168
14. B, p. 156
15. D, pp. 160-161
16. C, pp. 181-182
17. A, p. 158
18. A, p. 172
19. C, p. 181
20. C, p. 156
21. B, p. 156
22. D, p. 170
23. A, p. 174
24. A, p. 160

25. C, p. 173
26. C, p. 162
27. B, p. 161
28. C, p. 161
29. A, pp. 162-163
30. A, p. 172
31. C, p. 164
32. B, p. 164
33. D, p. 169
34. C, p. 181

Perceiving the World

Chapter Overview

Perception involves organizing sensations into meaningful patterns. Perceptions are hypotheses about sensory events or models of the world. Visual perceptions are stabilized by size, shape, and brightness constancies. The most basic perceptual pattern (in vision) is figure-ground organization. Sensations tend to be organized on the basis of nearness, similarity, continuity, closure, contiguity, and common region.

Depth perception depends on accommodation, convergence, retinal disparity, and various pictorial cues. The pictorial cues include linear perspective, relative size, light and shadow, overlap, texture gradients, aerial haze, and relative motion.

Learning, in the form of perceptual habits, influences perceptions. Perceptual judgments are related to stimulus context and to internal frames of reference, such as one's adaptation level. Perceptions are also greatly affected by attention, motives, values, and expectations. Perceptual learning can explain why illusions occur, but it cannot explain hallucinations. Hallucinations are different than sane hallucinations. People who experience sane hallucinations actually process stimuli from the environment. When we narrow our focus too much to one event, we may experience inattentional blindness to other stimuli. Selective attention and divided attention influence what information we are aware of at any moment. So do habituation, motives and values, and perceptual sets.

Parapsychology is the study of purported psi phenomena, including clairvoyance, telepathy, precognition, and psychokinesis. The bulk of the evidence to date is against the existence of extrasensory perception. Stage ESP is based on deception and tricks.

Because perceptions are reconstructions of events, eyewitness testimony can be unreliable. Perceptual accuracy can be improved by reality testing, dishabituation, actively paying attention, breaking perceptual habits, using broad frames of reference, and being aware of perceptual sets.

Learning Objectives

1. Define *perception* and describe the following constancies:

   a. size

   b. shape

   c. brightness

2. Give examples of the following as they relate to the organization of perception:

   a. figure-ground (include the concept of reversible figures)

   b. nearness

   c. similarity

   d. continuity

   e. closure (include the concept of illusory figures)

   f. contiguity

   g. common region

3. Describe the activities of an engineering psychologist. Include a discussion of the two components of effective design.

4. Explain what a perceptual hypothesis is and define and give an example of an ambiguous stimulus and an impossible figure.

5. Discuss depth perception and describe the research regarding this perceptual ability.

6. Describe the following cues for depth perception and indicate in each case whether the cue is monocular or binocular:

   a. accommodation

   b. convergence

   c. retinal disparity (include the term stereoscopic vision) and describe the special visual adaptations found among birds.

7. Describe the following two-dimensional, monocular, pictorial depth cues and give examples of how artists use them to give the appearance of three-dimensional space:

   a. linear perspective

   b. overlap

   c. relative size

   d. texture gradients

   e. height in the picture plane

   f. aerial perspective

   g. light and shadow

   h. relative motion (motion parallax)

8. Describe the phenomenon of the *moon illusion*. Include in your explanation the apparent distance hypothesis and a description of the work of the Kaufmans.

9. Define the terms *perceptual learning* and *perceptual habit* and explain how perceptual habits allow learning to affect perception and how the Ames room poses problems for organization and for a person's perceptual habits.

10. Describe the research which demonstrates the brain's sensitivity to perceptual features of the environment; discuss the effects of culture on this sensitivity; and explain how the results of the inverted vision experiments support the concept of perceptual habits and why active movement is so important to adapting to inverted vision.

11. Explain the concepts of *context*, *frames of reference*, and *adaptation level*; differentiate between illusions and hallucinations; and describe the *Charles Bonnet syndrome*, the stroboscopic movement illusion, the *Müller-Lyer* illusion, and the size-distance invariance.

12. Distinguish between selective attention and divided attention; list the factors that affect attention; and explain how inattentional blindness can affect what one perceives.

13. Differentiate habituation from sensory adaptation; describe the orientation response; and explain the boiled frog syndrome and how it may affect the ultimate survival of humans.

14. Explain how motives and perceptual expectancies may influence perception and describe bottom-up processing, top-down processing, perceptual sets, and perceptual categories.

15. Define *extrasensory perception, parapsychology, and psi phenomenon* and describe the following purported psychic abilities:

    a. clairvoyance

    b. telepathy

    c. precognition

    d. psychokinesis

16. Describe the research with Zener cards; explain why most psychologists remain skeptical about psi abilities and stage ESP; and state the best conclusion to make about *psi* events.

The following objectives are related to the material in the "Psychology in Action" section of your text.

1. Explain the phrase "We see what we believe" and why most eyewitness testimony is inaccurate (regardless of one's confidence). Include the concept of weapon focus.

2. Explain how a person can more accurately perceive the world. Include the terms *reality testing* and *dishabituation*; Maslow's theory of perceptual awareness; and the seven ways to become a better eyewitness to life.

RECITE AND REVIEW

What are perceptual constancies, and what is their role in perception?

Perceptual Constancies—Taming an Unruly World: Pages 189-190

1. Perception is the process of assembling sensations into _____ that provide a usable mental _____ of the world.

2. In vision, the retinal _____ changes from moment to moment, but the external world appears stable and undistorted because of _____ constancies.

3. In size and shape _____ , the perceived sizes and shapes of objects remain the same even though their retinal images change size and shape. The apparent brightness of objects remains stable (a property called brightness constancy) because each reflects a _____ proportion of light.

4. Perceptual constancies are partly native (_____) and partly empirical (_____).

What basic principles do we use to group sensations into meaningful patterns?

Perceptual Organization—Getting It All Together: Pages 191-195

1. The most basic organization of sensations is a division into figure and ground (_____ and _____). Reversible figures, however, allow figure-ground organization to be reversed.

2. A number of factors, identified by the Gestalt psychologists, contribute to the _____ of sensations. These are nearness, _____ , continuity, closure, contiguity, _____ region, and combinations of the preceding.

3. Stimuli near one another tend to be perceptually _____ together. So, too, do stimuli that are similar in _____ . Continuity refers to the fact that perceptions tend to be organized as simple, uninterrupted patterns.

4. Closure is the tendency to _____ a broken or incomplete pattern. Contiguity refers to nearness in _____ and space. Stimuli that fall in a defined area, or common region, also tend to be grouped together.

5. _____ psychologists are also known as human factors _____ . These specialists make machine _____ and controls compatible with human _____ and motor capacities.

6. The most effective _____ _____ engineering follows the principles of natural design.

7. Basic elements of line drawings, especially the edges of _____ and parallel edges, appear to be universally recognized.

8. A perceptual organization may be thought of as an _____ held until evidence contradicts it. Camouflage patterns disrupt perceptual _____ , especially figure-ground perceptions.

9. Perceptual organization shifts for ambiguous _____ , which may have more than one interpretation. An example is Necker's _____ . Impossible figures resist stable organization altogether.

How is it possible to see depth and judge distance?

Depth Perception—What If the World Were Flat? Pages 195-198

1. _____ perception is the ability to perceive three-dimensional space and judge distances.

2. Depth perception is present in basic form soon after _____ , as shown by testing with the visual cliff and other methods. As soon as infants become active _____ , they refuse to cross the visual cliff.

3. Depth perception depends on the muscular cues of accommodation (bending of the _____) and convergence (inward movement of the _____).

4. The area of binocular vision is _____ in some birds than in humans. However, birds and other animals may have extremely _____ fields of view.

Pictorial Cues for Depth—A Deep Topic: Pages 199-202

1. A number of pictorial _____ , which will work in _____ paintings, drawings, and photographs, also underlie normal depth perception.

2. Some pictorial cues are: linear perspective (the apparent convergence of _____ _____), relative size (more distant objects appear _____), height in the _____ plane, light and shadow (shadings of light), and overlap or interposition (one object overlaps another).

3. Additional pictorial cues include: texture gradients (textures become _____ in the distance), aerial haze (loss of color and detail at large distances), and relative _____ or _____ parallax (differences in the apparent movement of objects when a viewer is moving).

4. All the pictorial cues are monocular depth cues (only _____ _____ is needed to make use of them).

5. The moon illusion refers to the fact that the moon appears _____ near the horizon than it does when overhead.

6. The moon illusion appears to be explained by the apparent _____ hypothesis, which emphasizes the greater number of depth cues present when the moon is on the _____ .

What effect does learning have on perception?

Perceptual Learning—What If the World Were Upside Down? Pages 202-208

1. Perceptual _____ refers to the changes in the brain due to _____ that alters how we process sensory information.

2. Organizing and interpreting sensations is greatly influenced by learned perceptual _____ . An example is the Ames room, which looks rectangular but is actually distorted so that objects in the room appear to change _____ .

3. Sensitivity to perceptual _____ is also partly learned. Studies of inverted vision show that even the most basic organization is subject to a degree of change. Active _____ speeds adaptation to new perceptual environments.

4. European Americans can be described as individualistic as they tend to focus on the _____ and personal control. This focus influences their perceptual habits to pay attention to _____ in the environment rather than the surrounding ground.

5. East Asians can be described as collective as they tend to focus on _____ relationships and social responsibilities. This focus also influences East Asians' perceptual habits to pay _____ attention to the surrounding ground.

6. Perceptual judgments are almost always related to the _____ surrounding a stimulus, or to an internal frame of reference called the adaptation _____ , which is a personal _____ point for making judgments.

7. Perceptual _____ (misleading perceptions) differ from hallucinations (perceptions of nonexistent stimuli).

8. Illusions are often related to perceptual _____ . One of the most familiar of all illusions, the Müller-Lyer illusion, seems to be related to perceptual learning based on experience with box-shaped _____ and rooms.

9. Linear perspective, _____ invariance relationships, and mislocating the end-points of the _____ also contribute to the Müller-Lyer illusion.

10. Stereoscopic vision (_____ sight) relies on retinal disparity to determine the depth of objects that are within 50 feet of us.

11. People who have lost touch with reality may experience _____ that involve auditory, visual, touch, smell, or taste sensations created by the brain without proper environmental input.

12. " _____ hallucinations" are created by the brain to interpret sensory input received by partially _____ individuals who "see" objects appearing and disappearing in front of their eyes.

How is perception altered by attention, motives, values, and expectations?

Motives and Perception—May I Have Your . . . Attention! Pages 209-211

1. _____ attention refers to giving priority to some sensory messages while excluding others.

2. Attention acts like a _____ or narrowing of the information channel linking the senses to perception.

3. Attention may also be divided among various activities. Divided attention suggests that our _____ for storing and thinking about information is limited.

4. Attention is aroused by _____ stimuli, by repetition (with variation), by stimulus contrast, _____ , or incongruity.

5. _____ blindness refers to people's inability to _____ a stimulus that is right in front of their eyes because they were too busy focusing on another stimulus.

6. Attention is accompanied by an orientation response (OR). When a stimulus is repeated without _____ , the orientation response _____ , an effect known as habituation.

7. Personal motives and _____ often alter perceptions by changing the evaluation of what is seen or by altering attention to specific details.

Perceptual Expectancies—On Your Mark, Get Set: Pages 211-213

1. Perceptions may be based on _____ or bottom-up processing of information.

2. Bottom-up processing, perceptions begin with the organization of low-level _____ . In top-down processing, previous knowledge is used to rapidly _____ sensory information.

3. Attention, prior experience, suggestion, and motives combine in various ways to create perceptual sets, or _____ . A perceptual set is a readiness to perceive in a particular way, induced by strong expectations.

Is Extrasensory Perception Possible?

Extrasensory Perception—Do You Believe in Magic? Pages 213-216

1. Parapsychology is the study of purported _____ phenomena, including clairvoyance (perceiving events at a distance), _____ ("mind reading"), precognition (perceiving future events), and psychokinesis (mentally influencing inanimate objects).

2. Clairvoyance, telepathy, and precognition are purported types of extrasensory _____ .

3. Research in parapsychology remains controversial owing to a variety of problems. _____ and after-the-fact reinterpretation are problems with "natural" ESP episodes.

4. With no evidence supporting the existence of ESP, psychologists strongly suggest that people be _____ of those who claim to have _____ abilities. For example, the owner of the "Miss Cleo" TV-psychic operation made $1 billion from people who believed "Miss Cleo" was a psychic.

5. Many studies of ESP overlook the impact of statistically unusual outcomes that are no more than runs of _____ .

6. The bulk of the evidence to date is _____ the existence of ESP. Very few positive results in ESP research have been replicated (_____) by independent scientists.

7. Stage ESP is based on _____ and tricks.

How reliable are eyewitness reports?

Psychology in Action: Perception and Objectivity—Believing Is Seeing: Pages 217-220

1. Perception is an _____ reconstruction of events. This is one reason why eyewitness testimony is surprisingly _____ .

2. In many crimes, eyewitness accuracy is further damaged by weapon _____ . Similar factors, such as observer stress, brief exposure times, cross-racial inaccuracies, and the wording of questions can _____ eyewitness accuracy.

3. Perceptual accuracy is enhanced by reality _____ , dishabituation, and conscious efforts to pay _____ .

4. It is also valuable to break perceptual habits, to _____ frames of reference, to beware of perceptual sets, and to be aware of the ways in which motives and emotions influence perceptions.

CONNECTIONS

What are perceptual constancies, and what is their role in perception? Pages 189-190

1. _____ native perception
2. _____ empirical
3. _____ perception
4. _____ shape constancy
5. _____ brightness constancy

a. interpreting sensory input
b. interpretation based on prior knowledge
c. produced same brightness when light changes
d. same shape when viewed at various angles
e. natural and inborn perceptions

What basic principles do we use to group sensations into meaningful patterns? Pages 191-195

1. _____ continuity
2. _____ common region
3. _____ closure
4. _____ nearness
5. _____ reversible figure
6. _____ similarity

a.

b.

c.

d.

e.

f.

How is it possible to see depth and judge distance? Pages 195-202

1. _____ texture gradients
2. _____ stereoscopic vision
3. _____ convergence
4. _____ an impossible figure
5. _____ light and shadow
6. _____ relative size
7. _____ Necker's cube
8. _____ overlap
9. _____ retinal disparity
10. _____ linear perspective

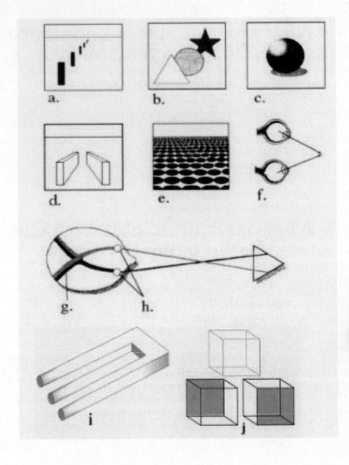

Perception

1. _____ binocular depth cue
2. _____ woodcock
3. _____ monocular depth cue
4. _____ mismatch
5. _____ visual cliff
6. _____ ponzo illusion

a. infant depth perception
b. convergence
c. stereoscopic vision
d. moon illusion
e. accommodation
f. 360 degree view

What effect does learning have on perception? Pages 202-208

1. _____ Zulu
2. _____ motion picture
3. _____ illusions
4. _____ perceptual habits
5. _____ hallucination
6. _____ sane hallucination

a. stroboscopic movement
b. diminished Müller-Lyer illusion
c. imaginary sensation
d. result from perceptual learning
e. partially blinded perception of images
f. misleading perception of real sensations

How is perception altered by attention, motives, values, and expectations? Pages 209-211

1. _____ top-down
2. _____ bottom-up
3. _____ selective attention
4. _____ inattention blindness
5. _____ orientation response
6. _____ advertising

a. bottle neck
b. perceptual expectancy
c. undetected stimulus
d. low-level features
e. double take
f. sex and anxiety

Is Extrasensory Perception Possible? How reliable are eyewitness reports? Pages 209-220

1. _____ dishabituation
2. _____ decline effect
3. _____ perceptual awareness
4. _____ Zener cards
5. _____ Uri Geller
6. _____ telepathy
7. _____ parapsychology
8. _____ psychokinesis
9. _____ Psi events
10. _____ psychic fraud

a. run of luck
b. study of ESP
c. mind reader
d. clairvoyance test
e. "Miss Cleo"
f. ability to move objects
g. surrender to experience
h. Zen and attention
i. stage ESP
j. J. B. Rhine

CHECK YOUR MEMORY

What are perceptual constancies, and what is their role in perception? Pages 189-190

1. Perception involves selecting, organizing, and integrating sensory information.

    TRUE or FALSE

2. Some perceptual abilities must be learned after sight is restored to the previously blind.

    TRUE or FALSE

3. Newborn babies show some evidence of size constancy.

    TRUE or FALSE

4. Houses and cars look like toys from a low-flying airplane because of shape constancy.

    TRUE or FALSE

5. Drunkenness impairs brightness constancy, but size and shape constancy are not usually affected.

    TRUE or FALSE

6. Brightness constancy does not apply to objects illuminated by different amounts of light.

    TRUE or FALSE

What basic principles do we use to group sensations into meaningful patterns? Pages 191-195

1. Basic figure-ground organization is learned at about age 2.

    TRUE or FALSE

2. Illusory figures are related to the principle of closure.

    TRUE or FALSE

3. Contiguity refers to our tendency to see lines as continuous.

    TRUE or FALSE

4. Common region refers to the tendency to see stimuli that are close together as one unit.

    TRUE or FALSE

5. A user-friendly camera must have displays and controls that are compatible with human sensory and motor capacities.

    TRUE or FALSE

6. Natural design minimizes feedback so that people are not distracted by unnecessary information.

   TRUE or FALSE

7. Pre-existing ideas actively guide our interpretation of sensations in many cases.

   TRUE or FALSE

8. Necker's cube and the "three-pronged widget" are impossible figures.

   TRUE or FALSE

9. Color boundaries on objects in drawings are intuitively understood by just about everyone.

   TRUE or FALSE

How is it possible to see depth and judge distance? Pages 195-202

1. Depth perception is partly learned and partly innate.

   TRUE or FALSE

2. Human depth perception typically emerges at about 4 months of age.

   TRUE or FALSE

3. Most infants, when coaxed by their mothers, will crawl cross the visual cliff.

   TRUE or FALSE

4. All depth cues are basically binocular.

   TRUE or FALSE

5. Accommodation and convergence are muscular depth cues.

   TRUE or FALSE

6. Accommodation acts as a depth cue primarily for distances greater than 4 feet from the eyes.

   TRUE or FALSE

7. Convergence acts as a depth cue primarily for distances less than 4 feet from the eyes.

   TRUE or FALSE

8. The brain is sensitive to mismatches in information received from the right and left eyes.

   TRUE or FALSE

9. Depth perception is actually as good when using just one eye as it is when both eyes are open.

   TRUE or FALSE

10. Pigeons, ducks, and hummingbirds can see ultraviolet light.

    TRUE or FALSE

11. With one eye closed, the pictorial depth cues no longer provide information about depth and distance.

    TRUE or FALSE

12. Changing the image size of an object implies that its distance from the viewer has changed, too.

    TRUE or FALSE

13. In a drawing, the closer an object is to the horizon line, the nearer it appears to be to the viewer.

    TRUE or FALSE

14. Aerial perspective is most powerful when the air is exceptionally clear.

    TRUE or FALSE

15. When an observer is moving forward, objects beyond the observer's point of fixation appear to move forward too.

    TRUE or FALSE

16. Accommodation is a binocular depth cue.

    TRUE or FALSE

17. Some familiarity with drawings is required to use overlap as a depth cue.

    TRUE or FALSE

18. The moon's image is magnified by the dense atmosphere near the horizon.

    TRUE or FALSE

19. More depth cues are present when the moon is viewed near the horizon.

    TRUE or FALSE

What effect does learning have on perception? Pages 202-211

1. A lack of relevant perceptual experience makes it difficult to judge upside-down faces.

    TRUE or FALSE

2. Stimuli that lie above the horizon line in a scene are more likely to be perceived as "figure" than as "ground."

    TRUE or FALSE

3. The Ames room is primarily used to test the effects of inverted vision.

    TRUE or FALSE

4. Cats who grow up surrounded by horizontal stripes are unusually sensitive to vertical stripes when they reach maturity.

    TRUE or FALSE

5. People who wear inverting goggles say that eventually the visual world turns right side up again.

   TRUE or FALSE

6. Divers must learn to compensate for visual distortions while underwater.

   TRUE or FALSE

7. Perception is most accurate during active interactions with one's surroundings.

   TRUE or FALSE

8. If your adaptation level for judging weight is 30 pounds, you would judge a 30-pound object as "heavy."

   TRUE or FALSE

9. Hearing voices when no one is speaking is an example of a perceptual illusion.

   TRUE or FALSE

10. Seeing images appearing and disappearing because one is partially blind can be described as "sane hallucination."

    TRUE or FALSE

11. Perceptual illusions are usually not noticeable until measurements reveal that our perceptions are inaccurate or distorted.

    TRUE or FALSE

12. According to Richard Gregory, the arrowhead-tipped line in the Müller-Lyer illusion looks like the outside corner of a building.

    TRUE or FALSE

13. Zulus rarely see round shapes and therefore fail to experience the Müller-Lyer illusion.

    TRUE or FALSE

How is perception altered by attention, motives, values, and expectations? Pages 209-213

1. Messages passing through the "bottleneck" of selective attention appear to prevent other messages from passing through.

   TRUE or FALSE

2. As skills become automated, they free mental capacity for other activities.

   TRUE or FALSE

3. Repetitious stimuli must vary a little to gain attention, otherwise repetition leads to habituation.

   TRUE or FALSE

4. Failing to see a pedestrian crossing a street because one is busy using a cell phone while driving is referred to as attentional blindness.

    TRUE or FALSE

5. Enlarged pupils and brain-wave changes typically accompany the OR.

    TRUE or FALSE

6. Humans are especially sensitive to slow, gradual changes that occur over very long time periods.

    TRUE or FALSE

7. Inattenional blindness refers to the fact that paying close attention to one stimulus can prevent a person from seeing other stimuli that are nearby.

    TRUE or FALSE

8. Emotional stimuli can shift attention away from other information.

    TRUE or FALSE

9. Analyzing information into small features and then building a recognizable pattern is called top-up processing.

    TRUE or FALSE

10. Perceptual sets are frequently created by suggestion.

    TRUE or FALSE

11. You could use a tachistoscope to flash stimuli on a screen for very brief periods.

    TRUE or FALSE

12. Labels and categories have been shown to have little real effect on perceptions.

    TRUE or FALSE

Is Extrasensory Perception Possible? Pages 213-216

1. Uri Geller was one of the first researchers in parapsychology to use the Zener cards.

    TRUE or FALSE

2. Psychokinesis is classified as a psi event, but not a form of ESP.

    TRUE or FALSE

3. Prophetic dreams are regarded as a form of precognition.

    TRUE or FALSE

4. Strange coincidences are strong evidence for the existence of ESP.

    TRUE or FALSE

5. The Zener cards eliminated the possibility of fraud and "leakage" of information in ESP experiments.

   TRUE or FALSE

6. "Miss Cleo" is one of the few people who truly have psychic abilities.

   TRUE or FALSE

7. "Psi missing" is perhaps the best current evidence for ESP.

   TRUE or FALSE

8. Stage ESP relies on deception, sleight of hand, and patented gadgets to entertain the audience.

   TRUE or FALSE

9. Belief in psi events has declined among parapsychologists in recent years.

   TRUE or FALSE

10. A skeptic of psi means that a person is unconvinced and is against the idea that psi exists.

    TRUE or FALSE

How reliable are eyewitness reports? Pages 217-220

1. In many ways we see what we believe, as well as believe what we see.

   TRUE or FALSE

2. The more confident an eyewitness is about the accuracy of his or her testimony, the more likely it is to be accurate.

   TRUE or FALSE

3. The testimony of crime victims is generally more accurate than the testimony of bystanders.

   TRUE or FALSE

4. Police officers and other trained observers are more accurate eyewitnesses than the average person.

   TRUE or FALSE

5. Victims tend to not notice detail information such as the appearance of their attacker because they fall prey to weapon focus.

   TRUE or FALSE

6. Reality testing is the process Abraham Maslow described as a "surrender" to experience.

   TRUE or FALSE

7. Perceptually, Zen masters have been shown to habituate more rapidly than the average person.

   TRUE or FALSE

FINAL SURVEY AND REVIEW

What are perceptual constancies, and what is their role in perception?

Perceptual Constancies—Taming an Unruly World: Pages 189-190

1. Perception is the process of assembling _____ into patterns that provide a usable _____ _____ of the world.

2. In vision, the _____ image changes from moment to moment, but the external world appears stable and undistorted because of perceptual _____ .

3. In size and shape constancy, the perceived sizes and shapes of objects remain the same even though their retinal images change size and shape. The apparent _____ of objects remains stable (a property called brightness constancy) because each reflects a constant _____ of _____ .

4. Perceptual constancies are partly _____ (inborn) and partly _____ (learned).

What basic principles do we use to group sensations into meaningful patterns?

Perceptual Organization—Getting It All Together: Pages 191-195

1. The most basic organization of sensations is a division into _____ and _____ (object and background).

2. A number of factors, identified by the _____ psychologists, contribute to the organization of sensations. These are _____ , similarity, continuity, _____ , contiguity, common region, and combinations of the preceding.

3. Stimuli near one another tend to be perceptually grouped together. So, too, do stimuli that are similar in appearance. _____ refers to the fact that perceptions tend to be organized as simple, uninterrupted patterns.

4. _____ refers to nearness in time and space. Stimuli that fall in a defined area, or common region, also tend to be grouped together.

5. Engineering psychologists are also known as _____ _____ engineers. These specialists make machine displays and _____ compatible with human sensory and _____ capacities.

6. The most effective human factors engineering follows the principles of _____ _____ .

7. Basic elements of line drawings, especially the edges of surfaces and _____ _____ , appear to be universally recognized.

8. A perceptual organization may be thought of as an hypothesis held until evidence contradicts it. _____ patterns disrupt perceptual organization, especially figure-ground perceptions.

9. Perceptual organization shifts for _____ stimuli, which may have more than one interpretation. An example is _____ cube. Impossible _____ resist stable organization altogether.

How is it possible to see depth and judge distance?

Depth Perception—What If the World Were Flat? Pages 195-198

1. Depth perception is the ability to perceive _____ space and judge distances.

2. Depth perception is present in basic form soon after birth, as shown by testing with the _____ _____ and other methods. As soon as infants become active crawlers they refuse to cross the deep side of the _____ _____ .

3. Depth perception depends on the muscular cues of _____ (bending of the lens) and _____ (inward movement of the eyes).

4. The area of _____ vision is smaller in some birds than in humans. However, birds and other animals may have extremely wide _____ _____ _____ .

Pictorial Cues for Depth—A Deep Topic: Pages 199-202

1. A number of _____ cues, which will work in flat paintings, drawings, and photographs, also underlie normal depth perception.

2. Some of these cues are: _____ _____ (the apparent convergence of parallel lines), relative size (more distant objects appear smaller), height in the picture plane, light and shadow (shadings of light), and overlap or _____ (one object overlaps another).

3. Additional pictorial cues include: texture _____ (textures become finer in the distance), aerial haze (loss of color and detail at large distances), and relative motion or motion _____ (differences in the apparent movement of objects when a viewer is moving).

4. All the pictorial cues are _____ depth cues (only one eye is needed to make use of them).

5. The moon illusion refers to the fact that the moon appears larger near the _____ .

6. The moon illusion appears to be explained by the _____ _____ hypothesis, which emphasizes the greater number of _____ _____ present when the moon is on the horizon.

What effect does learning have on perception?

Perceptual Learning—What If the World Were Upside Down? Pages 202-208

1. _____ _____ refers to the changes in the brain due to learning that alters how we process sensory information.

2. Organizing and interpreting sensations is greatly influenced by learned _____ _____ . An example is the _____ room, which looks rectangular but is actually distorted so that objects in the room appear to change size.

3. European Americans can be described as _____ as they tend to focus on the _____ and personal control. This focus influences their perceptual habits to pay attention to _____ in the environment rather than the surrounding ground.

4. East Asians can be described as _____ as they tend to focus on interpersonal relationships and _____ responsibilities. This focus also influences East Asians' perceptual habits to pay _____ attention to the surrounding ground.

5. Sensitivity to perceptual features is also partly learned. Studies of _____ vision show that even the most basic organization is subject to a degree of change. Active movement speeds _____ to new perceptual environments.

6. Perceptual judgments are almost always related to the context surrounding a stimulus, or to an internal _____ _____ _____ called the _____ level, which is a personal medium point for making judgments.

7. Perceptual _____ (misleading perceptions) differ from _____ (perceptions of nonexistent stimuli).

8. Illusions are often related to perceptual habits. One of the most familiar of all illusions, the _____ illusion, involves two equal-length lines tipped with arrowheads and V's. This illusion seems to be related to perceptual learning based on experience with box-shaped buildings and rooms.

9. Linear perspective, size-distance _____ relationships, and mislocating the _____ of the lines also contribute to the Müller-Lyer illusion.

10. _____ (three-dimensional sight) relies on retinal disparity to determine the depth of objects that are within 50 feet of us.

11. People who have lost touch with _____ may experience hallucinations that involve auditory, _____ , touch, smell, or taste sensations created by the brain without proper environmental input.

12. "_____ hallucinations" are created by the brain to interpret sensory input received by partially blind individuals who "see" objects appearing and disappearing in front of their eyes.

How is perception altered by attention, motives, values, and expectations?

Motives and Perception—May I Have Your . . . Attention! Pages 209-211

1. _____ _____ refers to giving priority to some sensory messages while excluding others.

2. Attention acts like a bottleneck or narrowing of the information _____ linking the senses to perception.

3. Attention may also be split among various activities. _____ attention suggests that our capacity for storing and thinking about information is limited.

4. Attention is aroused by intense stimuli, by repetition (with variation), by stimulus _____ , change, or _____ .

5. _____ blindness refers to people's inability to detect a stimulus that is right in front of their eyes because they were too busy focusing on another stimulus or activity.

6. Attention is accompanied by an _____ _____ (OR). When a stimulus is repeated without change, the OR decreases, an effect known as _____ .

7. Personal _____ and values often alter perceptions by changing the evaluation of what is seen or by altering attention to specific details.

Perceptual Expectancies—On Your Mark, Get Set: Pages 211-213

1. Perceptions may be based on top-down or bottom-up _____ of information.

2. _____ perceptions begin with the organization of low-level features. In _____ processing, previous knowledge is used to rapidly organize sensory information.

3. Attention, prior experience, suggestion, and motives combine in various ways to create _____ _____ , or expectancies. A _____ _____ is a readiness to perceive in a particular way, induced by strong expectations.

Is Extrasensory Perception Possible?

Extrasensory Perception—Do You Believe in Magic? Pages 213-216

1. _____ is the study of purported psi phenomena, including clairvoyance (perceiving events at a distance), telepathy ("mind reading"), _____ (perceiving future events), and psychokinesis (mentally influencing inanimate objects).

2. Clairvoyance, telepathy, and precognition are purported types of _____ perception.

3. Research in parapsychology remains controversial owing to a variety of problems. Coincidence and after-the-fact _____ are problems with "natural" ESP episodes.

4. With no evidence supporting the existence of ESP, psychologists strongly suggest that people be _____ of those who claim to have _____ abilities. For example, the owner of the "Miss Cleo" TV-psychic operation made $1 billion from people who believed "Miss Cleo" was a psychic.

5. Many studies of ESP overlook the impact of _____ unusual outcomes that are no more than runs of luck.

6. The bulk of the evidence to date is against the existence of ESP. Very few positive results in ESP research have been _____ (repeated) by independent scientists.

7. _____ ESP is based on deception and tricks.

How reliable are eyewitness reports?

Psychology in Action: Perception and Objectivity—Believing Is Seeing: Pages 217-220

1. Perception is an active _____ of events. This is one reason why eyewitness testimony is surprisingly inaccurate.

2. In many crimes, eyewitness accuracy is further damaged by _____ focus. Similar factors, such as observer _____ , brief exposure times, cross-racial inaccuracies, and the wording of questions can lower eyewitness accuracy.

3. Perceptual accuracy is enhanced by reality testing, _____ , and conscious efforts to pay attention.

4. It is also valuable to break _____ _____ , to broaden frames of reference, to beware of perceptual sets, and to be aware of the ways in which motives and emotions influence perceptions.

MASTERY TEST

1. The Ames room creates a conflict between
    a. horizontal features and vertical features
    b. attention and habituation
    c. top-down and bottom-up processing
    d. shape constancy and size constancy

2. Weapon focus tends to lower eyewitness accuracy because it affects
   a. selective attention
   b. the adaptation level
   c. perceptions of contiguity
   d. dishabituation

3. Stereograms create an illusion of depth by mimicking the effects of
   a. accommodation
   b. convergence
   c. retinal disparity
   d. stroboscopic motion

4. Which perceptual constancy is most affected by sitting in the front row at a movie theater?
   a. size constancy
   b. shape constancy
   c. brightness constancy
   d. depth constancy

5. The fact that American tourists in London tend to look in the wrong direction before stepping into crosswalks is based on
   a. habituation
   b. perceptual habits
   c. adaptation levels
   d. unconscious transference

6. When they look at drawings and photographs, people are more likely to notice unexpected objects. This is explained by the effects of _____ on perception.
   a. pictorial depth cues
   b. selective attention
   c. habituation
   d. figure-ground organization

7. Size constancy
   a. is strongest when objects are above the horizon line
   b. is affected by experience with seeing objects of various sizes
   c. requires that objects be illuminated by light of the same intensity
   d. all of the preceding

8. Adaptation to visual distortions is most rapid if people are allowed to
   a. remain immobile
   b. move actively
   c. move their eye muscles
   d. habituate their adaptation levels

9. Perceptual categories and perceptual expectancies tend to promote
    a. top-down processing
    b. bottom-up processing
    c. divided attention
    d. reality testing

10. Both internal frames of reference and external _____ alter the interpretation given to a stimulus.
    a. reconstructions
    b. bottlenecks
    c. accommodations
    d. contexts

11. Which of the following cues would be of greatest help to a person trying to thread a needle?
    a. light and shadow
    b. texture gradients
    c. linear perspective
    d. overlap

12. The American woodcock has a narrow band of _____ but an unusually wide

    _____.
    a. monocular vision, spectral sensitivity
    b. accommodation, field of view
    c. binocular vision, field of view
    d. spectral sensitivity, binocular range

13. Which of the following purported paranormal phenomena is not a form of ESP?
    a. clairvoyance
    b. telepathy
    c. precognition
    d. psychokinesis

14. Size-distance invariances contribute to which of the following?
    a. Müller-Lyer illusion
    b. the stroboscopic illusion
    c. perceptual hallucinations
    d. changes in a person's adaptation level

15. The visual cliff is used primarily to test infant
    a. size constancy
    b. figure-ground perception
    c. depth perception
    d. adaptation to spatial distortions

16. Which of the following organizational principles is based on nearness in time and space?
    a. continuity
    b. closure
    c. contiguity
    d. size constancy

17. Which of the following is both a muscular and a monocular depth cue?
    a. convergence
    b. relative motion
    c. aerial perspective
    d. accommodation

18. The problem with "natural" ESP occurrences is that it is usually impossible to rule out
    a. the fact that they are replicated
    b. the possibility that they are caused by habituation
    c. the ganzfeld effect
    d. coincidences

19. Which of the following is not part of the explanation of the Müller-Lyer illusion?
    a. aerial perspective
    b. accommodation
    c. living in a "square" culture
    d. mislocating the ends of the lines

20. The term _____ refers to our limited capacity for storing and thinking about information.
    a. selective attention
    b. habituated attention
    c. divided attention
    d. selective expectancy

21. A previously blind person has just had her sight restored. Which of the following perceptual experiences is she most likely to have?
    a. perceptual set
    b. size constancy
    c. linear perspective
    d. figure-ground

22. An artist manages to portray a face with just a few unconnected lines. Apparently the artist has capitalized on
    a. closure
    b. contiguity
    c. the reversible figure effect
    d. the principle of camouflage

23. The "boiled frog syndrome" is related to the idea that _____ elicit attention.
    a. repetition, habituation, and categories
    b. expectancies, constancies, and ambiguities
    c. change, contrast, and incongruity
    d. continuity, camouflage, and similarity

24. The most basic source of stereoscopic vision is
    a. accommodation
    b. retinal disparity
    c. convergence
    d. stroboscopic motion

25. Necker's cube is a good example of
    a. an ambiguous stimulus
    b. an impossible figure
    c. camouflage
    d. a binocular depth cue

26. Enlarged pupils, a pause in breathing, and increased blood flow to the head are associated with
    a. brightness constancy
    b. the onset of habituation
    c. reality testing
    d. an orientation response

27. Skeptics regard the decline effect as evidence that _____ occurred in an ESP test.
    a. replication
    b. cheating
    c. a run of luck
    d. leakage

28. Which of the following is a binocular depth cue?
    a. accommodation
    b. convergence
    c. linear perspective
    d. motion parallax

29. Ambiguous stimuli allow us to hold more than one perceptual
    a. gradient
    b. parallax
    c. constancy
    d. hypothesis

30. Increased perceptual awareness is especially associated with
    a. dishabituation
    b. unconscious transference
    c. high levels of stress
    d. stimulus repetition without variation

31. Effective, natural design provides
    a. clear feedback
    b. behavioral settings
    c. participative displays
    d. lifelike models

32. Joan, failing to see a pedestrian crossing the street because she is too busy using a cell phone, is an example of:
    a. attentional blindness.
    b. perceptual habits.
    c. inattentional blindness.
    d. apparent-distance hypothesis.

33. Megan screams out loud saying "insects are crawling everywhere!" when none are present and Hilda, who is partially blind, claims that people are disappearing and appearing in front of her eyes. Megan is experiencing _____ because she is seeing objects that are not present in her environment and Hilda is experiencing _____ since her brain in trying to seek meaningful patterns from her sensory input.
    a. hallucinations; "sane hallucinations"
    b. hallucinations; inattentional blindess
    c. illusions; extrasensory perception (ESP)
    d. none of the above

34. European Americans are to _____ as East Asians are to _____.
    a. collectivists; individualists
    b. individualists; collectivists
    c. collectivists; naturalists
    d. naturalists; individualists

LANGUAGE DEVELOPMENT - Perceiving the World

Word roots

The Greek word *stereos* means hard, firm, and solid. Since solids are three-dimensional, the term has come to suggest three-dimensionality in combination with other word roots, the word "stereoscopic," for example. Other words have developed in the English language that make use of the idea of hardness or firmness. For example, the term "stereotype" refers to hard or firmly fixed ideas.

What are perceptual constancies, and what is their role in perception?

Preview: Murder! (p. 189)

> (189) *passed out*: became unconscious

> (189) *integrates*: blends together

Perceptual Constancies—Taming an Unruly World (pp. 189-190)

> (189) *cataract*: clouding of the lens of the eye

> (189) *innate*: inborn; a biologically inherited ability

> (190) *jumble*: not organize

> (190) *Marilyn Monroe*: famous blonde movie actress (1926-1962)

> (190) *Madonna*: famous blonde popular singer, considered by some people to resemble Marilyn Monroe

> (190) *neon lamps*: type of electric lighting characterized by bright colors that glow

> (190) *hurdles*: difficulties, problems, barriers

What basic principles do we use to group sensations into meaningful patterns?

Perceptual Organization—Getting It All Together (pp. 191-195)

> (191) *Birds of a feather flock together*: just as birds of one type tend to stay together, so do people or things with similar characteristics group together

> (192) *camouflaged*: disguised, hidden

> (193) *culprit*: that which is causing something

> (194) *widget*: gadget, unnamed item considered as an example

> (194) *Papua New Guinea*: western Pacific nation that includes the eastern half of the island of New Guinea, north of Australia

How is it possible to see depth and judge distance?

Depth Perception—What If the World Were Flat? (pp. 195-198)

> (195) *shoot baskets*: play basketball

> (195) *thread a needle*: putting thread through the very small opening in a needle; the first step in sewing

> (195) *skydiving*: the sport of jumping out of an airplane with a parachute; here referring to the baby jumping off the table

> (195) *goggles*: large glasses or lenses

(196) *crash landings*: used to describe landings of airplanes under emergency conditions; here referring to the falls that babies take when they are first learning to crawl and walk

(196) *zap flies*: to kill flies

(197) *3-D movies*: a popular movie format in the 1950s where patrons wore special glasses to view specially-prepared movies; objects in the movies appeared to "pop out" to viewers

(197) *simulate*: copy or imitate

(197) *disparities*: differences

(198) *bird's eye view*: seeing the world from the perspective of a high-flying bird

(198) *acute stereoscopic vision*: outstanding depth perception

(198) *foxy*: clever, sly

(198) *holdover*: something that continues to exist from previous times

(198) *hitchhiker:* a person who asks for rides from passing cars or trucks

Pictorial Cues for Depth—A Deep Topic (pp. 199-202)

(199) *gauge*: measure

(199) *impart*: to show

(199) *Star Wars series*: series of famous science fiction movies

(199) *illusion*: a misleading image presented to vision

(200) *gradients*: gradual changes or variations

(200) *cobblestone street*: a street paved with round, flat stones

(200) *smog*: a combination of smoke and fog

(202) *wandering eye*: a condition in which an eye is constantly moving

What effect does learning have on perception?

Perceptual Learning—What If the World Were Upside Down? (pp. 202-208)

(202) *icons*: small images on a computer screen used to represent functions or programs

(202) *commands*: instructions one gives to a computer program

(203) *linebacker*: in football, a defensive player positioned behind the linemen

(203) *doctored*: altered, changed

(203) *ingrained*: innate, firmly fixed

(203) *grotesque*: bizarre, differing very much from what is normal

(203) *sleight of hand*: skill and dexterity used to trick the eye in stage magic

(203) *lopsided*: not symmetrical or balanced in shape

(204) *tuned*: pay attention to

(205) *grossly*: to a very large extent

(206) *"heavy"* (If you are an aging rock star, you will no doubt call everything *"heavy,"* man.): slang for "meaningful" or "significant"

(206) *snapshots*: a picture at a particular point in time

(208) *compensate*: neutralize the effect of; counterbalance

(208) *medium-priced meal*: an average cost for a meal

How is perception altered by attention, motives, values, and expectation?

Motives and Perception—May I Have Your . . . Attention! (pp. 209-211)

(209) *put others on hold:* temporarily ignore

(209) *bottleneck*: the relatively narrow area of a bottle; used here to indicate a slowdown in information

(209) *jumbo jet*: largest of jet aircraft

(209) *tuning the car's radio*: selecting a station on the radio

(209) *to capture attention*: to make one aware or take notice

(209) *dripping faucet*: water slowly coming from a faucet in drops

(210) *incongruity*: not conforming to the expected pattern, inconsistent

(210) *do a double take*: look, look away, and look back, stop and stare

(210) *are pushed* (other articles *are pushed* in ads): try very hard to sell

(211) *infatuated*: in love

(211) *swastika*: symbol used by Adolf Hitler in Nazi Germany, and so perceived as an anti-Semitic (anti-Jewish) symbol

Perceptual Expectancies—On Your Mark, Get Set (pp. 211-213)

(212) *starting blocks*: fixtures on the track where a runner places his or her feet prior to starting a race

(212) *backfires*: a loud banging noise made by a vehicle due to improper combustion

(212) *jump the gun*: start the race before the starting gun fires

(212) *punk*: a derogatory term for a juvenile delinquent, a young person who has been in trouble with the law

(212) *queer*: a derogatory term for a homosexual

(212) *bitch*: a derogatory term for a woman

Is extrasensory perception possible?

Extrasensory Perception—Do You Believe in Magic? (pp. 213-216)

(213) *psychics*: people who claim to be sensitive to nonphysical or supernatural forces and influences

(213) *purported*: supposed; claimed

(213) *prophetic*: predictive of the future

(214) *hunch*: guess

(214) *meticulous*: very careful and precise; detail oriented

(214) *plague the field*: to trouble

(214) *hits*: correct answers

(214) *Jamaican-accented*: a language accent that sounds like the person is from Jamaica

(215) *Zero. Zip. Nada*: words meaning "no outcome"

(215) *it is based on...patented gadgets*: tricks done by magicians and by those who practice ESP on stage use devices that can be bought in magic supply stores, such as trick playing cards or dice

(215) *sloppiness*: showing a lack of care

(216) *"die in the box" tests*: the person being tested is asked to guess which number is showing on a die (singular of dice) that is hidden in a box

(216) *A quick trip to a casino would allow the person to retire for life*: if a person really had ESP, he or she could gamble and be sure of winning lots of money

(216) *rampant*: widespread

(216) *intrepid*: fearless

How reliable are eyewitness reports?

Psychology in Action: Perception and Objectivity—Believing Is Seeing (pp. 217-220)

(217) *obscured*: hidden

(217) *pop of a flashbulb*: sound the flash of a camera makes

(217) *liability*: something that is to a person's disadvantage

(217) *infallible*: without mistakes

(217) *to put it bluntly*: to say plainly

(218) *degrade*: to break down

(218) *exonerated*: to be cleared of blame

(219) *surrender to experience*: have overconfidence in one's own experience

(219) *if you've seen one tree, you've seen them all*: the tendency to use a single example to generalize to all objects in a category

(220) ***"If the doors of perception were cleansed, man would see everything as it is, infinite."***: to see without judgment leads to an accurate view of the surrounding world

(220) *swayed*: influenced

Solutions

RECITE AND REVIEW

What are perceptual constancies, and what is their role in perception?

1. patterns; model
2. image; perceptual
3. constancy; constant
4. inborn; learned

What basic principles do we use to group sensations into meaningful patterns?

1. object; background
2. organization; similarity; common
3. grouped; appearance
4. complete; time
5. Engineering; engineers; displays; sensory
6. human; factors
7. surfaces
8. hypothesis; organization
9. stimuli; cube

How is it possible to see depth and judge distance?

1. Depth
2. birth; crawlers
3. lens; eyes
4. smaller; wide

Pictorial Cues for Depth—A Deep Topic: Pages 199-202

1. cues; flat
2. parallel; lines; smaller; picture
3. finer; motion; motion
4. one; eye
5. larger
6. distance; horizon

What effect does learning have on perception?

1. learning; learning
2. habits; size
3. features; movement
4. self; figures
5. interprersonal; more
6. context; level; medium
7. illusions
8. habits; buildings
9. size-distance; lines
10. three-dimensional
11. hallucinations
12. Sane; blind

How is perception altered by attention, motives, values, and expectations?

1. Selective
2. bottleneck
3. capacity
4. intense; change
5. Inattentional; detect
6. change; decreases
7. values

Perceptual Expectancies—On Your Mark, Get Set: Pages 211-213

1. top-down
2. features; organize
3. expectancies

Is Extrasensory Perception Possible?

1.	psi; telepathy	4.	skeptical; psychic	7.	deception
2.	perception	5.	luck		
3.	Coincidence	6.	against; repeated		

How reliable are eyewitness reports?

1.	active; inaccurate	3.	testing; attention
2.	focus; lower	4.	broaden

CONNECTIONS

What are perceptual constancies, and what is their role in perception? Pages 189-190

1.	E.	3.	A.	5.	C.
2.	B.	4.	D.		

What basic principles do we use to group sensations into meaningful patterns? Pages 191-195

1.	C.	3.	D.	5.	F.
2.	E.	4.	A.	6.	B.

How is it possible to see depth and judge distance? Pages 195-202

1.	E.	5.	C.	9.	H.
2.	G.	6.	A.	10.	D.
3.	F.	7.	J.		
4.	I.	8.	B.		

Perception

1.	B.	3.	E.	5.	A.
2.	F.	4.	C.	6.	D.

What effect does learning have on perception? Pages 202-208

1.	B.	3.	F.	5.	C.
2.	A.	4.	D.	6.	E.

How is perception altered by attention, motives, values, and expectations? Pages 209-211

1.	B.	3.	A.	5.	E.
2.	D.	4.	C.	6.	F.

Is Extrasensory Perception Possible? How reliable are eyewitness reports? Pages 209-220

1. H.	5. I.	9. J.
2. A.	6. C.	10. E.
3. G.	7. B.	
4. D.	8. F.	

CHECK YOUR MEMORY

What are perceptual constancies, and what is their role in perception? Pages 189-190

1. T	3. T	5. F
2. T	4. F	6. T

What basic principles do we use to group sensations into meaningful patterns? Pages 191-195

1. F	4. T	7. T
2. T	5. T	8. F
3. F	6. F	9. F

How is it possible to see depth and judge distance? Pages 195-202

1. T	8. T	15. T
2. T	9. F	16. F
3. F	10. T	17. F
4. F	11. F	18. F
5. T	12. T	19. T
6. F	13. F	
7. F	14. F	

What effect does learning have on perception? Pages 202-211

1. T	6. T	11. T
2. F	7. T	12. T
3. F	8. F	13. F
4. F	9. F	
5. F	10. T	

How is perception altered by attention, motives, values, and expectations? Pages 209-213

1. T	2. T	3. T

4. F	7. T	10. T
5. T	8. T	11. T
6. F	9. F	12. F

Is Extrasensory Perception Possible? Pages 213-216

1. F	5. F	9. T
2. T	6. F	10. F
3. T	7. F	
4. F	8. T	

How reliable are eyewitness reports? Pages 217-220

1. T	4. F	7. F
2. F	5. T	
3. F	6. F	

FINAL SURVEY AND REVIEW

What are perceptual constancies, and what is their role in perception?

1. sensations; mental; model	3. brightness; proportion; light
2. retinal; constancies	4. native; empirical

What basic principles do we use to group sensations into meaningful patterns?

1. figure; ground	4. Contiguity	7. parallel; edges
2. Gestalt; nearness; closure	5. human; factors; controls; motor	8. Camouflage
3. Closure	6. natural; design	9. ambiguous; Necker's; figures

How is it possible to see depth and judge distance?

1. three-dimensional	3. accommodation; convergence
2. visual; cliff; visual; cliff	4. binocular; fields; of; view

Pictorial Cues for Depth—A Deep Topic: Pages 199-202

1. pictorial	3. gradients; parallax	5. horizon
2. linear; perspective; interposition	4. monocular	6. apparent; distance; depth; cues

What effect does learning have on perception?

1. Perceptual; learning	4. collective; social; more	7. illusions; hallucinations
2. perceptual; habits; Ames	5. inverted; adaptation	8. Müller-Lyer
3. individualistic; self; figures	6. frame; of; reference; adaptation	9. invariance; end-points

10. Stereoscopic vision   11. reality; visual   12. Sane

How is perception altered by attention, motives, values, and expectations?

1. Selective; attention
2. channel
3. Divided

4. contrast; incongruity
5. Inattentional

6. orientation; response; habituation
7. motives

Perceptual Expectancies—On Your Mark, Get Set: Pages 211-213

1. processing

2. Bottom-up; top-down

3. perceptual; sets; perceptual; set

Is Extrasensory Perception Possible?

1. Parapsychology; precognition
2. extrasensory
3. reinterpretation

4. skeptical; psychic
5. statistically
6. replicated

7. Stage

How reliable are eyewitness reports?

1. reconstruction
2. weapon; stress

3. dishabituation
4. perceptual; habits

MASTERY TEST

How reliable are eyewitness reports?

1. D, p. 203
2. A, p. 218
3. C, p. 197
4. B, pp. 189-190
5. B, p. 202
6. B, p. 209
7. B, p. 189
8. B, p. 204
9. A, p. 211
10. D, pp. 205-206
11. D, p. 196
12. C, p. 198
13. D, p. 213

14. A, p. 207
15. C, p. 195
16. C, p. 191
17. D, p. 196
18. D, p. 214
19. A, pp. 207-208
20. C, p. 209
21. D, p. 191
22. A, p. 191
23. C, p. 210
24. B, p. 197
25. A, p. 192
26. D, p. 210

27. C, pp. 214-215
28. B, p. 196
29. D, p. 192
30. A, p. 219
31. A, p. 193
32. C, p. 210
33. A, p. 206
34. B, p. 205

States of Consciousness

Chapter Overview

Consciousness consists of everything you are aware of at a given instant. Altered states of consciousness (ASCs) differ significantly from normal waking consciousness. Many conditions produce ASCs, which frequently have culturally defined meanings.

Sleep is an innate biological rhythm characterized by changes in consciousness and brain activity. People who deprive themselves of sleep may experience sleep-deprivation psychosis. Hypersomnia is a common problem that adolescents have due to lack of sleep. Brain-wave patterns and sleep behaviors define four stages of sleep. The two most basic forms of sleep are rapid eye movement (REM) sleep and non-rapid eye movement (NREM) sleep. During REM sleep, the body's major muscles tend to be paralyzed. However, approximately 30 percent of individuals have experienced sleep paralysis outside of REM sleep referred to as hypnopompic hallucination upon awakening from their sleep. Dreams and nightmares occur primarily in REM sleep. Sleepwalking, sleeptalking, and night terrors are NREM events. Insomnia and other sleep disturbances are common, but generally treatable. REM rebound occurs when one is deprived of REM sleep the night before. Dreaming is emotionally restorative and it may help form adaptive memories. The psychodynamic view portrays dreams as a form of wish fulfillment; the activation-synthesis hypothesis says that dreaming is a physiological process with little meaning.

Hypnosis is characterized by narrowed attention and increased openness to suggestion. People vary in hypnotic susceptibility. Most hypnotic phenomena are related to the basic suggestion effect. Hypnosis can relieve pain and it has other useful effects, but it is not magic. Stage hypnotists simulate hypnosis in order to entertain. Similar to hypnotic suggestion, one might mentally "move" an object by using autosuggestion.

Sensory deprivation refers to any major reduction in external stimulation. Sensory deprivation also produces deep relaxation and a variety of perceptual effects. It can be used to help people enhance creative thinking and to change bad habits.

Psychoactive drugs are substances that alter consciousness. Most can be placed on a scale ranging from stimulation to depression, although some drugs are better classified as hallucinogens. The potential for abuse is high for drugs that lead to physical dependence, but psychological dependence can also be a serious problem. Drug abuse is often a symptom, rather than a cause, of personal maladjustment. It is supported by the immediate pleasure but delayed consequences associated with many psychoactive drugs, and by cultural values that encourage drug abuse.

Various strategies, ranging from literal to highly symbolic, can be used to reveal the meanings of dreams. Dreaming—especially lucid dreaming—can be a source of creativity and it may be used for problem solving and personal growth.

Learning Objectives

1. Define *consciousness, waking consciousness,* the *first-person experience,* and *altered state of consciousness (ASC) and* list causes of an ASC.

2. Describe some of the basic characteristics of sleep. Include what skills one is able to perform when asleep, sleep as a biological rhythm, and the concept of *microsleep.*

3. Describe the symptoms of two or three days of sleep deprivation and discuss temporary sleep deprivation psychosis.

4. Discuss the concept of sleep patterns. Include the characteristics of long and short sleepers, the relationship between age and sleep needs, and the brain's involvement in controlling sleep.

5. Explain the four stages of sleep, briefly describing the events in each stage.

6. Differentiate between the two basic states of sleep, REM and NREM and describe the symptoms of REM behavior disorder and the occurrence of hypnopompic hallucinations.

7. List factors that contribute to sleep problems in American society and describe the following sleep disturbances (Table 7.1):

   a. hypersomnia

   b. periodic limb movement syndrome

   c. restless legs syndrome

   d. sleep drunkenness

   e. sleep-wake schedule disorder.

8. List and describe the characteristics and treatments of the three types of insomnia.

9. Describe and differentiate between sleepwalking and sleeptalking and nightmares *vs.* night terrors. State three steps that can be used to eliminate nightmares.

10. Describe narcolepsy and cataplexy.

11. Describe the sleep disorder known as sleep apnea including its nature, cause, treatments, and relationship to SIDS. Describe some possible causes of SIDS and the sleep position which seems to minimize SIDS in infants.

12. Explain the relationship between REM sleep and dreaming; tell how many times per night most people dream and how long dreams usually last; discuss the cause and symptoms of REM rebound; and describe the possible functions of REM sleep, including its relationship to memory.

13. Explain how Calvin Hall and Sigmund Freud viewed dreams and discuss the activation-synthesis hypothesis concerning dreaming.

14. Define *hypnosis*; describe the history of hypnosis from Mesmer through its use today; explain how a person's hypnotic susceptibility can be determined; and list four factors common to all hypnotic techniques.

15. Explain how hypnosis may affect a person's willingness to act in a way that he or she would not normally act; define the basic suggestion effect; and describe the dissociation in awareness caused by hypnosis, including the concept of the hidden observer.

16. Explain six conclusions concerning what can and cannot be achieved with hypnosis and describe five features of the stage that are used by stage hypnotists to perform their acts.

17. Explain what sensory deprivation is and describe its positive and negative effects.

18. Define the term *psychoactive drug*; describe how various drugs affect the nervous system; differentiate physical dependence from psychological dependence; and describe five different patterns of drug use.

19. Describe the following frequently abused drugs in terms of their effects, possible medical uses, side-effects or long-term symptoms, organic damage potential, and potential for physical and/or psychological dependence:

    a. amphetamines (include the term *amphetamine psychosis*)

    b. cocaine (include the three signs of abuse)

    c. MDMA (Ecstasy)

    d. caffeine (include the term *caffeinism*)

    e. nicotine

    f. barbiturates

    g. GHB

    h. tranquilizers (include the concept of drug interaction)

    i. alcohol (include the concept of binge drinking)

    j. hallucinogens (including marijuana)

20. Explain the three phases in the development of a drinking problem; describe moderated drinking; and discuss the various treatment methods for alcoholism.

The following objective is related to the material in the "Psychology in Action" section of your text.

1. Explain how Freud, Hall, Cartwright, Perls, and Globus analyzed dreams; outline procedures for using dreams to improve creativity; and describe lucid dreaming. Include an explanation of Freud's four dream processes.

RECITE AND REVIEW

What is an altered state of consciousness?

State of Consciousness—The Many Faces of Awareness: Page 224

1. States of _____ that differ from normal, alert, _____ consciousness are called altered states of consciousness (ASCs).

2. ASCs involve distinct shifts in the quality and _____ of mental activity.

3. Altered states are especially associated with _____ and _____ , hypnosis, meditation, _____ deprivation, and psychoactive drugs.

4. Cultural conditioning greatly affects what altered states a person recognizes, seeks, considers _____ , and attains.

What are the effects of sleep loss or changes in sleep patterns?

Sleep—A Nice Place to Visit: Pages 224-228

1. Sleep is an innate biological _____ essential for _____ .

2. Higher animals and people deprived of sleep experience _____ microsleeps.

3. Moderate sleep loss mainly affects alertness and self-motivated performance on _____ or boring tasks.

4. Extended sleep _____ can (somewhat rarely) produce a _____ sleep-deprivation psychosis, marked by confusion, delusions, and possibly hallucinations.

5. _____ change during puberty increases adolescents need for _____ , which many lack since they tend to stay up late and get up early for school. This pattern causes them to experience hypersomnia (excessive daytime _____).

6. The "storm and stress" that adolescents experience may, in part, be caused by _____ of sleep.

7. Circadian _____ within the body are closely tied to sleep, activity levels, and energy cycles.

8. Sleep patterns show some flexibility, but 7 to 8 hours remains average. The unscheduled human sleep-waking cycle averages _____ hours and _____ minutes, but cycles of _____ and _____ tailor it to 24-hour days.

9. The amount of daily sleep _____ steadily from birth to old age and switches from multiple sleep-wake cycles to once-a-day sleep periods.

10. Adapting to _____ or _____ sleep cycles is difficult and inefficient for most people.

Are there different stages of sleep? How does dream sleep differ from dreamless sleep?

Stages of Sleep—The Nightly Roller-Coaster Ride: Pages 228-231

1. Sleepiness is associated with the accumulation of a sleep hormone in the _____ and spinal cord.

2. Sleep depends on which of _____ opposed sleep and waking systems in the _____ is dominant at any given moment.

3. Sleep occurs in _____ stages defined by changes in behavior and brain _____ recorded with an electroencephalograph (EEG).

4. Stage 1, _____ sleep, has small irregular brain waves. In stage 2, _____ spindles appear. _____ waves appear in stage 3. Stage 4, or deep sleep, is marked by almost pure delta waves.

5. Sleepers _____ between stages 1 and 4 (passing through stages 2 and 3) several times each night.

6. There are two basic sleep states, rapid eye _____ (REM) sleep and non-REM (NREM) sleep.

7. REM sleep is much more strongly associated with _____ than non-REM sleep is.

8. _____ and REMs occur mainly during stage 1 sleep, but usually not during the first stage 1 period.

9. Hypnopompic hallucinations occur when individuals experience sleep _____ upon awakening from sleep.

10. A day of _____ exertion generally leads to an increase in NREM sleep, which allows our body to recover from bodily fatigue. A day of _____ would lead to an increase in REM sleep.

11. Dreaming is accompanied by sexual and _____ arousal but relaxation of the skeletal _____ . People who move about violently while asleep may suffer from _____ behavior disorder.

What are the causes of sleep disorders and unusual sleep events?

Sleep Disturbances—Showing Nightly: Sleep Wars! Pages 231-235

1. Insomnia, which is difficulty in getting to sleep or staying asleep, may be _____ or chronic.

2. When insomnia is treated with drugs, sleep quality is often _____ and drug-dependency _____ may develop.

3. The amino acid tryptophan, found in bread, pasta, and other foods, helps promote _____ .

4. Behavioral approaches to managing insomnia, such as relaxation, sleep restriction, _____ control, and paradoxical _____ are quite effective.

5. _____ (somnambulism) and sleeptalking occur during NREM sleep in stages 3 and 4.

6. Night terrors occur in _____ sleep, whereas nightmares occur in _____ sleep.

7. Nightmares can be eliminated by the method called imagery _____ .

8. During sleep apnea, people repeatedly stop _____ . Apnea is suspected as one cause of _____ infant death syndrome (SIDS).

9. The first _____ months are critical for babies who are at risk for SIDS. Other factors include the baby being a _____ , breathing through an open _____ , having a mother who is a _____ , and having a crib that contains soft objects such as a pillow and quilts.

10. The phrase " _____ to sleep" refers to the safest position for most babies: their _____ .

Do dreams have meaning?

Dreams—A Separate Reality? Pages 235-237

1. People will experience REM _____ if they are deprived of REM sleep the night before.

2. People deprived of REM sleep showed an urgent need to _____ and mental disturbances the next day. However, total sleep loss seems to be more important than loss of a single sleep _____ .

3. One of the more important functions of REM sleep appears to be the processing of adaptive _____ .

4. Calvin Hall found that most dream content is about _____ settings, people, and actions. Dreams more often involve negative _____ than positive _____ .

5. The Freudian, or psychodynamic, view is that dreams express unconscious _____ , frequently hidden by dream symbols.

6. Allan Hobson and Robert McCarley's _____ -synthesis model portrays dreaming as a physiological process. The brain, they say, creates dreams to explain _____ and motor messages that occur during REM sleep.

How hypnosis is done, and what are its limitations

Hypnosis—Look into My Eyes: Pages 237-240

1. Hypnosis is an altered state characterized by narrowed attention and _____ suggestibility.

2. In the 1700s, Franz Mesmer (whose name is the basis for the term mesmerize) practiced "_____ magnetism," which was actually a demonstration of the power of _____ .

3. The term _____ was first used by James Braid, an English doctor.

4. People vary in hypnotic susceptibility; _____ out of 10 can be hypnotized, as revealed by scores on the Stanford Hypnotic Susceptibility _____ .

5. The core of hypnosis is the _____ suggestion effect—a tendency to carry out suggested actions as if they were involuntary. However, a hypnotized person will not perform behaviors that he or she deems to be _____ or repulsive.

6. Mentally moving an object back and forth, such as a ring that is dangling from a string you are holding, is the result of _____ (your own suggestive power made your hand move in small increments).

7. Hypnosis appears capable of producing relaxation, controlling _____ , and altering perceptions.

8. Stage hypnotism takes advantage of typical stage behavior, _____ suggestibility, responsive subjects, disinhibition, and _____ to simulate hypnosis.

How does sensory deprivation affect consciousness?

Sensory Deprivation—Life on a Sensory Diet: Pages 240-241

1. Sensory deprivation takes place when there is a major reduction in the amount or variety of sensory _____ available to a person.

2. Prolonged sensory deprivation is stressful and disruptive, leading to _____ distortions.

3. Brief or mild sensory deprivation can enhance sensory sensitivity and induce deep _____ .

4. Sensory deprivation also appears to aid the breaking of long-standing _____ and promotes creative thinking. This effect is the basis for Restricted Environmental Stimulation Therapy (REST).

What are the effects of the more commonly used psychoactive drugs?

Drug-Altered Consciousness—The High and Low of It: Pages 242-244

1. A psychoactive drug is a substance that affects the brain in ways that _____ consciousness.

2. Drugs alter the activities in the brain by _____ and blocking neurotransmitters (_____ that carry messages between neurons) to produce feelings of pleasure.

3. Most psychoactive drugs can be placed on a scale ranging from stimulation to _____ . Some, however, are best described as hallucinogens (drugs that alter _____ impressions).

4. Drugs may cause a physical dependence (_____) or a psychological dependence, or both.

5. Prolonged use of a drug can lead to drug tolerance (a _____ response to a drug) whereby the abuser must _____ the amount of a drug to receive the same desired effect.

6. Drug use can be classified as experimental, recreational, situational, intensive, and _____ . Drug abuse is most often associated with the last three.

Uppers—Amphetamines, Cocaine, MDMA, Caffeine, Nicotine: Pages 244-249

1. The physically addicting drugs are alcohol, amphetamines, barbiturates, cocaine, codeine, GHB, heroin, methadone, morphine, tobacco, and tranquilizers. All psychoactive drugs can lead to _____ dependence.

2. Amphetamines, known as "bennies," "dex," "go," and "_____," are synthetic stimulants that produce a rapid drug _____ . Abusers typically go on binges that last for several days until they "_____," suffering from _____ , confusion, depression, uncontrolled irritability, and aggression.

3. Stimulant drugs are readily abused because of the period of _____ that often follows stimulation. The greatest risks are associated with amphetamines, cocaine, MDMA, and nicotine, but even _____ can be a problem.

4. Methamphetamine, known as "_____," "speed," "meth," or "crystal," is cheaply produced in labs and can be snorted, _____ , or eaten.

5. Repeated use of amphetamine can cause brain damage and amphetamine _____ . Amphetamine psychosis can cause the abuser to act on their delusions and risk _____ -injury or injury to _____ .

6. Signs of cocaine abuse are: compulsive use, loss of _____ , and a disregard for _____ .

7. Users of MDMA are likely to risk an _____ in body temperature, liver damage, and unsafe sex. In addition, _____ brain cells may be damaged, which could increase levels of anxiety or depression.

8. MDMA or "_____," which is similar to amphetamine, has been linked with numerous deaths and with mental impairment.

9. Caffeine can be found in coffee, _____ , soft drinks, and chocolate. It stimulates the brain by _____ chemicals that inhibit nerve activities.

10. _____ includes the added risk of lung cancer, heart disease, and other health problems.

11. The smoking of cigarettes releases carcinogens (_____ -causing substances) in the air, which expose people to _____ smoke and places them at risk for developing lung cancer.

Downers—Sedatives, Tranquilizers, and Alcohol: Pages 249-253

1. Barbiturates are _____ drugs whose overdose level is close to the intoxication dosage, making them dangerous drugs. Common street names for barbiturates are "downers," " _____ heavens," " _____ hearts," "goofballs," " _____ ladies," and "rainbows."

2. The depressant drug _____ (gamma-hydroxybuyrate) can cause coma, breathing failure, and death in relatively low doses. GHB is commonly called "goop," "scoop," "max," or " _____ Home Boy."

3. Benzodiazepine tranquilizers, such as _____ , are used to lower anxiety. When abused, they have a strong _____ potential.

4. _____ , a tranquilizer, also known as "roofies" and the " _____ -rape drug," is odorless and tasteless and is sometimes used to spike drinks.

5. Mixing barbiturates and alcohol may result in a fatal _____ interaction (in which the joint effect of two drugs exceeds the effects of adding one drug's effects to the other's).

6. Every year in the United States, 75,000 people die of _____ -related deaths. Binge drinking (having _____ or more drinks in a short time) is responsible for 14,000 college student deaths a year.

7. Alcohol is the most heavily abused drug in common use today. The development of a drinking problem is usually marked by an _____ phase of increasing consumption, a crucial phase, in which a _____ drink can set off a chain reaction, and a chronic phase, in which a person lives to drink and drinks to live.

8. People who undergo detoxification (the _____ of poison) often experience unpleasant symptoms of drug _____ .

Marijuana—What's in the Pot? Pages 253-255

1. Marijuana ("pot," "herb," and " _____ ") is a hallucinogen subject to an _____ pattern similar to alcohol. Studies have linked chronic marijuana use with memory impairment, lung cancer, reproductive problems, immune system disorders, and other health problems.

2. _____ , the main active chemical in marijuana, accumulates in the cerebral cortex and reproductive organs.

3. Potential problems caused by frequent marijuana use are short-term _____ loss and a decline in learning, _____ , and thinking abilities. In addition, people who smoke _____ or more joints a week tend to score four points lower on IQ tests.

How are dreams used to promote personal understanding?

Psychology in Action: Exploring and Using Dreams: Pages 256-258

1. Freud held that the meaning of dreams is _____ by four dream _____ he called condensation, displacement, symbolization, and secondary elaboration.

2. Calvin Hall emphasizes the setting, cast, _____ , and emotions of a dream.

3. Rosalind Cartwright's view of dreams as feeling statements and Fritz Perls' technique of _____ for dream elements are also helpful.

4. Dreams may be used for _____ problem solving, especially when dream control is achieved through lucid dreaming (a dream in which the dreamer feels capable of normal thought and action).

CONNECTIONS

What is an altered state of consciousness? What are the effects of sleep loss or changes in sleep patterns? Pages 224-228

1. _____ hypersomnia
2. _____ Randy Gardner
3. _____ ASC
4. _____ microsleep
5. _____ short sleep cycles
6. _____ long sleepers
7. _____ sleep pattern
8. _____ circadian rhythms
9. _____ consciousness

a. over nine hours
b. few seconds of repeated sleep
c. biological clocks
d. sleep deprivation
e. 2 to 1 ratio of awake versus sleep
f. excessive sleepiness
g. mental awareness
h. daydreaming
i. infancy

Are there different stages of sleep? How does dream sleep differ from dreamless sleep? Pages 228-231

1. _____ alpha waves	a.	reflex muscle contraction
2. _____ beta waves	b.	images created upon awakening
3. _____ delta waves	c.	relaxed
4. _____ hypnic jerk	d.	sexual arousal
5. _____ hypnopompic hallucinations	e.	stage 2 of sleep
6. _____ sleep spindles	f.	stage 4 of sleep
7. _____ NREM sleep	g.	awake, alert
8. _____ REM sleep	h.	produces sleep stages 1–4

What are the causes of sleep disorders and unusual sleep events? Pages 232-235

1. _____ sleep drunkenness	a.	violent actions
2. _____ hypersomnia	b.	fatal to infants
3. _____ stimulus control	c.	remedy for insomnia
4. _____ nightmares	d.	slow awakening
5. _____ narcolepsy	e.	stages 3 and 4 of NREM
6. _____ SIDS	f.	sudden daytime REM sleep
7. _____ tryptophan	g.	during REM sleep
8. _____ REM behavior disorder	h.	sleep inducing foods
9. _____ drug-dependency insomnia	i.	excessive sleepiness
10. _____ sleepwalking	j.	sleep loss caused by *Nytol*

Do dreams have meaning? Pages 235-237

1. _____ integrate memories	a.	unconscious meanings
2. _____ dream symbols	b.	wish fulfillment
3. _____ REM rebound	c.	extra dream time
4. _____ activation-synthesis hypothesis	d.	reflect daily events
5. _____ Sigmund Freud	e.	function of REM sleep
6. _____ Calvin Hall	f.	neural firing triggering memories

How hypnosis is done, and what are its limitations? How does sensory deprivation affect consciousness? Pages 237-241

1. _____ mesmerize
2. _____ use tricks
3. _____ pain relief
4. _____ REST
5. _____ autosuggestion
6. _____ hypnagogic images

a. flotation tank
b. hypnotize
c. self-hypnosis
d. hypnosis effect
e. sensory deprivation visions
f. stage hypnosis

What are the effects of the more commonly used psychoactive drugs? Pages 242-255

1. _____ drug tolerance
2. _____ amphetamine
3. _____ dopamine
4. _____ nicotine
5. _____ carcinogen
6. _____ barbiturate
7. _____ AA
8. _____ alcohol treatment
9. _____ THC
10. _____ anhedonia

a. cocaine rush
b. cancer agent
c. addiction
d. sedative
e. hallucinogen
f. detoxification
g. loss of pleasure
h. stimulant
i. self-help group
j. insecticide

How are dreams used to promote personal understanding? Pages 256-258

1. _____ displacement
2. _____ symbolization
3. _____ secondary elaboration
4. _____ lucid dream
5. _____ condensation

a. redirect actions toward safer images
b. combining events into one image
c. nonliteral forms of dream content
d. feels awake while dreaming
e. add details to make dreams logical

CHECK YOUR MEMORY

What is an altered state of consciousness? Page 224

1. The quality and pattern of mental activity changes during an ASC.
   TRUE or FALSE

2. All people experience at least some ASCs.
   TRUE or FALSE

3. According to Thomas Nagel, through the use of objective studies of behavior and the first-person point of view, psychologists are able to understand the consciousness of animals.
   TRUE or FALSE

4. Both sensory overload and monotonous stimulation can produce ASCs.
   TRUE or FALSE

5. Almost every known religion has accepted some ASCs as desirable.
   TRUE or FALSE

What are the effects of sleep loss or changes in sleep patterns? Pages 224-228

1. Through sleep learning it is possible to master a foreign language.
   TRUE or FALSE

2. A total inability to sleep results in death.
   TRUE or FALSE

3. Even after extended sleep loss, most symptoms are removed by a single night's sleep.
   TRUE or FALSE

4. Hallucinations and delusions are the most common reaction to extended sleep deprivation.
   TRUE or FALSE

5. Physical changes during puberty increase adolescents' need for sleep.
   TRUE or FALSE

6. Without scheduled light and dark periods, human sleep rhythms would drift into unusual patterns.
   TRUE or FALSE

7. The average human sleep-wake cycle lasts 23 hours and 10 minutes.

   TRUE or FALSE

8. Short sleepers are defined as those who average less than 5 hours of sleep per night.

   TRUE or FALSE

9. Shortened sleep cycles, such as 3 hours of sleep to 6 hours awake, are more efficient than sleeping once a day.

   TRUE or FALSE

Are there different stages of sleep? How does dream sleep differ from dreamless sleep? Pages 228-231

1. Sleep is promoted by a chemical that accumulates in the bloodstream.

   TRUE or FALSE

2. Body temperature drops as a person falls asleep.

   TRUE or FALSE

3. A hypnic jerk is a sign of serious problems.

   TRUE or FALSE

4. Delta waves typically first appear in stage 2 sleep.

   TRUE or FALSE

5. About 45 percent of awakenings during REM periods produce reports of dreams.

   TRUE or FALSE

6. REM sleep occurs mainly in stages 3 and 4.

   TRUE or FALSE

7. REM sleep increases when a person is subjected to daytime stress.

   TRUE or FALSE

8. The average dream only lasts 3 to 4 minutes.

   TRUE or FALSE

9. Most people change positions in bed during REM sleep.

   TRUE or FALSE

10. REM behavior disorder causes people to briefly fall asleep and become paralyzed during the day.

    TRUE or FALSE

11. Approximately 30 percent of individuals have experienced hypnopompic hallucinations upon awakening from their sleep.

    TRUE or FALSE

What are the causes of sleep disorders and unusual sleep events? Pages 232-235

1. Bread, pasta, pretzels, cookies, and cereals all contain melatonin.

    TRUE or FALSE

2. Caffeine, alcohol, and tobacco can all contribute to insomnia.

    TRUE or FALSE

3. The two most effective behavioral treatments for insomnia are sleep restriction and stimulus control.

    TRUE or FALSE

4. Sleepwalking occurs during NREM periods, sleeptalking during REM periods.

    TRUE or FALSE

5. People who have NREM night terrors usually can remember very little afterward.

    TRUE or FALSE

6. Imagery rehearsal is an effective way to treat recurrent nightmares.

    TRUE or FALSE

7. REM sleep appears to help the brain process memories formed during the day.

    TRUE or FALSE

8. People who take barbiturate sleeping pills may develop drug-dependency insomnia.

    TRUE or FALSE

9. Newborn babies spend 8 or 9 hours a day in REM sleep.

    TRUE or FALSE

10. Sleep apnea does not increase the risk of having a heart attack. This is only a myth.

    TRUE or FALSE

Do dreams have meaning? Pages 235-237

1. REM rebound refers to people having more REM sleep when they do not get enough REM sleep the night before.

    TRUE or FALSE

2. The favorite dream setting is outdoors.
   TRUE or FALSE

3. People report feeling more negative emotions when they are awakened during REM sleep.
   TRUE or FALSE

4. Pleasant emotions are more common in dreams than unpleasant emotions.
   TRUE or FALSE

5. According to Freud, dreams represent thoughts and wishes expressed as images.
   TRUE or FALSE

6. The activation-synthesis hypothesis emphasizes the unconscious meanings of dream symbols.
   TRUE or FALSE

7. The activation-synthesis hypothesis does believe that dreams are created from memories or past experiences.
   TRUE or FALSE

How hypnosis is done, and what are its limitations? Pages 237-240

1. The Greek word hypnos means "magnetism."
   TRUE or FALSE

2. Only about 4 people out of 10 can be hypnotized.
   TRUE or FALSE

3. The "finger-lock" is an example of animal magnetism.
   TRUE or FALSE

4. Physical strength cannot be increased with hypnosis.
   TRUE or FALSE

5. Hypnosis is better at changing subjective experiences than behaviors.
   TRUE or FALSE

6. Stage hypnotists look for responsive volunteers who will cooperate and not spoil the show.
   TRUE or FALSE

7. Autosuggestion is used by people who believe they have psychic abilities.
   TRUE or FALSE

8. Hypnosis is not a valuable tool since its main purpose is entertainment.
   TRUE or FALSE

How does sensory deprivation affect consciousness? Pages 240-241

1. Sensory deprivation is almost always unpleasant, and it usually causes distorted perceptions.

   TRUE or FALSE

2. Sensory sensitivity temporarily increases after a period of sensory deprivation.

   TRUE or FALSE

3. Prolonged sensory deprivation produces deep relaxation.

   TRUE or FALSE

4. REST is a form of brainwashing used during the Vietnam war.

   TRUE or FALSE

What are the effects of the more commonly used psychoactive drugs? Pages 242-255

1. Abuse of any psychoactive drug can produce physical dependence.

   TRUE or FALSE

2. People who believe they have used too many drugs and feel they need to reduce their drug use are in need of professional help.

   TRUE or FALSE

3. Amphetamines are used to treat narcolepsy and hyperactivity.

   TRUE or FALSE

4. Amphetamine is more rapidly metabolized by the body than cocaine is.

   TRUE or FALSE

5. Ecstasy and amphetamine reduce the production of neurotransmitters in the brain.

   TRUE or FALSE

6. Cocaine ("coke" or "snow") produces feelings of alertness, euphoria, well-being, powerfulness, boundless energy, and pleasure.

   TRUE or FALSE

7. MDMA is chemically similar to amphetamine.

   TRUE or FALSE

8. MDMA is widely used by college students (1 in 20 students has tried Ecstasy).

   TRUE or FALSE

9. Disregarding consequences is a sign of cocaine abuse.

   TRUE or FALSE

10. Caffeine can increase the risk of miscarriage during pregnancy.

    TRUE or FALSE

11. Unlike other drugs, caffeine does not cause dependency or side effects.

    TRUE or FALSE

12. Twenty-five cigarettes could be fatal for a nonsmoker.

    TRUE or FALSE

13. Regular use of nicotine leads to drug tolerance, and often to physical addiction.

    TRUE or FALSE

14. Every cigarette reduces a smoker's life expectancy by 7 minutes.

    TRUE or FALSE

15. Secondary smoke only causes harm to the person who smokes, not those around them.

    TRUE or FALSE

16. In order to stop smoking, tapering off is generally more successful than quitting abruptly.

    TRUE or FALSE

17. One of the most effective ways to stop smoking is to schedule the number of cigarettes smoked each day.

    TRUE or FALSE

18. There have been no known deaths caused by barbiturate overdoses.

    TRUE or FALSE

19. GHB, a hallucinogen, can be easily purchased over the Internet.

    TRUE or FALSE

20. It is legal and safe to drive as long as blood alcohol level does not exceed .8.

    TRUE or FALSE

21. Drinking alone is a serious sign of alcohol abuse.

    TRUE or FALSE

22. To pace alcohol intake, you should limit drinking primarily to the first hour of a social event or party.

    TRUE or FALSE

23. Over 80 percent of fraternity and sorority members in the U.S. have engaged in binge drinking.

    TRUE or FALSE

24. Alcoholics Anonymous (AA) and Secular Organizations for Sobriety are organizations that seek to make money from drug abusers.

    TRUE or FALSE

25. Hallucinogens generally affect brain transmitter systems.

    TRUE or FALSE

26. THC receptors are found in large numbers in the cerebellum of the brain.

    TRUE or FALSE

27. People who smoke marijuana on a regular basis report that they are satisfied with their lives, earn more money, and are healthier than nonusers at the age of 29.

    TRUE or FALSE

28. Pregnant mothers who use marijuana may increase the risk that their babies will have trouble succeeding in goal-oriented tasks.

    TRUE or FALSE

29. Drug abuse is frequently part of general pattern of personal maladjustment.

    TRUE or FALSE

30. The negative consequences of drug use typically follow long after the drug has been taken.

    TRUE or FALSE

How are dreams used to promote personal understanding? Pages 256-258

1. Displacement refers to representing two or more people with a single dream image.

   TRUE or FALSE

2. Secondary elaboration is the tendency to make a dream more logical when remembering it.

   TRUE or FALSE

3. According to Calvin Hall, the overall emotional tone of a dream is the key to its meaning.

   TRUE or FALSE

4. Alcohol decreases REM sleep.

   TRUE or FALSE

5. It is basically impossible to solve daytime problems in dreams.

   TRUE or FALSE

6. Lucid dreams either occur or they don't; there is no way to increase their frequency.

   TRUE or FALSE

FINAL SURVEY AND REVIEW

What is an altered state of consciousness?

State of Consciousness—The Many Faces of Awareness: Page 224

1. States of awareness that differ from normal, alert, waking _____ are called altered states of _____ (ASCs).

2. ASCs involve distinct shifts in the quality and pattern of _____ _____ .

3. Altered states are especially associated with sleep and dreaming, _____ , meditation, sensory _____ , and psychoactive drugs.

4. _____ conditioning greatly affects what altered states a person recognizes, seeks, considers normal, and attains.

What are the effects of sleep loss or changes in sleep patterns?

Sleep—A Nice Place to Visit: Pages 224-228

1. Sleep is an _____ _____ rhythm essential for survival.

2. Higher animals and people deprived of sleep experience involuntary _____ (a brief shift to sleep patterns in the brain).

3. Moderate sleep loss mainly affects _____ and self-motivated performance on routine or boring tasks.

4. Extended sleep loss can (somewhat rarely) produce a temporary sleep-deprivation _____ , marked by confusion, _____ , and possibly hallucinations.

5. _____ change during puberty increases adolescents' need for sleep, which many lack since they tend to stay up late and get up early for school. This pattern causes them to experience _____ (excessive daytime sleepiness).

6. The "storm and stress" that adolescents experience may, in part, be caused by _____ of sleep.

7. _____ rhythms within the body are closely tied to sleep, activity levels, and energy cycles.

8. Sleep patterns show some flexibility, but 7 to 8 hours remains average. The unscheduled human _____ averages 24 hours and 10 minutes, but cycles of light and dark tailor it to 24-hour days.

9. The amount of daily sleep decreases steadily from birth to _____ _____ and switches from _____ sleep-wake cycles to once-a-day sleep periods.

10. Adapting to shorter or longer _____ _____ is difficult and inefficient for most people.

Are there different stages of sleep? How does dream sleep differ from dreamless sleep?

Stages of Sleep—The Nightly Roller-Coaster Ride: Pages 228-231

1. Sleepiness is associated with the accumulation of a sleep _____ in the brain and _____ _____ .

2. Sleep depends on which of two _____ sleep and waking _____ in the brain is dominant at any given moment.

3. Sleep occurs in 4 stages defined by changes in behavior and brain waves recorded with an _____ (EEG).

4. Stage 1, light sleep, has small irregular brain waves. In stage 2, sleep _____ appear. Delta waves appear in stage 3. Stage 4, or deep sleep, is marked by almost pure _____ _____ .

5. Sleepers alternate between stages _____ and _____ (passing through stages _____ and _____) several times each night.

6. There are two basic sleep states, _____ _____ movement (REM) sleep and non-REM (NREM) sleep.

7. _____ sleep is much more strongly associated with dreaming than _____ sleep is.

8. Dreams and REMs occur mainly during _____ sleep, but usually not during the first _____ period.

9. _____ hallucinations occur when individuals experience sleep paralysis upon _____ from sleep.

10. A day of physical exertion generally leads to an increase in _____ sleep, which allows our body to recover from bodily fatigue. A day of stress would lead to an increase in _____ sleep.

11. Dreaming is accompanied by sexual and emotional _____ but _____ of the skeletal muscles. People who move about violently while asleep may suffer from REM behavior _____ .

What are the causes of sleep disorders and unusual sleep events?

Sleep Disturbances—Showing Nightly: Sleep Wars! Pages 232-235

1. Insomnia, which is difficulty in getting to sleep or staying asleep, may be temporary or _____ .

2. When insomnia is treated with drugs, sleep quality is often lowered and drug- _____ insomnia may develop.

3. The amino acid _____ , found in bread, pasta, and other foods, helps promote sleep.

4. Behavioral approaches to managing insomnia, such as relaxation, sleep _____ , stimulus control, and _____ intention are quite effective.

5. Sleepwalking (_____) and sleeptalking occur during _____ sleep in stages 3 and 4.

6. Night terrors occur in _____ sleep, whereas nightmares occur in _____ sleep.

7. Nightmares can be eliminated by the method called _____ _____ .

8. During sleep _____ , people repeatedly stop breathing. _____ is suspected as one cause of sudden _____ _____ syndrome.

9. The first _____ months are critical for babies who are at risk for SIDS. Other factors include the baby being a _____ , breathing through an open _____ , having a mother who is a _____ , and having a crib that contains soft objects such as a pillow and quilts.

10. The phrase " _____ to sleep" refers to the safest position for most babies: their _____ .

Do dreams have meaning?

Dreams—A Separate Reality? Pages 235-237

1. People will experience _____ if they are deprived of REM sleep the night before.

2. People deprived of _____ sleep showed an urgent need to dream and _____ disturbances the next day. However, _____ amount of sleep loss seems to be more important than loss of a single sleep stage.

3. One of the more important functions of _____ _____ appears to be the processing of adaptive memories.

4. Calvin _____ found that most dream content is about familiar settings, people, and actions. Dreams more often involve _____ emotions than _____ emotions.

5. The Freudian, or _____ , view is that dreams express unconscious wishes, frequently hidden by dream _____ .

6. Allan Hobson and Robert McCarley's activation- _____ model portrays dreaming as a physiological process. The brain, they say, creates dreams to explain sensory and _____ messages that occur during REM sleep.

How hypnosis is done, and what are its limitations

Hypnosis—Look into My Eyes: Pages 237-240

1. Hypnosis is an altered state characterized by narrowed attention and increased _____ .

2. In the 1700s, Franz _____ (whose name is the basis for the term _____) practiced "animal magnetism," which was actually a demonstration of the power of suggestion.

3. The term hypnosis was first used by James _____ , an English doctor.

4. People vary in hypnotic susceptibility; 8 out of 10 can be hypnotized, as revealed by scores on the _____ Hypnotic Susceptibility Scale.

5. The core of hypnosis is the basic _____ effect—a tendency to carry out suggested actions as if they were _____ .

6. Mentally moving an object back and forth, such as a ring that is dangling from a string you are holding, is the result of _____ (your own suggestive power made your hand move in small increments).

7. Hypnosis appears capable of producing _____ , controlling pain, and altering perceptions.

8. _____ takes advantage of typical stage behavior, waking suggestibility, responsive subjects, disinhibition, and deception to _____ hypnosis.

How does sensory deprivation affect consciousness?

Sensory Deprivation—Life on a Sensory Diet: Pages 240-241

1. Sensory deprivation takes place when there is a major reduction in the amount or variety of _____ _____ available to a person.

2. _____ sensory deprivation is stressful and disruptive, leading to perceptual distortions.

3. Brief or mild sensory _____ can induce deep _____ .

4. Sensory deprivation also appears to aid the breaking of long-standing habits and promotes creative thinking. This effect is the basis for _____ _____ Stimulation Therapy (REST).

What are the effects of the more commonly used psychoactive drugs?

Drug-Altered Consciousness—The High and Low of It: Pages 242-244

1. A psychoactive drug is a substance that affects the brain in ways that alter _____ .

2. Drugs alter the activities in the brain by mimicking and blocking _____ (chemicals that carry messages between neurons) to produce feelings of pleasure.

3. Most psychoactive drugs can be placed on a scale ranging from _____ to _____ . Some, however, are best described as _____ (drugs that alter sensory impressions).

4. Drugs may cause a physical _____ (addiction) or a psychological _____ , or both.

5. Prolonged use of a drug can lead to drug _____ (a reduced response to a drug) whereby the abuser must _____ the amount of a drug to receive the same desired effect.

6. Drug use can be classified as experimental, _____ , situational, intensive, and compulsive. Drug abuse is most often associated with the last three.

Uppers—Amphetamines, Cocaine, MDMA, Caffeine, Nicotine: Pages 244-249

1. The _____ _____ drugs are alcohol, amphetamines, barbiturates, cocaine, codeine, GHB, heroin, methadone, morphine, tobacco, and tranquilizers. All psychoactive drugs can lead to psychological dependence.

2. Stimulant drugs are readily abused because of the period of depression that often follows stimulation. The greatest risks are associated with amphetamines, _____ , MDMA, and nicotine, but even caffeine can be a problem.

3. _____ , known as "bennies," "dex," "go," and "uppers," are synthetic stimulants that produce a rapid drug _____ .

4. _____ , known as "crank," "speed," "meth," or "crystal," is cheaply produced in labs and can be snorted, injected, or eaten.

5. Repeated use of amphetamine can cause brain damage and amphetamine _____ . Amphetamine psychosis can cause the abuser to act on their delusions and risk _____ -injury or injury to others.

6. Signs of cocaine abuse are: compulsive use, loss of _____ , and the disregard for _____ .

7. Users of MDMA are likely to risk an _____ in body temperature, liver damage, and unsafe sex. _____ brain cells may be damaged, which could increase anxiety level or lead to depression.

8. MDMA or "Ecstasy," which is similar to _____ , has been linked with numerous deaths and with _____ impairment.

9. _____ can be found in coffee, tea, soft drinks, and chocolate. It stimulates the brain by _____ chemicals that inhibit nerve activities.

10. Nicotine (smoking) includes the added risk of _____ _____ , heart disease, and other health problems.

11. The smoking of cigarettes releases _____ (cancer-causing substances) in the air, which expose people to secondhand smoke and places them at risk for developing lung cancer.

Downers—Sedatives, Tranquilizers, and Alcohol: Pages 249-253

1. Barbiturates are depressant drugs whose overdose level is close to the intoxication dosage, making them dangerous drugs. Common street names for _____ are "downers," "blue heavens," "purple hearts," "goofballs," "pink ladies," and "rainbows."

2. The _____ drug GHB (_____) can cause coma, breathing failure, and death in relatively low doses. _____ is commonly called "goop," "scoop," "max," or "Georgia Home Boy."

3. _____ tranquilizers, such as Valium, are used to lower anxiety. When abused, they have a strong addictive potential.

4. _____ , a tranquilizer, also known as "roofies" and the "date-rape drug," is odorless and tasteless and is sometimes used to spike drinks.

5. Mixing barbiturates and _____ may result in a fatal drug _____ (in which the joint effect of two drugs exceeds the effects of adding one drug's effects to the other's).

6. Every year in the United States, 75,000 people die of _____ -related deaths. _____ drinking (having five or more drinks in a short time) is responsible for 14,000 college student deaths a year.

7. _____ is the most heavily abused drug in common use today. The development of a drinking problem is usually marked by an initial phase of increasing consumption, a _____ phase, in which a single drink can set off a chain reaction, and a chronic phase, in which a person lives to drink and drinks to live.

8. People who undergo _____ (the removal of poison) often experience unpleasant symptoms of drug _____ .

Marijuana—What's in the Pot? Pages 253-255

1. Marijuana is a _____ subject to an abuse pattern similar to alcohol. Studies have linked chronic marijuana use with memory impairment, _____ cancer, reproductive problems, immune system disorders, and other health problems.

2. _____ , the main active chemical in marijuana, accumulates in the _____ cortex and reproductive organs.

3. Potential problems caused by frequent marijuana use are short-term _____ loss and decline in learning, _____ , and thinking abilities. In addition, people who smoke five or more joints a week tend to score four points _____ on IQ tests.

How are dreams used to promote personal understanding?

Psychology in Action: Exploring and Using Dreams: Pages 256-258

1. Freud held that the meaning of dreams is hidden by the dream processes he called _____ , displacement, symbolization, and _____ elaboration.

2. Calvin Hall emphasizes the setting, _____ , plot, and emotions of a dream.

3. Rosalind Cartwright's view of dreams as _____ statements and Fritz _____ technique of speaking for dream elements are also helpful.

4. Dreams may be used for creative problem solving, especially when dream control is achieved through _____ dreaming (a dream in which the dreamer feels capable of normal thought and action).

MASTERY TEST

1. Delirium, ecstasy, and daydreaming all have in common the fact that they are
   a. forms of normal waking consciousness
   b. caused by sensory deprivation
   c. perceived as subjectively real
   d. ASCs

2. The street drug GHB is
   a. chemically similar to morphine
   b. a depressant
   c. capable of raising body temperature to dangerous levels
   d. a common cause of sleep-deprivation psychosis

3. Which of the following does not belong with the others?
   a. nicotine
   b. caffeine
   c. cocaine
   d. codeine

4. Sleep spindles usually first appear in stage _____, whereas delta waves first appear in stage
   _____.
   a. 1, 2
   b. 2, 3
   c. 3, 4
   d. 1, 4

5. Which of the following is NOT one of the dream processes described by Freud?
   a. condensation
   b. illumination
   c. displacement
   d. symbolization

6. Which of the following most clearly occurs under hypnosis?
   a. unusual strength
   b. memory enhancement
   c. pain relief
   d. age regression

7. Alcohol, amphetamines, cocaine, and marijuana have in common the fact that they are all
   a. physically addicting
   b. psychoactive
   c. stimulants
   d. hallucinogens

8. Emotional arousal, blood pressure changes, and sexual arousal all primarily occur during
   a. REM sleep
   b. NREM sleep
   c. Delta sleep
   d. stage 4 sleep

9. The REST technique makes use of
   a. sensory deprivation
   b. hypodynamic imagery
   c. hallucinogens
   d. a CPAP mask

10. Mesmerism, hypnosis, hypnotic susceptibility scales, and stage hypnotism all rely in part on
    a. disinhibition
    b. rapid eye movements
    c. suggestibility
    d. imagery rehearsal

11. Shortened sleep-waking cycles overlook the fact that sleep
    a. must match a 3 to 1 ratio of time awake and time asleep
    b. is an innate biological rhythm
    c. is caused by a sleep-promoting substance in the blood
    d. cycles cannot be altered by external factors

12. Morning drinking appears during the _____ phase in the development of a drinking problem.
    a. initial
    b. crucial
    c. chronic
    d. rebound

13. Which of the following statements about sleep is true?
    a. Learning math or a foreign language can be accomplished during sleep.
    b. Some people can learn to do without sleep.
    c. Calvin Hall had hallucinations during a sleep deprivation experiment.
    d. Randy Gardner slept for 14 hours after ending his sleep deprivation.

14. Amphetamine is very similar in effects to
    a. narcotics and tranquilizers
    b. methaqualone
    c. codeine
    d. cocaine

15. Microsleeps would most likely occur
    a. in stage 4 sleep
    b. in a 3 to 1 ratio to microawakenings
    c. in conjunction with delusions and hallucinations
    d. during sleep deprivation

16. Sleepwalking, sleeptalking, and severe nightmares all have in common the fact that they
    a. are REM events
    b. are NREM events
    c. are sleep disorders
    d. can be controlled with imagery rehearsal

17. In its milder forms, sensory deprivation sometimes produces
    a. cataplectic images
    b. deep relaxation
    c. tryptophanic images
    d. REM symbolizations

18. The basic suggestion effect is closely related to
    a. hypnosis
    b. sensory enhancement after sensory deprivation
    c. hypersomnia
    d. the frequency of dreaming during REM sleep

19. A person who feels awake and capable of normal action while sleeping has experienced
    a. lucid dreaming
    b. the basic suggestion effect
    c. sleep drunkenness
    d. REM rebound

20. Which of the following is a hallucinogen?
    a. LSD
    b. THC
    c. hashish
    d. all of the preceding

21. The two most basic states of sleep are
    a. stage 1 sleep and stage 4 sleep
    b. REM sleep and NREM sleep
    c. Alpha sleep and Delta sleep
    d. Alpha sleep and hypnic sleep

22. Thinking and perception become dulled in the condition known as
    a. alcohol rebound
    b. alcohol apnea
    c. alcohol anhedonia
    d. alcohol myopia

23. Learning to use a computer would most likely be slowed if you were _____ each night.
    a. deprived of a half hour of NREM sleep
    b. allowed to engage in extra REM sleep
    c. prevented from dreaming
    d. awakened three times at random

24. By definition, compulsive drug use involves
    a. dependence
    b. experimentation
    c. repeated overdoses
    d. anhedonia

25. A particularly dangerous drug interaction occurs when _____ and _____ are combined.
    a. alcohol, amphetamine
    b. barbiturates, nicotine
    c. alcohol, barbiturates
    d. amphetamine, codeine

26. Narcolepsy is an example of
    a. a night terror
    b. a sleep disorder
    c. a tranquilizer
    d. an addictive drug

27. Sleep restriction and stimulus control techniques would most likely be used to treat
    a. insomnia
    b. narcolepsy
    c. sleepwalking
    d. REM behavior disorder

28. In addition to the nicotine they contain, cigarettes release
    a. dopamine
    b. tryptophan
    c. noradrenaline
    d. carcinogens

29. Disguised dream symbols are to psychodynamic dream theory as sensory and motor messages are to
    a. the Freudian theory of dreams
    b. the activation-synthesis hypothesis
    c. Fritz Perls' methods of dream interpretation
    d. paradoxical intention

30. Which is the most frequently used drug in North America?
    a. caffeine
    b. nicotine
    c. marijuana
    d. cocaine

31. Joan is 14 years old and is experiencing _____ throughout the day because she tends to stay up late and gets up early.
    a. insomnia
    b. narcolepsy
    c. hypersomnia
    d. hypnopompic

32. Gene was awakened throughout the night for a sleep study and did not receive enough REM sleep. The next night, he was allowed to sleep without interruption. Gene would be likely to experience
    a. insomnia
    b. REM rebound
    c. sleepwaking disorder
    d. REM behavior disorder

33. To impress his friends of his ability, Eric holds a string with a ring attached and mentally made the ring swing back and forth. Eric used _____, which means that as he thought about moving the ring, he made micromuscular movements with his fingers to move the string.
    a. autosuggestion
    b. telekinesis
    c. hypnotic susceptibility
    d. stimulus control

34. Nicotine and opiates stimulate the brain by _____ neurotransmitters.
    a. eliminating
    b. blocking
    c. suppressing
    d. mimicking

35. Upon awakening from sleep, Zack cannot move and as he struggles, he feels evil presences standing over him whispering to each other. Suddenly he hears screams coming from somewhere in his bedroom. Within moments, the evil presences disappear, Zack is able to move again, and realizes the screaming was from the radio. Zack just experienced
    a. a nightmare
    b. paradoxical hallucinations
    c. hypnopompic hallucinations
    d. lucid dreaming

LANGUAGE DEVELOPMENT - States of Consciousness

Word roots

Conscius is a Latin term meaning "knowing with others" (from *con*, a word meaning "with" or "together," and *scire*, a verb meaning "to know"). Several terms in the field of psychology use the English word "conscious" as a base for other words. Examples you will find in the text include consciousness, unconscious, and preconscious.

What is an altered state of consciousness?

Preview: A Visit to Several States (of Consciousness) (p. 224)

(224) *Aborigines*: original inhabitants of a region

(224) *peyote*: a primitive drug derived from an American cactus

(224) *stage fright*: fear of appearing before crowds to perform, give a speech, etc.

(224) *flotation chamber*: an enclosed box where a person can be isolated from most sensory inputs; the person literally "floats" in saline-saturated water and is cut off from sounds, smells, and other sensations as much as possible

(224) *joint*: marijuana cigarette

(224) *spare change*: money that bystanders will give to street performers or beggars

States of Consciousness—The Many Faces of Awareness (p. 224)

(224) *delirium*: a state of mental confusion accompanied by delusions, hallucinations, and illusions

(224) *euphoria*: a sense of well being; feeling happy and good all over

(224) *rave*: all night dance parties for young people

(224) *Mardi Gras*: a very large, crowded street party celebrated in New Orleans forty days before Easter

(224) *mosh pit:* slang term for an area at a music concert where audience members dance aggressively, often slamming themselves into one another

(224) *monotonous*: unchanging

(224) *highway hypnotism*: refers to the fact that drivers on long distance trips sometimes lose concentration due to the sameness of the road and scenery

(224) *hyperventilation*: excessive rate of respiration (breathing)

(224) *dehydration*: abnormal loss of body fluids

(225) *careen*: to sway from side to side as one flies quickly through the air

(225) *still-young night*: early in the night

(225) *echolocation*: using sounds to locate where objects are in the environment

(225) *revelation*: enlightenment, discovery of personal truth

(225) *madness*: archaic term for severe mental illness

(225) *possession by spirits*: the belief that an evil spirit (such as the devil) or the spirit of a dead person can inhabit the body of a living being

What are the effects of sleep loss or changes in sleep patterns?

Sleep—A Nice Place to Visit (pp. 224-228)

- (226) ***"The lion and the lamb shall lie down together"***: according to the Bible, at the end of the world enemies will become friends, even in the animal world
- (226) ***stupor***: a state of limited consciousness
- (226) ***macro***: large
- (226) ***disc jockey***: an announcer for a radio show that plays popular music
- (226) ***hallucinations***: imaginary perception of objects that do not exist in reality
- (226) ***spell disaster***: lead to a disaster
- (228) ***siesta***: nap
- (228) ***interns***: recent graduates of medical school (in this case) doing their first year of supervised practice; they tend to work long hours in hospital
- (228) ***tyrant***: absolute ruler

Are there different stages of sleep? How does dream sleep differ from dreamless sleep?

Stages of Sleep—The Nightly Roller-Coaster Ride (pp. 228-231)

- (228) ***the nightly roller coaster ride***: a roller coaster is an amusement park ride that causes the rider to go up and then quickly down steep inclines; here referring to the fact that sleep is characterized by stages, from the lightest (stage one) to the deepest (stage four)
- (228) ***see-saw back and forth***: going back and forth
- (228) ***shut down***: turn off; become inactive
- (230) ***iguana***: large tropical American lizard
- (230) ***hilarious***: very amusing or funny
- (230) ***escapades***: adventures
- (230) ***thrash***: to move or toss about
- (231) ***benign***: harmless
- (231) ***retard***: to slow down something

What are the causes of sleep disorders and unusual sleep events?

Sleep Disturbances—Showing Nightly: Sleep Wars (pp. 232-235)

(232) *Sleep Wars*: Coon is making reference to the popular science-fiction movie "Star Wars"

(232) *irony*: a result that is different, or the opposite, from what is expected

(232) *sedatives*: drugs that calm nervousness or excitement

(232) *sleeping-pill junkies*: people who are addicted to sleeping pills

(232) *weaned*: slowly removed from

(232) *rebound insomnia*: inability to sleep after one has stopped taking sleeping pills

(233) *paradoxical*: something that seems contradictory yet may still be true

(233) *blotting out*: to get rid of

(233) *strenuous*: vigorously active

(233) *drop the bomb*: to give bad news

(233) *eerie*: weird, strange

(233) *shuffling*: to move the feet by sliding along without raising the feet

(233) *immobilized*: incapable of movement

(233) *plague*: bother greatly

(234) *sage*: wise person

(234) *wood-sawing*: snoring

Do dreams have meaning?

Dreams—A Separate Reality? (pp. 235-237)

(235) *golden era*: period of great happiness, prosperity, and achievement

(235) *age-old questions*: questions that have been asked for a long time ago without clear answers

(235) *"off-line"*: not of primary or conscious processing

(236) *trivial*: of very little importance

How is hypnosis done, and what are its limitations?

Hypnosis—Look Into My Eyes (pp. 237-240)

(237) *animal magnetism*: a mysterious force that Mesmer claimed enabled him to hypnotize patients

(237) *coined*: created

(237) *susceptibility*: inability to resist

(238) *lethargic*: drowsy; lacking energy

(238) *bar*: prevent

(239) ***Ouija boards***: a game that involves one asking questions and with one's hands on a marker, moving around a board of letters to spell out answers

(240) ***disinhibits***: takes away inhibitions or restraints on behavior

(240) ***ham*** (brings out the *"ham"* in many people): actor; a person who overacts

How does sensory deprivation affect consciousness?

Sensory Deprivation—Life on a Sensory Diet (pp. 240-241)

(240) ***sensory deprivation***: being cut off from information normally received through the five senses

(240) ***solitary confinement***: kept alone in a prison cell

(240) ***lapses***: interruptions

(240) ***warping***: turning or twisting out of shape

What are the effects of the more commonly used psychoactive drugs?

Drug-Altered Consciousness—The High and Low of It (p. 242-244)

(243) ***Ecstasy***: relatively new, chemically-synthesized stimulant drug

(244) ***It's the hook that eventually snares the addict***: the drug produces good feelings that the person wants to repeat taking it again and again. The repeated behavior causes the person to become an addict

Uppers—Amphetamines, Cocaine, MDMA, Caffeine, Nicotine (pp. 244-249)

(244) ***uppers***: stimulant drugs

(245) ***illicit***: illegal

(245) ***speed freak***: a person addicted to stimulant drugs

(245) ***binges***: unrestrained use of drugs

(245) ***crash*** (after which they *"crash"*): hit a very low point

(245) ***paranoid delusions***: irrational beliefs that one is being persecuted; distrustfulness

(245) ***convulsions***: abnormal, violent, and involuntary contractions of the muscles

(246) ***heart arrhythmias***: irregular heartbeat

(246) ***adulterated***: mixed with other (often unknown) substances; made impure

(246) ***Seattle***: The capital city of the state of Washington; well-known for high consumption of coffee

(246) ***tremors***: uncontrollable shaking

(246) ***cysts***: closed sacs developing abnormally in a structure of the body

(246) *miscarriage*: failure to continue a pregnancy (loss of the fetus)

(247) *cold sweats*: chills caused by sweating due to anxiety, nervousness, or fear

(248) *urban cowboys and Skol bandits*: urban cowboys are men who live in cities, but attempt to act like cowboys (here by using chewing tobacco); Skol is a popular brand of chewing tobacco

(248) *snuff*: powdered tobacco to be inhaled, chewed, or placed against the gums

(248) *quit cold turkey*: stop smoking completely and suddenly instead of gradually

Downers—Sedatives, Tranquilizers, and Alcohol (pp. 249-253)

(249) *degrease your brain*: to slow down your brain's activity; to make it sluggish or slow moving

(249) *spike*: adding a mind-altering substance to someone's drink without his or her knowledge

(250) *aphrodisiac*: a substance that increases sexual performance or desire

(251) *myopia*: nearsightedness

(251) *blackouts*: periods of loss of consciousness or memory

(252) *compulsively*: uncontrollably

(252) *deteriorate*: become worse

(252) *wit* (as one *wit* once observed): an intelligent and funny person

(252) *dried out*: stopped drinking

(253) *premise*: something assumed or taken for granted

(253) *hit rock bottom*: reached the lowest point personally and emotionally

Marijuana—What's in the Pot? (pp. 253-255)

(253) *pot* (What's in the *pot*?): marijuana

(253) *resinous*: of leftover material

(253) *potent*: powerful

(253) *paranoia*: belief that one is being watched, pursued, or persecuted

(255) *veteran*: person with long experience

(255) *ebb and flow*: the coming and going

(255) *subsidize*: to support financially; to fund

How are dreams used to promote personal understanding?

Psychology in Action: Exploring and Using Dreams (pp. 256-258)

(256) *literal*: actual, obvious; exact meaning

(256) *exhibitionist:* a person who displays himself or herself indecently in public

(256) *insights*: self-knowledge

(257) *puns*: the humorous use of words in such a way as to suggest two or more meanings

(257) *twisting your arm*: making you do something that you would rather not do

(257) *transpire*: happen

(257) *intuitions*: something known or sensed without evident rational thought

(257) *tap*: gain access to

(258) *steep yourself*: immerse yourself; concentrate very hard

(258) *lucid*: having a clear understanding and awareness

(258) *clench*: close tightly

Solutions

RECITE AND REVIEW

What is an altered state of consciousness?

1. awareness; waking
2. pattern
3. sleep; dreaming; sensory
4. normal

What are the effects of sleep loss or changes in sleep patterns?

1. rhythm; survival
2. involuntary
3. routine
4. loss; temporary
5. Physical; sleep; sleepiness
6. lack
7. rhythms
8. 24; 10; light; dark
9. decreases
10. shorter; longer

Are there different stages of sleep? How does dream sleep differ from dreamless sleep?

1. brain
2. two; brain
3. 4; waves
4. light; sleep; Delta
5. alternate
6. movement
7. dreaming
8. Dreaming
9. paralysis
10. physical; stress
11. emotional; muscles; REM

What are the causes of sleep disorders and unusual sleep events?

1. temporary
2. lowered; insomnia
3. sleep
4. stimulus; intention
5. Sleepwalking
6. NREM; REM
7. rehearsal
8. breathing; sudden
9. six; preemie; mouth; teenager
10. *Back*backs

Do dreams have meaning?

1. rebound
2. dream; stage
3. memories
4. familiar; emotions; emotions
5. wishes
6. activation; sensory

How hypnosis is done, and what are its limitations

1. increased
2. animal; suggestion
3. hypnosis
4. 8; Scale
5. basic; immoral
6. autosuggestion
7. pain
8. waking; deception

How does sensory deprivation affect consciousness?

1. stimulation
2. perceptual
3. relaxation

4. habits

What are the effects of the more commonly used psychoactive drugs?

1. alter (affect or change)
2. mimicking; chemicals
3. depression; sensory
4. addiction
5. reduced; increase
6. compulsive

Uppers—Amphetamines, Cocaine, MDMA, Caffeine, Nicotine: Pages 244-249

1. psychological
2. uppers; tolerance; crash; fatigue
3. depression; caffeine
4. crank; injected
5. psychosis; self; others
6. control; consequences
7. increase; serotonergic
8. Ecstasy
9. tea; blocking
10. Nicotine (or Smoking)
11. cancer; second-hand

Downers—Sedatives, Tranquilizers, and Alcohol: Pages 249-253

1. depressant; blue; purple; pink
2. GHB; Georgia
3. Valium; addictive
4. Rohypnol; date
5. drug
6. alcohol; five
7. initial; single
8. removal; withdrawal

Marijuana—What's in the Pot? Pages 253-255

1. weed; abuse
2. THC
3. memory; attention; five

How are dreams used to promote personal understanding?

1. hidden; processes
2. plot
3. speaking
4. creative

CONNECTIONS

What is an altered state of consciousness? What are the effects of sleep loss or changes in sleep patterns? Pages 224-228

1. F.
2. D.
3. H.
4. B.
5. I.
6. A.
7. E.
8. C.
9. G.

Are there different stages of sleep? How does dream sleep differ from dreamless sleep? Pages 228-231

1. C.
2. G.
3. F.
4. A.
5. B.
6. E.
7. H.
8. D.

What are the causes of sleep disorders and unusual sleep events? Pages 232-235

1. D.	5. F.	9. J.
2. I.	6. B.	10. E.
3. C.	7. H.	
4. G.	8. A.	

Do dreams have meaning? Pages 235-237

1. E.	3. C.	5. B.
2. A.	4. F.	6. D.

How hypnosis is done, and what are its limitations? How does sensory deprivation affect consciousness? Pages 237-241

1. B.	3. D.	5. C.
2. F.	4. A.	6. E.

What are the effects of the more commonly used psychoactive drugs? Pages 242-255

1. C.	5. B.	9. E.
2. H.	6. D.	10. G.
3. A.	7. I.	
4. J.	8. F.	

How are dreams used to promote personal understanding? Pages 256-258

1. A.	3. E.	5. B.
2. C.	4. D.	

CHECK YOUR MEMORY

What is an altered state of consciousness? Page 224

1. T	3. T	5. T
2. T	4. T	

What are the effects of sleep loss or changes in sleep patterns? Pages 224-228

1. F	4. F	7. F
2. T	5. T	8. T
3. T	6. T	9. F

Are there different stages of sleep? How does dream sleep differ from dreamless sleep? Pages 228-231

1. F	5. F	9. F
2. T	6. F	10. F
3. F	7. T	11. T
4. F	8. F	

What are the causes of sleep disorders and unusual sleep events? Pages 232-235

1. F	5. T	9. T
2. T	6. T	10. F
3. T	7. T	
4. F	8. T	

Do dreams have meaning? Pages 235-237

1. T	4. F	7. T
2. F	5. T	
3. F	6. F	

How hypnosis is done, and what are its limitations? Pages 237-240

1. F	4. T	7. F
2. F	5. T	8. F
3. F	6. T	

How does sensory deprivation affect consciousness? Pages 240-241

1. F	3. F
2. T	4. F

What are the effects of the more commonly used psychoactive drugs? Pages 242-255

1. F	11. F	21. T
2. T	12. T	22. T
3. T	13. T	23. T
4. F	14. T	24. F
5. F	15. F	25. T
6. T	16. T	26. F
7. T	17. T	27. F
8. T	18. F	28. T
9. T	19. F	29. T
10. T	20. F	30. T

How are dreams used to promote personal understanding? Pages 256-258

1. F   3. F   5. F
2. T   4. T   6. F

FINAL SURVEY AND REVIEW

What is an altered state of consciousness?

1. consciousness; consciousness   3. hypnosis; deprivation
2. mental; activity   4. Cultural

What are the effects of sleep loss or changes in sleep patterns?

1. innate; biological   5. Physical; hypersomnia   9. old; age; multiple
2. microsleeps   6. lack   10. sleep; cycles
3. alertness   7. Circadian
4. psychosis; delusions   8. sleep-waking cycle

Are there different stages of sleep? How does dream sleep differ from dreamless sleep?

1. hormone; spinal; cord   5. 1; 4; 2; 3   9. Hypnopompic; awakening
2. opposed; systems   6. rapid; eye   10. NREM; REM
3. electroencephalograph   7. REM; non-REM   11. arousal; relaxation; disorder
4. spindles; delta; waves   8. stage 1; stage 1

What are the causes of sleep disorders and unusual sleep events?

1. chronic   5. somnambulism; NREM   9. six; preemie; mouth; teenager
2. dependency   6. NREM; REM   10. *Back*backs
3. tryptophan   7. imagery; rehearsal
4. restriction; paradoxical 8. apnea; Apnea; infant; death

Do dreams have meaning?

1. REM rebound   3. REM; sleep   5. psychodynamic; symbols
2. REM; mental; total 4. Hall; negative; positive 6. synthesis; motor

How hypnosis is done, and what are its limitations

1. suggestibility   4. Stanford   7. relaxation
2. Mesmer; mesmerize   5. suggestion; involuntary   8. Stage hypnotism; simulate
3. Braid   6. autosuggestion

How does sensory deprivation affect consciousness?

1. sensory; stimulation
2. Prolonged
3. deprivation; relaxation
4. Restricted; Environmental

What are the effects of the more commonly used psychoactive drugs?

1. consciousness
2. neurotransmitters
3. stimulation; depression; hallucinogens
4. dependence; dependence
5. tolerance; increase
6. recreational

Uppers—Amphetamines, Cocaine, MDMA, Caffeine, Nicotine: Pages 244-249

1. physically; addicting
2. cocaine
3. Amphetamines; tolerance
4. Methamphetamine
5. psychosis; self
6. control; consequences
7. increase; Serotonergic
8. amphetamine; mental
9. Caffeine; blocking
10. lung; cancer
11. carcinogens

Downers—Sedatives, Tranquilizers, and Alcohol: Pages 249-253

1. barbiturates
2. depressant; gamma-hydroxybuyrate; GHB
3. Benzodiazepine
4. Rohypnol
5. alcohol; interaction
6. alcohol; Binge
7. Alcohol; crucial
8. detoxification; withdrawal

Marijuana—What's in the Pot? Pages 253-255

1. hallucinogen; lung
2. THC; cerebral
3. memory; attention; lower

How are dreams used to promote personal understanding?

1. condensation; secondary
2. cast
3. feeling; Perls'
4. lucid

MASTERY TEST

How are dreams used to promote personal understanding?

1. D, p. 224
2. B, p. 249
3. D, p. 243
4. B, p. 229
5. B, p. 256
6. C, pp. 238-239
7. B, p. 242
8. A, p. 230
9. A, p. 241
10. C, p. 237
11. B, p. 227
12. A, p. 251
13. D, p. 226
14. D, p. 245
15. D, p. 226
16. C, p. 232
17. B, p. 241
18. A, p. 237
19. A, p. 258
20. D, p. 253
21. B, p. 230
22. D, p. 250
23. C, p. 226
24. A, p. 244

25. C, p. 249
26. B, p. 234
27. A, pp. 232-233
28. D, p. 247
29. B, p. 236

30. A, p. 246
31. C, p. 227
32. B, p. 235
33. A, p. 239
34. D, p. 244

35. C, p. 231

Conditioning and Learning

Chapter Overview

Learning is a relatively permanent change in behavior due to experience. Two basic forms of learning are classical conditioning and operant conditioning.

Classical conditioning is also called respondent or Pavlovian conditioning. Classical conditioning occurs when a neutral stimulus is associated with an unconditioned stimulus (which reliably elicits an unconditioned response). After many pairings of the NS and the US, the NS becomes a conditioned stimulus that elicits a conditioned response. Learning is reinforced during acquisition of a response. Withdrawing reinforcement leads to extinction (although some spontaneous recovery of conditioning may occur). It is apparent that stimulus generalization has occurred when a stimulus similar to the CS also elicits a learned response. In stimulus discrimination, people or animals learn to respond differently to two similar stimuli. Conditioning often involves simple reflex responses, but emotional conditioning is also possible.

In operant conditioning (or instrumental learning), the consequences that follow a response alter the probability that it will be made again. Positive and negative reinforcers increase responding; punishment suppresses responding; nonreinforcement leads to extinction. Various types of reinforcers and different patterns of giving reinforcers greatly affect operant learning. Four types of schedules of partial reinforcements are fixed ratio, variable ratio, fixed interval, and variable interval. Fix ratio produces a high response rate while variable interval produces a slow and steady response rate; it has a strong resistance to extinction.

Informational feedback (knowledge of results) also facilitates learning and performance. Antecedent stimuli (those that precede a response) influence operant learning, through stimulus generalization, discrimination, and stimulus control. Shaping, a form of operant conditioning, uses successive approximation to train animals to perform tricks.

Learning, even simple conditioning, is based on acquiring information. Higher level cognitive learning involves memory, thinking, problem solving, and language. At a simpler level, cognitive maps, latent learning, and discovery learning show that learning is based on acquiring information. Learning also occurs through observation and imitating models. Observational learning imparts large amounts of information that would be hard to acquire in other ways.

Operant principles can be applied to manage one's own behavior and to break bad habits. A mixture of operant principles and cognitive learning underlies self-regulated learning—a collection of techniques to improve learning in school.

Learning Objectives

1. Define *reinforcement* and explain its role in conditioning.

2. Describe the following terms as they apply to classical conditioning:

   a. neutral stimulus (NS)

   b. unconditioned stimulus (US)

   c. unconditioned response (UR)

   d. conditioned stimulus (CS)

   e. conditioned response (CR)

3. Explain how reinforcement occurs during the acquisition of a classically conditioned response. Explain higher order conditioning.

4. Describe and give examples of the following concepts as they relate to classical conditioning:

   a. extinction

   b. spontaneous recovery

   c. stimulus generalization

   d. stimulus discrimination

5. Contrast operant conditioning with classical conditioning. Briefly compare the differences between what is meant by the terms *reward* and *reinforcement*.

6. Explain how shaping occurs.

7. Compare and contrast positive reinforcement, negative reinforcement, and punishment, and give an example of each (including two types of punishment).

8. Discuss the way in which a secondary reinforcer becomes reinforcing.

9. Compare and contrast the effects of continuous and partial reinforcement.

10. Describe, give an example of, and explain the effects of the following schedules of partial reinforcement:

    a. fixed ratio (FR)

    b. variable ratio (VR)

    c. fixed interval (FI)

    d. variable interval (VI)

11. Explain the concept of *stimulus control*.

12. Describe the processes of *generalization* and *discrimination* as they relate to operant conditioning.

13. Explain how punishers can be defined by their effects on behavior.

14. List the three basic tools available to control simple learning.

15. List six guidelines which should be followed when using punishment.

16. Discuss three problems associated with punishment.

17. Define *cognitive learning*.

18. Describe the concepts of cognitive map and latent learning.

19. Discuss the factors which determine whether or not modeling or observational learning will occur.

20. Describe the experiment with children and the Bo-Bo doll that demonstrates the powerful effect of modeling on behavior.

The following objectives are related to the material in the "Psychology in Action" section of your text.

1. Briefly describe the seven steps in a behavioral self-management program.

2. Describe how self-recording and behavioral contracting can aid a self-management program.

3. Briefly describe eight strategies for self-regulated learning.

4. Describe the Premack principle.

RECITE AND REVIEW

What is learning?

What Is Learning—Does Practice Make Perfect? Pages 262-263

1. Learning is a relatively permanent change in _____ due to experience. To understand learning we must study antecedents (events that _____ responses) and consequences (events that _____ responses).

2. Classical, or respondent _____ , and instrumental or operant _____ are two basic types of learning.

3. In classical conditioning, a previously neutral _____ is associated with a stimulus that elicits a response. In operant conditioning, the pattern of voluntary _____ is altered by consequences.

4. Both types of conditioning depend on reinforcement. In classical conditioning, learning is _____ when a US follows the NS or CS. _____ reinforcement is based on the consequences that follow a response.

How does classical conditioning occur?

Classical Conditioning—Does the Name Pavlov Ring a Bell? Pages 263-265

1. Classical conditioning, studied by Ivan Pavlov, occurs when a _____ stimulus (NS) is associated with an unconditioned stimulus (US). The US triggers a reflex called the unconditioned _____ (UR).

2. If the NS is consistently paired with the US, it becomes a conditioned _____ (CS) capable of producing a response by itself. This response is a conditioned (_____) response (CR).

Principles of Classical Conditioning—Teach Your Little Brother to Salivate: Pages 265-267

1. During acquisition of classical conditioning, the conditioned stimulus must be consistently followed by the unconditioned _____ .

2. Higher-order conditioning occurs when a well-learned conditioned stimulus is used as if it were an unconditioned _____ , bringing about further learning.

3. When the CS is repeatedly presented alone, extinction takes place. That is, _____ is weakened or inhibited.

4. After extinction seems to be complete, a rest period may lead to the temporary reappearance of a conditioned _____ . This is called spontaneous recovery.

5. Through stimulus generalization, stimuli _____ to the conditioned stimulus will also produce a response.

6. Generalization gives way to _____ discrimination when an organism learns to respond to one stimulus, but not to similar stimuli.

7. From an informational view, conditioning creates expectancies (or expectations about events), which alter _____ patterns.

8. In classical conditioning, the CS creates an expectancy that the US will _____ it.

Does conditioning affect emotions?

Classical Conditioning in Humans—An Emotional Topic: Pages 267-269

1. Eye-blink conditioning can be used to detect _____ (a mental disorder that affects a person's ability to read, think, and recognize family members).

2. Conditioning applies to visceral or emotional responses as well as simple _____ . As a result, _____ emotional responses (CERs) also occur.

3. Irrational fears called phobias may be CERs that are extended to a variety of situations by _____ generalization.

4. The conditioning of emotional responses can occur vicariously (_____) as well as directly. Vicarious classical conditioning occurs when we _____ another person's emotional responses to a stimulus.

How does operant conditioning occur?

Operant Conditioning—Can Pigeons Play Ping-Pong? Pages 269-274

1. Operant conditioning (or instrumental _____) occurs when a voluntary action is followed by a reinforcer.

2. Reinforcement in operant conditioning _____ the frequency or probability of a response. This result is based on what Edward L. Thorndike called the law of _____ .

3. An operant reinforcer is any event that follows a _____ and _____ its probability.

4. Learning in operant conditioning is based on the expectation that a response will have a specific _____ .

5. To be effective, operant _____ must be _____ contingent.

6. Delay of reinforcement reduces its effectiveness, but long _____ of responses may be built up so that a _____ reinforcer maintains many responses.

7. Superstitious behaviors (unnecessary responses) often become part of _____ chains because they appear to be associated with reinforcement.

8. In a process called shaping, complex _____ responses can be taught by reinforcing successive approximations (ever closer matches) to a final desired response.

9. If an operant response is not reinforced, it may extinguish (disappear). But after extinction seems complete, it may temporarily reappear (spontaneous _____).

10. In positive reinforcement, _____ or a pleasant event follows a response. In negative reinforcement, a response that _____ discomfort becomes more likely to occur again.

11. Punishment _____ responding. Punishment occurs when a response is followed by the onset of an aversive event or by the removal of a positive event (response _____).

Are there different kinds of operant reinforcement?

Operant Reinforcers—What's Your Pleasure? Pages 274-278

1. Primary reinforcers are "natural," physiologically-based rewards. Intra-cranial stimulation of " _____ centers" in the _____ can also serve as a primary reinforcer.

2. Secondary reinforcers are _____ . They typically gain their reinforcing value by association with primary reinforcers or because they can be _____ for primary reinforcers. Tokens and money gain their reinforcing value in this way.

3. Human behavior is often influenced by social reinforcers, which are based on learned desires for attention and _____ from others.

4. Feedback, or knowledge of _____ , aids learning and improves performance.

5. Programmed instruction breaks learning into a series of small steps and provides immediate _____ .

6. Computer-assisted _____ (CAI) does the same, but has the added advantage of providing alternate exercises and information when needed.

7. Variations of _____ are instructional games and educational simulations.

How are we influenced by patterns of reward?

Partial Reinforcement—Las Vegas, a Human Skinner Box? Pages 278-280

1. Reward or reinforcement may be given continuously (after every _____), or on a schedule of _____ reinforcement. The study of schedules of reinforcement was begun by B. F. Skinner.

2. Partial reinforcement produces greater resistance to extinction. This is the partial reinforcement _____ .

3. The four most basic schedules of reinforcement are _____ ratio (FR), variable ratio (VR), _____ interval (FI), and variable interval (VI).

4. FR and VR schedules produce _____ rates of responding. An FI schedule produces moderate rates of responding with alternating periods of activity and inactivity. VI schedules produce _____ , steady rates of responding and strong resistance to extinction.

Stimulus Control—Red Light, Green Light: Pages 280-282

1. Stimuli that _____ a reinforced response tend to control the response on future occasions (stimulus control). The effect of stimulus control can be described as _____ a stimulus, performing a behavior, and getting a reward.

2. Two aspects of stimulus control are generalization and _____ .

3. In generalization, an operant response tends to occur when stimuli _____ to those preceding reinforcement are present.

4. In discrimination, responses are given in the presence of discriminative stimuli associated with reinforcement (_____) and withheld in the presence of stimuli associated with nonreinforcement (_____).

What does punishment do to behavior?

Punishment—Putting the Brakes on Behavior: Pages 282-286

1. A punisher is any consequence that _____ the frequency of a target behavior.

2. Punishment is most effective when it is _____ , consistent, and intense.

3. Mild punishment tends only to temporarily _____ responses that are also reinforced or were acquired by reinforcement.

4. Three basic tools used by teachers and parents to control behaviors are reinforcement, _____ , and punishment, which _____ responses, causes responses to be extinguished, and _____ responses, respectively.

5. Spanking a child _____ seem to show signs of long-term effects if it is backed up with supportive parenting techniques. However, if the spanking is severe, frequent, or paired with a harsh parenting technique, spanking may _____ damage a child.

6. The undesirable side effects of punishment include the conditioning of fear; the learning of _____ and avoidance responses; and the encouragement of aggression.

7. Reinforcement and nonreinforcement are better ways to change behavior than punishment. When punishment is used, it should be _____ and combined with reinforcement of alternate _____ .

What is cognitive learning?

Cognitive Learning—Beyond Conditioning: Pages 286-287

1. Cognitive learning involves higher mental processes, such as understanding, knowing, or anticipating. Evidence of cognitive learning is provided by cognitive _____ (internal representations of spatial relationships) and latent (hidden) _____ .

2. Discovery learning emphasizes insight and _____ , in contrast to rote learning.

Does learning occur by imitation?

Modeling—Do as I Do, Not as I Say: Pages 288-291

1. Much human learning is achieved through _____ , or modeling. Observational learning is influenced by the personal characteristics of the _____ and the success or failure of the _____ behavior.

2. Observational learning involves attention, remembering, _____ , and outcome of reproduction.

3. Television characters can act as powerful _____ for observational learning. Televised violence increases the likelihood of aggression by viewers.

4. People who play violent video games such as Mortal Kombat are prone to act _____ toward others.

How does conditioning apply to practical problems?

Psychology in Action: Behavioral Self-Management—A Rewarding Project: Pages 291-293

1. Operant principles can be readily applied to manage behavior in everyday settings. Self-management of behavior is based on self-reinforcement, self-recording, _____ , and behavioral contracting.

2. Prepotent, or frequent, high-probability _____ , can be used to reinforce low-frequency responses. This is known as the Premack _____ .

3. Attempts to break bad habits are aided by reinforcing alternate _____ , by extinction, breaking _____ chains, and _____ cues or antecedents.

4. In school, self-regulated _____ typically involves all of the following: setting learning _____ , planning learning strategies, using self-instruction, monitoring progress, evaluating yourself, reinforcing _____ , and taking corrective action when required.

CONNECTIONS

What is learning? How does classical conditioning occur? Pages 262-267

1. _____ respondent conditioning	a.	before responses
2. _____ antecedents	b.	Pavlov's CS
3. _____ meat powder	c.	after responses
4. _____ spontaneous recovery	d.	higher-order conditioning
5. _____ bell	e.	Pavlovian conditioning
6. _____ salivation	f.	US missing
7. _____ consequences	g.	reinforcement period
8. _____ expectancies	h.	UR
9. _____ CS used as US	i.	Pavlov's US
10. _____ desensitization	j.	extinction of fear
11. _____ extinction	k.	informational view
12. _____ acquisition	l.	incomplete extinction

Does conditioning affect emotions? How does operant conditioning occur? Pages 267-274

1. _____ response cost
2. _____ shaping
3. _____ negative reinforcement
4. _____ law of effect
5. _____ Skinner
6. _____ instrumental learning
7. _____ punishment
8. _____ phobia

a. operant conditioning
b. CER
c. losing privileges
d. learned reinforcer
e. increased responding
f. approximations
g. decreased responding
h. Edward Thorndike

Are there different kinds of operant reinforcement? Pages 274-278

1. _____ primary reinforcer
2. _____ secondary reinforcer
3. _____ tokens
4. _____ approval
5. _____ KR
6. _____ CAI

a. nonlearned reinforcer
b. social reinforcer
c. Chimp-O-Mat
d. educational simulations
e. feedback
f. conditioning chamber

How are we influenced by patterns of reward? Pages 278-282

1. _____ stimulus control
2. _____ continuous reinforcement
3. _____ partial reinforcement
4. _____ fixed ratio
5. _____ variable ratio
6. _____ variable interval
7. _____ fixed interval
8. _____ discriminative stimuli

a. resistance to extinction
b. reinforcement schedule
c. paper due every two weeks
d. S+ and S-
e. high response rate
f. antecedent stimuli
g. steady response rate
h. reinforce all correct responses

What does punishment do to behavior? Pages 282-286

1. _____ punishment
2. _____ avoidance learning
3. _____ severe punishment
4. _____ escape learning
5. _____ mild punishment
6. _____ fear and aggression

a. lying to prevent discomfort
b. side effects of punishment
c. suppresses a response
d. running away
e. weak effect
f. can stop a behavior permanently

What is cognitive learning? Does learning occur by imitation? How does conditioning apply to practical problems? Pages 286-293

1. _____ cognitive map
2. _____ Premack principle
3. _____ observational learning
4. _____ modeling
5. _____ self-recording
6. _____ rote learning
7. _____ televised violence
8. _____ discovery learning
9. _____ latent learning

a. insight
b. imitation
c. mental image of campus
d. learning through repetition
e. Albert Bandura
f. hidden learning
g. can produce aggression
h. self-management program
i. use repeated behavior as reinforcer

CHECK YOUR MEMORY

What is learning? Pages 262-263

1. Learning to press the buttons on a vending machine is based on operant conditioning.

   TRUE or FALSE

2. In classical conditioning, the consequences that follow responses become associated with one another.

   TRUE or FALSE

3. Getting compliments from friends could serve as reinforcement for operant learning.

   TRUE or FALSE

How does classical conditioning occur? Pages 263-267

1. Ivan Pavlov studied digestion and operant conditioning in dogs.

   TRUE or FALSE

2. Pavlov used meat powder to reinforce conditioned salivation to the sound of a bell.

   TRUE or FALSE

3. Many cancer patients unknowingly have undergone classical conditioning as they associate food eaten before receiving chemo treatments with the sickness generated by the treatments.

   TRUE or FALSE

4. To reduce the chances of developing an aversion to food before undergoing chemotherapy, cancer patients can flavor their food with hot pepper sauce.

   TRUE or FALSE

5. During successful conditioning, the NS becomes a CS.

   TRUE or FALSE

6. During acquisition, the CS is presented repeatedly without the US.

   TRUE or FALSE

7. The optimal delay between the CS and the US is 5 to 15 seconds.

   TRUE or FALSE

8. Spontaneous recovery occurs when a CS becomes strong enough to be used like a US.

   TRUE or FALSE

9. Discriminations are learned when generalized responses to stimuli similar to the CS are extinguished.

   TRUE or FALSE

Does conditioning affect emotions? Pages 267-269

1. Narrowing of the pupils in response to bright lights is learned in early infancy.

   TRUE or FALSE

2. Emotional conditioning involves autonomic nervous system responses.

   TRUE or FALSE

3. Stimulus generalization helps convert some CERs into phobias.

   TRUE or FALSE

4. Pleasant music can be used as a UR to create a CER.

   TRUE or FALSE

5. To learn a CER vicariously, you would observe the actions of another person and try to imitate them.

   TRUE or FALSE

6. Eye blink conditioning tends to occur faster than normal in people who are in the early stages of dementia.

   TRUE or FALSE

How does operant conditioning occur? Pages 269-274

1. In operant conditioning, learners actively emit responses.

   TRUE or FALSE

2. Rewards are the same as reinforcers.

   TRUE or FALSE

3. The Skinner box is primarily used to study classical conditioning.

   TRUE or FALSE

4. Reinforcement in operant conditioning alters how frequently involuntary responses are elicited.

   TRUE or FALSE

5. Operant reinforcers are most effective when they are response-contingent.

   TRUE or FALSE

6. Operant learning is most effective if you wait a minute or two after the response is over before reinforcing it.

   TRUE or FALSE

7. Response chains allow delayed reinforcers to support learning.

   TRUE or FALSE

8. Superstitious responses appear to be associated with reinforcement, but they are not.

   TRUE or FALSE

9. Teaching a pigeon to play Ping-Pong would most likely make use of the principle of response cost.

   TRUE or FALSE

10. Children who misbehave may be reinforced by attention from parents.

    TRUE or FALSE

11. Negative reinforcement is a type of punishment that is used to strengthen learning.

    TRUE or FALSE

12. Putting a pair of gloves on to stop the pain caused by the cold outside air is an example of negative reinforcement.

TRUE or FALSE

13. You have stopped offering advice to a friend because she turned distant every time you gave her advice is an example of punishment.

TRUE or FALSE

14. Both response cost and negative reinforcement decrease responding.

TRUE or FALSE

Are there different kinds of operant reinforcement? Pages 274-278

1. Food, water, grades, and sex are primary reinforcers.

TRUE or FALSE

2. ICS is a good example of a secondary reinforcer.

TRUE or FALSE

3. Social reinforcers are secondary reinforcers.

TRUE or FALSE

4. Attention and approval can be used to shape another person's behavior.

TRUE or FALSE

5. The effects of primary reinforcers may quickly decline as the person becomes satiated.

TRUE or FALSE

6. The Chimp-O-Mat accepted primary reinforcers and dispensed secondary reinforcers.

TRUE or FALSE

7. People are more likely to recycle used materials if they receive weekly feedback about how much they have recycled.

TRUE or FALSE

8. CAI is another term for informational feedback.

TRUE or FALSE

9. In sports, feedback is most effective when a skilled coach directs attention to important details.

TRUE or FALSE

10. The final level of skill and knowledge is almost always higher following CAI than it is with conventional methods.

TRUE or FALSE

How are we influenced by patterns of reward? Pages 278-282

1. Continuous reinforcement means that reinforcers are given continuously, regardless of whether or not responses are made.

TRUE or FALSE

2. An FR-3 schedule means that each correct response produces 3 reinforcers.

TRUE or FALSE

3. The time interval in FI schedules is measured from the last reinforced response.

TRUE or FALSE

4. In business, commissions and profit sharing are examples of FI reinforcement.

TRUE or FALSE

5. Antecedent stimuli tend to control when and where previously rewarded responses will occur.

TRUE or FALSE

6. Stimulus control refers to noticing an event occurring, performing a behavior, then getting a reward for the behavior.

TRUE or FALSE

7. Stimulus generalization is the primary method used to train dogs to detect contraband.

TRUE or FALSE

8. S+ represents a discriminative stimulus that precedes a nonreinforced response.

TRUE or FALSE

What does punishment do to behavior? Pages 282-286

1. Like reinforcement, punishment should be response-contingent.

TRUE or FALSE

2. Punishment is most effective if it is unpredictable.

TRUE or FALSE

3. Speeding tickets are an example of response cost.

TRUE or FALSE

4. Mild punishment causes reinforced responses to extinguish more rapidly.

   TRUE or FALSE

5. Generally, punishment should be the last resort for altering behavior.

   TRUE or FALSE

6. An apparatus known as a shuttle box is used to study escape and avoidance learning.

   TRUE or FALSE

7. Punishment does not have to be consistent to extinguish a behavior quickly as long as positive behaviors are reinforced.

   TRUE or FALSE

8. Spanking, even if it is backed up with a supportive parenting technique, is still emotionally damaging to most children.

   TRUE or FALSE

9. For humans, avoidance learning is reinforced by a sense of relief.

   TRUE or FALSE

10. Punishment frequently leads to increases in aggression by the person who is punished.

    TRUE or FALSE

What is cognitive learning? Pages 286-287

1. Cognitive learning involves thinking, memory, and problem solving.

   TRUE or FALSE

2. Animals learning their way through a maze memorize the correct order of right and left turns to make.

   TRUE or FALSE

3. Typically, reinforcement must be provided in order to make latent learning visible.

   TRUE or FALSE

4. In many situations, discovery learning produces better understanding of problems.

   TRUE or FALSE

5. Rote learning produces skills through insight and understanding.

   TRUE or FALSE

Does learning occur by imitation? Pages 288-291

1. Modeling is another term for discovery learning.

   TRUE or FALSE

2. After a new response is acquired through modeling, normal reinforcement determines if it will be repeated.

   TRUE or FALSE

3. Successful observational learning requires two steps: observing and reproducing the behavior.

   TRUE or FALSE

4. Children imitate aggressive acts performed by other people, but they are not likely to imitate cartoon characters.

   TRUE or FALSE

5. Violence on television causes children to be more violent.

   TRUE or FALSE

6. Playing violent video games tends to increase aggressive behavior in children and young adults.

   TRUE or FALSE

How does conditioning apply to practical problems? Pages 291-293

1. Choosing reinforcers is the first step in behavioral self-management.

   TRUE or FALSE

2. Self-recording can be an effective way to change behavior, even without using specific reinforcers.

   TRUE or FALSE

3. A prepotent response is one that occurs frequently.

   TRUE or FALSE

4. To use extinction to break a bad habit, you should remove, avoid, or delay the reinforcement that is supporting the habit.

   TRUE or FALSE

5. It is necessary to use cues or antecedents when breaking a bad habit.

   TRUE or FALSE

6. In a behavioral contract, you spell out what response chains you are going to extinguish.

   TRUE or FALSE

7. Self-regulated learners actively seek feedback in both formal and informal ways.

   TRUE or FALSE

FINAL SURVEY AND REVIEW

What is learning?

What Is Learning—Does Practice Make Perfect? Pages 262-263

1. Learning is a relatively permanent change in behavior due to experience. To understand learning we must study _____ (events that precede responses) and _____ (events that follow responses).

2. Classical, or _____ conditioning, and instrumental or _____ conditioning are two basic types of learning.

3. In classical conditioning, a previously _____ stimulus is associated with a stimulus that elicits a response. In operant conditioning, the pattern of voluntary responses is altered by _____ .

4. Both types of conditioning depend on _____ . In classical conditioning, learning is reinforced when a _____ follows the NS or CS. Operant reinforcement is based on the consequences that follow a response.

How does classical conditioning occur?

Classical Conditioning—Does the Name Pavlov Ring a Bell? Pages 263-265

1. Classical conditioning, studied by _____ _____ , occurs when a neutral stimulus (NS) is associated with an _____ stimulus (US). The US triggers a _____ called the unconditioned response (UR).

2. If the NS is consistently paired with the US, it becomes a _____ stimulus (CS) capable of producing a response by itself. This response is a _____ (learned) response (CR).

Principles of Classical Conditioning—Teach Your Little Brother to Salivate: Pages 265-267

1. During acquisition of classical conditioning, the conditioned stimulus must be consistently followed by the _____ _____ .

2. _____ conditioning occurs when a well-learned conditioned stimulus is used as if it were an unconditioned stimulus, bringing about further learning.

3. When the CS is repeatedly presented alone, _____ takes place. That is, conditioning is weakened or inhibited.

4. After extinction seems to be complete, a rest period may lead to the temporary reappearance of a conditioned response. This is called _____ .

5. Through stimulus _____ , stimuli similar to the conditioned stimulus will also produce a response.

6. Generalization gives way to stimulus _____ when an organism learns to respond to one stimulus, but not to similar stimuli.

7. From an _____ view, conditioning creates expectancies (or expectations about events), which alter response patterns.

8. In classical conditioning, the _____ creates an expectancy that the _____ will follow it.

Does conditioning affect emotions?

Classical Conditioning in Humans—An Emotional Topic: Pages 267-269

1. _____ conditioning can be used to detect dementia (a mental disorder that affects a person's ability to read, think, and recognize family members).

2. Conditioning applies to visceral or emotional responses as well as simple reflexes. As a result, conditioned _____ responses (CERs) also occur.

3. Irrational fears called _____ may be CERs that are extended to a variety of situations by stimulus _____ .

4. The conditioning of emotional responses can occur secondhand as well as directly. _____ classical conditioning occurs when we observe another person's emotional responses to a stimulus.

How does operant conditioning occur?

Operant Conditioning—Can Pigeons Play Ping-Pong? Pages 269-274

1. Operant conditioning (or _____ learning) occurs when a voluntary action is followed by a reinforcer.

2. Reinforcement in operant conditioning increases the frequency or _____ of a response. This result is based on what Edward L. _____ called the law of effect.

3. An operant reinforcer is any event that follows a _____ and _____ its probability.

4. Learning in operant conditioning is based on the _____ that a response will have a specific effect.

5. To be effective, operant reinforcement must be response _____ .

6. Delay of reinforcement _____ its effectiveness, but long chains of responses may be built up so that a single _____ maintains many responses.

7. _____ behaviors (unnecessary responses) often become part of response chains because they appear to be associated with reinforcement.

8. In a process called _____ , complex operant responses can be taught by reinforcing successive _____ (ever closer matches) to a final desired response.

9. If an operant response is not reinforced, it may _____ (disappear). But after extinction seems complete, it may temporarily reappear (_____ recovery).

10. In _____ reinforcement, reward or a pleasant event follows a response. In _____ reinforcement, a response that ends discomfort becomes more likely to occur again.

11. Punishment decreases responding. Punishment occurs when a response is followed by the onset of an _____ event or by the removal of a _____ event (response cost).

Are there different kinds of operant reinforcement?

Operant Reinforcers—What's Your Pleasure? Pages 274-278

1. _____ reinforcers are "natural," physiologically-based rewards. Intra-cranial _____ of "pleasure centers" in the brain can also serve as a primary reinforcer.

2. _____ reinforcers are learned. They typically gain their reinforcing value by association with _____ reinforcers or because they can be exchanged for _____ reinforcers. Tokens and money gain their reinforcing value in this way.

3. Human behavior is often influenced by _____ reinforcers, which are based on learned desires for attention and approval from others.

4. Feedback, or _____ of results, aids learning and improves performance.

5. Programmed _____ breaks learning into a series of small steps and provides immediate feedback.

6. _____ (CAI) does the same, but has the added advantage of providing alternate exercises and information when needed.

7. Variations of CAI are _____ games and _____ simulations.

How are we influenced by patterns of reward?

Partial Reinforcement—Las Vegas, a Human Skinner Box? Pages 278-280

1. Reward or reinforcement may be given continuously (after every response), or on a _____ of partial reinforcement. The study of schedules of reinforcement was begun by B. F. _____ .

2. Partial reinforcement produces greater resistance to _____ . This is the _____ reinforcement effect.

3. The four most basic schedules of reinforcement are fixed and variable _____ (FR and VR), and fixed and variable _____ (FI and VI).

4. _____ and _____ schedules produce high rates of responding. An _____ schedule produces moderate rates of responding with alternating periods of activity and inactivity. VI schedules produce slow, steady rates of responding and strong resistance to _____ .

Stimulus Control—Red Light, Green Light: Pages 280-282

1. Stimuli that precede a reinforced response tend to control the response on future occasions. This is called _____ _____ .

2. The effect of stimulus control can be described as _____ a stimulus, _____ a behavior, and getting a reward.

3. Two aspects of stimulus control are _____ and _____ .

4. In _____ , an operant response tends to occur when stimuli similar to those preceding reinforcement are present.

5. In _____ , responses are given in the presence of discriminative stimuli associated with reinforcement (S+) and withheld in the presence of stimuli associated with nonreinforcement (S−).

What does punishment do to behavior?

Punishment—Putting the Brakes on Behavior: Pages 282-286

1. A _____ is any consequence that decreases the frequency of a target behavior.

2. Punishment is most effective when it is immediate, _____ , and intense.

3. Mild punishment tends only to temporarily suppress responses that are also _____ in some way.

4. Three basic tools used by teachers and parents to control behaviors are _____ , nonreinforcement, and punishment, which _____ responses, causes responses to be _____ , and suppresses responses, respectively.

5. Spanking a child does not seem to show signs of long-term effects if it is backed up with _____ parenting techniques. However, if the spanking is severe, frequent, or paired with a harsh parenting technique, spanking may _____ damage a child.

6. The undesirable side effects of punishment include the conditioning of fear; the learning of escape and _____ responses; and the encouragement of _____ against others

7. _____ and _____ are better ways to change behavior than punishment.

What is cognitive learning?

Cognitive Learning—Beyond Conditioning: Pages 286-287

1. Cognitive learning involves higher mental processes, such as understanding, knowing, or anticipating. Evidence of cognitive learning is provided by _____ _____ (internal representations of spatial relationships) and _____ (hidden) learning.

2. Discovery learning emphasizes insight and understanding, in contrast to _____ learning.

Does learning occur by imitation?

Modeling—Do as I Do, Not as I Say: Pages 288-291

1. Much human learning is achieved through imitation, or _____ . _____ _____ is influenced by the personal characteristics of the model and the success or failure of the model's behavior.

2. _____ learning involves attention, remembering, reproduction, and outcome of reproduction.

3. Television characters can act as powerful models for _____ learning. Televised violence increases the likelihood of aggression by viewers.

4. People who play violent video games such as Mortal Kombat are prone to act _____ toward others.

How does conditioning apply to practical problems?

Psychology in Action: Behavioral Self-Management—A Rewarding Project: Pages 291-293

1. Operant principles can be readily applied to manage behavior in everyday settings. Self-management of behavior is based on self-reinforcement, self-recording, feedback, and behavioral _____ .

2. Prepotent, or frequent, high-probability responses, can be used to _____ low-frequency responses. This is known as the _____ principle.

3. Attempts to break bad habits are aided by reinforcing _____ responses, by extinction, breaking response _____ , and removing cues or _____ .

4. In school, self-regulated learning typically involves all of the following: setting learning goals, planning learning _____ , using self-instruction, monitoring progress, evaluating yourself, _____ successes, and taking corrective action when required.

MASTERY TEST

1. Tokens are a good example of
   a. secondary reinforcers
   b. the effects of ICS on behavior
   c. noncontingent reinforcers
   d. generalized reinforcers

2. The principle of feedback is of particular importance to
   a. CERs
   b. ICS
   c. CAI
   d. higher-order conditioning

3. As a coffee lover, you have become very efficient at carrying out the steps necessary to make a cup of espresso. Your learning is an example of
   a. response chaining
   b. spontaneous recovery
   c. vicarious reinforcement
   d. secondary reinforcement

4. To teach a pet dog to use a new dog door, it would be helpful to use
   a. the Premack principle
   b. shaping
   c. respondent conditioning
   d. delayed reinforcement

5. To test for the presence of classical conditioning you would omit the
   a. CS
   b. US
   c. CR
   d. S+

6. Which of the following does not belong with the others?
   a. Thorndike
   b. Skinner
   c. Pavlov
   d. instrumental learning

7. To teach a child to say "Please" when she asks for things, you should make getting the requested item
   a. the CS
   b. a token
   c. a negative reinforcer
   d. response-contingent

8. Money is to secondary reinforcer as food is to
   a. ICS
   b. prepotent responses
   c. primary reinforcer
   d. negative reinforcer

9. Whether a model is reinforced has a great impact on
   a. discovery learning
   b. latent learning
   c. observational learning
   d. self-regulated learning

10. One thing that classical and operant conditioning have in common is that both
    a. were discovered by Pavlov
    b. depend on reinforcement
    c. are affected by the consequences of making a response
    d. permanently change behavior

11. To shape the behavior of a teacher in one of your classes you would probably have to rely on
    a. tokens
    b. primary reinforcers
    c. negative attention seeking
    d. social reinforcers

12. The concept that best explains persistence at gambling is
    a. partial reinforcement
    b. continuous reinforcement
    c. fixed interval reinforcement
    d. fixed ratio reinforcement

13. Which of the following is NOT a common side effect of mild punishment?
    a. escape learning
    b. avoidance learning
    c. aggression
    d. accelerated extinction

14. With respect to televised violence it can be said that TV violence
    a. causes viewers to be more aggressive
    b. makes aggression more likely
    c. has no effect on the majority of viewers
    d. vicariously lowers aggressive urges

15. Which of the following types of learning is most related to the consequences of making a response?
    a. Pavlovian conditioning
    b. classical conditioning
    c. operant conditioning
    d. respondent conditioning

16. Which combination would most likely make a CER into a phobia?
    a. CER-discrimination
    b. CER-desensitization
    c. CER-response cost
    d. CER-generalization

17. Slower than normal eye blink conditioning is an early sign of
    a. two-factor avoidance learning
    b. escape learning
    c. vicarious extinction
    d. dementia

18. A loud, unexpected sound causes a startle reflex; thus, a loud sound could be used as a _____ in conditioning.
    a. NS
    b. CR
    c. UR
    d. US

19. Antecedents are to _____ as consequences are to _____.
    a. discriminative stimuli, reinforcers
    b. shaping, response chaining
    c. conditioned stimuli, cognitive maps
    d. punishment, negative reinforcement

20. The use of self-recording to change personal behavior is closely related to the principle of
    a. response chaining
    b. feedback
    c. two-factor reinforcement
    d. stimulus control

21. _____ typically only temporarily suppresses reinforced responses.
    a. Negative reinforcement
    b. Extinction
    c. Mild punishment
    d. Stimulus generalization

22. In general, the highest rates of responding are associated with
    a. delayed reinforcement
    b. variable reinforcement
    c. interval reinforcement
    d. fixed ratio reinforcement

23. A child who has learned, through classical conditioning, to fear sitting in a dentist's chair becomes frightened when he is placed in a barber's chair. This illustrates the concept of
    a. stimulus generalization
    b. spontaneous recovery
    c. higher-order discrimination
    d. vicarious conditioning

24. The informational view of learning places emphasis on the creation of mental
    a. expectancies
    b. reinforcement schedules
    c. contracts
    d. antecedents

25. For some adults, blushing when embarrassed or ashamed is probably a _____ first formed in childhood.
    a. conditioned stimulus
    b. CAI
    c. discriminative stimulus
    d. CER

26. Learning to obey traffic signals is related to the phenomenon called
    a. stimulus control
    b. spontaneous recovery
    c. avoidance learning
    d. modeling

27. To be most effective, punishment should be combined with
    a. response costs
    b. aversive stimuli
    c. delayed feedback
    d. reinforcement

28. Involuntary responses are to _____ conditioning as voluntary responses are to _____ conditioning.
    a. classical, respondent
    b. classical, operant
    c. operant, classical
    d. operant, instrumental

29. Negative attention seeking by children demonstrates the impact of _____ on behavior.
    a. operant extinction
    b. social reinforcers
    c. response costs
    d. prepotent responses

30. Which consequence increases the probability that a response will be repeated?
    a. punishment
    b. response cost
    c. nonreinforcement
    d. negative reinforcement

31. Successive approximations are used in _____ to train animals to perform tricks.
    a. observational conditioning
    b. classical conditioning
    c. shaping
    d. latent learning

32. Putting on a pair of gloves to stop your hands from hurting while working in the cold weather demonstrates
    a. positive reinforcement
    b. negative reinforcement
    c. punishment
    d. response cost

33. Wanting to do some light reading while his roommate drove, Cody picked up a magazine, and after a few minutes, Cody felt nauseated and had to stop reading. To avoid getting sick in the future, Cody no longer read while riding in a car. This illustrates
    a. positive reinforcement
    b. negative reinforcement
    c. punishment
    d. response cost

34. Introducing an energy tax to reduce people's tendency to waste energy or polluting the environment utilizes _____, a form of operant conditioning.
    a. positive reinforcement
    b. negative reinforcement
    c. punishment
    d. response cost

35. _____ gives students enough freedom and guidance to actively think and gain knowledge.
    a. Guided discovery
    b. Latent discovery
    c. Observational learning
    d. Classical learning

36. Which of the following is the correct sequence when using observational learning?
    a. attention, rewards, reproduction, and remembering
    b. attention, remembering, reproduction, and rewards
    c. rewards, remembering, attention, and reproduction
    d. remembering, rewards, attention, and reproduction

37. Increased aggression and violence among children and adolescents has been attributed to
    a. watching violent TV programs
    b. playing violent video games
    c. imitating others' aggressive behaviors
    d. all the preceding

38. Before going in for his first chemotherapy, Blake had a bread bowl crab soup from his favorite soup and sandwich shop. After his session, he got nauseous and vomits as a result of the chemotherapy. Since then, Blake cannot eat crab soup as it makes him nauseous. In this example, the unconditioned stimulus is _____ and the conditioned stimulus is _____.
    a. crab soup; nausea
    b. soup and sandwich shop; crab soup
    c. chemotherapy; crab soup
    d. chemotherapy; nausea

LANGUAGE DEVELOPMENT - Conditioning and Learning

Word roots

The word "operant" comes directly from Latin. It is the present participle of the Latin verb "operari," which means "to work." The word root is used in the type of learning called operant learning. Operant learning refers to spontaneous behavior, as opposed to behavior triggered by a specific stimulus (as in classical conditioning). In this and later chapters you will find words such as operant conditioning, operant response, and operant extinction. The term "operational definition" that we saw in an earlier chapter also derives from this root.

What is learning?

Preview: What Did You Learn in School Today? (p. 262)

   (262) *starving to death*: so hungry you feel you will die

What Is Learning—Does Practice Make Perfect? (pp. 262-263)

(262) ***bassoon***: a musical instrument

(262) ***incapacitated***: incapable of functioning normally

(263) ***snicker***: laugh in an unkind way

How does classical conditioning occur?

Classical Conditioning—Does the Name Pavlov Ring a Bell? (pp. 263-265)

(263) ***ring a bell*** (Does the Name Pavlov *Ring a Bell*?): Is it familiar to you?

(263) ***drooled***: salivated

(265) ***attracts***: draws something to it

Principles of Classical Conditioning—Teaching Your Little Brother to Salivate (p. 265-267)

(265) ***optimal***: maximum

(266) ***real hit***: very popular

(266) ***get a shot***: get an injection

(266) ***a catch in your breathing***: a short pause in breathing

(266) ***knockoffs***: imitations of famous-brand products

(266) ***hide in the closet***: avoid being found

(267) ***PlayStation Portable***: hand-held video game

Does conditioning affect emotions?

Classical Conditioning in Humans—An Emotional Topic (pp. 267-269)

(267) ***gut responses***: emotional responses, made without thinking

(268) ***"in the blink of an eye"***: this phrase has 2 meanings: in the future we can detect dementia very easily and quickly and the test can be done with the blinking of one eye.

How does operant conditioning occur?

Operant Conditioning—Can Pigeons Play Ping-Pong? (pp. 269-274)

(269) ***ping-pong***: table tennis

(270) ***rule of thumb***: guideline; practical method

(270) ***grooms***: cleans, licks itself

(271) **haphazardly**: marked by lack of plan, order, or direction

(271) **major league pitchers**: the players on major baseball teams who have the position of pitcher

(272) **superstitions**: beliefs or practices resulting from trust in magic or chance

(272) **get the large half of a wishbone**: refers to the practice in which two people pull on opposite sides of a chicken or turkey breastbone; the person who has the larger piece when the bone breaks is considered to be the one who will get what he or she wished for

(272) **walk under a ladder**: considered by some people to bring bad luck

(272) **better safe than sorry**: it's better to do everything possible to bring about a desired result than to fail

(272) **shapes up**: improves

(273) **throw tantrums**: yell, scream, or throw things in order to get what one wants

(273) **show off**: try to attract attention by one's behavior

(273) **scolding**: expressing disapproval

(273) **turns cold and distant**: one ignores and does not talk to another person.

(274) **parents who "ground" their teenage children**: parents who punish teenagers by forbidding them to go out

Are there different kinds of operant reinforcement?

Operant Reinforcers—What's Your Pleasure? (pp. 274-278)

(274) **double latte**: refers to a latte – a drink made with espresso and steamed milk -- made with 2 shots of espresso instead of 1

(275) **tokens**: something that can be exchanged for desired goods or services

(275) **tangible**: something that can be touched

(275) **poker chips**: tokens used in a card game to take the place of money

(275) **grab bag**: a bag that is filled with various small prizes that a child may reach in and pick a prize that he/she wants as a reward for being good

(275) **amenities**: things that provide material comfort

(275) **weekend passes**: permission to leave (in this case) the hospital for the weekend

(276) **check out their split ends**: examine the ends of one's hair (especially girls); a sign of boredom

(276) **toying with**: playing with; fingering aimlessly

(276) **furiously**: wildly

(276) **pick-off moves**: an advanced play used by the pitcher in a baseball game to keep a runner from stealing (taking) a base

(276) *acute chest pain*: sudden, sharp pain in the chest

(278) *vaporize an attacker*: make the attacker disappear; destroy the attacker

How are we influenced by patterns of reward?

Partial Reinforcement—Las Vegas, a Human Skinner Box? (pp. 278-280)

(279) *Las Vegas or a similar gambling mecca*: Las Vegas is a city where gambling is legal, so people who like to gamble (play for money) are attracted there; Mecca is a Moslem holy city to which Moslems make pilgrimages (a religious trip); therefore, a mecca is a place visited by many people

(279) *slot machines*: a device in a gambling casino into which a patron puts money and hopes to win a larger amount of money

(279) *payoff*: money won

(279) *Bingo!*: I won!; Bingo is a board game where the winner yells Bingo!

(279) *cleaned out*: lost all of one's money

(280) *piecework*: paid per job completed

(280) *treat*: something good to eat, like candy

(280) *persistent*: stubborn, determined

(280) *fanatic*: enthusiast

(280) *spurts*: brief periods of time

(280) *takes a break*: takes a rest from a job or task

(280) *saunters*: walks slowly

(280) *frenzy*: intense activity

(280) *Thanksgiving turkey*: the customary meal on the American holiday of Thanksgiving, celebrated in November

(280) *doggedly*: in a determined or persistent manner

(280) *bulldog tenacity*: bulldogs were bred to hold on to a bull's nose and not let go; therefore this means extreme stubbornness, refusal to give up

(280) *anglers*: men or women who fish

(281) *tailgating*: very closely following a car

Stimulus Control—Red Light, Green Light (pp. 280-282)

(281) *the presence of a police car brings about rapid reductions in driving speed...and, in Los Angeles, gun battles*: refers to the fact that some drivers on the freeways in Los Angeles have fired weapons at other drivers

(281) *feat*: accomplishment

(282) *contraband*: illegal items

(282) *baited*: substances planted to see if the dogs can detect them

What does punishment do to behavior?

Punishment—Putting the Brakes on Behavior (pp. 282-286)

(282) *Putting the Brakes on Behavior*: stopping behavior

(282) *reprimands*: scolding; expressions of disapproval

(282) *starved for attention*: badly needing and looking for attention

(283) *haphazardly*: marked by lack of plan, order, or direction

(283) *brute*: mean, insensitive person

(283) *incompatible*: not in accord with each other; not suitable for use together

(284) *rebuke*: yelling at a person because one disapproves of her/his actions

(284) *drawbacks*: undesirable effects

(285) *obnoxious*: very offensive or objectionable

(285) *dodge*: avoid

(285) *sidestep*: to avoid or go around

(285) *quell*: to end or put a stop to

(285) *silence may be golden*: the common saying "silence is golden" means that quiet moments are rare and should be enjoyed

(285) *sparing the rod*: a Biblical phrase meaning to not punish

What is cognitive learning?

Cognitive Learning—Beyond Conditioning (pp. 286-287)

(286) *navigate around the town*: move from place to place in your town

(286) *mental giant*: extremely intelligent

Does learning occur by imitation?

Modeling—Do as I Do, Not as I Say (pp. 288-291)

(288) *crochet*: a type of needlework done with a small hook

(288) *tune-up*: general adjustment of a car to improve performance

(288) *a large blowup "Bo-Bo the Clown" doll*: an inflatable life-sized plastic doll for children to play with

(289) *G-rated*: General audience; something anyone can watch

(289) *penchant*: habit, desire

(290) *desensitize*: to make less sensitive to something

How does conditioning apply to practical problems?

Psychology in Action: Behavioral Self-Management—A Rewarding Project (pp. 291-293)

(292) *fall short*: fail to reach your goal

(292) *sharp-edged humor*: harsh, often sarcastic

(292) *scramble*: mix up, put out of order

(292) *junk food*: food with little nutritional value

(293) *forfeit*: give up, lose

(293) *Ku Klux Klan*: a racist secret society in the U.S.; its members are opposed to minorities

(293) *American Nazi Party*: racist political group opposed to minorities, especially Jews

Solutions

RECITE AND REVIEW

What is learning?

1. behavior; precede; follow
2. conditioning; conditioning
3. stimulus; responses
4. reinforced; Operant

How does classical conditioning occur?

1. neutral; response
2. stimulus; learned

Principles of Classical Conditioning—Teach Your Little Brother to Salivate: Pages 265-267

1. stimulus
2. stimulus
3. conditioning
4. response
5. similar
6. stimulus
7. response
8. follow

Does conditioning affect emotions?

1. dementia
2. reflexes; conditioned
3. stimulus
4. secondhand; observe

How does operant conditioning occur?

1. learning
2. increases; effect
3. response; increases
4. effect
5. reinforcement; response
6. chains; single
7. response
8. operant
9. recovery
10. reward; ends
11. decreases; cost

Are there different kinds of operant reinforcement?

1. pleasure; brain
2. learned; exchanged
3. approval
4. results
5. feedback
6. instruction
7. CAI

How are we influenced by patterns of reward?

1. response; partial

2. effect   3. fixed; fixed   4. high; slow

Stimulus Control—Red Light, Green Light: Pages 280-282

1. precede; noticing
2. discrimination
3. similar
4. S+; S−

What does punishment do to behavior?

1. decreases
2. immediate
3. suppress
4. nonreinforcement; strengthens; suppresses
5. does not; emotionally
6. escape
7. mild; responses

What is cognitive learning?

1. maps; learning
2. understanding

Does learning occur by imitation?

1. imitation; model; model's
2. reproduction
3. models
4. aggressively

How does conditioning apply to practical problems?

1. feedback
2. responses; principle
3. responses; response; removing
4. learning; goals; successes

CONNECTIONS

What is learning? How does classical conditioning occur? Pages 262-267

1. E.
2. A.
3. I.
4. L.
5. B.
6. H.
7. C.
8. K.
9. D.
10. J.
11. F.
12. G.

Does conditioning affect emotions? How does operant conditioning occur? Pages 267-274

1. C.
2. F.
3. E.
4. H.
5. D.
6. A.
7. G.
8. B.

Are there different kinds of operant reinforcement? Pages 274-278

1. A.
2. F.
3. C.

4. B.	5. E.	6. D.

How are we influenced by patterns of reward? Pages 278-282

1. F.	4. E.	7. B.
2. H.	5. C.	8. D.
3. A.	6. G.	

What does punishment do to behavior? Pages 282-286

1. C.	3. F.	5. E.
2. A.	4. D.	6. B.

What is cognitive learning? Does learning occur by imitation? How does conditioning apply to practical problems? Pages 286-293

1. C.	4. B.	7. G.
2. I.	5. H.	8. A.
3. E.	6. D.	9. F.

CHECK YOUR MEMORY

What is learning? Pages 262-263

1. T	2. F	3. T

How does classical conditioning occur? Pages 263-267

1. F	4. F	7. F
2. T	5. T	8. F
3. T	6. F	9. T

Does conditioning affect emotions? Pages 267-269

1. F	3. T	5. F
2. T	4. F	6. T

How does operant conditioning occur? Pages 269-274

1. T	7. T	13. T
2. F	8. T	14. F
3. F	9. F	
4. F	10. T	
5. T	11. F	
6. F	12. T	

Are there different kinds of operant reinforcement? Pages 274-278

1.	F	5.	T	9.	T
2.	F	6.	F	10.	F
3.	T	7.	T		
4.	T	8.	F		

How are we influenced by patterns of reward? Pages 278-282

1.	F	4.	F	7.	F
2.	F	5.	T	8.	F
3.	T	6.	T		

What does punishment do to behavior? Pages 282-286

1.	T	5.	T	9.	T
2.	F	6.	T	10.	T
3.	T	7.	F		
4.	F	8.	F		

What is cognitive learning? Pages 286-287

1.	T	3.	T	5.	F
2.	F	4.	T		

Does learning occur by imitation? Pages 288-291

1.	F	3.	F	5.	F
2.	T	4.	F	6.	T

How does conditioning apply to practical problems? Pages 291-293

1.	F	4.	T	7.	T
2.	T	5.	F		
3.	T	6.	F		

FINAL SURVEY AND REVIEW

What is learning?

1. antecedents; consequences

2. respondent; operant   3. neutral; consequences   4. reinforcement; US

How does classical conditioning occur?

1. Ivan; Pavlov; unconditioned; reflex   2. conditioned; conditioned

Principles of Classical Conditioning—Teach Your Little Brother to Salivate: Pages 265-267

1. unconditioned; stimulus
2. Higher-order
3. extinction
4. spontaneous recovery
5. generalization
6. discrimination
7. informational
8. CS; US

Does conditioning affect emotions?

1. Eye-blink
2. emotional
3. phobias; generalization
4. Vicarious

How does operant conditioning occur?

1. instrumental
2. probability; Thorndike
3. response; increases
4. expectation
5. contingent
6. reduces; reinforcer
7. Superstitious
8. shaping; approximations
9. extinguish; spontaneous
10. positive; negative
11. aversive; positive

Are there different kinds of operant reinforcement?

1. Primary; stimulation
2. Secondary; primary; primary
3. social
4. knowledge
5. instruction
6. Computer-assisted instruction
7. instructional; educational

How are we influenced by patterns of reward?

1. schedule; Skinner
2. extinction; partial
3. ratio; interval
4. FR; VR; FI; extinction

Stimulus Control—Red Light, Green Light: Pages 280-282

1. stimulus; control
2. noticing; performing
3. generalization; discrimination
4. generalization
5. discrimination

What does punishment do to behavior?

1. punisher
2. consistent
3. reinforced
4. reinforcement; strengthens; extinguished
5. supportive; emotionally
6. avoidance; aggression
7. Reinforcement; nonreinforcement

What is cognitive learning?

1. cognitive; maps; latent

2. rote

Does learning occur by imitation?

1. modeling; Observational; learning

2. Observational

3. observational

4. aggressively

How does conditioning apply to practical problems?

1. contracting

2. reinforce; Premack

3. alternate; chains; antecedents

4. strategies; reinforcing

MASTERY TEST

How does conditioning apply to practical problems?

1. A, p. 275
2. C, p. 276
3. A, p. 272
4. B, p. 272
5. B, p. 264
6. C, pp. 269-270
7. D, p. 271
8. C, p. 274
9. C, p. 288
10. B, p. 262
11. D, p. 276
12. A, p. 279
13. D, pp. 284-285
14. B, p. 290
15. C, p. 263
16. D, p. 268
17. D, p. 268
18. D, p. 264
19. A, p. 262
20. B, p. 292
21. C, p. 283
22. D, p. 280
23. A, p. 281
24. A, p. 266
25. D, p. 267
26. A, p. 280
27. D, p. 284
28. B, p. 270
29. B, p. 276
30. D, p. 273
31. C, p. 272
32. B, p. 273
33. C, p. 273
34. D, p. 274
35. A, p. 287
36. B, p. 288
37. D, pp. 289-290
38. C, p. 265

Memory

Chapter Overview

Memory systems encode and store information for later retrieval. A popular model divides memory into three systems: sensory memory, short-term memory (STM), and long-term memory (LTM). Sensory memory stores exact copies of sensory information for very brief periods. STM is limited to about seven bits of information, but chunking and recoding allow more information to be stored. Short-term memories last only a limited time; however it can be extended through maintenance rehearsal. LTM has nearly unlimited storage and is relatively permanent. It undergoes updating, revision, constructive processing, and forgetting. Elaborative rehearsal ensures information is encoded in LTM. Specific types of information that people store in LTM is influenced by the culture in which they live.

Long-term memories can be further divided into declarative memories (which may be semantic or episodic) and procedural memories. Explicit memories are revealed by recall, recognition, and relearning tasks. Implicit memories are revealed by priming. Eidetic imagery (photographic memory) is fairly common in children, but rare among adults. Many people have internal memory images and some have exceptional memory based on internal imagery. Exceptional memory capacity is based on both learned strategies and natural abilities.

Forgetting is most rapid immediately after learning. Some "forgetting" is based on a failure to encode information. Short-term forgetting is partly explained by the decay (weakening) of memory traces. Some long-term forgetting may also occur this way. Some forgetting is related to a lack of memory cues. Much forgetting is related to interference among memories. Clinical psychologists believe that memories are sometimes repressed (unconsciously held out of awareness). Some also believe that repressed childhood memories of abuse can be "recovered." However, there is often no way to separate true memories from fantasies.

In the brain, memory traces (engrams) must be consolidated before they become relatively permanent. The hippocampus is a structure involved in memory consolidation. Information appears to be stored in the brain through changes in nerve cells. Long-term potentiation helps explain the formation of lasting memories. Electrical stimulation to certain parts of the brain (e.g., hippocampus) can decrease long-term potentiation.

Memory can be improved by the use of mnemonic systems and by attention to factors that affect memory, such as overlearning, serial position, organization, and the like.

Learning Objectives

1. Define *memory* and explain the three processes of memory.

2. Describe sensory memory, including how icons and echoes function in this memory system, and explain how information is transferred from sensory memory to short-term memory.

3. Describe short-term memory in terms of capacity, how information is encoded, permanence, and susceptibility to interference. Include the concept of working memory.

4. Describe long-term memory in terms of permanence, capacity and the basis on which information is stored; define *dual memo*ry; and explain how one's culture affects memory.

5. Explain the "magic number" seven; describe chunking; and explain how the two types of rehearsal affect memory.

6. Discuss the permanence of memory including the work of Penfield and the Loftuses.

7. Explain how memories are constructed. Include the concepts of constructive processing and pseudo-memories.

8. Discuss the effects of hypnosis on memory and how a cognitive interview can improve eyewitness memories.

9. Briefly describe how long-term memories are organized, including the network model and redintegrative memories.

10. Differentiate procedural (skill) memory from declarative (fact) memory and define and give examples of the two kinds of declarative memory (semantic and episodic).

11. Explain the tip-of-the tongue phenomenon (including the feeling of knowing).

12. Describe and give an example of each of the following ways of measuring memory:

    a. recall (include the serial position effect)

    b. recognition (compare to recall and include the concept of distractors)

    c. relearning (include the concept of savings)

13. Distinguish between explicit and implicit memories. Include a discussion of priming.

14. Describe the concepts of internal imagery and eidetic imagery and their effects on long-term memory and explain how these abilities are different from having an exceptional memory.

15. Explain Ebbinghaus's curve of forgetting.

16. Discuss the following explanations of forgetting:

    a. encoding failure

    b. decay of memory traces

    c. disuse (give three reasons to question this explanation)

    d. cue-dependent forgetting

    e. state-dependent learning

f. interference (list and explain the two types of interference and how they are investigated in the laboratory)

g. positive and negative transfer

h. repression (and differentiate it from suppression)

17. Describe the false memory syndrome.

18. Describe *flashbulb memories, retrograde* and *anterograde amnesia,* and the role of *consolidation* in memory, including the effects of ECS.

19. Name the structure in the brain that is responsible for switching information from STM to LTM. Include a discussion of the engram and the relationship between learning and transmitter chemicals.

20. Describe each of the following in terms of how it can improve memory:

a. knowledge of results

b. recitation

c. rehearsal

d. selection

e. organization

f. whole versus part learning

g. serial position effect

h. cues

i. overlearning

j. spaced practice

k. sleep

l. hunger

m. extension of memory intervals

n. review

o. strategies to aid recall, including the cognitive interview

The following objective is related to the material in the "Psychology in Action" section of your text.

1. Define *mnemonic;* explain the four basic principles of using mnemonics; and three techniques for using mnemonics to remember things in order.

RECITE AND REVIEW

Is there more than one type of memory?

Stages of Memory—Do You Have a Mind Like a Steel Trap? Or a Sieve? Pages 297-300

1. Memory is an active _____ . _____ is first encoded (changed into the form in which it will be retained).

2. Next it is _____ in memory. Later it must be retrieved to be put to use.

3. Humans appear to have _____ interrelated memory systems. These are sensory memory, _____ memory (STM), and _____ memory (LTM).

4. Sensory memory holds an _____ copy of what is seen or heard, in the form of an icon (_____) or echo (sound sensation).

5. Short-term memories tend to be stored as _____ . Long-term memories are stored on the basis of _____ , or importance.

6. STM acts as a _____ storehouse for small amounts of information. It provides a working memory where thinking, mental arithmetic, and the like take place. LTM acts as a _____ storehouse for meaningful information.

7. Cultural values impact the types of _____ we tend to store. American culture emphasizes the individual; therefore, American memories are _____ -focused. The Chinese culture emphasizes group membership; therefore, Chinese memories are of social events, which include _____ members, friends, and others.

What are the features of each type of memory?

Short-Term Memory—Do You Know the Magic Number? Pages 300-301

1. Sensory memory is exact, but very brief, lasting only a few _____ or less. Through selective attention, some information is transferred to _____ .

2. The digit-span test reveals that STM has an average upper limit of about 7 _____ of information. However, this can be extended by chunking, or recoding information into _____ units or groups.

3. The "_____ number" 7 (plus or minus 2) refers to the limitation of _____ memory discovered by George Miller. Nelson Cowan believes that the limitation of short-term memory is _____ than the "magic number" 7.

4. Short-term memories are brief and very sensitive to _____ , or interference; however, they can be prolonged by maintenance rehearsal (silent _____).

5. Elaborative rehearsal, which emphasizes meaning, helps transfer information from _____ to LTM. Elaborative rehearsal links new information with existing _____ .

Is there more than one type of long-term memory?

Long-Term Memory—Where the Past Lives: Pages 301-306

1. LTM seems to have an almost unlimited storage capacity. However, LTM is subject to constructive processing, or ongoing revision and _____ . As a result, people often have pseudo-memories (_____ memories) that they believe are true.

2. LTM is highly _____ to allow retrieval of needed information. The pattern, or structure, of memory networks is the subject of current memory research. Network _____ portray LTM as a system of linked ideas.

3. Redintegrative memories unfold as each added memory provides a cue for retrieving the next _____ . Seemingly forgotten memories may be reconstructed in this way.

4. Within long-term memory, declarative memories for _____ seem to differ from procedural memories for _____ .

5. _____ memories may be further categorized as semantic memories or episodic memories.

6. Semantic memories consist of basic factual knowledge that is almost immune to _____ .

7. Episodic memories record _____ experiences that are associated with specific times and places.

How is memory measured?

Measuring Memory—The Answer Is on the Tip of My Tongue: Pages 306-308

1. The tip-of-the-tongue _____ shows that memory is not an all-or-nothing event. Memories may be revealed by _____ , recognition, or relearning.

2. In recall, memory proceeds without specific cues, as in an _____ exam. Recall of listed information often reveals a serial position effect (_____ items on the list are most subject to errors).

3. A common test of _____ is the multiple-choice question. _____ is very sensitive to the kinds of distractors (wrong choices) used.

4. In relearning, "forgotten" material is learned again, and memory is indicated by a _____ score.

5. Recall, recognition, and relearning mainly measure explicit _____ that we are aware of having. Other techniques, such as priming, are necessary to reveal implicit _____ , which are unconscious.

What are "photographic" memories?

Exceptional Memory—Wizards of Recall: Pages 308-311

1. Eidetic imagery (photographic memory) occurs when a person is able to project an _____ onto an external surface. Such images allow brief, nearly complete recall by some children.

2. Eidetic imagery is rarely found in _____ . However, many adults have internal images, which can be very vivid and a basis for remembering.

3. Exceptional memory can be learned by finding ways to directly store information in _____ . Learning has no effect on the limits of _____ . Some people may have naturally superior memory abilities that exceed what can be achieved through learning.

What causes forgetting? How accurate are everyday memories?

Forgetting—Why We, Uh, Let's See; Why We, Uh . . . Forget! Pages 311-318

1. Forgetting and memory were extensively studied by Herman Ebbinghaus, whose _____ of forgetting shows that forgetting is typically most rapid immediately _____ learning.

2. Ebbinghaus used nonsense syllables to study memory. The forgetting of _____ material is much _____ than shown by his curve of forgetting.

3. Failure to encode _____ is a common cause of "forgetting."

4. Forgetting in sensory memory and STM probably reflects decay of memory _____ in the nervous system. Decay or _____ of memories may also account for some LTM loss, but most forgetting cannot be explained this way.

5. Often, forgetting is cue dependent. The power of cues to trigger memories is revealed by state-dependent _____ , in which bodily _____ at the time of learning and of retrieval affect memory.

6. Much _____ in both STM and LTM can be attributed to interference of memories with one another.

7. When recent learning _____ with retrieval of prior learning, retroactive interference has occurred. If old memories _____ with new memories, proactive interference has occurred.

8. Repression is the _____ of painful, embarrassing, or traumatic memories.

9. Repression is thought to be unconscious, in contrast to suppression, which is a _____ attempt to avoid thinking about something.

10. Experts are currently debating the validity of childhood memories of _____ that reappear after apparently being repressed for decades.

11. Independent evidence has verified that some recovered memories are _____ . However, others have been shown to be _____ .

12. In the absence of confirming or disconfirming _____ , there is currently no way to separate true memories from fantasies. Caution is advised for all concerned with attempts to retrieve supposedly hidden memories.

13. Flashbulb memories, which seem especially vivid, are created at emotionally significant times. While such memories may not be accurate, we tend to place great _____ in them.

What happens in the brain when memories are formed?

Memory Formation—Some "Shocking" Findings: Pages 318-321

1. Retrograde _____ and the effects of electroconvulsive _____ (ECS) may be explained by the concept of consolidation.

2. Consolidation theory holds that engrams (permanent _____) are formed during a critical period after learning. Until they are consolidated, long-term memories are easily destroyed.

3. The hippocampus is a _____ structure associated with the consolidation of memories.

4. The search within the brain for engrams has now settled on changes in individual _____ cells.

5. The best-documented changes are alterations in the amounts of transmitter _____ released by nerve cells.

6. Forming lasting memories depend on _____ potentiation which occurs when a connection between two brain cells grows stronger as they become more _____ at the same time. These cells will then respond more strongly to incoming messages from other cells.

How can memory be improved?

Improving Memory—Keys to the Memory Bank: Pages 321-323

1. Memory can be improved by using feedback, recitation, and rehearsal, by selecting and _____ information, and by using the progressive _____ method, spaced practice, overlearning, and active search strategies.

2. The effects of serial _____ , sleep, review, cues, and elaboration should also be kept in mind when studying or memorizing.

Psychology in Action: Mnemonics—Memory Magic: Pages 324-326

1. Mnemonic techniques avoid rote learning and work best during the _____ stages of learning.

2. Mnemonic systems, such as the _____ method, use mental images and unusual associations to link new information with familiar memories already stored in _____ . Such strategies give information personal meaning and make it easier to recall.

CONNECTIONS

Is there more than one type of memory? Pages 297-300

1. _____ storage
2. _____ encoding
3. _____ sensory memory
4. _____ echos and icons
5. _____ working memory

    a.   hard drive
    b.   STM
    c.   lasts for two to three seconds
    d.   keyboard
    e.   sensory memory

Connections

1. _____ selective attention
2. _____ long-term memory
3. _____ incoming information
4. _____ encoding for LTM
5. _____ sensory memory
6. _____ short-term memory
7. _____ rehearsal buffer

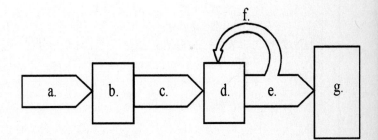

What are the features of each type of memory? Is there more than one type of long-term memory? Pages 300-306

1. _____ semantic memory
2. _____ long-term memory
3. _____ procedural memory
4. _____ sensory memory
5. _____ episodic memory
6. _____ short-term memory
7. _____ declarative memory

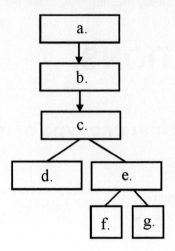

Connections Part II

1. _____ chunking
2. _____ skill memory
3. _____ revised memories
4. _____ seven information bits
5. _____ false memory
6. _____ memory structure

   a. magic number
   b. recoding
   c. constructive processing
   d. network model
   e. procedures
   f. pseudo-memory

How is memory measured? What are "photographic" memories? Pages 306-311

1. _____ relearning
2. _____ recall
3. _____ recognition memory
4. _____ false positive
5. _____ implicit memory
6. _____ memory prediction
7. _____ eidetic imagery
8. _____ serial position effect
9. _____ explicit memory

   a. retrieval of facts
   b. middle items are least recalled
   c. multiple-choice questions
   d. photographic memory
   e. conscious memories
   f. memories that are outside of awareness
   g. memory test
   h. feeling of knowing
   i. mistaken recognition

What causes forgetting? How accurate are everyday memories? Pages 311-318

1. _____ state dependent	a. WOL
2. _____ suppression	b. forgetting curve
3. _____ nonsense syllable	c. in same frame of mind
4. _____ repression	d. a stimulus linked to a memory
5. _____ cue-dependent memory	e. motivated forgetting
6. _____ interference	f. conscious forgetting
7. _____ Ebbinghaus	g. prevent retrieval of information

What happens in the brain when memories are formed? How can memory be improved? Pages 318-326

1. _____ memory trace	a. disuse of memory
2. _____ recitation	b. mnemonist
3. _____ amnesia	c. ECS
4. _____ memory expert	d. engram
5. _____ hippocampus	e. memory loss
6. _____ order of events	f. form a story
7. _____ decay	g. mental review
8. _____ spaced practice	h. summarize out loud
9. _____ erases memory	i. consolidation of memories
10. _____ rehearsal	j. study in short periods

CHECK YOUR MEMORY

Is there more than one type of memory? Pages 297-300

1. Incoming information must be encoded before it is stored in memory.

   TRUE or FALSE

2. Sensory memories last for a few minutes or less.

   TRUE or FALSE

3. A memory that cannot be retrieved has little value.

   TRUE or FALSE

4. Selective attention influences what information enters STM.

   TRUE or FALSE

5. Working memory is another name for sensory memory.

   TRUE or FALSE

6. Errors in long-term memory tend to focus on the sounds of words.

   TRUE or FALSE

7. Generally, the more you know, the more new information you can store in long-term memory.

   TRUE or FALSE

8. The type of memory people store is not affected by their cultural values.

   TRUE or FALSE

What are the features of each type of memory? Pages 300-301

1. For many kinds of information, STM can store an average of 5 bits of information.

   TRUE or FALSE

2. Nelson Cowan coined the term "magic number."

   TRUE or FALSE

3. Chunking recodes information into smaller units that are easier to fit into STM.

   TRUE or FALSE

4. The more times a short-term memory is rehearsed, the better its chance of being stored in LTM.

   TRUE or FALSE

5. On average, short-term memories last only about 18 minutes, unless they are rehearsed.

   TRUE or FALSE

6. Maintenance rehearsal keeps memories active in sensory memory.

   TRUE or FALSE

Is there more than one type of long-term memory? Pages 301-306

1. The surface of the brain records the past like a movie, complete with sound track.

   TRUE or FALSE

2. Long-term memory is *relatively* permanent as we tend to update, change, lose, or revise our old memories.

   TRUE or FALSE

3. Being confident about a memory tells little about the true accuracy of the memory.

   TRUE or FALSE

4. Long-term memories appear to be organized alphabetically for speedy access.

   TRUE or FALSE

5. False memory refers to having memories that never happened.

   TRUE or FALSE

6. Hypnosis increases false memories more than it does true ones.

   TRUE or FALSE

7. Recalling events from different viewpoints is part of doing a cognitive interview.

   TRUE or FALSE

8. Cognitive interview and standard questioning produce the same percentage of correct recall given by eyewitnesses.

   TRUE or FALSE

9. Knowing how to swing a golf club is a type of declarative memory.

   TRUE or FALSE

10. A person lacking declarative memory might still remember how to solve a mechanical puzzle.

    TRUE or FALSE

11. Semantic memories are almost immune to forgetting.

    TRUE or FALSE

12. Semantic memories are a type of declarative memory.

    TRUE or FALSE

13. Episodic memories have no connection to particular times and places.

    TRUE or FALSE

How is memory measured? Pages 306-308

1. Remembering the first sound of a name you are trying to recall is an example of the tip-of-the-tongue state.

   TRUE or FALSE

2. Tests of recognition require verbatim memory.

TRUE or FALSE

3. The serial position effect measures the strength of the feeling of knowing.

TRUE or FALSE

4. Recognition tends to be a more sensitive test of memory than recall.

TRUE or FALSE

5. False positives and distractors greatly affect the accuracy of relearning tests.

TRUE or FALSE

6. Recall, recognition, and relearning are used to measure explicit memories.

TRUE or FALSE

7. Priming is used to activate explicit (hidden) memories.

TRUE or FALSE

What are "photographic" memories? Pages 308-311

1. Eidetic images last for 30 seconds or more.

TRUE or FALSE

2. About 8 percent of all children have eidetic images.

TRUE or FALSE

3. Eidetic imagery becomes rare by adulthood.

TRUE or FALSE

4. Mr. S. (the mnemonist) had virtually unlimited eidetic imagery.

TRUE or FALSE

5. Practice in remembering one type of information increases the capacity of STM to store other types of information, too.

TRUE or FALSE

6. All contestants in the World Memory Championship performed poorly on tasks that prevented the use of learned strategies.

TRUE or FALSE

What causes forgetting? How accurate are everyday memories? Pages 311-318

1. Ebbinghaus chose to learn nonsense syllables so that they would all be the same length.

   TRUE or FALSE

2. Ebbinghaus's curve of forgetting levels off after 2 days, showing little further memory loss after that.

   TRUE or FALSE

3. Ebbinghaus's curve of forgetting only applies to memories of nonsense syllables.

   TRUE or FALSE

4. The magic card trick demonstrates our ability to focus and pay attention.

   TRUE or FALSE

5. Eyewitnesses are better at identifying members of other ethnic groups since they "look" different.

   TRUE or FALSE

6. Decay of memory traces clearly applies to information in STM.

   TRUE or FALSE

7. Disuse theories of forgetting answer the question: Have I been storing the information in the first place?

   TRUE or FALSE

8. The presence of memory cues almost always improves memory.

   TRUE or FALSE

9. Information learned under the influence of a drug may be best remembered when the drugged state occurs again.

   TRUE or FALSE

10. If you are in a bad mood, you are more likely to remember unpleasant events.

    TRUE or FALSE

11. Categorizing a person as a member of a group tends to limit the accuracy of memories about the person's appearance.

    TRUE or FALSE

12. Sleeping tends to interfere with retaining new memories.

    TRUE or FALSE

13. You learn information A and then information B. If your memory of B is lowered by having first learned A, you have experienced retroactive interference.

    TRUE or FALSE

14. Interference only applies to the initial stage of learning. Learned information is permanent and can be easily retrieved.

    TRUE or FALSE

15. Unconsciously forgetting painful memories is called negative transfer.

    TRUE or FALSE

16. A conscious attempt to put a memory out of mind is called repression.

    TRUE or FALSE

17. Elizabeth Loftus demonstrated the ease of implanting false memories by simply suggesting to Alan Alda that he does not like hard-boiled eggs, which he later avoided eating at a picnic.

    TRUE or FALSE

18. Suggestion and fantasy are elements of many techniques used in attempts to recover repressed memories.

    TRUE or FALSE

19. Unless a memory can be independently confirmed, there is no way to tell if it is real or not.

    TRUE or FALSE

20. Flashbulb memories tend to be formed when an event is surprising or emotional.

    TRUE or FALSE

21. The confidence we have in flashbulb memories is well placed—they are much more accurate than most other memories.

    TRUE or FALSE

What happens in the brain when memories are formed? Pages 318-321

1. Retrograde amnesia is a gap in memories of events preceding a head injury.

    TRUE or FALSE

2. People with damage to the hippocampus typically cannot remember events that occurred before the damage.

    TRUE or FALSE

3. In the early 1920s, Karl Lashley found the location of engrams in the brain.

    TRUE or FALSE

4. Storing memories alters the activity, structure, and chemistry of the brain.

    TRUE or FALSE

5. Enhancing memory is now possible by taking a memory pill.

   TRUE or FALSE

6. Electrically stimulating the hippocampus can decrease long-term potentiation.

   TRUE or FALSE

How can memory be improved? Pages 321-326

1. Recitation is a good way to generate feedback while studying.

   TRUE or FALSE

2. Elaborative rehearsal involving "why" questions improve memory.

   TRUE or FALSE

3. Overlearning is inefficient; you should stop studying at the point of initial mastery of new information.

   TRUE or FALSE

4. Massed practice is almost always superior to spaced practice.

   TRUE or FALSE

5. When learning, it helps to gradually extend how long you remember new information before reviewing it again.

   TRUE or FALSE

6. Roy G. Biv is a mnemonic for the notes on a musical staff.

   TRUE or FALSE

7. Many mnemonics make use of mental images or pictures.

   TRUE or FALSE

8. Mnemonics often link new information to familiar memories.

   TRUE or FALSE

9. The keyword method is superior to rote learning for memorizing vocabulary words in another language.

   TRUE or FALSE

FINAL SURVEY AND REVIEW

Is there more than one type of memory?

Stages of Memory—Do You Have a Mind Like a Steel Trap? Or a Sieve? Pages 297-300

1. Memory is an active system. Information is first _____ (changed into the form in which it will be retained).

2. Next it is stored in memory. Later it must be _____ to be put to use.

3. Humans appear to have 3 interrelated memory systems. These are _____ memory, _____ memory (STM), and long-term memory (LTM).

4. Sensory memory holds an exact copy of what is seen or heard, in the form of an _____ (image) or _____ (sound sensation).

5. _____ memories tend to be stored as sounds. _____ memories are stored on the basis of meaning, or importance.

6. _____ acts as a temporary storehouse for small amounts of information. It provides a _____ memory where thinking, mental arithmetic, and the like take place. LTM acts as a permanent storehouse for _____ information.

7. _____ values impact the types of memories we tend to store. American culture emphasizes the individual; therefore, American memories are _____ -focused. The Chinese culture emphasizes _____ membership; therefore, Chinese memories are of social events, which include family members, friends, and others.

What are the features of each type of memory?

Short-Term Memory—Do You Know the Magic Number? Pages 300-301

1. _____ memory is exact, but very brief, lasting only a few seconds or less. Through _____ _____ , some information is transferred to STM.

2. The _____ test reveals that STM has an average upper limit of about 7 bits of information. However, this can be extended by chunking, or _____ information into larger units or groups.

3. The " _____ " 7 (plus or minus 2) refers to the limitation of short-term memory discovered by George _____ . Nelson Cowan believes that the limitation of short-term memory is _____ than the "magic number" 7.

4. Short-term memories are brief and very sensitive to interruption or _____ ; however, they can be prolonged by _____ rehearsal (silent repetition).

5. _____ rehearsal, which emphasizes meaning, helps transfer information from STM to LTM.

Is there more than one type of long-term memory?

Long-Term Memory—Where the Past Lives: Pages 301-306

1. LTM seems to have an almost unlimited storage capacity. However, LTM is subject to _____ processing, or ongoing revision and updating. As a result, people often have _____ (false memories) that they believe are true.

2. LTM is highly organized to allow retrieval of needed information. The pattern, or structure, of memory _____ is the subject of current memory research. _____ models portray LTM as a system of linked ideas.

3. _____ memories unfold as each added memory provides a cue for retrieving the next memory. Seemingly forgotten memories may be reconstructed in this way.

4. Within long-term memory, _____ memories for facts seem to differ from _____ memories for skills.

5. Declarative memories may be further categorized as _____ memories or _____ memories.

6. _____ memories consist of basic factual knowledge that is almost immune to forgetting.

7. _____ memories record personal experiences that are associated with specific times and places.

How is memory measured?

Measuring Memory—The Answer Is on the Tip of My Tongue: Pages 306-308

1. The _____ -of-the- _____ state shows that memory is not an all-or-nothing event. Memories may be revealed by recall, _____ , or relearning.

2. In _____ , memory proceeds without specific cues, as in an essay exam. Remembering a list of information often reveals a _____ _____ effect (middle items on the list are most subject to errors).

3. A common test of recognition is the _____ -choice question. Recognition is very sensitive to the kinds of _____ (wrong choices) used.

4. In _____ , "forgotten" material is learned again, and memory is indicated by a savings score.

5. Recall, recognition, and relearning mainly measure _____ memories that we are aware of having. Other techniques, such as priming, are necessary to reveal _____ memories, which are unconscious.

What are "photographic" memories?

Exceptional Memory—Wizards of Recall: Pages 308-311

1. _____ (photographic memory) occurs when a person is able to project an image onto an external surface. Such images allow brief, nearly complete recall by some children.

2. _____ is rarely found in adults. However, many adults have internal images, which can be very vivid and a basis for remembering.

3. _____ memory can be learned by finding ways to directly store information in LTM. Learning has no effect on the _____ of STM. Some people may have naturally superior memory abilities that exceed what can be achieved through learning.

What causes forgetting? How accurate are everyday memories?

Forgetting—Why We, Uh, Let's See; Why We, Uh . . . Forget! Pages 311-318

1. Forgetting and memory were extensively studied by Herman _____ , whose curve of forgetting shows that forgetting is typically most rapid immediately after learning.

2. Ebbinghaus used _____ syllables to study memory. The forgetting of meaningful material is much slower than shown by his curve of forgetting.

3. Failure to _____ information is a common cause of "forgetting."

4. Forgetting in _____ memory and _____ probably reflects decay of memory traces in the nervous system. Decay or disuse of memories may also account for some _____ loss, but most forgetting cannot be explained this way.

5. Often, forgetting is _____ dependent. The power of _____ to trigger memories is revealed by _____ learning, in which bodily states at the time of learning and of retrieval affect memory.

6. Much forgetting in both STM and LTM can be attributed to _____ of memories with one another.

7. When recent learning interferes with retrieval of prior learning, _____ interference has occurred. If old memories interfere with new memories, _____ interference has occurred.

8. _____ is the forgetting of painful, embarrassing, or traumatic memories.

9. _____ is thought to be unconscious, in contrast to _____ , which is a conscious attempt to avoid thinking about something.

10. Experts are currently debating the validity of childhood memories of abuse that reappear after apparently being _____ for decades.

11. Independent evidence has verified that some _____ memories are true. However, others have been shown to be false.

12. In the absence of confirming or disconfirming evidence, there is currently no way to separate true memories from _____ . Caution is advised for all concerned with attempts to retrieve supposedly hidden memories.

13. _____ memories, which seem especially vivid, are created at emotionally significant times. While such memories may not be _____ , we tend to place great confidence in them.

What happens in the brain when memories are formed?

Memory Formation—Some "Shocking" Findings: Pages 318-321

1. _____ amnesia and the effects of _____ shock (ECS) may be explained by the concept of consolidation.

2. Consolidation theory holds that _____ (permanent memory _____ traces) are formed during a critical period after learning. Until they are _____ , long-term memories are easily destroyed.

3. The _____ is a brain structure associated with the consolidation of memories.

4. The search within the brain for engrams has now settled on changes in individual _____ _____ .

5. The best-documented changes are alterations in the amounts of _____ chemicals released by nerve cells.

6. _____ _____ occurs when a connection between two brain cells grow stronger as they become more active at the same time. These cells then respond more strongly to incoming messages from other cells. This process appears to affect the _____ of lasting memories.

How can memory be improved?

Improving Memory—Keys to the Memory Bank: Pages 321-323

1. Memory can be improved by using _____ (knowledge of results), recitation, and rehearsal, by _____ and organizing information, and by using the progressive part method, spaced practice, overlearning, and active _____ strategies.

2. The effects of _____ position, sleep, review, cues, and _____ (connecting new information to existing knowledge) should also be kept in mind when studying or memorizing.

Psychology in Action: Mnemonics—Memory Magic: Pages 324-326

1. Mnemonic techniques avoid _____ learning and work best during the _____ stages of learning.

2. _____ systems, such as the keyword method, use mental images and unusual associations to link new information with familiar memories already stored in LTM. Such strategies give information personal meaning and make it easier to recall.

MASTERY TEST

1. The meaning and importance of information has a strong impact on
   a. sensory memory
   b. eidetic memory
   c. long-term memory
   d. procedural memory

2. Pseudo-memories are closely related to the effects of
   a. repression
   b. suppression
   c. semantic forgetting
   d. constructive processing

3. The occurrence of _____ implies that consolidation has been prevented.
   a. retrograde amnesia
   b. hippocampal transfer
   c. suppression
   d. changes in the activities of individual nerve cells

4. Most of the techniques used to recover supposedly repressed memories involve
   a. redintegration and hypnosis
   b. suggestion and fantasy
   c. reconstruction and priming
   d. coercion and fabrication

5. Most daily memory chores are handled by
   a. sensory memory and LTM
   b. STM and working memory
   c. STM and LTM
   d. STM and declarative memory

6. Three key processes in memory systems are
   a. storage, organization, recovery
   b. encoding, attention, reprocessing
   c. storage, retrieval, encoding
   d. retrieval, reprocessing, reorganization

7. Procedural memories are to skills as _____ memories are to facts.
   a. declarative
   b. short-term
   c. redintegrative
   d. eidetic

8. An ability to answer questions about distances on a map you have seen only once implies that some memories are based on
   a. constructive processing
   b. redintegration
   c. internal images
   d. episodic processing

9. The first potential cause of forgetting that may occur is
   a. engram decay
   b. disuse
   c. cue-dependent forgetting
   d. encoding failure

10. The persistence of icons and echoes is the basis for
    a. sensory memory
    b. short-term memory
    c. long-term memory
    d. working memory

11. Priming is most often used to reveal
    a. semantic memories
    b. episodic memories
    c. implicit memories
    d. eidetic memories

12. "Projection" onto an external surface is most characteristic of
    a. sensory memories
    b. eidetic images
    c. flashbulb memories
    d. mnemonic images

13. Chunking helps especially to extend the capacity of
    a. sensory memory
    b. STM
    c. LTM
    d. declarative memory

14. There is presently no way to tell if a "recovered" memory is true or false unless independent _____ exists.
    a. evidence
    b. amnesia
    c. elaboration
    d. consolidation

15. Taking an essay test inevitably requires a person to use
    a. recall
    b. recognition
    c. relearning
    d. priming

16. A savings score is used in what memory task?
    a. recall
    b. recognition
    c. relearning
    d. priming

17. _____ rehearsal helps link new information to existing memories by concentrating on meaning.
    a. Redintegrative
    b. Constructive
    c. Maintenance
    d. Elaborative

18. Middle items are neither held in STM nor moved to LTM. This statement explains the
    a. feeling of knowing
    b. serial position effect
    c. tip-of-the-tongue state
    d. semantic forgetting curve

19. According to the curve of forgetting, the greatest decline in the amount recalled occurs during the
    _____ after learning.
    a. first hour
    b. second day
    c. third to sixth days
    d. retroactive period

20. Work with brain stimulation, truth serums, and hypnosis suggests that long-term memories are
    a. stored in the hippocampus
    b. relatively permanent
    c. unaffected by later input
    d. always redintegrative

21. Which of the following is most likely to improve the accuracy of memory?
    a. hypnosis
    b. constructive processing
    c. the serial position effect
    d. memory cues

22. To qualify as repression, forgetting must be
    a. retroactive
    b. proactive
    c. unconscious
    d. explicit

23. Which of the following typically is NOT a good way to improve memory?
    a. massed practice
    b. overlearning
    c. rehearsal
    d. recall strategies

24. A witness to a crime is questioned in ways that re-create the context of the crime and that provide many memory cues. It appears that she is undergoing
    a. retroactive priming
    b. the progressive part method
    c. retroactive consolidation
    d. a cognitive interview

25. One thing that is clearly true about flashbulb memories is that
    a. they are unusually accurate
    b. we place great confidence in them
    c. they apply primarily to public tragedies
    d. they are recovered by using visualization and hypnosis

26. One common mnemonic strategy is the
    a. serial position technique
    b. feeling of knowing tactic
    c. network procedure
    d. keyword method

27. A perspective that helps explain redintegrative memories is
    a. the feeling of knowing model
    b. recoding and chunking
    c. the network model
    d. mnemonic models

28. Which of the following is NOT considered a part of long-term memory?
    a. echoic memory
    b. semantic memory
    c. episodic memory
    d. declarative memory

29. You are very thirsty. Suddenly you remember a time years ago when you became very thirsty while hiking. This suggests that your memory is
    a. proactive
    b. state dependent
    c. still not consolidated
    d. eidetic

30. After memorizing 5 lists of words you recall less of the last list than a person who only memorized list number five. This observation is explained by
    a. reactive processing
    b. reconstructive processing
    c. proactive interference
    d. retroactive interference

31. On a TV game show, you are asked which way Lincoln's head faces on a penny. You are unable to answer correctly and you lose a large prize. Your memory failure is most likely a result of
    a. the serial position effect
    b. repression
    c. encoding failure
    d. priming

32. Who coined the term "magic number" 7 (plus or minus 2)?
    a. George Miller
    b. Nelson Cowan
    c. Herman Ebbinghaus
    d. Karl Lashley

33. People from the United States tend to recall memories that focus on what they did in a particular event while people from China tend to recall memories that focus on their interactions with family members and friends. Recalling different memories of similar events is the result of
    a. cultural influence
    b. mnemonic strategy
    c. eidetic imagery
    d. pseudo-memory

34. False memory is likely to occur if hypnosis is used in conjunction with
    a. a medical doctor conducting the procedure
    b. the presence of a loved one
    c. misleading questions
    d. both A and B

35. To reduce false identification from eyewitnesses, police should
    a. have witnesses view all the pictures of people at one time
    b. have witnesses view pictures of people one at a time
    c. use hypnosis since it has proven to be a reliable source data gathering
    d. not use eyewitness testimonies since they are not reliable

36. The tendency for eyewitnesses to better identity members of their own ethnic group than other groups is best explained by
    a. eidetic memory
    b. serial position effect
    c. sensory memory
    d. categorization effect

37. A card dealer asks you to silently pick out a card from the six cards laid out in front of you and to memorize it. Without knowing the card you picked, he takes your card away and presents to you the other five cards. To perform this trick properly, the dealer hopes that
    a. you failed to encode the other five cards as you memorize the card you picked
    b. you do have eidetic memory
    c. you believe that he can read your mind
    d. the serial position effect does influence your memory

38. To form lasting memories, the brain appears to use the mechanism of _____; a process that occurs when a connection between brain cells grow stronger as they become more active at the same time.
    a. encoding
    b. transience
    c. long-term potentiation
    d. elaboration

LANGUAGE DEVELOPMENT - Memory

Word roots

In Latin, *retro* refers to "backward" or "behind" and is a root word in two terms in this chapter (retroactive interference and retrograde amnesia). In Latin, *pro* means "for," and as a word root, it often suggests going forward. It is also part of two terms in this chapter (proactive interference and procedural memory), and it is also found as part of several other psychological terms in later chapters. In upcoming chapters, watch for programmed instruction, projective tests, projection, and prosocial behavior.

Is there more than one type of memory?

Preview: "What the Hell's Going on Here?" (p. 297)

>   (297) ***cross-country skiing***: snow skiing across large distances

>   (297) ***put yourself in Steven's shoes***: imagine you are Steven

>   (297) ***wiped out***: erased; taken away

Stages of Memory—Do You Have a Mind Like a Steel Trap? Or a Sieve? (p. 297-300)

(297) *a mind like a steel trap*: a very good memory

(297) *a mind like a sieve*: a very poor memory

(297) *a dusty storehouse*: a storage area that is not often used

(298) *fleeting*: passing quickly; not lasting

(298) *flurry*: a quick movement

(298) *dumped*: removed

(298) *mental scratch pad*: an area of the brain for writing and reading notes; it doesn't exist in a literal form, but is used here to represent working memory

(298) *aardvark*: a South African mammal that eats ants and termites

(298) *MTV*: a television station that plays music videos

(299) *hocked gem*: a gem that has been pawned or traded in

What are the features of each type of memory?

Short-Term Memory—Do You Know the Magic Number? (pp. 300-301)

(300) *IBM*: International Business Machines, a very large U.S.-based computer company

(300) *USN*: United States Navy

(300) *YMCA*: Young Men's Christian Association, an international organization that promotes the spiritual, social, and physical welfare of young men

Is there more than one type of long-term memory?

Long-Term Memory—Where the Past Lives (pp. 301-306)

(302) *quirks*: traits someone has that set him/her apart from other people

(303) *abducted*: kidnapped; taken against one's will

(303) *break the case*: solve the crime; find the criminals

(303) *to weave*: to form and connect by moving side to side

(303) *jogging*: to encourage remembering

(304) *hypothetical*: assumed as an example

(304) *unleashed a flood of*: having allowed an abundance of information to be released or come out all at once

(304) *touched off by*: is reached and recalled

(304) *encyclopedia*: a work in several volumes that contains information on all branches of knowledge

(305) *autobiographical*: historical events and records of one's life

How is memory measured?

Measuring Memory—The Answer Is on the Tip of My Tongue (pp. 306-308)

- (306) *drew a blank*: could not remember
- (306) *World Series*: a series of baseball games played each fall to decide the professional championship of the U.S.
- (306) *Hamlet*: a play written by William Shakespeare
- (307) *police lineups*: a line of people arranged for inspection by the victim or witness of a crime to help identify the criminal
- (308) *prime*: activate, stimulate
- (308) *nutritionists*: those who specialize in the study of proper eating, diets, and the way food is used in the body

What are "photographic" memories?

Exceptional Memory—Wizards of Recall (pp. 308-311)

- (309) *mnemonist*: a person who uses special techniques (mnemonics) to improve the memory
- (310) *avid*: passionate and enthusiastic
- (310) *phenomenal*: outstanding
- (310) *pi*: in geometry, the ratio of the circumference of a circle to its diameter
- (310) *diabolical*: extremely difficult or fiendish
- (311) *augment*: to expand

What causes forgetting? How accurate are everyday memories?

Forgetting—Why We, Uh, Let's See; Why We, Uh . . . Forget! (pp. 311-318)

- (311) *Vexing*: troublesome and problematic
- (312) *cramming*: studying a large amount of information in a short amount of time just before an examination
- (313) *senile*: showing a loss of mental abilities as a result of old age
- (313) *trivial*: of very little importance
- (314) *farfetched*: unbelievable
- (314) *scrapbook*: a blank book in which items such as newspaper articles or pictures are collected and kept

(314) *Vietnam Veterans Memorial*: a memorial in Washington, D.C. that consists of a black marble wall containing the names of all Americans who died in the Vietnam War

(314) *unleashes*: releases

(314) *rehashing old arguments*: going over the same points again and again

(316) *procrastinate*: put off; do later rather than immediately

(317) *deaden public sensitivity*: to reduce the public's concern

(317) *traumatic*: very disturbing or upsetting

(318) *Pearl Harbor attack*: the Japanese attack on American ships in Pearl Harbor (Hawaii) on December 7, 1941 that led the U.S. to enter World War II

(318) *John F. Kennedy*: President of the U.S. in the early '60s

(318) *Martin Luther King Jr.*: an African-American political figure who advocated peace and racial equality

(318) *the Challenger space shuttle disaster*: the spaceship that exploded shortly after take-off, killing everyone on board (January, 1986)

(318) *the Columbia space shuttle disaster*: the spaceship that disintegrated while reentering the earth's atmosphere, killing everyone on board (February, 2003)

(318) *crystallized*: formed and hardened

What happens in the brain when memories are formed?

Memory Formation—Some "Shocking" Findings (pp. 318-321)

(319) *"switching station"*: refers to the station at a railroad where trains are switched from one track to another, as memory switches from long term to short term

(320) *marine snail*: sea snail, as opposed to a land snail

(320) *circuit*: a path

How can memory be improved?

Improving Memory—Keys to the Memory Bank (pp. 321-323)

(321) *absent-minded*: having the tendency to be forgetful

(321) *boil down*: summarize

(322) *daunting*: overwhelming

(322) *jog*: trigger or revive

(322) *elaborate*: to expand with details

(322) **Carnegie Hall**: a famous New York City concert hall; it is a sign of success to be able to perform there

(323) **icing on your study cake**: being easy to review

(323) **eluded**: escaped from

(323) **recapturing**: bringing back

Psychology in Action: mnemonics—Memory Action (pp. 324-326)

(324) **budding**: inexperienced

(324) **port**: left side of a ship, boat, airplane, or space shuttle as one faces forward

(324) **starboard**: right side of a ship, boat, airplane, or space shuttle as one faces forward

(325) **Van Gogh**: Vincent Van Gogh (1853-1890), a well-known Dutch painter

(326) **orators**: those distinguished for their skill as public speakers

(326) **skeptical**: critical, not believing that everything you read is true

(326) **imp**: a playful and naughty being

Solutions

RECITE AND REVIEW

Is there more than one type of memory?

1. system; Information
2. stored
3. 3; short-term; long-term
4. exact; image
5. sounds; meaning
6. temporary; permanent
7. memories; self; family

What are the features of each type of memory?

1. seconds; STM
2. bits; larger
3. magic; short-term; lower
4. interruption; repetition
5. STM; memories

Is there more than one type of long-term memory?

1. updating; false
2. organized; models
3. memory
4. facts; skills
5. Declarative
6. forgetting
7. personal

How is memory measured?

1. state; recall
2. essay; middle
3. recognition; Recognition
4. savings
5. memories; memories

What are "photographic" memories?

1. image
2. adults
3. LTM; STM

What causes forgetting? How accurate are everyday memories?

1. curve; after
2. meaningful; slower
3. information
4. traces; disuse
5. learning; states
6. forgetting
7. interferes; interfere
8. forgetting
9. conscious
10. abuse
11. true; false
12. evidence
13. confidence

What happens in the brain when memories are formed?

1. amnesia; shock
2. memory traces
3. brain
4. nerve
5. chemicals
6. long-term; active

How can memory be improved?

1. organizing; part

2. position

Psychology in Action: Mnemonics—Memory Magic: Pages 324-326

1. initial   2. keyword; LTM

CONNECTIONS

Is there more than one type of memory? Pages 297-300

1. A.   3. C.   5. B.
2. D.   4. E.

Connections

1. C.   4. E.   7. F.
2. G.   5. B.
3. A.   6. D.

What are the features of each type of memory? Is there more than one type of long-term memory? Pages 300-306

1. F. or G.   4. A.   7. E.
2. C.   5. F. or G.
3. D.   6. B.

Connections Part II

1. B.   3. C.   5. F.
2. E.   4. A.   6. D.

How is memory measured? What are "photographic" memories? Pages 306-311

1. G.   4. I.   7. D.
2. A.   5. F.   8. B.
3. C.   6. H.   9. E.

What causes forgetting? How accurate are everyday memories? Pages 311-318

1. C.   4. E.   7. B.
2. F.   5. D.
3. A.   6. G.

What happens in the brain when memories are formed? How can memory be improved? Pages 318-326

1. D.	5. I.	9. C.
2. H	6. F.	10. G.
3. E.	7. A.	
4. B.	8. J	

CHECK YOUR MEMORY

Is there more than one type of memory? Pages 297-300

1. T	4. T	7. T
2. F	5. F	8. F
3. T	6. F	

What are the features of each type of memory? Pages 300-301

1. T	3. F	5. F
2. F	4. T	6. F

Is there more than one type of long-term memory? Pages 301-306

1. F	6. T	11. T
2. T	7. T	12. T
3. T	8. F	13. F
4. F	9. F	
5. T	10. T	

How is memory measured? Pages 306-308

1. T	4. T	7. F
2. F	5. F	
3. F	6. T	

What are "photographic" memories? Pages 308-311

1. T	3. T	5. F
2. T	4. F	6. F

What causes forgetting? How accurate are everyday memories? Pages 311-318

1. F	4. F	7. F
2. T	5. F	8. T
3. F	6. T	9. T

10. T	14. F	18. T
11. T	15. F	19. T
12. F	16. F	20. T
13. F	17. T	21. F

What happens in the brain when memories are formed? Pages 318-321

1. T	3. F	5. F
2. F	4. T	6. T

How can memory be improved? Pages 321-326

1. T	4. F	7. T
2. T	5. T	8. T
3. F	6. F	9. T

FINAL SURVEY AND REVIEW

Is there more than one type of memory?

1. encoded
2. retrieved
3. sensory; short-term
4. icon; echo
5. Short-term; Long-term
6. STM; working; meaningful
7. Cultural; self; group

What are the features of each type of memory?

1. Sensory; selective; attention
2. digit-span; recoding
3. magic number; Miller; lower
4. interference; maintenance
5. Elaborative

Is there more than one type of long-term memory?

1. constructive; pseudo-memories
2. networks; Network
3. Redintegrative
4. declarative; procedural
5. semantic; episodic
6. Semantic
7. Episodic

How is memory measured?

1. tip; tongue; recognition
2. recall; serial; position
3. multiple; distractors
4. relearning
5. explicit; implicit

What are "photographic" memories?

1. Eidetic imagery
2. Eidetic imagery
3. Exceptional; limits

What causes forgetting? How accurate are everyday memories?

1. Ebbinghaus
2. nonsense
3. encode

4. sensory; STM; LTM
5. cue; cues; state-dependent
6. interference
7. retroactive; proactive

8. Repression
9. Repression; suppression
10. repressed
11. recovered

12. fantasies
13. Flashbulb; accurate

What happens in the brain when memories are formed?

1. Retrograde; electroconvulsive
2. engrams; ; consolidated
3. hippocampus

4. nerve; cells
5. transmitter

6. Long-term; potentiation; formation

How can memory be improved?

1. feedback; selecting; search

2. serial; elaboration

Psychology in Action: Mnemonics—Memory Magic: Pages 324-326

1. rote; initial

2. Mnemonic

MASTERY TEST

Psychology in Action: Mnemonics—Memory Magic: Pages 324-326

1. C, p. 298
2. D, p. 302
3. A, p. 318
4. B, p. 317
5. C, p. 299
6. C, p. 297
7. A, p. 304
8. C, p. 308
9. D, p. 312
10. A, p. 298
11. C, p. 308
12. B, p. 308
13. B, p. 300
14. A, p. 317

15. A, p. 306
16. C, p. 307
17. D, p. 301
18. B, p. 306
19. A, p. 311
20. B, p. 301
21. D, p. 322
22. C, p. 316
23. A, p. 322
24. D, p. 303
25. B, p. 318
26. D, p. 325
27. C, p. 304
28. A, p. 305

29. B, p. 314
30. C, p. 315
31. C, pp. 312-313
32. A, p. 300
33. A, p. 299
34. C, p. 303
35. B, p. 307
36. D, p. 313
37. A, p. 312
38. C, p. 320

Cognition, Language, and Creativity

Chapter Overview

Thinking is the mental manipulation of images, concepts, and language (or symbols). Most people use internal images for thinking. Kinesthetic images come from remembered actions and implicit actions. A concept is a generalized idea of a class of objects or events. We learn concepts from positive and negative instances and from rules. Three types of concepts are conjunctive, relational, and disjunctive. Prototypes are often used to identify concepts.

Semantics is the study of meaning in language. Research has shown that words and their meanings greatly influence our thought processes. Language translates events into symbols, which are combined using the rules of grammar and syntax. True languages are productive. Studies suggest that primates are capable of some language use.

The solution to a problem may be arrived at mechanically (by trial and error or by rote). When a problem is solved using a rote method, an algorithm is used. Solutions by understanding usually begin with discovering the general properties of an answer. Next, functional solutions are proposed. Problem solving is frequently aided by heuristics, which narrow the search for solutions. When understanding leads to a rapid solution, it is said that insight has occurred. Three types of insights are selective encoding, selective combination, and selective comparison. Insight can be blocked by fixations.

Work on artificial intelligence has focused on computer simulations and expert systems. Computer simulations of human problem solving are usually based on a means-ends analysis. Human expertise is based on organized knowledge and acquired strategies.

Creative solutions are practical, sensible, and original. Creative thinking requires divergent thought, characterized by fluency, flexibility, and originality. Tests of creativity measure these qualities. Five stages often seen in creative problem solving are orientation, preparation, incubation, illumination, and verification. However, much creative work is simply based on incremental problem solving. Studies suggest that there is only a small positive correlation between IQ and creativity. Most creative people are not mentally disturbed, and most mentally disturbed people are not creative.

Intuitive thinking often leads to errors. Wrong conclusions may be drawn when an answer seems highly representative of what we already believe is true. A second problem is allowing emotions to determine our decisions. A third problem is ignoring the base rate of an event. Clear thinking is usually aided by stating or framing a problem in broad terms. Major sources of thinking errors include rigid mental sets, faulty logic, and over-simplifications. Various strategies, including brainstorming, tend to enhance creative problem solving.

Learning Objectives

1. Define *cognition* and list the three basic units of thought.

2. Describe mental imagery, synesthesia, and the properties of mental images; explain how both stored and created images may be used to solve problems (including how the size of a mental image may be important); and describe how kinesthetic imagery aids thinking.

3. Define the terms *concept* and *concept formation;* explain how they aid thought processes; and describe how they are learned.

4. Define the terms *conjunctive concept*, *relational concept*, *disjunctive concept*, and *prototype*.

5. Explain the difference between the denotative and the connotative meaning of a word or concept; describe how the connotative meaning of a word is measured; and discuss problems associated with social stereotypes and all-or-nothing thinking.

6. Explain how language aids thought, and define semantics.

7. Discuss bilingual education, including the concepts of additive and subtractive bilingualism and two-way bilingual education.

8. Briefly describe the following three requirements of a language and their related concepts and include a discussion of gestural languages:

   a. symbols

   b. phonemes

   c. morphemes

   d. grammar

   e. syntax

   f. transformational rules

   g. productivity

9. Explain the extent to which primates have been taught to use language and describe both the criticisms and practical value of attempts to teach language to primates.

10. Differentiate between mechanical problem-solving and problem-solving through understanding and discuss *heuristics* and how they aid problem-solving.

11. Tell how each of the following contribute to insight:

    a. selective encoding

    b. selective combination

    c. selective comparison

12. Explain and give examples of how fixation and functional fixedness block problem-solving and describe the four common barriers to creative thinking.

13. Define the term *artificial intelligence*; describe what it is based on and its potential uses and limitations; and explain how novices differ from experts.

14. Describe the following four kinds of thought:

    a. inductive

    b. deductive

    c. logical

    d. illogical

15. Describe the following characteristics of creative thinking:

    a. fluency

    b. flexibility

    c. originality

16. Explain the relationship of creativity to divergent and convergent thinking and discuss how fantasy (daydreams) are related to creativity. Include the two most common daydream themes.

17. List three characteristics of creativity other than divergent thinking and describe how the ability to think divergently can be measured.

18. Describe the five stages of creative thinking and discuss the five qualities which characterize creative persons.

19. Briefly discuss the use of syllogisms in logical thinking and explain the following three common intuitive thinking errors and include a brief description of what it means to have *wisdom*:

    a. representativeness (include representativeness heuristic)

    b. underlying odds (base rate)

    c. framing

The following objective is related to the material in the "Psychology in Action" section of your text.

1. Describe nine practical steps for encouraging creativity; describe the process of brainstorming and explain how it can be used to solve problems; and briefly discuss the creativity checklist and Csikszentmihalyi's recommendations about how to become more creative.

RECITE AND REVIEW

What is the nature of thought?

What is Thinking?—It's All in Your Head! Pages 330-331

1. Cognition is the _____ processing of information involving daydreaming, _____ solving, and reasoning.

2. Thinking is the manipulation of _____ representations of external problems or situations.

3. Three basic units of thought are images, concepts, and _____ or symbols.

In what ways are images related to thinking?

Mental Imagery—Does a Frog Have Lips? Pages 331-333

1. Most people have internal images of one kind or another. Images may be based on information stored in memory or they may be _____ .

2. Sometimes images cross normal _____ boundaries in a type of imagery called synesthesia.

3. The size of images used in problem solving may _____ . Images may be three-dimensional and they may be rotated in _____ to answer questions.

4. Many of the systems in the brain that are involved in processing _____ images work in reverse to create mental images.

5. Kinesthetic images are created by memories of _____ or by implicit (unexpressed) _____ . Kinesthetic sensations and micromovements seem to help structure thinking for many people.

How are concepts learned? Are there different kinds of concepts?

Concepts—I'm Positive, It's a Whatchamacallit: Pages 333-335

1. A concept is a generalized idea of a _____ of objects or events.

2. Forming concepts may be based on experiences with _____ and negative instances.

3. Concepts may also be acquired by learning rules that define the _____ .

4. Concepts may be classified as conjunctive (" _____ " concepts), disjunctive (" _____ " concepts), or relational concepts.

5. In practice, we frequently use prototypes (general _____ of the concept class) to identify concepts.

6. The denotative meaning of a word or concept is its dictionary _____ . Connotative meaning is _____ or emotional.

7. Connotative meaning can be measured with the semantic differential. Most connotative meaning involves the dimensions _____ , strong-weak, and active-passive.

8. Two common thinking errors are _____ thinking (thinking in black and white terms) and use of social stereotypes (inaccurate and oversimplified images of _____ _____).

What is the role of language in thinking? Can animals be taught to use language?

Language—Don't Leave Home Without It: Pages 336-340

1. Language allows events to be encoded into _____ for easy mental manipulation.

2. Thinking in language is influenced by meaning. The study of _____ is called semantics.

3. Language is built out of phonemes (basic speech _____) and morphemes (speech sounds collected into _____ units).

4. Learning a second _____ (bilingualism) during the elementary school years is most likely to benefit students who participate in _____ bilingual education.

5. Language carries meaning by combining a set of symbols or signs according to a set of _____ (grammar), which includes rules about word _____ (syntax).

6. Various sentences are created by applying transformation _____ to simple statements.

7. A true language is productive, and can be used to generate new ideas or possibilities. American Sign Language (ASL) and other _____ languages used by the deaf are true languages.

8. Animal communication is relatively limited because it lacks symbols that can be _____ easily.

9. Attempts to teach chimpanzees ASL and other nonverbal systems suggest to some that primates are capable of language use. However, others believe that the chimps are merely using _____ responses to get food and other reinforcers.

10. Studies that make use of lexigrams (_____ word-symbols) provide the best evidence yet of animal language use.

What do we know about problem solving?

Problem Solving—Getting an Answer in Sight: Pages 341-345

1. The solution to a problem may be found mechanically (by trial and error or by _____ application of rules). However, mechanical solutions are frequently inefficient or ineffective, except where aided by _____ .

2. Often a _____ solution is achieved through an algorithm, a _____ set of rules that always leads to a correct solution.

3. Solutions by understanding usually begin with discovery of the _____ properties of an answer. Next comes proposal of a number of functional _____ .

4. Problem solving is frequently aided by heuristics. These are strategies that typically _____ the search for solutions. The _____ strategy (identify, define, explore, act, look and learn) is a general heuristic.

5. When understanding leads to a rapid _____ , insight has occurred. Three elements of insight are _____ encoding, selective combination, and selective comparison.

6. The ability to apply _____ comparison (comparing old solutions to new problems) effectively can be influenced by our culture.

7. Insights and other problem solving attempts can be blocked by fixation (a tendency to repeat _____ solutions).

8. Functional fixedness is a common _____ , but emotional blocks, cultural values, learned conventions, and perceptual _____ are also problems.

What is Artificial Intelligence?

Artificial Intelligence—I Compute, Therefore I am: Pages 345-347

1. Artificial intelligence refers to any artificial _____ that can perform tasks that require _____ when done by people.

2. Two principal areas of artificial intelligence research are _____ simulations and expert systems.

3. Computer simulations of human problem solving are usually based on a means-ends _____ (finding ways to reduce the difference between the present state and the desired goal).

4. Expert human problem solving is based on organized _____ and acquired strategies, rather than some general improvement in thinking ability. Expertise also allows more automatic _____ of problems.

What is the nature of creative thinking?

Creative Thinking—Down Roads Less Traveled: Pages 347-352

1. _____ may be deductive or inductive, logical or illogical.

2. Creative thinking requires divergent thought, characterized by fluency, flexibility, and _____ . Creativity is also marked by problem _____ , the active discovery of problems to be solved.

3. To be creative, a solution must be _____ and sensible as well as original.

4. Daydreaming and _____ are a source of much divergent thinking. Two very common daydream plots are the conquering _____ and the suffering martyr.

5. Tests of _____ , such as the Unusual Uses Test, the Consequences Test, and the Anagrams Test, measure the capacity for divergent thinking.

6. Five stages often seen in creative problem solving are orientation, _____ , incubation, illumination, and verification.

7. Not all creative thinking fits this pattern. Much creative activity is based on incremental problem solving (many small _____).

8. Studies suggest that creative persons share a number of identifiable general traits, _____ abilities, thinking _____ , and personality characteristics. There is little or no correlation between IQ and creativity.

9. Many of history's most _____ artists, writers, poets, and composers suffered from mood disorders.

10. Most _____ people do not suffer from mental disorders, and most _____ disturbed people are not creative. However, there are a few exceptions in regard to _____ disorders. The relation between creativity and mood disorders may be due to the level of productivity during the manic state.

How accurate is intuition?

Logic and Intuition—Mental Shortcut? Or Dangerous Detour? Pages 352-355

1. Syllogisms can be evaluated for the _____ of their premises, the validity of the reasoning, and the truth of the _____ .

2. Intuitive thinking often leads to _____ . Wrong conclusions may be drawn when an answer seems highly representative of what we already believe is _____ . (That is, when people apply the representativeness heuristic.)

3. A second problem is allowing emotions such as _____ , hope, _____ , or disgust to guide _____ in decision making.

4. A third problem is ignoring the base rate (or underlying _____) of an event.

5. Clear thinking is usually aided by stating or framing a problem in _____ terms.

What can be done to promote creativity?

Psychology in Action: Enhancing Creativity—Brainstorms: Pages 356-359

1. Rigid mental sets are a major barrier to _____ thinking.

2. Creativity can be enhanced by defining problems _____ , by establishing a creative atmosphere, by allowing _____ for incubation, by seeking _____ input, and by looking for analogies.

3. Brainstorming, in which the production and criticism of ideas is kept _____ , also tends to enhance creative problem solving.

CONNECTIONS

What is the nature of thought? In what ways are images related to thinking? Pages 330-333

1. _____ cognition
2. _____ internal representation
3. _____ language
4. _____ mental rotation
5. _____ reverse vision
6. _____ synesthesia
7. _____ stored images
8. _____ kinesthetic imagery

a. imagined movements
b. remembered perceptions
c. brain imaging
d. mental expression
e. implicit actions
f. thinking
g. crossed senses
h. symbols and rules

How are concepts learned? Are there different kinds of concepts? Pages 333-335

1. _____ concept
2. _____ connotative meaning
3. _____ social stereotypes
4. _____ prototype
5. _____ denotative concept
6. _____ disjunctive concept
7. _____ relational concept
8. _____ conjunctive concept

a. objective meaning
b. mental class
c. ideal or model
d. semantic differential
e. two or more features
f. details of features and nearby area
g. at least one existing feature
h. faulty, oversimplified concepts

What is the role of language in thinking? Can animals be taught to use language? Pages 336-340

1. _____ word meanings
2. _____ additive bilingualism
3. _____ morpheme
4. _____ phoneme
5. _____ "hidden" grammar
6. _____ Washoe
7. _____ bilingual
8. _____ subtractive bilingualism
9. _____ Kanzi

a. meaningful unit
b. ASL
c. semantics
d. lexigrams
e. language sound
f. fluent in two languages
g. reduced competency in both languages
h. increased overall competency
i. transformation rules

What do we know about problem solving? What is Artificial Intelligence? Pages 341-347

1. _____ AI
2. _____ insight
3. _____ trial-and-error
4. _____ random search strategy
5. _____ expert versus novice
6. _____ heuristic
7. _____ understanding
8. _____ selective comparison
9. _____ fixation
10. _____ expert system

a. mechanical solution
b. thinking strategy
c. element of insight
d. knowledge plus rules
e. a clear, sudden solution
f. trial-and-error
g. Deep Blue
h. acquired strategies
i. blind to alternatives
j. deep comprehension

What is the nature of creative thinking? How accurate is intuition? What can be done to promote creativity? Pages 347-359

1. _____ fluency
2. _____ flexibility
3. _____ originality
4. _____ logical
5. _____ convergent thinking
6. _____ Anagrams Test
7. _____ cross-stimulation effect
8. _____ syllogism
9. _____ illumination
10. _____ brainstorming
11. _____ base rate
12. _____ intuition

a. analysis of logic
b. many types of solutions
c. one correct answer
d. follow explicit rule
e. moment of insight
f. underlying odds
g. quick and impulsive thought
h. many solutions
i. measures divergent thinking
j. novelty of solutions
k. domino effect of ideas
l. no idea is criticized

CHECK YOUR MEMORY

What is the nature of thought? Pages 330-331

1. Cognitive psychology is the study of sensation, memory, and learning.

TRUE or FALSE

2. Images, concepts, and language may be used to mentally represent problems.

TRUE or FALSE

3. Images are generalized ideas of a class of related objects or events.

TRUE or FALSE

4. Blindfolded chess players mainly use concepts to represent chess problems and solutions.

TRUE or FALSE

In what ways are images related to thinking? Pages 331-333

1. Mental images are used to make decisions, change feelings, and to improve memory.

TRUE or FALSE

2. Experiencing color sensations while listening to music is an example of mental rotation.

   TRUE or FALSE

3. Mental images may be used to improve memory and skilled actions.

   TRUE or FALSE

4. In an imagined space, it is easiest to locate objects placed above and below yourself.

   TRUE or FALSE

5. The visual cortex is activated when a person has a mental image.

   TRUE or FALSE

6. The more the image of a shape has to be rotated in space, the longer it takes to tell if it matches another view of the same shape.

   TRUE or FALSE

7. People who have good imaging abilities tend to score high on tests of creativity.

   TRUE or FALSE

8. The smaller a mental image is, the harder it is to identify its details.

   TRUE or FALSE

9. People with good synesthetic imagery tend to learn sports skills faster than average.

   TRUE or FALSE

How are concepts learned? Are there different kinds of concepts? Pages 333-335

1. Concept formation is typically based on examples and rules.

   TRUE or FALSE

2. Prototypes are very strong negative instances of a concept.

   TRUE or FALSE

3. "Greater than" and "lopsided" are relational concepts.

   TRUE or FALSE

4. Classifying things as absolutely right or wrong may lead to all-or-nothing thinking.

   TRUE or FALSE

5. The semantic differential is used to rate the objective meanings of words and concepts.

   TRUE or FALSE

6. Social stereotypes are accurate, oversimplified concepts people use to form mental images of groups of people.

TRUE or FALSE

What is the role of language in thinking? Can animals be taught to use language? Pages 336-340

1. Encoding is the study of the meanings of language.

TRUE or FALSE

2. The Stroop interference test shows that thought is greatly influenced by language.

TRUE or FALSE

3. People can easily name the color of the word without the meaning of the word interfering with their thought processing.

TRUE or FALSE

4. Morphemes are the basic speech sounds of a language.

TRUE or FALSE

5. Syntax is a part of grammar.

TRUE or FALSE

6. Noam Chomsky believes that a child who says, "I drinked my juice," has applied the semantic differential to a simple, core sentence.

TRUE or FALSE

7. Similar universal language patterns are found in both speech and gestural languages, such as ASL.

TRUE or FALSE

8. ASL has 600,000 root signs.

TRUE or FALSE

9. True languages are productive, thus ASL is not a true language.

TRUE or FALSE

10. If one is fluent in ASL, one can sign and understand other gestural languages such as Yiddish Sign.

TRUE or FALSE

11. Animal communication can be described as productive.

TRUE or FALSE

12. Chimpanzees have never learned to speak even a single word.

TRUE or FALSE

13. One of Sarah chimpanzee's outstanding achievements was mastery of sentences involving transformational rules.

    TRUE or FALSE

14. Some "language" use by chimpanzees appears to be no more than simple operant responses.

    TRUE or FALSE

15. Only a minority of the things that language-trained chimps "say" have anything to do with food.

    TRUE or FALSE

16. Language-trained chimps have been known to hold conversations when no humans were present.

    TRUE or FALSE

17. Kanzi's use of grammar is on a par with that of a 2-year-old child.

    TRUE or FALSE

What do we know about problem solving? Pages 341-345

1. Except for the simplest problems, mechanical solutions are typically best left to computers.

    TRUE or FALSE

2. An algorithm is a learned set of rules (grammar) for language.

    TRUE or FALSE

3. Karl Dunker's famous tumor problem could only be solved by trial-and-error.

    TRUE or FALSE

4. In solutions by understanding, functional solutions are usually discovered by use of a random search strategy.

    TRUE or FALSE

5. Working backward from the desired goal to the starting point can be a useful heuristic.

    TRUE or FALSE

6. In problem solving, rapid insights are more likely to be correct than those that develop slowly.

    TRUE or FALSE

7. Selective encoding refers to bringing together seemingly unrelated bits of useful information.

    TRUE or FALSE

8. An advantage of selective comparison is our ability to solve problems in all cultures.

    TRUE or FALSE

9. Functional fixedness is an inability to see new uses for familiar objects.

    TRUE or FALSE

10. Learned barriers in functional fixedness refer to our habits causing us to not identify other important elements of a problem.

TRUE or FALSE

What is Artificial Intelligence? Pages 345-347

1. In general, artificial intelligence lacks the creativity and common sense of human intelligence.
TRUE or FALSE

2. AI is frequently based on a set of rules applied to a body of information.
TRUE or FALSE

3. Computer simulations are used to test models of human cognition.
TRUE or FALSE

4. Most computer-based models of human problem solving rely on the principle of automatic processing.
TRUE or FALSE

5. Much human expertise is based on acquired strategies for solving problems.
TRUE or FALSE

6. Chess experts have an exceptional ability to remember the positions of chess pieces placed at random on a chessboard.
TRUE or FALSE

What is the nature of creative thinking? Pages 347-352

1. In inductive thinking, a general rule is inferred from specific examples.
TRUE or FALSE

2. Fluency and flexibility are measures of convergent thinking.
TRUE or FALSE

3. About half of our waking thoughts are occupied by daydreams.
TRUE or FALSE

4. Fantasy contributes to divergent thinking and creativity.
TRUE or FALSE

5. Creative thinkers typically apply reasoning and critical thinking to novel ideas after they produce them.
TRUE or FALSE

6. Creative ideas combine originality with feasibility.

   TRUE or FALSE

7. Creative problem solving temporarily stops during the incubation period.

   TRUE or FALSE

8. Much creative problem solving is incremental, rather than being based on sudden insights or breakthroughs.

   TRUE or FALSE

9. Creative people have an openness to experience and they have a wide range of knowledge and interests.

   TRUE or FALSE

10. An IQ score of 120 or above means that a person is creative.

    TRUE or FALSE

11. Most creative people like Vincent Van Gogh and Edgar Allan Poe tend to become insane later in life.

    TRUE or FALSE

12. Most people who are mentally ill are not especially creative. In fact, the more severely disturbed a person is, the less creative she or he is likely to be.

    TRUE or FALSE

13. The connection between mood swings and creativity may be mainly a matter of productivity.

    TRUE or FALSE

How accurate is intuition? Pages 352-355

1. It is possible to draw true conclusions using faulty logic.

   TRUE or FALSE

2. It is possible to draw false conclusions using valid logic.

   TRUE or FALSE

3. Intuition is a quick, impulsive insight into the true nature of a problem and its solution.

   TRUE or FALSE

4. To form accurate intuitive judgment of teachers, students must observe at least 20 minutes of the teacher's teaching ability.

   TRUE or FALSE

5. The probability of two events occurring together is lower than the probability of either one occurring alone.

   TRUE or FALSE

6. The representativeness heuristic is the strategy of stating problems in broad terms.
   TRUE or FALSE

7. Being logical, most people do not let their emotions interfere when making important decisions.
   TRUE or FALSE

8. Framing refers to the way in which a problem is stated or structured.
   TRUE or FALSE

9. People who are intelligent are also wise because they live their lives with openness and tolerance.
   TRUE or FALSE

What can be done to promote creativity? Pages 356-359

1. Creative problem solving involves defining problems as narrowly as possible.
   TRUE or FALSE

2. It is wise to allow time for incubation if you are seeking a creative solution to a problem.
   TRUE or FALSE

3. Exposure to creative models tends to increase creativity among observers.
   TRUE or FALSE

4. Delaying evaluation during the early stages of creative problem solving tends to lead to poor thinking.
   TRUE or FALSE

5. Asking yourself, "If the problem were edible, how would it taste?" is an example of restating a problem in a different way.
   TRUE or FALSE

6. Edward de Bono suggests that digging deeper with logic is a good way to increase your creativity.
   TRUE or FALSE

7. People who think creatively are typically unwilling to take risks; doing so just leads to deadends.
   TRUE or FALSE

8. The cross-stimulation effect is an important part of brainstorming in groups.
   TRUE or FALSE

FINAL SURVEY AND REVIEW

What is the nature of thought?

What is Thinking?—It's All in Your Head! Pages 330-331

1. _____ is the mental processing of information involving daydreaming, problem solving, and reasoning.

2. Thinking is the manipulation of internal _____ of external problems or situations.

3. Three basic units of thought are _____ , _____ , and language or _____ .

In what ways are images related to thinking?

Mental Imagery—Does a Frog Have Lips? Pages 331-333

1. Most people have internal images of one kind or another. Images may be based on _____ _____ in memory or they may be created.

2. Sometimes images cross normal sense boundaries in a type of imagery called _____ .

3. The _____ of images used in problem solving may change. Images may be three-dimensional and they may be _____ in space to answer questions.

4. Many of the systems in the _____ that are involved in processing _____ images work in reverse to create _____ images.

5. Kinesthetic images are created by memories of actions or by _____ (unexpressed) actions. Kinesthetic sensations and _____ seem to help structure thinking for many people.

How are concepts learned? Are there different kinds of concepts?

Concepts—I'm Positive, It's a Whatchamacallit: Pages 333-335

1. A concept is a _____ idea of a class of objects or events.

2. Forming concepts may be based on experiences with positive and _____ _____ .

3. Concepts may also be acquired by learning _____ that define the concept.

4. Concepts may be classified as _____ ("and" concepts), _____ (" _____ or" concepts), or relational concepts.

5. In practice, we frequently use _____ (general models of the concept class) to identify concepts.

6. The _____ meaning of a word or concept is its dictionary definition. _____ meaning is personal or emotional.

7. Connotative meaning can be measured with the _____ differential. Most connotative meaning involves the dimensions good-bad, _____ , and _____ .

8. Two common thinking errors are _____ thinking (thinking in black and white terms) and use of _____ (inaccurate and oversimplified images of social groups).

What is the role of language in thinking? Can animals be taught to use language?

Language—Don't Leave Home Without It: Pages 336-340

1. Language allows events to be _____ into symbols for easy mental manipulation.

2. Thinking in language is influenced by meaning. The study of meaning is called _____ .

3. Language is built out of _____ (basic speech sounds) and _____ (speech sounds collected into meaningful units).

4. Learning a second language (_____) during the elementary school years is most likely to benefit students who participate in _____ education.

5. Language carries meaning by combining a set of symbols or signs according to a set of rules (_____), which includes rules about word order (_____).

6. Various sentences are created by applying _____ rules to simple statements.

7. A true language is _____ , and can be used to generate new ideas or possibilities. _____ Language (ASL) and other gestural languages used by the deaf are true languages.

8. Animal communication is relatively limited because it lacks _____ that can be rearranged easily.

9. Attempts to teach chimpanzees ASL and other nonverbal systems suggest to some that _____ are capable of language use. However, others believe that the chimps are merely using operant responses to get food and other _____ .

10. Studies that make use of _____ (geometric word-symbols) provide the best evidence yet of animal language use.

What do we know about problem solving?

Problem Solving—Getting an Answer in Sight: Pages 341-345

1. The solution to a problem may be found _____ (by trial and error or by rote application of rules). However, _____ solutions are frequently inefficient or ineffective, except where aided by computer.

2. Often a rote solution is achieved through an _____ , a learned set of rules that always leads to a correct solution.

3. Solutions by _____ usually begin with discovery of the general properties of an answer. Next comes proposal of a number of _____ (workable) solutions.

4. Problem solving is frequently aided by _____ . These are strategies that typically narrow the search for solutions. The ideal strategy (_____ , define, _____ , act, look and learn) is a general heuristic.

5. When understanding leads to a rapid solution, _____ has occurred. Three elements of _____ are _____ , selective combination, and selective comparison.

6. The ability to apply selective comparison (comparing _____ solutions to new problems) effectively can be influenced by our _____ .

7. Insights and other problem solving attempts can be blocked by _____ (a tendency to repeat wrong solutions).

8. _____ fixedness is a common fixation, but emotional _____ , cultural _____ , learned conventions, and perceptual habits are also problems.

What is Artificial Intelligence?

Artificial Intelligence—I Compute, Therefore I am: Pages 345-347

1. Artificial intelligence refers to any _____ that can perform tasks that require intelligence when done by _____ .

2. Two principal areas of artificial intelligence research are computer simulations and _____ .

3. Computer simulations of human problem solving are usually based on a _____ analysis (finding ways to reduce the difference between the present state and the desired goal).

4. Expert human problem solving is based on _____ knowledge and acquired _____ , rather than some general improvement in thinking ability. Expertise also allows more _____ processing _____ of problems.

What is the nature of creative thinking?

Creative Thinking—Down Roads Less Traveled: Pages 347-352

1. Thinking may be deductive or _____ , _____ or illogical.

2. Creative thinking requires _____ thought, characterized by _____ , flexibility, and originality. Creativity is also marked by _____ , the active discovery of problems to be solved.

3. To be creative, a solution must be practical and sensible as well as _____ .

4. Daydreaming and fantasy are a source of much divergent thinking. Two very common daydream plots are the _____ hero and the suffering _____ .

5. Tests of creativity, such as the Unusual _____ Test, the Consequences Test, and the Anagrams Test, measure the capacity for _____ thinking.

6. Five stages often seen in creative problem solving are orientation, preparation, _____ , _____ , and verification.

7. Not all creative thinking fits this pattern. Much creative activity is based on _____ problem solving (many small steps).

8. Studies suggest that creative persons share a number of identifiable general traits, thinking abilities, thinking styles, and _____ characteristics. There is little or no _____ between IQ and creativity.

9. Many of history's most creative artists, writers, poets, and composers suffered from _____ disorders.

10. Most creative people do not suffer from _____ disorders, and most mentally disturbed people are not creative. However, there are a few exceptions in regard to _____ disorders. The relation between creativity and mood disorders may be due to the level of productivity during the _____ state.

How accurate is intuition?

Logic and Intuition—Mental Shortcut? Or Dangerous Detour? Pages 352-355

1. Syllogisms can be evaluated for the truth of their _____ , the validity of the _____ , and the truth of the conclusion.

2. Intuitive thinking often leads to errors. Wrong conclusions may be drawn when an answer seems highly _____ of what we already believe is true. (That is, when people apply the representativeness _____ .)

3. A second problem is allowing _____ such as fear, hope, anxiety, or disgust to guide thinking in _____ making.

4. A third problem is ignoring the _____ _____ (or underlying probability) of an event.

5. Clear thinking is usually aided by stating or _____ a problem in broad _____ terms.

What can be done to promote creativity?

Psychology in Action: Enhancing Creativity—Brainstorms: Pages 356-359

1. Rigid _____ are a major barrier to creative thinking.

2. Creativity can be enhanced by defining problems broadly, by establishing a creative atmosphere, by allowing time for _____ , by seeking varied _____ , and by looking for analogies.

3. _____ , in which the production and criticism of ideas is kept separate, also tends to enhance creative problem solving.

MASTERY TEST

1. The mark of a true language is that it must be
   a. spoken
   b. productive
   c. based on spatial grammar and syntax
   d. capable of encoding conditional relationships

2. Computer simulations and expert systems are two major applications of
   a. AI
   b. ASL
   c. brainstorming
   d. problem framing

3. Failure to wear automobile seat belts is an example of which intuitive thinking error?
   a. allowing too much time for incubation
   b. framing a problem broadly
   c. ignoring base rates
   d. recognition that two events occurring together are more likely than either one alone

4. One thing that images, concepts, and symbols all have in common is that they are
   a. morphemes
   b. internal representations
   c. based on reverse vision
   d. translated into micromovements

5. To decide if a container is a cup, bowl, or vase, most people compare it to
   a. a prototype
   b. its connotative meaning
   c. a series of negative instances
   d. a series of relevant phonemes

6. During problem solving, being "cold," "warm," or "very warm" is closely associated with
   a. insight
   b. fixation
   c. automatic processing
   d. rote problem solving

7. The Anagrams Test measures
   a. mental sets
   b. inductive thinking
   c. logical reasoning
   d. divergent thinking

8. "Either-or" concepts are
   a. conjunctive
   b. disjunctive
   c. relational
   d. prototypical

9. Which term does not belong with the others?
   a. selective comparison
   b. functional fixedness
   c. learned conventions
   d. emotional blocks

10. The IDEAL thinking strategy is basically a
    a. prototype
    b. heuristic
    c. functional solution
    d. form of intuitive thought

11. An incremental view of creative problem solving CONTRASTS most directly with which stage of creative thought?
    a. orientation
    b. preparation
    c. illumination
    d. verification

12. Daydreaming and fantasy are two principal sources of
    a. intuition
    b. divergent thinking
    c. feasible solutions
    d. selective comparison

13. The difference between prime beef and dead cow is primarily a matter of
    a. syntax
    b. conjunctive meaning
    c. semantics
    d. the productive nature of language

14. Synesthesia is an unusual form of
    a. imagery
    b. heuristic
    c. insight
    d. daydreaming

15. Which of the listed terms does NOT correctly complete this sentence: Insight involves selective
    _____.
    a. encoding
    b. combination
    c. comparison
    d. fixation

16. Which of the following is LEAST likely to predict that a person is creative?
    a. high IQ
    b. a preference for complexity
    c. fluency in combining ideas
    d. use of mental images

17. A major premise, minor premise, and conclusion are elements of
    a. brainstorming
    b. a syllogism
    c. selective comparison
    d. the representativeness heuristic

18. Language allows events to be _____ into _____.
    a. translated, concepts
    b. fixated, codes
    c. rearranged, lexigrams
    d. encoded, symbols

19. "A triangle must be a closed shape with three sides made of straight lines." This statement is an example of a
    a. prototype
    b. positive instance
    c. concept rule
    d. disjunctive concept

20. Fluency, flexibility, and originality are all measures of
    a. inductive thinking
    b. selective comparison
    c. intuitive framing
    d. divergent thinking

21. The form of imagery that is especially important in music, sports, dance, and martial arts is
    a. kinesthetic imagery
    b. synesthetic imagery
    c. prototypical imagery
    d. conjunctive imagery

22. Among animals trained to use language, Kanzi has been unusually accurate at
    a. using proper syntax
    b. substituting gestures for lexigrams
    c. expressing conditional relationships
    d. forming chains of operant responses

23. Random search strategies are most similar to
    a. selective encoding
    b. automatic processing
    c. trial-and-error problem solving
    d. the orientation phase of problem solving

24. Looking for analogies and delaying evaluation are helpful strategies for increasing
    a. divergent thinking
    b. convergent thinking
    c. functional fixedness
    d. concept formation

25. Comparing 2 three-dimensional shapes to see if they match is easiest if only a small amount of _____ is required.
    a. conceptual recoding
    b. mental rotation
    c. concept formation
    d. kinesthetic transformation

26. The good-bad dimension on the semantic differential is closely related to a concept's
    a. disjunctive meaning
    b. conjunctive meaning
    c. connotative meaning
    d. denotative meaning

27. Most computer models of human problem solving are based on some form of
    a. base rate framing
    b. means-ends analysis
    c. divergent search strategy
    d. representativeness heuristic

28. The directions "modify, magnify, rearrange, and suspend judgment" could be expected to aid a group engaged in
    a. a means-ends analysis
    b. base rate framing
    c. brainstorming
    d. solving delayed response problems

29. According to Noam Chomsky, surface sentences are created by applying _____ to simple sentences.
    a. encoding grammars
    b. transformation rules
    c. conditional prototypes
    d. selective conjunctions

30. The occurrence of an insight corresponds to which stage of creative thinking?
    a. verification
    b. incubation
    c. illumination
    d. fixation

31. "Try working backward from the desired goal to the starting point or current state." This advice describes a
    a. syllogism
    b. heuristic
    c. prototype
    d. dimension of the semantic differential

32. The _____ has demonstrated that people can quickly identify the color of a word if the word's meaning is similar to the word's color. This suggests that the meaning of words do influence our thoughts.
    a. memory task
    b. Stroop test
    c. Stanford-Binet Intelligence Scale
    d. American Sign Language

33. When one divides a number into another, step-by-step without the aid of a calculator, one is using a(an) _____ to find a solution.
    a. algorithm
    b. conceptual rule
    c. prototype
    d. Anagrams Test

34. Most American students were unable to solve a problem of how a chief can collect taxes without a scale to balance the right amount of gold coins each villager owes, whereas most Chinese students were able to since most Chinese students were familiar with a traditional story about weighing an elephant that is too big to be on a scale. This example illustrates which nature of insight?
    a. selective encoding
    b. selective combination
    c. selective comparison
    d. selective intuition

35. Most creative people do not suffer from mental disorders. However, an exception to this might include a few creative people who
    a. experience manic states
    b. express fantasy fulfillment
    c. seek attention
    d. both B and C

36. People who choose political candidates because they like them have fallen prey to which form of intuitive thinking error?
    a. representativeness
    b. emotions
    c. underlying odds
    d. framing

37. The immediate intuitive reactions to experience or the quickly making sense of thin slivers of experience can influence and help form carefully reasoned judgments of people. According to Malcolm Gladwell these reactions are the result of _____.
    a. social stereotypes
    b. divergence thinking
    c. discrimination
    d. the cognitive unconscious

LANGUAGE DEVELOPMENT - Cognition, Language, and Creativity

Word roots

The Latin word *vergere* means "to bend or turn." Using the Latin roots *con* (with) and *di* (apart), the English language has evolved to form two terms you will find used in this chapter: convergent (to turn with or merge together) and divergent (to turn apart or open).

What is the nature of thought?

Preview: Gizmos and Doohickeys (p. 330)

> (330) *gizmos and doohickeys*: names for machines or tools often used when the true name is unknown or not remembered
>
> (330) *wacky*: strange and unusual
>
> (330) *zany*: wild and crazy
>
> (330) *Einstein*: Albert Einstein (1879-1955), the physicist whose theories of relativity transformed physics and helped to create the atomic age
>
> (330) *Darwin*: Charles Darwin (1809-1882), the scientist who proposed the theory of evolution
>
> (330) *Mozart*: Wolfgang Amadeus Mozart (1756-1791), a famous Austrian composer and pianist
>
> (330) *Newton*: Sir Isaac Newton (1642-1727), the physicist and mathematician whose ideas created modern physics; he first described the Law of Gravity
>
> (330) *Michelangelo*: Michelangelo Buonarrotti (1475-1564), a famous Renaissance artist who created such famous works as the statue of David and the ceiling mural in the Sistine Chapel in Rome
>
> (330) *Galileo*: Galileo Galilei (1564-1642), the Italian astronomer and physicist who pioneered the use of the scientific experimental method and developed the first refracting telescope
>
> (330) *Madame Curie*: Marie Curie (1867-1934), the French chemist who first isolated the radioactive element radium; she was the first person to win two Nobel prizes
>
> (330) *Edison*: Thomas Alva Edison (1847-1931), the American inventor who conceived the electric light, phonograph, and microphone
>
> (330) *Martha Graham*: (1893-1991), a well-known American dancer and choreographer

What is Thinking?—It's All in Your Head! (pp. 330-331)

> (330) *frenzied cities*: fast-paced cities
>
> (330) *placid retreats*: calm, quiet places to go to get away from one's fast-paced life
>
> (331) *delve*: to dig deep into something

In what ways are images related to thinking?

Mental Imagery—Does a Frog Have Lips? (pp. 331-333)

> (332) *egg carton*: a box designed to hold one dozen eggs
>
> (332) *Lewis Carroll*: A pseudonym for Charles Lutwidge Dodgson, the famous English author who wrote <u>Alice in Wonderland</u> and <u>Through the Looking Glass</u>
>
> (333) *instant replay*: used in televised sports to repeat a play that has just taken place
>
> (333) *high points*: the most interesting parts of a game or event

How are concepts learned? Are there different kinds of concepts?

Concepts—I'm Positive, It's a Whatchamacallit: (pp. 333-335)

(333) *whatchamacallit*: what you may call it; used when the exact name for something cannot be remembered

(333) *daze*: state of confusion

(334) *punk music*: marked by extreme and often offensive expressions of social discontent

(334) *hip-hop*: a style of music and dance that derives from inner-city street culture; rap music is part of hip-hop

(334) *fusion*: a blending of jazz, rock, Latin, and improvisation to form a modern, smooth type of jazz

(334) *salsa*: popular music of Latin American origin combining rhythm and blues, jazz, and rock

(334) *heavy metal*: energetic and highly amplified rock music with a hard beat

(334) *grunge rock*: type of alternative rock music characterized by more distortion and slower tempos; it often incorporates elements of punk rock and heavy metal

(334) *rap*: characterized by lyrics that are spoken rather than sung

(334) *nudist*: person who wears no clothes in groups and special places (nudist camps)

(334) *movie censor*: person who gives ratings to movies depending on their sexual content and amount of violence

(334) *boils down*: narrows down; simplifies

(335) *conscientious*: extremely careful and attentive to details

(335) *nit-picky*: overly critical

(335) *muddled*: unclear; confused

What is the role of language in thinking? Can animals be taught to use language?

Language—Don't Leave Home Without It: (pp. 336-340)

(336) *marksmanship*: the art of shooting

(336) *bartending*: serving drinks at a bar

(336) *prime beef*: top grade cattle meat ready for consumption

(336) *incursion*: a hostile entrance into a territory

(336) *Bill Cosby*: a popular black comedian and situational comedy star

(336) *a rash of*: a huge spreading or increasing of something

(336) *circumcised*: having the foreskin of the penis removed

(337) *sink or swim*: one either fails completely or succeeds in an attempt at doing something

(338) *gestural*: using motions of the hands or body as a means of expression

(338) *mime*: to imitate actions without using words

(338) *pantomime*: dramatic presentation that uses no words, only action and gestures

(338) *remnant*: something that was once used to aid human survival, that is still with us, but is now unnecessary

(338) *embody*: to represent something

(339) *sucker* ("that *sucker* I saw yesterday..."): used as a general term to refer to a person or object (slang)

(339) *belch*: burp

(339) *gimme*: give me

(339) *wet* (Washoe once *"wet" on...*): urinated

(339) *make monkeys out of*: make fools of

(340) *plagued*: bothered, caused difficulties

(340) *on par*: on an equal level

What do we know about problem solving?

Problem Solving—Getting an Answer in Sight: (pp. 341-345)

(341) *rote*: use of memory, usually with little intelligence

(343) *hourglass*: an instrument for measuring time consisting of a glass container having two sections, one above the other; sand, water, or mercury runs from the upper section to the lower in one hour

(343) *hung up*: delayed, detained by

(345) *ambiguity*: possibility of several interpretations

(345) *frivolous*: not important enough or worthy of receiving attention

(345) *taboos*: restrictions imposed by social custom

What is Artificial Intelligence?

Artificial Intelligence—I Compute, Therefore I am: (pp. 345-347)

(346) *novices*: beginners; amateurs

(346) *stymied*: confused

(347) *eclipsed*: reduced in importance or reputation

What is the nature of creative thinking?

Creative Thinking—Down Roads Less Traveled: (pp. 347-352)

- (348) *detour*: a longer way than the direct route or usual procedure

- (348) *harebrained scheme*: foolish idea

- (348) *stroke of genius*: clever idea

- (349) *martyr:* great or constant sufferer

- (350) *saturate*: to fill up as much as possible

- (350) *incubation*: period during which ideas are developed

- (350) *futile*: useless

- (350) *goldsmith*: a craftsman who works with gold

- (351) *eccentric*: odd; strange

- (351) *introverted*: being wholly concerned with and interested in one's own mental life

- (351) *neurotic:* emotionally unstable or troubled by anxiety

- (351) *cultivate*: to increase in size or number by tending to it

- (351) *outlandish*: very out of the ordinary, strange

- (352) *the jury is out*: a judgment hasn't been made yet

- (352) *Ozzy Osbourne*: a well-known rock star; recently the star of a popular television series along with his wife and two children

How accurate is intuition?

Logic and Intuition—Mental Shortcut? Or Dangerous Detour? (pp. 352-355)

- (352) *flawed*: containing defects or errors

- (353) *pitfall*: a hidden danger or difficulty

- (354) *award custody*: when parents divorce, a judge will decide with which parent the child or children shall live

- (354) *shortcuts*: methods of doing something more directly and more quickly than usual

- (354) *short-circuit*: an event that reduces the effectiveness of something (thinking) because parts of the process involved were not completed

What can be done to promote creativity?

Psychology in Action: Enhancing Creativity—Brainstorms: (pp. 356-359)

(356) ***got caught on***: got stuck on a problem

(358) ***analogies***: similarities

(358) ***brainstorms***: sudden bright ideas

(358) ***barred***: prevented

(358) ***defer***: put off; postpone

(358) ***run amok***: behave in a totally wild or undisciplined manner

(358) ***suspend***: postpone while waiting for further information

Solutions

RECITE AND REVIEW

What is the nature of thought?

1. mental; problem
2. internal
3. language

In what ways are images related to thinking?

1. created
2. sense
3. change; space
4. visual
5. actions; actions

How are concepts learned? Are there different kinds of concepts?

1. class
2. positive
3. concept
4. and; either-or
5. models
6. definition; personal
7. good-bad
8. all-or-nothing; social; groups

What is the role of language in thinking? Can animals be taught to use language?

1. symbols
2. meaning
3. sounds; meaningful
4. language; two-way
5. rules; order
6. rules
7. gestural
8. rearranged
9. operant
10. geometric

What do we know about problem solving?

1. rote; computer
2. rote; learned
3. general; solutions
4. narrow; ideal
5. solution; selective
6. selective
7. wrong
8. fixation; habits

What is Artificial Intelligence?

1. system; intelligence
2. computer
3. analysis
4. knowledge; processing

What is the nature of creative thinking?

1. Thinking
2. originality; finding
3. practical
4. fantasy; hero
5. creativity
6. preparation
7. steps
8. thinking; styles
9. creative
10. creative; mentally; mood

How accurate is intuition?

1. truth; conclusion
2. errors; true
3. fear; anxiety; thinking
4. probability
5. broad

What can be done to promote creativity?

1. creative
2. broadly; time; varied
3. separate

CONNECTIONS

What is the nature of thought? In what ways are images related to thinking? Pages 330-333

1. F.
2. D.
3. H.
4. A.
5. C.
6. G.
7. B.
8. E.

How are concepts learned? Are there different kinds of concepts? Pages 333-335

1. B.
2. D.
3. H.
4. C.
5. A.
6. G.
7. F.
8. E.

What is the role of language in thinking? Can animals be taught to use language? Pages 336-340

1. C.
2. H.
3. A.
4. E.
5. J.
6. B.
7. F.
8. G.
9. D.

What do we know about problem solving? What is Artificial Intelligence? Pages 341-347

1. G.
2. E.
3. A.
4. F.
5. H.
6. B.
7. J.
8. C.
9. I.
10. D.

What is the nature of creative thinking? How accurate is intuition? What can be done to promote creativity? Pages 347-359

1. H.
2. B.
3. J.
4. D.
5. C.
6. I.
7. K.
8. A.
9. E.

10. L.   11. F.   12. G.

CHECK YOUR MEMORY

What is the nature of thought? Pages 330-331

1. F   3. F
2. T   4. F

In what ways are images related to thinking? Pages 331-333

1. T   4. T   7. T
2. F   5. T   8. T
3. T   6. T   9. F

How are concepts learned? Are there different kinds of concepts? Pages 333-335

1. T   3. T   5. F
2. F   4. T   6. F

What is the role of language in thinking? Can animals be taught to use language? Pages 336-340

1. F   8. F   15. T
2. T   9. F   16. T
3. F   10. F   17. T
4. F   11. F
5. T   12. F
6. F   13. F
7. T   14. T

What do we know about problem solving? Pages 341-345

1. T   5. T   9. T
2. F   6. T   10. F
3. F   7. F
4. F   8. F

What is Artificial Intelligence? Pages 345-347

1. T   3. T   5. T
2. T   4. F   6. F

What is the nature of creative thinking? Pages 347-352

1. T

2. F	6. T	10. F
3. T	7. F	11. F
4. T	8. T	12. T
5. T	9. T	13. T

How accurate is intuition? Pages 352-355

1. T	4. F	7. F
2. T	5. T	8. T
3. F	6. F	9. F

What can be done to promote creativity? Pages 356-359

1. F	4. F	7. F
2. T	5. T	8. T
3. T	6. F	

FINAL SURVEY AND REVIEW

What is the nature of thought?

1. Cognition
2. representations
3. images; concepts; symbols

In what ways are images related to thinking?

1. information; stored
2. synesthesia
3. size; rotated
4. brain; visual; mental
5. implicit; micromovements

How are concepts learned? Are there different kinds of concepts?

1. generalized
2. negative; instances
3. rules
4. conjunctive; disjunctive; either-
5. prototypes
6. denotative; Connotative
7. semantic; strong-weak; active-passive
8. all-or-nothing; social stereotypes

What is the role of language in thinking? Can animals be taught to use language?

1. encoded
2. semantics
3. phonemes; morphemes
4. bilingualism; two-way bilingual
5. grammar; syntax
6. transformation
7. productive; American Sign
8. symbols
9. primates; reinforcers
10. lexigrams

What do we know about problem solving?

1. mechanically; mechanical
2. algorithm
3. understanding; functional
4. heuristics; identify; explore
5. insight; insight; selective encoding

6. old; culture 　　　　7. fixation 　　　　8. Functional; blocks; values

What is Artificial Intelligence?

1. artificial system; people
2. expert systems
3. means-ends
4. organized; strategies; automatic;

What is the nature of creative thinking?

1. inductive; logical
2. divergent; fluency; problem finding
3. original
4. conquering; martyr
5. Uses; divergent
6. incubation; illumination
7. incremental
8. personality; correlation
9. mood
10. mental; mood; manic

How accurate is intuition?

1. premises; reasoning
2. representative; heuristic
3. emotions; decision
4. base; rate
5. framing;

What can be done to promote creativity?

1. mental sets
2. incubation; input
3. Brainstorming

MASTERY TEST

What can be done to promote creativity?

1. B, p. 338
2. A, pp. 345-346
3. C, p. 354
4. B, pp. 330-331
5. A, p. 334
6. A, p. 342
7. D, p. 349
8. B, p. 334
9. A, pp. 343; 345
10. B, p. 341
11. C, p. 350
12. B, p. 349
13. C, p. 336
14. A, p. 331
15. D, p. 343
16. A, p. 351
17. B, p. 352
18. D, p. 336
19. C, p. 334
20. D, p. 347
21. A, p. 333
22. A, p. 340
23. C, p. 341
24. A, p. 358
25. B, p. 331
26. C, p. 334
27. B, p. 346
28. C, p. 359
29. B, pp. 337-338
30. C, p. 350
31. B, p. 342
32. B, p. 336
33. A, p. 341
34. C, p. 343
35. A, p. 352
36. B, p. 354
37. D, p. 353

Intelligence

Chapter Overview

Intelligence refers to a general capacity to act purposefully, think rationally, and deal effectively with the environment. In practice, intelligence is operationally defined by creating tests. Aptitude tests measure a narrower range of abilities than general intelligence tests do. To be of value, an intelligence test must be reliable, valid, objective, and standardized.

The first practical individual intelligence test was assembled by Alfred Binet. A modern version is the *Stanford-Binet Intelligence Scales*. A second major intelligence test is the *Wechsler Adult Intelligence Scale*. Group intelligence tests are also available. Intelligence is expressed as an intelligence quotient (IQ) or as a deviation IQ. The distribution of IQ scores approximates a normal curve. There are no overall differences between males and females in tested intelligence. However a difference does exist when intelligence tests are applied to different cultural groups. Children are taught skills and values based on their culture. Due to these differences, cultural-fair intelligence tests have been implemented.

People with IQs in the gifted or "genius" range tend to be superior in many respects. By criteria other than IQ, a large proportion of children might be considered gifted or talented in one way or another. The terms mentally retarded and developmentally disabled apply to persons with an IQ below 70 or who lack various adaptive behaviors. About 50 percent of the cases of mental retardation are organic; the remaining cases are of undetermined cause (many are thought to be familial).

Newer approaches relate intelligence to the speed with which information is processed in the nervous system. In addition, people who possess metacognitive skills tend to be superior at thinking and problem solving. As a result, they also tend to be more intelligent. Many psychologists now believe that several distinct types of intelligence exist.

Studies of animals and family relationships in humans demonstrate that intelligence reflects the combined effects of heredity and environment. Traditional IQ tests often suffer from a degree of cultural bias. For this and other reasons, it is wise to remember that IQ is merely an index of intelligence and that intelligence is narrowly defined by most tests.

Learning Objectives

1. Describe the savant syndrome.

2. Describe Binet's role in intelligence testing; give a general definition of intelligence; and explain what an operational definition of intelligence is.

3. Define the term *aptitude* and briefly describe the three levels of aptitude testing.

4. Define the terms *reliability*, *validity*, *objective test*, and *test standardization*, as they relate to testing.

5. Describe the five cognitive factors measured by the *Stanford-Binet Intelligence Scales, Fifth Edition* (SB5) and explain how these cognitive factors may be viewed differently in other cultures.

6. Define mental age and chronological age; use examples to show how they are used to compute an intelligence quotient (IQ); and differentiate between this IQ (MA/CA x 100) and deviation IQs.

7. Explain how age affects the stability of intelligence scores and how aging affects intelligence. Define the term *terminal decline*.

8. Regarding the types of intelligence tests: a. distinguish the Wechsler tests from the Stanford-Binet tests; and b. distinguish between group and individual intelligence tests.

9. Explain the pattern of distribution of IQ scores observed in the general population; describe sex differences in intelligence; and explain the relationship between intelligence, grades, and occupations.

10. Describe Terman's study of gifted children; list five popular misconceptions concerning genius and their corrections; explain how Terman's successful subjects differed from the less successful ones; describe how gifted children are identified; and briefly discuss the GATE programs.

11. List two possible explanations for the exceptional abilities of autistic savants; state the dividing line between normal intelligence and retardation (or developmental disability); and describe the degrees of retardation.

12. Differentiate between familial and organic retardation and describe each of the following organic conditions:

    a. PKU

    b. microcephaly

    c. hydrocephaly

    d. cretinism

    e. Down syndrome

    f. fragile-*X* syndrome

13. Describe the studies that provide evidence for the hereditary view of intelligence and for the environmental view of intelligence. Include a discussion of the maze-bright, maze-dull rat study, the twin studies, the adoption studies, Skeels' and Nisbett's research, and the research on the effects of training thinking skills.

14. Describe the following new approaches to intelligence:

    a. the neural basis for intelligence and how speed of processing and inspection time are related to it

    b. Perkins' cognitive approach

c. Gardner's multiple intelligences

The following objectives are related to the material in the "Psychology in Action" section of your text.

1. Explain how IQ tests may be unfair to certain groups, and describe the term *culture-fair test*.

2. State the arguments against Hernstein's and Murray's claim of IQ differences among races being due to genetic inheritance.

3. State the arguments against Hernstein's and Murray's claim of IQ differences among races being due to genetic inheritance.

RECITE AND REVIEW

How do psychologists define intelligence? What are the qualities of a good psychological test?

Defining Intelligence—Intelligence Is . . . You Know, It's . . . : Pages 363-365

1. The first practical _____ _____ was assembled in 1904, in Paris, by Alfred Binet.

2. Intelligence refers to one's general capacity to act purposefully, think _____ , and deal effectively with the _____ .

3. In practice, writing an intelligence test provides an operational _____ of intelligence.

4. General _____ is distinguished from specific talents called aptitudes.

5. Aptitude tests measure a _____ range of abilities than general intelligence tests do.

6. Special _____ tests and multiple _____ tests (such as the *Scholastic Assessment Test*) are used to assess a person's capacities for learning various abilities.

7. To be of any value, a psychological test must be reliable (give _____ results).

8. Three types of reliability are test-retest, _____ -half, and equivalent- _____ .

9. A worthwhile test must also have validity, meaning that it _____ what it claims to _____ . Validity is often measured by comparing test scores to actual performance at work or in school.

10. Widely used intelligence tests are objective (they give the same result when scored by _____ _____).

11. Intelligence tests are also standardized (the same procedures are always used in giving the test, and _____ , or average scores, have been established so that scores can be interpreted).

What are typical IQ tests like?

Testing Intelligence—The IQ and You: Pages 365-370

1. A modern version of Binet's test is the *Stanford-Binet* _____ , *Fifth Edition*.

2. The Stanford-Binet measures _____ reasoning, general knowledge, quantitative reasoning, visual-spatial processing, and working _____ .

3. Intelligence is expressed in terms of an intelligence _____ (IQ). IQ is defined as mental age (MA) divided by chronological age (CA) and then multiplied by _____ . Mental age is the intellectual capacity of a group of people at a certain age and chronological age is a person's actual age.

4. An "average" IQ of _____ occurs when mental age _____ chronological age.

5. Modern IQ tests no longer calculate _____ directly. Instead, the final score reported by the test is a deviation IQ, which gives a person's _____ intellectual standing in his or her age group.

6. A second major intelligence test is the *Wechsler* _____ *Intelligence Scale, Third Edition* (WAIS-III). The WAIS-III measures both verbal and performance (_____) intelligence.

7. Intelligence tests have also been produced for use with _____ of people. A _____ test of historical interest is the *Army Alpha*.

8. One limitation of traditional intelligence testing is its _____ to other cultural groups. Because children from various cultures are taught different skills, _____ intelligence tests have been implemented to accurately assess individuals' intellectual abilities and to reduce biases.

9. The *Scholastic Assessment Test* (SAT), the *American College Test* (ACT), and the *College Qualifications Test* (CQT) are _____ scholastic aptitude tests. Although narrower in scope than IQ tests, they bear some similarities to them.

How do IQ scores relate to gender, age, and occupation?

Variations in Intelligence—The Numbers Game: Pages 368-371

1. IQ scores become fairly _____ at about age 6, and they become increasingly reliable thereafter.

2. On the average, IQ scores continue to gradually _____ until middle age. Later intellectual declines are moderate for most people until their _____ .

3. Shortly before _____ , a more significant terminal decline (sudden drop) in intelligence is often observed.

4. When graphed, the distribution (percentage of people receiving each score) of IQ scores approximates a normal (_____ -shaped) _____ .

5. There are no overall differences between males and females in tested _____ .

6. However, very small _____ differences may result from the intellectual skills our culture encourages males and females to develop.

7. IQ is related to school _____ and job status. The second association may be somewhat artificial because educational credentials are required for entry into many _____ .

What does IQ tell us about genius?

The Mentally Gifted—Smart, Smarter, Smartest: Pages 371-373

1. People with IQs above 140 are considered to be in the _____ or "genius" range.

2. Studies done by Lewis Terman showed that the gifted tend to be _____ in many respects, such as achievement, physical appearance, and mental health.

3. The most successful gifted persons tend to be those who are persistent and _____ to learn and succeed.

4. By criteria other than _____ , a large proportion of children might be considered gifted or talented in one way or another.

5. Intellectually gifted children often have difficulties in average classrooms and benefit from special _____ and Talented Education (GATE) programs.

6. Autistic savants have exceptional abilities in music, mechanics, _____ , and remembering names or _____ .

What causes mental retardation?

Mental Retardation—A Difference That Makes a Difference: Pages 373-376

1. The terms mentally _____ and developmentally disabled are applied to those whose IQ falls below _____ or who lack various adaptive behaviors.

2. Further classifications of retardation are: _____ (50-55 to 70), moderate (35-40 to 50-55), _____ (20-25 to 35-40), and profound (below 20-25).

3. About _____ percent of the cases of mental retardation are organic, being caused by _____ injuries, fetal damage, metabolic disorders, or genetic abnormalities. The remaining cases are of undetermined cause.

4. Many cases of subnormal intelligence are thought to be the result of familial retardation (a low level of _____ stimulation in the home, poverty, and poor nutrition).

5. Three specialized forms of _____ retardation are phenylketonuria (PKU), microcephaly (small headedness), and hydrocephaly (excess cerebrospinal fluid).

6. Two additional sources of retardation are cretinism (insufficient thyroid _____), and Down syndrome (presence of an extra _____).

7. The second most common form of genetic mental retardation is fragile-X _____ , a problem related to an abnormal area on the _____ chromosome.

How do heredity and environment affect intelligence?

Heredity and Environment—Super Rats and Family Trees: Pages 376-379

1. Studies of eugenics (selective _____ for desirable characteristics) in animals suggest that intelligence is influenced by heredity.

2. Studies of family relationships in humans, especially comparisons between fraternal twins and identical twins (who have identical _____), also suggest that intelligence is partly _____ .

3. However, environment is also important, as revealed by changes in tested intelligence induced by _____ environments and improved education.

4. Early childhood education programs such as Head Start provide longer-term stimulating intellectual experiences for _____ children.

5. An overall average increase of 15 IQ points during the last 30 years has been attributed to _____ factors such as improved education, nutrition, and technology (e.g., complexity of the Internet and computer software)

6. _____ therefore reflects the combined effects of heredity and environment.

How have views of intelligence changed in recent years?

New Approaches to Intelligence—Intelligent Alternatives: Pages 379-381

1. To an extent, intelligence may represent the brain's _____ and efficiency, which is revealed by tasks that measure the _____ of processing.

2. How smart a person is probably depends on his or her neural intelligence, experiential intelligence (specialized _____ and skills), and reflective intelligence (the ability to become aware of one's own _____ patterns).

3. Metacognitive skills involve an ability to manage one's own _____ and problem solving efforts.

4. Howard Gardner believes that _____ IQ tests define intelligence too narrowly. According to Gardner, intelligence consists of abilities in language, logic and _____ , _____ and spatial thinking, music, kinesthetic skills, intrapersonal skills, interpersonal skills, and naturalist skills.

Psychology in Action: How Intelligent Are Intelligent Tests?
Pages 381-385

1. Traditional IQ tests often suffer from a degree of cultural _____ that makes them easier for some groups and harder for others.

2. To reduce the influence of verbal skills, cultural background, and _____ level when measuring the IQ of people from another culture (e.g., China) or from a different background (e.g., poor community), culture- _____ tests have been implemented.

3. Culture-fair tests try to measure intelligence in ways that are not strongly affected by _____ background, but no test is entirely _____ -free.

4. Differences in the average IQ scores for various racial groups are based on environmental differences, not _____ .

5. _____ is merely an index of intelligence based tests that offer a narrow definition of intelligence.

CONNECTIONS

How do psychologists define intelligence? What are the qualities of a good psychological test? Pages 363-365

1. _____ standardization
2. _____ Binet
3. _____ aptitude
4. _____ reliable
5. _____ valid
6. _____ norm

a. legitimate measure
b. average score
c. capacity to learn
d. objective comparison
e. first intelligence test
f. consistent measure

What are typical IQ tests like? How do IQ scores relate to gender, age, and occupation? Pages 365-371

1. _____ IQ
2. _____ normal curve
3. _____ deviation IQ
4. _____ average IQ
5. _____ group test
6. _____ WAIS
7. _____ verbal reasoning
8. _____ memory test
9. _____ performance test
10. _____ mentally retarded

a. relative standing
b. absurdities
c. Wechsler test
d. block design
e. *Army Alpha*
f. bell shape
g. digit span
h. MA/CA * 100
i. IQ of 70
j. IQ of 100

What does IQ tell us about genius? What causes mental retardation? Pages 371-376

1. _____ Termites
2. _____ PKU
3. _____ adaptive behaviors
4. _____ hydrocephaly
5. _____ microcephaly
6. _____ GATE
7. _____ cretinism
8. _____ Down syndrome

a. phenylalanine
b. old parents
c. small head
d. deficient thyroid
e. gifted children
f. fluid in brain
g. Javits Gifted and Talented Children
h. basic survival skills

How do heredity and environment affect intelligence? How have views of intelligence changed in recent years? Pages 376-385

1. _____ general ability
2. _____ maze-bright
3. _____ multiple intelligence
4. _____ fraternal twins
5. _____ identical twins
6. _____ Head Start
7. _____ speed of processing

a. early childhood education program
b. "people smart" and "nature smart"
c. based on inspection time
d. smart rat
e. one egg
f. two eggs
g. g-factor

CHECK YOUR MEMORY

How do psychologists define intelligence? What are the qualities of a good psychological test? Pages 363-365

1. The savant syndrome refers to a person of normal intelligence who has a highly developed, but specific, mental ability.

    TRUE or FALSE

2. Alfred Binet's first test was designed to measure mechanical aptitude.

    TRUE or FALSE

3. Most psychologists list abstract reasoning ability as an important element of intelligence.

    TRUE or FALSE

4. A test of clerical aptitude would measure your capacity for learning to do office work.

    TRUE or FALSE

5. The SAT is a special aptitude test.

    TRUE or FALSE

6. A test is valid if it gives the same score, or close to the same score, when given to the same person on two separate occasions.

    TRUE or FALSE

7. To check for split-half reliability you would compare scores on two different versions of a test.

    TRUE or FALSE

8. Criterion validity is shown by comparing scores on a test to actual performance in the "real world."

    TRUE or FALSE

9. If a test is objective, then by definition it is fair.

    TRUE or FALSE

10. Standardizing a test helps ensure that it is the same for everyone who takes it.

    TRUE or FALSE

What are typical IQ tests like? Pages 365-370

1. Lewis Terman helped write the original Stanford-Binet intelligence test.

    TRUE or FALSE

2. The Stanford-Binet intelligence test measures three intelligence factors: knowledge, quantitative reasoning, and visual-spatial processing.

   TRUE or FALSE

3. The Stanford-Binet intelligence test does include a memory task (repeating a series of digits) to determine a person's ability to use his/her short-term memory.

   TRUE or FALSE

4. Mental age refers to average mental ability for a person of a given age.

   TRUE or FALSE

5. Mental age can't be higher than chronological age.

   TRUE or FALSE

6. IQ is equal to MA times CA divided by 100.

   TRUE or FALSE

7. An IQ will be greater than 100 when CA is larger than MA.

   TRUE or FALSE

8. Average intelligence is defined as an IQ from 90 to 109.

   TRUE or FALSE

9. Modern IQ tests give scores as deviation IQs.

   TRUE or FALSE

10. Being placed in the 84th percentile means that 16 percent of your peers received IQ scores higher than you and 84 percent have IQ scores lower than you.

    TRUE or FALSE

11. An advantage of the Stanford-Binet intelligence test is that it can be applied cross-culturally.

    TRUE or FALSE

12. The WISC is designed to test adult performance intelligence.

    TRUE or FALSE

13. The digit symbol task is considered a performance subtest of the WAIS.

    TRUE or FALSE

14. The Stanford-Binet, Wechsler's, and *Army Alpha* are all group intelligence tests.

    TRUE or FALSE

How do IQ scores relate to gender, age, and occupation? Pages 368-371

1. The correlation between IQ scores obtained at ages 2 and 18 is 3.1.

   TRUE or FALSE

2. On the average, changes in IQ are small after middle childhood.

   TRUE or FALSE

3. In a normal curve, a majority of scores are found near the average.

   TRUE or FALSE

4. An IQ above 130 is described as "bright normal."

   TRUE or FALSE

5. The correlation between IQ scores and school grades is .5.

   TRUE or FALSE

6. High IQ scores are strongly correlated with creativity.

   TRUE or FALSE

What does IQ tell us about genius? Pages 371-373

1. Only 12 people out of 100 score above 130 on IQ tests.

   TRUE or FALSE

2. Gifted children tend to get average IQ scores by the time they reach adulthood.

   TRUE or FALSE

3. Gifted persons are more susceptible to mental illness.

   TRUE or FALSE

4. Gifted persons are more likely to succeed in adulthood if they have a high degree of intellectual determination.

   TRUE or FALSE

5. Talking in complete sentences at age 2 is regarded as a sign of giftedness.

   TRUE or FALSE

6. Gifted children tend to become bored in classes designed for children of average abilities.

   TRUE or FALSE

7. The performances of many autistic savants appear to result from intense practice.

   TRUE or FALSE

8. Autistic savants who have unusual drawing abilities usually are also very advanced in the use of language.

TRUE or FALSE

What causes mental retardation? Pages 373-376

1. A person must have an IQ of 80 or below to be classified as mentally retarded.

TRUE or FALSE

2. The moderately retarded can usually learn routine self-help skills.

TRUE or FALSE

3. The borderline retarded are capable of living alone.

TRUE or FALSE

4. Familial retardation is a genetic condition that runs in families.

TRUE or FALSE

5. Mental retardation caused by birth injuries is categorized as an organic problem.

TRUE or FALSE

6. Phenylalanine is found in the artificial sweetener Aspartame.

TRUE or FALSE

7. Hydrocephaly cannot be treated.

TRUE or FALSE

8. Iodized salt has helped prevent cretinism.

TRUE or FALSE

9. The risk of having a Down syndrome child increases as the mother gets older, but is unaffected by the father's age.

TRUE or FALSE

10. Fragile-X males tend to be severely retarded as children but only mildly retarded during adulthood.

TRUE or FALSE

How do heredity and environment affect intelligence? Pages 376-379

1. The correlation between the IQs of unrelated people reared apart is 0.0.

TRUE or FALSE

2. The IQs of fraternal twins reared together are more similar than those of other siblings.

    TRUE or FALSE

3. The IQs of identical twins are more alike than those of fraternal twins.

    TRUE or FALSE

4. Adult intelligence is approximately 50 percent hereditary.

    TRUE or FALSE

5. The environmental influence on twins does include development inside their mother's womb before birth.

    TRUE or FALSE

6. Children adopted into higher status homes tend, on average, to have higher adult IQs.

    TRUE or FALSE

7. The increased complexity and use of video games, the Internet, and television programs have lowered the IQ score by 15 points over the last 30 years.

    TRUE or FALSE

8. IQ scores tend to rise the longer people stay in school.

    TRUE or FALSE

How have views of intelligence changed in recent years? Pages 379-385

1. The speed with which information is processed has been used as a measure of the speed and efficiency of the brain.

    TRUE or FALSE

2. Longer inspection times have been shown to correspond with higher intelligence.

    TRUE or FALSE

3. Experiential intelligence is a relatively fixed element of overall intelligence.

    TRUE or FALSE

4. Metacognitive skills are a major part of what is meant by reflective intelligence.

    TRUE or FALSE

5. Howard Gardner's theory of multiple intelligences states that traditional measures of language, logic, and math skills have little to do with intelligence.

    TRUE or FALSE

6. Gardner suggests that each of us has eight different types of intelligence such as being "people smart," "word smart," etc.

   TRUE or FALSE

7. Gardner is currently gathering evidence concerning a ninth intellectual capacity he calls existential intelligence.

   TRUE or FALSE

8. The g-factor is regarded by some psychologists as a sign that "general intelligence" underlies many different measures of intelligence.

   TRUE or FALSE

9. The Dove Test was designed to be culturally biased.

   TRUE or FALSE

10. The Stanford-Binet, Wechsler's, and the SAT are all culture-fair tests.

    TRUE or FALSE

11. Herrnstein and Murray, in their book, *The Bell Curve*, suggested that racial group differences in IQ were due to environmental influences, not genes.

    TRUE or FALSE

12. The book, *The Bell Curve* states that, as a group, African Americans score below average on IQ tests because they are more likely to attend poor-quality schools.

    TRUE or FALSE

13. The small difference in average IQ scores for African Americans and Anglo Americans is explained by cultural and environmental differences.

    TRUE or FALSE

14. IQ scores predict later career success.

    TRUE or FALSE

15. Standardized testing is used primarily to select people for school and employment.

    TRUE or FALSE

16. Changing intelligence tests would result in a change in the IQ scores of people taking the tests.

    TRUE or FALSE

FINAL SURVEY AND REVIEW

How do psychologists define intelligence? What are the qualities of a good psychological test?

Defining Intelligence—Intelligence Is . . . You Know, It's . . . : Pages 363-365

1. Intelligence refers to one's general capacity to act _____ , _____ rationally, and deal effectively with the environment.

2. In practice, writing an intelligence test provides an _____ definition of intelligence.

3. General intelligence is distinguished from specific talents called _____ .

4. _____ tests measure a narrower range of abilities than general intelligence tests do.

5. _____ aptitude tests and _____ aptitude tests (such as the *Scholastic Assessment Test*) are used to assess a person's capacities for _____ various abilities.

6. To be of any value, a psychological test must be _____ (give consistent results).

7. Three types of reliability are _____ , split-half, and _____ -forms.

8. A worthwhile test must also have _____ , meaning that it measures what it claims to measure. _____ is often measured by comparing test scores to actual _____ at work or in school.

9. Widely used intelligence tests are _____ (they give the same result when scored by different people).

10. Intelligence tests are also _____ (the same procedures are always used in giving the test, and norms, or average scores, have been established so that _____ can be interpreted).

What are typical IQ tests like?

Testing Intelligence—The IQ and You: Pages 365-370

1. The first practical intelligence test was assembled in 1904, in Paris, by _____ _____ .

2. A modern version of Binet's test is the _____ *Intelligence* _____ *Scales, Fifth Edition.*

3. The Stanford-Binet measures fluid reasoning, general knowledge, _____ reasoning, _____ -spatial processing, and working memory.

4. Intelligence is expressed in terms of an intelligence quotient (IQ). IQ is defined as _____ _____ (MA) divided by _____ _____ (CA) and then multiplied by 100. Mental age is the _____ capacity of a group of people at a certain age and chronological age is a person's actual age in years.

5. An "average" IQ of 100 occurs when _____ age equals _____ age.

6. Modern IQ tests no longer calculate IQs directly. Instead, the final score reported by the test is a _____ _____ , which gives a person's relative intellectual standing in his or her age group.

7. A second major intelligence test is the _____ *Adult Intelligence Scale, Third Edition* (WAIS-III). The WAIS-III measures both _____ and performance (nonverbal) intelligence.

8. Intelligence tests have also been produced for use with groups of people. A group test of historical interest is the _____ _____ .

9. One limitation of traditional intelligence testing is its applicability to various _____ groups. Because children from various cultures are taught different skills, _____ intelligence tests have been implemented to accurately assess individuals' intellectual abilities and to reduce biases.

10. The *Scholastic Assessment Test* (SAT), the *American College Test* (ACT), and the *College Qualifications Test* (CQT) are group _____ _____ tests. Although narrower in scope than IQ tests, they bear some similarities to them.

How do IQ scores relate to gender, age, and occupation?

Variations in Intelligence—The Numbers Game: Pages 368-371

1. IQ scores become fairly stable at about age _____ , and they become increasingly _____ thereafter.

2. On the average, IQ scores continue to gradually increase until middle age. Later intellectual _____ are moderate for most people until their 70s.

3. Shortly before death, a more significant _____ _____ (sudden drop) in intelligence is often observed.

4. When graphed, the _____ (percentage of people receiving each score) of IQ scores approximates a _____ (bell-shaped) curve.

5. There are no overall _____ between males and females in tested intelligence.

6. However, very small gender differences may result from the intellectual skills our _____ encourages males and females to develop.

7. IQ is related to school grades and _____ _____ . The second association may be somewhat artificial because _____ credentials are required for entry into many occupations.

What does IQ tell us about genius?

The Mentally Gifted—Smart, Smarter, Smartest: Pages 371-373

1. People with IQs above _____ are considered to be in the gifted or "genius" range.

2. Studies done by Lewis _____ showed that the _____ tend to be superior in many respects, such as achievement, physical appearance, and mental health.

3. The most _____ gifted persons tend to be those who are persistent and motivated to learn and succeed.

4. By criteria other than IQ, a large proportion of children might be considered _____ or _____ in one way or another.

5. Intellectually gifted children often have difficulties in average classrooms and benefit from special Gifted and Talented _____ (GATE) programs.

6. Autistic _____ have exceptional abilities in music, mechanics, math, and remembering names or numbers.

What causes mental retardation?

Mental Retardation—A Difference That Makes a Difference: Pages 373-376

1. The terms mentally retarded and _____ disabled are applied to those whose IQ falls below 70 or who lack various adaptive behaviors.

2. Further classifications of retardation are: mild (50-55 to 70), _____ (35-40 to 50-55), severe (20-25 to 35-40), and _____ (below 20-25).

3. About 50 percent of the cases of mental retardation are _____ , being caused by birth injuries, fetal damage, metabolic disorders, or _____ abnormalities. The remaining cases are of undetermined cause.

4. Many cases of subnormal intelligence are thought to be the result of _____ retardation (a low level of intellectual stimulation in the home, poverty, and poor nutrition).

5. Three specialized forms of organic retardation are _____ (PKU), _____ (small headedness), and hydrocephaly (excess cerebrospinal fluid).

6. Two additional sources of retardation are _____ (insufficient thyroid hormone), and _____ syndrome (presence of an extra chromosome).

7. The second most common form of genetic mental retardation is _____ syndrome, a problem related to an abnormal area on the X or female _____ .

How do heredity and environment affect intelligence?

Heredity and Environment—Super Rats and Family Trees: Pages 376-379

1. Studies of _____ (selective breeding for desirable characteristics) in animals suggest that intelligence is influenced by heredity.

2. Studies of family relationships in humans, especially comparisons between _____ twins and _____ twins, also suggest that intelligence is partly hereditary.

3. However, _____ is also important, as revealed by changes in tested intelligence induced by stimulating _____ and improved education.

4. Early childhood _____ programs such as Head Start provide longer-term stimulating intellectual experiences for disadvantaged children.

5. An overall average increase of 15 IQ points during the last 30 years has been attributed to _____ factors such as improved education, nutrition, and _____ (e.g., the complexity of the Internet and computer software)

6. Intelligence therefore reflects the combined effects of _____ and _____ .

How have views of intelligence changed in recent years?

New Approaches to Intelligence—Intelligent Alternatives: Pages 379-381

1. To an extent, intelligence may represent the _____ speed and efficiency, which is revealed by tasks that measure the speed of _____ .

2. How smart a person is probably depends on his or her _____ intelligence, experiential intelligence (specialized knowledge and skills), and reflective intelligence (the ability to become aware of one's own thinking patterns).

3. _____ skills involve an ability to manage one's own thinking and problem solving efforts.

4. Howard _____ believes that traditional IQ tests define intelligence too narrowly. According to Gardner, intelligence consists of abilities in _____ , logic and math, visual and spatial thinking, _____ , kinesthetic skills, intrapersonal skills, interpersonal skills, and naturalist skills.

Psychology in Action: How Intelligent Are Intelligent Tests: Pages 381-385

1. Traditional IQ tests often suffer from a degree of _____ bias that makes them easier for some groups and harder for others.

2. _____ tests try to measure intelligence in ways that are not strongly affected by cultural background, but no test is entirely culture-free.

3. Differences in the average IQ scores for various racial groups are based on _____ differences, not heredity.

4. IQ is merely an _____ of intelligence based tests that offer a narrow definition of intelligence.

MASTERY TEST

1. The largest number of people are found in which IQ range?
   a. 80-89
   b. 90-109
   c. 110-119
   d. below 70

2. Questions that involve copying geometric shapes would be found in which ability area of the SB5?
   a. fluid reasoning
   b. quantitative reasoning
   c. visual-spatial processing
   d. working memory

3. The *Scholastic Assessment Test* is really a
   a. special aptitude test
   b. multiple aptitude test
   c. general intelligence test
   d. test of performance intelligence

4. It is unlikely that a developmentally disabled person would benefit from
   a. a sheltered workshop
   b. supervised education
   c. a GATE program
   d. learning self-help skills

5. Which of the following is NOT a group test?
   a. SAT
   b. ACT
   c. WAIS
   d. *Army Alpha*

6. On the average, the smallest changes in IQ would be expected between the ages of
   a. 2 and 10
   b. 10 and 15
   c. 2 and 18
   d. 30 and 40

7. A combination of high ability and general retardation is found in
   a. autistic savants
   b. Down syndrome
   c. the adapted developmentally disabled
   d. maze-bright retardation

8. The distribution of IQ scores closely matches
    a. an inverted U curve
    b. a normal curve
    c. a g-factor curve
    d. Bell's percentiles

9. Which of the following is fixed at birth?
    a. IQ
    b. genes
    c. giftedness
    d. MA

10. Speed of neural processing has been measured by using a/an _____ task.
    a. inspection time
    b. reflective
    c. metacognitive
    d. g-factor

11. Separate collections of verbal and performance subtests are a feature of the
    a. WAIS
    b. *Dove Test*
    c. CQT
    d. SAT

12. Fourteen nations have shown large average IQ gains in a single generation. These findings support the idea that intelligence is influenced by
    a. eugenics
    b. environment
    c. genetics
    d. the hereditary g-factor

13. Mental retardation is formally defined by deficiencies in
    a. aptitudes and self-help skills
    b. intelligence and scholastic aptitudes
    c. language and spatial thinking
    d. IQ and adaptive behaviors

14. A 12-year-old child, with an IQ of 100, must have an MA of
    a. 100
    b. 12
    c. 10
    d. 15

15. The *Stanford-Binet Intelligence Scale* was based on the work of Binet and
    a. Terman
    b. Wechsler
    c. Gardner
    d. Feuerstein

16. A test deliberately written to be culturally biased is the
    a. WAIS
    b. SB5
    c. Dove Test
    d. SOMPA test battery

17. A person's relative intellectual standing in his or her age group is revealed by
    a. the age quotient
    b. the digit symbol index
    c. chronological age
    d. deviation IQ

18. The age of parents may affect the risks of having a child suffering from
    a. familial retardation
    b. phenylketonuria
    c. Down syndrome
    d. the savant syndrome

19. Traditional intelligence tests are especially good at predicting
    a. career success
    b. performance in school
    c. creative achievement
    d. which children will benefit from eugenic programs

20. The validity of a test could be assessed by comparing
    a. scores earned on one occasion to scores earned on another
    b. scores based on the first half of the test to scores based on the second half
    c. scores on two equivalent forms of the test
    d. scores on the test to an external criterion of performance

21. Creating an intelligence test provides a/an _____ definition of intelligence.
    a. valid
    b. reliable
    c. operational
    d. chronological

22. For large groups, the greatest similarity in IQs would be expected between
    a. identical twins
    b. fraternal twins
    c. siblings reared together
    d. parents and their children

23. Both the *Scholastic Assessment Test* and the *Law School Admissions Test* are
    a. tests of general intelligence
    b. standardized aptitude tests
    c. culture-fair tests of verbal comprehension
    d. objective performance tests

24. An intelligence test specifically designed for use with children is the
    a. WAIS-C
    b. Dove Test
    c. WISC-III
    d. *Savant Developmental Scale*

25. Which statement about gifted persons is TRUE?
    a. They tend to be shy and socially withdrawn.
    b. They tend to be smaller and weaker than average.
    c. They have above average mental health records.
    d. They must score above 160 on IQ tests to be considered gifted.

26. Instrumental Enrichment is to _____ as eugenics is to _____.
    a. environment, genetics
    b. genetics, selective breeding
    c. culture fairness, genetics
    d. intelligence, culture

27. A type of retardation that appears to be based largely on the effects of poor environment is
    a. Down syndrome
    b. microcephaly
    c. PKU
    d. familial retardation

28. The idea that children can be gifted in ways other than having a high IQ is in agreement with
    a. Feuerstein's Instrumental Enrichment program
    b. Dove's Counterbalance model of intelligence
    c. Gardner's eight intelligences
    d. Hernstein and Murray's bell curve model

29. Culture-fair tests attempt to measure intelligence without being affected by a person's
    a. verbal skills
    b. cultural background
    c. educational level
    d. all the preceding

30. Which of the five Stanford-Binet Intelligence Scales measures how well people can imagine and correctly determine their location by following written instructions?
    a. fluid reasoning
    b. visual-spatial processing
    c. knowledge
    d. working memory

31. Winnie took an IQ test and she is ranked in the 97th percentile. Without knowing her actual IQ score, you can assume that
    a. she is smarter than 97 percent of the people who took the test
    b. she and 97 percent of the others who took the test have the same IQ scores
    c. she is smarter than 3 percent of the people who took the test
    d. 97 percent of the people who took the test are smarter than Winnie

32. The argument that people from different regions and cultures are taught to understand the world differently by using different kinds of knowledge and mental abilities suggests that a _____ is necessary to measure intelligence accurately.
    a. Stanford-Binet Intelligence Scale
    b. culture-fair test
    c. SAT
    d. WAIS

33. An average increase of 15 IQ points during the last 30 years has been attributed to
    a. an increase in the complexity of the Internet and computer software
    b. people working harder and playing less
    c. an increase in intelligent people having more children
    d. none of the above

LANGUAGE DEVELOPMENT - Intelligence

Word roots

The Latin word *norma* was the name given to a carpenter's square. This term contributed to several English words that refer to something being standard or typical. Examples used in this text include: norm, normal, normality, abnormal, and abnormality.

How do psychologists define intelligence? What are the qualities of a good psychological test?

Preview: What Day Is It? (p. 363)

> (363) *island of brilliance. . . in a sea of retardation*: displaying an extraordinary talent or skill while other mental capabilities are developmentally retarded

> (363) *wheel of fortune* (Is intelligence determined by the genetic "*wheel of fortune*"...?): the wheel of fortune is a large wheel which is spun and prizes are won depending on where the wheel stops spinning; thus the author is referring to the theory that the genes inherited from one's parents determine one's intelligence

Defining Intelligence—Intelligence Is…You Know, It's…(pp. 363-365)

> (363) *genius*: an exceptionally intelligent person

> (363) *a flash of brilliance*: an insightful moment

> (363) *heated debate*: intense discussion and sometimes disagreement

> (364) *clerical work*: work as a secretary, data clerk, or other similar jobs

> (364) *deranged*: insane

> (365) *testy*: irritable

What are typical IQ tests like?

Testing Intelligence—The IQ and You (p. 365-370)

> (365) *Stanford University*: a highly-respected university in California

> (368) *innate intelligence*: intelligence one is born with

> (368) *rote*: memorization

> (369) *foreshadowed*: having shown or predicted an incident before it occurs

> (369) *military inductees*: persons drafted or who enlisted in the armed forces

How do IQ scores relate to gender, age, and occupation?

Variations in Intelligence—The Numbers Game (pp. 368-371)

> (371) *real-world success*: success in the world outside of the school environment; practical success

What does IQ tell us about genius?

The Mentally Gifted—Smart, Smarter, Smartest (pp. 371-373)

(371) ***Early ripe means later rot; the gifted tend to fizzle out as adults***: a fruit or plant that matures earlier will rot earlier; in the same way, the misconception is that the gifted will mature early but later lose their special abilities

(371) ***eggheads***: slang for intellectuals, or very intelligent people

(371) ***nerds***: slang, derogatory word for intellectual people

(372) ***persevere***: persist in spite of opposition

(372) ***blossom***: come forth; to develop

(372) ***precocious***: developed earlier than normal

(372) ***shortchange***: cheat

(372) ***show-off***: one who thinks that he or she knows all the answers

(372) ***smart aleck***: one who wants to be the center of attention

What causes mental retardation?

Mental Retardation—A Difference That Makes a Difference (pp. 373-376)

(373) ***prodigious***: extraordinary

(373) ***harbors embers of mental brilliance that intense practice could fan into full flame***: we each may have unrealized potential that could be turned into major ability if we worked at it

(374) ***institutions***: secure, hospital-like settings for persons with profound mental retardation or very severe mental illness

(374) ***PCBs***: polychlorinated biphenyls, often found in soil and are suspected cancer-causing agents

(375) ***color blindness***: the inability to distinguish colors; the world is seen in shades of grey

How do heredity and environment affect intelligence?

Heredity and Environment—Super Rats and Family Trees (pp. 376-379)

(376) ***rat chow***: rat food

(376) ***siblings***: brothers and sisters

(377) ***inflate***: artificially increase

(377) ***orphanage***: a state-operated house where children without parents or relatives to take care of them live until they are adopted

(378) ***both camps***: groups on either side of the issue

How have views of intelligence changed in recent years?

New Approaches to Intelligence—Intelligent Alternatives (pp. 379-381)

(379) *flurry*: a quick movement

(379) *swift*: quick thinking

(379) *brainy*: slang term for smart

(380) *reflective*: able to think in depth about something

(380) *intricate*: complicated

(380) *forge*: form, bring into being

(380) *medicine man*: healer and spiritual leader in Native American, Central and South American tribal groups; shaman

(380) *organic farmer*: farmer who doesn't use chemical pesticides or fertilizers

(381) *cultivate*: to encourage

Psychology in Action: How Intelligent Are Intelligence Tests? (p. 381-385)

(383) *inflammatory claim*: a statement that intends to produce strong feelings

(384) *arbitrary*: based on individual preference or convenience

(384) *overhaul*: to completely rework, redesign

(384) *two-edged sword*: can be used in more than one way; can have both positive and negative results

Solutions

RECITE AND REVIEW

How do psychologists define intelligence? What are the qualities of a good psychological test?

1. intelligence; test
2. rationally; environment
3. definition
4. intelligence
5. narrower
6. aptitude; aptitude
7. consistent
8. split; forms
9. measures; measure
10. different; people
11. norms

What are typical IQ tests like?

1. *Intelligence Scales*
2. fluid; memory
3. quotient; 100
4. 100; equals
5. IQs; relative
6. *Adult*nonverbal
7. groups; group
8. applicability; cultural-fair
9. group

How do IQ scores relate to gender, age, and occupation?

1. stable
2. increase; 70s
3. death
4. bell; curve
5. intelligence
6. gender
7. grades; occupations

What does IQ tell us about genius?

1. gifted
2. superior
3. motivated
4. IQ
5. Gifted
6. math; numbers

What causes mental retardation?

1. retarded; 70
2. mild; severe
3. 50; birth
4. intellectual
5. organic
6. hormone; chromosome
7. syndrome; X or female

How do heredity and environment affect intelligence?

1. breeding
2. genes; hereditary
3. stimulating
4. disadvantaged
5. environmental
6. Intelligence

How have views of intelligence changed in recent years?

1. speed; speed

2. knowledge; thinking   3. thinking   4. traditional; math; visual

Psychology in Action: How Intelligent Are Intelligent Tests? Pages 381-385

1. bias
2. educational; fair
3. cultural; culture
4. genetics (or heredity)
5. IQ

CONNECTIONS

How do psychologists define intelligence? What are the qualities of a good psychological test? Pages 363-365

1. D.
2. E.
3. C.
4. F.
5. A.
6. B.

What are typical IQ tests like? How do IQ scores relate to gender, age, and occupation? Pages 365-371

1. H.
2. F.
3. A.
4. J.
5. E.
6. C.
7. B.
8. G.
9. D.
10. I.

What does IQ tell us about genius? What causes mental retardation? Pages 371-376

1. E.
2. A.
3. H.
4. F.
5. C.
6. G.
7. D.
8. B.

How do heredity and environment affect intelligence? How have views of intelligence changed in recent years? Pages 376-385

1. G.
2. D.
3. B.
4. F.
5. E.
6. A.
7. C.

CHECK YOUR MEMORY

How do psychologists define intelligence? What are the qualities of a good psychological test? Pages 363-365

1. F
2. F
3. T

4.	T	7.	F	10.	T
5.	F	8.	T		
6.	F	9.	F		

What are typical IQ tests like? Pages 365-370

1.	T	7.	F	13.	T
2.	F	8.	T	14.	F
3.	T	9.	T		
4.	T	10.	T		
5.	F	11.	F		
6.	F	12.	F		

How do IQ scores relate to gender, age, and occupation? Pages 368-371

1.	F	3.	T	5.	T
2.	T	4.	F	6.	F

What does IQ tell us about genius? Pages 371-373

1.	F	4.	T	7.	T
2.	F	5.	T	8.	F
3.	F	6.	T		

What causes mental retardation? Pages 373-376

1.	F	5.	T	9.	F
2.	T	6.	T	10.	F
3.	T	7.	F		
4.	F	8.	T		

How do heredity and environment affect intelligence? Pages 376-379

1.	T	4.	T	7.	F
2.	T	5.	T	8.	T
3.	T	6.	T		

How have views of intelligence changed in recent years? Pages 379-385

1.	T	7.	T	13.	T
2.	F	8.	T	14.	F
3.	F	9.	T	15.	T
4.	T	10.	F	16.	T
5.	F	11.	F		
6.	F	12.	F		

FINAL SURVEY AND REVIEW

How do psychologists define intelligence? What are the qualities of a good psychological test?

1. purposefully; think
2. operational
3. aptitudes
4. Aptitude

5. Special; multiple; learning
6. reliable
7. test-retest; equivalent
8. validity; Validity; performance

9. objective
10. standardized; scores

What are typical IQ tests like?

1. Alfred; Binet
2. *Stanford-Binet*;
3. quantitative; visual

4. mental; age; chronological; age; intellectual
5. mental; chronological
6. deviation; IQ

7. *Wechsler*verbal
8. *Army*; *Alpha*
9. cultural; culture-fair
10. scholastic; aptitude

How do IQ scores relate to gender, age, and occupation?

1. 6; reliable
2. declines
3. terminal; decline

4. distribution; normal
5. differences
6. culture

7. job; status; educational

What does IQ tell us about genius?

1. 140
2. Terman; gifted

3. successful
4. gifted; talented

5. Education
6. savants

What causes mental retardation?

1. developmentally
2. moderate; profound
3. organic; genetic

4. familial
5. phenylketonuria; microcephaly
6. cretinism; Down

7. fragile-X; chromosome

How do heredity and environment affect intelligence?

1. eugenics
2. fraternal; identical

3. environment; environments
4. education

5. environmental; technology
6. heredity; environment

How have views of intelligence changed in recent years?

1. brain's; processing

2. neural   3. Metacognitive   4. Gardner; language; music

Psychology in Action: How Intelligent Are Intelligent Tests: Pages 381-385

1. cultural
2. Culture-fair
3. environmental
4. index

MASTERY TEST

Psychology in Action: How Intelligent Are Intelligent Tests: Pages 381-385

1. B, p. 370
2. C, p. 366
3. B, p. 370
4. C, p. 372
5. C, p. 369
6. D, pp. 368-369
7. A, p. 373
8. B, p. 370
9. B, p. 378
10. A, p. 379
11. A, p. 369

12. B, p. 377
13. D, p. 373
14. B, p. 367
15. A, p. 365
16. C, p. 382
17. D, p. 368
18. C, p. 375
19. B, pp. 371; 384
20. D, p. 365
21. C, p. 364
22. A, p. 376

23. B, p. 384
24. C, p. 369
25. C, p. 371
26. A, pp. 376-377
27. D, p. 374
28. C, p. 380
29. D, p. 383
30. B, p. 366
31. A, p. 368
32. B, p. 383
33. A, pp. 377-378

Motivation and Emotion

Chapter Overview

Motivation typically involves needs, drives, goals, and goal attainment. Three types of motives are primary motives, stimulus motives, and secondary motives. Most primary motives maintain homeostasis.

Hunger is influenced by the stomach, blood sugar levels, metabolism in the liver, fat stores in the body, activity in the hypothalamus, diet, and other factors. Body Mass Index (BMI) measures one's body fat. A BMI value of 25 or more should be a cause for concern since obesity has been linked to heart disease, high blood pressure, stroke, diabetes, and premature death. External cues within our environment have increased the obesity problem and frequency of eating disorders in America. Anorexia and bulimia are serious and sometimes fatal problems. Behavioral dieting uses self-control techniques to change basic eating patterns and habits.

Thirst and other basic motives are affected by many factors, but they are primarily controlled by the hypothalamus. Pain avoidance is episodic and partially learned. The sex drive is non-homeostatic. To some extent, it is influenced by hormone levels in the body.

The stimulus motives include drives for information, exploration, manipulation, and sensory input. Drives for stimulation are partially explained by arousal theory. The desired level of arousal or stimulation is measured by the Sensation-Seeking Scale and those scoring high on the Sensation-Seeking Scale tend to engage in high-risk behaviors. Optimal performance on a task usually occurs at moderate levels of arousal. Test anxiety is caused by a mixture of excessive worrying and heightened physiological arousal, which can be reduced through preparation, relaxation, rehearsal, and restructuring thoughts.

Circadian rhythms are closely tied to sleep, activity, and energy cycles, which impact our daily performance. Time changes in our schedule can increase errors in our performance as our circadian rhythms adjust to the new time change. Melatonin, a hormone secreted by the pineal gland, can ease the adjustment of jet lag.

Social motives, which are learned, account for much of the diversity of human motivation. The need for achievement is a social motive correlated with success in many situations. Self-confidence also affects motivation by influencing the types of challenges that one takes.

Maslow's hierarchy of motives categorizes needs as basic or growth oriented. Self-actualization, the highest and most fragile need, is reflected in meta-needs. In many situations, extrinsic motivation can lower intrinsic motivation, enjoyment, and creativity.

Emotions are linked to basic adaptive behaviors. Other major elements of emotion are bodily changes, emotional expressions, and emotional feelings. Physiological changes during emotion are caused by adrenaline and the autonomic nervous system (ANS). The sympathetic branch of the ANS arouses the body and the parasympathetic branch quiets it. A polygraph measures a person's general emotional arousal through changes in heart rate, blood pressure, breathing, and galvanic skin response.

Basic emotional expressions are unlearned. Facial expressions are central to emotion. Body gestures and movements (body language) also express feelings. A variety of theories and hypotheses have been proposed to explain emotion: the James-Lange theory, the Cannon-Bard theory, Schachter's Cognitive Theory of Emotion, attribution theory, and the facial feedback hypothesis.

Emotional intelligence involves a combination of skills, such as self-awareness, empathy, self-control, and an understanding of how to use emotions. For success in many situations, emotional intelligence is as important as IQ. Martin Seligman proposed that genuinely happy people are people who have cultivated their natural strengths into their lives to help to buffer against misfortunes.

Learning Objectives

1. Define *motivation*.

2. Describe a motivational sequence using the need reduction model; explain how the incentive value of a goal can affect motivation; and describe how incentive value is related to internal need.

3. List and describe the three types of motives and give an example of each.

4. Define *homeostasis*.

5. Discuss why hunger cannot be fully explained by the contractions of an empty stomach and describe the relationship of each of the following to hunger:

    a. blood sugar

    b. liver

    c. hypothalamus:

        i)   feeding system (lateral hypothalamus)
        ii) satiety system (ventromedial hypothalamus)
        iii) blood sugar regulator (paraventricular nucleus)

    d. GLP-1

6. Explain how each of the following is related to overeating and obesity and include a brief discussion of body mass index and explain how it is calculated:

    a. a person's set point

    b. the release of leptin

    c. external eating cues

    d. dietary content

    e. emotionality

7. Explain the paradox of "yo-yo" dieting and describe what is meant by behavioral dieting and how these techniques can enable you to control your weight.

8. Describe the impact of cultural factors and taste on hunger and explain how taste aversions are acquired.

9. Describe the essential features of the eating disorders of anorexia nervosa and bulimia nervosa; explain what causes them; and what treatment is available for them. Include a brief discussion of the relationship of culture and ethnicity to dieting and preferred body size.

10. Name the brain structure that appears to control thirst (as well as hunger) and differentiate extracellular and intracellular thirst.

11. Explain how the drive to avoid pain and the sex drive differ from other primary drives and include a brief explanation of the non-homeostatic nature of the sex drive.

12. Describe the evidence for the existence of stimulus drives for exploration, manipulation, curiosity, and stimulation; explain the arousal theory of motivation and the characteristics of high and low sensation-seekers; describe the inverted U function; and relate arousal to the Yerkes-Dodson law.

13. Describe the two major components of test anxiety and describe four ways to reduce it.

14. Explain how circadian rhythms affect energy levels, motivation, and performance. Include an explanation of how and why shift work and jet lag may adversely affect a person and how to minimize the effects of shifting one's rhythms, including the use of melatonin.

15. Use the ideas of Solomon's opponent-process theory to explain how a person might learn to like hazardous, painful, or frightening pursuits.

16. Define the *need for achievement* (nAch) and differentiate it from the need for power; relate this need for achievement to risk taking; explain the influences of drive and determination in the success of high achievers; and list seven steps to enhance self-confidence.

17. List (in order) the needs found in Maslow's hierarchy of motives; distinguish between basic needs and growth needs; explain why Maslow's lower (physiological) needs are considered prepotent; and define and give examples of meta-needs.

18. Distinguish between intrinsic and extrinsic motivation, and explain how each type of motivation may affect a person's interest in work, leisure activities, and creativity.

19. Explain how emotions aid survival; describe the three major elements of emotions; list the eight primary emotions proposed by Plutchik; explain how a person may experience two opposite emotions simultaneously; and state which side of the brain processes positive versus negative emotions and what effect the amygdala has on emotion.

20. Describe, in general, the effects of the sympathetic and parasympathetic branches of the ANS during and after emotion; explain how the *parasympathetic rebound* may be involved in cases of sudden death; and discuss the limitations of lie detector (polygraph) in detecting "lies" and what it actually measures.

21. Discuss Darwin's view of human emotion; differentiate between Duchenne smiles and forced smiles; describe cultural and gender differences in emotions and emotional expressions; and discuss *kinesics*,

including the emotional messages conveyed by facial expressions and body language and the behavioral clues to lying, such as illustrators versus emblems.

22. Describe and give examples of the following theories of emotion:

    a.   James-Lange theory

    b.   Cannon-Bard theory

    c.   Schachter's cognitive theory

    d.   the effects of attribution on emotion

    e.   the facial feedback hypothesis

    f.   the role of appraisal in the contemporary model of emotion.

The following objective is related to the material in the "Psychology in Action" section of your text.

1. Describe the concept of emotional intelligence and its five skills and briefly discuss the benefits of positive emotions.

RECITE AND REVIEW

What is motivation? Are there different types of motives?

Motivation—Forces that Push and Pull: Pages 388-390

1. Motives _____ (begin), sustain (perpetuate), and direct _____ .

2. Motivation typically involves the sequence _____ , drive, _____ , and goal attainment (need reduction).

3. Behavior can be activated either by needs (_____) or by goals (_____).

4. The attractiveness of a _____ and its ability to initiate action are related to its incentive value (its value above and beyond its capacity to fill a _____).

5. Three principal types of motives are primary motives, stimulus motives, and _____ motives.

6. Most _____ motives operate to maintain a _____ state of bodily equilibrium called homeostasis.

What causes hunger? Overeating? Eating disorders?

Hunger—Pardon Me, My Hypothalamus Is Growling: Pages 390-397

1. Hunger is influenced by a complex interplay between distention (fullness) of the _____ , lowered levels of glucose (_____), metabolism in the _____ , and fat stores in the body.

2. The most direct control of eating is exerted by the hypothalamus, which has areas that act like feeding (_____) and satiety (_____) systems for hunger and eating.

3. The lateral hypothalamus acts as a _____ system; the ventromedial hypothalamus is part of a _____ system; the paraventricular nucleus influences both hunger and satiety.

4. Other factors influencing hunger are the set point for the proportion of _____ in the body, external eating cues, the attractiveness and variety of _____ .

5. A body mass index is a measure of body fat that is calculated by dividing body _____ squared over body _____ multiplied by 703.

6. A BMI of _____ or higher should be a cause for concern since obesity is linked to heart disease, high blood pressure, stroke, diabetes, and premature death.

7. Because of the limitations of traditional dieting, changing basic eating patterns and _____ is usually more effective.

8. Behavioral _____ brings about such changes by use of self-control techniques.

9. A successful behavioral dieting approach begins with committing oneself to weight loss, _____ , counting _____ , developing techniques to control overeating, and charting one's progress.

10. Hunger is also influenced by emotions, learned _____ preferences and _____ aversions (such as bait shyness in animals), and cultural values.

11. Anorexia nervosa (self-inflicted _____) and bulimia nervosa (_____ and purging) are two prominent eating disorders.

12. Treatments for anorexia begin with medical diet to restore weight and health then advance to _____ .

13. Both eating disorders tend to involve conflicts about self-image, self-control, and _____ .

Is there more than one type of thirst? In what ways are pain avoidance and the sex drive unusual?

Primary Motives Revisited—Thirst, Sex, and Pain: Pages 397-399

1. Like hunger, thirst and other basic motives are affected by a number of _____ factors, but are primarily under the central control of the hypothalamus in the _____ .

2. Thirst may be either intracellular (when _____ is lost from inside _____) or extracellular (when _____ is lost from the spaces between _____).

3. Pain avoidance is unusual because it is episodic (associated with particular conditions) as opposed to cyclic (occurring in regular _____).

4. Pain avoidance and pain tolerance are partially _____ (influenced by training).

5. The sex drive in many lower animals is related to estrus (or "heat") in _____ . The sex drive is unusual in that it is non-homeostatic (both its _____ and its reduction are sought).

6. Sex _____ in both males and females may be related to bodily levels of androgens.

How does arousal relate to motivation?

Stimulus Drives—Skydiving, Horror Movies, and the Fun Zone: Pages 399-403

1. The stimulus drives reflect needs for information, exploration, manipulation, and _____ input.

2. Drives for stimulation are partially explained by arousal theory, which states that an ideal level of _____ will be maintained if possible.

3. The desired level of _____ or stimulation varies from person to person, as measured by the *Sensation-Seeking Scale* (SSS).

4. Individuals from America, Israel, and Ireland tend to score _____ on the Sensation-Seeking Scale and they are likely to engage in high-risk behaviors.

5. Optimal performance on a task usually occurs at _____ levels of arousal. This relationship is described by an inverted U function.

6. The Yerkes-Dodson law further states that for _____ tasks the ideal arousal level is higher, and for _____ tasks it is lower.

7. Test anxiety is caused by a combination of _____ worrying and heightened physiological arousal, which can be reduced with better _____ , relaxation, _____ , and restructuring thoughts.

8. Circadian _____ within the body are closely tied to sleep, activity levels, and energy cycles. Time zone travel and shift work can seriously disrupt _____ and bodily rhythms.

9. If you anticipate a _____ in body rhythms, you can gradually preadapt to your new _____ over a period of days.

10. Body rhythms and _____ cycles are strongly influenced by the release of melatonin, a _____ produced at night by the pineal gland.

What are social motives? Why are they important?

Learned Motives—The Pursuit of Excellence: Pages 404-406

1. _____ motives are learned through socialization and cultural conditioning.

2. Opponent-process theory, which states that strong _____ tend to be followed by an opposite _____ , explains some acquired motives.

3. One of the most prominent social motives is the _____ for achievement (nAch).

4. High nAch is correlated with _____ in many situations, with occupational choice, and with moderate _____ taking.

5. Self-confidence affects _____ because it influences the challenges you will undertake, the _____ you will make, and how long you will _____ when things don't go well.

6. To enhance self-confidence, one should do the following: Set goals that are specific, _____ , and attainable, advance in _____ steps, find a role model, get expert instructions, and get _____ support.

Are some motives more basic than others?

Motives in Perspective—A View from the Pyramid: Pages 406-409

1. Maslow's hierarchy (rank ordering) of motives categorizes needs as _____ and growth oriented.

2. _____ needs in the hierarchy are assumed to be prepotent (dominant) over _____ needs.

3. _____ -actualization, the highest and most fragile need, is reflected in meta- _____ .

4. In many situations, extrinsic motivation (that which is induced by obvious _____ rewards) can reduce intrinsic motivation, enjoyment, and creativity.

What happens during emotion?

Inside an Emotion—How Do You Feel? Pages 409-411

1. Emotions are linked to many basic adaptive _____ , such as attacking, retreating, feeding, and reproducing.

2. Other major elements of emotion are physiological changes in the body, emotional expressions, and emotional _____ .

3. The following are considered to be primary emotions: fear, surprise, _____ , disgust, _____ , anticipation, joy, and trust (acceptance). Other emotions seem to represent mixtures of the primaries.

Can "Lie Detectors" really detect lies?

Physiology and Emotion—Arousal, Sudden Death, and Lying: Pages 411-414

1. Physical changes associated with emotion are caused by the action of adrenaline, a _____ released into the bloodstream, and by activity in the autonomic _____ (ANS).

2. The sympathetic _____ of the ANS is primarily responsible for arousing the body, the parasympathetic _____ for quieting it.

3. Sudden death due to prolonged and intense emotion is probably related to parasympathetic _____ (excess activity). Heart attacks caused by sudden intense emotion are more likely due to sympathetic _____ .

4. The polygraph, or "lie detector," measures _____ by monitoring heart rate, blood pressure, breathing rate, and the galvanic skin response (GSR).

5. Asking a series of _____ and irrelevant questions may allow the detection of _____ , but overall, the accuracy of the lie detector has been challenged by many researchers.

6. A polygraph makes use of such _____ questions as "Have you ever stolen anything from your place of work?" to increase the person's anxiety level. Their answers will be compared to other _____ questions for which the police are seeking answers.

7. Infrared face scans and the use of _____ in analyzing brain activity are possible alternative techniques to polygraph testing.

How accurately do "body language" and the face express emotions?

Expressing Emotions—Making Faces and Talking Bodies: Pages 414-417

1. Basic emotional expressions, such as smiling or baring one's teeth when angry, appear to be

   _____ .

2. Facial expressions of _____ , anger, disgust, _____ , and happiness are recognized by people of all cultures.

3. In Western culture, women are encouraged to express such emotions as _____ , fear, _____ , and guilt, and men are expected to express _____ and hostility.

4. Body gestures and movements (body language) also express _____ , mainly by communicating emotional _____ .

5. Three dimensions of _____ expressions are pleasantness-unpleasantness, attention-rejection, and activation.

6. The study of _____ is known as kinesics.

How do psychologists explain emotions?

Theories of Emotion—Several Ways To Fear a Bear: Pages 417-421

1. The James-Lange theory of emotion says that emotional experience _____ an awareness of the bodily reactions of emotion.

2. In contrast, the Cannon-Bard theory says that bodily reactions and emotional experience occur

   _____ _____ _____ _____ and that emotions are organized in

   the brain.

3. Schachter's cognitive theory of emotion emphasizes the importance of _____ , or

   interpretations, applied to feelings of bodily arousal.

4. Also important is the process of attribution, in which bodily _____ is attributed to a particular

   person, object, or situation.

5. Research on attribution theory has shown that physical arousal (e.g., an _____ heart rate from

   exercise or fear) can be _____ to different sources such as attraction or love for someone.

6. The facial feedback hypothesis holds that sensations and information from emotional _____

   help define what emotion a person is feeling.

7. Making faces does influence _____ and bodily activities through the _____

   nervous system.

8. Contemporary views of emotion place greater emphasis on how _____ are appraised. Also, all

   of the elements of emotion are seen as interrelated and interacting.

What does it mean to have "emotional intelligence"?

Psychology in Action: Emotional Intelligence—The Fine Art of Self-control: Pages 422-423

1. Emotional intelligence involves the following skills: _____ -awareness, empathy,

   _____ -control, and an understanding of how to use _____ .

2. Emotionally intelligent people are good at reading facial expressions, tone of voice, and other signs of

   _____ .

3. They also use their _____ to enhance thinking and decision making.

4. _____ emotions are not just a luxury. They tend to encourage personal growth and social

   connection.

5. Martin Seligman believes people can achieve genuine happiness by optimizing their natural

    _____ , such as _____ , originality, humor, _____ , and generosity,

    to buffer them against misfortunes.

CONNECTIONS

What is motivation? Are there different types of motives?
Pages 388-390

1. _____ incentive value
2. _____ motivational model
3. _____ need
4. _____ homeostasis
5. _____ secondary motives

a. internal deficiency
b. goal desirability
c. learned goals
d. need reduction
e. steady state

What causes hunger? Overeating? Eating disorders? Pages
390-397

1. _____ ventromedial hypothalamus
2. _____ lateral hypothalamus
3. _____ paraventricular nucleus

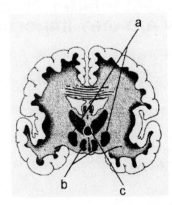

Connections Part II

1. _____ satiety system	a.	weight/height^2 x 703
2. _____ taste aversion	b.	classical condition
3. _____ set point	c.	thermostat for fat level
4. _____ hunger and satiety	d.	lateral hypothalamus
5. _____ body mass index	e.	yo-yo dieting
6. _____ weight cycling	f.	paraventricular nucleus
7. _____ changes eating habits	g.	ventromedial hypothalamus
8. _____ feeding system	h.	behavioral dieting

Is there more than one type of thirst? In what ways are pain avoidance and the sex drive unusual? Pages 397-399

1. _____ episodic drive	a.	weight/height^2 x 703
2. _____ non-homeostatic	b.	result from diarrhea
3. _____ intracellular thirst	c.	drive to avoid incidences of pain
4. _____ extracellular thirst	d.	human sex drive
5. _____ estrus	e.	result from too much salt intake

How does arousal relate to motivation? What are social motives? Why are they important? Pages 399-406

1. _____ melatonin	a.	standards of excellence
2. _____ heightened physiological arousal	b.	sensation seekers
3. _____ nAch	c.	impaired test performance
4. _____ self-confidence	d.	high in nAch
5. _____ SSS	e.	mixture of arousal and performance
6. _____ moderate risk takers	f.	24-hour day cycle
7. _____ circadian rhythm	g.	sleep induced hormone
8. _____ inverted U function	h.	believing that one can succeed

Are some motives more basic than others? Pages 406-409

1. _____ safety and security
2. _____ basic needs
3. _____ love and belonging
4. _____ self-actualization
5. _____ physiological needs
6. _____ esteem and self-esteem
7. _____ growth needs

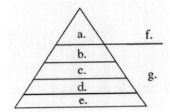

What happens during emotion? Can "Lie Detectors" really detect lies? Pages 409-414

1. _____ adrenaline
2. _____ parasympathetic rebound
3. _____ Robert Plutchik
4. _____ irrelevant questions
5. _____ polygraph
6. _____ sympathetic branch
7. _____ relevant questions
8. _____ mood

a. eight primary emotions
b. arousal-producing hormone
c. "Did you murder Hensley?"
d. nonemotional questions
e. prolonged mild emotion
f. fight or flight
g. intense emotional overreaction
h. lie detection

How accurately do "body language" and the face express emotions? How do psychologists explain emotions? What does it mean to have "emotional intelligence"? Pages 414-423

1. _____ anxiety
2. _____ sadness
3. _____ authentic happiness
4. _____ James-Lange theory
5. _____ body language
6. _____ facial blend
7. _____ self-awareness
8. _____ Schachter's cognitive theory
9. _____ emotional intelligence

a. arousal + label then emotions
b. bodily arousal then emotions
c. mixing 2+ facial emotions
d. appraisal of loss
e. appraisal of threat
f. kinesics
g. emotional skills
h. in tune with own feelings
i. emphasize natural strengths

CHECK YOUR MEMORY

What is motivation? Are there different types of motives? Pages 388-390

1. The terms need and drive are used interchangeably to describe motivation.

   TRUE or FALSE

2. Incentive value refers to the "pull" of valued goals.

   TRUE or FALSE

3. Primary motives are based on needs that must be met for survival.

   TRUE or FALSE

4. Much of the time, homeostasis is maintained by automatic reactions within the body.

   TRUE or FALSE

What causes hunger? Overeating? Eating disorders? Pages 390-397

1. Cutting the sensory nerves from the stomach abolishes hunger.

   TRUE or FALSE

2. Lowered levels of glucose in the blood can cause hunger.

   TRUE or FALSE

3. The body's hunger center is found in the thalamus.

   TRUE or FALSE

4. The paraventricular nucleus is sensitive to neuropeptide Y.

   TRUE or FALSE

5. Both glucagon-like peptide 1 (GLP-1) and leptin act as stop signals that inhibit eating.

   TRUE or FALSE

6. BMI is an estimation of body fat.

   TRUE or FALSE

7. Dieting speeds up the body's metabolic rate.

   TRUE or FALSE

8. People who diet intensely every other day lose as much weight as those who diet moderately every day.

   TRUE or FALSE

9. Exercise makes people hungry and tends to disrupt dieting and weight loss.

   TRUE or FALSE

10. External cues have little impact on one's tendency to overeat.

    TRUE or FALSE

11. The fast-food industry promotes healthy and tasty products that have contributed to the problem of obesity.

    TRUE or FALSE

12. "Yo-yo dieting" refers to repeatedly losing and gaining weight through the process of bingeing and purging.

    TRUE or FALSE

13. Behavioral dieting changes habits without reducing the number of calories consumed.

    TRUE or FALSE

14. Charting daily progress is a basic behavioral dieting technique.

    TRUE or FALSE

15. The incentive value of foods is largely determined by cultural values.

    TRUE or FALSE

16. Taste aversions may be learned after longer time delays than in other forms of classical conditioning.

    TRUE or FALSE

17. Taste aversions tend to promote nutritional imbalance.

    TRUE or FALSE

18. Many victims of anorexia nervosa overestimate their body size.

    TRUE or FALSE

19. Over time anorexics lose their appetite and do not feel hungry.

    TRUE or FALSE

20. Treatment for anorexia begins with counseling.

    TRUE or FALSE

Is there more than one type of thirst? In what ways are pain avoidance and the sex drive unusual? Pages 397-399

1. Bleeding, vomiting, or sweating can cause extracellular thirst.
   TRUE or FALSE

2. Intracellular thirst is best satisfied by a slightly salty liquid.
   TRUE or FALSE

3. Tolerance for pain is largely unaffected by learning.
   TRUE or FALSE

4. Castration of a male animal typically abolishes the sex drive.
   TRUE or FALSE

5. Getting drunk *decreases* sexual desire, arousal, pleasure, and performance.
   TRUE or FALSE

How does arousal relate to motivation? Pages 399-403

1. It is uncomfortable to experience both very high and very low levels of arousal.
   TRUE or FALSE

2. Disinhibition and boredom susceptibility are characteristics of sensation-seeking persons.
   TRUE or FALSE

3. Individuals who score high on the Sensation-Seeking Scales do not engage in high-risk behaviors such as substance abuse.
   TRUE or FALSE

4. For nearly all activities, the best performance occurs at high levels of arousal.
   TRUE or FALSE

5. Test anxiety is a combination of arousal and excessive worry.
   TRUE or FALSE

6. Being overprepared is a common cause of test anxiety.
   TRUE or FALSE

7. Changes in body temperature are closely related to circadian rhythms.
   TRUE or FALSE

8. Adapting to rapid time zone changes is easiest when a person travels east, rather than west.
   TRUE or FALSE

What are social motives? Why are they important? Pages 404-406

1. Opponent-process theory assumes that emotional responses habituate when activities are repeated.
    TRUE or FALSE

2. The need for achievement refers to a desire to have impact on other people.
    TRUE or FALSE

3. People high in nAch generally prefer "long shots" or "sure things."
    TRUE or FALSE

4. Benjamin Bloom found that high achievement is based as much on hard work as it is on talent.
    TRUE or FALSE

5. For many activities, self-confidence is one of the most important sources of motivation.
    TRUE or FALSE

Are some motives more basic than others? Pages 406-409

1. Maslow's hierarchy of needs places self-esteem at the top of the pyramid.
    TRUE or FALSE

2. Maslow believed that needs for safety and security are more potent than needs for love and belonging.
    TRUE or FALSE

3. Meta-needs are the most basic needs in Maslow's hierarchy.
    TRUE or FALSE

4. Maslow believed that most people are motivated to seek esteem, love and security rather than self-actualization.
    TRUE or FALSE

5. Intrinsic motivation occurs when obvious external rewards are provided for engaging in an activity.
    TRUE or FALSE

6. People are more likely to be creative when they are intrinsically motivated.
    TRUE or FALSE

7. Emotions help people survive by bonding with each other as they socialize and work together.
    TRUE or FALSE

8. Happy, positive moods are as equally adaptive as negative moods in influencing creativity, efficiency, and helpfulness to others.
    TRUE or FALSE

What happens during emotion? Pages 409-411

1. Most physiological changes during emotion are related to the release of adrenaline into the brain.
   TRUE or FALSE

2. Robert Plutchik's theory lists contempt as a primary emotion.
   TRUE or FALSE

3. For most students, elevated moods tend to occur on Saturdays and Tuesdays.
   TRUE or FALSE

4. Positive emotions are processed mainly in the left hemisphere of the brain.
   TRUE or FALSE

5. The brain area called the amygdala specializes in producing fear.
   TRUE or FALSE

Can "Lie Detectors" really detect lies? Pages 411-414

1. The sympathetic branch of the ANS is under voluntary control and the parasympathetic branch is involuntary.
   TRUE or FALSE

2. The parasympathetic branch of the ANS slows the heart and lowers blood pressure.
   TRUE or FALSE

3. Most sudden deaths due to strong emotion are associated with the traumatic disruption of a close relationship.
   TRUE or FALSE

4. Although not 100% accurate, infrared face scans are 50% better at detecting lies than polygraph tests.
   TRUE or FALSE

How accurately do "body language" and the face express emotions? Pages 414-417

1. The polygraph measures the body's unique physical responses to lying.
   TRUE or FALSE

2. Only a guilty person should react emotionally to irrelevant questions.
   TRUE or FALSE

3. Control questions used in polygraph exams are designed to make almost everyone anxious.

TRUE or FALSE

4. The lie detector's most common error is to label innocent persons guilty.

TRUE or FALSE

5. Children born deaf and blind express emotions with their faces in about the same way as other people do.

TRUE or FALSE

6. An authentic, or Duchenne, smile involves the muscles near the corners of a person's eyes, not just the mouth.

TRUE or FALSE

7. The "A-okay" hand gesture means "everything is fine" around the world.

TRUE or FALSE

8. Facial blends mix two or more basic expressions.

TRUE or FALSE

9. Liking is expressed in body language by leaning back and relaxing the extremities.

TRUE or FALSE

10. Gestures such as rubbing hands, twisting hair, and biting lips are consistently related to lying.

TRUE or FALSE

11. People from Asian cultures are more likely to express anger in public than people from Western cultures.

TRUE or FALSE

12. In Western cultures, men tend to be more emotionally expressive than women.

TRUE or FALSE

How do psychologists explain emotions? Pages 417-421

1. The James-Lange theory of emotion says that we see a bear, feel fear, are aroused, and then run.

TRUE or FALSE

2. The Cannon-Bard theory states that emotion and bodily arousal occur at the same time.

TRUE or FALSE

3. According to Schachter's cognitive theory, arousal must be labeled in order to become an emotion.

TRUE or FALSE

4. Attribution theory predicts that people are most likely to "love" someone who does not agitate, anger, and frustrate them.

TRUE or FALSE

5. Making facial expressions can actually cause emotions to occur and alter physiological activities in the body.

   TRUE or FALSE

6. Emotional appraisal refers to deciding if your own facial expressions are appropriate for the situation you are in.

   TRUE or FALSE

7. Suppressing emotions can impair thinking and memory because a lot of energy must be devoted to self-control.

   TRUE or FALSE

8. Moving toward a desired goal is associated with the emotion of happiness.

   TRUE or FALSE

9. Emotional intelligence refers to the ability to use primarily the right cerebral hemisphere to process emotional events.

   TRUE or FALSE

What does it mean to have "emotional intelligence"? Pages 422-423

1. People who excel in life tend to be emotionally intelligent.

   TRUE or FALSE

2. People who are empathetic are keenly tuned in to their own feelings.

   TRUE or FALSE

3. People who are emotionally intelligent know what causes them to feel various emotions.

   TRUE or FALSE

4. Negative emotions can be valuable because they impart useful information to us.

   TRUE or FALSE

5. Positive emotions produce urges to be creative, to explore, and to seek new experiences.

   TRUE or FALSE

6. Martin Seligman believes that to be genuinely happy, people must cultivate their own natural strengths.

   TRUE or FALSE

7. A first step toward becoming emotionally intelligent is to pay attention to and value your feelings and emotional reactions.

   TRUE or FALSE

FINAL SURVEY AND REVIEW

What is motivation? Are there different types of motives?

Motivation—Forces that Push and Pull: Pages 388-390

1. Motives initiate (begin), _____ (perpetuate), and _____ activities.

2. Motivation typically involves the sequence need, _____ , goal, and goal _____ (need reduction).

3. Behavior can be activated either by _____ (push) or by _____ (pull).

4. The attractiveness of a goal and its ability to initiate action are related to its _____ _____ .

5. Three principal types of motives are _____ motives, _____ motives, and _____ motives.

6. Most primary motives operate to maintain a steady state of bodily equilibrium called _____ .

What causes hunger? Overeating? Eating disorders?

Hunger—Pardon Me, My Hypothalamus Is Growling: Pages 390-397

1. Hunger is influenced by a complex interplay between _____ (fullness) of the stomach, lowered levels of _____ , metabolism in the liver, and fat stores in the body.

2. The most direct control of eating is exerted by the _____ , which has areas that act like feeding (start) and _____ (stop) systems for hunger and eating.

3. The _____ hypothalamus acts as a feeding system; the _____ hypothalamus is part of a satiety system; the paraventricular _____ influences both hunger and satiety.

4. Other factors influencing hunger are the _____ _____ for the proportion of fat in the body, external eating _____ , the attractiveness and variety of diet.

5. A _____ (BMI) is a measure of body _____ which is calculated by dividing body height squared over body weight multiplied by 703.

6. A BMI of _____ or higher should be a cause for concern since obesity is linked to _____ disease, high blood pressure, _____ , diabetes, and premature death.

7. Because of the limitations of traditional dieting, changing basic _____ patterns and habits is usually more effective.

8. _____ dieting brings about such changes by use of _____ -control techniques.

9. A successful behavioral dieting approach begins with committing oneself to weight loss, _____ , counting _____ , developing techniques to control overeating, and charting one's progress.

10. Hunger is also influenced by emotions, learned taste preferences and taste _____ (such as _____ _____ in animals), and cultural values.

11. _____ nervosa (self-inflicted starvation) and _____ nervosa (gorging and purging) are two prominent eating disorders.

12. Treatments for anorexia begin with _____ diet then advance to counseling.

13. Both eating disorders tend to involve conflicts about _____ , self-control, and anxiety.

Is there more than one type of thirst? In what ways are pain avoidance and the sex drive unusual?

Primary Motives Revisited—Thirst, Sex, and Pain: Pages 397-399

1. Like hunger, thirst and other basic motives are affected by a number of bodily factors, but are primarily under the central control of the _____ in the brain.

2. Thirst may be either _____ (when fluid is lost from inside cells) or _____ (when fluid is lost from the spaces between cells).

3. Pain avoidance is unusual because it is _____ (associated with particular conditions) as opposed to _____ (occurring in regular cycles).

4. Pain _____ and pain _____ are partially learned.

5. The sex drive in many lower animals is related to _____ (or "heat") in females. The sex drive is unusual in that it is non- _____ (both its arousal and its reduction are sought).

6. Sex drive in both males and females may be related to bodily levels of _____ .

How does arousal relate to motivation?

Stimulus Drives—Skydiving, Horror Movies, and the Fun Zone: Pages 399-403

1. The _____ drives reflect needs for information, _____ , manipulation, and sensory input.

2. Drives for stimulation are partially explained by _____ , which states that an ideal level of physical arousal will be maintained if possible.

3. The desired level of arousal or stimulation varies from person to person, as measured by the _____ *Scale*.

4. Individuals from America, Israel, and Ireland tend to score high on the Sensation-Seeking Scale and they are likely to engage in _____ behaviors.

5. Optimal performance on a task usually occurs at moderate levels of arousal. This relationship is described by an _____ function.

6. The _____ law further states that for simple tasks the ideal arousal level is higher, and for complex tasks it is lower.

7. Test anxiety is caused by a combination of excessive _____ and heightened physiological _____ , which can be reduced with better preparation, relaxation, rehearsal, and restructuring thoughts.

8. _____ rhythms within the body are closely tied to sleep, activity levels, and energy cycles. Travel across _____ and shift work can seriously disrupt sleep and bodily rhythms.

9. If you anticipate a change in body rhythms, you can gradually _____ to your new schedule over a period of days.

10. Body rhythms and sleep cycles are strongly influenced by the release of _____ , a hormone produced at night by the _____ gland.

What are social motives? Why are they important?

Learned Motives—The Pursuit of Excellence: Pages 404-406

1. Social motives are learned through _____ and cultural conditioning.

2. _____ theory, which states that strong emotions tend to be followed by an opposite emotion, explains some acquired motives.

3. One of the most prominent social motives is the need for _____ (nAch).

4. _____ nAch is correlated with success in many situations, with occupational choice, and with moderate risk taking.

5. _____ affects motivation because it influences the challenges you will undertake, the effort you will make, and how long you will persist when things don't go well.

6. To enhance self- _____ , one should do the following: Set goals that are specific, _____ , and attainable, advance in small steps, find a role model, get expert instructions, and get _____ support.

Are some motives more basic than others?

Motives in Perspective—A View from the Pyramid: Pages 406-409

1. Maslow's _____ (rank ordering) of motives categorizes needs as basic and _____ oriented.

2. Lower needs in the hierarchy are assumed to be _____ (dominant) over higher needs.

3. Self- _____ , the highest and most fragile need, is reflected in _____ -needs.

4. In many situations, _____ motivation (that which is induced by obvious external rewards) can reduce _____ motivation, enjoyment, and creativity.

What happens during emotion?

Inside an Emotion—How Do You Feel? Pages 409-411

1. Emotions are linked to many basic _____ behaviors, such as attacking, retreating, feeding, and reproducing.

2. Other major elements of emotion are physiological changes in the body, emotional _____ , and emotional feelings.

3. The following are considered to be _____ emotions: fear, surprise, sadness, disgust, anger, anticipation, joy, and trust (acceptance).

Can "Lie Detectors" really detect lies?

Physiology and Emotion—Arousal, Sudden Death, and Lying: Pages 411-414

1. Physical changes associated with emotion are caused by the action of _____ , a hormone released into the bloodstream, and by activity in the _____ nervous system (ANS).

2. The _____ branch of the ANS is primarily responsible for arousing the body, the _____ branch for quieting it.

3. Sudden death due to prolonged and intense emotion is probably related to _____ rebound (excess activity). Heart attacks caused by sudden intense emotion are more likely due to _____ arousal.

4. The _____ , or "lie detector," measures emotional _____ arousal by monitoring heart rate, blood pressure, breathing rate, and the galvanic skin response (GSR).

5. Asking a series of _____ and _____ questions may allow the detection of lying, but overall, the accuracy of the lie detector has been challenged by many researchers.

6. A _____ makes use of such control questions as "Have you ever stolen anything from your place of work?" to increase the person's anxiety level. Their answers will be compared to other _____ questions.

7. _____ _____ scans and the use of fMRI in analyzing brain activity are possible alternative techniques to the polygraph testing.

How accurately do "body language" and the face express emotions?

Expressing Emotions—Making Faces and Talking Bodies: Pages 414-417

1. Basic emotional _____ , such as smiling or baring one's teeth when angry, appear to be unlearned.

2. _____ expressions of fear, anger, disgust, sadness, and happiness are recognized by people of all cultures.

3. In Western culture, _____ are encouraged to express such emotions as sadness, fear, shame, and guilt, and _____ are expected to express anger and hostility.

4. Body gestures and movements (body language) also express _____ , mainly by communicating emotional tone.

5. Three dimensions of facial expressions are pleasantness-unpleasantness, attention-rejection, and _____ .

6. The study of body language is known as _____ .

How do psychologists explain emotions?

Theories of Emotion—Several Ways To Fear a Bear: Pages 417-421

1. The _____ -Lange theory of emotion says that emotional experience follows an awareness of the bodily reactions of emotion.

2. In contrast, the _____ -Bard theory says that bodily reactions and emotional experience occur at the same time and that emotions are organized in the brain.

3. Schachter's _____ theory of emotion emphasizes the importance of labels, or interpretations, applied to feelings of bodily _____ .

4. Also important is the process of _____ , in which bodily arousal is attributed to a particular person, object, or situation.

5. Research on attribution theory has shown that _____ _____ (e.g., increased heart rate from exercise or fear) can be attributed to different sources such as attraction or love for someone.

6. The _____ _____ hypothesis holds that sensations and information from emotional expressions help define what emotion a person is feeling.

7. Making faces does influence _____ and bodily activities through the _____ nervous system.

8. Contemporary views of emotion place greater emphasis on how situations are _____ (evaluated). Also, all of the elements of emotion are seen as interrelated and interacting.

What does it mean to have "emotional intelligence"?

Psychology in Action: Emotional Intelligence—The Fine Art of Self-control: Pages 422-423

1. Emotional _____ involves the following skills: self-awareness, _____ , self-control, and an understanding of how to use emotions.

2. Emotionally intelligent people are good at reading _____ expressions, tone of _____ , and other signs of emotion.

3. They also use their feelings to enhance _____ and _____ making.

4. Positive emotions are not just a luxury. They tend to encourage personal _____ and _____ connection.

5. Martin Seligman believes people can achieve genuine _____ by optimizing their natural _____ , such as kindness, originality, humor, optimism, and generosity, to buffer them against misfortunes.

MASTERY TEST

1. Which of the following is NOT one of the signs of emotional arousal recorded by a polygraph?
   a. heart rate
   b. blood pressure
   c. pupil dilation
   d. breathing rate

2. Plain water is most satisfying when a person has _____ thirst.
   a. intracellular
   b. hypothalamic
   c. extracellular
   d. homeostatic

3. We have a biological tendency to associate an upset stomach with foods eaten earlier. This is the basis for the development of
   a. taste aversions
   b. yo-yo dieting
   c. bulimia
   d. frequent weight cycling

4. Strong external rewards tend to undermine
   a. extrinsic motivation
   b. intrinsic motivation
   c. prepotent motivation
   d. stimulus motivation

5. Activity in the ANS is directly responsible for which element of emotion?
   a. emotional feelings
   b. emotional expressions
   c. physiological changes
   d. misattributions

6. Empathy is a major element of
   a. nAch
   b. intrinsic motivation
   c. emotional intelligence
   d. the sensation-seeking personality

7. Motivation refers to the ways in which activities are initiated, sustained, and
   a. acquired
   b. valued
   c. directed
   d. aroused

8. The psychological state or feeling we call thirst corresponds to which element of motivation?
   a. need
   b. drive
   c. deprivation
   d. incentive value

9. People who score high on the SSS generally prefer
   a. low levels of arousal
   b. moderate levels of arousal
   c. high levels of arousal
   d. the middle of the V function

10. Which facial expression is NOT recognized by people of all cultures?
    a. anger
    b. disgust
    c. optimism
    d. fear

11. Learning to weaken eating cues is useful in
    a. self-selection feeding
    b. yo-yo dieting
    c. rapid weight cycling
    d. behavioral dieting

12. People who score high on tests of the need for achievement tend to be:
    a. motivated by power and prestige
    b. moderate risk takers
    c. sensation seekers
    d. attracted to longshots

13. Which theory holds that emotional feelings, arousal, and behavior are generated simultaneously in the brain?
    a. James-Lange
    b. Cannon-Bard
    c. cognitive
    d. attribution

14. Compared with people in North America, people in Asian cultures are less likely to express which emotion?
    a. anger
    b. jealousy
    c. curiosity
    d. fear

15. Binge eating is most associated with
    a. bulimia nervosa
    b. bait shyness
    c. low levels of NPY
    d. anorexia nervosa

16. Goals that are desirable are high in
    a. need reduction
    b. incentive value
    c. homeostatic valence
    d. motivational "push"

17. _____ is to pain avoidance as _____ is to the sex drive.
    a. Non-homeostatic, episodic
    b. Episodic, non-homeostatic
    c. Non-homeostatic, cyclic
    d. Cyclic, non-homeostatic

18. A specialist in kinesics could be expected to be most interested in
    a. facial blends
    b. circadian rhythms
    c. sensation seeking
    d. primary motives

19. Coping statements are a way to directly correct which part of test anxiety?
    a. overpreparation
    b. under-arousal
    c. excessive worry
    d. compulsive rehearsal

20. Drives for exploration and activity are categorized as
    a. primary motives
    b. secondary motives
    c. stimulus motives
    d. extrinsic motives

21. Sudden death following a period of intense fear may occur when _____ slows the heart to a stop.
    a. a sympathetic overload
    b. adrenaline poisoning
    c. opponent-process feedback
    d. a parasympathetic rebound

22. People who enjoy skydiving and ski jumping are very likely high in
    a. parasympathetic arousal
    b. extrinsic motivation
    c. their desires to meet meta-needs
    d. the trait of sensation seeking

23. You could induce eating in a laboratory rat by activating the
    a. lateral hypothalamus
    b. corpus callosum
    c. rat's set point
    d. ventromedial hypothalamus

24. People think cartoons are funnier if they see them while holding a pen crosswise in their teeth. This observation supports
    a. the James-Lange theory
    b. the Cannon-Bard theory
    c. Schachter's cognitive theory
    d. the facial feedback hypothesis

25. Basic biological motives are closely related to
    a. nAch
    b. homeostasis
    c. activity in the thalamus
    d. levels of melatonin in the body

26. Self-actualization is to _____ needs as safety and security are to _____ needs.
    a. growth, basic
    b. basic, meta-
    c. prepotent, basic
    d. meta-, extrinsic

27. Which of the following is NOT a core element of emotion?
    a. physiological changes
    b. emotional expressions
    c. emotional feelings
    d. misattributions

28. The effects of a "supermarket diet" on eating are related to the effects of _____ on eating.
    a. anxiety
    b. incentive value
    c. metabolic rates
    d. stomach distention

29. According to the Yerkes-Dodson law, optimum performance occurs at _____ levels of arousal for simple tasks and _____ levels of arousal for complex tasks.
    a. higher, lower
    b. lower, higher
    c. minimum, high
    d. average, high

30. Contemporary models of emotion place greater emphasis on _____, or the way situations are evaluated.
    a. appraisal
    b. attribution
    c. feedback
    d. emotional tone

31. A _____ (BMI) measures one's body fat by applying the formula: weight/height^2 x 703.
    a. Body Magnitude Indicator
    b. Basic Magnitude Indicator
    c. Body Mass Index
    d. Basic Mass Index

32. Which statement correctly explains why there is an obesity problem in the United States?
    a. The all-you-can-eat dining halls and restaurants tempt people to overeat.
    b. Although the food industry has made dinner easier to cook and buy, the food is high in fat and sugar.
    c. Overeating during large meals increases one's body set point.
    d. All the preceding

33. Although in some parts of the world, eating monkey eyes is considered a delicacy, to Americans it is not. This difference in preference is largely influenced by
    a. cultural values
    b. primary motives
    c. the availability of taste buds
    d. overdeveloped hypothalamus

34. Bev placed herself on a strict diet of eating no other fruits except for grapefruit. Eventually, she began to crave other fruits and could not stand seeing, smelling, or tasting another grapefruit. One explanation for Bev's strong dislike of grapefruit is her body was trying to avoid nutritional imbalance by producing
    a. positive reinforcement
    b. a taste aversion
    c. shaping
    d. purging

35. The causes of anorexia have been attributed to
    a. unrealistic comparison of body image to others
    b. seeking control
    c. distorted body image
    d. all the preceding

36. Variables that aid our survival include _____ moods, which help us make better decisions and be more helpful, efficient, and creative. The ability to understand and display _____ expressions such as anger helps us communicate with others.
    a. primary, universal
    b. negative, natural
    c. positive, facial
    d. natural, primary

37. The National Academy of Sciences has concluded that polygraph tests should not be used to screen _____ since the test tends to label honest people dishonest.
    a. immigrants
    b. employees
    c. government officials
    d. mentally disturbed people

38. According to Martin Seligman, to be genuinely happy, one must
    a. optimize one's natural strengths
    b. focus on fixing one's weaknesses
    c. strengthen negative emotions to better understand positive emotions
    d. balance both negative and positive emotions

39. Two possible alternative techniques for detecting lies over polygraph testing are infrared face scans and _____.
    a. X-Ray
    b. fMRI
    c. high score on the SSS
    d. low score on the nAch

LANGUAGE DEVELOPMENT – Motivation and Emotion

Word roots

The Latin verb *movere* means "to move." The English word "move" comes from this root. One form of movere is *motivus* (moving). Several psychological and biological terms derive from this root. Examples you will find include motivation and motive.

What is motivation? Are there different types of motives?

Preview: The Sun Sets Twice in Utah (p. 388)

   (388) *vista*: a view, scenery

   (388) *spice of life*: that which makes life exciting

Motivation—Forces That Push and Pull (pp. 388-390)

   (388) *depletion*: lessening or loss

   (389) *incentives*: motivating factors

   (389) *in the eye of the beholder*: according to each person; each person will measure the value in their own way

What causes hunger? Overeating? Eating disorders?

Hunger—Pardon Me, That's Just My Hypothalamus Growling (pp. 390- 397)

(390) *hunger pangs*: extreme feeling of hunger

(390) *inflated conclusion*: an exaggerated and incorrect conclusion

(391) *balloon up*: to gain weight very rapidly

(392) *when your "spare tire" is well inflated*: when you have too much excess weight across your midsection

(392) *obesity*: extreme overweight

(392) *stigma*: mark or sign of shame

(394) *battle of the bulge*: efforts to control overeating and obesity

(395) *threshold*: a set point or amount; a dividing line

(395) *predators*: animals that hunt and kill for food

(395) *coyote*: wild canine that resembles a wolf or large dog

(395) *tainted*: contaminated; having something bad added

(395) *lithium chloride*: a liquid poison

(395) *protect roadrunners from the Wile E. Coyote*: in a well-known children's cartoon television show, Wile E. Coyote attempts by trickery to capture and eat the Roadrunner (a type of desert bird that runs fast)

(396) *gorge*: eat to excess

Is there more than one type of thirst? In what ways are pain avoidance and the sex drive unusual?

Primary Motives Revisited—Thirst, Sex, and Pain (pp. 397-399)

(398) *Gatorade*: a drink that is taken especially after exercise to help restore minerals lost through perspiration

(399) *copulate*: have sex

How does arousal relate to motivation?

Stimulus Drives—Skydiving, Horror Movies, and the Fun Zone (pp. 399-403)

(399) *skydiving*: the sport of jumping from an airplane with a parachute

(401) *bungee jumping*: a sport requiring a person to jump off a point of great height with his/her legs tied to a strong elastic rope to prevent him/her from hitting the water or ground below as the rope pulls him/her back a few feet

(401) *sprinters*: runners who compete in short, fast races

(402) *groggy*: sleepy

(402) *shift work*: working schedule that frequently changes, for example, from day to evening to night, then back to day

(402) *jet lag*: condition characterized by fatigue and irritability that occurs following long flights through several different time zones

(402) *bathing*: soaking up

(402) *Chernobyl*: city in former U.S.S.R. where a nuclear power plant accident occurred, injuring and killing many people

(402) *Three-Mile Island*: location of a U.S. nuclear power plant accident

(403) *synchronization*: happening at the same time

(403) *burned the midnight oil*: stayed up late studying

What are social motives? Why are they important?

Learned Motives—The Pursuit of Excellence (pp. 404-406)

(404) *marathons*: long-distance foot-races, usually of 26 miles

(404) *sauna*: a dry heat bath

(404) *seasoned*: experienced

(405) *exploit*: to use to one's own advantage

(406) *prodigies*: highly talented people, especially children

(406) *eminent*: prominent, famous

(406) *ingredients*: characteristics

(406) *elite*: finest, best

(406) *talent will surface*: talent (inborn skill) will eventually become obvious

(406) *emulate*: to model your actions after someone you admire

Are some motives more basic than others?

Motives in Perspective—A View From the Pyramid (pp. 406-409)

(407) *drudgery*: dull and fatiguing work

(408) *bribed*: paid to act a certain way

(408) *"under the gun"*: working under intense pressure

What happens during emotion?

Inside an Emotion—How Do You Feel? (pp. 409-411)

(409) *stage fright*: fear of appearing before crowds to perform, give a speech, etc.

(409) *choking up*: fail to perform effectively because of fear

(409) *butterflies*: feeling of nervousness

(409) *contorts*: twisting of the face into unusual shapes

(410) *recoil:* to pull back quickly in a reflexive move

(410) *Blue Monday*: because Monday is the beginning of the work and school week, it is a "blue," or sad day

Can lie detectors really detect lies?

Physiology and Emotion—Arousal, Sudden Death, and Lying (pp. 411-414)

(411) *prowler*: a person moving about secretly, as in search of things to steal

(413) *be thrown off* (the polygraph may *be thrown off*): give inaccurate readings

How accurately do "body language" and the face express emotion?

Expressing Emotions—Making Faces and Talking Bodies (pp. 414-417)

(416) *Halloween*: celebrated on October 31; children wear masks and costumes and go to neighbors' houses asking for candy

(416) *You're an ass*!: telling someone he or she is a stupid or disagreeable person (usually considered vulgar)

(417) *chameleon*: lizard that can rapidly change skin color to blend in with the surroundings

(417) *mimic*: copy

(417) *slumping*: assume a drooping posture; bending over

(417) *shifty eyes*: indicating a tricky nature

(417) *squirming*: twisting about; moving around

How do psychologists explain emotions?

Theories of Emotion—Several Ways to Fear a Bear (pp. 417-421)

(418) *slapstick*: type of comedy

(418) *added an interesting wrinkle*: contributed something new

(419) *on the sly*: secretly

(419) *suspension bridge*: a bridge, river, or canyon that has its roadway hanging from cables anchored on each side

(419) *chasm*: deep hole in the earth

(419) *ingenious*: very clever

(419) *billboard*: a large panel displaying outdoor advertising

(420) *snarling*: growling

(420) *lunged*: rushed forward suddenly

(421) *demeaned*: lowered a person's pride or self-respect

What does it mean to have "emotional intelligence"?

Psychology in Action: Emotional Intelligence—The Fine Art of Self Control (pp. 422-423)

(422) *empathy*: the ability to share in another's thoughts and emotions

(422) *sabotage*: ruin future chances of accomplishing something

(422) *amplify*: to make big, enlarge

(423) *altruism*: concern for others

Solutions

RECITE AND REVIEW

What is motivation? Are there different types of motives?

1. initiate; activities
2. need; goal
3. push; pull
4. goal; need
5. secondary
6. primary; steady

What causes hunger? Overeating? Eating disorders?

1. stomach; sugar; liver
2. start; stop
3. feeding; satiety
4. fat; diet
5. height; weight
6. 25
7. habits
8. dieting
9. exercise; calories
10. taste; taste
11. starvation; gorging
12. counseling
13. anxiety

Is there more than one type of thirst? In what ways are pain avoidance and the sex drive unusual?

1. bodily; brain
2. fluid; cells; fluid; cells
3. cycles
4. learned
5. females; arousal
6. drive

How does arousal relate to motivation?

1. sensory
2. physical arousal
3. arousal
4. high
5. moderate
6. simple; complex
7. excessive; preparation; rehearsal
8. rhythms; sleep
9. change; schedule
10. sleep; hormone

What are social motives? Why are they important?

1. Social
2. emotions; emotion
3. need
4. success; risk
5. motivation; effort; persist
6. challenging; small; social

Are some motives more basic than others?

1. basic

2. Lower; higher	3. Self; needs	4. external

What happens during emotion?

1. behaviors	2. feelings	3. sadness; anger

Can "Lie Detectors" really detect lies?

1. hormone; nervous system	4. emotional arousal	7. fMRI
2. branch; branch	5. relevant; lying	
3. rebound; arousal	6. control; critical	

How accurately do "body language" and the face express emotions?

1. unlearned	3. sadness; shame; anger	5. facial
2. fear; sadness	4. feelings; tone	6. body language

How do psychologists explain emotions?

1. follows	4. arousal	7. emotions; autonomic
2. at; the; same; time	5. increased; attributed	8. situations
3. labels	6. expressions	

What does it mean to have "emotional intelligence"?

1. self; self; emotions	3. feelings (or emotions)	5. strengths; kindness; optimism
2. emotion	4. Positive	

CONNECTIONS

What is motivation? Are there different types of motives? Pages 388-390

1. B.	3. A.	5. C.
2. D.	4. E.	

What causes hunger? Overeating? Eating disorders? Pages 390-397

1. B.	2. A.	3. C.

Connections Part II

1. G.	4. F.	7. H.
2. B.	5. A.	8. D.
3. C.	6. E.	

Is there more than one type of thirst? In what ways are pain avoidance and the sex drive unusual? Pages 397-399

1. C.	3. E.	5. B.
2. D.	4. A.	

How does arousal relate to motivation? What are social motives? Why are they important? Pages 399-406

1. G.	4. H.	7. F.
2. C.	5. B.	8. E.
3. A.	6. D.	

Are some motives more basic than others? Pages 406-409

1. D.	4. A.	7. F.
2. G.	5. E.	
3. C.	6. B.	

What happens during emotion? Can "Lie Detectors" really detect lies? Pages 409-414

1. B.	4. D.	7. C.
2. G.	5. H.	8. E.
3. A.	6. F.	

How accurately do "body language" and the face express emotions? How do psychologists explain emotions? What does it mean to have "emotional intelligence"? Pages 414-423

1. E.	4. B.	7. H.
2. D.	5. F.	8. A.
3. I.	6. C.	9. G.

CHECK YOUR MEMORY

What is motivation? Are there different types of motives? Pages 388-390
1. F

2. T	3. T	4. T

What causes hunger? Overeating? Eating disorders? Pages 390-397

1. F	9. F	17. F
2. T	10. F	18. T
3. F	11. F	19. F
4. T	12. F	20. F
5. T	13. F	
6. T	14. T	
7. F	15. T	
8. T	16. T	

Is there more than one type of thirst? In what ways are pain avoidance and the sex drive unusual? Pages 397-399

1. T	3. F	5. T
2. F	4. T	

How does arousal relate to motivation? Pages 399-403

1. T	4. F	7. T
2. T	5. T	8. F
3. F	6. F	

What are social motives? Why are they important? Pages 404-406

1. T	3. F	5. T
2. F	4. T	

Are some motives more basic than others? Pages 406-409

1. F	4. T	7. T
2. T	5. F	8. F
3. F	6. T	

What happens during emotion? Pages 409-411

1. F	3. F	5. T
2. F	4. T	

Can "Lie Detectors" really detect lies? Pages 411-414

1. F

2. T   3. T   4. F

How accurately do "body language" and the face express emotions? Pages 414-417

1. F	5. T	9. F
2. F	6. T	10. F
3. T	7. F	11. F
4. T	8. T	12. F

How do psychologists explain emotions? Pages 417-421

1. F	4. F	7. T
2. T	5. T	8. T
3. T	6. F	9. F

What does it mean to have "emotional intelligence"? Pages 422-423

1. T	4. T	7. T
2. F	5. T	
3. T	6. T	

FINAL SURVEY AND REVIEW

What is motivation? Are there different types of motives?

1. sustain; direct
2. drive; attainment
3. needs; goals
4. incentive; value
5. primary; stimulus; secondary
6. homeostasis

What causes hunger? Overeating? Eating disorders?

1. distention; glucose
2. hypothalamus; satiety
3. lateral; ventromedial; nucleus
4. set; point; cues
5. body mass index; fat
6. 25; heart; stroke
7. eating
8. Behavioral; self
9. exercise; calories
10. aversions; bait; shyness
11. Anorexia; bulimia
12. medical
13. self-image

Is there more than one type of thirst? In what ways are pain avoidance and the sex drive unusual?

1. hypothalamus
2. intracellular; extracellular
3. episodic; cyclic
4. avoidance; tolerance
5. estrus; homeostatic
6. androgens

How does arousal relate to motivation?

1. stimulus; exploration
2. arousal theory
3. *Sensation-Seeking*

4. high-risk
5. inverted U
6. Yerkes-Dodson

7. worrying; arousal
8. Circadian; time zones
9. preadapt

10. melatonin; pineal

What are social motives? Why are they important?

1. socialization
2. Opponent-process

3. achievement
4. High

5. Self-confidence
6. confidence; challenging; social

Are some motives more basic than others?

1. hierarchy; growth
2. prepotent

3. actualization; meta
4. extrinsic; intrinsic

What happens during emotion?

1. adaptive

2. expressions

3. primary

Can "Lie Detectors" really detect lies?

1. adrenaline; autonomic
2. sympathetic; parasympathetic
3. parasympathetic; sympathetic

4. polygraph;
5. relevant; irrelevant
6. polygraph; critical

7. Infrared; face

How accurately do "body language" and the face express emotions?

1. expressions
2. Facial

3. women; men
4. feelings

5. activation
6. kinesics

How do psychologists explain emotions?

1. James
2. Cannon
3. cognitive; arousal

4. attribution
5. physical; arousal
6. facial; feedback

7. emotions; autonomic
8. appraised

What does it mean to have "emotional intelligence"?

1. intelligence; empathy
2. facial; voice

3. thinking; decision
4. growth; social

5. happiness; strengths

MASTERY TEST

What does it mean to have "emotional intelligence"?

1. C, p. 412
2. A, p. 398
3. A, p. 395

4. B, p. 407
5. C, p. 411
6. C, p. 422

7. C, p. 388
8. B, p. 388
9. C, p. 400

10. C, pp. 415-416
11. D, p. 394
12. B, p. 400
13. B, p. 418
14. A, p. 414
15. A, p. 396
16. B, p. 389
17. B, p. 398
18. A, p. 416
19. C, p. 402

20. C, p. 389
21. D, p. 411
22. D, p. 401
23. A, p. 391
24. D, p. 420
25. B, p. 390
26. A, p. 406
27. D, p. 409
28. B, pp. 389; 395
29. A, pp. 400-401

30. A, p. 420
31. C, p. 393
32. D, pp. 393-394
33. A, p. 395
34. B, p. 395
35. D, p. 396
36. C, p. 409
37. B, p. 414
38. A, p. 423
39. B, p. 413

Gender and Sexuality

Chapter Overview

A person's sex is determined by a combination of genetic sex, gonadal sex, hormonal sex, genital sex, and gender identity. The development of primary and secondary sexual characteristics is influenced by androgens and estrogens. Hormonal imbalance before birth may cause a person to develop ambiguous sexual anatomy or become an intersexual. Corrective surgery can be performed to give the genitals a male or female appearance. Prenatal hormones may exert a biological biasing effect that combines with social factors to influence psychosexual development.

On most psychological dimensions, men and women are more alike than they are different. Social factors are especially apparent in learned gender identity and the effects of gender roles. Gender roles often lead to gender role stereotypes that can be seen in the amount of money males and females earn. When females violate gender norms by performing tasks that are traditionally male, they are less liked. Gender role socialization accounts for most observed male/female differences beginning at the age of three when children participate in sex-segregated play. Psychological androgyny is related to greater personal adaptability.

"Normal" sexual behavior is defined differently by various cultures. There is little difference in male and female sexual responsiveness. The difference lies in the subjective feelings of arousal in which females tend to focus more on their emotional responses to erotic cues. Contrary to belief, high amounts of alcohol consumption and many drugs actually decrease sexual desire, arousal, pleasure, and performance. Sexual orientation refers to whether a person is heterosexual, homosexual, or bisexual. A combination of hereditary, biological, social, and psychological influences combine to produce one's sexual orientation. Some theorists believe that evolutionarily, homosexuality may have developed to reduce competition among men for female mates.

Human sexual response can be divided into four phases: (1) excitement; (2) plateau; (3) orgasm; and (4) resolution, which apply to both males and females.

Atypical sexual behavior can produce troubling sexual disorders such as pedophilia and fetishism. Such disorders are called paraphilias.

Attitudes toward sexual behavior have grown more liberal, but actual changes in behavior have been more gradual. People who are sexually active, even with one person, may increase their risk of getting STDs, including the HIV virus, if they do not practice safe sex and have indirect sex with others through their partner's indiscretion. During the last 20 years there has been a steady increase in the incidence of sexually transmitted diseases, which has altered patterns of sexual behavior.

The principal problems in sexual adjustment are desire disorders, arousal disorders, orgasm disorders, and sexual pain disorders. Behavioral methods and counseling techniques can alleviate each problem. However, communication skills that foster and maintain intimacy are the real key to successful relationships.

Learning Objectives

1. Distinguish between the terms *sex* and *gender*; differentiate primary from secondary sex characteristics; and define the following terms:

   a. menarche

   b. ovulation

   c. menopause

   d. gonads

   e. estrogens

   f. androgens

   g. testosterone

2. List and describe the five dimensions of sex and explain how a person's sex develops. Include in your discussion a description of these conditions:

   a. androgen insensitivity

   b. intersexual person

   c. androgenital syndrome

   d. biological biasing effect

3. Differentiate gender identity from gender role; explain how gender identity is formed; and discuss the effects of socialization on gender roles, including gender role stereotypes, cultural variations, instrumental and expressive behaviors, and androgyny.

4. Define *erogenous zone* and *sexual script*; discuss the differences between males and females in their degree of arousal and their sex drives; describe the effects of alcohol, castration, and aging on the sex drive; and discuss the normality and acceptability of masturbation.

5. Define the term *sexual orientation;* discuss the various types of sexual orientation; describe the combination of influences that appears to produce homosexuality; and characterize the emotional adjustment of homosexuals versus heterosexuals.

6. List in order and briefly describe the four phases of sexual response in men and women and state the basic differences in sexual response styles of men and women.

7. Explain the difference between public and private standards of sexual behavior and what sets true sexual deviations apart from other sexual activity and list and define eight behavior patterns (paraphilias) that fit the definition of sexual deviation. Include a discussion of exhibitionism, including who the offenders are, why they do it, and how one's reactions may encourage them.

8. Describe pedophilia (child molestation) including who does it, what the offenders are like, and the factors that affect the seriousness of the molestation. Include seven ways to recognize molestation from a child's behavior; six tactics of molesters; and ways to prevent children from being molested.

9. Describe the changes that have taken place in sexual attitudes and behavior in the last 50 years; discuss how the pace of the "revolution" seems to have slowed recently; and explain what is meant by the phrase *slow death of the double standard.*

10. Define *acquaintance or "date" rape* and discuss its effects; explain how gender role stereotyping may encourage the act of rape; differentiate forcible rape from date rape; and explain why rape is not viewed by experts as primarily a sexual act.

11. Explain the cause of, methods of transmission, and ways of preventing AIDS and other STDs.

The following objectives are related to the material in the "Psychology in Action" section of your text.

1. Describe the following sexual problems including the nature, cause, and treatment of each:

    a. Desire Disorders

        i)   hypoactive sexual desire
        ii) sexual aversion

    b. Arousal Disorders

        i)   male erectile disorder
        ii) female sexual arousal disorder

    c. Orgasm Disorders

        i)   female orgasmic disorder
        ii) male orgasmic disorder
        iii) premature ejaculation

    d. Sexual Pain Disorders

        i)   dyspareunia
        ii) vaginismus

2. List four elements of a healthy sexual relationship and seven guidelines for effective communication between husbands and wives.

RECITE AND REVIEW

What are the basic dimensions of sex? How does one's sense of maleness or femaleness develop?

Sexual Development—Circle One: *XX* or *XY*: Pages 427-434

1. Physical differences between males and females can be divided into _____ and _____ sexual characteristics.

2. Primary sexual characteristics are the _____ and internal reproductive organs.

3. Secondary sexual characteristics are bodily features such as breast development, body _____ , and facial hair.

4. Reproductive maturity in females is signaled by menarche (the onset of _____). Soon after, ovulation (the release of _____ , or eggs) begins.

5. The development of sexual characteristics is influenced by androgens (_____ sex hormones) and estrogens (_____ sex hormones) secreted by the gonads (sex _____).

6. A person's sex can be broken down into genetic sex, gonadal sex, _____ sex, genital sex, and _____ identity.

7. Sexual development begins with _____ sex (*XX* or *XY* chromosomes). Two *X* chromosomes normally produce a _____ ; an *X* plus a *Y* produces a _____ .

8. During prenatal sexual development, the presence of testosterone produces _____ genitals; an absence of testosterone produces _____ genitals.

9. Androgen insensitivity, exposure to progestin, and the androgenital _____ result in _____ ambiguities called intersexualism.

10. Many researchers believe that prenatal _____ can exert a biological biasing _____ that combines with social factors present after birth to influence psychosexual development.

11. On most psychological dimensions, men and women are more _____ than they are _____ .

12. Surgical _____ with hormone therapy can alter the genital _____ and secondary sex characteristics for intersexuals (children with _____ sexual anatomy) to either male or female. However, these factors alone do not determine gender identity; socialization is also important.

13. Social factors are especially apparent in learned gender identity (a private sense of _____ or _____) and the effect of gender roles (patterns of behavior defined as male or female within a particular culture).

14. Gender identity, which is based to a large extent on labeling, usually becomes stable by age _____ or _____ years.

15. Gender roles contribute to the development of _____ stereotypes (oversimplified beliefs about the nature of men and women) that often distort perceptions about the kinds of occupations for which men and women are suited.

16. As a result of gender role _____ , for every $1.00 men earn in business, academia, medicine, law, sports, and politics, white _____ earn $.75, black _____ earn $.67, and Latino women earn $.54.

17. Another effect of gender role _____ is that women are _____ liked by their peers for violating _____ norms, such as holding a job that as been defined as traditionally "male."

18. Culture determines the gender _____ of males and females in each society.

19. _____ socialization (learning gender roles) seems to account for most observed male/female differences.

20. Parents tend to encourage _____ in instrumental behaviors and _____ in expressive behaviors.

21. By age _____ , _____ -segregated playing can be seen in boys and girls: Boys play _____ games that focus on superheroes, and girls play _____ games that focus on house-related activities.

What is psychological androgyny (and is it contagious)?

Androgyny—Are You Masculine, Feminine, or Androgynous? Pages 434-436

1. Androgyny is measured with the *Bem* _____ *Inventory (BSRI)*.

2. Research conducted by Sandra Bem indicates that roughly one third of all persons are androgynous (they possess both _____ and _____ traits).

3. Being _____ means that a person is independent and assertive.

4. Being _____ means that a person is nurturant and interpersonally oriented.

5. Psychological _____ appears related to greater adaptability or flexibility in behavior.

What are the most typical patterns of human sexual behavior?

Sexual Behavior—Mapping the Erogenous Zone: Pages 436-438

1. Sexual behavior, including orgasm (sexual _____) is apparent soon after birth and expressed in various ways throughout life.

2. Sexual arousal is related to stimulation of the body's erogenous zones (areas that produce erotic _____), but cognitive elements such as _____ and images are equally important.

3. "Normal" sexual behavior is defined differently by various _____ . Also, each person uses learned sexual scripts (plots or mental plans) to guide sexual behavior.

4. There is little difference in sexual _____ between males and females.

5. Research suggests that both women and men are equal in physiological sexual _____ but differ in the _____ feelings of arousal. Women's sexual arousal is linked to their _____ responses to cues and acknowledgment from their partners of their needs and preferences.

6. Evidence suggests that the sex drive peaks at a _____ age for females than it does for males, although this difference is diminishing.

7. Sex _____ in both males and females may be related to bodily levels of androgens. As testosterone levels decline with _____ , so does _____ drive; both males and females can take testosterone supplements to restore it.

8. The belief that alcohol and other drugs enhance sex drive is a _____ . Alcohol is a depressant, which in large doses tends to _____ sexual desire, arousal, pleasure, and performance. Other drugs like _____ , amyl nitrite, barbiturates, cocaine, Ecstasy, LSD, and marijuana tend to _____ sexual responses.

9. Nocturnal _____ are a normal, but relatively minor, form of sexual release.

10. _____ (removal of the gonads) may or may not influence sex drive in humans, depending on how sexually experienced a person is. Sterilization (a vasectomy or tubal ligation) does not alter sex drive.

11. There is a gradual _____ in the frequency of sexual intercourse with increasing age.

12. Masturbation is a normal, harmless behavior practiced by a large percentage of the population. For many, masturbation is an important part of sexual self- _____ .

Sexual Orientation—Who Do You Love? Pages 438-440

1. Sexual orientation refers to one's degree of emotional and erotic attraction to members of the same _____ , opposite _____ , or both _____ .

2. A person may be heterosexual, _____ , or bisexual.

3. A combination of hereditary, biological, social, and psychological influences combine to produce one's _____ _____ .

4. Research conducted on _____ orientation or behavior by neurobiologists suggests a _____ link between mothers and children. Other theorists believe that homosexuality may have developed to _____ the male and female competition for sexual partners.

5. A national survey suggests that of every 100 people, _____ identify themselves as homosexual or _____ .

6. However, gay men and lesbians are frequently affected by homophobia (fear of _____) and heterosexism (the belief that heterosexuality is more natural than homosexuality).

7. As a group, homosexual men and women do not differ psychologically from _____ .

To what extent do males and females differ in sexual response?

Human Sexual Response—Sexual Interactions: Pages 440-442

1. In a series of landmark studies, William _____ and Virginia Johnson directly observed sexual response in a large number of adults.

2. Human sexual response can be divided into four phases: (1) _____ ; (2) plateau; (3) _____ ; and (4) resolution.

3. There do not appear to be any differences between "vaginal _____ " and "clitoral _____ " in the female.

4. Males experience a refractory period after _____ and ejaculation. Only 5 percent of men are multi-orgasmic.

5. Both males and females may go through all four stages in _____ or five minutes. But during lovemaking, most females typically take longer than this, averaging from 10 to 20 minutes.

6. Mutual _____ has been abandoned by most sex counselors as the ideal in lovemaking.

7. Fifteen percent of women are consistently _____ -orgasmic, and at least 48 percent are capable of _____ orgasm.

What are the most common sexual disorders?

Atypical Sexual Behavior—Trench Coats, Whips, Leathers, and Lace: Pages 442-444

1. Definitions of sexual deviance are highly _____ . Many "sexually deviant" behaviors are acceptable in private or in some _____ .

2. Sexual _____ that often cause difficulty are called paraphilias.

3. Some paraphilias include: pedophilia (sex with children), _____ (sexual arousal associated with inanimate objects), voyeurism (viewing the genitals of others without their permission), and _____ (displaying the genitals to unwilling viewers).

4. Other paraphilias are: transvestic fetishism (achieving sexual arousal by wearing clothing of the opposite sex), sexual _____ (deriving sexual pleasure from inflicting pain), sexual _____ (desiring pain as part of the sex act), and frotteurism (sexually touching or rubbing against a nonconsenting person).

5. Exhibitionists are rarely dangerous and can best be characterized as sexually _____ and immature.

6. The effects of child molestation vary greatly, depending on the _____ of the molestation and the child's relationship to the molester.

7. Children who have been _____ may display such signs as fear of being seen _____ , anxiety, _____ , or discomfort to references of _____ behaviors and express low self-esteem or self-worth.

8. Child molesters tend to gain access to children through caretaking _____ and bring them to their homes. Some tactics molesters use to lull children are bribing them with _____ , encouraging them to talk about sex, and using threats to gain _____ .

Have recent changes in attitudes affected sexual behavior?

Attitudes and Sexual Behavior—The Changing Sexual Landscape: Pages 444-447

1. Attitudes toward sexual behavior, especially the behavior of others, have become more liberal, but actual changes in sexual _____ have been more gradual.

2. Another change has been _____ and more frequent sexual activity among adolescents and young adults, including larger percentages of people who have premarital _____ .

3. Also evident are a greater acceptance of _____ sexuality and a narrowing of differences in male and female patterns of sexual _____ . In other words, the double standard is fading.

4. Acquaintance (_____) rape and _____ -supportive myths and attitudes remain major problems.

5. _____ is primarily a violent crime of aggression rather than a sex crime.

What impacts have sexually transmitted diseases had on sexual behavior?

STDs and Safer Sex—Choice, Risk, and Responsibility: Pages 447-450

1. Based on a recent study, approximately _____ percent of sexually active teenage _____ reported that they do not believe they will get _____ transmitted diseases (STDs) because their partners _____ show symptoms of STDs.

2. People who are sexually _____ , even with only one person, may still be engaging in risky sex from _____ contact with others through their partner's indiscretion.

3. During the last 20 years there has been a steady increase in the incidence of sexually transmitted _____ (STDs).

4. Part of this increase is due to the emergence of _____ deficiency syndrome (AIDS) caused by the human immunodeficiency _____ (HIV).

5. STDs have had a sizable impact on patterns of sexual behavior, including increased awareness of high- _____ behaviors and some curtailment of _____ taking.

6. It is predicted that over the next 20 to 30 years, the dominant group of individuals that will spread the _____ virus are heterosexuals, and unless preventions are taken, _____ million people will die of AIDS.

What are the most common sexual adjustment problems? How are they treated?

Psychology in Action: Sexual Problems—When Pleasure Fades: Pages 450-455

1. The principal problems in sexual adjustment are _____ disorders, arousal disorders, orgasm disorders, and sexual _____ disorders.

2. Desire disorders include hypoactive _____ _____ (a loss of sexual desire) and _____ aversion (fear or disgust about engaging in sex).

3. Arousal disorders include _____ erectile disorder and _____ sexual arousal disorder.

4. Approximately 40 percent of _____ disorders result from psychogenic causes (having _____ or emotional origin) rather than physical illnesses, diseases, or _____ to the penis.

5. Both males and females have similar causes for sexual _____ disorder, which include anxiety, _____ toward their partner, depression, stress, _____ experiences, having a strict religious background, and distrust of men or women.

6. To _____ a healthy relationship through communication, people should _____ gunnysacking each other, be open about their feelings, not _____ each other's characteristics, not be mind readers, and try to understand the other's perspectives.

7. Orgasm disorders are male orgasmic disorder (retarded _____), premature _____ , and female orgasm disorder (an inability to reach orgasm during lovemaking).

8. Sexual pain disorders are dyspareunia (_____ intercourse) and vaginismus (_____ of the vagina).

9. Behavioral methods such as sensate _____ and the squeeze technique have been developed to alleviate each problem. In addition, counseling can be quite helpful.

10. However, most sexual adjustment problems are closely linked to the general health of a couple's _____ .

11. For this reason, communication skills that foster and maintain _____ are the key to successful relationships.

CONNECTIONS

What are the basic dimensions of sex? How does one's sense of maleness or femaleness develop? What is psychological androgyny (and is it contagious)? Pages 427-436

1. _____ pelvic bone
2. _____ urethra
3. _____ labia minora
4. _____ ovary
5. _____ vagina
6. _____ uterus
7. _____ rectum
8. _____ fallopian tube
9. _____ clitoris
10. _____ labia majora
11. _____ urinary bladder
12. _____ cervix

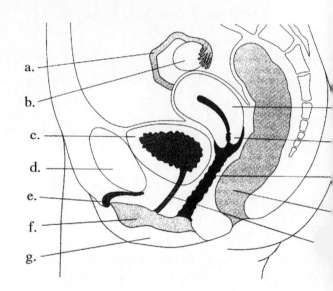

Connections

1. _____ Cowper's gland
2. _____ glans penis
3. _____ urethra
4. _____ seminal vesicle
5. _____ vas deferens
6. _____ pelvic bone
7. _____ urinary bladder
8. _____ testis
9. _____ rectum
10. _____ urethral orifice
11. _____ epididymis
12. _____ prostate

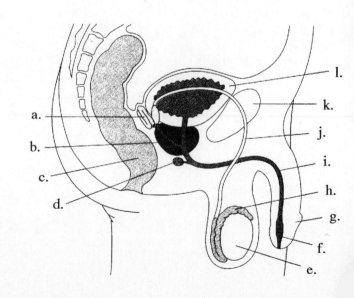

Connections Part II

1. _____ androgen
2. _____ estrogen
3. _____ genetic sex
4. _____ gonadal sex
5. _____ hermaphroditism
6. _____ gender identity
7. _____ gender role
8. _____ menopause
9. _____ menarche
10. _____ androgyny

a. ovaries or testes
b. cultural pattern
c. self-perception
d. female hormone
e. man-woman
f. XX or XY
g. androgenital syndrome
h. ending of menstruation
i. onset of menstruation
j. testosterone

What are the most typical patterns of human sexual behavior? Pages 436-440

1. _____ masturbation
2. _____ homophobia
3. _____ heterosexual
4. _____ homosexual
5. _____ bisexual
6. _____ sex drive
7. _____ sterilization
8. _____ erogenous zone
9. _____ castration
10. _____ sexual script

a. attracted to both sexes
b. attracted to opposite sex
c. attracted to same sex
d. safest sex
e. infertility
f. testical removal
g. fear of homosexuality
h. motivation for intercourse
i. dialogue for sexual behavior
j. productive of pleasure

To what extent do males and females differ in sexual response? What are the most common sexual disorders? Have recent changes in attitudes affected sexual behavior? Pages 440-447

1. _____ voyeurism
2. _____ excitement phase
3. _____ pedophilia
4. _____ exhibitionism
5. _____ acquaintance rape
6. _____ orgasm

a. date rape
b. "flashing"
c. "peeping"
d. child molesting
e. sexual climax
f. signs of sexual arousal

What impacts have sexually transmitted diseases had on sexual behavior? What are the most common sexual adjustment problems? How are they treated? Pages 447-455

1. _____ orgasmic disorder
2. _____ STD
3. _____ psychogenic
4. _____ gunnysacking
5. _____ safer sex practices
6. _____ dyspareunia

a. "dumping" saved-up complaints
b. genital pain from intercourse
c. inability to reach orgasm
d. psychological origin
e. using a condom
f. AIDS

CHECK YOUR MEMORY

What are the basic dimensions of sex? How does one's sense of maleness or femaleness develop? Pages 427-434

1. Primary sexual characteristics involve differences in the reproductive organs and the breasts.

   TRUE or FALSE

2. The term menarche refers to the ending of regular monthly fertility cycles in females.

   TRUE or FALSE

3. The female gonads are the ovaries.

   TRUE or FALSE

4. Cowper's glands are female reproductive structures.

   TRUE or FALSE

5. All individuals normally produce both androgens and testosterones.

   TRUE or FALSE

6. Transsexuals are persons who have had their genetic sex altered medically.

   TRUE or FALSE

7. Without testosterone, a human embryo will develop into a female.

   TRUE or FALSE

8. Androgen insensitivity results in the development of female genitals.

   TRUE or FALSE

9. Surgical reconstruction determines intersexuals' gender identity by altering their ambiguous genital appearance to be either male or female.

   TRUE or FALSE

10. Differences in male and female scores on the SAT have declined in recent years.

    TRUE or FALSE

11. Observed differences in the abilities of males and females are based on averages; they tell nothing about a particular person.

    TRUE or FALSE

12. Gender identity refers to all the behaviors that are defined as male or female by one's culture.

    TRUE or FALSE

13. Babies are perceived differently and treated differently when they are labeled as males than when they are labeled as females.

    TRUE or FALSE

14. Due to gender role stereotyping, women today are liked more by their peers for successfully holding a job that has been defined as traditionally "male."

    TRUE or FALSE

15. Women continue to receive unequal pay for work comparable to that of men.

    TRUE or FALSE

16. Women of all ethnic groups receive the same unequal pay of $.75 for every $1.00 men earn.

    TRUE or FALSE

17. Even though their culture is quite different, the sex roles of Tchambuli men and women are almost identical to those in North America.

    TRUE or FALSE

18. Boys are allowed to roam over wider areas than girls are.

    TRUE or FALSE

19. Expressive behaviors are those that directly express a person's desire to attain a goal.

    TRUE or FALSE

20. Sex-segregated play means that boys and girls do not play with each other.

    TRUE or FALSE

What is psychological androgyny (and is it contagious)? Pages 434-436

1. The BSRI consists of 20 masculine traits and 20 feminine traits.

   TRUE or FALSE

2. About 50 percent of all people who take the BSRI are scored as androgynous.

   TRUE or FALSE

3. Masculine men and feminine women consistently choose to engage in sex-appropriate activities.

   TRUE or FALSE

4. Masculine men find it difficult to accept support from others.

   TRUE or FALSE

5. Androgynous persons tend to be more satisfied with their lives than non-androgynous persons are.

   TRUE or FALSE

What are the most typical patterns of human sexual behavior? Pages 436-440

1. Sexual scripts determine when, where, and with whom we are likely to express sexual feelings.

   TRUE or FALSE

2. Women are less physically aroused by erotic stimuli than men are.

   TRUE or FALSE

3. Research suggests that women and men are equal in the level of physiological sexual arousal but differ in the subjective feelings of arousal.

   TRUE or FALSE

4. Differences between male and female sexuality are accurately perceived by the general public.

   TRUE or FALSE

5. Women may engage in sexual activity at any time during their menstrual cycles.

   TRUE or FALSE

6. More women than men have sexual dreams that result in orgasm.

   TRUE or FALSE

7. As testosterone levels decline with age, females can take testosterone supplements to restore their sex drive.

   TRUE or FALSE

8. Alcohol and other drugs enhance sexual desire, arousal, and pleasure.

   TRUE or FALSE

9. Drunkenness lowers sexual arousal and performance.

   TRUE or FALSE

10. Sterilization tends to abolish the sex drive in the sexually inexperienced.

    TRUE or FALSE

11. Masturbation typically ends soon after people get married.

    TRUE or FALSE

12. The average frequency of sexual intercourse declines dramatically between the ages of 30 and 39.

    TRUE or FALSE

13. Your sexual orientation is revealed, in part, by who you have erotic fantasies about.

    TRUE or FALSE

14. Gay males are converted to homosexuality during adolescence by other homosexuals.

    TRUE or FALSE

15. Sexual orientation is a very stable personal characteristic.

    TRUE or FALSE

16. Sexual orientation is influenced by heredity.

    TRUE or FALSE

17. Hormone imbalances cause most instances of homosexuality and bisexuality.

    TRUE or FALSE

18. Fifteen percent of men and 13 percent of women identify themselves as homosexual.

    TRUE or FALSE

19. A national survey suggests that of every 100 people, seven identify themselves as homosexual or bisexual.

    TRUE or FALSE

20. Evolutionists suggested that homosexuality may have developed to reduce male competition for female mates.

    TRUE or FALSE

21. Homosexual persons tend to discover their sexual orientation at a later age than heterosexual persons do.

    TRUE or FALSE

To what extent do males and females differ in sexual response? Pages 440-442

1. Masters and Johnson's data on human sexuality was restricted to questionnaires and interviews.
   TRUE or FALSE

2. During the excitement phase of sexual response, the nipples become erect in both males and females.
   TRUE or FALSE

3. In males, orgasm is always accompanied by ejaculation.
   TRUE or FALSE

4. Almost all women experience a short refractory period after ejaculation.
   TRUE or FALSE

5. Both orgasm and resolution tend to last longer in females than they do in males.
   TRUE or FALSE

6. Contemporary research has confirmed that clitoral orgasms are an inferior form of sexual response.
   TRUE or FALSE

7. Women tend to go through the phases of sexual response more slowly than men do.
   TRUE or FALSE

8. One woman in 3 does not experience orgasm during the first year of marriage.
   TRUE or FALSE

What are the most common sexual disorders? Pages 442-444

1. Oral sex and masturbation are formally classified as paraphilias.
   TRUE or FALSE

2. Frotteurism refers to sex with children.
   TRUE or FALSE

3. Most exhibitionists are male and married.
   TRUE or FALSE

4. An exhibitionist who approaches closer than arm's length may be dangerous.
   TRUE or FALSE

5. In the majority of cases of child molesting, the offender is an acquaintance or relative of the child.
   TRUE or FALSE

6. Child molesting is especially likely to be harmful if the molester is someone the child deeply trusts.

   TRUE or FALSE

7. Child molesters tend to kidnap children on playgrounds in parks when caretakers are not looking.

   TRUE or FALSE

Have recent changes in attitudes affected sexual behavior? Pages 444-447

1. In recent decades the gap between sexual values and actual behavior has narrowed.

   TRUE or FALSE

2. A majority of young adults continue to believe that premarital sex is unacceptable.

   TRUE or FALSE

3. The incidence of extramarital sex has not changed much in the last 40 years.

   TRUE or FALSE

4. The majority of men and women have sexual experiences before marriage.

   TRUE or FALSE

5. About 12 percent of all adult Americans are sexually abstinent.

   TRUE or FALSE

6. Women who are raped usually asked for trouble by wearing sexy clothes.

   TRUE or FALSE

7. One woman in 70 will be raped in her lifetime.

   TRUE or FALSE

8. The majority of rapists are friends or acquaintances of the victim.

   TRUE or FALSE

9. Males high in sex role stereotyping are more aroused by stories about rape than males low in sex role stereotyping.

   TRUE or FALSE

What impacts have sexually transmitted diseases had on sexual behavior? Pages 447-450

1. Many people suffering from STDs are asymptomatic.

   TRUE or FALSE

2. People who are sexually active with one partner do not have to worry about STDs or indirect sexual contact with others.

   TRUE or FALSE

3. Teenage girls today are well educated about STDs and understand that they may get STDs if they are sexually active.

   TRUE or FALSE

4. The first symptoms of AIDS may not appear for up to 7 years.

   TRUE or FALSE

5. HIV infections are spread by direct contact with body fluids.

   TRUE or FALSE

6. The AIDS epidemic has dramatically altered the sexual behavior of college students.

   TRUE or FALSE

7. Most women who contract the HIV virus today do so through intravenous drug use.

   TRUE or FALSE

8. It is unwise to count on a partner for protection from HIV infection.

   TRUE or FALSE

9. Gonorrhea can be prevented by vaccination.

   TRUE or FALSE

10. Hepatitis B can be prevented by vaccination.

    TRUE or FALSE

11. Chlamydia is now the most common STD among men.

    TRUE or FALSE

12. Heterosexuals are predicted to be the main group of people to spread the HIV virus in the next 20 years.

    TRUE or FALSE

13. In the United States, three million people die each year from AIDS, and worldwide five million people die each year.

    TRUE or FALSE

What are the most common sexual adjustment problems? How are they treated? Pages 450-455

1. In a desire disorder the person desires sex, but does not become sexually aroused.

   TRUE or FALSE

2. A person who is repelled by sex and seeks to avoid it suffers from a sexual aversion.

   TRUE or FALSE

3. Men suffering from primary erectile dysfunction have never had an erection.

   TRUE or FALSE

4. The squeeze technique is the most commonly recommended treatment for erectile disorders.

   TRUE or FALSE

5. The majority of erectile dysfunctions are psychogenic.

   TRUE or FALSE

6. The causes of erectile disorders include physical illnesses, diseases, and damage to the penis.

   TRUE or FALSE

7. Males' sexual arousal disorder is caused by physical illnesses, and females' sexual arousal disorder is caused by traumatic childhood experiences.

   TRUE or FALSE

8. Treatment for female sexual arousal disorder usually involves sensate focus.

   TRUE or FALSE

9. Female orgasmic disorder is the female equivalent of premature ejaculation in the male.

   TRUE or FALSE

10. Both males and females can experience dyspareunia.

    TRUE or FALSE

11. Masters and Johnson regard all sexual problems as mutual, or shared by both parties.

    TRUE or FALSE

12. Gunnysacking is an important communication skill that all couples should master.

    TRUE or FALSE

13. Rather than telling your partner what he or she thinks, you should ask her or him.

    TRUE or FALSE

FINAL SURVEY AND REVIEW

What are the basic dimensions of sex? How does one's sense of maleness or femaleness develop?

Sexual Development—Circle One: *XX* or *XY*: Pages 427-434

1. Physical differences between males and females can be divided into primary and secondary

   _____ _____ .

2. _____ refers to the genitals and _____ reproductive organs.

3. _____ refers to bodily features such as breast development in females, body shape, and

   facial _____ .

4. Reproductive maturity in females is signaled by _____ (the onset of menstruation). Soon

   after, _____ (the release of the eggs) begins.

5. The development of sexual characteristics is influenced by _____ (male sex hormones) and

   _____ (female sex hormones) secreted by the _____ (sex glands).

6. A person's sex can be broken down into _____ sex, _____ sex, hormonal sex,

   _____ sex, and gender identity.

7. Sexual development begins with genetic sex (XX or XY _____). Two _____ s

   normally produce a female; an _____ plus a _____ produces a male.

8. During prenatal sexual development, the presence of _____ produces male _____ ;

   its absence produces female _____ .

9. _____ insensitivity, exposure to progestin, and the androgenital syndrome result in sexual

   ambiguities called _____ .

10. Many researchers believe that _____ hormones can exert a biological _____ effect

    that combines with social factors present after birth to influence psychosexual development.

11. On most _____ dimensions, men and women are more alike than they are different.

12. _____ _____ with hormone therapy can alter the genital appearance and secondary

    sex characteristics for _____ (children with ambiguous sexual anatomy) to either male or

    female. However, these factors alone do not determine gender identity; _____ is also important.

13. Social factors are especially apparent in learned _____ _____ (a private sense of

    maleness or femaleness) and the effect of _____ _____ (patterns of behavior defined

    as male or female within a particular culture).

14. Gender identity, which is based to a large extent on _____ , usually becomes stable by age 3 or 4 years.

15. Gender roles contribute to the development of gender role _____ (oversimplified beliefs about the nature of men and women) that often distort perceptions about the kinds of occupations for which men and women are suited.

16. As a result of gender role _____ , for every $1.00 men earn in business, academia, medicine, law, sports, and politics, white women earn $. _____ , black women earn $. _____ , and Latino women earn $. _____ .

17. Another effect of gender role _____ is that _____ are less liked by their peers for violating gender norms when they hold a job that as been defined as traditionally "male."

18. _____ determines gender roles of males and females in each society.

19. Gender role _____ (learning gender roles) seems to account for most observed male/female differences.

20. Parents tend to encourage boys in _____ behaviors (goal-directed actions) and girls in _____ (emotional) behaviors.

21. By age three, _____ play can be seen in boys and girls: Boys play outdoor games that focus on superheroes, and girls play indoor games that focus on house-related activities.

What is psychological androgyny (and is it contagious)?

Androgyny—Are You Masculine, Feminine, or Androgynous? Pages 434-436

1. Androgyny is measured with the _____ *Sex Role Inventory (BSRI)*.

2. Research conducted by Sandra Bem indicates that roughly one _____ of all persons are androgynous (they possess both masculine and feminine traits).

3. Being masculine means that a person is _____ and assertive.

4. Being feminine means that a person is _____ (helpful and comforting) and interpersonally oriented.

5. Psychological androgyny appears related to greater _____ or flexibility in behavior.

What are the most typical patterns of human sexual behavior?

Sexual Behavior—Mapping the Erogenous Zone: Pages 436-438

1. Sexual behavior, including _____ (sexual climax) is apparent soon after birth and expressed in various ways throughout life.

2. Sexual arousal is related to stimulation of the body's _____ zones (areas that produce erotic pleasure), but _____ elements such as thoughts and images are equally important.

3. "Normal" sexual behavior is defined differently by various cultures. Also, each person uses learned sexual _____ (plots or mental _____) to guide sexual behavior.

4. There is little _____ in sexual _____ between males and females.

5. Research suggests that _____ women and men are _____ in physiological sexual arousal but _____ in the subjective feelings of arousal. Women's sexual arousal is linked to their emotional responses to cues and acknowledgment from their partners of their needs and preferences.

6. Evidence suggests that the sex drive peaks at a later age for _____ than it does for _____ , although this difference is diminishing.

7. Sex drive in both males and females may be related to bodily levels of _____ . As testosterone levels decline with age, so does _____ drive; both males and females can take _____ supplements to restore it.

8. The belief that alcohol and other drugs _____ sex drive is a myth. Alcohol is a depressant, which in large doses tends to _____ sexual desire, arousal, pleasure, and performance. Other drugs like amphetamines, amyl nitrite, barbiturates, cocaine, Ecstasy, LSD, and marijuana tend to impair sexual responses.

9. _____ orgasms, which occur during sleep, are a normal form of sexual release.

10. Castration (removal of the gonads) may or may not influence sex drive in humans, depending on how sexually experienced a person is. _____ (a vasectomy or tubal ligation) does not alter sex drive.

11. There is a gradual decline (or decrease) in the _____ of sexual intercourse with increasing age. However, many elderly persons remain sexually active and great variations exist at all ages.

12. _____ is a normal, harmless behavior practiced by a large percentage of the population. For many, it is an important part of sexual self- discovery.

Sexual Orientation—Who Do You Love? Pages 438-440

1. Sexual _____ refers to one's degree of emotional and erotic attraction to members of the same sex, opposite sex, or both sexes.

2. A person may be _____ , homosexual, or bisexual.

3. A combination of _____ , biological, _____ , and psychological influences combine to produce one's sexual orientation.

4. Research conducted on sexual _____ or behavior by neurobiologists suggests a genetic link between _____ and children. Other theorists believe that homosexuality may have developed to _____ the male and female competition for sexual partners.

5. A national survey suggests that of every 100 people, 7 identify themselves as _____ or bisexual.

6. However, gay men and lesbians are frequently affected by _____ (fear of homosexuality) and _____ (the belief that heterosexuality is more natural than homosexuality).

7. As a group, _____ men and women do not differ psychologically from _____ .

To what extent do males and females differ in sexual response?

Human Sexual Response—Sexual Interactions: Pages 440-442

1. In a series of landmark studies, William Masters and Virginia _____ directly observed sexual response in a large number of adults.

2. Human sexual response can be divided into four phases: (1) excitement; (2) _____ ; (3) orgasm; and (4) _____ .

3. There do not appear to be any differences between " _____ orgasms" and " _____ orgasms" in the female.

4. Males experience a _____ period after orgasm and ejaculation. Only 5 percent of men are multi- _____ .

5. Both males and females may go through all four stages in 4 or 5 minutes. But during lovemaking, most _____ typically take longer than this, averaging from 10 to 20 minutes.

6. _____ orgasm has been abandoned by most sex counselors as the ideal in lovemaking.

7. _____ percent of women are consistently _____ , and at least 48 percent are capable of multiple orgasm.

What are the most common sexual disorders?

Atypical Sexual Behavior—Trench Coats, Whips, Leathers, and Lace: Pages 442-444

1. Definitions of sexual deviance are highly subjective. Many " _____ _____ " behaviors are acceptable in private or in some cultures.

2. Sexual deviations that often cause difficulty are called _____ (destructive deviations in sexual preferences or behavior).

3. Some paraphilias include: _____ (sex with children), fetishism (sexual arousal associated with inanimate objects), _____ (viewing the genitals of others without their permission), and exhibitionism (displaying the genitals to unwilling viewers).

4. Other are: _____ fetishism (achieving sexual arousal by wearing clothing of the opposite sex), sexual sadism (deriving sexual pleasure from inflicting pain), sexual masochism (desiring pain as part of the sex act), and _____ (sexually touching or rubbing against a nonconsenting person).

5. _____ ("flashers") are rarely dangerous and can best be characterized as sexually inhibited and immature.

6. The effects of child molestation vary greatly, depending on the severity of the _____ and the child's _____ to the molester.

7. _____ who have been molested may display such signs as fear of being seen _____ , anxiety, shame, or discomfort to references of _____ behaviors and express low self-esteem or self-worth.

8. Child molesters tend to gain access to children through _____ opportunities and bring them to their homes. Some tactics molesters use to lull children are _____ them with gifts, encouraging them to _____ about sex, and using threats to gain compliance.

Have recent changes in attitudes affected sexual behavior?

Attitudes and Sexual Behavior—The Changing Sexual Landscape: Pages 444-447

1. _____ toward sexual behavior, especially the behavior of others, have become more _____ , but actual changes in sexual behavior have been more gradual.

2. Another change has been earlier and more frequent sexual activity among adolescents and young adults, including larger percentages of people who have _____ intercourse.

3. Also evident are a greater acceptance of female sexuality and a narrowing of differences in male and female patterns of sexual behavior. In other words, the _____ _____ is fading.

4. _____ (date) rape and rape-supportive _____ and attitudes remain major problems.

5. Rape is primarily a violent crime of _____ rather than a sex crime.

What impacts have sexually transmitted diseases had on sexual behavior?

STDs and Safer Sex—Choice, Risk, and Responsibility: Pages 447-450

1. Based on a recent study, approximately 90 percent of _____ teenage girls reported that they do not believe they will get _____ diseases (STDs) because their partners did not show symptoms of STDs.

2. People who are sexually active, even with only one person, may still be engaging in _____ sex from indirect _____ with others through their partner's indiscretion.

3. During the last 20 years there has been a steady increase in the incidence of _____ _____ diseases (STDs).

4. Part of this increase is due to the emergence of acquired immune _____ syndrome (AIDS) caused by the human _____ virus (HIV).

5. _____ have had a sizable impact on patterns of sexual behavior, including increased awareness of high-risk behaviors and some curtailment of risk taking.

6. It is predicted that over the next 20 to 30 years, the dominant group of individuals that will spread the HIV virus are _____ , and unless preventions are taken, 65 million people will die of _____ .

What are the most common sexual adjustment problems? How are they treated?

Psychology in Action: Sexual Problems—When Pleasure Fades: Pages 450-455

1. The principal problems in sexual adjustment are desire disorders, _____ disorders, _____ disorders, and sexual pain disorders.

2. Desire disorders include _____ sexual desire (a loss of sexual desire) and sexual _____ (fear or disgust about engaging in sex).

3. Arousal disorders include male _____ disorder and female sexual _____ disorder.

4. Approximately 40 percent of _____ disorders result from _____ causes (having psychological or emotional origin) rather than physical illnesses, diseases, or damage to the penis.

5. Both males and females have similar causes for sexual _____ disorder, which include _____ , hostility toward their partner, depression, stress, childhood experiences, having a _____ religious background, and distrust of men or women.

6. To maintain a _____ relationship through communication, people should _____ gunnysacking each other, be open about their _____ , not attack each other's _____ , not be mind readers, and try to understand the other's perspectives.

7. Orgasm disorders are male orgasmic disorder (_____ ejaculation), _____ ejaculation, and female _____ disorder (an inability to reach orgasm during lovemaking).

8. Sexual pain disorders are _____ (painful intercourse) and _____ (muscle spasms of the vagina).

9. Behavioral methods such as _____ focus and the _____ technique have been developed to alleviate each problem. In addition, counseling can be quite helpful.

10. However, most sexual _____ problems are closely linked to the general health of a couple's relationship.

11. For this reason, _____ skills that foster and maintain intimacy are the key to successful relationships.

MASTERY TEST

1. The strength of the sex drive in both men and women increases when _____ levels are higher in the body.
   a. testosterone
   b. progestin
   c. ovulin
   d. androgenin

2. Worldwide, the main source of HIV infection is
   a. heterosexual sex
   b. homosexual sex
   c. intravenous drug use
   d. blood transfusions

3. Boys are encouraged to be strong, aggressive, dominant, and achieving through the process of
   a. biological biasing
   b. sexual orienting
   c. gender adaptation
   d. gender role socialization

4. Before birth, a genetic male will develop as a female if which condition exists?
   a. excessive progestin
   b. an androgen insensitivity
   c. the androgenital syndrome
   d. the testes produce testosterone

5. One of the greatest changes in attitudes toward sex is a tolerance for
   a. teenage pregnancies
   b. the sexual behavior of others
   c. the double standard
   d. STDs

6. The squeeze technique is typically used to treat
   a. dyspareunia
   b. vaginismus
   c. female sexual arousal disorder
   d. premature ejaculation

7. In a female, gonadal sex is determined by the presence of
   a. estrogens
   b. androgens
   c. ovaries
   d. a vagina and uterus

8. A policeman who accepts emotional support from others, especially from women, would most likely be scored as _____ on the BSRI.
   a. masculine
   b. feminine
   c. androgynous
   d. expressive-nurturant

9. Which of the following is POOR advice for couples who want to communicate effectively and maintain intimacy?
   a. Avoid gunnysacking.
   b. Avoid expressing anger.
   c. Don't try to win.
   d. Don't be a mind-reader.

10. The aspect of sex that is essentially formed by age 4 is
    a. gender identity
    b. gender roles
    c. sexual scripting
    d. psychological androgyny

11. In a female, broadening of the hips and breast development are
    a. primary sexual characteristics
    b. secondary sexual characteristics
    c. caused by the release of androgens
    d. associated with the presence of a Y chromosome

12. The first two phases of the sexual response cycle are
    a. excitement, arousal
    b. arousal, orgasm
    c. excitement, plateau
    d. stimulation, arousal

13. A special danger in the transmission of STDs is that many people are _____ at first.
    a. not infectious
    b. androgynous
    c. androgenital
    d. asymptomatic

14. The presence of a Y chromosome is associated with
    a. intersexualism
    b. prenatal testosterone
    c. menarche
    d. the presence of progestin

15. With respect to the behaviors parents encourage in their children, which is a correct match?
    a. controlling-female
    b. goal-oriented-female
    c. expressive-male
    d. instrumental-male

16. Which condition is LEAST likely to lower sexual performance?
    a. sterilization
    b. castration
    c. extreme alcohol intoxication
    d. sexual aversion

17. Prenatally masculinized females tend to be tomboys during childhood, an observation that supports the
    a. biological biasing effect
    b. estrogen paradox
    c. view that gender is genetically determined
    d. idea that gender role socialization is dominant

18. Which of the following increases the likelihood that a man will commit rape?
    a. drinking alcohol
    b. being high in gender role stereotyping
    c. belief in rape myths
    d. all of the preceding

19. Gender role _____ treat learned gender role differences as if they were real gender differences.
    a. labels
    b. behavior patterns
    c. stereotypes
    d. templates

20. Regarding sexual response it can be said that
    a. orgasm and resolution tend to last longer in women
    b. a short refractory period occurs just before orgasm in males
    c. some women skip the arousal phase of the cycle
    d. men are incapable of having second orgasms

21. The decline of the double standard refers to abandoning different standards for
    a. risky sex and "safe" sex
    b. heterosexual relationships and homosexual relationships
    c. sexuality before and after marriage
    d. male and female sexual behavior

22. Declines in the differences in male and female scores on the SAT call into question which concept?
    a. the androgenital syndrome
    b. the biological biasing effect
    c. gender role socialization
    d. gender identity

23. When expectations of a friendly first date clash with an attempted seduction the problem can be attributed to differences in
    a. gender roles
    b. erogenous confrontation
    c. gender myths
    d. sexual scripts

24. Which statement concerning sexual orientation is TRUE?
    a. Sexual orientation is partly hereditary
    b. Homosexuality is caused by a hormone imbalance
    c. Sexual orientation can be changed fairly easily
    d. Heterosexual persons tend to discover their sexual orientation at a later date than homosexual persons do

25. Pedophilia, fetishism, and sadism are classified as
    a. the three basic forms of child molestation
    b. STDs
    c. paraphilias
    d. hormonal disorders

26. All but one of the following is a rape myth. Which is NOT a myth?
    a. Women who get raped ask for it in one way or another.
    b. A majority of rapes are committed by a friend or acquaintance of the victim.
    c. Women who are sexually active are usually lying if they say they were raped.
    d. Many women who are raped secretly enjoy it.

27. Which of the following diseases is currently untreatable?
    a. gonorrhea
    b. chlamydia
    c. syphilis
    d. hepatitis B

28. The male sexual disorder that corresponds most closely to female sexual arousal disorder is
    a. sexual aversion
    b. erectile disorder
    c. premature ejaculation
    d. dyspareunia

29. Surgical reconstruction can alter genital appearances to either male or female for _____ or children with ambiguous sexual anatomy.
    a. pedophilia
    b. sexual masochism
    c. sexual sadism
    d. intersexuals

30. Women earn approximately $.54 to $.75 for every $1.00 men earn is the result of
    a. gender identity
    b. gender role stereotyping
    c. sexual orientation
    d. androgen insensitivity

31. To restore sex drive due to aging, both men and women can
    a. increase their sexual activities
    b. take estrogen supplements
    c. take testosterone supplements
    d. eat oysters and drink wine

32. At an early age, boys play outdoor games with other boys that focus on who's the boss, and girls play indoor games with other girls that focus on house-related activities and cooperation. This difference is the result of
    a. gender role socialization
    b. sex-segregated play
    c. instrumental versus expressive behaviors
    d. all the preceding

33. Research suggests that women who have violated _____ are _____ by their peers when they hold a job that has been defined as traditionally "male."
    a. gender norms; less liked
    b. sexual scripts; well liked
    c. cultural norms; supported
    d. biological biasing; harassed

34. Research suggests that physiological sexual arousal for men and women is _____, but their subjective feelings of arousal are _____.
    a. equal; different
    b. different; equal
    c. culturally defined; biologically defined
    d. easily measured; not measurable

35. Evolution theorists believe that homosexuality was developed
    a. to reduce male competition for female sexual partners
    b. to explain why certain men were not physically capable of performing "manly" duties
    c. as a result of hormonal imbalance
    d. as a result of survival of the fittest

36. Which of the following is NOT a tactic used by child molesters?
    a. use the chat room on the Internet to encourage children to talk about sex
    b. bribe children with gifts
    c. use threats to gain children's compliance
    d. have partners to help lure children to their homes

37. The performance gap between men and women can be traced back to
    a. heredity
    b. women being told they cannot outperform men
    c. availability of resources allocated to men versus women
    d. women too busy taking care of their family to maintain their physical skills

38. A recent study found that as high as _____ of teenage girls who are sexually active do not believe that they will get STDs because their partners did not exhibit any symptoms of STDs.
    a. 90 percent
    b. 70 percent
    c. 45 percent
    d. 35 percent

39. Cocaine and large doses of alcohol _____ sexual desire, arousal, pleasure, and performance.
    a. increase
    b. decrease
    c. do not affect
    d. enhance men's

LANGUAGE DEVELOPMENT - Gender and Sexuality

Word roots

The Greek word *homos* means "same" and is a root in such English words as homogenize and homonym. In this chapter, this root is part of several terms that refer to behavior involving the same sex: homosexuality, homosexual, homoerotic, and homophobic.

What are the basic dimensions of sex? How does one's sense of maleness or femaleness develop?

Preview: That Magic Word (p. 427)

(427) ***transsexual***: person who undergoes surgery to modify the sex organs to have them appear the same as those of the opposite sex

(427) ***ambiguities***: uncertainties

Sexual Development—Circle One: *XX* or *XY*? (pp. 427-434)

(431) *tomboys*: girls who prefer the company and the activities of boys

(431) *mired*: stuck

(431) *battle of the sexes*: implies fighting for superiority between men and women

(431) *left-brained*: preference for using the left hemisphere of the brain

(431) *right-brained*: preference for using the right hemisphere of the brain

(432) *running in place*: running, but not getting anywhere

(432) *hobbled:* to make movement difficult

(433) *effeminate:* displaying female characteristics of expressiveness and emotional behavior

What is psychological androgyny (and is it contagious)?

Androgyny—Are You Masculine, Feminine, or Androgynous? (pp. 434-436)

(434) *gullible*: believe everything you hear

(434) *seminal*: original and influential work

(434) *asexuality*: lack of sexual interest for both the same sex (homosexuality) and the opposite sex (heterosexuality)

(434) *dust begins to settle*: after the debate has subsided

What are the most typical patterns of human sexual behavior?

Sexual Behavior—Mapping the Erogenous Zone (pp. 436-438)

(436) *spontaneously*: arising from a natural feeling or momentary impulse

(436) *urological exam*: an inspection of the genital and urinary track of men

(436) *plot*: story

(436) *agendas*: plans of things that need to be done

(436) *macho fantasy*: a fantasy contrived by men that depicts male sexual desires

(436) *sexual prop*: a tool, such as sexy outfits that males and females wear, to enhance sexual arousal

(437) *dandy*: very good and fine

(437) *curb*: to control and reduce

(438) *use it or lose it*: suggests that if one is sexually active, there is a tendency to remain sexually active; not being sexually active can lead to a loss of sexual desire

(438) *one more item on the menu*: masturbation is just one more way to have sexual pleasure

Sexual Orientation—Who Do You Love? (pp. 438-440)

(438) *nil*: none

(439) *gay*: homosexual

(439) *lesbians*: female homosexual persons

To what extent do females and males differ in sexual response?

Human Sexual Responses—Sexual Interactions (pp. 440-442)

(441) *ebb*: to decline

(442) *flaccid*: not erect; limp

(442) *potency*: ability to engage in sexual intercourse; somewhat archaic term

What are the most common sexual disorders?

Atypical Sexual Behavior—Trench Coats, Whips, Leather, and Lace (pp. 442-444)

(442) *trench coats*: In a rare form of exhibitionism, exhibitionists may wear raincoats (trench coats) with no clothing under the coat

(443) *child molestation (child molesting)*: sexual abuse of children

(443) *despicable*: worthy of disgust or contempt

(443) *perverts*: those who engage in sexually deviant behavior

(443) *puritanical*: extremely strict in morals; refers to the Puritans of the 16th and 17th centuries who favored extreme moral strictness

(443) *fondling*: caressing, touching

(443) *fidgeting*: moving around restlessly or nervously

(443) *online*: accessing and using the Internet

(443) *lull*: to slowly convince

(443) *chat rooms*: sites on the Internet where individuals may type messages that will be seen by everyone in the "room" at that time

Have recent changes in attitudes affected sexual behavior?

Attitudes and Sexual Behavior—The Changing Sexual Landscape (pp. 444-447)

(444) *jock itch*: ringworm; or itching in the crotch area

(444) *Victorian era*: the time period when Queen Victoria reigned in England (1837-1901), characterized by excessive modesty regarding sexual matters

(445) *liberalization*: the encouragement of individuals to have the maximum freedom to express their opinions and ideas

(445) *albeit*: although

(445) *cohabitation*: living together as if married

(445) *preludes*: introductions, preparation

(445) *sowed some wild oats*: engaged in sexual intercourse with casual partners

(445) *tacitly*: implied or indicated indirectly

(445) *mores*: moral attitudes

(446) *condones*: pardons or overlooks

(446) *debase*: to lower in value or dignity

(447) *sodomized*: forced to engage in anal sexual intercourse

What impacts have sexually transmitted diseases had on sexual behavior?

STDs and Safer Sex—Choice, Risk, and Responsibility (pp. 447-450)

(447) *ambivalence*: uncertainty

(448) *incubation*: period between the infection of an individual and the appearance of symptoms of disease

(448) *hemophiliacs*: those who have a blood disease characterized by delayed clotting of the blood and resulting tendency to bleed easily

(448) *gambling with their lives*: putting their life at risk

(448) *condom*: thin sheath for the penis, usually made of latex, used for contraception and for the prevention of STDs

(449) *clueless*: lacking an understanding

(449) *monogamous relationships*: intimate relationships with one partner only

(449) *Russian roulette*: the practice of spinning the cylinder of a gun loaded with one bullet, pointing the gun at one's head, and pulling the trigger; here it means taking extreme risks with one's health

(449) *contraceptives*: devices or medicines to prevent pregnancy

(449) *"the pill"*: oral medication taken to prevent pregnancy

(449) *endearment*: affection

What are the most common sexual adjustment problems? How are they treated?

Psychology in Action: Sexual Problems—When Pleasure Fades (pp. 450-455)

(451) *performance demands*: perceptions by the male that he must perform sexually

(451) *vicious cycle*: in this case, the inability to sustain an erection leads to anxiety about having an erection, which in turn contributes to the inability to sustain an erection

(451) *fixing the "hydraulics" of erectile problems*: trying to find solutions to the problem of increasing blood flow and pressure to the penis

(452) *side effects*: unwanted consequences of taking medications

(453) *phobic*: reaction based on irrational fear

(453) *take their toll*: have a negative effect

(454) *bridges to sexual satisfaction*: ways by which one can have sexual pleasure

(454) *hitting below the belt*: being unfair and hurtful

(454) *mind reading*: attempting to know what another person is thinking without actually asking him or her

(455) *haven*: a safe place

Solutions

RECITE AND REVIEW

What are the basic dimensions of sex? How does one's sense of maleness or femaleness develop?

1. primary; secondary
2. genitals
3. shape
4. menstruation; ova
5. male; female; glands
6. hormonal; gender
7. genetic; female; male
8. male; female
9. syndrome; sexual
10. hormones; effect
11. alike; different
12. reconstruction; appearance; ambiguous
13. maleness; femaleness
14. 3; 4
15. gender role
16. stereotypes; women; women
17. stereotyping; less; gender
18. roles
19. Gender role
20. boys; girls
21. three; sex; outdoor; indoor

What is psychological androgyny (and is it contagious)?

1. *Sex Role*
2. masculine; feminine
3. masculine
4. feminine
5. androgyny

What are the most typical patterns of human sexual behavior?

1. climax
2. pleasure; thoughts
3. cultures
4. responsiveness
5. arousal; subjective; emotional
6. later
7. drive; age; sex
8. myth; decrease; amphetamines; impair
9. orgasms
10. Castration
11. decline (or decrease)
12. discovery

Sexual Orientation—Who Do You Love? Pages 438-440

1. sex; sex; sexes
2. homosexual
3. sexual; orientation
4. sexual; genetic; reduce
5. seven; bisexual
6. homosexuality
7. heterosexuals

To what extent do males and females differ in sexual response?

1. Masters
2. excitement; orgasm
3. orgasms; orgasms
4. orgasm
5. 4
6. orgasm
7. multi; multiple

What are the most common sexual disorders?

1. subjective; cultures
2. deviations
3. fetishism; exhibitionism
4. sadism; masochism
5. inhibited
6. severity

7. molested; nude; shame; sexual   8. opportunities; gifts; compliance

Have recent changes in attitudes affected sexual behavior?

1. behavior
2. earlier; intercourse
3. female; behavior
4. date; rape
5. Rape

What impacts have sexually transmitted diseases had on sexual behavior?

1. 90; girls; sexually; did not
2. active; indirect
3. diseases
4. acquired immune; virus
5. risk; risk
6. HIV; 65

What are the most common sexual adjustment problems? How are they treated?

1. desire; pain
2. sexual; desire; sexual
3. male; female
4. erectile; psychological; damage
5. arousal; hostility; childhood
6. maintain; avoid; attack
7. ejaculation; ejaculation
8. painful; muscle spasms
9. focus
10. relationship
11. intimacy

CONNECTIONS

What are the basic dimensions of sex? How does one's sense of maleness or femaleness develop? What is psychological androgyny (and is it contagious)? Pages 427-436

1. D.
2. H.
3. F.
4. B.
5. J.
6. L.
7. I.
8. A.
9. E.
10. G.
11. C.
12. K.

Connections

1. D.
2. G.
3. I.
4. A.
5. J.
6. K.
7. L.
8. E.
9. C.
10. F.
11. H.
12. B.

Connections Part II

1. J.
2. D.
3. F.
4. A.
5. G.
6. C.
7. B.
8. H.
9. I.
10. E.

What are the most typical patterns of human sexual behavior? Pages 436-440

1. D.	5. A.	9. F.
2. G.	6. H.	10. I.
3. B.	7. E.	
4. C.	8. J.	

To what extent do males and females differ in sexual response? What are the most common sexual disorders? Have recent changes in attitudes affected sexual behavior? Pages 440-447

1. C.	3. D.	5. A.
2. F.	4. B.	6. E.

What impacts have sexually transmitted diseases had on sexual behavior? What are the most common sexual adjustment problems? How are they treated? Pages 447-455

1. C.	3. D.	5. E.
2. F.	4. A.	6. B.

CHECK YOUR MEMORY

What are the basic dimensions of sex? How does one's sense of maleness or femaleness develop? Pages 427-434

1. F	9. F	17. F
2. F	10. T	18. T
3. T	11. T	19. F
4. F	12. F	20. T
5. F	13. T	
6. F	14. F	
7. T	15. T	
8. T	16. F	

What is psychological androgyny (and is it contagious)? Pages 434-436

1. F	3. T	5. T
2. F	4. T	

What are the most typical patterns of human sexual behavior? Pages 436-440

1. T	2. F	3. T

4. F	10. F	16. T
5. T	11. F	17. F
6. F	12. F	18. F
7. T	13. T	19. T
8. F	14. F	20. T
9. T	15. T	21. T

To what extent do males and females differ in sexual response? Pages 440-442

1. F	4. F	7. T
2. T	5. T	8. T
3. F	6. F	

What are the most common sexual disorders? Pages 442-444

1. F	4. T	7. T
2. F	5. T	
3. T	6. T	

Have recent changes in attitudes affected sexual behavior? Pages 444-447

1. T	4. T	7. F
2. F	5. T	8. T
3. T	6. F	9. T

What impacts have sexually transmitted diseases had on sexual behavior? Pages 447-450

1. T	6. F	11. F
2. F	7. F	12. T
3. F	8. T	13. F
4. T	9. F	
5. T	10. T	

What are the most common sexual adjustment problems? How are they treated? Pages 450-455

1. F	6. F	11. T
2. T	7. F	12. F
3. T	8. T	13. T
4. F	9. F	
5. T	10. T	

FINAL SURVEY AND REVIEW

What are the basic dimensions of sex? How does one's sense of maleness or femaleness develop?

1. sexual; characteristics
2. Primary sexual characteristics; internal
3. Secondary sexual characteristics; hair
4. menarche; ovulation
5. androgens; estrogens; gonads
6. genetic; gonadal; genital
7. chromosomes; X; X; Y
8. testosterone; genitals; genitals
9. Androgen; intersexualism
10. prenatal; biasing
11. psychological
12. Surgical; reconstruction; intersexuals; socialization
13. gender; identity; gender; roles
14. labeling
15. stereotypes
16. stereotypes; 75; 67; 54
17. stereotyping; women
18. Culture
19. socialization
20. instrumental; expressive
21. sex-segregated

What is psychological androgyny (and is it contagious)?

1. *Bem*
2. third
3. independent
4. nurturant
5. adaptability

What are the most typical patterns of human sexual behavior?

1. orgasm
2. erogenous; cognitive
3. scripts; plans
4. difference; behavior
5. both; equal; differ
6. females; males
7. androgens; sex; testosterone
8. enhance; decrease
9. Nocturnal
10. Sterilization
11. frequency
12. Masturbation

Sexual Orientation—Who Do You Love? Pages 438-440

1. orientation
2. heterosexual
3. hereditary; social
4. orientation; mothers; reduce
5. homosexual
6. homophobia; heterosexism
7. homosexual; heterosexuals

To what extent do males and females differ in sexual response?

1. Johnson
2. plateau; resolution
3. vaginal; clitoral
4. refractory; orgasmic
5. females
6. Mutual
7. Fifteen; multi-orgasmic

What are the most common sexual disorders?

1. sexually; deviant
2. paraphilias
3. pedophilia; voyeurism
4. transvestic; frotteurism
5. Exhibitionists
6. molestation; relationship
7. Children; nude; sexual
8. caretaking; bribing; talk

Have recent changes in attitudes affected sexual behavior?

1. Attitudes; liberal
2. premarital
3. double; standard

4. Acquaintance; myths   5. aggression

What impacts have sexually transmitted diseases had on sexual behavior?

1. sexually active; sexually transmitted

2. risky; contact

3. sexually; transmitted

4. deficiency; immunodeficiency

5. STDs

6. heterosexuals; AIDS

What are the most common sexual adjustment problems? How are they treated?

1. arousal; orgasm

2. hypoactive; aversion

3. erectile; arousal

4. erectile; psychogenic

5. arousal; anxiety; strict

6. healthy; avoid; feelings; characteristics

7. retarded; premature; orgasm

8. dyspareunia; vaginismus

9. sensate; squeeze

10. adjustment

11. communication

MASTERY TEST

What are the most common sexual adjustment problems? How are they treated?

1. A, p. 437

2. A, p. 449

3. D, p. 433

4. B, p. 430

5. B, p. 444

6. D, p. 453

7. C, p. 429

8. C, p. 434

9. B, p. 454

10. A, p. 430

11. B, p. 427

12. C, p. 441

13. D, p. 447

14. B, p. 429

15. D, p. 433

16. A, p. 437

17. A, pp. 430-431

18. D, pp. 445-446

19. C, p. 432

20. A, p. 442

21. D, p. 445

22. B, p. 431

23. D, p. 436

24. A, p. 439

25. C, p. 443

26. B, p. 446

27. D, p. 447

28. B, p. 451

29. D, p. 430

30. B, p. 432

31. C, p. 437

32. D, p. 433

33. A, p. 432

34. A, p. 436

35. A, p. 439

36. D, p. 443

37. C, p. 431

38. A, p. 447

39. B, p. 437

Personality

Chapter Overview

Personality refers to unique and enduring behavior patterns. Character is personality evaluated. Temperament refers to the hereditary and physiological aspects of one's emotional nature. Personality traits are lasting personal qualities. Personality types are categories defined by groups of shared traits. Behavior is also influenced by self-concept. Personality theories combine various ideas and principles to explain personality.

Allport's trait theory classifies traits as common, individual, cardinal, central, or secondary. Cattell's trait theory attributes visible surface traits to the existence of 16 underlying source traits. The five-factor model reduces traits to 5 dimensions. Traits appear to interact with situations to determine behavior. Behavioral genetics suggests that heredity influences personality traits. Twin studies suggest that heredity accounts for 25 percent -50 percent of the variability in personality traits.

Like other psychodynamic approaches, Sigmund Freud's psychoanalytic theory emphasizes unconscious forces and conflicts within the personality. The neo-Freudian theorists retained many of Freud's basic ideas, but modified some of them or added to them. Behavioral theories of personality emphasize learning, conditioning, and the immediate effects of the environment. Social learning theory adds cognitive elements, such as perception, thinking, expectancies, and understanding, to the behavioral view. Many differences between males and females are based on social learning. Humanistic theory emphasizes subjective experiences and needs for self-actualization. Positivistic theory focuses on characteristics that contribute to a person's well-being and life satisfaction.

Techniques typically used to assess personality are interviews, direct observation, rating scales, questionnaires, and projective tests.

Shyness is a mixture of social inhibition and social anxiety. It is marked by heightened public self-consciousness and a tendency to regard one's shyness as a lasting trait. Shyness can be lessened by changing self-defeating beliefs and by improving social skills.

Learning Objectives

1. Define the term *personality* and explain how personality differs from character and temperament.

2. Describe the trait approach and the type approach to personality; discuss the stability of personality; describe the characteristics of introverts and extroverts; and explain the disadvantages of the type approach.

3. Explain the terms *self-concept* and *self-esteem* and how they affect behavior and personal adjustment and explain the differences in the basis of self-esteem in Eastern and Western cultures.

4. Define the term *personality theory* and describe the different psychological perspectives regarding personality theory covered in your text.

5. Describe the following trait theories:

   a. Eysenck and the ancient Greeks

   b. Rentfrow and Gosling's musical personalities

   c. Gordon Allport

   d. Raymond Cattell

   e. the Five-Factor Model of Personality

6. Explain trait-situation interaction; define behavioral genetics; explain how twin studies are used to assess the relative contribution of heredity and environment to a person's personality; and discuss how the similarities in the personalities of twins can be explained.

7. Discuss Freud's view of personality development, including:

   a. the three parts of the personality

   b. neurotic and moral anxiety

   c. the three levels of awareness

   d. the psychosexual stages and fixation

   e. the positive and negative aspects of Freud's theory

8. Define the term *neo-Freudian*; explain why many of Freud's followers eventually disagreed with him; and describe the theories of each of the following: Alfred Adler, Karen Horney, and Carl Jung.

9. Explain how learning theorists (behaviorists) view the structure of personality. Include in your discussion the terms *situational determinants, habit, drive, cue, response, and reward.*

10. Explain how learning theory and social learning theory differ and describe the role of social reinforcement in personality development. Include in your discussion a description of these terms: *psychological situation, expectancy, reinforcement value, self-efficacy,* and *self-reinforcement.*

11. Using the behavioristic view of development, explain why feeding, toilet training, sex training, and learning to express anger or aggression may be particularly important to personality formation; and describe the role of imitation and identification in personality development.

12. Briefly explain how the humanists set themselves apart from the Freudian and behaviorist viewpoints or personality; describe Maslow's concept of self-actualization and the characteristics of self-actualizers; explain what helps and hinders self-actualization; list eight steps to promote self-actualization; and describe the six human strengths that contribute to well-being and life satisfaction.

13. Discuss Rogers' views of the normal or fully functioning individual; define his terms: *self, self-concept, incongruence, ideal self; conditions of worth, organismic valuing, positive self-regard,* and *unconditional positive regard*; and explain how possible selves help translate our hopes, dreams, and fears and ultimately direct our future behavior.

14. Compare and contrast in general terms the strengths and weaknesses of the trait, psychoanalytic, behavioristic, social learning, and humanistic theories of personality.

15. Discuss the following assessment techniques in terms of purpose, method, advantages, and limitations:

    a. structured, unstructured, and diagnostic interviews (include the halo effect)

    b. direct observation (combined with rating scales, behavioral assessment, and situational testing)

    c. personality questionnaires (including the MMPI-2)

    d. honesty tests

    e. projective tests (include the Rorschach and the TAT)

16. Describe the personality characteristics of sudden murderers, and explain how their characteristics are related to the nature of their homicidal actions.

The following objective is related to the material in the "Psychology in Action" section of your text.

1. List and describe the three elements of shyness; state what usually causes shyness; compare the personality of the shy and not-shy; and list and discuss the four self-defeating beliefs that can lead to shyness and possible ways to counteract these beliefs.

RECITE AND REVIEW

How do psychologists use the term personality? What core concepts make up the psychology of personality?

The Psychology of Personality—Do You Have Personality? Pages 459-463

1. Personality is made up of one's unique and relatively stable _____ patterns.

2. Character is personality that has been judged or _____ . That is, it is the possession of desirable qualities.

3. Temperament refers to the _____ and physiological aspects of one's emotional nature.

4. Personality traits are lasting personal qualities that are inferred from _____ .

5. A personality type is a style of personality defined by having a group of related _____ or similar characteristics.

6. Two widely recognized personality _____ are an introvert (shy, self-centered person) and an extrovert (bold, outgoing person).

7. Behavior is influenced by self-concept, which is a person's perception of his or her own _____ traits.

8. Culture determines how people go about developing and maintaining _____ (self-evaluation): People with high self-esteem are confident, _____ , and self-respecting, and people with low self-esteem are insecure, _____ , and lack confidence.

9. _____ theories combine interrelated assumptions, ideas, and principles to explain personality.

10. Five major types of personality theories are: _____ , psychodynamic, behavioristic, _____ learning, and humanistic.

Are some personality traits more basic or important than others?

The Trait Approach—Describe Yourself in 18,000 Words or Less: Pages 463-468

1. Research has found a link between personality characteristics and _____ . For example, people who value aesthetic experiences, have good _____ skills, and are liberal and tolerant of others tend to prefer jazz, _____ , classical, and folk music.

2. Trait _____ attempt to specify qualities of personality that are most lasting or characteristic of a person.

3. Gordon Allport made useful distinctions between common traits (which are shared by most members of a culture) and _____ traits (characteristics of a single person).

4. Allport also identified cardinal traits (a trait that influences nearly all of a person's activities), central traits (core traits of personality), and _____ traits (superficial traits).

5. The theory of Raymond Cattell attributes visible _____ traits to the existence of 16 underlying source traits (which he identified using factor _____).

6. Source traits are measured by the *Sixteen* _____ _____ *Questionnaire (16 PF)*.

7. The outcome of the 16 PF and other personality tests may be graphically presented as a _____ profile.

8. The five-factor model of personality reduces traits to 5 _____ dimensions of personality.

9. The five factors are: extroversion, _____ , conscientiousness, neuroticism, and openness to _____ .

10. _____ interact with situations to determine behavior.

11. Behavioral genetics is the study of _____ behavioral traits.

12. Heredity is responsible for 25 to 50 percent of the variation in personality _____ .

13. Studies of separated _____ twins suggest that heredity contributes significantly to adult personality traits. Overall, however, personality is shaped as much, or more by differences in environment.

How do psychodynamic theories explain personality?

Psychoanalytic Theory—Id Came to Me in a Dream and Psychodynamic Theories—Freud's Descendants: Pages 468-474

1. Psychodynamic theories focus on the inner workings of personality, especially hidden or _____ forces and internal conflicts.

2. According to Sigmund Freud's psychoanalytic theory, personality is made up of the id, _____ , and superego.

3. The id operates on the pleasure _____ . The ego is guided by the reality _____ .

4. The _____ is made up of the conscience and the ego ideal.

5. Libido, derived from the _____ instincts, is the primary _____ running the personality.

6. Conflicts within the personality may cause neurotic _____ or moral _____ and motivate use of ego-defense mechanisms.

7. The personality operates on three levels, the _____ , preconscious, and unconscious.

8. The id is completely _____ ; the ego and superego can operate at all three levels of awareness.

9. The Freudian view of personality development is based on a series of psychosexual _____ : the _____ , anal, phallic, and genital.

10. Fixations (unresolved emotional conflicts) at any stage can leave a lasting imprint on _____ .

11. Freud's theory pioneered the idea that feeding, toilet training, and early sexual experiences leave an imprint on _____ .

12. During the phallic stage of Freud's _____ stages of development, boys must confront and resolve the _____ complex and girls must confront and resolve the Electra complex.

13. Freud's theory has been influential toward the understanding of personality development for several reasons: He suggested that adult personality is formed during the _____ years of a person's life; he identified feeding, _____ training, and early sexual experiences as critical events; and he indicated that development proceeds in _____ .

14. Personality theorists who altered or revised Freud's ideas are called neo- _____ . Three prominent members of this group are Alfred Adler, Karen Horney, and Carl Jung.

What do behaviorists emphasize in their approach to personality?

Learning Theories of Personality—Habit I Seen You Before? Pages 474-479

1. Behavioral theories of personality emphasize _____ , conditioning, and immediate effects of the environment.

2. Learning theorists generally stress the effects of prior learning and _____ determinants of behavior.

3. Learning theorists John Dollard and Neal Miller consider _____ the basic core of personality. _____ express the combined effects of drive, cue, response, and _____ .

4. _____ learning theory adds cognitive elements, such as perception, thinking, and understanding to the behavioral view of personality.

5. Examples of social learning concepts are the _____ situation (the situation as it is perceived), expectancies (expectations about what effects a response will have), and reinforcement _____ (the subjective value of a reinforcer or activity).

6. Albert Bandura believes one's self-efficacy (belief in our _____ to produce a desired outcome) is an important aspect of expectancy. He also believes that self-efficacy beliefs influence the _____ and situations we choose to get into.

7. Some social learning theorists treat "conscience" as a case of _____ -reinforcement.

8. The behavioristic view of personality development holds that social reinforcement in four situations is critical. The critical situations are _____ , toilet or cleanliness training, sex training, and _____ or aggression training.

9. Identification (feeling emotionally connected to a person) and _____ (mimicking another person's behavior) are of particular importance in sex (or gender) training.

How do humanistic theories differ from other perspectives?

Humanistic Theory—Peak Experiences and Personal Growth and Personality Theory—Overview and Comparison: Pages 479-483

1. Humanistic theory views human nature as _____ , and emphasizes subjective experience, _____ choice, and needs for self-actualization.

2. Abraham Maslow's study of self-actualizers identified characteristics they share, ranging from efficient perceptions of reality to frequent _____ (temporary moments of self-actualization).

3. The process of self-actualization involves multiple steps, some of which include being willing to change, taking _____ , examining one's motives, getting involved, and making use of _____ experiences.

4. A person's well-being and life _____ are linked to six human strengths: wisdom and knowledge, _____ , humanity, justice, _____ , and transcendence.

5. Carl Rogers' theory views the _____ as an entity that emerges when experiences that match the self- _____ are symbolized (admitted to consciousness), while those that are incongruent are excluded.

6. The incongruent person has a highly unrealistic _____ and/or a mismatch between the _____ and the ideal self.

7. The congruent or _____ functioning person is flexible and open to experiences and feelings.

8. In the development of personality, humanists are primarily interested in the emergence of a _____ and in self-evaluations.

9. As parents apply conditions of _____ (standards used to judge thoughts, feelings, and actions) to a child, the child begins to do the same.

10. Internalized conditions of worth contribute to incongruence, they damage _____ self-regard, and they disrupt the organismic _____ process.

How do psychologists measure personality?

Personality Assessment—Psychological Yardsticks: Pages 483-487

1. Techniques typically used for personality assessment are _____ , observation, questionnaires, and projective _____ .

2. Structured and unstructured _____ provide much information, but they are subject to _____ bias and misperceptions. The halo effect may also _____ accuracy.

3. Direct observation, sometimes involving situational tests, behavioral assessment, or the use of _____ scales, allows evaluation of a person's actual _____ .

4. Personality questionnaires, such as the _____ _____ *Personality Inventory-2 (MMPI-2)*, are objective and _____ , but their validity is open to question.

5. Honesty tests, which are essentially personality _____ , are widely used by businesses to make hiring decisions. Their validity is hotly debated.

Projective Tests of Personality—Inkblots and Hidden Plots and Sudden Murderers—A Research Example: Pages 487-490

1. Projective tests ask a subject to project thoughts or feelings onto an ambiguous _____ or unstructured situation.

2. The *Rorschach*, or _____ test, is a well-known projective technique. A second is the _____ *Apperception Test (TAT)*.

3. The validity and objectivity of projective tests are quite _____ . Nevertheless, projective techniques are considered useful by many clinicians, particularly as part of a _____ battery.

What causes shyness? What can be done about it?

Psychology in Action: Barriers and Bridges—Understanding Shyness: Pages 490-493

1. Shyness is a mixture of _____ inhibition and _____ anxiety.

2. Shy persons tend to lack social skills and they feel social anxiety (because they believe they are being _____ by others).

3. Shy persons also have a self-defeating bias in their _____ (they tend to blame _____ for social failures).

4. Shyness is marked by heightened _____ self-consciousness (awareness of oneself as a _____ object) and a tendency to regard shyness as a lasting trait.

5. Shyness can be lessened by changing self-defeating _____ and by improving _____ skills.

CONNECTIONS

How do psychologists use the term personality? What core concepts make up the psychology of personality? Pages 459-463

1. _____ character
2. _____ trait
3. _____ Type A
4. _____ Introverts or extroverts
5. _____ melancholic
6. _____ choleric
7. _____ temperament
8. _____ phlegmatic
9. _____ sanguine

a. heart attack risk
b. hot-tempered
c. personality judged
d. cheerful
e. sluggish
f. sad, gloomy
g. lasting personal quality
h. Carl Jung
i. hereditary part of personality

Are some personality traits more basic or important than others? How do psychodynamic theories explain personality? Pages 463-474

1. _____ trait situation	a. mouth
2. _____ behavior genetics	b. pride
3. _____ 16 PF	c. genitals
4. _____ Big Five	d. female conflict
5. _____ common traits	e. male conflict
6. _____ Thanatos	f. death instinct
7. _____ Eros	g. elimination
8. _____ conscience	h. life instinct
9. _____ ego ideal	i. guilt
10. _____ oral stage	j. pleasure principle
11. _____ anal stage	k. twin studies
12. _____ phallic stage	l. interaction
13. _____ id	m. source traits
14. _____ Oedipus complex	n. culturally typical
15. _____ Electra complex	o. universal dimensions

What do behaviorists emphasize in their approach to personality? How do humanistic theories differ from other perspectives? Pages 474-483

1. _____ reward	a. anticipation
2. _____ subjective experience	b. self-actualization
3. _____ expectancy	c. learned behavior pattern
4. _____ unconditional positive regards	d. positive reinforcer
5. _____ situational determinants	e. external causes
6. _____ habits	f. self-image = ideal self
7. _____ Karen Horney	g. unshakable love
8. _____ Carl Rogers	h. private perceptions of reality
9. _____ Carl Jung	i. fully functioning person
10. _____ Abraham Maslow	j. belief in one's capability
11. _____ self-efficacy	k. archetypes
12. _____ congruence	l. basic anxiety

How do psychologists measure personality? What causes shyness? What can be done about it? Pages 483-493

1.	_____ validity scale		a.	Rorschach
2.	_____ social anxiety		b.	integrity at work
3.	_____ MMPI		c.	interview problem
4.	_____ inkblot		d.	personality questionnaire
5.	_____ private self-consciousness		e.	faking good
6.	_____ situational test		f.	Shoot Don't Shoot
7.	_____ public self-consciousness		g.	view self as social object
8.	_____ honesty test		h.	focus on inner feelings
9.	_____ self-defeating bias		i.	distortion in thinking
10.	_____ halo effect		j.	evaluation fears

CHECK YOUR MEMORY

How do psychologists use the term personality? What core concepts make up the psychology of personality? Pages 459-463

1. The term personality refers to charisma or personal style.

   TRUE or FALSE

2. Personality is a person's relatively stable pattern of attitudes.

   TRUE or FALSE

3. Character refers to the inherited "raw material" from which personality is formed.

   TRUE or FALSE

4. A person with genuine high self-esteem has a tendency to accurately appraise his/her own strengths and weaknesses.

   TRUE or FALSE

5. In Asian cultures, self-esteem is strongly tied to personal achievement, rather than group success.

   TRUE or FALSE

6. Traits are stable or lasting qualities of personality, displayed in most situations.

   TRUE or FALSE

7. Personality traits typically become quite stable by age 30 with the exception of conscientiousness and agreeability.

   TRUE or FALSE

8. Paranoid, dependent, and antisocial personalities are regarded as personality types.

   TRUE or FALSE

9. Two major dimensions of Eysenck's personality theory are stable-unstable and calm-moody.

   TRUE or FALSE

10. Trait theories of personality stress subjective experience and personal growth.

    TRUE or FALSE

Are some personality traits more basic or important than others? Pages 463-468

1. Extroverted students tend to study in noisy areas of the library.

   TRUE or FALSE

2. Peter Rentfrow and Samuel Gosling found that one's preference to music is linked to personality characteristics.

   TRUE or FALSE

3. People who are cheerful, conventional, extroverted, and reliable tend to prefer blues, jazz, and classical music.

   TRUE or FALSE

4. Nearly all of a person's activities can be traced to one or two common traits.

   TRUE or FALSE

5. Roughly 7 central traits are needed, on the average, to describe an individual's personality.

   TRUE or FALSE

6. Allport used factor analysis to identify central traits.

   TRUE or FALSE

7. The 16 PF is designed to measure surface traits.

   TRUE or FALSE

8. Judging from scores on the 16 PF, airline pilots have traits that are similar to creative artists.

   TRUE or FALSE

9. As one of the Big Five factors, neuroticism refers to having negative, upsetting emotions.

   TRUE or FALSE

10. Extreme perfectionism typically lowers performance at school and elsewhere.

    TRUE or FALSE

11. The expression of personality traits tends to be influenced by external situations.

    TRUE or FALSE

12. Similarities between reunited identical twins show that personality is mostly shaped by genetics.

    TRUE or FALSE

13. Intelligence, some mental disorders, temperament, and personality traits are all influenced by heredity.

    TRUE or FALSE

14. Studies of identical twins show that personality traits are approximately 70 percent hereditary.

    TRUE or FALSE

15. Some of the coincidences shared by identical twins appear to be based on the fallacy of positive instances.

    TRUE or FALSE

16. Unrelated people can share amazingly similar personality characteristics due to their age, gender, and living conditions.

    TRUE or FALSE

How do psychodynamic theories explain personality? Pages 468-474

1. Freud described the id, ego, and superego as "little people" that manage the human psyche.

   TRUE or FALSE

2. The id is totally unconscious.

   TRUE or FALSE

3. The ego is guided by the pleasure principle.

   TRUE or FALSE

4. The superego is the source of feelings of guilt and pride.

   TRUE or FALSE

5. Threats of punishment from the Thanatos cause moral anxiety.

   TRUE or FALSE

6. Oral-dependent persons are gullible.

   TRUE or FALSE

7. Vanity and narcissism are traits of the anal-retentive personality.

   TRUE or FALSE

8. According to Freud, boys experience the Oedipus complex and girls experience the Electra complex.

TRUE or FALSE

9. The genital stage occurs between the ages of 3 and 6, just before latency.

TRUE or FALSE

10. Boys are more likely to develop a strong conscience if their fathers are affectionate and accepting.

TRUE or FALSE

11. Freud regarded latency as the most important stage of psychosexual development.

TRUE or FALSE

12. Erik Erikson's psychosocial stages were derived, in part, from Freud's psychosexual stages.

TRUE or FALSE

13. Alfred Adler believed that we are driven by basic anxiety to move toward, against, or away from others.

TRUE or FALSE

14. According to Jung, people strive for superiority by creating a unique style of life.

TRUE or FALSE

15. Jung called the male principle the animus.

TRUE or FALSE

What do behaviorists emphasize in their approach to personality? Pages 474-479

1. Behaviorists view personality as a collection of learned behavior patterns.

TRUE or FALSE

2. Behaviorists attribute our actions to prior learning and specific situations.

TRUE or FALSE

3. Behaviors are influenced by an interaction between the situation and previously gained knowledge.

TRUE or FALSE

4. Knowing the consistent ways people respond to certain situations allows us to predict their personality characteristics.

TRUE or FALSE

5. According to Dollard and Miller, habits are acquired through observational learning.

TRUE or FALSE

6. Cues are signals from the environment that guide responses.

TRUE or FALSE

7. An expectancy refers to the anticipation that making a response will lead to reinforcement.

    TRUE or FALSE

8. Self-reinforcement is highly related to one's self-esteem.

    TRUE or FALSE

9. People who are depressed tend to engage in a high rate of self-reinforcement to make themselves feel better.

    TRUE or FALSE

10. Social reinforcement is based on attention and approval from others.

    TRUE or FALSE

11. In elementary school, boys typically get more attention from teachers than girls do.

    TRUE or FALSE

How do humanistic theories differ from other perspectives? Pages 479-483

1. Humanists believe that humans are capable of free choice.

    TRUE or FALSE

2. To investigate self-actualization, Maslow studied eminent men and women exclusively.

    TRUE or FALSE

3. Self-actualizers usually try to avoid task centering.

    TRUE or FALSE

4. Personal autonomy is a characteristic of the self-actualizing person.

    TRUE or FALSE

5. People who live happy and meaningful lives are people who possess the traits characteristic of a self-actualizer and express such human strengths as courage, justice, and temperance.

    TRUE or FALSE

6. Information inconsistent with one's self-image is described as incongruent.

    TRUE or FALSE

7. Images of our possible selves are derived from our hopes, fears, fantasies, and goals.

    TRUE or FALSE

8. Poor self-knowledge is associated with high self-esteem because people do not have to think about their own faults.

    TRUE or FALSE

9. Congruence represents a close correspondence between self-image, the ideal self, and the true self.
   TRUE or FALSE

10. Images of possible selves typically cause feelings of incongruence.
    TRUE or FALSE

11. Rogers believed that organismic valuing is healthier than trying to meet someone else's conditions of worth.
    TRUE or FALSE

How do psychologists measure personality? Pages 483-490

1. Planned questions are used in a structured interview.
   TRUE or FALSE

2. Computers are sometimes used to do diagnostic interviews at psychological clinics.
   TRUE or FALSE

3. The halo effect may involve either a positive or a negative impression.
   TRUE or FALSE

4. Personality questionnaires are used to do behavioral assessments.
   TRUE or FALSE

5. Judgmental firearms training is a type of honesty test.
   TRUE or FALSE

6. Items on the MMPI-2 were selected for their ability to identify persons with psychiatric problems.
   TRUE or FALSE

7. The validity scale of the MMPI-2 is used to rate Type A behavior.
   TRUE or FALSE

8. The psychasthenia scale of the MMPI-2 detects the presence of phobias and compulsive actions.
   TRUE or FALSE

9. It is very easy to fake responses to a projective test.
   TRUE or FALSE

10. The TAT is a situational test.
    TRUE or FALSE

11. Habitually violent prison inmates are aggressive and over-controlled.
    TRUE or FALSE

What causes shyness? What can be done about it? Pages 491-493

1. Shyness is closely related to private self-consciousness.

   TRUE or FALSE

2. Not-shy persons believe that external situations cause their occasional feelings of shyness.

   TRUE or FALSE

3. The odds of meeting someone interested in socializing are about the same wherever you are.

   TRUE or FALSE

4. Open-ended questions help keep conversations going.

   TRUE or FALSE

FINAL SURVEY AND REVIEW

How do psychologists use the term personality? What core concepts make up the psychology of personality?

The Psychology of Personality—Do You Have Personality? Pages 459-463

1. _____ is made up of one's unique and relatively stable behavior _____ .

2. _____ is personality that has been judged or evaluated. That is, it is the possession of desirable qualities.

3. _____ refers to the hereditary and physiological aspects of one's emotional nature.

4. Personality _____ are lasting personal qualities that are inferred from behavior.

5. A personality _____ is a style of personality defined by having a group of related traits or similar characteristics.

6. Two widely recognized personality types are an _____ (shy, self-centered person) and an _____ (bold, outgoing person).

7. Behavior is influenced by _____ , which is a person's perception of his or her own personality traits.

8. _____ determines how people go about developing and maintaining self-esteem (self-evaluation): People with _____ self-esteem are confident, proud, and self-respecting, and people with _____ self-esteem are insecure, self-critical, and lack confidence.

9. Personality _____ combine interrelated assumptions, ideas, and principles to explain personality.

10. Five major types of personality theories are: trait, _____ , behavioristic, social learning, and _____ .

Are some personality traits more basic or important than others?

The Trait Approach—Describe Yourself in 18,000 Words or Less: Pages 463-468

1. Research has found a link between _____ characteristics and music. For example, people who value _____ experiences, have good _____ skills, and are liberal and tolerant of others tend to prefer jazz, blues, classical, and folk music.

2. _____ theories attempt to specify qualities of personality that are most lasting or characteristic of a person.

3. Gordon _____ made useful distinctions between _____ traits (which are shared by most members of a culture) and individual traits (characteristics of a single person).

4. He also identified _____ traits (a trait that influences nearly all of a person's activities), _____ traits (core traits of personality), and secondary traits (superficial traits).

5. The theory of Raymond _____ attributes visible surface traits to the existence of 16 underlying _____ traits (which he identified using _____ analysis).

6. _____ _____ are measured by the Sixteen Personality Factor Questionnaire (16 PF).

7. The outcome of the 16 PF and other personality tests may be graphically presented as a trait _____ .

8. The _____ model of personality reduces traits to 5 universal dimensions of personality.

9. They are: _____ , agreeableness, conscientiousness, _____ , and openness to experience.

10. Traits _____ with _____ to determine behavior.

11. _____ _____ is the study of inherited behavioral traits.

12. Heredity is responsible for _____ to _____ percent of the variation in personality traits.

13. Studies of separated identical twins suggest that _____ contributes significantly to adult personality traits. Overall, however, personality is shaped as much, or more by differences in _____ .

How do psychodynamic theories explain personality?

Psychoanalytic Theory—Id Came to Me in a Dream and Psychodynamic Theories—Freud's Descendants: Pages 468-474

1. Psychodynamic theories focus on the inner workings of _____ , especially hidden or unconscious forces and internal _____ .

2. According to Sigmund Freud's _____ theory, personality is made up of the _____ , ego, and _____ .

3. The id operates on the _____ principle. The ego is guided by the _____ principle.

4. The superego is made up of the _____ and the _____ ideal.

5. _____ , derived from the life _____ , is the primary energy running the personality.

6. Conflicts within the personality may cause _____ anxiety or _____ anxiety and motivate use of ego-defense mechanisms.

7. The personality operates on three levels, the conscious, _____ , and _____ .

8. The _____ is completely unconscious; the _____ and _____ can operate at all three levels of awareness.

9. The Freudian view of personality development is based on a series of _____ stages: the oral, anal, _____ , and genital.

10. _____ (unresolved emotional conflicts) at any stage can leave a lasting imprint on personality.

11. Freud's theory pioneered the idea that _____ , _____ training, and early sexual experiences leave an imprint on personality.

12. During the _____ stage of Freud's psychosexual stages of development, _____ must confront and resolve the Oedipus complex and _____ must confront and resolve the Electra complex.

13. Freud's theory has been influential toward the understanding of personality development for several reasons: He suggested that _____ personality is formed during the first few years of a person's life; he identified feeding, toilet training, and early sexual experiences as _____ events; and he indicated that development proceeds in _____ .

14. Personality theorists who altered or revised Freud's ideas are called _____ -Freudians. Three prominent members of this group are Alfred _____ , Karen Horney, and Carl _____ .

What do behaviorists emphasize in their approach to personality?

Learning Theories of Personality—Habit I Seen You Before? Pages 474-479

1. _____ theories of personality emphasize learning, conditioning, and immediate effects of the environment.

2. Learning theorists generally stress the effects of prior learning and situational _____ of behavior.

3. Learning theorists John Dollard and Neal Miller consider habits the basic core of personality. Habits express the combined effects of _____ , _____ , response, and reward.

4. Social learning theory adds _____ elements, such as perception, thinking, and understanding to the behavioral view of personality.

5. Examples of social learning concepts are the psychological situation (the situation as it is perceived), _____ (expectations about what effects a response will have), and _____ value (the subjective value of a reinforcer or activity).

6. Albert Bandura believes one's self- _____ (belief in our ability to produce a desired outcome) is an important aspect of _____ . He also believes that _____ beliefs influence the activities and situations we choose to get into.

7. Some social learning theorists treat "conscience" as a case of self- _____ .

8. The behavioristic view of personality development holds that social reinforcement in four situations is critical. The critical situations are feeding, _____ , sex training, and anger or _____ training.

9. _____ (feeling emotionally connected to a person) and imitation (mimicking another person's behavior) are of particular importance in sex (or gender) training.

How do humanistic theories differ from other perspectives?

Humanistic Theory—Peak Experiences and Personal Growth and Personality Theory—Overview and Comparison: Pages 479-483

1. Humanistic theory views human nature as good, and emphasizes _____ experience, free choice, and needs for self- _____ .

2. Abraham _____ study of self- _____ identified characteristics they share, ranging from efficient perceptions of reality to frequent peak experiences.

3. The process of self- _____ involves multiple steps, some of which include being willing to change, taking responsibility, examining one's motives, getting involved, and making use of positive experiences.

4. A person's well- _____ and life satisfaction are linked to six human _____ : wisdom and knowledge, courage, humanity, justice, temperance, and transcendence.

5. Carl Rogers' theory views the self as an entity that emerges when experiences that match the self-image are _____ (admitted to consciousness), while those that are _____ are excluded.

6. The _____ person has a highly unrealistic self-image and/or a mismatch between the self-image and the _____ self.

7. The _____ or fully functioning person is flexible and open to experiences and feelings.

8. In the development of personality, humanists are primarily interested in the emergence of a self-image and in _____ .

9. As parents apply _____ of worth (standards used to judge thoughts, feelings, and actions) to a child, the child begins to do the same.

10. Internalized _____ _____ _____ contribute to incongruence, they damage

positive self-regard, and they disrupt the _____ valuing process.

How do psychologists measure personality?

Personality Assessment—Psychological Yardsticks: Pages 483-487

1. Techniques typically used for personality assessment are interviews, direct _____ ,

questionnaires, and _____ tests.

2. Structured and _____ interviews provide much information, but they are subject to interviewer

_____ and misperceptions. The halo effect may also lower accuracy.

3. Direct observation, sometimes involving _____ tests, behavioral _____ , or the use

of rating scales, allows evaluation of a person's actual behavior.

4. Personality questionnaires, such as the Minnesota Multiphasic _____ _____ -2

(MMPI-2), are objective and reliable, but their _____ is open to question.

5. _____ tests, which are essentially personality questionnaires, are widely used by businesses

to make hiring decisions.

Projective Tests of Personality—Inkblots and Hidden Plots and Sudden Murderers—A Research Example: Pages 487-490

1. _____ tests ask subjects to react to an ambiguous stimulus or unstructured situation.

2. The _____ , or inkblot test, is a well-known projective technique. A second is the Thematic

_____ Test (TAT).

3. The _____ and objectivity of projective tests are quite low. Nevertheless, projective

techniques are considered useful by many clinicians, particularly as part of a test _____ .

What causes shyness? What can be done about it?

Psychology in Action: Barriers and Bridges—Understanding Shyness: Pages 491-493

1. Shyness is a mixture of social _____ and social anxiety.

2. Shy persons tend to lack social _____ and they feel social anxiety (because they believe they are being evaluated by others).

3. Shy persons also have a _____ bias in their thinking (they tend to blame themselves for social failures).

4. Shyness is marked by heightened public self- _____ (awareness of oneself as a _____ object) and a tendency to regard shyness as a lasting _____ .

5. Shyness can be lessened by changing _____ beliefs and by improving social _____ .

MASTERY TEST

1. The hereditary aspects of a person's emotional nature define his or her
   a. character
   b. personality
   c. cardinal traits
   d. temperament

2. Two parts of the psyche that operate on all three levels of awareness are the
   a. id and ego
   b. ego and superego
   c. id and superego
   d. id and ego ideal

3. The four critical situations Miller and Dollard consider important in the development of personality are feeding, toilet training,
   a. sex, and aggression
   b. cleanliness, and language
   c. attachment, and imitation
   d. social learning

4. Scales that rate a person's tendencies for depression, hysteria, paranoia, and mania are found on the
   a. MMPI-2
   b. Rorschach
   c. TAT
   d. 16 PF

5. In the five-factor model, people who score high on openness to experience are
   a. intelligent
   b. extroverted
   c. choleric
   d. a personality type

6. Jung regarded mandalas as symbols of the
   a. animus
   b. anima
   c. self archetype
   d. persona

7. Maslow used the term _____ to describe the tendency to make full use of personal potentials.
   a. full functionality
   b. self-potentiation
   c. ego-idealization
   d. self-actualization

8. Studies of reunited identical twins support the idea that
   a. personality traits are 70 percent hereditary and 30 percent learned
   b. childhood fixations influence the expression of personality traits in adulthood
   c. personality traits are altered by selective mating
   d. personality is shaped at least as much by environment as by heredity

9. A person's perception of his or her own personality is the core of
   a. temperament
   b. source traits
   c. self-concept
   d. trait-situation interactions

10. Which of the following concepts is NOT part of Dollard and Miller's behavioral model of personality?
    a. drive
    b. expectancy
    c. cue
    d. reward

11. The terms structured and unstructured apply most to
    a. the halo effect
    b. interviews
    c. questionnaires
    d. honesty tests

12. Feelings of pride come from the _____, a part of the _____.
    a. libido, conscience
    b. ego ideal, superego
    c. reality principle, superego
    d. superego, ego

13. Four types of temperament recognized by the early Greeks are: melancholic, choleric, phlegmatic and
    a. sanguine
    b. sardonic
    c. sagittarian
    d. sagacious

14. Freud believed that boys identify with their fathers in order to resolve the _____ conflict.
    a. Animus
    b. Electra
    c. Oedipus
    d. Persona

15. Maslow regarded peak experiences as temporary moments of
    a. task-centering
    b. congruent selfhood
    c. self-actualization
    d. organismic valuing

16. Ambiguous stimuli are used primarily in the
    a. MMPI-2
    b. Shoot-Don't-Shoot Test
    c. Rorschach
    d. 16 PF

17. A person who is generally extroverted is more outgoing in some situations than in others. This observation supports the concept of
    a. trait-situation interactions
    b. behavioral genetic determinants
    c. situational fixations
    d. possible selves

18. Allport's concept of central traits is most closely related to Cattell's
    a. surface traits
    b. source traits
    c. secondary traits
    d. cardinal traits

19. According to Freud, tendencies to be orderly, obstinate, and stingy are formed during the _____ stage.
    a. genital
    b. anal
    c. oral
    d. phallic

20. Which of the following is NOT part of Carl Rogers' view of personality?
    a. possible selves
    b. organismic valuing
    c. conditions of worth
    d. congruence

21. Rating scales are primarily used in which approach to personality assessment?
    a. projective testing
    b. direct observation
    c. questionnaires
    d. the TAT technique

22. Which theory of personality places the greatest emphasis on the effects of the environment?
    a. trait
    b. psychodynamic
    c. behavioristic
    d. humanistic

23. Freudian psychosexual stages occur in the order:
    a. oral, anal, genital, phallic
    b. oral, phallic, anal, genital
    c. genital, oral, anal, phallic
    d. oral, anal, phallic, genital

24. Rogers described mismatches between one's self-image and reality as a state of
    a. moral anxiety
    b. incongruence
    c. basic anxiety
    d. negative symbolization

25. All but one of the following are major elements of shyness; which does not apply?
    a. private self-consciousness
    b. social anxiety
    c. self-defeating thoughts
    d. belief that shyness is a lasting trait

26. People who all grew up in the same culture would be most likely to have the same _____ traits.
    a. cardinal
    b. common
    c. secondary
    d. source

27. A trait profile is used to report the results of
    a. the 16 PF
    b. situational tests
    c. the TAT
    d. the inkblot test

28. An emphasis on the situational determinants of actions is a key feature of _____ theories of personality.
    a. psychodynamic
    b. projective
    c. behaviorist
    d. humanist

29. The behavioral concept most closely related to the superego is
    a. psychological situation
    b. self-reinforcement
    c. reinforcement value
    d. self-concept

30. Which two personality characteristics continue to increase as people age?
    a. creativity and organization
    b. conscientiousness and agreeability
    c. affection and trust
    d. irritability and disorganization

31. People who prefer hip-hop, soul, and electronic music tend to
    a. be talkative and forgiving
    b. value aesthetic experiences
    c. be conservative
    d. enjoy taking risks

32. Jill was invited to go snowboarding, an activity she has not done before. Jill believes she has the ability to learn snowboarding and keep up with her friends because she is a fast learner. Bandura would say that Jill is high in
    a. self-actualizing
    b. organismic valuing
    c. congruence
    d. self-efficacy

33. _____ psychologists believe that one's well-being and life satisfaction are influenced by six personality traits, including courage, temperance, and transcendence.
    a. Behavioral
    b. Positive
    c. Psychodynamic
    d. Learning

34. In Asian cultures, _____ tends to be more strongly related to group membership and the success of the group.
    a. temperament
    b. character
    c. self-esteem
    d. moral anxiety

LANGUAGE DEVELOPMENT - Personality

Word roots

Freud used Latin terms to help define the parts of the personality that he proposed. In Latin, *id* means "it" (the third person singular neuter pronoun) while *ego* means "I" (the first person singular pronoun). He combined *ego* with other words to form other psychoanalytic terms found in this chapter (superego and ego ideal).

How do psychologists use the term personality? What core concepts make up the psychology of personality?

Preview: The Hidden Essence (p. 459)

(459) *dilapidated*: falling apart

(459) *hooting and whooping*: yelling with pleasure and excitement

(459) *lumberjack*: logger; one who cuts trees for lumber

(459) *zaniest*: silliest; exhibits odd and often comical behavior

The Psychology of Personality—Do You Have Personality (pp. 459-463)

(459) *charisma*: special magnetic charm or appeal

(459) *keep your bearings*: understand the text; keep your orientation

(460) *inferred*: resulted from, deduced from observation

(460) *hip-hop type*: a type that derives from inner-city street culture; it includes rap music and a style of dress and dance

(460) *techno geek*: a person who spends much of his or her time with technical things such as computers

(462) *arrogance*: too much pride and sense of self-importance

(462) *plagues*: continually troubles

(462) *hotshot*: a person who displays great skills and abilities

(462) *bask in the glow*: enjoy the good feelings

(462) *sketches*: samples of drawings

(462) *pumped up*: made to feel good, strong, and competent

(462) *collectivism*: philosophy that everyone works together for the good of the group; welfare of the group is more important than individual desires

Are some personality traits more basic or important than others?

The Trait Approach—Describe Yourself in 18,000 Words or Less (pp. 463-468)

(463) *uninhibited*: not restrained by social norms; informal

(463) *pessimistic (pessimism)*: the tendency to emphasize the worst possible outcome

(463) *aesthetic*: pleasing and nice to look at

(464) *Hopi of Northern Arizona*: a Native American tribe found primarily in the American southwest

(465) *spiteful*: malicious, nasty

(466) *off-color jokes*: improper or inappropriate jokes that can be offensive

(466) *boisterous*: being loud, wild, and disorderly in behavior

(467) *reared apart*: raised in separate homes

(467) *nervous tics*: nervous habits or actions

(467) *excels*: is good at; performs well at

(467) *sizable effect*: to have a considerable effect, or to influence greatly

(467) *wired in*: unchangeable

(468) *astute*: observant

(468) *rival*: be competitive with

(468) *similarities blaze brightly*: more attention is paid to the similarities than to the differences

How do psychodynamic theories explain personality?

Psychoanalytic Theory—Id Came to Me in a Dream (pp. 468-472)

(468) *animate*: to give life to

(469) *censor*: one who represses or forbids unacceptable notions or ideas

(469) *postulated*: to have claimed without proof

(469) *chaotic*: confused; totally disorganized

(470) *executive*: the one in charge

(470) *clamors*: the act of demanding

(470) *go for it*: go after what you want; do it

(470) *sublimate*: to redirect an urge toward a more socially accepted activity

(471) *hang-up*: problem; barrier

(471) *they swallow things easily*: this statement has two references: individuals in the oral stage seek pleasure by swallowing things and these individuals have the tendency to believe anything told to them even if the information is false.

(471) *passive*: inactive and not showing feeling or interest

(471) *showered with gifts*: being given lots of gifts

(471) *forte:* originally a musical term meaning loud or strong, it is also used to mean strength or one's specialty

(472) *Oedipus*: character in a Greek tragedy who unknowingly married his mother and killed his father

(472) *Electra*: character in a Greek tragedy who killed her mother

(472) *on hold*: postponed; put off until a later time

(472) *embrace*: believes in; holds to be true

Psychodynamic Theories—Freud's Descendants (pp. 472-474)

(472) *carry-over*: continuation

(472) *offshoot*: development; derivation

(473) *withdrawing*: removing oneself from social contact

(473) *loner*: one who avoids social contact with others

(473) *incestuous*: having to do with sexual relations between two people who are closely related

(474) *obstinate*: being stubborn

What do behaviorists emphasize in their approach to personality?

Learning Theories of Personality—Habit I Seen You Before? (pp. 474-479)

(475) *Data of Star Trek*: a human robot character in the popular futuristic *Star Trek* television series

(476) *goad*: something that urges or stimulates into action

(477) *aghast*: horrified

(477) *with joyful abandon*: in an unrestrained manner; free and careless

(478) *vicariously*: experienced indirectly

(478) *arbitrary*: selected at random or without reason

(478) *scoldings*: expressing disapproval

(478) *rebukes*: yelling at a person because one disapproves of her/his actions

(478) *unwittingly*: not intentionally

(478) *submissive*: allowing oneself to be governed by another

(478) *assault*: physical confrontation

(478) *"shop 'til you drop"*: going shopping until one is exhausted and does not have the energy to move anymore

How do humanistic theories differ from other perspectives?

Humanistic Theory—Peak Experiences and Personal Growth (pp. 479-482)

(479) *inherently*: involved in the framework or essential character of something

(479) *blossom*: come forth; to develop

(479) *facet*: an area or component

(479) *mission*: purpose or goal

(479) *"innocence of vision"*: experiencing and seeing the same object like it was seen for the first time

(480) *wry*: ironically humorous

(480) *exaltation*: great happiness

(480) *gauge*: measure

(480) *gleaned from*: gathered information from

(481) *seething*: boiling

(481) *gulf*: a space or an opening

(482) *grossly obese*: extremely overweight

(482) *gut-level response*: arising from one's innermost self, instinctual

(482) *"prized"*: valued; thought of as important

Personality Theories—Overview and Comparison (pp. 482-483)

(483) *fared*: worked out; succeeded

(483) *telling*: revealing; effective

How do psychologists measure personality?

Personality Assessment—Psychological Yardsticks (pp. 484-487)

(484) *sized up*: evaluated; measured

(484) *swayed*: influenced

(484) *ski bum*: a person who spends a great deal of time on the ski slopes

(484) *accentuate*: make more obvious

(486) *split-second*: very fast

(486) *satirize*: to make fun of

(487) *cynicism*: the belief that selfishness motivates human actions

(487) *fake*: to deliberately answer in a misleading manner

(488) *predispose*: influence

(488) *brushes with the law*: illegal actions

Projective Tests of Personality—Inkblots and Hidden Plots (pp. 487-489)

(489) *bereaved*: grieving

(489) *ambiguous*: able to be interpreted in more than one way

Sudden Murderers—A Research Example (p. 490)

(490) *someone you could easily push around*: someone who is easily bullied or influenced by others

(490) *belittlement*: causing to seem little or less

(490) *amnesia*: temporary loss of memory

What causes shyness? What can be done about it?

Psychology in Action: Barriers and Bridges—Understanding Shyness (pp. 491-493)

(491) *wrapped up*: too focused on oneself

(492) *see through*: to understand beyond the surface level

(492) *stage fright*: fear of appearing before crowds to perform, give a speech, etc.

(492) *broken the ice*: concluded an introduction; became acquainted

Solutions

RECITE AND REVIEW

How do psychologists use the term personality? What core concepts make up the psychology of personality?

1. behavior
2. evaluated
3. hereditary
4. behavior
5. traits
6. types
7. personality
8. self-esteem; proud; self-critical
9. Personality
10. trait; social

Are some personality traits more basic or important than others?

1. music; verbal; blues
2. theories
3. individual
4. secondary
5. surface; analysis
6. *Personality*; *Factor*
7. trait
8. universal
9. agreeableness; experience
10. Traits
11. inherited
12. traits
13. identical

How do psychodynamic theories explain personality?

1. unconscious
2. ego
3. principle; principle
4. superego
5. life; energy
6. anxiety; anxiety
7. conscious
8. unconscious
9. stages; oral
10. personality
11. personality
12. psychosexual; Oedipus
13. first few ; toilet; stages
14. Freudians

What do behaviorists emphasize in their approach to personality?

1. learning
2. situational
3. habits; Habits; reward
4. Social
5. psychological; value
6. ability; activities
7. self
8. feeding; anger
9. imitation

How do humanistic theories differ from other perspectives?

1. good; free
2. peak experiences
3. responsibility; positive
4. satisfaction; courage; temperance
5. self; image
6. self-image; self-image
7. fully
8. self-image
9. worth
10. positive; valuing

How do psychologists measure personality?

1. interviews; tests
2. interviews; interviewer; lower
3. rating; behavior

4. *Minnesota*; *Multiphasic*reliable   5. questionnaires

Projective Tests of Personality—Inkblots and Hidden Plots and Sudden Murderers—A Research Example: Pages 487-490

1. stimulus   2. inkblot; *Thematic*   3. low; test

What causes shyness? What can be done about it?

1. social; social   3. thinking; themselves   5. beliefs; social
2. evaluated   4. public; social

CONNECTIONS

How do psychologists use the term personality? What core concepts make up the psychology of personality? Pages 459-463

1. C.   4. H.   7. I.
2. G.   5. F.   8. E.
3. A.   6. B.   9. D.

Are some personality traits more basic or important than others? How do psychodynamic theories explain personality? Pages 463-474

1. L.   6. F.   11. G.
2. K.   7. H.   12. C.
3. M.   8. I.   13. J.
4. O.   9. B.   14. E.
5. N.   10. A.   15. D.

What do behaviorists emphasize in their approach to personality? How do humanistic theories differ from other perspectives? Pages 474-483

1. D.   5. E.   9. K.
2. H.   6. C.   10. B.
3. A.   7. L.   11. J.
4. G.   8. I.   12. F.

How do psychologists measure personality? What causes shyness? What can be done about it? Pages 483-493

1. E.   5. H.   9. I.
2. J.   6. F.   10. C.
3. D.   7. G.
4. A.   8. B.

CHECK YOUR MEMORY

How do psychologists use the term personality? What core concepts make up the psychology of personality? Pages 459-463

1. F	5. F	9. F
2. F	6. T	10. F
3. F	7. T	
4. T	8. T	

Are some personality traits more basic or important than others? Pages 463-468

1. T	7. F	13. T
2. T	8. F	14. F
3. F	9. T	15. T
4. F	10. T	16. T
5. T	11. T	
6. F	12. F	

How do psychodynamic theories explain personality? Pages 468-474

1. F	6. T	11. F
2. T	7. F	12. T
3. F	8. T	13. F
4. T	9. F	14. F
5. F	10. T	15. T

What do behaviorists emphasize in their approach to personality? Pages 474-479

1. T	5. F	9. F
2. T	6. T	10. T
3. T	7. T	11. T
4. T	8. T	

How do humanistic theories differ from other perspectives? Pages 479-483

1. T	5. T	9. T
2. F	6. T	10. F
3. F	7. T	11. T
4. T	8. F	

How do psychologists measure personality? Pages 483-490

1. T	2. T	3. T

4. F	7. F	10. F
5. F	8. T	11. F
6. T	9. F	

What causes shyness? What can be done about it? Pages 491-493

| 1. F | 3. F |
| 2. T | 4. T |

FINAL SURVEY AND REVIEW

How do psychologists use the term personality? What core concepts make up the psychology of personality?

1. Personality; patterns	5. type	9. theories
2. Character	6. introvert; extrovert	10. psychodynamic; humanistic
3. Temperament	7. self-concept	
4. traits	8. Culture; high; low	

Are some personality traits more basic or important than others?

1. personality; aesthetic; verbal	6. Source; traits	11. Behavioral; genetics
2. Trait	7. profile	12. 25; 50
3. Allport; common	8. five-factor	13. heredity; environment
4. cardinal; central	9. extroversion; neuroticism	
5. Cattell; source; factor	10. interact; situations	

How do psychodynamic theories explain personality?

1. personality; conflicts	7. preconscious; unconscious	13. adult; critical; stages
2. psychoanalytic; id; superego	8. id; ego; superego	14. neo; Adler; Jung
3. pleasure; reality	9. psychosexual; phallic	
4. conscience; ego	10. Fixations	
5. Libido; instincts	11. feeding; toilet	
6. neurotic; moral	12. phallic; boys; girls	

What do behaviorists emphasize in their approach to personality?

1. Behavioral	5. expectancies; reinforcement	8. toilet or cleanliness training; aggression
2. determinants	6. efficacy; expectancy; self-efficacy	9. Identification
3. drive; cue	7. reinforcement	
4. cognitive		

How do humanistic theories differ from other perspectives?

1. subjective; actualization

2. Maslow's; actualizers
3. actualization
4. being; strengths
5. symbolized; incongruent
6. incongruent; ideal
7. congruent
8. self-evaluations
9. conditions
10. conditions; of; worth; organismic

How do psychologists measure personality?

1. observation; projective
2. unstructured; bias
3. situational; assessment
4. Personality; Inventory; validity
5. Honesty

Projective Tests of Personality—Inkblots and Hidden Plots and Sudden Murderers—A Research Example: Pages 487-490

1. Projective
2. Rorschach; Apperception
3. validity; battery

What causes shyness? What can be done about it?

1. inhibition
2. skills
3. self-defeating
4. consciousness; social; trait
5. self-defeating; skills

MASTERY TEST

What causes shyness? What can be done about it?

1. D, p. 459
2. B, p. 471
3. A, p. 477
4. A, p. 487
5. A, p. 465
6. C, p. 474
7. D, p. 479
8. D, p. 467
9. C, p. 461
10. B, p. 475
11. B, p. 484
12. B, p. 470
13. A, p. 462
14. C, p. 472
15. C, p. 480
16. C, p. 488
17. A, p. 466
18. B, p. 464
19. B, p. 471
20. A, pp. 481-482
21. B, p. 485
22. C, p. 483
23. D, p. 471
24. B, p. 481
25. A, p. 491
26. B, p. 464
27. A, p. 464
28. C, p. 475
29. B, p. 476
30. B, p. 460
31. A, p. 463
32. D, p. 476
33. B, p. 480
34. C, p. 462

Health, Stress, and Coping

Chapter Overview

Health psychologists study behavioral risk factors and health-promoting behaviors. Various "lifestyle" diseases are directly related to unhealthy personal habits. To reduce lifestyle diseases, people are encouraged to adopt health-promoting behaviors, such as getting regular exercise, controlling smoking and alcohol use, maintaining a balanced diet, getting good medical care, and managing stress. In addition to health-promoting behaviors, early prevention programs and community health campaigns have been implemented. Stress is also a major risk factor. At work, prolonged stress can lead to burnout. Emotional appraisals greatly affect our stress reactions and coping attempts. Traumatic stressors, such as violence, torture, or natural disasters, tend to produce severe stress reactions.

Frustration and conflict are common sources of stress. Major behavioral reactions to frustration include persistence, more vigorous responding, circumvention, direct aggression, displaced aggression, and escape or withdrawal. Five major types of conflict are approach-approach, avoidance-avoidance, approach-avoidance, double approach-avoidance, and multiple approach-avoidance.

Anxiety, threat, or feelings of inadequacy frequently lead to the use of defense mechanisms. Common defense mechanisms include compensation, denial, fantasy, intellectualization, isolation, projection, rationalization, reaction formation, regression, repression, and sublimation. Learned helplessness explains some depression and some failures to cope with threat. Mastery training acts as an antidote to helplessness.

A large number of life changes can increase susceptibility to illness. However, immediate health is more closely related to the severity of daily hassles or microstressors. Intense or prolonged stress may cause psychosomatic problems. The medical model assumes that health and illness are caused by complex biological and physical sources within one's body. An alternative model, the biopsychosocial model, suggests an interplay of biological, psychological, and social factors influencing one's health and illnesses. Biofeedback may be used to combat stress and psychosomatic illnesses. People with Type A personalities run a heightened risk of suffering a heart attack. People with hardy personality traits are resistant to stress and tend to maintain positive emotions that promote creativity, seek new experiences, and appreciate life. Direct or imagined social support from family, friends, and pets can also reduce stress. The body reacts to stress in a pattern called the general adaptation syndrome (G.A.S.). In addition, stress may lower the body's immunity to disease.

The *College Life Stress Inventory*, which is similar to the SRRS, can be used to rate the amount of stress an undergraduate student has experienced. A number of coping skills can be applied to manage stress. Most focus on bodily effects, ineffective behaviors, and upsetting thoughts. Meditation can also be used to reduce stress. Two benefits of meditation are its ability to interrupt anxious thoughts and its ability to elicit the relaxation response.

Learning Objectives

1. Define the terms health *psychology* and *behavioral medicine*.

2. List twelve behavioral risk factors that can adversely affect one's health; and describe the disease-prone personality.

3. Briefly describe the relationship between health-promoting behaviors and longevity; explain how health psychologists work to lessen behavioral risks to health, including the impact of refusal-skills training and community health programs; and define *wellness* and list five characteristics of it.

4. Explain the similarity between your body's stress reaction and emotion; and list five aspects of stress that make it more intense and damaging. Include the definitions of *stress* and *pressure*.

5. Define burnout; describe the three aspects of the problem; and explain ways that burnout can be reduced.

6. Give an example of how primary and secondary appraisal are used in coping with a threatening situation; and explain how the perception of control of a stressor influences the amount of threat felt.

7. Differentiate problem-focused coping from emotion-focused coping; explain how they may help or hinder each other; and describe the impact of traumatic stress and ways to cope with reactions to severe stress.

8. List and describe: the two different kinds of frustration, four factors that increase frustration, five common reactions to frustration (see Fig. 15.3); explain how scapegoating is a special form of displaced aggression; explain how a *stereotyped response* differs from persistence; and discuss three effective ways to avoid frustration.

9. Describe and give an example of each of the following four types of conflict: approach-approach, avoidance-avoidance, approach-avoidance (include the terms *ambivalence* and *partial approach*), and double approach-avoidance (include the term *vacillation*); and discuss four strategies for coping with conflict.

10. Define the term *defense mechanism*; discuss the positive value of defense mechanisms; and describe the following defense mechanisms and give an example of each:

    a. denial

    b. repression

    c. reaction formation

    d. regression

    e. projection

    f. rationalization

g. compensation

h. sublimation

11. Describe the development of learned helplessness; relate this concept to attribution and depression; list problems that contribute to depression among college students and the danger signs of depression; and discuss how helplessness may be unlearned and depression can be combated.

12. Discuss the relationship between life changes and long-term health; describe the SRRS; and explain how hassles are related to immediate health and how acculturative stress can cause problems.

13. Distinguish between *psychosomatic disorders* and *hypochondria*; list the causes of psychosomatic disorders; compare the biopsychosocial model of health to the traditional medical model; and briefly discuss biofeedback in terms of the process involved and its possible applications.

14. Differentiate between Type A and Type B personalities; list strategies for reducing hostility; describe a hardy personality and how this personality views the world; and explain how being optimist and happy and having social support are related to stress reduction.

15. Explain the concept of the General Adaptation Syndrome; list and describe its three stages; and describe how stress affects the immune system. Include the definition of *psychoneuroimmunology*.

The following objectives are related to the material in the "Psychology in Action" section of your text.

1. Define the term *stress management;* and briefly discuss the College Life Stress Inventory.

2. List the three responses that are triggered by stress; and discuss the stress management techniques that can be used to diminish or break the cycle of stress responses.

RECITE AND REVIEW

What is health psychology? How does behavior affect health?

Health Psychology—Here's to Your Good Health: Pages 497-500

1. Health psychologists are interested in _____ that helps maintain and promote health. The related field of behavioral medicine applies psychology to _____ treatment and problems.

2. Most people today die from lifestyle diseases caused by unhealthy personal _____ .

3. Studies have identified a number of behavioral risk factors, which increase the chances of _____ or injury.

4. A general disease-prone personality pattern also raises the risk of _____ .

5. Health-promoting _____ tend to maintain good health. They include practices such as getting regular exercise, controlling _____ and alcohol use, maintaining a balanced _____ , getting good medical care, avoiding _____ deprivation, and managing stress.

6. Health psychologists attempt to promote wellness (a positive state of _____) through community health _____ that educate people about risk factors and healthful behaviors.

What is stress? What factors determine its severity?

Stress—Thrill or Threat? Pages 501-505

1. Stress occurs when we are forced to _____ or adapt to external demands.

2. Stress is more damaging in situations involving pressure (responding at full capacity for long periods), a lack of _____ , unpredictability of the stressor, and _____ or repeated emotional shocks.

3. In _____ settings, prolonged stress can lead to burnout, marked by emotional _____ , depersonalization (detachment from others), and reduced personal accomplishment.

4. The _____ (initial) appraisal of a situation greatly affects our emotional response to it. Stress reactions, in particular, are related to an appraisal of _____ .

5. During a _____ appraisal some means of coping with a situation is selected. Coping may be either problem-focused (managing the situation) or emotion-focused (managing one's emotional reactions) or both.

6. _____ is intensified when a situation is perceived as a threat and when a person does not feel competent to cope with it.

7. Traumatic _____ , such as violence, torture, or natural disasters, tend to produce severe _____ reactions.

8. Traumatic _____ leave people feeling threatened, vulnerable, and with the sense that they are losing control over their _____ .

9. Severe or _____ traumatic _____ can leave people with lasting emotional handicaps called stress disorders.

What causes frustration and what are typical reactions to it?

Frustration—Blind Alleys and Lead Balloons: Pages 505-507

1. Frustration is the negative emotional state that occurs when progress toward a _____ is _____ . Sources of frustration may be external or personal.

2. External frustrations are based on delay, failure, rejection, loss, and other direct blocking of motives. Personal frustration is related to _____ characteristics over which one has little control.

3. Frustrations of all types become more _____ as the strength, urgency, or importance of the blocked motive increases.

4. Major behavioral reactions to frustration include persistence, more _____ responding, and circumvention of barriers.

5. Other reactions to frustration are _____ aggression, displaced aggression (including scapegoating), and escape, or _____ .

6. Ways of _____ with frustration include identifying its source, determining if the source is manageable, and deciding if _____ the source is worth the effort.

Are there different types of conflict? How do people react to conflict?

Conflict—Yes, No, Yes, No, Yes, No, Well, Maybe: Pages 507-510

1. _____ occurs when we must choose between contradictory alternatives.

2. Three basic types of conflict are approach-approach (choice between two _____ alternatives), avoidance-avoidance (both alternatives are _____), and approach-avoidance (a goal or activity has both positive and negative aspects).

3. Approach-approach conflicts are usually the _____ to resolve.

4. Avoidance conflicts are _____ to resolve and are characterized by inaction, indecision, freezing, and a desire to escape (called _____ the field).

5. People usually remain in approach-avoidance conflicts, but fail to fully resolve them. Approach-avoidance conflicts are associated with ambivalence (_____ feelings) and _____ approach.

6. More complex conflicts are: double approach-avoidance (both alternatives have _____ and _____ qualities) and multiple approach-avoidance (several alternatives each have good and bad qualities).

7. Vacillation (wavering between choices) is the most common reaction to double _____ conflicts.

8. Managing conflicts effectively involves not making hasty decisions, trying out a few _____ at a time, looking for _____ , and sticking with the choice.

What are defense mechanisms?

Psychological Defense—Mental Karate? Pages 510-512

1. Anxiety, threat, or feelings of _____ frequently lead to the use of psychological defense mechanisms. These are habitual strategies used to avoid or reduce anxiety.

2. A number of defense mechanisms have been identified, including denial, fantasy, intellectualization, isolation, projection, rationalization, _____ formation, regression, and _____ (motivated forgetting).

3. Two defense mechanisms that have some _____ qualities are compensation and sublimation.

What do we know about coping with feelings of helplessness and depression?

Learned Helplessness—Is There Hope? Pages 512-515

1. Learned helplessness is a learned inability to overcome obstacles or to _____ punishment.

2. Learned helplessness explains the failure to cope with some threatening situations. The symptoms of learned helplessness and depression are nearly _____ .

3. Mastery _____ and hope act as antidotes to helplessness.

4. Nearly _____ percent of all college students suffer from depression due to being _____ from their families, lacking the basic skills necessary for _____ success, abusing alcohol, and feeling they are missing out on life.

5. Depression (a state of deep sadness or despondency) is a serious emotional problem. Actions and thoughts that counter feelings of helplessness tend to _____ depression.

How is stress related to health and disease?

Stress and Health—Unmasking a Hidden Killer: Pages 515-524

1. Work with the *Social Readjustment Rating Scale (SRRS)* indicates that a large number of life _____ units (LCUs) can increase susceptibility to _____ or illness.

2. Immediate health is more closely related to the intensity and severity of daily annoyances, known as _____ or microstressors.

3. Intense or prolonged stress may damage the body in the form of psychosomatic disorders (illnesses in which _____ factors play a part).

4. Psychosomatic (mind-body) disorders have no connection to hypochondria, the tendency to imagine that one has a _____ .

5. The medical model suggests one's health and illness are caused by _____ and physical sources within one's body and the _____ model suggests that three factors–biological, psychological, and social–influence one's health and illness.

6. During biofeedback training, bodily processes are _____ and converted to a signal that indicates what the body is doing.

7. Biofeedback allows alteration of many bodily activities. It shows promise for promoting _____ , self-regulation, and for treating some psychosomatic illnesses.

8. People with Type A (_____ attack prone) personalities are competitive, striving, and frequently angry or hostile, and they have a chronic sense of _____ urgency.

9. _____ and hostility are especially likely to increase the chances of heart attack.

10. People who have traits of the hardy personality seem to be resistant to _____ , even if they also have Type A traits.

11. People who have a hardy personality tend to be _____ and have _____ emotions such as joy, interest, and contentment. These factors reduce bodily arousal and help people find _____ solutions when they are stressed.

12. Unlike pessimists, optimists tend to deal with their problems head on, are less likely to be _____ and anxious, believe they will _____ , and take better care of themselves.

13. Stress can be reduced through the mechanism of _____ support by allowing people to seek assistance and to share _____ events with friends and families.

14. Thinking about a person who provides _____ or having a _____ present can reduce one's level of stress.

15. The body reacts to stress in a series of stages called the _____ adaptation syndrome (G.A.S.).

16. The stages of the G.A.S. are alarm, resistance, and exhaustion. The G.A.S. contributes to the development of _____ disorders.

17. Stress weakens the immune system and lowers the body's resistance to _____ .

What are the best strategies for managing stress?

Psychology in Action: Stress Management: Pages 525-528

1. Most stress management skills focus on one of three areas: bodily effects, ineffective _____ , and upsetting _____ .

2. Bodily effects can be managed with exercise, meditation, progressive _____ , and guided _____ .

3. Meditation is a self-control technique that can be used to reduce _____ .

4. Benefits of _____ are its ability to interrupt anxious thoughts and its ability to promote relaxation.

5. The impact of ineffective behavior can be remedied by slowing down, getting organized, striking a balance between "good stress" and _____ , accepting your limits, and seeking social support.

6. A good way to control upsetting thoughts is to replace negative self-statements with _____ coping statements.

CONNECTIONS

What is health psychology? How does behavior affect health? What is stress? What factors determine its severity? Pages 497-505

1. _____ risk factors
2. _____ problem-focused coping
3. _____ wellness
4. _____ burnout
5. _____ tobacco
6. _____ refusal skills
7. _____ primary appraisal
8. _____ managing stress
9. _____ disease-prone personality
10. _____ stress reaction

a. well-being
b. people who are depressed
c. health-promoting behavior
d. leading cause of death
e. lifestyle diseases
f. smoking prevention
g. ANS arousal
h. plans to reduce stress
i. "Am I in trouble?"
j. job stress

What causes frustration and what are typical reactions to it? Are there different types of conflict? How do people react to conflict? Pages 505-510

1. _____ frustration
2. _____ displaced aggression
3. _____ apathy
4. _____ External frustration
5. _____ avoidance-avoidance
6. _____ approach-avoidance
7. _____ approach-approach

a. blocked motive
b. psychological escape
c. scapegoat
d. ambivalence
e. deciding on two negative alternatives
f. deciding on two positive alternatives
g. distress caused by outside sources

What are defense mechanisms? What do we know about coping with feelings of helplessness and depression? Pages 510-515

1. _____ compensation
2. _____ denial
3. _____ fantasy
4. _____ intellectualization
5. _____ isolation
6. _____ projection
7. _____ rationalization
8. _____ reaction formation
9. _____ regression
10. _____ repression
11. _____ sublimation

a. fulfilling unmet desires in imagined activities
b. separating contradictory thoughts into "logic-tight" mental compartments
c. preventing actions by exaggerating opposite behavior
d. justifying your behavior by giving reasonable but false reasons for it
e. unconsciously preventing painful thoughts from entering awareness
f. counteracting a real or imagined weakness by seeking to excel
g. retreating to an earlier level of development
h. attributing one's own shortcomings or unacceptable impulses to others
i. protecting oneself from an unpleasant reality by refusing to perceive it
j. working off unacceptable impulses in constructive activities
k. thinking about threatening situations in impersonal terms

Connections

1. _____ defense mechanism
2. _____ feeling despondent
3. _____ learned helplessness
4. _____ mastery training

a. depression
b. Sigmund Freud
c. hope
d. shuttle box

How is stress related to health and disease? What are the best strategies for managing stress? Pages 515-528

1. _____ College Life Stress Inventory	a.	LCU
2. _____ SRRS	b.	mind-body
3. _____ hassle	c.	self-regulation
4. _____ hardy personality	d.	cardiac personality
5. _____ psychosomatic	e.	alarm reaction
6. _____ modifying ineffective behavior	f.	stress resistant
7. _____ Type A	g.	microstressor
8. _____ biofeedback	h.	stress rating scale
9. _____ coping statements	i.	Keep It Simple (K.I.S.)
10. _____ G.A.S.	j.	stress inoculation

CHECK YOUR MEMORY

What is health psychology? How does behavior affect health? Pages 497-500

1. Heart disease, lung cancer, and stroke are typical lifestyle diseases.

   TRUE or FALSE

2. A person who is overweight doubles the chance of dying from cancer or heart disease.

   TRUE or FALSE

3. One can expect to lose up to 20 years of life expectancy if he/she is overweight by the age of 20.

   TRUE or FALSE

4. Illicit use of drugs is the second most common cause of death in the United States, after smoking.

   TRUE or FALSE

5. Behavioral risk factors such as smoking, poor diet, or alcohol abuse are linked to infectious diseases.

   TRUE or FALSE

6. People with disease-prone personalities are depressed, anxious, and hostile.

   TRUE or FALSE

7. Unhealthy lifestyles typically involve multiple risks.

   TRUE or FALSE

8. Maintaining a healthy diet means a person must live on a high-protein diet consisting of tofu and wheat grain.

   TRUE or FALSE

9. Moderation in drinking refers to having three to five drinks per day.

   TRUE or FALSE

10. School-based prevention programs have successfully increased teens' negative attitudes toward smoking.

    TRUE or FALSE

11. Community health campaigns provide refusal skills training to large numbers of people.

    TRUE or FALSE

12. Wellness can be described as an absence of disease.

    TRUE or FALSE

What is stress? What factors determine its severity? Pages 501-505

1. Unpleasant activities produce stress, whereas pleasant activities do not.

   TRUE or FALSE

2. Initial reactions to stressors are similar to those that occur during strong emotion.

   TRUE or FALSE

3. Short-term stresses rarely do any damage to the body.

   TRUE or FALSE

4. Unpredictable demands increase stress.

   TRUE or FALSE

5. Pressure occurs when we are faced with a stressor we can control.

   TRUE or FALSE

6. Burnout is especially a problem in helping professions.

   TRUE or FALSE

7. The opposite of burnout is positive job engagement.

   TRUE or FALSE

8. Stress is often related to the meaning a person places on events.

   TRUE or FALSE

9. The same situation can be a challenge or a threat, depending on how it is appraised.

TRUE or FALSE

10. In a secondary appraisal, we decide if a situation is relevant or irrelevant, positive or threatening.

TRUE or FALSE

11. When confronted by a stressor, it is best to choose one type of coping—problem focused or emotion focused.

TRUE or FALSE

12. Emotion-focused coping is best suited to managing stressors you cannot control.

TRUE or FALSE

13. A distressed person may distract herself by listening to music, taking a walk to relax, or seeking emotional support from others. Such strategies illustrate problem-focused coping.

TRUE or FALSE

14. Nightmares, grief, flashbacks, nervousness, and depression are common reactions to traumatic stress.

TRUE or FALSE

15. It is possible to have stress symptoms from merely witnessing traumatically stressful events on television.

TRUE or FALSE

16. An excellent way to cope with traumatic stress is to stop all of your daily routines and isolate yourself from others.

TRUE or FALSE

What causes frustration and what are typical reactions to it? Pages 505-507

1. Delays, rejections, and losses are good examples of personal frustrations.

TRUE or FALSE

2. Varied responses and circumvention attempt to directly destroy or remove barriers that cause frustration.

TRUE or FALSE

3. Scapegoating is a good example of escape or withdrawal.

TRUE or FALSE

4. Abuse of drugs can be a way of psychologically escaping frustration.

TRUE or FALSE

5. Persistence must be flexible before it is likely to aid a person trying to cope with frustration.

    TRUE or FALSE

Are there different types of conflict? How do people react to conflict? Pages 507-510

1. Approach-approach conflicts are fairly easy to resolve.

    TRUE or FALSE

2. Indecision, inaction, and freezing are typical reactions to approach-approach conflicts.

    TRUE or FALSE

3. People find it difficult to escape approach-avoidance conflicts.

    TRUE or FALSE

4. Wanting to eat, but not wanting to be overweight, creates an approach-approach conflict.

    TRUE or FALSE

5. People are very likely to vacillate when faced with a double approach-avoidance conflict.

    TRUE or FALSE

What are defense mechanisms? Pages 510-512

1. Defense mechanisms are used to avoid or distort sources of threat or anxiety.

    TRUE or FALSE

2. Denial is a common reaction to bad news, such as learning that a friend has died.

    TRUE or FALSE

3. In reaction formation, a person fulfills unmet desires in imagined achievements.

    TRUE or FALSE

4. A child who becomes homesick while visiting relatives may be experiencing a mild regression.

    TRUE or FALSE

5. Denial and repression are the two most positive of the defense mechanisms.

    TRUE or FALSE

What do we know about coping with feelings of helplessness and depression? Pages 512-515

1. The deep depression experienced by prisoners of war appears to be related to learned helplessness.

   TRUE or FALSE

2. Learned helplessness occurs when events appear to be uncontrollable.

   TRUE or FALSE

3. Attributing failure to lasting, general factors, such as personal characteristics, tends to create the most damaging feelings of helplessness.

   TRUE or FALSE

4. Mastery training restores feelings of control over the environment.

   TRUE or FALSE

5. At any given time, 52 to 61 percent of all college students are experiencing the symptoms of depression.

   TRUE or FALSE

6. Making a daily schedule will only emphasize the goals that a person cannot accomplish and will push him/her deeper into depression.

   TRUE or FALSE

7. Depression is more likely when students find it difficult to live up to idealized images of themselves.

   TRUE or FALSE

8. Writing rational answers to self-critical thoughts can help counteract feelings of depression.

   TRUE or FALSE

How is stress related to health and disease? Pages 515-524

1. Scores on the SRRS are expressed as life control units.

   TRUE or FALSE

2. A score of 300 LCUs on the SRRS is categorized as a major life crisis.

   TRUE or FALSE

3. According to the SRRS, being fired at work involves more LCUs than divorce does.

   TRUE or FALSE

4. Microstressors tend to predict changes in health 1 to 2 years after the stressful events took place.

   TRUE or FALSE

5. Psychosomatic disorders involve actual damage to the body or damaging changes in bodily functioning.

   TRUE or FALSE

6. A person undergoing biofeedback can sleep if he or she desires—the machine does all the work.

   TRUE or FALSE

7. Type B personalities are more than twice as likely to suffer heart attacks as Type A personalities.

   TRUE or FALSE

8. People with the hardy personality type tend to see life as a series of challenges.

   TRUE or FALSE

9. People with a hardy personality have had to cope with many adversities and therefore have a negative view of life.

   TRUE or FALSE

10. Both men and women will seek social support when they are stressed.

    TRUE or FALSE

11. Thinking about a supportive person or having a pet present can help lower one's stress level.

    TRUE or FALSE

12. In the stage of resistance of the G.A.S., people have symptoms of headache, fever, fatigue, upset stomach, and the like.

    TRUE or FALSE

13. Serious health problems tend to occur when a person reaches the stage of exhaustion in the G.A.S.

    TRUE or FALSE

14. Stress management training can actually boost immune system functioning.

    TRUE or FALSE

15. Happiness and high levels of arousal due to stress have been shown to strengthen the immune system's response.

    TRUE or FALSE

What are the best strategies for managing stress? Pages 525-528

1. Concern about being pregnant is the most stressful item listed on the College Life Stress Inventory.

   TRUE or FALSE

2. The harder you try to meditate the more likely you are to succeed.

   TRUE or FALSE

3. Exercising for stress management is most effective when it is done daily.

   TRUE or FALSE

4. Guided imagery is used to reduce anxiety and promote relaxation.

   TRUE or FALSE

5. Merely writing down thoughts and feelings about daily events can provide some of the benefits of social support.

   TRUE or FALSE

6. To get the maximum benefits, coping statements should be practiced in actual stressful situations.

   TRUE or FALSE

7. Persistence must be flexible before it is likely to aid a person trying to cope with frustration.

   TRUE or FALSE

8. Humor increases anxiety and emotional distress because it put problems into perspective for individuals.

   TRUE or FALSE

FINAL SURVEY AND REVIEW

What is health psychology? How does behavior affect health?

Health Psychology—Here's to Your Good Health: Pages 497-500

1. Health psychologists are interested in behavior that helps maintain and promote health. The related field of _____ _____ applies psychology to medical treatment and problems.

2. Most people today die from _____ diseases caused by unhealthy personal habits.

3. Studies have identified a number of behavioral _____ , which increase the chances of disease (or illness) or injury.

4. A general _____ personality pattern also raises the risk of illness (or disease).

5. Health- _____ behaviors tend to maintain good health. They include practices such as getting regular exercise, controlling smoking and alcohol use, maintaining a balanced diet, getting good medical care, avoiding sleep _____ , and managing _____ .

6. Health psychologists attempt to promote _____ (a positive state of health) through _____ _____ campaigns that educate people about risk factors and healthful behaviors.

What is stress? What factors determine its severity?

Stress—Thrill or Threat? Pages 501-505

1. Stress occurs when we are forced to adjust or _____ to external _____ .

2. Stress is more damaging in situations involving _____ (responding at full capacity for long periods), a lack of control, unpredictability of the _____ , and intense or repeated emotional shocks.

3. In work settings, prolonged stress can lead to _____ , marked by emotional exhaustion, _____ (detachment from others), and reduced personal accomplishment.

4. The primary _____ of a situation greatly affects our emotional response to it. Stress reactions, in particular, are related to an _____ of threat.

5. During a secondary appraisal some means of coping with a situation is selected. Coping may be either _____ -focused (managing the situation) or _____ -focused (managing one's emotional reactions) or both.

6. Stress is intensified when a situation is perceived as a _____ and when a person does not feel _____ to cope with it.

7. _____ stressors, such as violence, torture, or natural disasters, tend to produce severe stress reactions.

8. Traumatic stresses leave people feeling threatened, vulnerable, and with the sense that they are losing _____ over their lives.

9. Severe or repeated traumatic stress can leave people with lasting emotional handicaps called _____ _____ .

What causes frustration and what are typical reactions to it?

Frustration—Blind Alleys and Lead Balloons: Pages 505-507

1. _____ is the negative emotional state that occurs when progress toward a goal is blocked. Sources of frustration may be external or _____ .

2. _____ frustrations are based on delay, failure, rejection, loss, and other direct blocking of motives. _____ frustration is related to personal characteristics over which one has little control.

3. Frustrations of all types become more intense as the strength, urgency, or importance of the _____ _____ increases.

4. Major behavioral reactions to frustration include _____ , more vigorous responding, and _____ of barriers.

5. Other reactions to frustration are direct aggression, _____ aggression (including _____), and escape, or withdrawal.

6. Ways of coping with _____ include identifying its source, determining if the source is _____ , and deciding if changing the source is worth the effort.

Are there different types of conflict? How do people react to conflict?

Conflict—Yes, No, Yes, No, Yes, No, Well, Maybe: Pages 507-510

1. Conflict occurs when we must choose between _____ alternatives.

2. Three basic types of conflict are _____ (choice between two positive alternatives), _____ (both alternatives are negative), and approach-avoidance (a goal or activity has both positive and negative aspects).

3. _____ conflicts are usually the easiest to resolve.

4. _____ conflicts are difficult to resolve and are characterized by inaction, indecision, freezing, and a desire to escape (called leaving the field).

5. People usually remain in approach-avoidance conflicts, but fail to fully resolve them. Approach-avoidance conflicts are associated with _____ (mixed feelings) and partial approach.

6. More complex conflicts are: _____ approach-avoidance (both alternatives have positive and negative qualities) and _____ approach-avoidance (several alternatives each have good and bad qualities).

7. _____ (wavering between choices) is the most common reaction to double approach-avoidance conflicts.

8. Managing _____ effectively involves not making _____ decisions, trying out a few possibilities at a time, looking for compromises, and sticking with the choice.

What are defense mechanisms?

Psychological Defense—Mental Karate? Pages 510-512

1. Anxiety, threat, or feelings of inadequacy frequently lead to the use of psychological _____ _____ . These are habitual strategies used to avoid or reduce _____ .

2. A number of defense mechanisms have been identified, including _____ (refusing to perceive an unpleasant reality), fantasy, intellectualization, isolation, projection, _____ (justifying one's behavior), reaction formation, regression, and repression.

3. Two defense mechanisms that have some positive qualities are _____ and _____ .

What do we know about coping with feelings of helplessness and depression?

Learned Helplessness—Is There Hope? Pages 512-515

1. Learned _____ is a learned inability to overcome obstacles or to avoid _____ .

2. The symptoms of learned helplessness and _____ are nearly identical.

3. _____ training and hope act as antidotes to helplessness.

4. Nearly 80 percent of all _____ students suffer from _____ due to being isolated from their families, lacking basic skills necessary for academic success, abusing alcohol, and feeling they are missing out on life.

5. _____ (a state of deep sadness or despondency) is a serious emotional problem. Actions and thoughts that counter feelings of helplessness tend to reduce depression.

How is stress related to health and disease?

Stress and Health—Unmasking a Hidden Killer: Pages 515-524

1. Work with the _____ _____ _____ Scale (SRRS) indicates that a large number of life change units (LCUs) can increase susceptibility to accident or illness.

2. Immediate health is more closely related to the intensity and severity of daily annoyances, known as hassles or _____ .

3. Intense or prolonged stress may damage the body in the form of _____ disorders (illnesses in which psychological factors play a part).

4. _____ (mind-body) disorders have no connection to _____ , the tendency to imagine that one has a disease.

5. The _____ model suggests one's health and illness are caused by biological and physical sources within one's body and the biopsychosocial model suggests that three factors– _____ , _____ , and _____ –influences one's health and illnesses.

6. During _____ training, bodily processes are monitored and converted to a _____ that indicates what the body is doing.

7. Biofeedback allows alteration of many bodily activities. It shows promise for promoting relaxation, self- _____ , and for treating some psychosomatic illnesses.

8. People with _____ _____ (heart attack prone) personalities are competitive, striving, and frequently _____ or hostile, and they have a chronic sense of time urgency.

9. Anger and hostility are especially likely to increase the chances of _____ _____ .

10. People who have traits of the _____ personality seem to be resistant to stress, even if they also have Type A traits.

11. People who have a _____ personality tend to be optimists and have _____ emotions such as joy, interest, and contentment. These factors _____ bodily arousal and help people find creative solutions when they are stressed.

12. Unlike pessimists, _____ tend to deal with their problems head on, are _____ likely to be stressed and anxious, believe they _____ succeed, and take better care of themselves.

13. Stress can be _____ through the mechanism of social support by allowing people to seek assistance and to share positive _____ with friends and families.

14. Thinking about a _____ who provides support or having a pet present can _____ one's level of stress.

15. The body reacts to stress in a series of stages called the _____ _____ _____ (G.A.S.).

16. The stages of the G.A.S. are _____ , resistance, and exhaustion. The G.A.S. contributes to the development of psychosomatic disorders.

17. Stress weakens the _____ system and lowers the body's resistance to disease (or illness).

What are the best strategies for managing stress?

Psychology in Action: Stress Management: Pages 525-528

1. Most stress management skills focus on one of three areas: bodily effects, _____ behavior, and _____ thoughts.

2. Bodily effects can be managed with exercise, meditation, _____ relaxation, and _____ imagery.

3. The impact of ineffective behavior can be remedied by slowing down, getting organized, striking a balance between "good stress" and relaxation, accepting your _____ , and seeking _____ support.

4. A good way to control upsetting thoughts is to replace _____ self-statements with positive _____ statements.

5. _____ is a self-control technique that can be used to reduce stress.

6. Benefits of meditation are its ability to interrupt anxious thoughts and its ability to promote _____ .

MASTERY TEST

1. When stressful events appear to be uncontrollable, two common reactions are
    a. apathy and double-approach conflict
    b. helplessness and depression
    c. assimilation and marginalization
    d. psychosomatic disorders and hypochondria

2. The *College Life Stress Inventory* is most closely related to the
    a. SRRS
    b. G.A.S.
    c. K.I.S.
    d. *Disease-Prone Personality Scale*

3. We answer the question "Am I okay or in trouble" when making
    a. negative self-statements
    b. coping statements
    c. a primary appraisal
    d. a secondary appraisal

4. Which of the following is NOT a major symptom of burnout?
    a. emotional exhaustion
    b. depersonalization
    c. reduced accomplishment
    d. dependence on co-workers

5. A child who displays childish speech and infantile play after his parents bring home a new baby shows signs of
    a. compensation
    b. reaction formation
    c. regression
    d. sublimation

6. Persistent but inflexible responses to frustration can become
    a. stereotyped behaviors
    b. imagined barriers
    c. negative self-statements
    d. sublimated and depersonalized

7. The leading cause of death in the United States is
    a. tobacco
    b. diet/inactivity
    c. alcohol
    d. infection

8. Both mountain climbing and marital strife
   a. are behavioral risk factors
   b. are appraised as secondary threats
   c. cause stress reactions
   d. produce the condition known as pressure

9. LCUs are used to assess
   a. burnout
   b. social readjustments
   c. microstressors
   d. what stage of the G.A.S. a person is in

10. Sujata is often ridiculed by her boss, who also frequently takes advantage of her. Deep inside, Sujata has come to hate her boss, yet on the surface she acts as if she likes him very much. It is likely that Sujata is using the defense mechanism called
    a. reaction formation
    b. Type B appraisal
    c. problem-focused coping
    d. sublimation

11. Lifestyle diseases are of special interest to _____ psychologists.
    a. health
    b. community
    c. wellness
    d. psychosomatic

12. Which of the following is NOT characteristic of the hardy personality?
    a. commitment
    b. a sense of control
    c. accepting challenge
    d. repression

13. Unhealthy lifestyles are marked by the presence of a number of
    a. health refusal factors
    b. behavioral risk factors
    c. cultural stressors
    d. Type B personality traits

14. The most effective response to a controllable stressor is
    a. problem-focused coping
    b. emotion-focused coping
    c. leaving the field
    d. depersonalization

15. Delay, rejection, failure, and loss are all major causes of
    a. pressure
    b. frustration
    c. conflict
    d. helplessness

16. There is evidence that the core lethal factor of Type A behavior is
    a. time urgency
    b. anger and hostility
    c. competitiveness and ambition
    d. accepting too many responsibilities

17. A person is caught between "the frying pan and the fire" in an _____ conflict.
    a. approach-approach
    b. avoidance-avoidance
    c. approach-avoidance
    d. double appraisal

18. Which of the following is NOT one of the major health-promoting behaviors listed in the text?
    a. do not smoke
    b. get adequate sleep
    c. get regular exercise
    d. avoid eating between meals

19. Ambivalence and partial approach are very common reactions to what type of conflict?
    a. approach-approach
    b. avoidance-avoidance
    c. approach-avoidance
    d. multiple avoidance

20. Which of the following terms does not belong with the others?
    a. Type A personality
    b. stage of exhaustion
    c. displaced aggression
    d. psychosomatic disorder

21. Coping statements are a key element in
    a. stress inoculation
    b. the K.I.S. technique
    c. guided imagery
    d. refusal skills training

22. Which of the following factors typically minimizes the amount of stress experienced?
    a. predictable stressors
    b. repeated stressors
    c. uncontrollable stressors
    d. intense stressors

23. Scapegoating is closely related to which response to frustration?
    a. leaving the field
    b. displaced aggression
    c. circumvention
    d. reaction formation

24. The study of the ways in which stress and the immune system affect susceptibility to disease is called
    a. neuropsychosymptomology
    b. immunohypochondrology
    c. psychosomatoneurology
    d. psychoneuroimmunology

25. Refusal skills training is typically used to teach young people how to
    a. avoid drug use
    b. cope with burnout
    c. resist stressors at home and at school
    d. avoid forming habits that lead to heart disease

26. Which combination is most relevant to managing bodily reactions to stress?
    a. social support, self pacing
    b. exercise, social support
    c. exercise, negative self-statements
    d. progressive relaxation, guided imagery

27. Stress reactions are most likely to occur when a stressor is viewed as a _____ during the
    _____.
    a. pressure, primary appraisal
    b. pressure, secondary appraisal
    c. threat, primary appraisal
    d. threat, secondary appraisal

28. External symptoms of the body's adjustment to stress are least visible in which stage of the G.A.S?
    a. alarm
    b. regulation
    c. resistance
    d. exhaustion

29. A perceived lack of control creates a stressful sense of threat when combined with a perceived
    a. sense of time urgency
    b. state of sublimation
    c. need to change secondary risk factors
    d. lack of competence

30. Stress, smoking, and overeating are related to each other in that they are behavioral
    a. hassles
    b. risk factors
    c. sources of burnout
    d. causes of depersonalization

31. Behavioral risk factors such as smoking cigarettes, drinking alcohol, and overeating have been linked to
    a. Type B personality
    b. infectious diseases
    c. high life expectancy
    d. hardy personality

32. Consuming no more than one to two alcoholic drinks per day, exercising three to four times a week, and eating a healthy diet are
    a. stress-induced behaviors
    b. behavioral risk factors
    c. health-promoting behaviors
    d. factors that increase heart disorders

33. Shane likes to listen to his favorite music and taking long walks in the park to relax when he is distressed or stressed. Shane's method involves
    a. defense mechanism
    b. reaction formation
    c. problem focused coping
    d. emotion focused coping

34. People with a _____ personality tend to be optimistic and have positive emotions that help them reduce and find creative solutions to stress.
    a. realistic
    b. Type A
    c. hardy
    d. high-strung

35. Real or imagined social support and encouragement from _____ can reduce one's level of stress.
    a. family members
    b. friends
    c. pets
    d. all the preceding

36. Which factor reduces one's stress or emotional distress?
    a. humor
    b. smoking
    c. high blood pressure
    d. approach-avoidance

37. Lisa's doctor suggested that her disorder has three contributing causes: biological, psychological, and social. Which model of explanation is her doctor relying on to diagnose and treat Lisa's disorder?
    a. medical
    b. biopsychosocial
    c. cognitive-behavioral
    d. cultural

LANGUAGE DEVELOPMENT - Health, Stress, and Coping

Word roots

The Greek word *hypo* means "under" and, when combined with other terms, also means "beneath" or "lowered." For example, the terms "hypochondriac" and "hypochondriasis" come from "hypochondria," an old anatomical term that once referred to the area under the ribs (*khondros* in ancient Greek means "cartilage"). Other examples of the use of the root word "hypo" found in this text are: hypothesis, hypothalamus, hypopituitary, hypothyroidism, hypoglycemia, and hypoactive.

What is health psychology? How does behavior affect health?

Preview: Taylor's (Not So Very) Fine Adventure (p. 497)

> (497) *make-or-break*: an event or activity that can determine success or failure in some aspect of one's life
>
> (497) *one-finger salute*: an impolite gesture with the middle finger used to indicate anger or disgust
>
> (497) *swarming*: to hurriedly move as a group in one area
>
> (497) *darted*: moved suddenly and quickly
>
> (497) *colossal*: huge
>
> (497) *bronchitis*: respiratory illness centered in the lungs

Health Psychology—Here's to Your Good Health (pp. 497-500)

> (497) *bedevil*: to torment, create great distress
>
> (497) *in the long run*: eventually
>
> (498) *plaque*: fatty substances deposited in the inner layers of the arteries
>
> (498) *sermon*: lecture or talk by minister or priest

(499) *silent killer*: a deadly disease with little or no outward warning signs

(499) *teetotaler*: a person who drinks very little alcohol; an inexperienced drinker who gets drunk very quickly

(499) *curb*: to cut back; to limit oneself

(499) *lethal*: deadly

(500) *immunize* (attempts to *"immunize"* youths): give them information that will keep them safe, just as immunizations are given to keep people from getting sick

(500) *mass media*: television, radio, newspapers

(500) *labor of love*: a job or activity that one cares about greatly

What is stress? What factors determine its severity?

Stress—Thrill or Threat? (pp. 500-505)

(501) *takes a toll*: has a negative or harmful effect

(502) *apathetic*: showing little or no feeling or concern

(502) *detachment*: state of being uninvolved, uninterested

(503) *appraise*: determine the severity of

(503) *the enforcer*: a reference to a person who might use physical threat to collect a debt

(504) *Ground Zero*: the place where the twin towers of the World Trade Center stood

(505) *shortchanges*: making it less effective

What causes frustration and what are typical reactions to it?

Frustration—Blind Alleys and Lead Balloons (pp. 505-507)

(505) *blind alleys and lead balloons*: blind alleys lead nowhere; balloons made of lead would not fly; therefore both are symbols of frustration

(505) *impede*: slow; make difficult

(505) *T-bone*: a beef steak

(505) *"the straw that broke the camel's back"*: a common saying that means the last negative event in a series of negative events

(506) *nomadic*: wandering; having no permanent home

(506) *retaliate*: to get revenge

(506) *hitchhike*: to travel from place to place by getting free rides from motorists

(507) *futile*: useless

Are there different types of conflict? How do people react to conflict?

Conflict—Yes, No, Yes, No, Yes, No, Well, Maybe (pp. 507-510)

> (507-508) ***"the devil and the deep blue sea," "the frying pan and the fire"***: both are common sayings that mean one has to choose between two equally unpleasant choices

> (508) ***tampered***: interfered

> (508) ***billow in***: great waves (in this case, of smoke) flowing in

What are defense mechanisms?

Psychological Defense—Mental Karate? (pp. 510-512)

> (510) ***tightwad***: someone who is very careful about spending his/her money

> (511) ***throws a temper tantrum***: has an emotional display of anger or frustration

> (511) ***go belly-up***: stop working

> (511) ***the last straw***: the final event in a series of difficulties

> (511) ***pumping iron***: lifting heavy weights in order to build muscle

> (512) ***Freud would have had a field day***: would have been pleased with all of the possibilities

What do we know about coping with feelings of helplessness and depression?

Learned Helplessness—Is There Hope? (pp. 512-515)

> (512) ***concentration camps***: places of imprisonment for soldiers and others during the Vietnam War and other wars

> (513) ***blunted***: dulled and uninterested

> (514) ***blue***: sad

> (514) ***down***: in a low mood

> (514) ***blown it***: failed

How is stress related to health and disease?

Stress and Health—Unmasking a Hidden Killer (pp. 515-524)

> (516) ***foreclosure***: the claim of ownership of a property such as a home when no payment has been made over time

(516) **"To be forewarned is to be forearmed"**: a common saying meaning that if one knows about a danger ahead of time, one can prepare against it

(517) **take it easy**: relax

(517) **hives**: an allergic disorder that causes the skin to itch and break out in bumps

(517) **rheumatoid arthritis**: disease characterized by pain, stiffness, and swelling of the joints

(520) **chafe**: become irritated by

(520) **bottled up**: kept inside

(521) **lets you down**: disappoints you

(522) **melodramatic**: exaggerated; overly dramatic

(523) **spleen**: organ that destroys red blood cells, stores blood, and produces white blood cells

(523) **lymph nodes**: rounded masses of lymph tissue (lymph is a fluid that bathes the tissues and contains white blood cells)

(524) **bereavement**: state of grieving after the death of a loved one

(524) **double whammy**: being attacked by two things at once

What are the best strategies for managing stress?

Psychology in Action: Stress Management (pp. 525-528)

(526) **uptight**: tense, nervous

(527) **get blown out of proportion**: become exaggerated in importance

(527) **loafing**: resting; relaxing

(527) **browsing**: looking over casually

(527) **puttering**: moving or acting aimlessly or idly; engaging in trivial tasks

(528) **psyched up**: psychologically ready; prepared

(528) **antidotes**: remedies

Solutions

RECITE AND REVIEW

What is health psychology? How does behavior affect health?

1. behavior; medical
2. habits
3. disease (or illness)
4. illness (or disease)
5. behaviors; smoking; diet; sleep
6. health; campaigns

What is stress? What factors determine its severity?

1. adjust
2. control; intense
3. work; exhaustion
4. primary; threat
5. secondary
6. Stress
7. stressors; stress
8. stresses; lives
9. repeated; stress

What causes frustration and what are typical reactions to it?

1. goal; blocked
2. personal
3. intense
4. vigorous
5. direct; withdrawal
6. coping; changing

Are there different types of conflict? How do people react to conflict?

1. Conflict
2. positive; negative
3. easiest
4. difficult; leaving
5. mixed; partial
6. positive; negative
7. approach-avoidance
8. possibilities; compromises

What are defense mechanisms?

1. inadequacy
2. reaction; repression
3. positive

What do we know about coping with feelings of helplessness and depression?

1. avoid
2. identical
3. training
4. 80; isolated ; academic
5. reduce

How is stress related to health and disease?

1. change; accident
2. hassles
3. psychological
4. disease
5. biological; biopsychosocial
6. monitored
7. relaxation
8. heart; time
9. Anger
10. stress
11. optimists; positive; creative
12. stressed; succeed
13. social; positive
14. support; pet
15. general
16. psychosomatic
17. disease (or illness)

What are the best strategies for managing stress?

1.	behavior; thoughts	3.	stress	5.	relaxation
2.	relaxation; imagery	4.	meditation	6.	positive

CONNECTIONS

What is health psychology? How does behavior affect health? What is stress? What factors determine its severity? Pages 497-505

1.	E.	5.	D.	9.	B.
2.	H.	6.	F.	10.	G.
3.	A.	7.	I.		
4.	J.	8.	C.		

What causes frustration and what are typical reactions to it? Are there different types of conflict? How do people react to conflict? Pages 505-510

1.	A.	4.	G.	7.	F.
2.	C.	5.	E.		
3.	B.	6.	D.		

What are defense mechanisms? What do we know about coping with feelings of helplessness and depression? Pages 510-515

1.	F.	5.	B.	9.	G.
2.	I.	6.	H.	10.	E.
3.	A.	7.	D.	11.	J.
4.	K.	8.	C.		

Connections

1.	B.	3.	D.
2.	A.	4.	C.

How is stress related to health and disease? What are the best strategies for managing stress? Pages 515-528

1.	H.	5.	B.	9.	J.
2.	A.	6.	I.	10.	E.
3.	G.	7.	D.		
4.	F.	8.	C.		

CHECK YOUR MEMORY

What is health psychology? How does behavior affect health? Pages 497-500

1. T	5. T	9. F
2. T	6. T	10. T
3. T	7. T	11. F
4. F	8. F	12. F

What is stress? What factors determine its severity? Pages 501-505

1. F	7. T	13. F
2. T	8. T	14. T
3. T	9. T	15. T
4. T	10. F	16. F
5. F	11. F	
6. T	12. T	

What causes frustration and what are typical reactions to it? Pages 505-507

1. F	3. F	5. T
2. F	4. T	

Are there different types of conflict? How do people react to conflict? Pages 507-510

1. T	3. T	5. T
2. F	4. F	

What are defense mechanisms? Pages 510-512

1. T	3. F	5. F
2. T	4. T	

What do we know about coping with feelings of helplessness and depression? Pages 512-515

1. T	4. T	7. T
2. T	5. F	8. T
3. T	6. F	

How is stress related to health and disease? Pages 515-524

1. F	3. F	5. T
2. T	4. F	6. F

7. F	10. F	13. T
8. T	11. T	14. T
9. F	12. F	15. F

What are the best strategies for managing stress? Pages 525-528

1. F	4. T	7. T
2. F	5. T	8. F
3. T	6. T	

FINAL SURVEY AND REVIEW

What is health psychology? How does behavior affect health?

1. behavioral; medicine
2. lifestyle
3. risk factors
4. disease-prone
5. promoting; deprivation; stress
6. wellness; community; health

What is stress? What factors determine its severity?

1. adapt; demands
2. pressure; stressor
3. burnout; depersonalization
4. appraisal; appraisal
5. problem; emotion
6. threat; competent
7. Traumatic
8. control
9. stress; disorders

What causes frustration and what are typical reactions to it?

1. Frustration; personal
2. External; Personal
3. blocked; motive
4. persistence; circumvention
5. displaced; scapegoating
6. frustration; manageable

Are there different types of conflict? How do people react to conflict?

1. contradictory
2. approach-approach; avoidance-avoidance
3. Approach-approach
4. Avoidance
5. ambivalence
6. double; multiple
7. Vacillation
8. conflicts; hasty

What are defense mechanisms?

1. defense; mechanisms; anxiety
2. denial ; rationalization
3. compensation; sublimation

What do we know about coping with feelings of helplessness and depression?

1. helplessness; punishment
2. depression
3. Mastery
4. college; depression
5. Depression

How is stress related to health and disease?

1. Social; Readjustment; Rating
2. microstressors
3. psychosomatic

4. Psychosomatic; hypochondria
5. medical; biological; psychological; social
6. biofeedback; signal
7. regulation
8. Type; A; angry
9. heart; attack
10. hardy
11. hardy; positive; reduce
12. optimists; less; will
13. reduced; events
14. person; reduce
15. general; adaptation; syndrome
16. alarm
17. immune

What are the best strategies for managing stress?

1. ineffective; upsetting
2. progressive; guided
3. limits; social
4. negative; coping
5. Meditation
6. relaxation

MASTERY TEST

What are the best strategies for managing stress?

1. B, pp. 512-513
2. A, p. 525
3. C, p. 503
4. D, p. 502
5. C, p. 511
6. A, p. 507
7. A, p. 498
8. C, p. 501
9. B, p. 515
10. A, p. 511
11. A, p. 496
12. D, p. 510
13. B, p. 496
14. A, p. 504
15. B, p. 505
16. B, p. 520
17. B, pp. 507-508
18. D, p. 499
19. C, p. 508
20. C, pp. 518; 520; 522
21. A, p. 528
22. A, p. 501
23. B, p. 506
24. D, p. 523
25. A, p. 500
26. D, p. 527
27. C, p. 503
28. C, p. 522
29. D, p. 503
30. B, p. 497
31. B, p. 499
32. C, p. 499
33. D, p. 504
34. C, p. 522
35. D, p. 523
36. A, p. 528
37. B, p. 519

Psychological Disorders

Chapter Overview

Abnormal behavior is defined by subjective discomfort, deviation from statistical norms, social nonconformity, and cultural or situational contexts. Disordered behavior is also maladaptive. Major types of psychopathology are described by DSM-IV-TR. Risk factors contributing to psychopathology include social, family, psychological, and biological factors. Psychopathology is not isolated to Western societies. Every culture recognizes the existence of psychological disorders. In the United States, insanity is a legal term, not a mental disorder.

Personality disorders are deeply ingrained maladaptive personality patterns, such as the antisocial personality. In addition to maladaptive patterns of behaviors, personality disorders are diagnosed and differentiated based on the degree of impairment. Ranging from moderate to severe impairment, some personality disorders are narcissistic, histrionic, borderline, and schizotypal.

Anxiety disorders, dissociative disorders, and somatoform disorders are characterized by high levels of anxiety, rigid defense mechanisms, and self-defeating behavior patterns. Anxiety disorders include generalized anxiety disorder, panic disorder (with or without agoraphobia), agoraphobia, specific phobia, social phobia, obsessive-compulsive disorders, and posttraumatic or acute stress disorders. Dissociative disorders may take the form of amnesia, fugue, or identity disorder (multiple personality). Somatoform disorders center on physical complaints that mimic disease or disability.

Psychodynamic explanations of anxiety disorders emphasize unconscious conflicts. The humanistic approach emphasizes faulty self-images. The behavioral approach emphasizes the effects of learning, particularly avoidance learning. The cognitive approach stresses maladaptive thinking patterns.

Psychosis is a break in contact with reality. Persons suffering from delusional disorders have delusions of grandeur, persecution, infidelity, romantic attraction, or physical disease. The most common delusional disorder is paranoid psychosis. Schizophrenia is the most common psychosis. Four types of schizophrenia are: disorganized, catatonic, paranoid, and undifferentiated. Explanations of schizophrenia emphasize environmental stress, inherited susceptibility, and biochemical abnormalities.

Mood disorders involve disturbances of emotion. Two moderate mood disorders are dysthymic disorder and cyclothymic disorder. Major mood disorders include bipolar disorders and major depressive disorder. Seasonal affective disorder is another common form of depression. Biological, psychoanalytic, cognitive, and behavioral theories of depression have been proposed. Heredity is clearly a factor in susceptibility to mood disorders. Labeling someone with a disorder rather than the problems that people experience can dramatically influence how people with mental disorders are treated. They often are faced with prejudice and discrimination, denied jobs and housing, and accused of crimes they did not commit.

Basic approaches to treating psychological disorders are psychotherapy and medical therapies. Suicide is statistically related to such factors as age, sex, and marital status. However, in individual cases the potential for suicide is best identified by a desire to escape, unbearable psychological pain, frustrated psychological needs, and a constriction of options. Suicide can sometimes be prevented by the efforts of family, friends, and mental health professionals.

Learning Objectives

1. Indicate the magnitude of mental health problems in this country; and define psychopathology.

2. Describe the following ways of viewing normality, including the shortcoming(s) of each: subjective discomfort, statistical definitions, social nonconformity, situational context, and cultural relativity; explain why more women than men are treated for psychological problems; and indicate the two core features of abnormal behavior.

3. Explain the functions of the DSM-IV-TR; and generally describe each of the following categories of mental disorders found in the DSM-IV-TR, and include a description of the outdated term neurosis and explain why it was dropped from use:

    a. psychotic disorders

    b. organic mental disorders

    c. substance related disorders

    d. mood disorders

    e. anxiety disorders

    f. somatoform disorders

    g. dissociative disorders

    h. personality disorders

    i. sexual and gender identity disorders

4. List the four general categories of risk factors for mental disorders; and explain how culture affects the labeling and incidence of mental disorders and give examples.

5. Distinguish the term insanity from a mental disorder.

6. List and briefly describe the ten different types of personality disorders (see Table 16.4). Include an indepth discussion of the distinctive characteristics, causes, and treatment of the antisocial personality.

7. Outline the general features and characteristics of anxiety-related problems and differentiate this category from an anxiety disorder. State what is usually meant when the term nervous breakdown is used.

8. Generally describe each of the following conditions:

    a.   anxiety disorders:

        i)   generalized anxiety disorder
        ii) panic disorder
        iii) agoraphobia
        iv) specific phobia
        v)   social phobia
        vi) obsessive-compulsive disorder
        vii) acute stress disorder
        viii) post-traumatic stress disorder

    b.   dissociative disorders:

        i)   dissociative amnesia
        ii) dissociative fugue
        iii) dissociative identity disorder

    c.   somatoform disorders:

        i)   hypochondriasis
        ii) somatization disorder
        iii) pain disorder
        iv) conversion disorder

9.   Discuss how each of the major perspectives in psychology view anxiety disorders:

    a.   psychodynamic

    b.   humanistic (Rogers)

    c.   humanistic-existential

    d.   behavioral (include the terms self-defeating paradox, avoidance learning, and anxiety reduction hypothesis)

    e.   cognitive

10. List and explain the five major characteristics of psychotic disorders, including a description of the different types of delusions and the most common types of hallucinations.

11. Define the terms organic psychosis and dementia and give examples; and discuss Alzheimer's disease, including its incidence, symptoms, and types of neurological damage.

12. Describe the main feature of delusional disorders; and discuss five types of delusional disorders.

13. Generally describe schizophrenia, including its frequency, typical age of onset, and symptoms; list and describe the four major types of schizophrenia; explain how paranoid delusional disorder and paranoid schizophrenia differ; and describe the general relationship between psychosis and violence.

14. Describe the roles of the following three areas as causes of schizophrenia, explain how CT, MRI, and PET scans contribute to the study of abnormal brain activity, and describe the stress-vulnerability model:

    a.   environment

        i)   prenatal problems and birth complications

   ii) psychological trauma

   iii) disturbed family environment

   iv) deviant communication patterns

b. heredity

c. brain chemistry

   i) dopamine

   ii) glutamate

15. State the incidence and characteristics of mood disorders, especially depression, in the general population; describe the characteristics of the moderate mood disorders: dysthymia and cyclothymia; describe the characteristics of the three major mood disorders: major depression, bipolar I and bipolar II; and explain the differences between the moderate and major mood disorders.

16. Describe the possible explanations for depression; briefly discuss the symptoms of maternity blues and postpartum depression; and describe seasonal affective disorder (SAD), its five major symptoms, and its treatment.

17. Explain why caution is necessary when using psychiatric labels. Briefly describe Rosenhan's pseudo-patient study, and explain how his observations relate to the idea of labeling.

The following objectives are related to the material in the "Psychology in Action" section of your text.

1. Discuss how each of the following factors affects suicide rate:

a. season

b. sex

c. age

d. income

e. marital status

2. Describe the conditions which typically precede suicide and why people try to kill themselves; list the twelve warning signs of suicide and the four common characteristics of suicidal thoughts and feelings; and explain how you can help prevent suicide.

RECITE AND REVIEW

How is normality defined, and what are the major psychological disorders?

Normality—What Is Normal? Pages 532-535

1. *Psychopathology* refers to mental _____ themselves or to psychologically _____ behavior.

2. Formal definitions of abnormality usually take into account subjective _____ (private feelings of suffering or unhappiness).

3. Statistical definitions define abnormality as an extremely _____ or _____ score on some dimension or measure.

4. Social nonconformity is a failure to follow societal _____ for acceptable conduct.

5. Frequently, the _____ or situational context that a behavior takes place in affects judgments of normality and abnormality.

6. _____ of the preceding definitions are relative standards.

7. A key element in judgments of disorder is that a person's _____ must be maladaptive (it makes it difficult for the person to _____ to the demands of daily life.

8. A _____ disorder is a significant impairment in psychological functioning.

Classifying Mental Disorders—Problems by the Book: Pages 535-540

1. Major disorders and categories of psychopathology are described in the *Diagnostic and Statistical* _____ *of* _____ *Disorders* (DSM-IV-TR).

2. Psychotic disorders are characterized by a retreat from _____ , by hallucinations and delusions, and by _____ withdrawal.

3. Organic mental disorders are problems caused by _____ injuries and _____ .

4. Substance related disorders are defined as abuse of or dependence on _____ - or behavior-altering _____ .

5. Mood disorders involve disturbances in affect, or _____ .

6. Anxiety disorders involve high levels of fear or _____ and distortions in behavior that are _____ related.

7. Somatoform disorders involve physical symptoms that mimic physical _____ or injury for which there is no identifiable _____ .

8. Dissociative disorders include cases of sudden amnesia, multiple _____ , or episodes of depersonalization.

9. Personality disorders are deeply ingrained, unhealthy _____ patterns.

10. Sexual and gender disorders include _____ identity disorders, paraphilias, and _____ dysfunctions.

11. In the past, the term *neurosis* was used to describe milder, _____ related disorders. However, the term is fading from use.

12. Psychological disorders are recognized in every _____ . For example, Native Americans who are preoccupied with death and the deceased have _____ sickness, and East Asians who experience intense anxiety that their penis, vulva, or nipples are receding into their bodies have _____ disorder.

13. Insanity is a _____ term defining whether a person may be held responsible for his or her actions. Sanity is determined in _____ on the basis of testimony by expert witnesses.

What is a personality disorder?

Personality Disorders—Blueprints for Maladjustment: Pages 540-542

1. People with borderline _____ disorder tend to react to ordinary criticisms by feeling rejected and _____ , which then causes them to respond with anger, self-hatred, and _____ .

2. Personality disorders are deeply ingrained _____ personality patterns.

3. The personality disorders are: antisocial, avoidant, _____ , dependent, histrionic, narcissistic, obsessive- _____ paranoid, schizoid, and schizotypal.

4. Antisocial persons (sociopaths) seem to lack a _____ . They are _____ shallow and manipulative.

5. Possible causes attributed to people with antisocial _____ disorder include emotional deprivation, neglect, _____ abuse as children, and boredom due to receiving little stimulation from the environment.

6. People with _____ -compulsive disorder are plagued with images or thoughts that they cannot force out of _____ . To reduce anxiety caused by these constantly occurring images and thoughts, they are compelled to _____ irrational acts.

What problems result when a person suffers high levels of anxiety?

Anxiety-Based Disorders—When Anxiety Rules: Pages 542-547

1. The term *nervous breakdown* has no formal meaning. However, "emotional breakdowns" do correspond somewhat to adjustment disorders, in which the person is overwhelmed by ongoing _____ .

2. Anxiety disorders include generalized anxiety disorder (chronic _____ and worry) and panic disorder (anxiety attacks, panic, free- _____ anxiety).

3. Panic disorder may occur with or without agoraphobia (fear of _____ places, unfamiliar situations, or leaving the _____).

4. Other anxiety disorders are agoraphobia and _____ phobia (irrational fears of specific objects or situations).

5. In the anxiety disorder called social phobia, the person fears being _____ , evaluated, embarrassed, or humiliated by others in _____ situations.

6. Obsessive-compulsive disorders (obsessions and compulsions), and posttraumatic stress disorder or acute stress disorder (emotional disturbances triggered by severe _____) are also classified as _____ disorders.

7. Dissociative disorders may take the form of dissociative amnesia (loss of _____ and personal identity) or _____ fugue (flight from familiar surroundings).

8. A more dramatic problem is dissociative identity disorder, in which a person develops _____ personalities.

9. Somatoform disorders center on physical complaints that mimic _____ or disability.

10. In hypochondriasis, persons think that they have specific diseases, when they are, in fact _____ .

11. In a somatization disorder, the person has numerous _____ complaints. The person repeatedly seeks medical _____ for these complaints, but no organic problems can be found.

12. Somatoform pain refers to discomfort for which there is no identifiable _____ cause.

13. In conversion disorders, actual symptoms of disease or disability develop but their causes are really _____ .

14. Anxiety disorders, dissociative disorders, and somatoform disorders all involve high levels of _____ , rigid _____ mechanisms, and self-defeating behavior patterns.

How do psychologists explain anxiety-based disorders?

Anxiety and Disorder—Four Pathways to Trouble: Pages 547-549

1. The psychodynamic approach emphasizes _____ conflicts within the personality as the cause of disabling anxiety.

2. The humanistic approach emphasizes the effects of a faulty _____ .

3. The behavioral approach emphasizes the effects of previous _____ , particularly avoidance _____ .

4. Some patterns in anxiety disorders can be explained by the _____ reduction hypothesis, which states that immediate _____ from anxiety rewards self-defeating behaviors.

5. According to the cognitive view, distorted _____ patterns cause anxiety disorders.

What are the general characteristics of psychotic disorders?

Psychotic Disorders—Life in the Shadow of Madness: Pages 549-551

1. Psychosis is a _____ in contact with reality.

2. Some common types of delusions are depressive, _____ , grandeur, _____ , persecution, and reference.

3. Psychosis is marked by delusions, _____ (false sensations), and sensory changes.

4. Other symptoms of psychosis are disturbed emotions, disturbed communication, and _____ disintegration.

5. An organic psychosis is based on known injuries or _____ of the brain.

6. The most common _____ problem is dementia, a serious mental impairment in old age caused by deterioration of the _____ .

7. One of the common causes of _____ is Alzheimer's disease.

How do delusional disorders differ from other forms of psychosis?

Delusional Disorders—An Enemy Behind Every Tree: Page 551-552

1. A diagnosis of delusional disorder is based primarily on the presence of _____ .

2. Delusions may concern grandeur, _____ (harassment or threat), infidelity, _____ attraction, or physical disease.

3. The most common delusional disorder is paranoid psychosis. Because they often have intense and irrational delusions of _____ , paranoids may be violent if they believe they are threatened.

What forms does schizophrenia take? What causes it?

Schizophrenia—Shattered Reality: Pages 552-558

1. Schizophrenia is distinguished by a _____ between _____ and emotion, and by delusions, hallucinations, and communication difficulties.

2. Disorganized schizophrenia is marked by extreme _____ disintegration and silly, bizarre, or obscene behavior. _____ impairment is usually extreme.

3. Catatonic schizophrenia is associated with stupor, _____ (inability to speak), _____ flexibility, and odd postures. Sometimes violent and agitated behavior also occurs.

4. In paranoid schizophrenia (the most common type), outlandish delusions of grandeur and _____ are coupled with psychotic symptoms and personality breakdown.

5. Undifferentiated schizophrenia is the term used to indicate a _____ of clear-cut patterns of disturbance.

6. Current explanations of schizophrenia emphasize a combination of environmental _____ , inherited susceptibility, and biochemical _____ in the body or brain.

7. A number of environmental factors appear to increase the risk of developing schizophrenia. These include viral _____ during the mother's pregnancy and _____ complications.

8. Early psychological _____ (psychological injury or shock) and a disturbed _____ environment, especially one marked by deviant communication, also increase the risk of schizophrenia.

9. Studies of _____ and other close relatives strongly support heredity as a major factor in schizophrenia.

10. Recent biochemical studies have focused on abnormalities in brain _____ substances, especially glutamate and dopamine and their receptor sites.

11. Current explanations of schizophrenia emphasize a combination of environmental _____ , inherited susceptibility, and biochemical _____ in the body or brain.

12. Other known causes that induce schizophrenic symptoms are the hallucinogenic drug _____ and stress, which affect _____ and dopamine levels in the brain.

13. Additional abnormalities in brain structure or _____ have been detected in schizophrenic brains by the use of CT scans, MRI scans, and PET scans.

14. The dominant explanation of schizophrenia is the _____ -vulnerability model.

What are mood disorders? What causes depression?

Mood Disorders—Peaks and Valleys and Disorders in Perspective—Psychiatric Labeling: Pages 558-563

1. Mood disorders primarily involve disturbances of mood or _____ .

2. Long-lasting, though relatively moderate, _____ is called a dysthymic disorder.

3. Chronic, though moderate, swings in mood between _____ and _____ are called a cyclothymic disorder.

4. In a bipolar I disorder the person alternates between extreme mania and _____ .

5. In a bipolar II disorder the person is mostly _____ , but has had at least one episode of hypomania (mild _____).

6. The problem known as major depressive disorder involves extreme sadness and despondency, but no evidence of _____ .

7. Major mood disorders more often appear to be endogenous (produced from _____) rather than reactions to _____ events.

8. Postpartum depression is a mild to moderate depressive disorder that affects many women after they give birth. Postpartum depression is more serious than the more common _____ .

9. _____ affective disorder (SAD), which occurs during the _____ months, is another common form of depression. SAD is typically treated with phototherapy.

10. Biological, psychoanalytic, cognitive, and _____ theories of depression have been proposed. Heredity is clearly a factor in susceptibility to mood disorders.

11. Factors that influence the development of depression include being a woman, _____ , not being married, having limited _____ , high levels of _____ , and feelings of hopelessness.

12. David Rosenhan demonstrated the damaging effects of _____ a person with a disorder in our society. They are stigmatized, _____ jobs and housing, and accused of _____ that they did not commit.

13. Treatments for psychological disorders range from hospitalization and _____ to drug therapy. Individuals diagnosed with a major disorder do respond well to drugs and psychotherapy while individuals diagnosed with _____ mental disorders can be treated successfully.

Why do people commit suicide? Can suicide be prevented?

Psychology in Action: Suicide—Lives on the Brink: Pages 563-566

1. _____ is statistically related to such factors as age, sex, and marital status.

2. Major risk factors for suicide include _____ or _____ abuse, a prior attempt, depression, hopelessness, antisocial behavior, suicide by relatives, shame, failure, or rejection, and the availability of a _____ .

3. In individual cases the potential for suicide is best identified by a desire to _____ , unbearable psychological pain, frustrated psychological needs, and a constriction of _____ .

4. Suicidal _____ usually precede suicide threats, which progress to suicide attempts.

5. Suicide can often be prevented by the efforts of family, friends, and mental health professionals to establish _____ and rapport with the person, and by gaining day-by-day commitments from her or him.

CONNECTIONS

How is normality defined, and what are the major psychological disorders? Pages 532-540

1.	_____ DSM-IV-TR	a.	culturally recognized disorder
2.	_____ drapetomania	b.	physical symptoms
3.	_____ mood disorder	c.	legal problem
4.	_____ somatoform disorder	d.	outdated term
5.	_____ insanity	e.	sexual deviation
6.	_____ organic disorder	f.	diagnostic manual
7.	_____ neurosis	g.	fear of germs
8.	_____ paraphilia	h.	brain pathology
9.	_____ amok	i.	mania or depression

What is a personality disorder? Pages 540-542

1.	_____ dependent personality	a.	self-importance
2.	_____ histrionic personality	b.	rigid routines
3.	_____ narcissistic personality	c.	submissiveness
4.	_____ antisocial personality	d.	little emotion
5.	_____ obsessive-compulsive	e.	attention seeking
6.	_____ schizoid personality	f.	unstable self-image
7.	_____ avoidant personality	g.	odd, disturbed thinking
8.	_____ borderline personality	h.	suspiciousness
9.	_____ paranoid personality	i.	fear of social situations
10.	_____ schizotypal personality	j.	no conscience

What problems result when a person suffers high levels of anxiety? How do psychologists explain anxiety-based disorders? Pages 542-549

1. _____ cognitive explanation	a. afraid to leave the house
2. _____ psychodynamic explanation	b. fears being observed
3. _____ behavioral explanation	c. conversion disorder
4. _____ adjustment disorder	d. one month after extreme stress
5. _____ generalized anxiety	e. caused by unconscious forces
6. _____ panic disorder	f. within weeks after extreme stress
7. _____ agoraphobia	g. sudden attacks of fear
8. _____ specific phobia	h. self-defeating thoughts
9. _____ social phobia	i. chronic worry
10. _____ humanistic-existential	j. fears objects or activities
11. _____ PTSD	k. maladaptive pattern of behavior
12. _____ acute stress disorder	l. dissociation
13. _____ glove anesthesia	m. faulty self-image and no meaning in life
14. _____ fugue	n. normal life stress

What are the general characteristics of psychotic disorders? How do delusional disorders differ from other forms of psychosis? Pages 549-552

1. _____ psychosis	a. retreat from reality
2. _____ hallucinations	b. false belief
3. _____ delusion	c. believing a celebrity loves him/her
4. _____ Alzheimer's disease	d. believing one has great talents
5. _____ jealous type	e. believing one's body is diseased
6. _____ erotomatic type	f. believing one's partner is unfaithful
7. _____ persecution type	g. believing one is being spied on
8. _____ somatic type	h. dementia
9. _____ grandiose type	i. imaginary sensations

What forms does schizophrenia take? What causes it? Pages 552-558

1. _____ disorganized type
2. _____ catatonic type
3. _____ undifferentiated type
4. _____ paranoid type
5. _____ psychological trauma
6. _____ twin studies
7. _____ dopamine
8. _____ stress-vulnerability

a. displaying rigidity, delusions, and disorganization
b. incoherence, bizarre thinking
c. biological and environmental influences
d. genetics of schizophrenia
e. grandeur or persecution
f. chemical messenger
g. risk factor for schizophrenia
h. stuporous or agitated

What are mood disorders? What causes depression? Why do people commit suicide? Can suicide be prevented? Pages 558-566

1. _____ postpartum depression
2. _____ bipolar I
3. _____ bipolar II
4. _____ endogenous
5. _____ suicide
6. _____ phototherapy
7. _____ SAD
8. _____ social stigma

a. produced from within
b. depression and hypomania
c. depression after childbirth
d. light treatment
e. leads to prejudice
f. desire to end all pains
g. winter depression
h. severe mania and depression

CHECK YOUR MEMORY

How is normality defined, and what are the major psychological disorders? Pages 532-540

1. Psychopathology refers to the study of mental disorders and to disorders themselves.

   TRUE or FALSE

2. One out of every 10 persons will require mental hospitalization during his or her lifetime.

   TRUE or FALSE

3. Statistical definitions do not automatically tell us where to draw the line between normality and abnormality.

    TRUE or FALSE

4. To understand how social norms define normality, a person could perform a mild abnormal behavior in public to observe the public's reaction.

    TRUE or FALSE

5. Cultural relativity refers to making personal judgments about another culture's practices.

    TRUE or FALSE

6. All cultures classify people as abnormal if they fail to communicate with others.

    TRUE or FALSE

7. Drapetomania, childhood masturbation, and nymphomania are considered mental disorders listed in the DSM-IV-TR.

    TRUE or FALSE

8. Gender is a common source of bias in judging normality.

    TRUE or FALSE

9. Being a persistent danger to oneself or others is regarded as a clear sign of disturbed psychological functioning.

    TRUE or FALSE

10. Poverty, abusive parents, low intelligence, and head injuries are risk factors for mental disorder.

    TRUE or FALSE

11. "Organic mental disorders" is one of the major categories in DSM-IV-TR.

    TRUE or FALSE

12. Keel and Klump believe that bulimia occurs primarily in Western cultures.

    TRUE or FALSE

13. *Koro, locura, dhat*, and *zar* are brain diseases that cause psychosis.

    TRUE or FALSE

14. Multiple personality is a dissociative disorder.

    TRUE or FALSE

15. Neurosis is a legal term, not a type of mental disorder.

    TRUE or FALSE

What is a personality disorder? Pages 540-542

1. The "emotional storms" experienced by people with borderline personality disorder is a normal process about which they and their friends have a clear understanding.

    TRUE or FALSE

2. Histrionic persons are preoccupied with their own self-importance.

    TRUE or FALSE

3. Personality disorders usually appear suddenly in early adulthood.

    TRUE or FALSE

4. The schizoid person shows little emotion and is uninterested in relationships with others.

    TRUE or FALSE

5. "Psychopath" is another term for the borderline personality.

    TRUE or FALSE

6. Sociopaths usually have a childhood history of emotional deprivation, neglect, and abuse.

    TRUE or FALSE

7. Antisocial behavior typically declines somewhat after age 20.

    TRUE or FALSE

8. Antisocial personality disorders are often treated successfully with drugs.

    TRUE or FALSE

What problems result when a person suffers high levels of anxiety? Pages 542-547

1. Anxiety is an emotional response to an ambiguous threat.

    TRUE or FALSE

2. Adjustment disorders occur when severe stresses outside the normal range of human experience push people to their breaking points.

    TRUE or FALSE

3. Sudden, unexpected episodes of intense panic are a key feature of generalized anxiety disorder.

    TRUE or FALSE

4. A person who fears he or she will have a panic attack in public places or unfamiliar situations suffers from acrophobia.

    TRUE or FALSE

5. Arachnophobia, claustrophobia, and pathophobia are all specific phobias.
    TRUE or FALSE

6. Many people who have an obsessive-compulsive disorder are checkers or cleaners.
    TRUE or FALSE

7. PTSD is a psychological disturbance lasting more than one month after exposure to severe stress.
    TRUE or FALSE

8. Multiple personality is a dissociative disorder.
    TRUE or FALSE

9. Multiple personality is the most common form of schizophrenia.
    TRUE or FALSE

10. Depersonalization and fusion are the goals of therapy for dissociative identity disorders.
    TRUE or FALSE

11. The word somatoform means "body form."
    TRUE or FALSE

12. An unusual lack of concern about the appearance of a sudden disability is a sign of a conversion reaction.
    TRUE or FALSE

How do psychologists explain anxiety-based disorders? Pages 547-549

1. Anxiety disorders appear to be partly hereditary.
    TRUE or FALSE

2. The psychodynamic approach characterizes anxiety disorders as a product of id impulses that threaten a loss of control.
    TRUE or FALSE

3. Carl Rogers interpreted emotional disorders as the result of a loss of meaning in one's life.
    TRUE or FALSE

4. Disordered behavior is paradoxical, because it makes the person more anxious and unhappy in the long run.
    TRUE or FALSE

5. The cognitive view attributes anxiety disorders to distorted thinking that leads to avoidance learning.
    TRUE or FALSE

What are the general characteristics of psychotic disorders? Pages 549-551

1. The most common psychotic delusion is hearing voices.

   TRUE or FALSE

2. People with depressive delusions believe that they are depressed but that they do not need therapy.

   TRUE or FALSE

3. Even a person who displays flat affect may continue to privately feel strong emotion.

   TRUE or FALSE

4. Extremely psychotic behavior tends to occur in brief episodes.

   TRUE or FALSE

5. Severe brain injuries or diseases sometimes cause psychoses.

   TRUE or FALSE

6. Children must eat leaded paint flakes before they are at risk for lead poisoning.

   TRUE or FALSE

7. Roughly 80 percent of all cases of Alzheimer's disease are genetic.

   TRUE or FALSE

How do delusional disorders differ from other forms of psychosis? Pages 551-552

1. In delusional disorders, people have auditory hallucinations of grandeur or persecution.

   TRUE or FALSE

2. Delusions of persecution are a key symptom of paranoid psychosis.

   TRUE or FALSE

3. A person who believes that his body is diseased and rotting has an erotomanic type of delusional disorder.

   TRUE or FALSE

4. Delusional disorders are common and are easily treated with drugs.

   TRUE or FALSE

What forms does schizophrenia take? What causes it? Pages 552-558

1. One person out of 100 will become schizophrenic.

   TRUE or FALSE

2. Schizophrenia is the most common dissociative psychosis.

   TRUE or FALSE

3. Individuals who are mentally ill are, on average, no more violent than normal individuals.

   TRUE or FALSE

4. Silliness, laughter, and bizarre behavior are common in disorganized schizophrenia.

   TRUE or FALSE

5. Periods of immobility and odd posturing are characteristic of paranoid schizophrenia.

   TRUE or FALSE

6. At various times, patients may shift from one type of schizophrenia to another.

   TRUE or FALSE

7. Exposure to influenza during pregnancy produces children who are more likely to become schizophrenic later in life.

   TRUE or FALSE

8. If one identical twin is schizophrenic, the other twin has a 46 percent chance of also becoming schizophrenic.

   TRUE or FALSE

9. Excess amounts of the neurotransmitter substance PCP are suspected as a cause of schizophrenia.

   TRUE or FALSE

10. The brains of schizophrenics tend to be more responsive to dopamine than the brains of normal persons.

    TRUE or FALSE

11. PET scans show that activity in the frontal lobes of schizophrenics tends to be abnormally low.

    TRUE or FALSE

12. At least three schizophrenic patients out of four are completely recovered 10 years after being diagnosed.

    TRUE or FALSE

13. The stress-vulnerability model suggests that psychotic disorders are caused by a combination of environment and heredity.

    TRUE or FALSE

What are mood disorders? What causes depression? Pages 558-563

1. The two most basic types of mood disorder are bipolar I and bipolar II.

    TRUE or FALSE

2. In bipolar disorders, people experience both mania and depression.

    TRUE or FALSE

3. If a person is moderately depressed for at least two weeks, a dysthymic disorder exists.

    TRUE or FALSE

4. A cyclothymic disorder is characterized by moderate levels of depression and manic behavior.

    TRUE or FALSE

5. Endogenous depression appears to be generated from within, with little connection to external events.

    TRUE or FALSE

6. Behavioral theories of depression emphasize the concept of learned helplessness.

    TRUE or FALSE

7. Overall, women are twice as likely as men are to become depressed.

    TRUE or FALSE

8. Having limited education, experiencing high levels of stress, not being married, and feeling hopeless are some characteristics that increase a woman's chance of being depressed.

    TRUE or FALSE

9. Research indicates that heredity does not play a role in major mood disorder.

    TRUE or FALSE

10. Postpartum depression typically lasts from about two months to a year after giving birth.

    TRUE or FALSE

11. SAD is most likely to occur during the winter, in countries lying near the equator.

    TRUE or FALSE

12. Phototherapy is used to treat SAD successfully 80 percent of the time.

    TRUE or FALSE

13. Labeling a person with a disorder when they do not have it does not harm them in any way.

    TRUE or FALSE

14. People who have been successfully treated for a mental disorder are no longer a threat to society and, therefore, are not stigmatized like criminals.

    TRUE or FALSE

Why do people commit suicide? Can suicide be prevented? Pages 563-566

1. The greatest number of suicides during a single day takes place at New Year's.

   TRUE or FALSE

2. More men than women complete suicide.

   TRUE or FALSE

3. Suicide rates steadily decline after young adulthood.

   TRUE or FALSE

4. Most suicides involve despair, anger, and guilt.

   TRUE or FALSE

5. People who threaten suicide rarely actually attempt it—they're just crying wolf.

   TRUE or FALSE

6. Only a minority of people who attempt suicide really want to die.

   TRUE or FALSE

7. The risk of attempted suicide is high if a person has a concrete, workable plan for doing it.

   TRUE or FALSE

FINAL SURVEY AND REVIEW

How is normality defined, and what are the major psychological disorders?

Normality—What Is Normal? Pages 532-535

1. _____ refers to mental disorders themselves or to psychologically unhealthy behavior.

2. Formal definitions of abnormality usually take into account _____ discomfort (private feelings of suffering or unhappiness).

3. _____ definitions define abnormality as an extremely high or low score on some dimension or measure.

4. _____ is a failure to follow societal standards for acceptable conduct.

5. Frequently, the cultural or situational _____ that a behavior takes place in affects judgments of normality and abnormality.

6. All of the preceding definitions are _____ standards.

7. A key element in judgments of disorder is that a person's behavior must be _____ (it makes it difficult for the person to adapt to the demands of daily life).

8. A mental disorder is a significant impairment in _____ functioning.

Classifying Mental Disorders—Problems by the Book: Pages 535-540

1. Major disorders and categories of psychopathology are described in the _____ *and* _____ *Manual of Mental Disorders* (DSM-IV-TR).

2. _____ disorders are characterized by a retreat from reality, by _____ and delusions, and by social withdrawal.

3. _____ mental disorders are problems caused by brain injuries and diseases.

4. _____ disorders are defined as abuse of or dependence on mood- or behavior-altering drugs.

5. _____ disorders involve disturbances in _____ , or emotion.

6. _____ disorders involve high levels of fear or anxiety and distortions in behavior that are anxiety related.

7. _____ disorders involve physical symptoms that mimic physical disease or injury for which there is no identifiable cause.

8. _____ disorders include cases of sudden _____ , multiple personality, or episodes of depersonalization.

9. _____ disorders are deeply ingrained, unhealthy personality patterns.

10. Sexual and gender disorders include gender _____ disorders, paraphilias, and sexual _____ .

11. In the past, the term _____ was used to describe milder, anxiety related disorders. However, the term is fading from use.

12. Psychological disorders are recognized in every culture. For example, Native Americans who are preoccupied with death and the deceased have _____ , and _____ who experience intense anxiety that their penis, vulva, or nipples are receding into their bodies have Koro disorder.

13. _____ is a legal term defining whether a person may be held responsible for his or her actions. Sanity is determined in court on the basis of testimony by expert witnesses.

What is a personality disorder?

Personality Disorders—Blueprints for Maladjustment: Pages 540-542

1. People with _____ personality disorder tend to react to ordinary criticisms by feeling rejected and abandoned, which then causes them to respond with anger, self-hatred, and _____ .

2. Personality disorders are deeply _____ maladaptive personality patterns.

3. The personality disorders are: antisocial, avoidant, borderline, _____ , histrionic, narcissistic, obsessive-compulsive, _____ , schizoid, and _____ .

4. _____ persons (sociopaths) seem to lack a conscience. They are emotionally shallow and _____ .

5. Possible causes attributed to people with _____ personality disorder include _____ deprivation, neglect, physical abuse as _____ , and boredom due to receiving little stimulation from the environment.

6. People with _____ disorder are plagued with images or thoughts that they cannot force out of awareness. To reduce _____ caused by these constant occurring images and thoughts, they are compelled to repeat irrational acts.

What problems result when a person suffers high levels of anxiety?

Anxiety-Based Disorders—When Anxiety Rules: Pages 542-547

1. Anxiety disorders, _____ disorders, and _____ disorders all involve high levels of anxiety, rigid defense mechanisms, and self-defeating behavior patterns.

2. The term nervous _____ has no formal meaning. However, people do experience _____ disorders, in which the person is overwhelmed by ongoing life stresses.

3. Anxiety disorders include _____ anxiety disorder (chronic anxiety and worry) and _____ disorder (anxiety attacks, panic, free-floating anxiety).

4. Panic disorder may occur with or without _____ (fear of public places, unfamiliar situations, or leaving the home).

5. Other anxiety disorders are _____ (fear of public places, _____ situations, or leaving the home) and specific phobia (irrational fears of specific objects or situations).

6. In the anxiety disorder called _____ _____ , the person fears being observed, _____ , embarrassed, or humiliated by others in social situations.

7. _____ -compulsive disorders and _____ stress disorder (PTSD) or _____ stress disorder (emotional disturbances triggered by severe stress) are also classified as anxiety disorders.

8. Dissociative disorders may take the form of dissociative _____ (loss of memory and personal identity) or dissociative _____ (confused identity and flight from familiar surroundings).

9. A more dramatic problem is dissociative _____ _____ , in which a person develops multiple personalities.

10. _____ disorders center on physical complaints that mimic disease or disability.

11. In _____ , persons think that they have specific diseases, when they are, in fact healthy.

12. In a _____ disorder, the person has numerous physical complaints. The person repeatedly seeks medical treatment for these complaints, but no organic problems can be found.

13. _____ _____ refers to discomfort for which there is no identifiable physical cause.

14. In _____ disorders, actual symptoms of disease or disability develop but their causes are really psychological.

How do psychologists explain anxiety-based disorders?

Anxiety and Disorder—Four Pathways to Trouble: Pages 547-549

1. The _____ approach emphasizes unconscious conflicts within the personality as the cause of disabling anxiety.

2. The _____ approach emphasizes the effects of a faulty self-image.

3. The _____ approach emphasizes the effects of previous learning, particularly _____ learning.

4. Some patterns in anxiety disorders can be explained by the anxiety _____ hypothesis, which states that immediate relief from anxiety rewards _____ behaviors.

5. According to the _____ view, distorted thinking patterns cause anxiety disorders.

What are the general characteristics of psychotic disorders?

Psychotic Disorders—Life in the Shadow of Madness: Pages 549-551

1. _____ is a break in contact with _____ .

2. Some common types of _____ are depressive, somatic, grandeur, influence, persecution, and reference.

3. Psychosis is marked by _____ (false beliefs), hallucinations, and _____ changes.

4. Other symptoms of psychosis are disturbed emotions, disturbed _____ , and personality _____ .

5. An _____ psychosis is based on known injuries or diseases of the brain.

6. The most common organic problem is _____ , a serious mental impairment in old age caused by deterioration of the brain.

7. One of the common causes of dementia is _____ disease.

How do delusional disorders differ from other forms of psychosis?

Delusional Disorders—An Enemy Behind Every Tree: Page 551-552

1. A _____ of _____ disorder is based primarily on the presence of delusions.

2. Delusions may concern _____ (personal importance), persecution, infidelity, romantic attraction, or physical _____ .

3. The most common delusional disorder is _____ psychosis. Because they often have intense and irrational delusions of persecution, paranoids may be _____ if they believe they are threatened.

What forms does schizophrenia take? What causes it?

Schizophrenia—Shattered Reality: Pages 552-558

1. Schizophrenia is distinguished by a split between thought and _____ , and by delusions, hallucinations, and _____ difficulties.

2. _____ schizophrenia is marked by extreme personality _____ and silly, bizarre, or obscene behavior. Social impairment is usually extreme.

3. _____ schizophrenia is associated with stupor, mutism (inability to speak), waxy _____ , and odd postures. Sometimes violent and agitated behavior also occurs.

4. In _____ schizophrenia (the most common type), outlandish delusions of _____ and persecution are coupled with psychotic symptoms and personality breakdown.

5. _____ schizophrenia is the term used to indicate a lack of clear-cut patterns of disturbance.

6. Current explanations of schizophrenia emphasize a combination of _____ stress, inherited susceptibility, and _____ abnormalities in the body or brain.

7. A number of _____ factors appear to increase the risk of developing schizophrenia. These include viral infection during the mother's pregnancy and birth complications.

8. Early _____ trauma (psychological injury or shock) and a disturbed family environment, especially one marked by _____ communication, also increase the risk of schizophrenia.

9. Studies of twins and other close relatives strongly support _____ as a major factor in schizophrenia.

10. Recent biochemical studies have focused on abnormalities in brain transmitter substances, especially glutamate and _____ and their _____ sites.

11. Current explanations of schizophrenia emphasize a combination of _____ stress, inherited susceptibility, and _____ abnormalities in the body or brain.

12. Other known causes that induce _____ symptoms are the _____ drug PCP and stress, which affect glutamate and dopamine levels in the brain.

13. Additional abnormalities in brain structure or activity have been detected in schizophrenic brains by the use of _____ scans, _____ scans, and _____ scans.

14. The dominant explanation of schizophrenia is the stress- _____ model.

What are mood disorders? What causes depression?

Mood Disorders—Peaks and Valleys and Disorders in Perspective—Psychiatric Labeling: Pages 558-563

1. Mood disorders primarily involve disturbances of _____ or emotion.

2. Long-lasting, though relatively moderate, depression is called a _____ disorder.

3. Chronic, though moderate, swings in mood between depression and elation are called a _____ disorder.

4. In a _____ disorder the person alternates between extreme _____ and depression.

5. In a _____ disorder the person is mostly depressed, but has had at least one episode of _____ (mild mania).

6. The problem known as _____ _____ disorder involves extreme sadness and despondency, but no evidence of mania.

7. _____ depression is a mild to moderate depressive disorder that affects many women after they give birth. It is more serious than the more common maternity blues.

8. Major mood disorders more often appear to be _____ (produced from within) rather than reactions to external events.

9. Seasonal _____ disorder (SAD), which occurs during the winter months, is another common form of depression. SAD is typically treated with _____ (exposure to bright light).

10. _____ , psychoanalytic, _____ , and behavioral theories of depression have been proposed. Heredity is clearly a factor in susceptibility to mood disorders.

11. Factors that influence the development of _____ include being a woman, Latina, not being married, having limited education, high levels of stress, and feelings of _____ .

12. David Rosenhan demonstrated the damaging effects of _____ a person with a disorder in our society. They are _____ , denied jobs and housing, and accused of crimes that they did not commit.

13. Treatments for psychological disorders range from hospitalization and _____ to drug therapy. Individuals diagnosed with a major disorder do respond well to _____ and psychotherapy while individuals diagnosed with _____ mental disorders can be treated successfully.

Why do people commit suicide? Can suicide be prevented?

Psychology in Action: Suicide—Lives on the Brink: Pages 563-566

1. Suicide is _____ related to such factors as age, sex, and marital status.

2. Major _____ _____ for suicide include alcohol or drug abuse, a prior attempt, depression, hopelessness, _____ behavior, suicide by relatives, shame, failure, or rejection, and the availability of a firearm.

3. In individual cases the potential for suicide is best identified by a desire to escape, unbearable psychological _____ , _____ psychological needs, and a constriction of options.

4. Suicidal thoughts usually precede suicide _____ , which progress to suicide _____ .

5. Suicide can often be prevented by the efforts of family, friends, and mental health professionals to establish communication and _____ with the person, and by gaining day-by-day _____ from her or him.

MASTERY TEST

1. The difference between an acute stress disorder and PTSD is
   a. how long the disturbance lasts
   b. the severity of the stress
   c. whether the anxiety is free-floating
   d. whether dissociative behavior is observed

2. A person is at greatest risk of becoming schizophrenic if he or she has
   a. schizophrenic parents
   b. a schizophrenic fraternal twin
   c. a schizophrenic mother
   d. a schizophrenic sibling

3. A core feature of all abnormal behavior is that it is
   a. statistically extreme
   b. associated with subjective discomfort
   c. ultimately maladaptive
   d. marked by a loss of contact with reality

4. Excess amounts of dopamine in the brain, or high sensitivity to dopamine provides one major explanation for the problem known as
   a. PTSD
   b. schizophrenia
   c. major depression
   d. SAD

5. The descriptions "acro," and "claustro," and "pyro" refer to
   a. common obsessions
   b. specific phobias
   c. free-floating anxieties
   d. hypochondriasis

6. Glove anesthesia strongly implies the existence of a _____ disorder.
   a. organic
   b. depersonalization
   c. somatization
   d. conversion

7. In the stress-vulnerability model of psychosis, vulnerability is primarily attributed to
   a. heredity
   b. exposure to influenza
   c. psychological trauma
   d. disturbed family life

8. A patient believes that she has a mysterious disease that is causing her body to "rot away." What type of symptom is she suffering from?
   a. bipolar
   b. delusion
   c. neurosis
   d. cyclothymic

9. Phototherapy is used primarily to treat
   a. postseasonal depression
   b. SAD
   c. catatonic depression
   d. affective psychoses

10. Psychopathology is defined as an inability to behave in ways that
   a. foster personal growth and happiness
   b. match social norms
   c. lead to personal achievement
   d. do not cause anxiety

11. Which of the following is NOT characteristic of suicidal thinking?
   a. desires to escape
   b. psychological pain
   c. frustrated needs
   d. too many options

12. Fear of using the rest room in public is
   a. a social phobia
   b. an acute stress disorder
   c. a panic disorder
   d. an adjustment disorder

13. A person who displays personality disintegration, waxy flexibility, and delusions of persecution suffers from _____ schizophrenia.
   a. disorganized
   b. catatonic
   c. paranoid
   d. undifferentiated

14. You find yourself in an unfamiliar town and you can't remember your name or address. It is likely that you are suffering from
   a. paraphilia
   b. Alzheimer's disease
   c. a borderline personality disorder
   d. a dissociative disorder

15. A major problem with statistical definitions of abnormality is
   a. calculating the normal curve
   b. choosing dividing lines
   c. that they do not apply to groups of people
   d. that they do not take norms into account

16. DSM-IV-TR primarily describes and classifies _____ disorders.
    a. mental
    b. organic
    c. psychotic
    d. cognitive

17. A person who is a frequent "checker" may have which disorder?
    a. agoraphobia
    b. somatization
    c. free-floating fugue
    d. obsessive-compulsive

18. The most direct explanation for the anxiety reducing properties of self-defeating behavior is found in
    a. an overwhelmed ego
    b. avoidance learning
    c. the loss of meaning in one's life
    d. the concept of existential anxiety

19. A person with a(an) _____ personality disorder might be described as "charming" by people who don't know the person well.
    a. avoidant
    b. schizoid
    c. antisocial
    d. dependent

20. One of the most powerful situational contexts for judging the normality of behavior is
    a. culture
    b. gender
    c. statistical norms
    d. private discomfort

21. A person who is manic most likely suffers from a(an) _____ disorder.
    a. anxiety
    b. somatoform
    c. organic
    d. mood

22. The principal problem in paranoid psychosis is
    a. delusions
    b. hallucinations
    c. disturbed emotions
    d. personality disintegration

23. A problem that may occur with or without agoraphobia is
    a. dissociative disorder
    b. somatoform disorder
    c. panic disorder
    d. obsessive-compulsive disorder

24. Hearing voices that do not exist is an almost sure sign of a _____ disorder.
    a. psychotic
    b. dissociative
    c. personality
    d. delusional

25. A conversion reaction is a type of _____ disorder.
    a. somatoform
    b. dissociative
    c. obsessive-compulsive
    d. postpartum

26. The existence, in the past, of "disorders" such as "drapetomania" and "nymphomania" suggests that judging normality is greatly affected by
    a. gender
    b. cultural disapproval
    c. levels of functioning
    d. subjective discomfort

27. Which of the following terms does NOT belong with the others?
    a. neurosis
    b. somatoform disorder
    c. personality disorder
    d. dissociative disorder

28. Threats to one's self-image are a key element in the _____ approach to understanding anxiety and disordered functioning.
    a. Freudian
    b. humanistic
    c. existential
    d. behavioral

29. Which of the following is NOT classified as an anxiety disorder?
    a. adjustment disorder
    b. panic disorder
    c. agoraphobia
    d. obsessive-compulsive disorder

30. Cyclothymic disorder is most closely related to
    a. neurotic depression
    b. major depressive disorder
    c. bipolar disorder
    d. SAD

31. Pretending to possess a delusional disorder (schizophrenia) by walking around campus on a sunny day with a raincoat on and holding an open umbrella over one's head and, when inside, continuing to hold the open umbrella over one's head is a way to
    a. understand how social norms define normality
    b. determine how normality is defined
    c. test cultural relativism
    d. all the preceding

32. A person who sometimes is friendly, charming, impulsive, moody, extremely sensitive to ordinary criticisms, and suicidal has the _____ personality disorder.
    a. dependent
    b. borderline
    c. dissociative
    d. narcissistic

33. A person who is "blind" to signs that would disgust others, charming, lacks a conscience, and feels no guilt, shame, fear, loyalty, or love has the _____ personality disorder.
    a. histrionic
    b. schizoid
    c. avoidant
    d. antisocial

34. Which of the following is NOT a type of delusion?
    a. avoidant
    b. depressive
    c. reference
    d. influence

35. Which of the following statements is true of delusional disorders?
    a. The disorders are common and easily treated
    b. The main feature is a deeply held false belief
    c. Symptoms include perceiving sensations that do not exist (e.g., seeing insects crawling under their skin)
    d. The disorder is genetically linked

36. Which of the following is NOT a cause of schizophrenia?
    a. Malnutrition during pregnancy and exposure to influenza
    b. Females are more vulnerable to developing schizophrenic disorder
    c. Psychological trauma during childhood increases the risk
    d. Sensitivity to neurotransmitters dopamine and glutamate

37. Knowing that Lloyd is suffering from bipolar disorder and currently is undergoing treatment, Joan assumes that he will relapse sooner or later and, therefore, refuses to hire him as a delivery person. Joan's reaction and response to Lloyd's application reflects the impact of
    a. labeling a person with a disorder rather than the problem
    b. prejudice and discrimination
    c. stigmatism
    d. all the preceding

LANGUAGE DEVELOPMENT - Psychological Disorders

Word roots

Skhizein in Greek means "split." In addition to such English words as "schism," the names for several mental disorders discussed in this chapter derive from this root: schizoid, schizotypal, and schizophrenia. The term schizophrenia evolved from two Greek words, *skhizein* (split) and *phren* (mind). (*Phren* itself gave rise to the term "phrenology," which was found in an earlier chapter.)

How is normality defined, and what are the major psychological disorders?

Preview: Beware the Helicopters (p. 532)

> (532) *incapacitated*: incapable of functioning normally

> (532) *psychoses*: basic mental derangements characterized by loss of contact with reality

Normality—What Is Normal? (pp. 532-535)

> (532) *"That guy is really wacko. His porch lights are dimming." "Yeah, the butter's sliding off his waffle. I think he's ready to go postal."*: slang expressions for "crazy" and "insane" (which are themselves slang words for mental illness)

> (532) *snap judgments*: hurried decisions

> (532) *anguish*: distress; suffering; sorrow

> (532) *on top of the world*: great; wonderful

> (533) *where to draw the line*: where to find the dividing point between two positions

> (533) *facet*: an area or component

> (534) *histrionic*: very emotional; displaying emotion to gain attention

> (535) *commitment*: sending someone involuntarily to a mental institution

Classifying Mental Disorders—Problems by the Book (pp. 535-540)

> (536) *hyperactive*: excess activity

> (537) *ingrained*: innate, firmly fixed

(537) *exhibitionism*: sexual stimulation through the exposure of one's genitalia to others to obtain shock

(537) *fetishism*: erotic fixation on an object or bodily part

(537) *maladies*: illnesses

(538) *apathetic*: showing little or no feeling or concern

(538) *empirical*: based on careful observation or experience

(538) *mastery*: ability, knowledge of an area

(539) *voyeurism*: practice of seeking sexual stimulation by observing unsuspecting others who are unclothed or engaging in intercourse

What is a personality disorder?

Personality Disorders—Blueprints for Maladjustment (pp. 540-542)

(540) *gouging*: forcing out with the thumb

(542) *bat an eyelash*: show a response

What problems result when a person suffers high levels of anxiety?

Anxiety-Based Disorders—When Anxiety Rules (pp. 542-547)

(543) *just around the corner*: about to happen soon

(543) *clammy*: damp

(544) *jingle*: short verse or song used repetitively with commercials to fix them in your memory

(545) *recluse*: hermit; one who prefers to be alone

(546) *hooch*: building where members of the military live; barracks

(546) *flamboyant*: elaborate or colorful behavior; showy

How do psychologists explain anxiety-based disorders?

Anxiety and Disorder—Four Pathways to Trouble (pp. 547-549)

(547) *wary*: cautious

(548) *perfectionists*: people who must have and do everything "just right"

What are the general characteristics of psychotic disorders?

Psychotic Disorders—Life in the Shadow of Madness (pp. 549-551)

(550) *I can't handle it*: inability to cope with life's difficulties

(550) *chaotic*: confused; totally disorganized

(550) *"word salad"*: the result of not following the proper use of grammar when speaking English; when one constructs sentences in a seemingly random manner.

(551) *atrophy*: wasting away; decreased in size

How do delusional disorders differ from other psychotic disorders?

Delusional Disorders—An Enemy Behind Every Tree (pp. 551-552)

(551) *maligned*: to be criticized, smeared

(552) *crank letter*: irrational, eccentric letter

(552) *the Mafia*: organized crime group

What forms does schizophrenia take? What causes it?

Schizophrenia—Shattered Reality (pp. 552-558)

(552) *stuporous*: mental apathy and dullness

(552) *mutism*: inability to speak

(554) *Jeffrey Dahmer*: convicted murderer, who drugged his victims, sexually molested them after death, and removed and ate their body parts, which he kept stored in a refrigerator

(555) *heinous*: evil; horrible

(555) *enigma*: puzzle

(555) *laden*: full of

(555) *prying*: looking for information; being nosy

(556) *PCP ("angel dust")*: a psychedelic drug that causes vivid mental imagery

(556) *fissuring*: divisions among the lobes of the brain

(558) *vulnerability*: open to influence; easily hurt

(558) *"recipe" for psychosis*: a description for generating psychosis

(558) *"ingredients" (for psychosis)*: list of factors that contribute to psychosis

What are mood disorders? What causes depression?

Mood Disorders—Peaks and Valleys (pp. 558-562)

(558) *down and out:* weakened or incapable; depressed

(559) *bleak:* lacking warm or cheerful qualities

(559) *despondency:* depression

(561) *cabin fever:* extreme irritability and restlessness resulting from living in isolation or within a confined indoor area for a long period

(561) *foreboding:* feeling that something harmful or bad is going to happen

Disorder in Perspective—Psychiatric Labeling (pp. 562-563)

(562) *pseudo:* false; pretended

(562) *phony:* fake; false

(562) *checking up on:* investigating

(562) *grappling:* struggling and trying to cope

(562) *stigma:* mark or sign of shame

Why do people commit suicide? Can suicide be prevented?

Psychology in Action: Suicide—Lives on the Brink (pp. 563-566)

(564) *fallacy:* false belief

(565) *rapport:* a good relationship or closeness

(565) *tip the scales:* have a deciding influence

(565) *on the verge:* on the edge of danger

Solutions

RECITE AND REVIEW

How is normality defined, and what are the major psychological disorders?

1. disorders; unhealthy
2. discomfort
3. high; low
4. standards
5. cultural
6. All
7. behavior; adapt
8. mental

Classifying Mental Disorders—Problems by the Book: Pages 535-540

1. *Manual*; *Mental*
2. reality; social
3. brain; diseases
4. mood; drugs
5. emotion
6. anxiety; anxiety
7. disease; cause
8. personality
9. personality
10. gender; sexual
11. anxiety
12. culture; Ghost ; Koro
13. legal; court

What is a personality disorder?

1. personality; abandoned; impulsiveness
2. maladaptive
3. borderline; compulsive,
4. conscience; emotionally
5. personality; physical
6. obsessive; awareness; repeat

What problems result when a person suffers high levels of anxiety?

1. life stresses
2. anxiety; floating
3. public; home
4. specific
5. observed; social
6. stress; anxiety
7. memory; dissociative
8. multiple
9. disease
10. healthy
11. physical; treatment
12. physical
13. psychological
14. anxiety; defense

How do psychologists explain anxiety-based disorders?

1. unconscious
2. self-image
3. learning; learning
4. anxiety; relief
5. thinking

What are the general characteristics of psychotic disorders?

1. break
2. somatic; influence
3. hallucinations
4. personality
5. diseases
6. organic; brain
7. dementia

How do delusional disorders differ from other forms of psychosis?

1. delusions
2. persecution; romantic
3. persecution

What forms does schizophrenia take? What causes it?

1. split; thought
2. personality; Social
3. mutism; waxy
4. persecution
5. lack
6. stress; abnormalities
7. infection; birth
8. trauma; family
9. twins
10. transmitter
11. stress; abnormalities
12. PCP; glutamate
13. activity
14. stress

What are mood disorders? What causes depression?

1. emotion
2. depression
3. depression; elation
4. depression
5. depressed; mania
6. mania
7. within; external
8. maternity blues
9. Seasonal; winter
10. behavioral
11. Latina; education; stress
12. labeling; denied; crimes
13. psychotherapy; milder

Why do people commit suicide? Can suicide be prevented?

1. Suicide
2. alcohol; drug; firearm
3. escape; options
4. thoughts
5. communication

CONNECTIONS

How is normality defined, and what are the major psychological disorders? Pages 532-540

1. F.
2. A.
3. I.
4. B.
5. C.
6. H.
7. D.
8. E.
9. G.

What is a personality disorder? Pages 540-542

1. C.
2. E.
3. A.
4. J.
5. B.
6. D.
7. I.
8. F.
9. H.
10. G.

What problems result when a person suffers high levels of anxiety? How do psychologists explain anxiety-based disorders? Pages 542-549

1. H.
2. E.
3. K.

4.	N.	8.	J.	12.	F.
5.	I.	9.	B.	13.	C.
6.	G.	10.	M.	14.	L.
7.	A.	11.	D.		

What are the general characteristics of psychotic disorders? How do delusional disorders differ from other forms of psychosis? Pages 549-552

1.	A.	4.	H.	7.	G.
2.	I.	5.	F.	8.	E.
3.	B.	6.	C.	9.	D.

What forms does schizophrenia take? What causes it? Pages 552-558

1.	B.	4.	E.	7.	F.
2.	H.	5.	G.	8.	C.
3.	A.	6.	D.		

What are mood disorders? What causes depression? Why do people commit suicide? Can suicide be prevented? Pages 558-566

1.	C.	4.	A.	7.	G.
2.	H.	5.	F.	8.	E.
3.	B.	6.	D.		

CHECK YOUR MEMORY

How is normality defined, and what are the major psychological disorders? Pages 532-540

1.	T	6.	T	11.	F
2.	F	7.	F	12.	T
3.	T	8.	T	13.	F
4.	T	9.	T	14.	T
5.	F	10.	T	15.	F

What is a personality disorder? Pages 540-542

1.	F	4.	T	7.	F
2.	F	5.	F	8.	F
3.	F	6.	T		

What problems result when a person suffers high levels of anxiety? Pages 542-547

1.	T	5.	T	9.	F
2.	F	6.	T	10.	F
3.	F	7.	T	11.	T
4.	F	8.	T	12.	T

How do psychologists explain anxiety-based disorders? Pages 547-549

1.	T	3.	F	5.	F
2.	T	4.	T		

What are the general characteristics of psychotic disorders? Pages 549-551

1.	F	4.	T	7.	F
2.	F	5.	T		
3.	T	6.	F		

How do delusional disorders differ from other forms of psychosis? Pages 551-552

1.	F	3.	F
2.	T	4.	F

What forms does schizophrenia take? What causes it? Pages 552-558

1.	T	6.	T	11.	T
2.	F	7.	T	12.	F
3.	T	8.	T	13.	T
4.	T	9.	F		
5.	F	10.	T		

What are mood disorders? What causes depression? Pages 558-563

1.	F	7.	T	13.	F
2.	T	8.	T	14.	F
3.	F	9.	F		
4.	T	10.	T		
5.	T	11.	F		
6.	T	12.	T		

Why do people commit suicide? Can suicide be prevented? Pages 563-566

1.	T	3.	F	5.	F
2.	T	4.	T	6.	T

7. T

FINAL SURVEY AND REVIEW

How is normality defined, and what are the major psychological disorders?

1. *Psychopathology*
2. subjective
3. Statistical
4. Social nonconformity
5. context
6. relative
7. maladaptive
8. psychological

Classifying Mental Disorders—Problems by the Book: Pages 535-540

1. *Diagnostic; Statistical*
2. Psychotic; hallucinations
3. Organic
4. Substance related
5. Mood; affect
6. Anxiety
7. Somatoform
8. Dissociative; amnesia
9. Personality
10. identity; dysfunctions
11. neurosis
12. Ghost sickness; East Asians
13. Insanity

What is a personality disorder?

1. borderline; impulsiveness
2. ingrained
3. dependent; paranoid; schizotypal
4. Antisocial; manipulative
5. antisocial; emotional; children
6. obsessive-compulsive; anxiety

What problems result when a person suffers high levels of anxiety?

1. dissociative; somatoform
2. breakdown; adjustment
3. generalized; panic
4. agoraphobia
5. agoraphobia; objects or
6. social; phobia; evaluated
7. Obsessive; posttraumatic; acute
8. amnesia; fugue
9. identity; disorder
10. Somatoform
11. hypochondriasis
12. somatization
13. Somatoform; pain
14. conversion

How do psychologists explain anxiety-based disorders?

1. psychodynamic
2. humanistic
3. behavioral; avoidance
4. reduction; self-defeating
5. cognitive

What are the general characteristics of psychotic disorders?

1. Psychosis; reality
2. delusions
3. delusions; sensory
4. communication; disintegration
5. organic
6. dementia
7. Alzheimer's

How do delusional disorders differ from other forms of psychosis?

1. diagnosis; delusional

2. grandeur; disease   3. paranoid; violent

What forms does schizophrenia take? What causes it?

1. emotion; communication
2. Disorganized; disintegration
3. Catatonic; flexibility
4. paranoid; grandeur
5. Undifferentiated
6. environmental; biochemical
7. environmental
8. psychological; deviant
9. heredity
10. dopamine; receptor
11. environmental; biochemical
12. schizophrenic; hallucinogenic
13. CT; MRI ; PET
14. vulnerability

What are mood disorders? What causes depression?

1. mood
2. dysthymic
3. cyclothymic
4. bipolar I; mania
5. bipolar II; hypomania
6. major; depressive
7. Postpartum
8. endogenous
9. affective; phototherapy
10. Biological; cognitive
11. depression; hopelessness
12. labeling; stigmatized
13. psychotherapy; drugs; milder

Why do people commit suicide? Can suicide be prevented?

1. statistically
2. risk; factors; antisocial
3. pain; frustrated
4. threats; attempts
5. rapport; commitments

MASTERY TEST

Why do people commit suicide? Can suicide be prevented?

1. A, p. 545
2. A, p. 555
3. C, p. 534
4. B, p. 556
5. B, p. 544
6. D, p. 547
7. A, p. 558
8. B, p. 549
9. B, p. 561
10. A, p. 532
11. D, p. 565
12. A, p. 544
13. D, pp. 553-555
14. D, p. 546
15. B, p. 533
16. A, p. 535
17. D, p. 545
18. B, p. 548
19. C, pp. 541-542
20. A, p. 533
21. D, p. 536
22. A, p. 522
23. C, p. 543
24. A, p. 549
25. A, pp. 546-547
26. B, pp. 532-534
27. A, p. 537
28. B, p. 548
29. A, p. 543
30. C, p. 559
31. D, pp. 532-534
32. B, p. 540
33. D, pp. 541-542
34. A, p. 549
35. B, p. 549
36. B, pp. 555-556
37. D, p. 562

Therapies

Chapter Overview

Psychotherapies may be classified as individual, group, insight, action, directive, nondirective, time-limited, positive, or supportive, and combinations of these. Primitive and superstitious approaches to mental illness have included trepanning and demonology. More humane treatment began in 1793 with the work of Philippe Pinel in Paris.

Freudian psychoanalysis seeks to release repressed thoughts and emotions from the unconscious. Brief psychodynamic therapy has largely replaced traditional psychoanalysis.

Client-centered (or person-centered) therapy is a nondirective humanistic technique dedicated to creating an atmosphere of growth. Existential therapies focus on the meaning of life choices. Gestalt therapy attempts to rebuild thinking, feeling, and acting into connected wholes.

Behavior therapists use behavior modification techniques such as aversion therapy, systematic desensitization, operant shaping, extinction, and token economies. The tension-release method teaches people to recognize tensed muscles and learn to relax them. Of the various behavioral techniques, desensitization has been the most successful form of treatment to reduce fears, anxiety, and psychological pain.

Cognitive therapists attempt to change troublesome thought patterns. Major distortions in thinking include selective perception, overgeneralization, and all-or-nothing thinking. In rational-emotive behavior therapy, clients learn to recognize and challenge their own irrational beliefs.

Group therapies, such as psychodrama and family therapy, may be based on individual therapy methods or special group techniques. Sensitivity groups, encounter groups, and large-group awareness trainings also try to promote constructive changes.

All psychotherapies offer a caring relationship, emotional rapport, a protected setting, catharsis, explanations for one's problems, a new perspective, and a chance to practice new behaviors. Many basic counseling skills underlie the success of therapies. Successful therapists also include clients' cultural beliefs and traditions. Research has found that behavioral, cognitive-behavioral, and drug therapies are the most effective methods for treating obsessive-compulsive disorders. Because of the high cost of mental health services, future therapy may include short-term therapy; solution-focused; problem-solving approaches; master's-level practitioners; Internet services; telephone counseling; and self-help groups.

Three medical approaches to the treatment of psychological disorders are pharmacotherapy, electroconvulsive therapy, and psychosurgery. When using drugs as a form of treatment, patients must be aware of the trade-offs between the benefits and risks of drug use. Most professionals recommend using limited amounts of ECT with drug therapy to treat depression. When other therapeutic techniques are not effective at reducing mental illness symptoms, deep lesioning is considered.

Mental hospitalization can serve as a treatment for psychological disorders. Prolonged hospitalization has been discouraged by deinstitutionalization and by partial-hospitalization policies. Community mental health centers attempt to prevent mental health problems before they become serious.

Cognitive and behavioral techniques such as covert sensitization, thought stopping, covert reinforcement, and desensitization can aid self-management. In most communities, competent therapists can be located through public sources or by referrals.

Learning Objectives

1. Define *psychotherapy*; describe each of the following approaches to therapy and discuss what a person can expect as possible outcomes from psychotherapy:

   a. individual therapy

   b. group therapy

   c. insight therapy

   d. action therapy

   e. directive therapy

   f. non-directive therapy

   g. time-limited therapy

   h. supportive therapy

2. Briefly describe the history of the treatment of psychological problems, including trepanning, demonology, exorcism, ergotism, and the work of Pinel.

3. Discuss the development of psychoanalysis and its four basic techniques; name and describe the therapy that is frequently used today instead of psychoanalysis; and describe the criticism that helped prompt the switch, including the concept of spontaneous remission.

4. Discuss the following humanistic approaches to therapy: client-centered therapy, existential therapy, and Gestalt therapy. Contrast the humanistic approaches to psychoanalysis; and compare the three humanistic approaches to each other.

5. Discuss the advantages and disadvantages of telephone therapy, cybertherapy, and videoconferencing therapy; and describe what the APA recommends should be the extent of their activities.

6. Contrast the goal of behavior therapy with the goal of insight therapies; and define *behavior modification* and state its basic assumption.

7. Explain the relationship of aversion therapy to classical conditioning; and describe how aversion therapy can be used to stop bad habits and maladaptive behaviors.

8. Explain how relaxation, reciprocal inhibition, and use of a hierarchy, are combined to produce systematic desensitization; and describe how desensitization therapy, vicarious desensitization therapy; virtual reality exposure; and eye movement desensitization (EMDR) are used to treat anxiety disorders, such as phobias and post-traumatic stress disorder.

9. List and briefly describe the seven operant principles most frequently used by behavior therapists; explain how nonreinforcement and time out can be used to bring about extinction of a maladaptive behavior; and describe a token economy.

10. Explain what sets a cognitive therapist apart from other action therapists; describe three thinking errors which Beck said underlies depression and what can be done to correct such thinking; and discuss Ellis' rational-emotive behavior therapy and the three core ideas which serve as the basis of most irrational beliefs.

11. List the advantages of group therapy; briefly describe each of the following group therapies and include the concept of the therapy placebo effect:

    a. psychodrama (include role-playing, role reversal, and mirror technique)

    b. family therapy

    c. group awareness training (include sensitivity groups, encounter groups, and large group awareness training)

12. Discuss the effectiveness and strengths of each type of psychotherapy (see Table 17.2); describe the rate at which doses of therapy help people improve; and list the eight goals of psychotherapy and how they are accomplished. Include a description of a culturally-skilled therapist and the future of psychotherapy.

13. List and briefly describe the nine points or tips which can help a person when counseling a friend.

14. Describe the three types of somatic therapy, including the advantages and disadvantages of the therapy, its effects, and the types of disorders for which each is most useful:

    a. pharmacotherapy and the three major classes of drugs (see Table 17.4)

    b. electoconvulsive therapy (ECT)

    c. psychosurgery (prefrontal lobotomy and deep lesioning techniques)

15. Describe the role of hospitalization and partial hospitalization in the treatment of psychological disorders; explain what deinstitutionalization is and how halfway houses have attempted to help in the treatment of mental health; and discuss the roles of community mental health centers.

The following objectives are related to the material in the "Psychology in Action" section of your text.

1. Describe how covert sensization, thought stopping, and covert reinforcement can be used to reduce unwanted behavior.

2. Give an example of how you can overcome a common fear or break a bad habit using the steps given for desensitization.

3. List four indicators that may signal the need for professional psychological help and six methods a person can use for finding a therapist (see Table 17.5); and describe how one can choose a psychotherapist, including the concepts of peer counselors and self-help groups.

4. Summarize what is known about the importance of the personal qualities of the therapist and the client for successful therapy; and list six psychotherapy danger signals.

RECITE AND REVIEW

How do psychotherapies differ? How did psychotherapy originate?

Psychotherapy—Getting Better by the Hour: Pages 570-571

1. Psychotherapy is any psychological technique used to facilitate _____ changes in a person's personality, _____ , or adjustment.

2. _____ therapies seek to produce personal understanding. Action therapies try to directly change troublesome thoughts, feelings, or behaviors.

3. Directive therapists provide strong _____ . Nondirective therapists assist, but do not _____ their clients.

4. Supportive therapies provide on-going support, rather than actively promoting personal _____ .

5. Positive therapists seek to enhance _____ growth by nurturing _____ traits in individuals rather than trying to "fix" weakness.

6. Therapies may be conducted either individually or in groups, and they may be _____ limited (restricted to a set number of sessions).

Origins of Therapy—Bored Skulls and Hysteria on the Couch: Pages 571-572

1. Primitive approaches to mental illness were often based on _____ .

2. Trepanning involved boring a hole in the _____ .

3. Demonology attributed mental disturbance to supernatural forces and prescribed _____ as the cure.

4. In some instances, the actual cause of bizarre behavior may have been ergotism or _____ fungus _____ .

5. More humane treatment began in 1793 with the work of Philippe Pinel who created the first _____ in Paris.

Is Freudian psychoanalysis still used?

Psychoanalysis—Expedition into the Unconscious: Pages 572-574

1. Sigmund Freud's psychoanalysis was the first formal _____ .

2. Psychoanalysis was designed to treat cases of hysteria (physical symptoms without known _____ causes).

3. Psychoanalysis seeks to release repressed thoughts, memories, and emotions from the _____ and resolve _____ conflicts.

4. The psychoanalyst uses _____ association, _____ analysis, and analysis of resistance and transference to reveal health-producing insights.

5. Freud believed that in order to uncover the individual's unconscious _____ and feelings, a psychoanalyst must conduct _____ analysis to discover the _____ content that is expressed through the manifest content of a person's dream.

6. _____ psychodynamic therapy (which relies on psychoanalytic theory but is brief and focused) is as effective as other major therapies.

7. Some critics have argued that traditional psychoanalysis may frequently receive credit for _____ remissions of symptoms. However, psychoanalysis has been shown to be better than no treatment at all.

What are the major humanistic therapies?

Humanistic Therapies—Restoring Human Potential: Pages 574-576

1. _____ therapies try to help people live up to their potentials and to give tendencies for mental health to emerge.

2. Carl Rogers' client-centered (or _____ -centered) therapy is nondirective and is dedicated to creating an atmosphere of _____ .

3. In client-centered therapy, unconditional _____ regard, _____ (feeling what another is feeling), authenticity, and reflection are combined to give the client a chance to solve his or her own problems.

4. Existential therapies focus on the end result of the _____ one makes in life.

5. Clients in existential therapy are encouraged through confrontation and encounter to exercise free _____ , to take responsibility for their _____ , and to find _____ in their lives.

6. The goal of Gestalt therapy is to rebuild thinking, feeling, and acting into connected _____ and to help clients break through emotional blocks.

7. Frederick Perls' Gestalt therapy emphasizes immediate _____ of thoughts and feelings and discourages people from dwelling on what they ought to do.

Therapy at a Distance—Psych Jockeys and Cybertherapy: Pages 576-577

1. Media psychologists, such as those found on the radio, are supposed to restrict themselves to _____ listeners, rather than actually doing _____ .

2. Telephone therapists and cybertherapists working on the _____ may or may not be competent. Even if they are, their effectiveness may be severely limited.

3. In an emerging approach called telehealth, _____ is being done at a distance, through the use of videoconferencing (two-way _____ links).

What is behavior therapy? How is behavior therapy used to treat phobias, fears, and anxieties?

Behavior Therapy—Healing by Learning: Pages 578-582

1. Behavior therapists use various behavior modification techniques that apply _____ principles to change human behavior.

2. Classical conditioning is a basic form of _____ in which existing reflex responses are _____ with new conditioned stimuli.

3. In aversion therapy, classical conditioning is used to associate maladaptive behavior with _____ or other aversive events in order to inhibit undesirable responses.

4. To be most effective, aversive _____ must be response-contingent (closely connected with responses).

5. In desensitization, gradual _____ and reciprocal inhibition break the link between fear and particular situations.

6. Classical conditioning also underlies _____ desensitization, a technique used to reduce fears, phobias, and anxieties.

7. Typical steps in desensitization are: Construct a fear hierarchy; learn to produce total _____ ; and perform items on the hierarchy (from least to most disturbing).

8. Desensitization may be carried out in real settings or it may be done by vividly _____ scenes from the fear hierarchy.

9. The tension-release method allows individuals, through practice, to _____ their bodies' tensed muscles and to learn to _____ them on command.

10. Desensitization is also effective when it is administered vicariously; that is, when clients watch _____ perform the feared responses.

11. In a newly developed technique, virtual _____ exposure is used to present _____ stimuli to patients undergoing desensitization.

12. Another new technique called eye-movement desensitization shows promise as a treatment for traumatic _____ and _____ disorders.

What role does reinforcement play in behavior therapy?

Operant Therapies—All the World Is a Skinner Box? Pages 582-584

1. Behavior modification also makes use of operant principles, such as positive reinforcement, nonreinforcement, extinction, punishment, shaping, stimulus _____ , and _____ out.

2. Nonreward can extinguish troublesome behaviors. Often this is done by simply identifying and eliminating _____ .

3. Time out is an extinction technique in which attention and approval are withheld following undesirable _____ .

4. Time out can also be done by _____ a person from the setting in which misbehavior occurs, so that it will not be reinforced.

5. Attention, approval, and concern are subtle _____ that are effective at _____ human behaviors.

6. To apply positive reinforcement and operant shaping, symbolic rewards known as tokens are often used. Tokens allow _____ reinforcement of selected target _____ .

7. Full-scale use of _____ in an institutional setting produces a token economy.

8. Toward the end of a token economy program, patients are shifted to social rewards such as recognition and _____ .

Can therapy change thoughts and emotions?

Cognitive Therapy—Think Positive! Pages 584-586

1. Cognitive therapy emphasizes changing _____ patterns that underlie emotional or behavioral problems.

2. Aaron Beck's cognitive therapy for depression corrects major distortions in thinking, including _____ perception, overgeneralization, and all-or-nothing _____ .

3. The goals of cognitive therapy are to correct distorted thinking and/or teach improved coping _____ .

4. In a variation of cognitive therapy called rational-emotive behavior therapy (REBT), clients learn to recognize and challenge their own irrational _____ , which lead to upsetting consequences.

5. Some _____ beliefs that lead to conflicts are: I am worthless if I am not loved, I should be _____ competent, I should _____ on others who are stronger than I am, and it is easier for me to avoid difficulties than to face them.

Can psychotherapy be done with groups of people?

Group Therapy—People Who Need People: Pages 586-588

1. Group therapy may be a simple extension of _____ methods or it may be based on techniques developed specifically for groups.

2. In psychodrama, individuals use _____ playing, _____ reversals, and the mirror technique to gain insight into incidents resembling their real-life problems.

3. In family therapy, the family group is treated as a _____ so that the entire _____ system is changed for the better.

4. Although they are not literally _____ , sensitivity groups and encounter groups attempt to encourage positive personality change.

5. In recent years, commercially offered large-group awareness _____ have become popular.

6. The therapeutic benefits of large-group techniques are questionable and may reflect nothing more than a _____ placebo effect.

What do various therapies have in common?

Psychotherapy—An Overview: Pages 588-592

1. After eight therapy sessions, _____ percent of all patients showed an improvement, and after _____ therapy sessions, 75 percent of all patients improved.

2. To alleviate personal problems, all psychotherapies offer a caring relationship and _____ rapport in a protected _____ .

3. All therapies encourage catharsis and they provide explanations for the client's _____ .

4. In addition, psychotherapy provides a new perspective and a chance to practice new _____ .

5. Psychotherapy in the future may include short-term therapy, _____ -focused approaches, _____ -help groups, Internet services, _____ counseling, paraprofessional, and master's-level practitioners.

6. Many basic _____ skills are used in therapy. These include listening actively and helping to clarify the problem.

7. Effective therapists also focus on feelings and avoid giving unwanted _____ .

8. It helps to accept the person's perspective, to reflect thoughts and feelings, and to be patient during _____ .

9. In counseling it is important to use _____ questions when possible and to maintain confidentiality.

10. Therapists must establish rapport and include the patients' _____ beliefs and practices when treating them.

How do psychiatrists treat psychological disorders?

Medical Therapies—Psychiatric Care: Pages 592-596

1. Three _____ (bodily) approaches to treatment of psychosis are pharmacotherapy (use of _____), electroconvulsive therapy (ECT) (brain shock for the treatment of depression), and psychosurgery (surgical alteration of the _____).

2. Pharmacotherapy is done with _____ tranquilizers (anti-anxiety drugs), antipsychotics (which reduce delusions and _____), and antidepressants (_____ elevators).

3. All psychiatric drugs involve a trade-off between _____ and benefits.

4. ECT and _____ , especially prefrontal lobotomy, once received great acclaim for their effectiveness but recently have _____ support from professionals.

5. If psychosurgery is necessary, deep _____ , where a small targeted area in the brain is _____ , is the preferred alternative to a lobotomy.

6. _____ hospitalization is considered a form of treatment for mental disorders.

7. Prolonged hospitalization has been discouraged by deinstitutionalization (reduced use of commitment to treat mental disorders) and by _____ -hospitalization policies.

8. Half-way _____ within the community can help people make the transition from a hospital or institution to _____ living.

9. Community mental health centers were created to help avoid or minimize _____ .

10. Community mental health centers also have as their goal the prevention of mental health problems through education, consultation, and _____ intervention.

How are behavioral principles applied to everyday problems? How could a person find professional help?

Psychology in Action: Self-Management and Finding Professional Help: Pages 596-601

1. In covert sensitization, aversive _____ are used to discourage unwanted behavior.

2. Thought stopping uses mild _____ to prevent upsetting thoughts.

3. Covert reinforcement is a way to encourage desired _____ by mental rehearsal.

4. Desensitization pairs _____ with a hierarchy of upsetting images in order to lessen fears.

5. In most communities, a competent and reputable therapist can usually be located through public sources of information or by a _____ .

6. Practical considerations such as _____ and qualifications enter into choosing a therapist. However, the therapist's personal characteristics are of equal importance.

7. Self-help _____ , made up of people who share similar problems, can sometimes add valuable support to professional treatment.

CONNECTIONS

How do psychotherapies differ? How did psychotherapy originate? Is Freudian psychoanalysis still used? Pages 570-574

1. _____ positive therapy
2. _____ trepanning
3. _____ exorcism
4. _____ ergotism
5. _____ Pinel
6. _____ free association
7. _____ Freud
8. _____ dream analysis
9. _____ transference
10. _____ spontaneous remission

a. tainted rye
b. old relationships
c. hysteria
d. waiting list control
e. Bicêtre
f. latent content
g. possession
h. enhanced personal strength
i. release of evil spirits
j. saying anything on mind

What are the major humanistic therapies? Pages 574-577

1. _____ telephone therapy
2. _____ authenticity
3. _____ unconditional positive regards
4. _____ rephrasing
5. _____ distance therapy
6. _____ existentialist
7. _____ Rogers
8. _____ Gestalt therapy

a. reflection
b. client centered
c. no facades
d. being in the world
e. lack visual cues
f. telehealth
g. whole experiences
h. unshakable personal acceptance

What is behavior therapy? How is behavior therapy used to treat phobias, fears, and anxieties? Pages 578-582

1. _____ behavior modification
2. _____ unconditional response
3. _____ virtual reality exposure
4. _____ vicarious desensitization
5. _____ desensitization
6. _____ EMDR
7. _____ rapid smoking

a. unlearned reaction
b. easing post-traumatic stress
c. secondhand learning
d. applied behavior analysis
e. aversion therapy
f. fear hierarchy
g. computer-generated fear images

What role does reinforcement play in behavior therapy? Can therapy change thoughts and emotions? Pages 582-586

1. _____ overgeneralization
2. _____ cognitive therapy
3. _____ time-out
4. _____ REBT
5. _____ target behaviors

a. operant extinction
b. token economy
c. Aaron Beck
d. thinking error
e. irrational beliefs

Can psychotherapy be done with groups of people? What do various therapies have in common? How do psychiatrists treat psychological disorders? Pages 586-596

1. _____ psychodrama
2. _____ family therapy
3. _____ sensitivity group
4. _____ encounter group
5. _____ media psychologist
6. _____ therapeutic alliance
7. _____ catharsis
8. _____ pharmacotherapy
9. _____ ECT
10. _____ psychosurgery

a. public education
b. enhanced self-awareness
c. emotional release
d. causes of memory loss
e. prefrontal lobotomy
f. systems approach
g. drug therapy
h. role reversals
i. caring relationship
j. intense interactions

How are behavioral principles applied to everyday problems? How could a person find professional help? Pages 596-601

1. _____ covert reinforcement
2. _____ unethical practices
3. _____ qualified therapist ·
4. _____ covert sensitization
5. _____ self-help group

   a. positive imagery
   b. shared problems
   c. aversive imagery
   d. therapist encourages dependency
   e. American Psychiatrist Association

CHECK YOUR MEMORY

How do psychotherapies differ? How did psychotherapy originate? Pages 570-572

1. A goal of positive therapy is to "fix" a person's weaknesses to enhance their personal strength.

   TRUE or FALSE

2. A particular psychotherapy could be both insight- and action-oriented.

   TRUE or FALSE

3. With the help of psychotherapy, chances of improvement are fairly good for phobias and low self-esteem.

   TRUE or FALSE

4. Psychotherapy is sometimes used to encourage personal growth for people who are already functioning well.

   TRUE or FALSE

5. Personal autonomy, a sense of identity, and feelings of personal worth are elements of mental health.

   TRUE or FALSE

6. Trepanning was really an excuse to kill people since none of the patients survived.

   TRUE or FALSE

7. Exorcism sometimes took the form of physical torture.

   TRUE or FALSE

8. Trepanning was the most common treatment for ergotism.

   TRUE or FALSE

9. Pinel was the first person to successfully treat ergotism.

   TRUE or FALSE

10. The problem Freud called hysteria is now called a somatoform disorder.

    TRUE or FALSE

Is Freudian psychoanalysis still used? Pages 572-574

1. During free association, patients try to remember the earliest events in their lives.

   TRUE or FALSE

2. Freud called transference "the royal road to the unconscious."

   TRUE or FALSE

3. Using dream analysis, a therapist seeks to uncover the latent content or symbolic meaning of a person's dreams.

   TRUE or FALSE

4. The manifest content of a dream is its surface or visible meaning.

   TRUE or FALSE

5. In an analysis of resistance, the psychoanalyst tries to understand a client's resistance to forming satisfying relationships.

   TRUE or FALSE

6. Therapists use direct interviewing as part of brief psychodynamic therapy.

   TRUE or FALSE

7. If members of a waiting list control group improve at the same rate as people in therapy, it demonstrates that the therapy is effective.

   TRUE or FALSE

What are the major humanistic therapies? Pages 574-577

1. Through client-centered therapy, Carl Rogers sought to explore unconscious thoughts and feelings.

   TRUE or FALSE

2. The client-centered therapist does not hesitate to react with shock, dismay, or disapproval to a client's inappropriate thoughts or feelings.

   TRUE or FALSE

3. In a sense, the person-centered therapist acts as a psychological mirror for clients.

   TRUE or FALSE

4. Existential therapy emphasizes our ability to freely make choices.

   TRUE or FALSE

5. According to the existentialists, our choices must be courageous.

   TRUE or FALSE

6. Existential therapy emphasizes the integration of fragmented experiences into connected wholes.

   TRUE or FALSE

7. Fritz Perls was an originator of telehealth.

   TRUE or FALSE

8. Gestalt therapy may be done individually or in a group.

   TRUE or FALSE

9. Gestalt therapists urge clients to intellectualize their feelings.

   TRUE or FALSE

10. The APA suggests that media psychologists should discuss only problems of a general nature.

    TRUE or FALSE

11. Under certain conditions, telephone therapy can be as successful as face-to-face therapy.

    TRUE or FALSE

12. The problem with doing therapy by videoconferencing is that facial expressions are not available to the therapist or the client.

    TRUE or FALSE

What is behavior therapy? How is behavior therapy used to treat phobias, fears, and anxieties? Pages 578-582

1. Behavior modification, or applied behavior analysis, uses classical and operant conditioning to directly alter human behavior.

   TRUE or FALSE

2. Aversion therapy is based primarily on operant conditioning.

   TRUE or FALSE

3. For many children, the sight of a hypodermic needle becomes a conditioned stimulus for fear because it is often followed by pain.

   TRUE or FALSE

4. Rapid smoking creates an aversion because people must hyperventilate to smoke at the prescribed rate.

   TRUE or FALSE

5. About one half of all people who quit smoking begin again.

   TRUE or FALSE

6. In aversion therapy for alcohol abuse, the delivery of shock must appear to be response-contingent to be most effective.

   TRUE or FALSE

7. Poor generalization of conditioned aversions to situations outside of therapy can be a problem.

   TRUE or FALSE

8. During desensitization, the steps of a hierarchy are used to produce deep relaxation.

   TRUE or FALSE

9. Relaxation is the key ingredient of reciprocal inhibition.

   TRUE or FALSE

10. Clients typically begin with the most disturbing item in a desensitization hierarchy.

    TRUE or FALSE

11. Desensitization is most effective when people are directly exposed to feared stimuli.

    TRUE or FALSE

12. The tension-release method is used to produce deep relaxation.

    TRUE or FALSE

13. Live or filmed models are used in vicarious desensitization.

    TRUE or FALSE

14. During eye-movement desensitization, clients concentrate on pleasant, calming images.

    TRUE or FALSE

What role does reinforcement play in behavior therapy? Pages 582-584

1. Operant punishment is basically the same thing as nonreinforcement.

   TRUE or FALSE

2. Shaping involves reinforcing ever closer approximations to a desired response.

   TRUE or FALSE

3. An undesirable response can be extinguished by reversing stimulus control.

   TRUE or FALSE

4. Misbehavior tends to decrease when others ignore it.

   TRUE or FALSE

5. To be effective, tokens must be tangible rewards, such as slips of paper or poker chips.
   TRUE or FALSE

6. The value of tokens is based on the fact that they can be exchanged for other reinforcers.
   TRUE or FALSE

7. A goal of token economies is to eventually switch patients to social reinforcers.
   TRUE or FALSE

Can therapy change thoughts and emotions? Pages 584-586

1. Cognitive therapy is especially successful in treating depression.
   TRUE or FALSE

2. Depressed persons tend to magnify the importance of events.
   TRUE or FALSE

3. Cognitive therapy is as effective as drugs for treating many cases of depression.
   TRUE or FALSE

4. Stress inoculation is a form of rational-emotive behavior therapy.
   TRUE or FALSE

5. The A in the ABC analysis of REBT stands for "anticipation."
   TRUE or FALSE

6. The C in the ABC analysis of REBT stands for "consequence."
   TRUE or FALSE

7. According to REBT, you would hold an irrational belief if you believe that you should depend on others who are stronger than you.
   TRUE or FALSE

Can psychotherapy be done with groups of people? Pages 586-588

1. The mirror technique is the principal method used in family therapy.
   TRUE or FALSE

2. Family therapists try to meet with the entire family unit during each session of therapy.
   TRUE or FALSE

3. A "trust walk" is a typical sensitivity group exercise.

   TRUE or FALSE

4. Sensitivity groups attempt to tear down defenses and false fronts.

   TRUE or FALSE

5. Large-group awareness training has been known to create emotional crises where none existed before.

   TRUE or FALSE

What do various therapies have in common? Pages 588-592

1. Half of all people who begin psychotherapy feel better after 8 sessions.

   TRUE or FALSE

2. Emotional rapport is a key feature of the therapeutic alliance.

   TRUE or FALSE

3. Therapy gives clients a chance to practice new behaviors.

   TRUE or FALSE

4. An increase in short-term therapy, telephone counseling, and self-help groups in the future is likely the result of the high cost of mental health services.

   TRUE or FALSE

5. Regarding the future of psychotherapy, experts predict that the use of psychoanalysis will increase.

   TRUE or FALSE

6. Regarding the future of psychotherapy, experts predict that there will be an increase in the use of short-term therapy.

   TRUE or FALSE

7. Competent counselors do not hesitate to criticize clients, place blame when it is deserved, and probe painful topics.

   TRUE or FALSE

8. "Why don't you . . . Yes, but . . ." is a common game used to avoid taking responsibility in therapy.

   TRUE or FALSE

9. Closed questions tend to be most helpful in counseling another person.

   TRUE or FALSE

10. A necessary step toward becoming a culturally skilled therapist is to adopt the culture of your clients as your own.

    TRUE or FALSE

How do psychiatrists treat psychological disorders? Pages 592-596

1. Major mental disorders are primarily treated with psychotherapy.

   TRUE or FALSE

2. When used for long periods of time, major tranquilizers can cause a neurological disorder.

   TRUE or FALSE

3. Two percent of all patients taking clozaril suffer from a serious blood disease.

   TRUE or FALSE

4. ECT treatments are usually given in a series of 20 to 30 sessions, occurring once a day.

   TRUE or FALSE

5. ECT is most effective when used to treat depression.

   TRUE or FALSE

6. To reduce a relapse, antidepressant drugs are recommended for patients with depression following ECT treatment.

   TRUE or FALSE

7. The prefrontal lobotomy is the most commonly performed type of psychosurgery today.

   TRUE or FALSE

8. Psychosurgeries performed by deep lesioning can be reversed if necessary.

   TRUE or FALSE

9. In the approach known as partial hospitalization, patients live at home.

   TRUE or FALSE

10. Admitting a person to a mental institution is the first step to treating the disorder.

    TRUE or FALSE

11. Deinstitutionalization increased the number of homeless persons living in many communities.

    TRUE or FALSE

12. Most half-way houses are located on the grounds of mental hospitals.

    TRUE or FALSE

13. Crisis intervention is typically one of the services provided by community mental health centers.

    TRUE or FALSE

14. Most people prefer to seek help from a professional doctor over a paraprofessional because of their approachability.

    TRUE or FALSE

How are behavioral principles applied to everyday problems? How could a person find professional help? Pages 596-601

1. To do covert sensitization, you must first learn relaxation exercises.

    TRUE or FALSE

2. Disgusting images are used in thought stopping.

    TRUE or FALSE

3. Covert reinforcement should be visualized before performing steps in a fear hierarchy.

    TRUE or FALSE

4. Approximately 50 percent of all American households had someone who received mental health treatment.

    TRUE or FALSE

5. Significant changes in your work, relationships, or use of drugs or alcohol can be signs that you should seek professional help.

    TRUE or FALSE

6. Marital problems are the most common reason for seeing a mental health professional.

    TRUE or FALSE

7. For some problems, paraprofessional counselors and self-help groups are as effective as professional psychotherapy.

    TRUE or FALSE

8. All major types of psychotherapy are about equally successful.

    TRUE or FALSE

9. All therapists are equally qualified and successful at treating mental disorders.

    TRUE or FALSE

FINAL SURVEY AND REVIEW

How do psychotherapies differ? How did psychotherapy originate?

Psychotherapy—Getting Better by the Hour: Pages 570-571

1. _____ is any psychological technique used to facilitate positive changes in a person's

    _____ , behavior, or adjustment.

2. Insight therapies seek to produce personal understanding. _____ therapies try to directly change troublesome thoughts, feelings, or behaviors.

3. _____ therapists provide strong guidance. _____ therapists assist, but do not guide their clients.

4. _____ therapies provide on-going support, rather than actively promoting personal change.

5. _____ therapists seek to enhance personal growth by nurturing positive traits in individuals rather than trying to _____ weakness.

6. Therapies may be conducted either _____ or in groups, _____ they may be time limited (restricted to a set number of sessions).

Origins of Therapy—Bored Skulls and Hysteria on the Couch: Pages 571-572

1. _____ approaches to mental illness were often based on superstition.

2. _____ involved boring a hole in the skull.

3. _____ attributed mental disturbance to supernatural forces and prescribed exorcism as the cure.

4. In some instances, the actual cause of bizarre behavior may have been _____ , a type of _____ poisoning.

5. More humane treatment began in 1793 with the work of Philippe _____ who created the first mental hospital in Paris.

Is Freudian psychoanalysis still used?

Psychoanalysis—Expedition into the Unconscious: Pages 572-574

1. Sigmund _____ _____ was the first formal psychotherapy.

2. Psychoanalysis was designed to treat cases of _____ (physical symptoms without known physical causes).

3. Psychoanalysis seeks to release _____ thoughts, memories, and emotions from the unconscious and resolve unconscious conflicts.

4. Freud believed that in order to uncover the individual's _____ desires and feelings, a psychoanalyst must conduct _____ analysis to discover the latent content of a person's dream.

5. The psychoanalyst uses free _____ , dream analysis, and analysis of _____ and transference to reveal health-producing insights.

6. Brief _____ therapy (which relies on _____ theory but is brief and focused) is as effective as other major therapies.

7. Some critics have argued that traditional psychoanalysis may frequently receive credit for spontaneous _____ of symptoms. However, psychoanalysis has been shown to be better than no treatment at all.

What are the major humanistic therapies?

Humanistic Therapies—Restoring Human Potential: Pages 574-576

1. Humanistic therapies try to help people live up to their _____ and to give tendencies for mental health to emerge.

2. Carl _____ client-centered (or person-centered) therapy is _____ and is dedicated to creating an atmosphere of growth.

3. In client-centered therapy, _____ positive regard, empathy, authenticity, and _____ (restating thoughts and feelings) are combined to give the client a chance to solve his or her own problems.

4. _____ therapies focus on the end result of the choices one makes in life.

5. Clients in existential therapy are encouraged through _____ and _____ to exercise free will, to take responsibility for their choices, and to find meaning in their lives.

6. The goal of Perl's approach is to rebuild thinking, feeling, and acting into connected wholes and to help clients break through _____ _____ .

7. Frederick Perls' _____ therapy emphasizes immediate awareness of thoughts and feelings and discourages people from dwelling on what they ought to do.

Therapy at a Distance—Psych Jockeys and Cybertherapy: Pages 576-577

1. _____ psychologists, such as those found on the radio, are supposed to restrict themselves to educating listeners, rather than actually doing therapy.

2. Telephone therapists and _____ working on the Internet may or may not be competent. Even if they are, their effectiveness may be severely limited.

3. In an emerging approach called _____ , therapy is being done at a distance, through the use of _____ (two-way audio-video links).

What is behavior therapy? How is behavior therapy used to treat phobias, fears, and anxieties?

Behavior Therapy—Healing by Learning: Pages 578-582

1. _____ therapists use various behavior _____ techniques that apply learning principles to change human behavior.

2. _____ conditioning is a basic form of learning in which existing _____ responses are associated with new conditioned stimuli.

3. In _____ therapy, classical conditioning is used to associate maladaptive behavior with pain or other aversive events in order to inhibit undesirable responses.

4. To be most effective, aversive stimuli must be _____ (closely connected with responses).

5. In desensitization, gradual adaptation and reciprocal _____ break the link between fear and particular situations.

6. Classical conditioning also underlies systematic _____ , a technique used to reduce fears, phobias, and anxieties.

7. Typical steps in desensitization are: Construct a fear _____ ; learn to produce total relaxation; and perform items on the _____ (from least to most disturbing).

8. Desensitization may be carried out in real settings or it may be done by vividly imagining scenes from the _____ _____ .

9. The _____ -release method allows individuals, through practice, to recognize their bodies' tensed _____ and to learn to relax them on command.

10. Desensitization is also effective when it is administered _____ ; that is, when clients watch models perform the feared responses.

11. In a newly developed technique, _____ reality _____ is used to present fear stimuli to patients undergoing desensitization.

12. Another new technique called _____ desensitization shows promise as a treatment for traumatic memories and stress disorders.

What role does reinforcement play in behavior therapy?

Operant Therapies—All the World Is a Skinner Box? Pages 582-584

1. Behavior modification also makes use of _____ principles, such as positive reinforcement, nonreinforcement, _____ (eliminating responses), _____ (molding responses), shaping, stimulus control, and time out.

2. _____ can extinguish troublesome behaviors. Often this is done by simply identifying and eliminating reinforcers.

3. Time out is an _____ technique in which attention and approval are withheld following undesirable responses.

4. Time out can also be done by removing a person from the _____ in which misbehavior occurs, so that it will not be _____ .

5. Attention, approval, and concern are subtle _____ that are effective at maintaining human _____ .

6. To apply positive reinforcement and operant shaping, symbolic rewards known as _____ are often used. Tokens allow immediate reinforcement of selected _____ behaviors.

7. Full-scale use of tokens in an institutional setting produces a _____ _____ .

8. Toward the end of a token economy program, patients are shifted to _____ rewards such as recognition and approval.

Can therapy change thoughts and emotions?

Cognitive Therapy—Think Positive! Pages 584-586

1. _____ therapy emphasizes changing thinking patterns that underlie emotional or behavioral problems.

2. Aaron _____ therapy for depression corrects major distortions in thinking, including selective perception, _____ , and all-or-nothing thinking.

3. The goals of cognitive therapy are to correct distorted thinking and/or teach improved _____ skills.

4. In a variation called _____ therapy (REBT), clients learn to recognize and challenge their own irrational beliefs, which lead to upsetting consequences.

5. Some irrational _____ that lead to conflicts are: I am _____ if I am not loved, I should be completely competent, I should _____ on others who are stronger than I am, and it is easier for me to avoid difficulties than to face them.

Can psychotherapy be done with groups of people?

Group Therapy—People Who Need People: Pages 586-588

1. _____ therapy may be a simple extension of individual methods or it may be based on techniques developed specifically for _____ .

2. In _____ , individuals use role playing, role _____ , and the mirror technique to gain insight into incidents resembling their real-life problems.

3. In _____ therapy, the _____ group is treated as a unit so that the entire family system is changed for the better.

4. Although they are not literally psychotherapies, sensitivity groups and _____ groups attempt to encourage positive personality change.

5. In recent years, commercially offered large-group _____ trainings have become popular.

6. The therapeutic benefits of large-group techniques are questionable and may reflect nothing more than a therapy _____ effect.

What do various therapies have in common?

Psychotherapy—An Overview: Pages 588-592

1. After _____ therapy sessions, 50 percent of all patients showed an improvement, and after 26 therapy sessions, _____ percent of all patients improved.

2. To alleviate personal problems, all psychotherapies offer a caring relationship and emotional _____ in a _____ setting.

3. All therapies encourage _____ (emotional release) and they provide explanations for the client's problems.

4. In addition, psychotherapy provides a new _____ and a chance to practice new behaviors.

5. _____ in the future may include _____ -term therapy, solution-focused approaches, self-help groups, _____ services, telephone counseling, paraprofessional, and _____ -level practitioners.

6. Many basic counseling skills are used in therapy. These include listening _____ and helping to _____ the problem.

7. Effective therapists also focus on _____ and avoid giving unwanted advice.

8. It helps to accept the person's _____ , to _____ thoughts and feelings, and to be patient during silences.

9. In counseling it is important to use open questions when possible and to maintain _____ .

10. Therapists must establish rapport and include their patients' _____ beliefs and traditional practices when treating them.

How do psychiatrists treat psychological disorders?

Medical Therapies—Psychiatric Care: Pages 592-596

1. Three somatic approaches to treatment of psychosis are _____ (use of drugs), _____ therapy (ECT), and psychosurgery.

2. Pharmacotherapy is done with minor tranquilizers (anti-anxiety drugs), _____ (which reduce delusions and hallucinations), and _____ (mood elevators).

3. All psychiatric drugs involve a trade-off between risks and _____ .

4. _____ therapy (ECT) and psychosurgery, especially prefrontal lobotomy, once received great acclaim for their _____ but recently have lost support from professionals.

5. If psychosurgery is necessary, _____ , where a small targeted area in the brain is destroyed, is the preferred alternative to a lobotomy.

6. _____ hospitalization is considered a form of treatment for mental _____ .

7. Prolonged hospitalization has been discouraged by _____ (reduced use of commitment to treat mental disorders) and by partial-hospitalization policies.

8. _____ houses within the community can help people make the transition from a hospital or institution to independent living.

9. _____ _____ health centers were created to help avoid or minimize hospitalization.

10. These centers have as their goal the _____ of mental health problems through education, consultation, and crisis _____ .

How are behavioral principles applied to everyday problems? How could a person find professional help?

Psychology in Action: Self-Management and Finding Professional Help: Pages 596-601

1. In _____ sensitization, aversive images are used to discourage unwanted behavior.

2. _____ uses mild punishment to prevent upsetting thoughts.

3. Covert _____ is a way to encourage desired responses by mental rehearsal.

4. _____ pairs relaxation with a hierarchy of upsetting images in order to lessen fears.

5. In most communities, a _____ and reputable therapist can usually be located through public sources of information or by a referral.

6. Practical considerations such as cost and qualifications enter into choosing a therapist. However, the therapist's _____ _____ are of equal importance.

7. _____ groups, made up of people who share similar _____ , can sometimes add valuable support to professional treatment.

MASTERY TEST

1. To demonstrate that spontaneous remissions are occurring, you could use a
    a. patient-defined hierarchy
    b. waiting list control group
    c. target behavior group
    d. short-term dynamic correlation

2. In desensitization, relaxation is induced to block fear, a process known as
    a. systematic adaptation
    b. vicarious opposition
    c. stimulus control
    d. reciprocal inhibition

3. Role reversals and the mirror technique are methods of
    a. psychodrama
    b. person-centered therapy
    c. family therapy
    d. brief psychodynamic therapy

4. One thing that both trepanning and exorcism have in common is that both were used
    a. to treat ergotism
    b. by Pinel in the Bicêtre Asylum
    c. to remove spirits
    d. to treat cases of hysteria

5. Unconditional positive regard is a concept particularly associated with
    a. Beck
    b. Frankl
    c. Perls
    d. Rogers

6. Many of the claimed benefits of large-group awareness trainings appear to represent a therapy
    _____ effect.
    a. remission
    b. education
    c. placebo
    d. transference

7. Personal change is LEAST likely to be the goal of
    a. supportive therapy
    b. action therapy
    c. desensitization
    d. humanistic therapy

8. Inducing seizures is a standard part of using
   a. Gestalt therapy
   b. antidepressants
   c. ECT
   d. cybertherapy

9. Which counseling behavior does not belong with the others listed here?
   a. paraphrasing
   b. judging
   c. reflecting
   d. active listening

10. In psychoanalysis, the process most directly opposite to free association is
    a. resistance
    b. transference
    c. symbolization
    d. remission

11. Identification of target behaviors is an important step in designing
    a. a desensitization hierarchy
    b. activating stimuli
    c. token economies
    d. encounter groups

12. A person who wants to lose weight looks at a dessert and visualizes maggots crawling all over it. The person is obviously using
    a. systematic adaptation
    b. covert sensitization
    c. stress inoculation
    d. systematic desensitization

13. Which of the following is NOT a humanistic therapy?
    a. client-centered
    b. Gestalt
    c. existential
    d. cognitive

14. Not many emergency room doctors drive without using their seatbelts. This observation helps explain the effectiveness of
    a. systematic desensitization
    b. aversion therapy
    c. covert reinforcement
    d. the mirror technique

15. Telephone counselors have little chance of using which element of effective psychotherapy?
    a. empathy
    b. nondirective reflection
    c. the therapeutic alliance
    d. accepting the person's frame of reference

16. Which of the following is a self-management technique?
    a. thought stopping
    b. vicarious reality exposure
    c. REBT
    d. EMDR

17. A good example of a nondirective insight therapy is _____ therapy.
    a. client-centered
    b. Gestalt
    c. psychoanalytic
    d. brief psychodynamic

18. Which statement about psychotherapy is true?
    a. Most therapists are equally successful.
    b. Most techniques are equally successful.
    c. Therapists and clients need not agree about the goals of therapy.
    d. Effective therapists instruct their clients not to discuss their therapy with anyone else.

19. Analysis of resistances and transferences is a standard feature of
    a. client-centered therapy
    b. Gestalt therapy
    c. REBT
    d. psychoanalysis

20. Both classical and operant conditioning are the basis for
    a. desensitization
    b. token economies
    c. behavior therapy
    d. aversion therapy

21. Rational-emotive behavior therapy is best described as
    a. insight, nondirective, individual
    b. insight, supportive, individual
    c. action, supportive, group
    d. action, directive, individual

22. Deep lesioning is a form of
    a. ECT
    b. psychosurgery
    c. pharmacotherapy
    d. PET

23. Identifying and removing rewards is a behavioral technique designed to bring about
    a. operant shaping
    b. extinction
    c. respondent aversion
    d. token inhibition

24. Culturally skilled therapists must be aware of their own cultural backgrounds, as well as
    a. the percentage of ethnic populations in the community
    b. that of their clients
    c. the importance of maintaining confidentiality
    d. the life goals of minorities

25. A behavioral therapist would treat acrophobia with
    a. desensitization
    b. aversion therapy
    c. covert sensitization
    d. cybertherapy

26. Which technique most closely relates to the idea of nondirective therapy?
    a. confrontation
    b. dream analysis
    c. role reversal
    d. reflection

27. Fifty percent of psychotherapy patients say they feel better after the first _____ sessions.
    a. 4
    b. 8
    c. 12
    d. 20

28. Overgeneralization is a thinking error that contributes to
    a. depression
    b. somatization
    c. phobias
    d. emotional reprocessing

29. Death, freedom, and meaning are special concerns of
    a. REBT
    b. cognitive therapy
    c. existential therapy
    d. psychodrama

30. An intense awareness of present experience and breaking through emotional impasses is the heart of
    a. action therapy
    b. Gestalt therapy
    c. time-limited therapy
    d. REBT

31. The ABCs of REBT stand for
    a. anticipation, behavior, conduct
    b. action, behavior, conflict
    c. activating experience, belief, consequence
    d. anticipation, belief, congruent experience

32. Which of the following in NOT a "distance therapy"?
    a. REBT
    b. telephone therapy
    c. cybertherapy
    d. telehealth

33. Virtual reality exposure is a type of
    a. psychodrama
    b. ECT therapy
    c. cognitive therapy
    d. desensitization

34. ECT is most often used to treat
    a. psychosis
    b. anxiety
    c. hysteria
    d. depression

35. Which of the following is most often associated with community mental health programs?
    a. pharmacotherapy
    b. covert reinforcement
    c. crisis intervention
    d. REBT

36. Which of the following method(s) effectively treats obsessive-compulsive disorder?
    a. behavioral
    b. cognitive-behavioral
    c. pharmacology
    d. all of the preceding

37. Which therapy's main purpose is to enhance people's personal strengths rather than try to fix their weakness?
    a. supportive
    b. positive
    c. insight
    d. directive

38. An element of positive mental health that therapists seek to promote is
    a. dependency on therapist
    b. a sense of identity
    c. personal autonomy and independence
    d. both B and C

39. Which theory relies on dream analysis to uncover the unconscious roots of neurosis?
    a. existential
    b. psychoanalytic
    c. client-centered
    d. telehealth

40. _____ has been one of the most successful behavioral therapies for reducing fears, anxieties, and psychological pains.
    a. Vicarious desensitization
    b. Virtual reality exposure
    c. Eye-movement desensitization
    d. Desensitization

41. Research suggests that, as a solution to handling people with mental illness, mental hospitals in our society are being replaced by
    a. a full-time live-in nurse
    b. placing them in jail
    c. medicating the mentally ill until they reach 65 years old
    d. allowing the mentally ill to take care of themselves

42. "There is always a perfect solution to human problems and it is awful if this solution is not found" is a typical _____ statement.
    a. irrational belief
    b. self-awareness
    c. health-promoting
    d. response-contingent

43. Experts predict that, in the near future, traditional forms of psychotherapy will be replaced by short-term, solution-focused, telephone, and self-help group therapy. This is a reflection of
    a. the lack of time available in people's busy life to seek mental health services
    b. fewer people needing mental health services
    c. societal pressures to reduce costs in mental health services
    d. people being afraid to reveal their mental illness

LANGUAGE DEVELOPMENT – Therapies

Word roots

Therapeia in Greek means "treatment" and is derived from another Greek word, *therapeuein* (to attend, nurse, or administer treatment to). Two important terms in this chapter derive from this root: therapy and psychotherapy.

How do psychotherapies differ? How did psychotherapy originate?

Preview: Cold Terror on a Warm Afternoon (p. 570)

> (570) ***come to grips***: understand and accept

> (570) ***alleviate***: reduce; lessen

Psychotherapy—Getting Better by the Hour (pp. 570-571)

> (571) ***"major overhaul"***: complete repair

Origins of Therapy—Bored Skulls and Hysteria on the Couch (pp. 571-572)

> (571) ***witchcraft***: use of sorcery or magic by a person (a witch) believed to have such power

> (571) ***wizards***: persons believed to be skilled in magic

> (572) ***squalid***: dirty; filthy

> (572) ***psychoanalysis is the "granddaddy" of more modern psychotherapies***: psychoanalysis is the first and oldest form of psychotherapy from which others are descended

Is Freudian psychoanalysis still used?

Psychoanalysis—Expedition Into the Unconscious (p. 572-574)

> (573) ***impotence***: inability to perform sexually

What are the major humanistic therapies?

Humanistic Therapies—Restoring Human Potential (pp. 574-576)

(574) *atmosphere of growth*: conditions that will allow the patient to improve

(575) *futile*: hopeless

(575) *dire*: desperate; terrible

(575) *brush with death*: a dangerous situation that could have been fatal

(576) *stop intellectualizing*: stop analyzing the situation

Therapy at a Distance—Psych Jockeys and Cybertherapy (pp. 576-577)

(576) *psych jockeys*: radio psychologists; because music announcers on the radio are called "disc jockeys," Coon calls radio psychologists "psych jockeys"

(576) *cybertherapy*: psychology via computer

(576) *videoconferencing*: communication through a two-way set-up that involves video (through the use of television or computer monitors), audio (through speakerphones or computer speakers), and microphones

(576) *on-line*: accessing and using the Internet

(576) *legitimate*: certified

(577) *anonymous*: unidentified

(577) *intercepted*: read or found out by others

(577) *cybershrinks*: online psychologists or counselors

(577) *link*: connection

What is behavior therapy? How is behavior therapy used to treat phobias, fears, and anxieties?

Behavior Therapy—Healing by Learning (pp. 578-582)

(578) *feelers*: antennas

(578) *covert*: hidden

(578) *aversion*: intense dislike

(579) *interminable*: never ending or continuous

(580) *vicarious*: to experience something through another person

(580) *claustrophobia*: fear of small, closed-in spaces, such as closets

(581) *flashbacks*: remembered images of events from the past

(581) *wishful thinking*: wanting something so much that one interprets reality in such a way as to support one's desires

(581) **berserk**: crazy; derives from "berserker," a particularly fierce type of early Norse warrior

What role does reinforcement play in behavior therapy?

Operant Therapies—All the World Is a Skinner Box (pp. 582-584)

(582) **slot machine**: a device in a gambling casino into which a patron puts money and hopes to win a larger amount of money

(582) **industrial settings**: factories

(583) **subsided**: lessened

(583) **sheepishly**: in an embarrassed or timid manner

(583) **mute**: not speaking

(583) **incentive**: motivating factors

Can therapy change thoughts and emotions?

Cognitive Therapy—Think Positive! (pp. 584-586)

(584) **self-defeating**: in opposition to one's self

(585) **I must be a total zero**: I must be worthless

(585) **dumped**: abruptly broke a relationship with

(585) **easy as A-B-C**: easy as learning the alphabet

(586) **self-talk**: what people tell themselves

Can psychotherapy be done with groups of people?

Group Therapy—People Who Need People (pp. 586-588)

(586) **role-play**: pretend to be another

(586) **reenacts**: acts out something that occurred previously

(587) **distorted**: unclear; misinterpreted

(587) **human potential**: belief that humans have the potential to be fully alive and functioning at the highest level possible

What can various therapies have in common?

Psychotherapy—An Overview (pp. 588-592)

  (588) *tricky*: difficult

  (589) *rapport*: a good relationship

  (589) *sanctuary*: a safe place

  (590) *eclectic*: a combination of very different styles

  (590) *ambiguity*: possibility of several interpretations

  (590) *distilled*: extracted or taken from

  (591) *catharsis*: getting rid of one's problems through the process of purging by releasing emotions

  (591) *down about school*: unmotivated or depressed about school

  (591) *hassling*: annoying, bothering

  (592) *has it in for me*: is against me; doesn't like me

  (592) *gossip*: to share personal information with someone about other people

How do psychiatrists treat psychological disorders?

Medical Therapies—Psychiatric Care (pp. 592-596)

  (593) *bad spot*: difficult situation

  (594) *"vegetable"*: a person whose brain only functions to the degree of keeping the body alive; he/she is not conscious and no longer has higher brain functions

  (594) *stupor*: a state of limited consciousness

  (595) *joined the ranks of the homeless*: become homeless

  (595) *warehouses*: huge buildings that store merchandise not needed for immediate use; Coon is suggesting that mental hospitals were once used as a place to store patients that society did not want around

  (595) *wavering*: unreliable

  (595) *been there*: have had similar experiences

How are behavioral principles applied to everyday problems? How could a person find professional help?

Psychology in Action: Self-Management and Finding Professional Help (pp. 596-601)

  (596) *snake oil*: in the past, traveling salesmen sold "tonics," or fake medicine, supposedly made from a variety of ingredients (such as snake oil) to cure illnesses

(597) *curb*: to control or restrain

(597) *grossed out*: disgusted

(597) *maggots*: fly larvae

(597) *put yourself down*: criticize yourself harshly

(597) *with conviction*: with force

(598) *vividly*: clearly

(599) *dismayed*: upset; alarmed

(599) *outreach clinics*: clinics usually set up in neighborhoods to make it easier for people to access health care

(600) *integrity*: honesty

(600) *terminate*: end; stop

Solutions

RECITE AND REVIEW

How do psychotherapies differ? How did psychotherapy originate?

1. positive; behavior
2. Insight
3. guidance; guide
4. change
5. personal; positive
6. time

Origins of Therapy—Bored Skulls and Hysteria on the Couch: Pages 571-572

1. superstition
2. skull
3. exorcism
4. ergot; poisoning
5. mental hospital

Is Freudian psychoanalysis still used?

1. psychotherapy
2. physical
3. unconscious; unconscious
4. free; dream
5. desires; dream; latent
6. Brief
7. spontaneous

What are the major humanistic therapies?

1. Humanistic
2. person; growth
3. positive; empathy
4. choices
5. will; choices; meaning
6. wholes
7. awareness

Therapy at a Distance—Psych Jockeys and Cybertherapy: Pages 576-577

1. educating; therapy
2. Internet
3. therapy; audio-video

What is behavior therapy? How is behavior therapy used to treat phobias, fears, and anxieties?

1. learning
2. learning; associated
3. pain
4. stimuli
5. adaptation
6. systematic
7. relaxation
8. imagining
9. recognize; relax
10. models
11. reality; fear
12. memories; stress

What role does reinforcement play in behavior therapy?

1. control; time
2. reinforcers
3. responses
4. removing
5. reinforcers; maintaining
6. immediate; behaviors
7. tokens
8. approval

Can therapy change thoughts and emotions?

1. thinking
2. selective; thinking
3. skills
4. beliefs
5. irrational; completely; depend

Can psychotherapy be done with groups of people?

1. individual
2. role; role
3. unit ; family
4. psychotherapies
5. trainings
6. therapy

What do various therapies have in common?

1. 50; 26
2. emotional; setting
3. problems
4. behaviors
5. solution; self; telephone
6. counseling
7. advice
8. silences
9. open
10. traditional

How do psychiatrists treat psychological disorders?

1. somatic; drugs; brain
2. minor; hallucinations; mood
3. risks
4. psychosurgery; lost
5. lesioning; destroyed
6. Mental or Psychiatric
7. partial
8. houses; independent
9. hospitalization
10. crisis

How are behavioral principles applied to everyday problems? How could a person find professional help?

1. images
2. punishment
3. responses
4. relaxation
5. referral
6. cost (or fees)
7. groups

CONNECTIONS

How do psychotherapies differ? How did psychotherapy originate? Is Freudian psychoanalysis still used? Pages 570-574

1. H.
2. I.
3. G.
4. A.
5. E.
6. J.
7. C.
8. F.
9. B.
10. D.

What are the major humanistic therapies? Pages 574-577

1. E.
2. C.
3. H.
4. A.
5. F.
6. D.
7. B.
8. G.

What is behavior therapy? How is behavior therapy used to treat phobias, fears, and anxieties? Pages 578-582

1. D.	4. C.	7. E.
2. A.	5. F.	
3. G.	6. B.	

What role does reinforcement play in behavior therapy? Can therapy change thoughts and emotions? Pages 582-586

1. D.	3. A.	5. B.
2. C.	4. E.	

Can psychotherapy be done with groups of people? What do various therapies have in common? How do psychiatrists treat psychological disorders? Pages 586-596

1. H.	5. A.	9. D.
2. F.	6. I.	10. E.
3. B.	7. C.	
4. J.	8. G.	

How are behavioral principles applied to everyday problems? How could a person find professional help? Pages 596-601

1. A.	3. E.	5. B.
2. D.	4. C.	

CHECK YOUR MEMORY

How do psychotherapies differ? How did psychotherapy originate? Pages 570-572

1. F	5. T	9. F
2. T	6. F	10. T
3. T	7. T	
4. T	8. F	

Is Freudian psychoanalysis still used? Pages 572-574

1. F	4. T	7. F
2. F	5. F	
3. T	6. T	

What are the major humanistic therapies? Pages 574-577

1.	F	5.	T	9.	F
2.	F	6.	F	10.	T
3.	T	7.	F	11.	T
4.	T	8.	T	12.	F

What is behavior therapy? How is behavior therapy used to treat phobias, fears, and anxieties? Pages 578-582

1.	T	7.	T	13.	T
2.	F	8.	F	14.	F
3.	T	9.	T		
4.	F	10.	F		
5.	T	11.	T		
6.	T	12.	T		

What role does reinforcement play in behavior therapy? Pages 582-584

1.	F	4.	T	7.	T
2.	T	5.	F		
3.	F	6.	T		

Can therapy change thoughts and emotions? Pages 584-586

1.	T	4.	F	7.	T
2.	T	5.	F		
3.	T	6.	T		

Can psychotherapy be done with groups of people? Pages 586-588

1.	F	3.	T	5.	T
2.	F	4.	F		

What do various therapies have in common? Pages 588-592

1.	T	5.	F	9.	F
2.	T	6.	T	10.	F
3.	T	7.	F		
4.	T	8.	T		

How do psychiatrists treat psychological disorders? Pages 592-596

1.	F	6.	T	11.	T
2.	T	7.	F	12.	F
3.	T	8.	F	13.	T
4.	F	9.	T	14.	F
5.	T	10.	F		

How are behavioral principles applied to everyday problems? How could a person find professional help? Pages 596-601

1. F		4. T		7. T	
2. F		5. T		8. T	
3. F		6. F		9. F	

FINAL SURVEY AND REVIEW

How do psychotherapies differ? How did psychotherapy originate?

1. Psychotherapy; personality
2. Action
3. Directive; Nondirective
4. Supportive
5. Positive; "fix"
6. individually; and

Origins of Therapy—Bored Skulls and Hysteria on the Couch: Pages 571-572

1. Primitive
2. Trepanning
3. Demonology
4. ergotism; fungus
5. Pinel

Is Freudian psychoanalysis still used?

1. Freud's; psychoanalysis
2. hysteria
3. repressed
4. unconscious; dream
5. association; resistance
6. psychodynamic; psychoanalytic
7. remissions

What are the major humanistic therapies?

1. potentials
2. Rogers'; nondirective
3. unconditional; reflection
4. Existential
5. confrontation; encounter
6. emotional; blocks
7. Gestalt

Therapy at a Distance—Psych Jockeys and Cybertherapy: Pages 576-577

1. Media
2. cybertherapists
3. telehealth; videoconferencing

What is behavior therapy? How is behavior therapy used to treat phobias, fears, and anxieties?

1. Behavior; modification
2. Classical; reflex
3. aversion
4. response-contingent
5. inhibition
6. desensitization
7. hierarchy; hierarchy
8. fear; hierarchy
9. tension; muscles
10. vicariously
11. virtual; exposure
12. eye-movement

What role does reinforcement play in behavior therapy?

1. operant; extinction ; punishment
2. Nonreward
3. extinction
4. setting; reinforced
5. reinforcers; behaviors
6. tokens; target
7. token; economy
8. social

Can therapy change thoughts and emotions?

1. Cognitive
2. Beck's; overgeneralization
3. coping
4. rational-emotive behavior
5. beliefs; worthless; depend

Can psychotherapy be done with groups of people?

1. Group; groups
2. psychodrama; reversals
3. family; family
4. encounter
5. awareness
6. placebo

What do various therapies have in common?

1. eight; 75
2. rapport; protected
3. catharsis
4. perspective
5. Psychotherapy; short; Internet ; master's
6. actively; clarify
7. feelings
8. perspective; reflect
9. confidentiality
10. cultural

How do psychiatrists treat psychological disorders?

1. pharmacotherapy; electroconvulsive
2. antipsychotics; antidepressants
3. benefits
4. Electroconvulsive; effectiveness
5. deep lesioning
6. Psychiatric; disorders
7. deinstitutionalization
8. Half-way
9. Community; mental
10. prevention; intervention

How are behavioral principles applied to everyday problems? How could a person find professional help?

1. covert
2. Thought stopping
3. reinforcement
4. Desensitization
5. competent
6. personal; characteristics
7. Self-help; problems

MASTERY TEST

How are behavioral principles applied to everyday problems? How could a person find professional help?

1. B, p. 573
2. D, p. 579
3. A, pp. 586-587
4. C, pp. 571-572
5. D, p. 574
6. C, pp. 587-588
7. A, p. 571
8. C, p. 593
9. B, p. 591
10. A, pp. 572-573
11. C, p. 583
12. B, p. 597

13. D, pp. 574-575

14. B, p. 578

15. C, pp. 576; 589

16. A, p. 597

17. A, p. 574

18. B, p. 600

19. D, p. 573

20. C, p. 578

21. D, pp. 570; 585-586

22. B, p. 594

23. B, p. 582

24. B, p. 590

25. A, p. 579

26. D, pp. 570; 574-575

27. B, p. 588

28. A, p. 584

29. C, p. 575

30. B, p. 576

31. C, p. 585

32. A, pp. 576-577

33. D, p. 580

34. D, p. 593

35. C, p. 595

36. D, p. 588

37. B, p. 571

38. D, p. 571

39. B, pp. 572-573

40. D, pp. 580-581

41. B, p. 595

42. A, p. 585

43. C, p. 590

Social Behavior

Chapter Overview

Social psychology is the study of individual behavior in social situations. Social roles, status, group structure, norms, and group cohesiveness influence interpersonal behavior. Group cohesiveness is strong for in-group members who tend to attribute positive traits to members of the group. Negative qualities tend to be attributed to out-group members.

Attribution theory summarizes how we make inferences about behavior. The fundamental attributional error is to ascribe the actions of others to internal causes. Because of an actor-observer bias, we tend to attribute our own behavior to external causes.

The need to affiliate is related to needs for approval, support, friendship, information, and desires to reduce anxiety or uncertainty. Social comparison theory holds that we affiliate to evaluate our actions, feelings, and abilities. Interpersonal attraction is increased by physical proximity, frequent contact, physical attractiveness, competence, and similarity. Self-disclosure, which follows a reciprocity norm, occurs more when two people like one another. According to social exchange theory, we tend to maintain relationships that are profitable. Romantic love can be distinguished from liking by the use of attitude scales. Adult love relationships tend to mirror patterns of emotional attachment observed in infancy and early childhood. Evolutionary psychology attributes human mating patterns to the reproductive challenges faced by men and women since the dawn of time.

Social influence refers to alterations in behavior brought about by the behavior of others. Examples are conformity, groupthink, and obedience to authority. Social influence is also related to five types of social power: reward power, coercive power, legitimate power, referent power, and expert power. Compliance with direct requests is another means by which behavior is influenced. Three types of compliance techniques are foot-in-the-door, door-in-the-face, and low-ball. Knowing that salespeople use these compliance techniques, customers could conduct a background search on the product and compare prices to other stores before making a commitment.

Self-assertion, as opposed to aggression, involves clearly stating one's wants and needs to others. It is a method to reduce the pressure to conform, obey, and comply with others' suggestions. Learning to be assertive is accomplished by role-playing, rehearsing assertive actions, overlearning, and use of specific techniques, such as the "broken record."

Learning Objectives

1. Define social *psychology*.

2. Define the following terms and include a description of Zimbardo's prison experiment and an explanation of how norms are formed using the idea of the autokinetic effect:

   a. culture

   b. social roles

   c. ascribed role

   d. achieved role

   e. role conflict

   f. group structure

   g. group cohesiveness

   h. status

   i. norm

3. Define *personal space* and *proxemics*; and describe the four basic interpersonal zones and the nature of the interactions that occur in each.

4. Define *attribution;* state the difference between external and internal causes; explain how the consistency and distinctiveness of a person's behavior affects the attributions others make about the person; and discuss six other factors affecting attribution.

5. Explain how self-handicapping protects a person who has a fragile self-image.

6. Explain what the fundamental attribution error is. Include the concept of the actor-observer bias in making attributions.

7. State the needs that appear to be satisfied by affiliation; and describe the research indicating humans have a need to affiliate.

8. Describe social comparison theory.

9. List and describe the factors that affect interpersonal attraction. Include a description of homogamy.

10. Explain self-disclosure; discuss the effects of varying degrees of disclosure on interpersonal relationships; and explain the difference in gendered friendships.

11. Describe the social exchange theory as it relates to interpersonal relationships.

12. Describe Rubin's studies of romantic love; and discuss the differences between loving and liking and between male and female friendships (including the term *mutual absorption* and the three different love/attachment styles).

13. Define the term *evolutionary psychology;* and describe how it explains the different mating preferences of males and females.

14. State the meaning of *social influence* and give examples of it; describe Asch's experiment on conformity; explain how groupthink may contribute to poor decision-making and list ways to prevent it; and describe how group sanctions and unanimity affect conformity.

15. List and describe the five sources of social power.

16. Describe Milgram's study of obedience; and identify the factors which affect the degree of obedience.

17. Explain how compliance differs from simple conformity; describe the following methods of gaining compliance: foot-in-the-door, door-in-the-face, and low-ball technique; and discuss the research that deals with passive compliance and how it applies to everyday behavior.

The following objective is related to the material in the "Psychology in Action" section of your text.

1. Describe assertiveness training; describe the concept of self-assertion and contrast it with aggression; and explain how a person can learn to be more assertive using rehearsal, role-playing, overlearning, and the broken record technique.

RECITE AND REVIEW

How does group membership affect individual behavior?

Humans in a Social Context—People, People, Everywhere: Pages 605-608

1. Social psychology studies how individuals behave, think, and feel in _____ situations.

2. Culture provides a broad social context for our behavior. One's position in _____ defines a variety of roles to be played.

3. _____ , which may be achieved or ascribed, are particular behavior patterns associated with social positions.

4. When two or more _____ roles are held, role conflict may occur.

5. The Stanford _____ experiment showed that destructive roles may override individual motives for behavior.

6. Positions within _____ typically carry higher or lower levels of status. High status is associated with special privileges and respect.

7. Two dimensions of a group are group structure (network of _____ , communication pathways, and power) and group cohesiveness (members' desire to _____ in the group). Group cohesion is strong for _____ members.

8. Members of the _____ identify themselves based on a combination of dimensions such as nationality, _____ , age, _____ , income, etc. People tend to attribute _____ traits to members of their in-group and negative traits to members of the _____ .

9. Norms are _____ of conduct enforced (formally or informally) by _____ .

10. The autokinetic effect (the illusion of _____ in a stationary light in a darkened room) has been used to demonstrate that norms rapidly form even in _____ groups.

What unspoken rules govern the use of personal space?

Personal Space—Invisible Boundaries: Pages 608-609

1. The study of _____ is called proxemics.

2. Four basic spatial zones around each person's body are intimate distance (0-18 inches), _____ distance (1.5-4 feet), _____ distance (4-12 feet), and public distance (12 feet or more).

3. Norms for the use of personal space vary considerably in various _____ .

How do we perceive the motives of others, and the causes of our own behavior?

Social Perception—Behind the Mask: Pages 609-612

1. Attribution theory is concerned with how we make inferences about the _____ of behavior.

2. Behavior can be attributed to internal _____ or external _____ .

3. To infer _____ we take into account the _____ , the object of the action, and the setting in which the action occurs.

4. The _____ of behavior on different occasions and its distinctiveness (whether it occurs only in certain circumstances) affect the attributions we make.

5. Situational demands tend to cause us to discount _____ causes as explanations of someone's behavior.

6. Consensus in behavior (in which many people act alike) implies that their behavior has an _____ cause.

7. The fundamental attributional _____ is to ascribe the actions of others to _____ causes. This is part of the actor-observer bias, in which we ascribe the behavior of others to _____ causes, and our own behavior to _____ causes.

8. Self-handicapping involves arranging excuses for poor _____ as a way to protect your self-image or self-esteem.

Why do people affiliate?

The Need for Affiliation—Come Together: Pages 612-613

1. The need to affiliate is tied to needs for _____ , support, friendship, and _____ .

2. Additionally, research indicates that we sometimes affiliate to _____ anxiety and uncertainty.

3. Social comparison theory holds that we affiliate to _____ our actions, feelings, and abilities.

4. Social _____ are also made for purposes of self-protection and self-enhancement.

5. Downward _____ are sometimes used to make us feel better when faced with a threat. Upward _____ may be used for self-improvement.

What factors influence interpersonal attraction?

Interpersonal Attraction—Social Magnetism? Pages 613-615

1. Interpersonal attraction is increased by physical proximity (_____) and frequent _____ .

2. Initial acquaintance and _____ are influenced by physical attractiveness (beauty), competence (high ability), and _____ (being alike).

3. A large degree of _____ on many dimensions is characteristic of _____ selection, a pattern called homogamy.

4. Self-disclosure (_____ oneself to others) occurs to a greater degree if two people like one another.

5. Self-disclosure follows a reciprocity _____ : Low levels of self-disclosure are met with low levels in return, whereas moderate self-disclosure elicits more personal replies.

6. Overdisclosure tends to inhibit _____ by others.

7. According to social exchange theory, we tend to maintain relationships that are profitable; that is, those for which perceived _____ exceed perceived _____ .

Loving and Liking—Dating, Rating, Mating: Pages 616-618

1. Romantic love can be distinguished from liking by the use of attitude scales. Dating couples _____ and _____ their partners but only _____ their friends.

2. Romantic love is also associated with greater _____ absorption between people.

3. Adult _____ relationships tend to mirror patterns of emotional attachment observed in infancy and early childhood.

4. _____ , avoidant, and ambivalent patterns can be defined on the basis of how a person approaches romantic and affectionate relationships with others.

5. Evolutionary psychology attributes human _____ patterns to the differing reproductive challenges faced by men and women since the dawn of time.

6. David Buss's study on human mating patterns showed that men prefer _____ and physically attractive partners, and women prefer _____ partners who are industrious, high in status, and _____ successful.

What have social psychologists learned about conformity, social power, obedience, and compliance?

Social Influence—Follow the Leader: Pages 619-621

1. Social influence refers to alterations in _____ brought about by the behavior of _____ .

2. Conformity to group pressure is a familiar example of social influence. Virtually everyone _____ to a variety of broad social and cultural _____ .

3. Conformity pressures also exist within small _____ . The famous Asch experiments demonstrated that various _____ sanctions encourage conformity.

4. Groupthink refers to compulsive conformity in group _____ . Victims of groupthink seek to maintain each other's approval, even at the cost of critical thinking.

Social Power—Who Can Do What to Whom? Obedience—Would You Electrocute a Stranger? Pages 621-624

1. Social influence is also related to five types of _____ reward power, coercive power, legitimate power, referent power, and expert power.

2. Obedience to _____ has been investigated in a variety of experiments, particularly those by Stanley Milgram.

3. _____ in Milgram's studies decreased when the victim was in the same room, when the victim and subject were face to face, when the authority figure was absent, and when others refused to obey.

Compliance—A Foot in the Door: Pages 624-626

1. Compliance with direct _____ by a person who has little or no social _____ is another means by which behavior is influenced.

2. Three strategies for inducing compliance are the _____ -in-the-door technique, the door-in-the- _____ approach, and the low-ball technique.

3. To _____ the odds with salespeople, one should know a rough _____ of the product, get the negotiated price in _____ , and compare the negotiated price with other stores to get the best deal.

4. Recent research suggests that in addition to excessive obedience to _____ , many people show a surprising passive compliance to unreasonable _____ .

How does self-assertion differ from aggression?

Psychology in Action: Assertiveness Training—Standing Up for Your Rights: Pages 627-628

1. Self-assertion involves clearly stating one's _____ and _____ to others.

2. Aggression expresses one's feelings and desires, but it _____ others.

3. Non-assertive behavior is self- _____ and inhibited.

4. Learning to be _____ is accomplished by role-playing and rehearsing assertive actions.

5. Self-assertion is also aided by overlearning (practice that _____ after initial mastery of a skill) and use of specific techniques, such as the "broken record" (_____ a request until it is acknowledged).

CONNECTIONS

How does group membership affect individual behavior? Pages 605-608

1. _____ culture
2. _____ ascribed role
3. _____ achieved role
4. _____ status
5. _____ cohesiveness
6. _____ norm
7. _____ autokinetic

a. privilege and importance
b. rule or standard
c. way of life
d. self-moving
e. assigned role
f. degree of attraction
g. voluntary role

What unspoken rules govern the use of personal space? How do we perceive the motives of others, and the causes of our own behavior? Pages 608-612

1. _____ intimate distance	a. impairing performance
2. _____ personal distance	b. social inference
3. _____ social distance	c. 0-18 inches
4. _____ public distance	d. 12 feet plus
5. _____ attribution	e. 1.5-4 feet
6. _____ fundamental attribution error	f. 4-12 feet
7. _____ self-handicapping	g. overestimate internal causes

Why do people affiliate? What factors influence interpersonal attraction? Pages 612-618

1. _____ proximity	a. relating self to others
2. _____ halo effect	b. generalized impression
3. _____ competency	c. rewards minus costs
4. _____ reciprocity	d. return in kind
5. _____ need to affiliate	e. a person's proficiency
6. _____ social comparison	f. affinity to others
7. _____ interpersonal attraction	g. desire to associate
8. _____ social exchange	h. nearness

What have social psychologists learned about conformity, social power, obedience, and compliance? How does self-assertion differ from aggression? Pages 619-628

1. _____ foot-in-the-door	a. rewards and punishments
2. _____ assertiveness	b. matching behavior
3. _____ conformity	c. self-assertion technique
4. _____ group sanctions	d. salesperson's tactic
5. _____ obedience	e. honest expression
6. _____ broken record	f. following authority
7. _____ compliance	g. yielding to requests

CHECK YOUR MEMORY

How does group membership affect individual behavior? Pages 605-608

1. The average number of first-name acquaintance links needed to connect two widely separated strangers is about 70 people.

   TRUE or FALSE

2. Language and marriage customs are elements of culture.

   TRUE or FALSE

3. *Son*, *husband*, and *teacher* are achieved roles.

   TRUE or FALSE

4. The Stanford prison experiment investigated the impact of the roles "prisoner" and "guard."

   TRUE or FALSE

5. Group cohesion refers to the dimensions that define a group such as ethnicity, age, or religion.

   TRUE or FALSE

6. A group could have a high degree of structure but low cohesiveness.

   TRUE or FALSE

7. "Us and them" refers to members of the in-group perceiving themselves as one unit and everyone else as the out-group.

   TRUE or FALSE

8. Persons of higher status are more likely to touch persons of lower status than the reverse.

   TRUE or FALSE

9. Women are more likely to touch men than men are to touch women.

   TRUE or FALSE

10. The more trash that is visible in public places, the more likely people are to litter.

    TRUE or FALSE

11. An autokinetic light appears to move about the same distance for everyone who observes it.

    TRUE or FALSE

What unspoken rules govern the use of personal space? Pages 608-609

1. Most people show signs of discomfort when someone else enters their personal space without permission.

    TRUE or FALSE

2. The Dutch sit closer together when talking than the English do.

    TRUE or FALSE

3. Social distance basically keeps people within arm's reach.

    TRUE or FALSE

4. Formal interactions tend to take place in the 4 to 12 foot range.

    TRUE or FALSE

How do we perceive the motives of others, and the causes of our own behavior? Pages 609-612

1. The deliberateness of another person's behavior affects the attributions we make about it.

    TRUE or FALSE

2. If someone always salts her food before eating, it implies that her behavior has an external cause.

    TRUE or FALSE

3. Situational demands lead us to discount claims that a person's behavior is externally caused.

    TRUE or FALSE

4. A strong consensus in the behavior of many people implies that their behavior is externally caused.

    TRUE or FALSE

5. Getting drunk is a common form of self-handicapping.

    TRUE or FALSE

6. Attributing the actions of others to external causes is the most common attributional error.

    TRUE or FALSE

7. Good performances by women are more often attributed to luck than skill.

    TRUE or FALSE

Why do people affiliate? Pages 612-613

1. The need to affiliate is a basic human characteristic.
    TRUE or FALSE

2. People who are frightened prefer to be with others who are in similar circumstances.
    TRUE or FALSE

3. Social comparisons are used to confirm objective evaluations and measurements.
    TRUE or FALSE

4. Useful social comparisons are usually made with persons similar to ourselves.
    TRUE or FALSE

5. Some social comparisons are made for self-protection.
    TRUE or FALSE

6. Downward social comparisons are typically made for self-improvement.
    TRUE or FALSE

What factors influence interpersonal attraction? Pages 613-618

1. Interpersonal attraction to someone takes weeks to develop.
    TRUE or FALSE

2. Nearness has a powerful impact on forming friendships.
    TRUE or FALSE

3. Physical proximity leads us to think of people as competent, and therefore worth knowing.
    TRUE or FALSE

4. The halo effect is the tendency to generalize a positive or negative first impression to other personal characteristics.
    TRUE or FALSE

5. Physical attractiveness is closely associated with intelligence, talents, and abilities.
    TRUE or FALSE

6. Physical attractiveness has more influence on women's fates than men's.
    TRUE or FALSE

7. Homogamy, marrying someone who is like oneself, does not apply to unmarried couples.
    TRUE or FALSE

8. The risk of divorce is higher than average for couples who have large differences in age and education.

   TRUE or FALSE

9. In choosing mates, women rank physical attractiveness as the most important feature.

   TRUE or FALSE

10. Self-disclosure is a major step toward friendship.

    TRUE or FALSE

11. Overdisclosure tends to elicit maximum self-disclosure from others.

    TRUE or FALSE

12. Self-disclosure through an Internet chat room can lead to genuine, face-to-face friendship.

    TRUE or FALSE

13. Male friendships tend to be activity-based; women's friendships tend to be based on shared feelings and confidences.

    TRUE or FALSE

14. The personal standard used to judge the acceptability of a social exchange is called the comparison level.

    TRUE or FALSE

15. The statement, "I find it easy to ignore _____'s faults" is an item on the Liking Scale.

    TRUE or FALSE

16. People with an avoidant attachment style tend to form relationships that are marked by mixed emotions.

    TRUE or FALSE

17. Where their mates are concerned, men tend to be more jealous over a loss of emotional commitment than they are over sexual infidelities.

    TRUE or FALSE

18. Although women tend to give "polite" answers about men's infidelity, privately, they are just as angry as men are about infidelity.

    TRUE or FALSE

What have social psychologists learned about conformity, social power, obedience, and compliance? Pages 619-626

1. Conformity situations occur when a person becomes aware of differences between his or her own behavior and that of a group.

   TRUE or FALSE

2. Most subjects in the Asch conformity experiments suspected that they were being deceived in some way.
   TRUE or FALSE

3. Seventy-five percent of Asch's subjects yielded to the group at least once.
   TRUE or FALSE

4. People who are anxious are more likely to conform to group pressure.
   TRUE or FALSE

5. Groupthink is more likely to occur when people emphasize the task at hand, rather than the bonds between group members.
   TRUE or FALSE

6. Rejection, ridicule, and disapproval are group norms that tend to enforce conformity.
   TRUE or FALSE

7. A unanimous majority of 3 is more powerful than a majority of 8 with 1 person dissenting.
   TRUE or FALSE

8. If you identify with a particular person, that person has referent power with respect to your behavior.
   TRUE or FALSE

9. Milgram's famous shock experiment was done to study compliance and conformity.
   TRUE or FALSE

10. Over half of Milgram's "teachers" went all the way to the maximum shock level.
    TRUE or FALSE

11. Being face-to-face with the "learner" had no effect on the number of subjects who obeyed in the Milgram experiments.
    TRUE or FALSE

12. People are less likely to obey an unjust authority if they have seen others disobey.
    TRUE or FALSE

13. The foot-in-the-door effect is a way to gain compliance from another person.
    TRUE or FALSE

14. The low-ball technique involves changing the terms that a person has agreed to, so that they are less desirable from the person's point of view.
    TRUE or FALSE

15. Using the door-in-the-face strategy is an effective way to even the odds with salespeople for using the low-ball technique.
    TRUE or FALSE

How does self-assertion differ from aggression? Pages 627-628

1. Many people have difficulty asserting themselves because they have learned to be obedient and "good."
    TRUE or FALSE

2. Self-assertion involves the rights to request, reject, and retaliate.
    TRUE or FALSE

3. Aggression does not take into account the rights of others.
    TRUE or FALSE

4. Overlearning tends to lead to aggressive responses.
    TRUE or FALSE

5. In order to be assertive, you should never admit that you were wrong.
    TRUE or FALSE

6. If someone insults you, an assertive response should include getting the person to accept responsibility for his or her aggression.
    TRUE or FALSE

FINAL SURVEY AND REVIEW

How does group membership affect individual behavior?

Humans in a Social Context—People, People, Everywhere: Pages 605-608

1. _____ _____ studies how individuals behave, think, and feel in social situations.

2. _____ provides a broad social context for our behavior. One's position in groups defines a variety of _____ to be played.

3. Social roles, which may be _____ or _____ , are particular behavior patterns associated with social positions.

4. When two or more contradictory roles are held, role _____ may occur.

5. The _____ prison experiment showed that destructive _____ may override individual motives for behavior.

6. Positions within groups typically carry higher or lower levels of _____ . _____ _____ is associated with special privileges and respect.

7. Two dimensions of a group are group _____ (network of roles, communication pathways, and power) and group _____ (members' desire to remain in the group). Group cohesion is strong for _____ members.

8. Members of the _____ identify themselves based on a combination of dimensions such as nationality, ethnicity, age, religion, income, etc. People tend to attribute _____ traits to members of their in-group and _____ traits to members of the out-group.

9. _____ are standards of conduct enforced (formally or informally) by groups.

10. The _____ effect (the illusion of movement in a _____ light in a darkened room) has been used to demonstrate that _____ rapidly form even in temporary groups.

What unspoken rules govern the use of personal space?

Personal Space—Invisible Boundaries: Pages 608-609

1. The study of personal space is called _____ .

2. Four basic spatial zones around each person's body are _____ distance (0-18 inches), personal distance (1.5-4 feet), social distance (4-12 feet), and _____ distance (12 feet or more).

3. _____ for the use of personal space vary considerably in various cultures.

How do we perceive the motives of others, and the causes of our own behavior?

Social Perception—Behind the Mask: Pages 609-612

1. _____ theory is concerned with how we make inferences about the causes of behavior.

2. Behavior can be attributed to _____ causes or _____ causes.

3. To infer causes we take into account the actor, the _____ of the action, and the _____ in which the action occurs.

4. The consistency of behavior on different occasions and its _____ (whether it occurs only in certain circumstances) affect the attributions we make.

5. _____ demands tend to cause us to _____ (downgrade) internal causes as explanations of someone's behavior.

6. _____ in behavior (in which many people act alike) implies that their behavior has an external cause.

7. The _____ _____ error is to ascribe the actions of others to internal causes. This is part of the _____ bias, in which we ascribe the behavior of others to internal causes, and our own behavior to external causes.

8. _____ involves arranging excuses for poor performance as a way to protect your self-image or self-esteem.

Why do people affiliate?

The Need for Affiliation—Come Together: Pages 612-613

1. The _____ to _____ is tied to needs for approval, support, friendship, and information.

2. Additionally, research indicates that we sometimes affiliate to reduce _____ and uncertainty.

3. Social _____ theory holds that we affiliate to evaluate our actions, feelings, and abilities.

4. Social comparisons are also made for purposes of self- _____ and self-enhancement.

5. _____ comparisons are sometimes used to make us feel better when faced with a threat. _____ comparisons may be used for self-improvement.

What factors influence interpersonal attraction?

Interpersonal Attraction—Social Magnetism? Pages 613-615

1. Interpersonal attraction is increased by physical _____ (nearness) and frequent contact.

2. Initial acquaintance and attraction are influenced by _____ attractiveness (beauty), _____ (high ability), and similarity.

3. A large degree of similarity on many dimensions is characteristic of mate selection, a pattern called

   _____ .

4. _____ (revealing oneself to others) occurs to a greater degree if two people like one another.

5. Self-disclosure follows a _____ norm: Low levels of self-disclosure are met with low levels in return, whereas moderate self-disclosure elicits more personal replies.

6. _____ tends to inhibit self-disclosure by others.

7. According to social _____ theory, we tend to maintain relationships that are _____ ; that is, those for which perceived rewards exceed perceived costs.

Loving and Liking—Dating, Rating, Mating: Pages 616-618

1. Romantic love can be distinguished from liking by the use of _____ _____ . Dating couples like and love their partners but only like their friends.

2. Romantic love is also associated with greater mutual _____ between people.

3. Adult love relationships tend to mirror patterns of emotional _____ observed in infancy and early childhood.

4. Secure, _____ (noncommittal), and _____ (conflicted) patterns can be defined on the basis of how a person approaches romantic and affectionate relationships with others.

5. _____ psychology attributes human mating patterns to the differing _____ challenges faced by men and women since the dawn of time.

6. David Buss's study on human mating patterns showed that _____ prefer younger and physically attractive partners, and _____ prefer older partners who are industrious, high in status, and _____ successful.

What have social psychologists learned about conformity, social power, obedience, and compliance?

Social Influence—Follow the Leader: Pages 619-621

1. _____ refers to alterations in behavior brought about by the behavior of others.

2. _____ to group pressure is a familiar example of social influence. Virtually everyone conforms to a variety of broad social and _____ norms.

3. Conformity pressures also exist within small groups. The famous _____ experiments demonstrated that various group _____ encourage conformity.

4. _____ refers to compulsive conformity in group decision making. Its victims seek to maintain each other's approval, even at the cost of critical thinking.

Social Power—Who Can Do What to Whom? Obedience—Would You Electrocute a Stranger? Pages 621-624

1. Social influence is also related to five types of social power: _____ power, _____ power (based on an ability to punish), legitimate power, referent power, and expert power.

2. _____ to authority has been investigated in a variety of experiments, particularly those by Stanley _____ .

3. Obedience in his studies _____ when the victim was in the same room, when the victim and subject were face to face, when the _____ figure was absent, and when others refused to obey.

Compliance—A Foot in the Door: Pages 624-626

1. _____ with direct requests by a person who has little or no social power is another means by which behavior is influenced.

2. Three strategies for inducing compliance are the foot-in-the- _____ technique, the _____ -in-the-face approach, and the _____ technique.

3. To _____ the odds with salespeople, one should know a rough _____ of the product, get the negotiated price in _____ , and compare the negotiated price with other stores to get the best deal.

4. Recent research suggests that in addition to excessive obedience to authority, many people show a surprising _____ compliance to unreasonable requests.

How does self-assertion differ from aggression?

Psychology in Action: Assertiveness Training—Standing Up for Your Rights: Pages 627-628

1. _____ involves clearly stating one's wants and needs to others.

2. _____ expresses one's feelings and desires, but it hurts others.

3. _____ behavior is self-denying and inhibited.

4. Learning to be assertive is accomplished by _____ and rehearsing assertive actions.

5. Self-assertion is also aided by _____ (practice that continues after initial mastery of a skill) and use of specific techniques, such as the " _____ _____ " (repeating a request until it is acknowledged).

MASTERY TEST

1. Homogamy is directly related to which element of interpersonal attraction?
   a. competence
   b. similarity
   c. beauty
   d. proximity

2. Being an agent of an accepted social order is the basis for _____ power.
   a. coercive
   b. legitimate
   c. referent
   d. compliant

3. Suspicion and reduced attraction are associated with
   a. reciprocity
   b. self-disclosure
   c. competence and proximity
   d. overdisclosure

4. We expect people to be respectful and polite at funerals because of
   a. situational demands
   b. the door-in-the-face effect
   c. attributional discounting
   d. self-handicapping

5. Conflicting feelings of anger, affection, doubt, and attraction are characteristic of what attachment style?
   a. avoidant
   b. ambivalent
   c. compliant
   d. kinetic

6. Which of the following is an assertiveness technique?
   a. foot-in-the-door
   b. calm absorption
   c. door-in-the-face
   d. broken record

7. Using social comparison for self-protection typically involves
   a. external attributions
   b. comparisons with group norms
   c. downward comparisons
   d. comparison with a person of higher ability

8. "President of the United States" is
   a. an ascribed role
   b. an achieved role
   c. a structural norm
   d. a cohesive role

9. Where attribution is concerned, wants, needs, motives, or personal characteristics are perceived as
   a. external causes
   b. situational attributions
   c. discounted causes
   d. internal causes

10. Asch is to _____ experiments as Milgram is to _____ experiments.
    a. compliance, assertion
    b. conformity, obedience
    c. autokinetic, social power
    d. groupthink, authority

11. Social psychology is the scientific study of how people
    a. behave in the presence of others
    b. form into groups and organizations
    c. form and maintain interpersonal relationships
    d. make inferences about the behavior of others

12. "A person who first agrees with a small request is later more likely to comply with a larger demand." This summarizes the
    a. low-ball technique
    b. set-the-hook technique
    c. door-in-the-face effect
    d. foot-in-the-door effect

13. Large desks in business offices almost ensure that interactions with others take place at
    a. ascribed distance
    b. social distance
    c. personal distance
    d. public distance

14. Comparison level is an important concept in
    a. social comparison theory
    b. social exchange theory
    c. evolutionary psychology
    d. social compliance theory

15. Group structure involves all but one of the following elements. Which does NOT belong?
    a. roles
    b. communication pathways
    c. allocation of power
    d. social comparisons

16. A "guard" in the Stanford prison experiment who discovers that one of the "prisoners" is a friend would very likely experience
    a. role conflict
    b. a change in status
    c. groupthink
    d. a shift to coercive power

17. Groupthink is a type of _____ that applies to decision making in groups.
    a. conformity
    b. social comparison
    c. social power
    d. obedience

18. If procrastinating on school assignments helps protect your self-image, you have used procrastination as a type of
    a. double standard
    b. attributional error
    c. self-handicapping
    d. situational demand

19. When two people view an autokinetic light at the same time, their estimates of movement
    a. polarize
    b. normalize
    c. cohere
    d. converge

20. In Milgram's studies, the smallest percentage of subjects followed orders when
    a. the teacher and learner were in the same room
    b. the teacher received orders by phone
    c. the teacher and learner were face to face
    d. the experiment was conducted off campus

21. The most basic attributional error is to attribute the behavior of others to _____ causes, even when they are caused by _____ causes.
    a. inconsistent, consistent
    b. internal, external
    c. random, distinctive
    d. situational, personal

22. In an experiment, most women waiting to receive a shock preferred to wait with others who
    a. were about to be shocked
    b. did not share their fears
    c. were trained to calm them
    d. had been shocked the day before

23. Evolutionary theories attribute mate selection, in part, to the _____ of past generations.
    a. food-gathering habits
    b. tribal customs
    c. maternal instincts
    d. reproductive success

24. The "what is beautiful is good" stereotype typically does NOT include the assumption that physically attractive people are more
    a. likable
    b. intelligent
    c. honest
    d. mentally healthy

25. Which of the following gives special privileges to a member of a group?
    a. convergent norms
    b. high cohesiveness
    c. actor-observer bias
    d. high status

26. When situational demands are strong we tend to discount _____ causes as a way of explaining another person's behavior.
    a. public
    b. internal
    c. legitimate
    d. external

27. When we are subjected to conformity pressures, the _____ of a majority is more important than the number of people in it.
    a. unanimity
    b. cohesion
    c. proximity
    d. comparison level

28. Distressed couples tend to _____ their partner's actions to negative motives.
    a. discount
    b. compare
    c. coerce
    d. attribute

29. Which of the following factors does NOT increase interpersonal attraction?
    a. competence
    b. overdisclosure
    c. proximity
    d. similarity

30. _____ consists of a network of roles, communication pathways, and power in a group.
    a. Group cohesiveness
    b. Group structure
    c. Group norm
    d. Group goal

31. Members of the _____ are people who share similar values, goals, interest, and identify themselves as belonging to a same group.
    a. in-group
    b. out-group
    c. pepgroup
    d. essential group

32. Which tactic should one use to get someone to voluntarily comply with a request?
    a. foot-in-the-door
    b. door-in-the-face
    c. high-ball
    d. both A and B

33. Kyle has taken a psychology class and is aware of the tactics that salespeople use to hook customers into buying their products. He reviewed the cost of a car model that he is interested in from a consumer's reports guide. Having a general idea of a price, Kyle can negotiate with the salesperson, and after getting a quote from a salesperson, Kyle should
    a. buy the car immediately because the salesperson is offering him a good deal
    b. tell the salesperson he has changed his mind and does not need a new car
    c. tell the salesperson he cannot afford it
    d. leave the store and compare the quoted price to other car dealers

LANGUAGE DEVELOPMENT - Social Behavior

Word roots

The Latin word *ambi* means "both." It has been combined over time with other roots to form many English words, several used in the field of psychology. Examples you will find in this chapter and elsewhere in the text include: ambidextrous, ambidexterity, ambiguous, ambiguity, and ambivalent.

How does group membership affect individual behavior?

Preview: We Are Social Animals (p. 605)

(605) *No man is an island, entire of itself*: "No man is an island, entire of itself" is a line from a well-known poem by the 16th-17th century English writer John Donne. It means that each person needs others, and each person's actions have an effect on others.

(605) *tapestry*: heavy, reversible textile that has designs or pictures woven into it

(605) *samplers*: brief introductions

Humans in Social Context—People, People, Everywhere (pp. 605-608)

(606) *streamline*: simplify

(606) *flunk*: fail

(606) *simulated*: pretend; faked

(606) *demeaning*: degrading

(607) *lax*: not strict

(608) *convergence*: come together; agree

(608) *party animals*: people who thoroughly enjoy partying, often at the exclusion of other responsibilities

What unspoken rules govern the use of personal space?

Personal Space—Invisible Boundaries (pp. 608-609)

> (609) *impromptu*: unplanned; unrehearsed

How do we perceive the motives of others, and the causes of our own behavior?

Social Perception—Behind the Mask (pp. 609-612)

> (609) *inferences*: guesses
>
> (610) *grubbies*: old, unattractive clothes
>
> (610) *potions*: liquids
>
> (610) *in droves*: in large numbers
>
> (610) *tuba*: large brass musical instrument that makes a deep sound
>
> (610) *Sousa march*: reference to the music of John Philip Sousa; marches are pieces of music with a strong beat suitable for marching
>
> (611) *loaded*: drunk
>
> (611) *half-hearted effort*: not trying as hard as one could or should
>
> (611) *procrastinating*: putting off something that must be done
>
> (611) *cheapskates*: stingy, miserly people
>
> (611) *Ye Olde Double Standard*: the old double standard; the idea that there is one set of rules to be applied to women, and a different set of rules for men
>
> (611) *dog the heels*: pursue; harass; annoy

Why do people affiliate?

The Need for Affiliation—Come Together (pp. 612-613)

> (612) *ominously*: in a threatening or alarming way
>
> (612) *"misery loves company"*: a common saying meaning those in an unpleasant situation like to be with others in the same situation
>
> (612) *rampant*: widespread
>
> (613) *cuts your hours*: reduces one's working schedule

What factors influence interpersonal attraction?

Interpersonal Attraction—Social Magnetism? (pp. 613-615)

- (613) ***"birds of a feather flock together"***: just as birds of one type tend to stay together, so do people or things with similar characteristics group together

- (613) ***"familiarity breeds contempt"***: a common saying meaning that the more one knows about a person, the less one likes that person

- (613) ***opposites attract***: the belief that persons with opposite personalities, interests, values, etc. will be attracted to one another

- (613) ***"absence makes the heart grow fonder"***: a common saying meaning that if friends or lovers are separated they will grow fonder of each other

- (613) ***folklore***: traditional customs, stories, or sayings of a people

- (614) ***halo***: in art, a circle of light around the head of a person that indicates holiness, goodness, or virtuousness; in psychology, the tendency to rate a person too high or too low on the basis of a single trait

- (614) ***shallow***: not deep; not looking for deeper and meaningful explanations

- (614) ***close to the vest***: keeping it to one's self

- (615) ***back off***: become more reserved, less friendly

- (615) ***Sports Illustrated***: a popular magazine devoted to sports

- (615) ***bicker***: to argue

Loving and Liking—Dating, Rating, and Mating (pp. 616-618)

- (616) ***had some rough spots***: having been in difficult situations

- (616) ***stormy and troubled***: in reference to relationships, when a couple experiences stress, difficulties, and the threat of breaking up

- (616) ***ambivalent***: having both positive and negative feelings toward something

- (617) ***aloof***: reserved; distant

- (617) ***turmoil***: a confusing and unpredictable state or situation

- (617) ***infidelity***: unfaithfulness

- (618) ***trophy wives***: wives chosen primarily for their physical attractiveness so men can "show them off"

- (618) ***sire***: to be the father of

- (618) ***allies***: friends

What have social psychologists learned about conformity, social power, obedience, and compliance?

Social Influence—Follow the Leader (pp. 619-621)

(619) *lethal*: deadly

(619) *yielded*: conformed

(619) *erred*: made a mistake

(620) *dissenter*: one who disagrees

(620) *rock the boat*: disturb the situation; make changes

(620) *Columbia space shuttle disaster*: reference to the space shuttle accident that killed all the astronauts on board in February, 2003

(620) *Mars Climate Orbiter*: signals from the orbiter probe were lost as it entered orbit around Mars; no signal has been detected since

(620) *devil's advocate*: one who argues in support of the less accepted or approved alternative

(620) *deadlock*: a situation where no one is willing to change his/her decision; therefore, the situation has come to a complete stop and is not moving forward

(620) *meltdowns*: nuclear power accidents

(620) *ridicule*: teasing someone or making them the object of laughter

(620) *sanctions*: rules or laws

(620) *in your corner*: on your side; supportive of you

Social Power—Who Can Do What to Whom? (p. 621)

(621) *disperse*: spread apart

(621) *exert*: force

(621) *programmers*: people who develop computer software

(621) *bumper sticker*: a sticker that one puts on the back of any car or vehicle that has a short message on it

Obedience—Would You Electrocute a Stranger? (pp. 621-624)

(621) *electrocute*: to kill by electric shock

(622) *provocative*: tending to stimulate or excite interest

(622) *shabby*: run down; poorly kept

(623) *knuckle under*: submit

(623) *sanctioned massacres*: authorized slaying of large masses of people at one time

(624) *fortitude*: courage; strength

Compliance—A Foot in the Door (pp. 624-626)

(624) *notorious*: very well known

(624) *bump the price up*: increase the price

(625) *drive a hard bargain*: make a good business deal, favorable to one's self

(625) *rebuffs*: rejections; criticisms

(626) *accosted*: spoken to in a challenging or aggressive way

(626) *ripe targets*: the object (i.e., women) is set to be taken advantage of, attacked

How does self-assertion differ from aggression?

Psychology in Action: Assertiveness Training—Standing Up for Your Rights (pp. 627-628)

(627) *making a scene*: exhibiting anger or improper behavior

(627) *carbonized*: charred or burnt

(627) *pent-up*: held in; unexpressed

(627) *flustered*: confused; agitated

(627) *broken record*: repetition of one phrase over and over

(628) *defective*: faulty; lacking in some essential ingredient

(628) *folksy*: old-fashioned; out of date

Solutions

RECITE AND REVIEW

How does group membership affect individual behavior?

1. social
2. groups
3. Social roles
4. contradictory
5. prison
6. groups
7. roles; remain; in-group
8. in-group; ethnicity; religion; positive; out-group
9. standards; groups
10. movement; temporary

What unspoken rules govern the use of personal space?

1. personal space
2. personal; social
3. cultures

How do we perceive the motives of others, and the causes of our own behavior?

1. causes
2. causes; causes
3. causes; actor
4. consistency
5. internal
6. external
7. error; internal; internal; external
8. performance

Why do people affiliate?

1. approval; information
2. reduce
3. evaluate
4. comparisons
5. comparisons; comparisons

What factors influence interpersonal attraction?

1. nearness; contact
2. attraction; similarity
3. similarity; mate
4. revealing
5. norm
6. self-disclosure
7. rewards; costs

Loving and Liking—Dating, Rating, Mating: Pages 616-618

1. like; love; like
2. mutual
3. love
4. Secure
5. mating
6. younger; older; economically

What have social psychologists learned about conformity, social power, obedience, and compliance?

1. behavior; others

2. conforms ; norms   3. groups; group   4. decision making

Social Power—Who Can Do What to Whom? Obedience—Would You Electrocute a Stranger? Pages 621-624

1. social power: 2. authority   3. Obedience

Compliance—A Foot in the Door: Pages 624-626

1. requests; power   3. even; price; writing
2. foot; face   4. authority; requests

How does self-assertion differ from aggression?

1. wants; needs   3. denying   5. continues; repeating
2. hurts   4. assertive

CONNECTIONS

How does group membership affect individual behavior? Pages 605-608

1. C.   4. A.   7. D.
2. E.   5. F.
3. G.   6. B.

What unspoken rules govern the use of personal space? How do we perceive the motives of others, and the causes of our own behavior? Pages 608-612

1. C.   4. D.   7. A.
2. E.   5. B.
3. F.   6. G.

Why do people affiliate? What factors influence interpersonal attraction? Pages 612-618

1. H.   4. D.   7. F.
2. B.   5. G.   8. C.
3. E.   6. A.

What have social psychologists learned about conformity, social power, obedience, and compliance? How does self-assertion differ from aggression? Pages 619-628

1. D.   3. B.   5. F.
2. E.   4. A.   6. C.

7. G.

CHECK YOUR MEMORY

How does group membership affect individual behavior? Pages 605-608

1. F	5. F	9. F
2. T	6. T	10. T
3. F	7. T	11. F
4. T	8. T	

What unspoken rules govern the use of personal space? Pages 608-609

1. T	3. F
2. F	4. F

How do we perceive the motives of others, and the causes of our own behavior? Pages 609-612

1. F	4. T	7. T
2. F	5. T	
3. F	6. F	

Why do people affiliate? Pages 612-613

1. T	3. F	5. T
2. T	4. T	6. F

What factors influence interpersonal attraction? Pages 613-618

1. F	7. F	13. T
2. T	8. T	14. T
3. F	9. F	15. F
4. T	10. T	16. F
5. F	11. F	17. F
6. T	12. T	18. T

What have social psychologists learned about conformity, social power, obedience, and compliance? Pages 619-626

1. T	6. F	11. F
2. F	7. T	12. T
3. T	8. T	13. T
4. T	9. F	14. T
5. F	10. T	15. F

How does self-assertion differ from aggression? Pages 627-628

1. T
2. F
3. T
4. F
5. F
6. T

FINAL SURVEY AND REVIEW

How does group membership affect individual behavior?

1. Social; psychology
2. Culture; roles
3. achieved; ascribed
4. conflict
5. Stanford; roles
6. status; High; status
7. structure; cohesiveness; in-group
8. in-group; positive; negative
9. Norms
10. autokinetic; stationary; norms

What unspoken rules govern the use of personal space?

1. proxemics
2. intimate; public
3. Norms

How do we perceive the motives of others, and the causes of our own behavior?

1. Attribution
2. internal; external
3. object; setting
4. distinctiveness
5. Situational; discount
6. Consensus
7. fundamental; attributional; actor-observer
8. Self-handicapping

Why do people affiliate?

1. need; affiliate
2. anxiety
3. comparison
4. protection
5. Downward; Upward

What factors influence interpersonal attraction?

1. proximity
2. physical; competence
3. homogamy
4. Self-disclosure
5. reciprocity
6. Overdisclosure
7. exchange; profitable

Loving and Liking—Dating, Rating, Mating: Pages 616-618

1. attitude; scales
2. absorption
3. attachment
4. avoidant; ambivalent
5. Evolutionary; reproductive
6. men; women; economically

What have social psychologists learned about conformity, social power, obedience, and compliance?

1. Social influence

2. Conformity; cultural   3. Asch; sanctions   4. Groupthink

Social Power—Who Can Do What to Whom? Obedience—Would You Electrocute a Stranger? Pages 621-624

1. reward; coercive   2. Obedience; Milgram   3. decreased; authority

Compliance—A Foot in the Door: Pages 624-626

1. Compliance   3. even; price; writing

2. door; door; low-ball   4. passive

How does self-assertion differ from aggression?

1. Self-assertion   3. Non-assertive   5. overlearning; broken; record

2. Aggression   4. role-playing

MASTERY TEST

How does self-assertion differ from aggression?

1. B, p. 614	13. B, p. 608	25. D, pp. 606-607
2. B, p. 621	14. B, p. 615	26. B, p. 610
3. D, p. 614	15. D, pp. 606-607	27. A, p. 620
4. A, p. 610	16. A, p. 606	28. D, p. 610
5. B, p. 617	17. A, p. 620	29. B, p. 614
6. D, p. 627	18. C, p. 611	30. B, p. 606
7. C, p. 613	19. D, p. 608	31. A, p. 606
8. B, p. 605	20. B, p. 623	32. D, p. 624
9. D, p. 609	21. B, p. 610	33. D, p. 625
10. B, pp. 619; 622	22. A, p. 612	
11. A, p. 605	23. D, p. 617	
12. D, p. 624	24. C, p. 614	

Attitudes, Culture, and Human Relations

Chapter Overview

Attitudes have a belief component, an emotional component, and an action component. Attitudes may be formed by direct contact, interaction with others, child-rearing, group pressures, peer group influences, the mass media, and chance conditioning. Attitudes are measured by open-ended interviews, social distance scales, and attitude scales. Attitude change is related to reference group membership, to deliberate persuasion, and to personal experiences. Effective persuasion occurs when characteristics of the communicator, the message, and the audience are well matched. Cognitive dissonance theory explains how attitudes are maintained and changed. Brainwashing is forced attitude change. Many cults recruit new members with high-pressure techniques similar to brainwashing. Members are expected to give their loyalty and be obedient to a leader of the cult.

Prejudice is a negative attitude held toward out-group members. Prejudice can be attributed to scapegoating, personal prejudice, group norms, and authoritarian personality traits. Intergroup conflict leads to hostility and stereotyping. Status inequalities tend to build prejudices. Equal-status contact and superordinate goals tend to reduce these problems.

Ethologists blame aggression on instincts. Biological explanations emphasize brain mechanisms and physical factors. Aggression tends to follow frustration, especially when aggression cues are present. Social learning theory relates aggressive behavior to the influence of aggressive models. Students who plan to commit violence in school might disrupt classes, fight, join gangs, destroy property, get frustrated easily, react with extreme anger to criticism, blame others for their troubles, and use drugs.

Four decision points that must be passed before we give help to others are: noticing, defining an emergency, taking responsibility, and selecting a course of action. Helping is less likely at each point when other potential helpers are present. Giving help tends to encourage others to help too.

Multiculturalism is an attempt to give equal status to different ethnic, racial, and cultural groups. To reduce conflict and misunderstanding between members of different ethnic groups, one can do the following: Be aware of stereotyping, seek individuating information, beware of just-world beliefs, understand that race is a social construction, look for commonalities, and set examples for others. Cultural awareness is a key element in promoting greater social harmony.

Learning Objectives

1. Define *attitude*; describe the belief, emotional, and action components of an attitude; and list and give examples of six ways in which attitudes are acquired.

2. Explain three reasons why people may exhibit discrepancies between attitudes and behavior and how conviction affects attitudes; and briefly describe the following techniques for measuring attitudes: open-ended interview, social distance scale, and attitude scale.

3. Differentiate between reference groups and membership groups.

4. Define *persuasion;* describe the three factors in understanding the success or failure of persuasion; list nine conditions that encourage attitude change; and explain the effects of role playing as a way to change attitudes.

5. Explain cognitive dissonance theory; list five strategies for reducing dissonance (see Table 19.1); and describe the effect of reward or justification on dissonance.

6. Differentiate between brainwashing and other persuasive techniques; describe the techniques used in brainwashing; indicate how permanent the attitude changes brought about by brainwashing are; and describe how cults are able to recruit, convert, and retain their members.

7. Define and differentiate *prejudice* and *discrimination*; explain how scapegoating relates to prejudice; and distinguish between personal and group prejudices.

8. Describe the characteristic beliefs (including ethnocentrism and dogmatism) and childhood experiences of the authoritarian personality.

9. Present the major characteristics of social stereotypes and indicate how they may lead to intergroup conflicts. Include a description of symbolic prejudice.

10. Explain how status inequalities may lead to the development of stereotypes and how equal-status contact may reduce intergroup tension. Give an example of each situation.

11. Define *superordinate goals* and include an explanation of how they can reduce conflict and hostility; and explain how a jigsaw classroom utilizes superordinate goals and helps reduce prejudice.

12. Define *aggression*; and discuss the role of each of the following in aggressive behavior and include a brief description of the results of studies on the relationship between aggressive pornography and aggression of males toward females:

    a. instincts

    b. biology

    c. frustration-aggression hypothesis

    d. frustration, in the form of aversive stimuli

    e. weapons effect

    f. social learning theory

13. Explain how television may serve as a disinhibiting factor with respect to aggression; present evidence to support the viewpoint that watching television can cause a desensitization to violence; list six ways in which parents can buffer the impact of television on children's behavior; and explain how watching television can also increase prosocial behavior.

14. Explain the basic principle of anger control; describe five strategies for controlling anger; list at least eight signs that indicate a student may be prone to school violence; and describe antidotes to school violence.

15. Give an example of bystander apathy; explain how the presence of other people can influence apathy; describe four conditions that need to exist before bystanders are likely to give help; discuss how heightened and empathetic arousal affect helping behavior; and state three ways in which prosocial behavior can be encouraged.

The following objective is related to the material in the "Psychology in Action" section of your text.

1. Define the term *multiculturalism*; discuss eight ways in which a person can become more tolerant; and explain how a person can develop cultural awareness.

RECITE AND REVIEW

What are attitudes? How are they acquired? How are attitudes measured and changed?

Attitudes—Beliefs+Emotion+Action: Pages 632-634

1. Attitudes are learned tendencies to respond in a _____ or _____ way.

2. Attitudes are made up of a belief component, an emotional component, and an _____ component.

3. Attitudes may be formed by _____ contact, interaction with others, the effects of _____ -rearing practices, and social pressures from group membership.

4. Peer group influences, the mass _____ , and _____ conditioning (accidental learning) also appear to be important in attitude formation.

5. The _____ consequences of actions, how we think others will _____ our actions, and habits all influence whether attitudes are converted to actions.

6. Attitudes held with conviction are most likely to be _____ in behavior.

7. One way of measuring attitudes is the open-ended _____ , in which a person freely states his or her views.

8. A social distance scale is a rating of the degree of _____ a person would be willing to have with a member of another _____ .

9. Attitude scales are a collection of statements with which people express _____ or _____ .

Under what conditions is persuasion most effective? What is cognitive dissonance? What does it have to do with attitudes and behavior?

Attitude Change—Why the "Seekers" Went Public: Pages 634-636

1. People tend to change their attitudes to match those of their reference group (a group the person _____ with and refers to for guidance).

2. Effective persuasion occurs when characteristics of the communicator, the _____ , and the audience are well matched.

3. In general, a likable and believable communicator who repeats a credible message that arouses _____ in the audience and states clear-cut _____ will be persuasive.

4. Significant personal experiences (which may be engineered through role-playing) tend to _____ attitudes.

5. One reason for this is that maintaining and changing attitudes is closely related to needs for _____ in thoughts and actions. Cognitive dissonance theory explains the dynamics of such needs.

6. Cognitive dissonance occurs when there is a _____ between thoughts or between thoughts and actions.

7. The amount of reward or justification (reasons) for one's actions influences whether _____ occurs.

8. We are motivated to _____ dissonance when it occurs, often by changing beliefs or attitudes.

Is brainwashing actually possible? How are people converted to cult membership?

Forced Attitude Change—Brainwashing and Cults: Pages 636-639

1. Brainwashing is a form of _____ attitude change. It depends on control of the target person's total environment.

2. Three steps in brainwashing are unfreezing (loosening) old attitudes and beliefs, _____ , and refreezing (rewarding and strengthening) new attitudes and beliefs.

3. Many cults recruit new members with high-pressure indoctrination techniques resembling

   _____ .

4. Cults attempt to catch people when they are vulnerable. Then they combine isolation, displays of

   _____ , discipline and rituals, intimidation, and escalating commitment to bring about

   _____ .

What causes prejudice and intergroup conflict? What can be done about these problems?

Prejudice—Attitudes that Injure: Pages 639-641

1. Prejudice is a _____ attitude held toward members of various out-groups.

2. Racism, ageism, and sexism are specific types of prejudice based on race, age, and _____ .

3. One theory attributes prejudice to scapegoating, which is a type of displaced _____ .

4. A second account says that prejudices may be held for personal reasons such as direct threats to a person's well being (personal prejudice) or simply through adherence to group _____ (group prejudice).

5. Prejudiced individuals tend to have an authoritarian or dogmatic _____ , characterized by rigidity, inhibition, intolerance, and _____ -simplification.

6. Authoritarians tend to be very ethnocentric (they use their own _____ as a basis for judging all others).

Intergroup Conflict—The Roots of Prejudice: Pages 641-647

1. Intergroup _____ gives rise to hostility and the formation of social stereotypes (over-simplified images of members of various groups).

2. Symbolic prejudice, or prejudice expressed in _____ ways, is common today.

3. _____ inequalities (differences in power, prestige, or privileges) tend to build prejudices.

4. In-group beliefs of superiority, _____ , vulnerability, and distrust are common variables that promote _____ between groups.

5. Equal-status contact (social interaction on an equal footing) tends to _____ prejudice.

6. Superordinate _____ (those that rise above all others) usually reduce intergroup conflict.

7. On a small scale, jigsaw _____ (which encourage cooperation through _____ interdependence) have been shown to be an effective way of combating prejudice.

How do psychologists explain human aggression?

Aggression—The World's Most Dangerous Animal: Pages 647-652

1. Ethologists explain aggression as a natural expression of inherited _____ .

2. Biological explanations emphasize brain mechanisms and physical factors that _____ the threshold (trigger point) for aggression.

3. According to the frustration- _____ hypothesis, frustration and _____ are closely linked.

4. Frustration is only one of many aversive _____ that can arouse a person and make aggression more likely. Aggression is especially likely to occur when _____ cues (stimuli associated with aggression) are present.

5. Social learning theory has focused attention on the role of aggressive _____ in the development of aggressive behavior.

6. Aggressive _____ on television encourage aggression because they desensitize (lower the sensitivity of) _____ to violence and disinhibit (remove restraints against) aggressive impulses.

7. Students who plan to _____ violence in school might disrupt classes, fight, join gangs, _____ property, get _____ easily, react with _____ anger to criticism, blame others for their troubles, and use drugs.

8. To _____ anger, aggression, and violence, parents should _____ children, avoid hitting children, be consistent in disciplining children, and teach children _____ ways to solve problems.

Why are bystanders so often unwilling to help in an emergency?

Prosocial Behavior—Helping Others: Pages 653-655

1. Prosocial behavior is _____ , constructive, or altruistic toward others.

2. Bystander apathy is the unwillingness of bystanders to offer _____ to others during emergencies.

3. Four decision points that must be passed before a person gives help are: _____ , defining an emergency, taking responsibility, and selecting a course of action.

4. Helping is _____ likely at each point when other potential helpers are present.

5. Helping is encouraged by general arousal, empathic _____ , being in a good mood, low effort or _____ , and perceived similarity between the victim and the helper.

6. Altruistic behaviors can be seen in people who perform acts of _____ by saving people from various disasters, _____ their kidneys and blood, volunteering for the Peace Corps, and _____ children's games.

7. A method to _____ negative stereotypes is to use individuating information, which requires getting to know someone on an _____ and personal level.

What can be done to lower prejudice and promote social harmony?

Psychology in Action: Multiculturalism—Living with Diversity: Pages 656-658

1. Multiculturalism is an attempt to give _____ status to different ethnic, racial, and cultural groups.

2. To _____ prejudice, one can do the following: Be _____ of stereotyping, seek individuating information, beware of _____ -world beliefs, understand that race is a _____ construction, look for commonalities, and set examples for others.

3. Greater tolerance can be encouraged by neutralizing stereotypes with individuating information (which helps see others as _____).

4. Tolerance comes from looking for commonalties with others and by avoiding the effects of just-world _____ , self-fulfilling prophecies, and _____ competition.

5. _____ awareness is a key element in promoting greater social harmony. It refers to _____ one's understanding of how people from different cultures and religious backgrounds practice their _____ and traditions to _____ misunderstanding, stereotyping, and prejudice.

CONNECTIONS

What are attitudes? How are they acquired? How are attitudes measured and changed? Pages 632-634

1. _____ attitude
2. _____ Mrs. Keech
3. _____ misdirected letter
4. _____ conviction
5. _____ chance conditioning
6. _____ social distance

a. belief plus strong emotion
b. doomsday group
c. attitude-behavior test
d. allowed contact
e. belief + emotion + action
f. coincidence

Under what conditions is persuasion most effective? What is cognitive dissonance? What does it have to do with attitudes and behavior? Is brainwashing actually possible? How are people converted to cult membership? Pages 634-639

1. _____ persuasion
2. _____ message
3. _____ reference group
4. _____ communicator
5. _____ dissonance
6. _____ cult
7. _____ brainwashing
8. _____ unfreeze
9. _____ Festinger

a. uncomfortable clash
b. cognitive dissonance theory
c. thought reform
d. relay the message
e. Heaven's Gate
f. change attitude with arguments
g. standard for comparison
h. loosen former ties
i. content of argument

What causes prejudice and intergroup conflict? What can be done about these problems? Pages 639-647

1. _____ scapegoat
2. _____ authoritarianism
3. _____ implicit association test
4. _____ ethnocentric
5. _____ dogmatism
6. _____ discrimination
7. _____ stereotype
8. _____ symbolic prejudice
9. _____ superordinate

a. unequal treatment
b. aggression target
c. modern bias
d. above all others
e. F scale
f. group-centered
g. unwarranted certainty
h. simplified image
i. reveals hidden prejudices

How do psychologists explain human aggression? Pages 647-652

1. _____ prosocial
2. _____ ethology
3. _____ weapons effect
4. _____ desensitization
5. _____ mean world
6. _____ disinhibition

a. instincts
b. television perspective
c. reduced emotional sensitivity
d. remove inhibition
e. aggression cue
f. altruistic

Why are bystanders so often unwilling to help in an emergency? What can be done to lower prejudice and promote social harmony? Pages 653-658

1. _____ social competition
2. _____ spreading the accountability
3. _____ bystander apathy
4. _____ just-world beliefs
5. _____ bystander intervention
6. _____ empathic arousal
7. _____ multiculturalism

a. taking responsibility
b. feeling someone's anguish
c. group rivalry
d. Kitty Genovese
e. diffusion of responsibility
f. "tossed salad"
g. she gets what she deserves

CHECK YOUR MEMORY

What are attitudes? How are they acquired? How are attitudes measured and changed? Pages 632-634

1. Attitudes predict and direct future actions.

   TRUE or FALSE

2. The misdirected letter technique was used to measure the belief component of attitudes toward the Irish.

   TRUE or FALSE

3. What you think about the object of an attitude makes up its belief component.

   TRUE or FALSE

4. Attitudes are only composed of our positive or negative opinions of others. They do not include a behavioral component.

   TRUE or FALSE

5. If both parents belong to the same political party, their child probably will too.

   TRUE or FALSE

6. A person who deviates from the majority opinion in a group tends to be excluded from conversation.

   TRUE or FALSE

7. Heavy TV viewers feel safer than average because they spend so much time in security at home.

   TRUE or FALSE

8. An attitude held with conviction is more likely to be acted upon.

   TRUE or FALSE

9. In an open-ended interview, people respond to a series of statements for and against a particular issue.

   TRUE or FALSE

10. A social distance scale is used to measure attitudes toward members of various social groups.

    TRUE or FALSE

11. Five-point rating scales are frequently used in open-ended attitude interviews.

    TRUE or FALSE

Under what conditions is persuasion most effective? What is cognitive dissonance? What does it have to do with attitudes and behavior? Pages 634-636

1. Our attitudes are more likely to match those held by members of our reference groups than our membership groups.

   TRUE or FALSE

2. Persuasion refers to a deliberate attempt to change a person's reference groups.

   TRUE or FALSE

3. Persuasion is less effective if the message appeals to the emotions.

   TRUE or FALSE

4. For a poorly informed audience, persuasion is more effective if only one side of the argument is presented.

   TRUE or FALSE

5. A persuasive message should not be repeated; doing so just weakens its impact.

   TRUE or FALSE

6. Emotional experiences can alter attitudes, even if the experience is created by role-playing.

   TRUE or FALSE

7. Acting contrary to one's attitudes or self-image causes cognitive dissonance.

   TRUE or FALSE

8. Public commitment to an attitude or belief makes it more difficult to change.

   TRUE or FALSE

9. Romantic couples reduce the dissonance caused by their partner's faults by ignoring them.

   TRUE or FALSE

10. The greater the reward or justification for acting contrary to one's beliefs, the greater the cognitive dissonance felt.

TRUE or FALSE

11. Dissonance is especially likely to be felt when a person causes an undesired event to occur.

TRUE or FALSE

Is brainwashing actually possible? How are people converted to cult membership? Pages 636-639

1. Roughly 16 percent of American POWs in the Korean war signed false confessions.

TRUE or FALSE

2. True brainwashing requires a captive audience.

TRUE or FALSE

3. In brainwashing, the target person is housed with other people who hold the same attitudes and beliefs that he or she does.

TRUE or FALSE

4. In most cases, the effects of brainwashing are very resistant to further change.

TRUE or FALSE

5. Cult leaders, like David Koresh, use brainwashing as a technique to persuade people to conform.

TRUE or FALSE

6. A cult is a group in which the belief system is more important than the leader who espouses it.

TRUE or FALSE

7. Cults play on emotions and discourage critical thinking.

TRUE or FALSE

8. Cult members are typically isolated from former reference groups.

TRUE or FALSE

What causes prejudice and intergroup conflict? What can be done about these problems? Pages 639-647

1. Sexism is a type of prejudice.

TRUE or FALSE

2. The implicit association test reveals people's tendency to harbor hidden prejudicial views of others even when they explicitly deny it.

    TRUE or FALSE

3. The term *racial profiling* refers to giving preferential treatment to some students seeking admission to college.

    TRUE or FALSE

4. Scapegoating is a prime example of discrimination.

    TRUE or FALSE

5. A person who views members of another group as competitors for jobs displays group prejudice.

    TRUE or FALSE

6. Authoritarian persons tend to be prejudiced against all out-groups.

    TRUE or FALSE

7. The F in F scale stands for fanatic.

    TRUE or FALSE

8. An authoritarian would agree that people can be divided into the weak and the strong.

    TRUE or FALSE

9. Dogmatic personalities are found at both ends of the political spectrum.

    TRUE or FALSE

10. Social stereotypes can be positive as well as negative.

    TRUE or FALSE

11. People who feel they are being evaluated in terms of a stereotype tend to become anxious, which can lower their performance and seemingly confirm the stereotype.

    TRUE or FALSE

12. Children as young as age three have begun to show signs of racial bias.

    TRUE or FALSE

13. Beliefs on superiority, injustice, and distrust are common variables that tend to promote conflict among members of the in-group.

    TRUE or FALSE

14. Symbolic prejudice occurs when people understand the causes of prejudice and do not discriminate against minorities.

    TRUE or FALSE

15. Symbolic prejudice is the most obvious and socially unacceptable form of bigotry.

    TRUE or FALSE

16. Images of national enemies tend to humanize the inhabitants of other countries, making them seem less threatening.

TRUE or FALSE

17. The key to creating prejudice in Jane Elliot's experiment was her use of scapegoating to cause group conflict.

TRUE or FALSE

18. Equal-status contact tends to reduce prejudice and stereotypes.

TRUE or FALSE

19. Superordinate groups help people of opposing groups to see themselves as members of a single larger group.

TRUE or FALSE

20. Prejudice tends to be reduced when members of groups that have higher status offer to reward members of other groups for cooperating.

TRUE or FALSE

How do psychologists explain human aggression? Pages 647-652

1. Over 75 percent of all married persons physically attack their spouses at one time or another.
   TRUE or FALSE

2. Ethologists argue that humans learn to be aggressive by observing aggressive behavior in lower animals.
   TRUE or FALSE

3. Specific areas of the brain are capable of initiating or ending aggression.
   TRUE or FALSE

4. Intoxication tends to raise the threshold for aggression, making it more likely.
   TRUE or FALSE

5. Higher levels of the hormone testosterone are associated with more aggressive behavior by both men and women.
   TRUE or FALSE

6. The frustration-aggression hypothesis says that being aggressive is frustrating.
   TRUE or FALSE

7. People exposed to aversive stimuli tend to become less sensitive to aggression cues.
   TRUE or FALSE

8. Murders are less likely to occur in homes where guns are kept.

   TRUE or FALSE

9. Social learning theorists assume that instinctive patterns of human aggression are modified by learning.

   TRUE or FALSE

10. American Quakers have adopted a nonviolent way of life as a way to inhibit aggression.

    TRUE or FALSE

11. According to Leonard Eron, children learn aggression from direct contact with other children and not from indirect contact of viewing TV programs that shows aggressive behaviors.

    TRUE or FALSE

12. To discourage violence, parents should get themselves and their children involved in community-related activities.

    TRUE or FALSE

13. The erotic content of pornography is usually more damaging than the aggressive content.

    TRUE or FALSE

14. Aggressive crimes in TV dramas occur at a much higher rate than they do in real life.

    TRUE or FALSE

15. Preferring violent TV programs at age 8 predicts higher levels of violent behavior at age 19.

    TRUE or FALSE

16. Prosocial TV programs have little effect on viewer behavior.

    TRUE or FALSE

17. An important element of anger control is looking at upsetting situations as problems to be solved.

    TRUE or FALSE

18. A student who is easily frustrated and reacts with extreme anger to criticism or disappointments has a heightened risk of engaging in school violence.

    TRUE or FALSE

19. Children who see violence in the community tend to be less likely to engage in violence themselves.

    TRUE or FALSE

Why are bystanders so often unwilling to help in an emergency? Pages 653-655

1. In the Kitty Genovese murder, no one called the police until after the attack was over.

   TRUE or FALSE

2. In an emergency, the more potential helpers present, the more likely a person is to get help.

   TRUE or FALSE

3. The first step in giving help is to define the situation as an emergency.

   TRUE or FALSE

4. Emotional arousal, especially empathic arousal, lowers the likelihood that one person will help another.

   TRUE or FALSE

5. You are more likely to help a person who seems similar to yourself.

   TRUE or FALSE

6. In many emergency situations it can be more effective to shout "Fire!" rather than "Help!"

   TRUE or FALSE

What can be done to lower prejudice and promote social harmony? Pages 656-658

1. Multiculturalism is an attempt to blend multiple ethnic backgrounds into one universal culture.

   TRUE or FALSE

2. A study conducted in Canada found that increasing interaction among different groups only increases negative stereotypes of both groups.

   TRUE or FALSE

3. Members of major groups in the United States rated themselves better than other groups to enhance their self-esteem.

   TRUE or FALSE

4. The emotional component of prejudicial attitudes may remain even after a person intellectually renounces prejudice.

   TRUE or FALSE

5. Both prejudiced and nonprejudiced people are equally aware of social stereotypes.

   TRUE or FALSE

6. Individuating information forces us to focus mainly on the labels attached to a person.

   TRUE or FALSE

7. From a scientific point of view, "race" is a matter of social labeling, not a biological reality.

   TRUE or FALSE

8. People who hold just-world beliefs assume that people generally get what they deserve.

   TRUE or FALSE

9. Every major ethnic group rates itself better than other groups.

    TRUE or FALSE

10. The statement "Don't judge somebody until you know them. The color of their skin doesn't matter" is an example of a way to promote understanding in an ethnically diverse group of people.

    TRUE or FALSE

FINAL SURVEY AND REVIEW

What are attitudes? How are they acquired? How are attitudes measured and changed?

Attitudes—Beliefs+Emotion+Action: Pages 632-634

1. Attitudes are _____ _____ to respond in a positive or negative way.

2. Attitudes are made up of a _____ component, an _____ component, and an action component.

3. Attitudes may be formed by direct _____ , interaction with others, the effects of child-rearing practices, and social pressures from _____ _____ .

4. _____ group influences, the mass media, and chance _____ (accidental learning) also appear to be important in attitude formation.

5. The immediate _____ of actions, how we think others will evaluate our actions, and _____ all influence whether attitudes are converted to actions.

6. Attitudes held with _____ are most likely to be expressed in behavior.

7. One way of measuring attitudes is the _____ interview, in which a person freely states his or her views.

8. A _____ scale is a rating of the degree of contact a person would be willing to have with a member of another group.

9. _____ are a collection of statements with which people express agreement or disagreement.

Under what conditions is persuasion most effective? What is cognitive dissonance? What does it have to do with attitudes and behavior?

Attitude Change—Why the "Seekers" Went Public: Pages 634-636

1. People tend to change their attitudes to match those of their _____ group (a group the person identifies with and refers to for guidance).

2. Effective persuasion occurs when characteristics of the _____ , the message, and the _____ are well matched.

3. In general, a likable and believable _____ who repeats a credible message that arouses emotion in the _____ and states clear-cut conclusions will be persuasive.

4. Significant personal experiences (which may be engineered through _____) tend to change attitudes.

5. One reason for this is that maintaining and changing attitudes is closely related to needs for consistency in thoughts and actions. Cognitive _____ theory explains the dynamics of such needs.

6. Cognitive _____ occurs when there is a clash between _____ or between thoughts and actions.

7. The amount of _____ or _____ (reasons) for one's actions influences whether dissonance occurs.

8. We are motivated to reduce dissonance when it occurs, often by changing _____ or _____ , rather than behavior.

Is brainwashing actually possible? How are people converted to cult membership?

Forced Attitude Change—Brainwashing and Cults: Pages 636-639

1. Brainwashing is a form of forced attitude change. It depends on _____ of the target person's total _____ .

2. Three steps in brainwashing are _____ (loosening) old attitudes and beliefs, changing, and _____ (rewarding and strengthening) new attitudes and beliefs.

3. Many cults recruit new members with high-pressure _____ techniques resembling brainwashing.

4. Cults attempt to catch people when they are vulnerable. Then they combine isolation, displays of affection, discipline and _____ , intimidation, and escalating _____ to bring about conversion.

What causes prejudice and intergroup conflict? What can be done about these problems?

Prejudice—Attitudes that Injure: Pages 639-641

1. Prejudice is a negative attitude held toward members of various _____ .

2. _____ , _____ , and _____ are specific types of prejudice based on race, age, and gender.

3. One theory attributes prejudice to _____ , which is a type of _____ aggression.

4. A second account says that prejudices may be held for personal reasons such as direct threats to a person's well being (_____ prejudice) or simply through adherence to group norms (_____ prejudice).

5. Prejudiced individuals tend to have an _____ or dogmatic personality, characterized by rigidity, inhibition, intolerance, and over-simplification.

6. Authoritarians tend to be very _____ (they use their own group as a basis for judging all others).

Intergroup Conflict—The Roots of Prejudice: Pages 641-647

1. Intergroup conflict gives rise to hostility and the formation of _____ _____ (over-simplified images of members of various groups).

2. _____ prejudice, or prejudice expressed in disguised ways, is common today.

3. Status _____ (differences in power, prestige, or privileges) tend to build prejudices.

4. _____ beliefs of superiority, injustice, vulnerability, and distrust are common variables that promote _____ between groups.

5. _____ contact (social interaction on an equal footing) tends to reduce prejudice.

6. _____ goals (those that rise above all others) usually reduce intergroup conflict.

7. On a small scale, _____ classrooms (which encourage cooperation through mutual _____) have been shown to be an effective way of combating prejudice.

How do psychologists explain human aggression?

Aggression—The World's Most Dangerous Animal: Pages 647-652

1. _____ explain aggression as a natural expression of inherited instincts.

2. Biological explanations emphasize brain mechanisms and physical factors that lower the _____ (trigger point) for aggression.

3. According to the _____ -aggression hypothesis, _____ and aggression are closely linked.

4. Frustration is only one of many _____ stimuli that can arouse a person and make aggression more likely. Aggression is especially likely to occur when aggression _____ (stimuli associated with aggression) are present.

5. _____ _____ theory has focused attention on the role of aggressive models in the development of aggressive behavior.

6. Aggressive models on television encourage aggression because they _____ (lower the sensitivity of) viewers to violence and _____ (remove restraints against) aggressive impulses.

7. Students who plan to commit _____ in school might disrupt classes, fight, join gangs, destroy property, get _____ easily, react with _____ anger to criticism, blame others for their troubles, and use drugs.

8. To _____ anger, aggression, and violence, parents should supervise children, _____ hitting children, be consistent in disciplining children, and teach children _____ ways to solve problems.

Why are bystanders so often unwilling to help in an emergency?

Prosocial Behavior—Helping Others: Pages 653-655

1. Prosocial behavior is helpful, constructive, or _____ toward others.

2. Bystander _____ is the unwillingness of bystanders to offer help to others during emergencies.

3. Four decision points that must be passed before a person gives help are: noticing, defining an _____ , taking _____ , and selecting a course of action.

4. Helping is less likely at each point when other _____ _____ are present.

5. Helping is encouraged by general arousal, _____ arousal, being in a good mood, low effort or risk, and perceived _____ between the victim and the helper.

6. _____ behaviors can be seen in people who perform acts of heroism by _____ people from various disasters, _____ their kidneys and blood, volunteering for the Peace Corps, and coaching children's games.

7. A method to reduce negative stereotypes is to use _____ information, which requires getting to know someone on an individual and personal level.

What can be done to lower prejudice and promote social harmony?

Psychology in Action: Multiculturalism—Living with Diversity: Pages 656-658

1. _____ is an attempt to give equal status to different ethnic, racial, and cultural groups.

2. To reduce prejudice, one can do the following: Be _____ of stereotyping, seek individuating information, beware of _____ -world beliefs, understand that race is a _____ construction, look for commonalities, and set examples for others.

3. Greater tolerance can be encouraged by neutralizing stereotypes with _____ information (which helps see others as individuals).

4. Tolerance comes from looking for commonalties with others and by avoiding the effects of _____ beliefs, _____ prophecies, and social competition.

5. Cultural _____ is a key element in promoting greater social harmony. It refers to increasing one's _____ of how people from different cultures and religious backgrounds practice their beliefs and traditions to prevent misunderstanding, _____ , and prejudice.

MASTERY TEST

1. The weapons effect refers to the fact that weapons can serve as aggression
   a. thresholds
   b. cues
   c. models
   d. inhibitors

2. The Seekers' renewed conviction and interest in persuading others after the world failed to end can be explained by the
   a. social competition hypothesis
   b. frustration-persuasion hypothesis
   c. group's just-world beliefs
   d. theory of cognitive dissonance

3. One thing that reduces the chances that a bystander will give help in an emergency is
   a. heightened arousal
   b. empathic arousal
   c. others who could help
   d. similarity to the victim

4. The misdirected letter technique is a way to demonstrate the _____ component of an attitude.
   a. emotional
   b. belief
   c. action
   d. reactive

5. One consequence of seeing aggression portrayed on TV is a loss of emotional response, called
   a. disinhibition
   b. disassociation
   c. deconditioning
   d. desensitization

6. If you are speaking to a well-informed audience, it is important to _____ if you want to persuade them.
   a. repeat your message
   b. give both sides of the argument
   c. be likable
   d. appeal to their emotions

7. Which view of human aggression is most directly opposed to that of the ethologists?
   a. social learning
   b. brain mechanisms
   c. sociobiological
   d. innate releaser

8. Development of a mean world view is usually associated with which source of attitudes?
   a. child rearing
   b. mass media
   c. chance conditioning
   d. group membership

9. Research suggests that the most damaging element of pornography is the
   a. erotic content
   b. nudity
   c. aggressive content
   d. impersonality

10. Creating superordinate goals is an important way to
    a. reduce group conflict
    b. break the frustration-aggression link
    c. promote bystander intervention
    d. reverse self-fulfilling prophecies

11. Children who learn good manners by watching television demonstrate that TV can promote
    a. disinhibition
    b. prosocial behavior
    c. deconditioning
    d. superordinate behavior

12. A person who is dogmatic and politically conservative would be most likely to score high on the
    a. R Scale
    b. Individuation Inventory
    c. Social Competition Scale
    d. F Scale

13. A major problem with the ethological view of human aggression is that
    a. labeling a behavior does not explain it
    b. aversive stimuli alter the threshold for aggression
    c. it assumes that aggression begets aggression
    d. it assumes that aggression is related to biological processes

14. The Bennington College study showed that attitudes are not affected very much by
    a. membership groups
    b. child-rearing
    c. reference groups
    d. chance conditioning

15. Students who were paid to lie about a boring task experienced the most dissonance and changed their ratings the most when they were
    a. paid $1
    b. paid $10
    c. paid $20
    d. asked to help lure other students into the experiment

16. A key element in the effectiveness of jigsaw classrooms is
    a. deindividuation
    b. the promotion of self-fulfilling prophecies
    c. mutual interdependence
    d. selecting competent student leaders

17. A good antidote for social stereotyping is
    a. adopting just-world beliefs
    b. creating self-fulfilling prophecies
    c. accepting status inequalities
    d. seeking individuating information

18. A learned tendency to respond to people and objects in positive or negative ways. This defines a(an)
    a. opinion
    b. belief
    c. attitude
    d. social distance scale

19. An important difference between brainwashing and other types of persuasion is that brainwashing
    a. requires a captive audience
    b. is almost always permanent
    c. changes actions, not attitudes and beliefs
    d. is reversed during the refreezing phase

20. The effects of frustration on aggression are most like the effects of _____ on aggression.
    a. social learning
    b. prosocial models
    c. defining an emergency
    d. aversive stimuli

21. A negative attitude toward eggplant would be best explained by _____ if you were ill the first time you tried it.
    a. chance conditioning
    b. attitudinal freezing
    c. scapegoating
    d. dogmatic association

22. The top three categories on which social stereotypes are based are
    a. employment, age, race
    b. age, race, income
    c. race, national origin, income
    d. gender, age, race

23. Status inequalities are to _____ as equal-status contact is to _____.
    a. dependence, independence
    b. discrimination, stereotyping
    c. prejudice, tolerance
    d. aggression, individuation

24. Your actions are most likely to agree with one of your attitudes when
    a. the actions reverse an old habit
    b. the attitude is held with conviction
    c. you know that others disagree with your position
    d. you score high on an attitude scale

25. Conversion to membership in a cult usually involves
    a. depression, disorientation, and intimidation
    b. a series of emotional disturbances similar to post-traumatic stress
    c. loyalty tests and unfreezing
    d. a progression from small to large commitments

26. If it is easier for Anglo Americans to get automobile insurance than it is for African Americans, then African Americans have experienced
    a. discrimination
    b. scapegoating
    c. ethnocentrism
    d. personal prejudice

27. The presence of other potential helpers reduces the likelihood that a bystander will offer help in an emergency during which decision point?
    a. noticing
    b. defining an emergency
    c. taking responsibility
    d. all of the decision points

28. You mark a 5-point scale after reading a series of statements on the issue of rent control. Obviously you are completing an
    a. attitude differential
    b. attitude scale
    c. R scale
    d. attitudinal distance test

29. Racism expressed in a disguised form, so that it appears to be socially acceptable, is called _____ prejudice.
    a. secondary
    b. subjective
    c. silent
    d. symbolic

30. In April 1993 in Waco, Texas, David Koresh used a mixture of manipulation, isolation, deception, and fear to gain absolute loyalty and obedience from a group of followers who ultimately committed suicide at his request. This is an example of
    a. brainwashing
    b. scapegoating
    c. desensitization
    d. discrimination

31. Beliefs concerning superiority, injustice, vulnerability, and distrust are common variables that promote
    a. cooperation from out-group members
    b. cooperation from in-group members
    c. hostilities between out-group members
    d. hostilities within in-group members

32. When a white candidate is given "the benefit of the doubt" on his/her abilities to perform a task and is hired for a position for which other black candidates are qualified, is an example of
    a. symbolic prejudice
    b. modern racism
    c. justice
    d. both A and B

33. Which theory combines learning principles with cognitive processes, socialization, and modeling to explain human behavior?
    a. social learning
    b. individuating information
    c. existential
    d. multiculturalism

34. Students who are disruptive, get into fights, destroy property, react with extreme anger to criticism, blame others for their troubles, and use drugs are exhibiting signs that they might
    a. commit violent acts toward others
    b. commit suicide
    c. join the Peace Corps
    d. none of the above

35. Billy's new neighbor is from Pakistan. Because Billy wants to avoid misunderstandings and conflict when he meets and talks to his neighbor, he attends a cultural event sponsored by the Pakistani student club at his university. Billy is attempting to
    a. set an example for others in his neighborhood
    b. increase his cultural awareness of other's culture
    c. reduce stereotypes and prejudicial views of others
    d. all the preceding

LANGUAGE DEVELOPMENT - Attitudes, Culture, and Human Relations

Word roots

The suffix "ism" derives from the Greek *ismos* and the Latin *ismus*, which in Greek, then Latin, and now in English is an ending added to nouns to denote a condition, quality, or practice. Many terms in this text make use of this word ending. Among the many examples are these words: structuralism, functionalism, behaviorism, humanism, racism, sexism, ageism, heterosexism, ethnocentrism, dogmatism, multiculturalism, and determinism.

What are attitudes? How are they acquired? How are attitudes measured and changed?

Preview: Doomsday for the Seekers (p. 632)

> (632) *doomsday group*: a group who believes that the end of the world is coming soon

Attitudes—Belief + Emotion + Action (pp. 632-634)

> (632) *affirmative action*: action that provides equal opportunity (in employment, college admissions, etc.) to members of all ethnic and social groups

(632) *euthanasia*: mercy killing or assisted suicide for persons with terminal illness

(632) *death penalty*: punishment for a crime where the sentence is death

(632) *gun control*: attempts to legislate the possession of guns

(632) *orient*: to make familiar

(634) *unduly*: being excessive, unjustifiable

(634) *smog*: a combination of smoke and fog; air pollution

(634) *National Guard*: a militia force recruited by each state in the U.S., equipped by the federal government, and called into active duty in the case of national or state emergencies

(634) *male chauvinist*: a person who believes men are superior to women and speaks and behaves accordingly

(634) *socialized medicine*: the provision of medical services for everyone in the country and paid for by the government through taxation

Under what conditions is persuasion most effective? What is cognitive dissonance? What does it have to do with attitudes and behavior?

Attitude—Why the "Seekers" Went Public (pp. 634-636)

(634) *blitz*: intensive campaign

(636) *frugal*: avoiding unnecessary purchases; thrifty

(636) *egotistical*: self-centered

(636) *free spirit*: independent

(636) *family barge*: the family car, typically considered old, large, inefficient (and probably ugly)

(636) *antiquated*: old

(636) *gas-guzzler*: not fuel efficient

(636) *lure*: to draw someone away from their normal path

Is brainwashing actually possible? How are people converted to cult membership?

Forced Attitude Change—Brainwashing and Cults (pp. 636-639)

(637) *Branch Dravidian tragedy*: the self-destruction of the religious cult led by David Koresh in Waco, Texas in April, 1993

(637) *Heaven's Gate*: cult based on the idea that extraterrestrial beings would take the group members away in a UFO if they left their bodies behind (committed suicide); this event was to take place

at the time of the appearance of the Hale-Bopp comet in 1997, at which time the members committed group suicide

(637) ***POW***: prisoner of war

(637) ***lulled***: calmed

(637) ***rigid***: stiff and inflexible

(637) ***primed***: prepared

(637) ***allegiance***: loyalty

(637) ***infallible***: without mistakes

(637) ***sexual mores***: norms for sexual behaviors (e.g., when, with whom, where, and how to have sexual encounters)

(637) ***errant***: misbehaving, not following orders

(637) ***escalating***: increasing

(637) ***indoctrinating***: intense teaching and instruction intended to convert a person's basic beliefs

(637) ***succumbed***: to have yielded

(638) ***posttraumatic stress disorder***: cognitive, emotional, behavioral, and physiological effects occurring after a trauma or tragedy in one's life

What causes prejudice and intergroup conflict? What can be done about these problems?

Prejudice—Attitudes That Injure (pp. 639-641)

(639) ***racial profiling***: identified on the basis of racial characteristics

(639) ***rude awakening***: unpleasant realization

(641) ***anti-Semitism***: prejudice against Jews

(641) ***out-groups***: minority groups

(641) ***fascism***: tendency toward strong autocratic or dictatorial control

(641) ***close-minded***: not willing to accept or try out new ideas

(641) ***covet***: to wish for; to desire

(641) ***dogmatic***: a steadfast certainty of belief or opinion

(641) ***bigotry***: prejudice

Intergroup Conflict—The Roots of Prejudice (pp. 641-647)

(641) ***jarring***: disturbing

(641) ***strife***: clashes and conflict

(641) *blue-collar worker*: workers in trades, industrial settings, and manual labor; refers to the blue work shirts many such workers wear on the job

(641) *redneck*: derogatory term for a white, Southern or Western (Rocky Mountain states), rural, and working-class person

(643) *amassed*: gathered

(643) *the benefit of the doubt*: overlooking problems or deficits

(643) *pushy*: overly aggressive

(643) *standoffish*: cold and reserved

(644) *genocide*: the systematic, planned destruction of an entire race or political or social group

(644) *moral high ground*: the superior moral position

(644) *wanton*: without reason; unjustifiable

(644) *slurs*: insults

(645) *baited*: teased or taunted into action

(645) *free-for-all*: brawl or fight

(645) *we're all in the same boat*: we are all in the same situation

(646) *jigsaw puzzle*: a puzzle consisting of small, irregularly cut pieces that are to be fitted together to form a picture

(646) *accessories*: people who contribute as assistants in the committing of an offense

How do psychologists explain human aggression?

Aggression—The World's Most Dangerous Animal (pp. 647-652)

(647) *Homo sapiens*: human beings

(647) *killer instinct*: innate desire to kill

(647) *the Arapesh, the Senoi, and the Navajo*: the Arapesh and Senoi are tribes in Malaysia; the Navajo refers to a Native American tribe

(647) *Eskimo*: native people of northern Canada, Greenland, Alaska, and eastern Siberia

(648) *legacy*: something that has come from the past; passed down from one's ancestors

(648) *trappings*: signs and indications of

(649) *pipe-bombing*: using a type of homemade bomb for destructive purposes

(649) *95-mile-an-hour beanballs*: baseball pitches aimed at the head of the person who is at bat

(650) *erotic*: materials tending to arouse sexual desire

(650) *X-rated*: labeled as having a high level of sexual content

(650) *mugging*: attacking and robbing an unsuspecting person

(650) *gut wrenching*: emotionally difficult

(650) *begets*: causes or produces

(650) *prizefight*: boxing match for money

(650) *drain off*: to empty out or remove

(650) *spiral (of aggression)*: increasing in severity, frequency

(651) *pulling the plug*: unplugging the TV from the outlet

(651) *Barney and Friends, Sesame Street, and Mr. Roger's Neighborhood*: popular educational programs for children

(651) *altruistic*: characterized by unselfish regard for the welfare of others

(652) *dysfunctional*: not operating or not operating properly

Why are bystanders so often unwilling to help in an emergency?

Prosocial Behavior—Helping Others (pp. 653-655)

(653) *sparsely traveled*: very little traffic

(654) *fake each other out*: fool each other by showing false emotion

(654) *keyed-up*: prepared and ready to act

(654) *feel for*: care about

What can be done to lower prejudice and promote social harmony?

Psychology in Action: Multiculturalism—Living With Diversity (pp. 656-658)

(656) *tossed salad*: all the ingredients (people in this case) are together but keep their original identity

(656) *melting pot*: all the ingredients (people in this case) are blended together, and individual identity is lost

(656) *forsake*: give up or abandon

(657) *fabled town of Lake Woebegone*: the hypothetical town described by host Garrison Keeler on National Public Radio (NPR)

(657) *emulating*: imitating

(657) *buffer*: protect

(657) *boycott*: refusal to have dealings with a store or some other institution in order to express disapproval

(657) ***Confucian-steeped Korean culture***: Korean culture is greatly influenced by the teachings of Confucius, a Chinese philosopher

(658) ***Orthodox Jews***: Jews who strictly apply the principles and regulations of the Torah and Talmud (Jewish sacred book and traditions) to modern living

(658) ***kosher***: following the rules specified by Jewish law (usually refers to eating and food preparation)

Solutions

RECITE AND REVIEW

What are attitudes? How are they acquired? How are attitudes measured and changed?

1. positive; negative
2. action
3. direct; child
4. media; chance
5. immediate; evaluate
6. expressed
7. interview
8. contact; group
9. agreement; disagreement

Under what conditions is persuasion most effective? What is cognitive dissonance? What does it have to do with attitudes and behavior?

1. identifies
2. message
3. emotion; conclusions
4. change
5. consistency
6. clash
7. dissonance
8. reduce

Is brainwashing actually possible? How are people converted to cult membership?

1. forced
2. changing
3. brainwashing
4. affection; conversion

What causes prejudice and intergroup conflict? What can be done about these problems?

1. negative
2. gender (or sex)
3. aggression
4. norms
5. personality; over
6. group

Intergroup Conflict—The Roots of Prejudice: Pages 641-647

1. conflict
2. disguised
3. Status
4. injustice; hostilities
5. reduce
6. goals
7. classrooms; mutual

How do psychologists explain human aggression?

1. instincts
2. lower
3. aggression; aggression
4. stimuli; aggression
5. models
6. models; viewers
7. commit; destroy; frustrated; extreme
8. minimize; supervise; nonaggressive

Why are bystanders so often unwilling to help in an emergency?

1. helpful

2. help
3. noticing

4. less
5. arousal; risk

6. heroism; donating; coaching
7. reduce; individual

What can be done to lower prejudice and promote social harmony?

1. equal
2. reduce; aware; just; social

3. individuals
4. beliefs; social

5. Cultural; increasing; beliefs; prevent

CONNECTIONS

What are attitudes? How are they acquired? How are attitudes measured and changed? Pages 632-634

1. E.
2. B.

3. C.
4. A.

5. F.
6. D.

Under what conditions is persuasion most effective? What is cognitive dissonance? What does it have to do with attitudes and behavior? Is brainwashing actually possible? How are people converted to cult membership? Pages 634-639

1. F.
2. I.
3. G.

4. D.
5. A.
6. E.

7. C.
8. H.
9. B.

What causes prejudice and intergroup conflict? What can be done about these problems? Pages 639-647

1. B.
2. E.
3. I.

4. F.
5. G.
6. A.

7. H.
8. C.
9. D.

How do psychologists explain human aggression? Pages 647-652

1. F.
2. A.

3. E.
4. C.

5. B.
6. D.

Why are bystanders so often unwilling to help in an emergency? What can be done to lower prejudice and promote social harmony? Pages 653-658

1. C.
2. E.
3. D.

4. G.
5. A.
6. B.

7. F.

CHECK YOUR MEMORY

What are attitudes? How are they acquired? How are attitudes measured and changed? Pages 632-634

1. T	5. T	9. F
2. F	6. T	10. T
3. T	7. F	11. F
4. F	8. T	

Under what conditions is persuasion most effective? What is cognitive dissonance? What does it have to do with attitudes and behavior? Pages 634-636

1. T	5. F	9. F
2. F	6. T	10. F
3. F	7. T	11. T
4. T	8. T	

Is brainwashing actually possible? How are people converted to cult membership? Pages 636-639

1. T	4. F	7. T
2. T	5. T	8. T
3. F	6. F	

What causes prejudice and intergroup conflict? What can be done about these problems? Pages 639-647

1. T	9. T	17. F
2. T	10. T	18. T
3. F	11. T	19. T
4. F	12. T	20. F
5. F	13. F	
6. T	14. F	
7. F	15. F	
8. T	16. F	

How do psychologists explain human aggression? Pages 647-652

1. F	7. F	13. F
2. F	8. F	14. T
3. T	9. F	15. T
4. F	10. T	16. F
5. T	11. F	17. T
6. F	12. T	18. T

19. F

Why are bystanders so often unwilling to help in an emergency? Pages 653-655

1. T	3. F	5. T
2. F	4. F	6. T

What can be done to lower prejudice and promote social harmony? Pages 656-658

1. F	5. T	9. T
2. F	6. F	10. T
3. T	7. T	
4. T	8. T	

FINAL SURVEY AND REVIEW

What are attitudes? How are they acquired? How are attitudes measured and changed?

1. learned; tendencies	4. Peer; conditioning	7. open-ended
2. belief; emotional	5. consequences; habits	8. social distance
3. contact; group; membership	6. conviction	9. Attitude scales

Under what conditions is persuasion most effective? What is cognitive dissonance? What does it have to do with attitudes and behavior?

1. reference	4. role-playing	7. reward; justification
2. communicator; audience	5. dissonance	8. beliefs; attitudes
3. communicator; audience	6. dissonance; thoughts	

Is brainwashing actually possible? How are people converted to cult membership?

1. control; environment	3. indoctrination
2. unfreezing; refreezing	4. rituals; commitment

What causes prejudice and intergroup conflict? What can be done about these problems?

1. out-groups	3. scapegoating; displaced	5. authoritarian
2. Racism; ageism; sexism	4. personal; group	6. ethnocentric

Intergroup Conflict—The Roots of Prejudice: Pages 641-647
1. social; stereotypes

2. Symbolic
3. inequalities

4. In-group; hostilities
5. Equal-status

6. Superordinate
7. jigsaw; interdependence

How do psychologists explain human aggression?

1. Ethologists
2. threshold
3. frustration; frustration

4. aversive; cues
5. Social; learning
6. desensitize; disinhibit

7. violence; frustrated; extreme
8. minimize; avoid; nonaggressive

Why are bystanders so often unwilling to help in an emergency?

1. altruistic
2. apathy
3. emergency; responsibility

4. potential; helpers
5. empathic; similarity
6. Altruistic; saving; donating

7. individuating

What can be done to lower prejudice and promote social harmony?

1. Multiculturalism
2. aware; just; social

3. individuating
4. just-world; self-fulfilling

5. awareness; understanding; stereotyping

MASTERY TEST

What can be done to lower prejudice and promote social harmony?

1. B, p. 648
2. D, p. 636
3. C, p. 654
4. C, p. 632
5. D, p. 650
6. B, p. 635
7. A, pp. 647; 649
8. B, p. 633
9. C, p. 650
10. A, p. 645
11. B, pp. 651-652
12. D, p. 641
13. A, p. 647

14. A, p. 634
15. A, p. 636
16. C, p. 646
17. D, p. 656
18. C, p. 632
19. A, p. 637
20. D, p. 648
21. A, p. 633
22. D, p. 641
23. C, pp. 644-645
24. B, p. 634
25. D, p. 638
26. A, p. 639

27. D, pp. 653-654
28. B, p. 634
29. D, p. 642
30. A, p. 637
31. C, p. 641
32. D, p. 642
33. A, p. 649
34. A, p. 652
35. D, pp. 656-657

Applied Psychology

Chapter Overview

Applied psychologists attempt to solve practical problems. Some major applied specialties are: clinical and counseling, industrial-organizational, environmental, educational, legal, and sports psychology.

Industrial-organizational psychologists are interested in the problems people face at work. They specialize in personnel psychology and human relations at work. Personnel psychologists try to match people with jobs by combining job analysis with various tests and selection procedures. Two basic approaches to business and industrial management are scientific management (Theory X) and human relations (Theory Y) approaches. Healthy organizations express concern for the well-being of their employees by promoting trust, promoting open confrontation to avoid "desk rage," empowering their employees, and encouraging cooperation.

Environmental psychologists study the effects of behavioral settings, physical or social environments, and human territoriality, among many other major topics. The question of whether human activities cause harm to the environment is being debated by two worldviews: the traditional Western view and the ecological worldview. Over-population is a major world problem, often reflected at an individual level in crowding. Environmental psychologists are solving many practical problems—from noise pollution to architectural design.

Educational psychologists seek to understand how people learn and teachers instruct. They are particularly interested in teaching styles and teaching strategies. Two of the basic types of teaching styles are direct instruction which includes lecture, demonstration, and rote practice and open teaching which involves active teacher-student discussion. As schools have become increasingly diverse, a third teaching style has emerged; the Universal Design for Instruction makes use of different instructional methods to accommodate the different needs of students.

The psychology of law includes courtroom behavior and other topics that pertain to the legal system. Psychologists serve various consulting and counseling roles in legal, law enforcement, and criminal justice settings.

Sports psychologists seek to enhance sports performance and the benefits of sports participation. A careful task analysis of sports skills is a major tool for improving coaching and performance. The psychological dimension contributes greatly to peak performance.

Communication at work can be improved by following a few simple guidelines for effective speaking and listening.

Learning Objectives

1. Define the term *applied psychology*.

2. List the two main areas of interest of industrial-organizational psychology.

3. Describe the activities of personnel psychologists by defining or describing the following areas and related concepts:

   a. job analysis (include the concept of critical incidents)

   b. biodata (include the concepts of personal interviews and the halo effect)

   c. vocational interest test

   d. aptitude test (include multi-media computerized tests)

   e. assessment center (include situational judgement tests, in-basket tests, and leaderless group discussion).

4. Differentiate scientific management styles (Theory X) from human relations approaches (Theory Y) to management including work efficiency and psychological efficiency; and define the terms *participative management*, *management by objectives*, *self-managed teams*, and *quality circles*.

5. List eight factors that seem to contribute the most to job satisfaction; and explain the concept of flextime and how it is related to job satisfaction.

6. Describe the four basic coping styles in making career decisions.

7. Explain the purpose and results of job enrichment.

8. Explain what is meant by *organizational culture* and *organizational citizenship*.

9. Explain the goals of environmental psychology, including the three types of environments or settings of interest; and describe how people exhibit territoriality.

10. Discuss the results of animal experiments on the effects of overcrowding and the possible implications for humans; differentiate between crowding and density; and discuss the concept of attentional overload and the effects of noise pollution.

11. List and describe four ways people can be encouraged to preserve the environment.

12. Explain how environmental assessments and architectural psychology can be used to solve environmental problems.

13. Describe the goals of educational psychology; define the term *teaching strategy*; differentiate direct instruction from open teaching; and explain the basic ideas of the Universal Design for Instruction.

14. Discuss the psychology of law and identify topics of special interest; list several problems in jury behavior; describe the process of scientific jury selection; and explain what a "death-qualified jury" is.

15. Explain the ways in which a sports psychologist might contribute to peak performance by an athlete; differentiate between a motor skill and a motor program; list six rules that can aid skill learning; and describe *flow*.

The following objective is related to the material in the "Psychology in Action" section of your text.

1. List and explain ten ways to improve communication skills; and list and describe six ways to be a good listener.

RECITE AND REVIEW

How is psychology applied in business and industry?

Industrial-Organizational Psychology—Psychology at Work: Pages 662-666

1. Applied psychology refers to the use of psychological principles and research methods to solve _____ .

2. Major applied specialties include clinical and _____ psychology.

3. Other applied areas are related to business, such as _____ /organizational psychology.

4. Psychology is also applied to problems that arise in the environment, in education, in law, and in _____ .

5. Industrial-organizational psychologists are interested in the problems people face at _____ and within organizations.

6. Typically they specialize in personnel psychology and human _____ at work.

7. Personnel psychologists try to match people with _____ by combining _____ analysis with a variety of selection procedures.

8. To effectively match people with jobs, it is important to identify critical incidents (situations with which _____ employees must be able to cope).

9. Personnel selection is often based on gathering biodata (detailed _____ information about an applicant).

10. The traditional _____ interview is still widely used to select people for jobs. However, interviewers must be aware of the halo effect and other sources of _____ .

11. Standardized psychological _____ , such as vocational interest inventories, aptitude tests, and multi-media _____ tests, are mainstays of personnel selection.

12. In the assessment center approach, in-depth _____ of job candidates are done by observing them in simulated _____ situations.

13. Two popular assessment center techniques are the in-basket test, and leaderless _____ discussions.

Theories of Management—What Works at Work? Pages 666-670

1. Two basic approaches to business and industrial management are scientific management (Theory _____) and human relations approaches (Theory _____).

2. Theory _____ is most concerned with work efficiency (productivity), whereas, Theory _____ emphasizes psychological efficiency (good human relations).

3. Two common Theory _____ methods are participative management and _____ by objectives.

4. Recently, many companies have given employees more autonomy and responsibility by creating self-managed _____ .

5. Below the management level, employees may be encouraged to become more involved in their work by participating in _____ circles.

6. Job satisfaction is related to _____ , and it usually affects absenteeism, morale, employee turnover, and other factors that affect overall business efficiency.

7. Job satisfaction is usually enhanced by _____ oriented job enrichment.

8. An active, vigilant coping style is most likely to produce good _____ decisions.

9. Workers who fit comfortably within the _____ of a business typically show good organizational citizenship.

10. "Desk rage" (workplace _____) occurs from job-related _____ , work-related conflicts, people feeling that they have been treated _____ , and people perceiving that their self-esteem is threatened.

11. _____ organizations express concerns for the well-being of their employees by promoting trust, open _____ of problems, employee _____ and participation, cooperation, and full use of human potential.

What have psychologists learned about the effects of our physical and social environments?

Environmental Psychology—Life in the Big City: Pages 670-678

1. Environmental psychologists are interested in the effects of behavioral _____ , physical or _____ environments, and human territoriality, among many other major topics.

2. Territorial behavior involves defining a space as one's own, frequently by placing _____ markers (signals of ownership) in it.

3. Over-population is a major world problem, often reflected at an individual level in _____ .

4. Animal experiments indicate that excessive crowding can be unhealthy and lead to _____ and pathological behaviors.

5. However, human research shows that psychological feelings of _____ do not always correspond to density (the number of people in a given space).

6. One major consequence of _____ is attentional overload (stress caused when too many demands are placed on a person's attention).

7. Toxic or poisoned environments, pollution, excess consumption of natural resources, and other types of environmental _____ pose serious threats to future _____ .

8. Human activities greatly impact the environment by _____ its resources, producing global warming, and introducing _____ concentrations of _____ pollutants.

9. The traditional _____ view holds that _____ are superior to all living creatures, that the environment has _____ resources, and that advanced technology can solve any problem.

In contrast, the _____ worldview holds that humans are _____ with other living creatures and the environment has limited resources.

10. Recycling can be encouraged by monetary _____ , removing barriers, persuasion, obtaining public commitment, _____ setting, and giving feedback.

11. In many cases, solutions to environmental problems are the result of doing a careful _____ assessment (an analysis of the effects environments have on behavior).

12. Architectural psychology is the study of the effects _____ have on behavior and the design of _____ using _____ principles.

How has psychology improved education?

Educational Psychology—An Instructive Topic: Pages 679-680

1. Educational psychologists seek to understand how people _____ and teachers _____ .

2. An effective teaching strategy involves _____ preparation, stimulus presentation, the learner's _____ , reinforcement, evaluation of the learner's progress, and periodic review.

3. They are particularly interested in teaching styles, such as direct instruction (_____ and demonstrations) and open teaching (active student-teacher _____).

4. The Universal Design for Instruction makes use of different _____ methods such as a lecture, a podcast of the lecture, a group activity, or an Internet discussion.

What does psychology reveal about juries and court verdicts?

Psychology and Law—Judging Juries: Pages 680-682

1. The psychology of law includes studies of courtroom behavior and other topics that pertain to the _____ system.

2. Studies of mock juries (_____ juries) show that jury decisions are often far from _____ .

3. Psychologists are sometimes involved in jury _____ . Demographic information, a community survey, nonverbal behavior, and looking for authoritarian _____ traits may be used to select jurors.

Can psychology enhance athletic performance?

Sports Psychology—The Athletic Mind: Pages 682-685

1. Sports psychologists seek to enhance sports performance and the benefits of sports _____ .

2. A careful task analysis breaks _____ _____ into their subparts.

3. Motor skills are the core of many sports performances. Motor skills are nonverbal _____ chains assembled into a smooth sequence.

4. Motor skills are guided by internal _____ plans or models called motor programs.

5. _____ performances are associated with the flow experience, an unusual mental state.

6. Top athletes typically _____ their arousal level so that it is appropriate for the task. They also focus _____ on the task and mentally rehearse it beforehand.

7. Most top athletes use various self-regulation strategies to _____ their performances and make necessary adjustments.

What can be done to improve communication at work?

Psychology in Action: Improving Communication at Work: Pages 686-688

1. To improve communication at work you should state your message _____ and precisely.

2. Try to avoid overuse of obscure vocabulary, jargon, _____ , and loaded words.

3. Learn and use people's _____ . Be polite, but not servile.

4. Be expressive when you _____ . Pay attention to nonverbal cues and the messages they send.

5. To be a good listener, you should _____ pay attention.

6. Try to identify the speaker's purpose and core _____ .

7. Suspend evaluation while listening but check your _____ frequently and note nonverbal information.

CONNECTIONS

How is psychology applied in business and industry? Pages 662-670

1. _____ defensive-avoidant style
2. _____ I/O psychology
3. _____ Flextime
4. _____ Biodata
5. _____ critical incident
6. _____ Kuder
7. _____ in-basket test
8. _____ Theory X
9. _____ quality circle
10. _____ Theory Y

a. poor career decisions
b. vocational interests
c. essential work problem
d. variable schedule
e. work efficiency
f. personal history
g. work and organizations
h. psychological efficiency
i. discussion group
j. typical work problems

What have psychologists learned about the effects of our physical and social environments? Pages 670-678

1. _____ feedback
2. _____ spatial norm
3. _____ territorial marker
4. _____ density
5. _____ social traps
6. _____ noise pollution
7. _____ architectural psychology
8. _____ environmental psychology
9. _____ community psychology
10. _____ proxemics

a. intrusive sounds
b. pollution
c. persons in area
d. study of personal space norms
e. public distance
f. ownership signal
g. tragedy of the commons
h. solution for overcrowded buildings
i. information about effects
j. mental health

How has psychology improved education? What does psychology reveal about juries and court verdicts? Pages 679-682

1. _____ direct instruction
2. _____ open teaching
3. _____ jury selection
4. _____ death-qualified jury
5. _____ mock jury

a. favoring death penalty
b. better for facts
c. simulated trial
d. avoid authoritarian personality
e. better for thinking

Can psychology enhance athletic performance? What can be done to improve communication at work? Pages 682-688

1. _____ jargon
2. _____ motor program
3. _____ loaded word
4. _____ mental practice
5. _____ sports psychology
6. _____ cognitive map
7. _____ peak performance

a. coaching styles
b. imagined performance
c. movement plan
d. flow
e. communication barrier
f. mental area plan
g. strong emotional meaning

CHECK YOUR MEMORY

How is psychology applied in business and industry? Pages 662-670

1. Applied psychology can be defined as the use of learning principles to change undesirable human behavior.

   TRUE or FALSE

2. Psychological research has shown that the best fire alarm is a recorded voice.

   TRUE or FALSE

3. During a fire in a high-rise building, you should use the elevators, rather than the stairwell, so that you can leave as quickly as possible.

   TRUE or FALSE

4. Personnel psychology is a specialty of I-O psychologists.

   TRUE or FALSE

5. The basic idea of flextime is that employees can work as many or as few hours a week as they choose.

    TRUE or FALSE

6. One way of doing a job analysis is to interview expert workers.

    TRUE or FALSE

7. To have an effective interview, one should focus on direct efforts (emphasizing positive traits and past successes) rather than indirect efforts (wearing cologne and flattering the interviewer).

    TRUE or FALSE

8. Impression management refers to employers seeking to certify their authority through appearances (wearing jackets and ties).

    TRUE or FALSE

9. Critical incidents are serious employee mistakes identified by doing a job analysis.

    TRUE or FALSE

10. Use of biodata is based on the idea that past behavior predicts future behavior.

    TRUE or FALSE

11. Because of their many shortcomings, personal interviews are fading from use as a way of selecting job applicants.

    TRUE or FALSE

12. The halo effect is a major problem in aptitude testing.

    TRUE or FALSE

13. Excessive self-promotion tends to lower the ratings candidates receive in job interviews.

    TRUE or FALSE

14. "I would prefer to read a good book," is the kind of statement typically found on aptitude tests.

    TRUE or FALSE

15. Multi-media computerized tests seek to present realistic work situations to job candidates.

    TRUE or FALSE

16. Leaderless quality circles are a typical task applicants face in assessment centers.

    TRUE or FALSE

17. Theory X assumes that workers enjoy autonomy and accept responsibility.

    TRUE or FALSE

18. The main benefit of a Theory X management style is a high level of psychological efficiency among workers.

    TRUE or FALSE

19. Participative management aims to make work a cooperative effort.

TRUE or FALSE

20. Quality circles are typically allowed to choose their own methods of achieving results as long as the group is effective.

TRUE or FALSE

21. Job satisfaction comes from a good fit between work and a person's interests, needs, and abilities.

TRUE or FALSE

22. Job enrichment involves assigning workers a large number of new tasks.

TRUE or FALSE

23. A hypervigilant style usually leads to the best career decisions.

TRUE or FALSE

24. People who display organizational citizenship tend to contribute in ways that are not part of their job description.

TRUE or FALSE

25. "Desk rage" at work is associated with job stresses, threats to one's self-esteem, and conflicts with other workers.

TRUE or FALSE

26. A healthy organization encourages their employees to openly confront their problems.

TRUE or FALSE

What have psychologists learned about the effects of our physical and social environments? Pages 670-678

1. A study of the pace of life found that the three fastest cities in the U.S. are Boston, New York, and Los Angeles.

TRUE or FALSE

2. Environmental psychologists study physical environments rather than social environments.

TRUE or FALSE

3. The traditional Western view holds that people are depleting earth's resources and destroying the environment.

TRUE or FALSE

4. The ecological worldview holds that humans should not waste the limited resources available on earth.

TRUE or FALSE

5. A dance is a behavioral setting.

   TRUE or FALSE

6. Saving a place at a theater is a type of territorial behavior.

   TRUE or FALSE

7. Burglars tend to choose houses to break into that have visible territorial markers.

   TRUE or FALSE

8. World population doubled between 1950 and 1987. By 2040, 12 billion people will populate the earth.

   TRUE or FALSE

9. In Calhoun's study of overcrowding in a rat colony, food and water rapidly ran out as the population increased.

   TRUE or FALSE

10. High densities invariably lead to subjective feelings of crowding.

    TRUE or FALSE

11. Stress is most likely to result when crowding causes a loss of control over a person's immediate social environment.

    TRUE or FALSE

12. People suffering from attentional overload tend to ignore nonessential events and their social contacts are superficial.

    TRUE or FALSE

13. Exposure to toxic hazards increases the risk of mental disease, as well as physical problems.

    TRUE or FALSE

14. Long-corridor dormitories reduce feelings of crowding and encourage friendships.

    TRUE or FALSE

15. Providing feedback about energy consumption tends to promote conservation of resources.

    TRUE or FALSE

16. Direct monetary rewards have little or no effect on whether or not people recycle.

    TRUE or FALSE

How has psychology improved education? Pages 679-680

1. Reinforcement, evaluation, and spaced review are elements of a teaching strategy.

   TRUE or FALSE

2. Students of direct instruction do a little better on achievement tests than students of open teaching do.

TRUE or FALSE

3. Students of open instruction tend to be better at thinking and problem solving than students of direct instruction.

TRUE or FALSE

4. The Universal Design for Instruction makes use of one instructional method that all students can understand.

TRUE or FALSE

What does psychology reveal about juries and court verdicts? Pages 680-682

1. In court, attractive defendants are less likely to be found guilty than unattractive persons.

TRUE or FALSE

2. Jurors are supposed to take into account the severity of the punishment that a defendant faces, but many don't.

TRUE or FALSE

3. Scientific jury selection is only used in laboratory studies—the practice isn't allowed in real jury trials.

TRUE or FALSE

4. Demographic information consists of the most prominent personality traits a person displays.

TRUE or FALSE

5. All members of a death-qualified jury must be opposed to the death penalty.

TRUE or FALSE

Can psychology enhance athletic performance? Pages 682-685

1. Peak performances in sports require both mental and physical training.

TRUE or FALSE

2. Distance running tends to reduce anxiety, tension, and depression.

TRUE or FALSE

3. The most accurate marksmen are those who learn to pull the trigger just as their heart beats.

TRUE or FALSE

4. Motor programs adapt complex movements to changing conditions.

   TRUE or FALSE

5. Verbal rules add little to learning a sports skill; you should concentrate on lifelike practice.

   TRUE or FALSE

6. To enhance motor skill learning, feedback should call attention to correct responses.

   TRUE or FALSE

7. Mental practice refines motor programs.

   TRUE or FALSE

8. The top athletes in most sports are the ones who have learned how to force the flow experience to occur.

   TRUE or FALSE

9. Better athletes often use imagery, relaxation techniques, and fixed routines to control their arousal levels.

   TRUE or FALSE

What can be done to improve communication at work? Pages 686-688

1. Effective communication addresses the who, what, when, where, how, and why of events.

   TRUE or FALSE

2. Ambiguous messages are desirable because they leave others room to disagree.

   TRUE or FALSE

3. Jargon is an acceptable means of communication as long as you are sure that listeners are familiar with it.

   TRUE or FALSE

4. True politeness puts others at ease.

   TRUE or FALSE

5. To add credibility to your message, you should learn to speak very slowly and deliberately.

   TRUE or FALSE

6. Arriving late for meetings is a form of communication.

   TRUE or FALSE

7. To be a good listener, learn to evaluate each sentence as it is completed.

   TRUE or FALSE

8. Good listening improves communication as much as effective speaking does.

   TRUE or FALSE

FINAL SURVEY AND REVIEW

How is psychology applied in business and industry?

Industrial-Organizational Psychology—Psychology at Work: Pages 662-666

1. Applied psychology refers to the use of psychological _____ and _____ methods to solve practical problems.

2. Major applied specialties include _____ and _____ psychology.

3. Other applied areas are related to business, such as industrial/ _____ psychology.

4. Psychology is also applied to problems that arise in the natural and social _____ , in _____ , in law, and in sports.

5. _____ psychologists are interested in the problems people face at work and within organizations.

6. Typically they specialize in _____ psychology (testing, selecting, and promoting employees) and human relations at work.

7. _____ psychologists try to match people with jobs by combining job _____ with a variety of selection procedures.

8. To effectively match people with jobs, it is important to identify _____ incidents (situations with which competent employees must be able to cope).

9. Personnel selection is often based on gathering _____ (detailed biographical information about an applicant).

10. The traditional personal _____ is still widely used to select people for jobs. However, interviewers must be aware of the _____ effect and other sources of bias.

11. Standardized psychological tests, such as _____ interest inventories, _____ tests, and multi-media computerized tests, are mainstays of personnel selection.

12. In the _____ approach, in-depth evaluations of job candidates are done by observing them in simulated work situations.

13. Two popular assessment center techniques are the in- _____ test, and _____ group discussions.

Theories of Management—What Works at Work? Pages 666-670

1. Two basic approaches to business and industrial management are _____ management (Theory X) and _____ _____ approaches (Theory Y).

2. Theory X is most concerned with work _____ (productivity), whereas, Theory Y emphasizes _____ efficiency (good human relations).

3. Two common Theory Y methods are _____ management and management by _____ .

4. Recently, many companies have given employees more autonomy and responsibility by creating _____ teams.

5. Below the management level, employees may be encouraged to become more involved in their work by participating in _____ _____ .

6. Job _____ is related to productivity, and it usually affects absenteeism, _____ , employee turnover, and other factors that affect overall business efficiency.

7. Job satisfaction is usually enhanced by Theory Y oriented job _____ .

8. An active, _____ coping style is most likely to produce good career decisions.

9. Workers who fit comfortably within the culture of a business typically show good organizational _____ .

10. " _____ " (workplace anger) occurs from _____ -related stresses, work-related conflicts, people feeling that they have been treated unfairly, and people perceiving that their self-esteem is threatened.

11. _____ organizations express concerns for the well-being of their employees by promoting trust, _____ confrontation of problems, employee empowerment and _____ , cooperation, and full use of human potential.

What have psychologists learned about the effects of our physical and social environments?

Environmental Psychology—Life in the Big City: Pages 670-678

1. _____ psychologists are interested in the effects of _____ settings, physical or social environments, and human territoriality, among many other major topics.

2. Territorial behavior involves defining a space as one's own, frequently by placing territorial _____ (signals of ownership) in it.

3. _____ is a major world problem, often reflected at an individual level in crowding.

4. Animal experiments indicate that excessive _____ can be unhealthy and lead to abnormal and pathological behaviors.

5. However, human research shows that psychological feelings of crowding do not always correspond to _____ (the number of people in a given space).

6. One major consequence of crowding is _____ _____ (stress caused when too many demands are placed on a person's attention).

7. Toxic or poisoned environments, _____ , excess consumption of natural _____ , and other types of environmental damage pose serious threats to future generations.

8. Human _____ greatly impact the environment by _____ its resources, producing global warming, and introducing unhealthy concentrations of _____ pollutants.

9. The _____ view holds that humans are superior to all living creatures, that the environment has unlimited resources, and that advance technology can solve any problem. In contrast, the _____ holds that humans are interdependent with other living creatures and the environment has limited resources.

10. Recycling can be encouraged by _____ rewards, removing barriers, persuasion, obtaining public _____ , goal setting, and giving feedback.

11. In many cases, solutions to environmental problems are the result of doing a careful environmental _____ (an analysis of the effects environments have on behavior).

12. _____ psychology is the study of the effects buildings have on behavior and the design of buildings using psychological principles.

How has psychology improved education?

Educational Psychology—An Instructive Topic: Pages 679-680

1. _____ psychologists seek to understand how people learn and teachers instruct.

2. An effective teaching _____ involves learner preparation, stimulus presentation, the learner's response, _____ , evaluation of the learner's progress, and periodic _____ .

3. They are particularly interested in teaching styles, such as _____ (lecture and demonstrations) and _____ teaching (active student-teacher _____).

4. The _____ Design for Instruction makes use of different instructional methods such as a lecture, a podcast of the lecture, a group activity, or an Internet discussion.

What does psychology reveal about juries and court verdicts?

Psychology and Law—Judging Juries: Pages 680-682

1. The psychology of _____ includes studies of courtroom behavior and other topics that pertain to the legal system.

2. Studies of _____ juries (simulated juries) show that jury decisions are often far from objective.

3. Psychologists are sometimes involved in jury selection. _____ information (population data), a community survey, nonverbal behavior, and looking for _____ personality traits may be used to select jurors.

Can psychology enhance athletic performance?

Sports Psychology—The Athletic Mind: Pages 682-685

1. Sports psychologists seek to enhance sports _____ and the benefits of sports participation.

2. A careful _____ _____ breaks sports skills into their subparts.

3. _____ skills are the core of many sports performances. Motor skills are nonverbal response _____ assembled into a smooth sequence.

4. Motor skills are guided by internal mental plans or models called _____ _____ .

5. Peak performances are associated with the _____ experience, an unusual _____ state.

6. Top athletes typically adjust their _____ level so that it is appropriate for the task. They also focus attention on the task and mentally _____ it beforehand.

7. Most top athletes use various self-regulation _____ to evaluate their performances and make necessary adjustments.

What can be done to improve communication at work?

Psychology in Action: Improving Communication at Work: Pages 686-688

1. To improve communication at work you should state your _____ clearly and precisely.

2. Try to avoid overuse of obscure _____ , _____ , (inside lingo) slang, and loaded words.

3. Learn and use people's names. Be _____ , but not servile.

4. Be _____ when you speak. Pay attention to _____ cues and the messages they send.

5. To be a good _____ , you should actively pay _____ .

6. Try to identify the speaker's _____ and core message.

7. Suspend _____ while listening but check your understanding frequently and note nonverbal information.

MASTERY TEST

1. Praise and feedback make up what part of a teaching strategy?
   a. learner preparation
   b. stimulus presentation
   c. reinforcement
   d. review

2. Which is POOR advice for learning motor skills?
   a. Observe a skilled model.
   b. Learn only nonverbal information.
   c. Get feedback.
   d. Avoid learning artificial parts of a task.

3. Which of the following would be a question for applied psychology?
   a. How does conditioning occur?
   b. How can eyewitness memory be improved?
   c. What are the most basic personality traits?
   d. Do athletes have unusual personality profiles?

4. Signs are placed on a recycling container each week showing how many aluminum cans were deposited during the previous week. This practice dramatically increases recycling, showing the benefits of using _____ to promote recycling.
   a. feedback
   b. public commitment
   c. consumer symbolization
   d. persuasion

5. Psychological efficiency is promoted by
   a. scientific management
   b. Theory Y
   c. time-and-motion studies
   d. progressive pay schedules

6. In court, being attractive does NOT help a defendant avoid being found guilty when
   a. a majority of jurors are also attractive
   b. the defendant is a man
   c. the defendant is over age 30
   d. being attractive helped the person commit a crime

7. Which of the following is NOT a specialty of I-O psychologists?
   a. personnel psychology
   b. theories of management
   c. human relations
   d. architectural psychology

8. Dividing long-corridor dormitories into two living areas separated by a lounge
   a. makes residents feel more crowded, not less
   b. decreases social contacts
   c. increases energy consumption
   d. decreases stress

9. You leave a book on a table in the library to save your place. The book is a territorial
   a. display
   b. marker
   c. strategy
   d. control

10. When professional golfer Jack Nicklaus talks about "watching a movie" in his head before each shot, he is referring to the value of _____ for enhancing sports performance.
    a. mental practice
    b. self-regulation
    c. skilled modeling
    d. task analysis

11. What cognitive maps, behavioral settings, and crowding have in common is that all
    a. are studied by community psychologists
    b. produce attentional overload
    c. are studied by environmental psychologists
    d. are characteristics of Type A cities

12. Potentials for learning the skills used in various occupations are measured by
    a. interest tests
    b. aptitude tests
    c. in-basket tests
    d. cognitive mapping

13. To encourage creative thinking by students, a teacher would be wise to use
    a. direct instruction
    b. demonstrations as well as lectures
    c. open teaching
    d. spaced review

14. A good job analysis should identify
    a. critical incidents
    b. compatible controls
    c. motor programs
    d. essential biodata

15. High _____ is experienced as crowding when it leads to a loss of _____ one's immediate environment.
    a. overload, attention to
    b. density, control over
    c. stimulation, interest in
    d. arousal, contact with

16. Studies of flextime would most likely be done by a _____ psychologist.
    a. community
    b. environmental
    c. I-O
    d. consumer

17. The halo effect is a problem in
    a. collecting biodata
    b. scoring interest inventories
    c. conducting interviews
    d. aptitude testing

18. Mental practice is one way to improve
    a. motor programs
    b. the flow experience
    c. the accuracy of cognitive maps
    d. job satisfaction

19. Joan has been given a specific sales total to meet for the month, suggesting that she works for a company that uses
    a. quality circles
    b. job enrichment
    c. flexi-quotas
    d. management by objectives

20. Which of the following is NOT recommended for people who want to be effective listeners in the workplace?
    a. Identify the speaker's purpose.
    b. Evaluate as you listen.
    c. Check your understanding.
    d. Attend to nonverbal messages.

21. Planning, control, and orderliness are typical of _____ management.
    a. Theory X
    b. participative
    c. Theory Y
    d. enriched

22. A psychologist who checks demographic information, does a community survey, and looks for authoritarian traits is most likely
    a. a personnel psychologist
    b. doing a community mental health assessment
    c. a consumer welfare advocate
    d. a legal consultant

23. A very important element of job enrichment is
    a. switching to indirect feedback
    b. increasing worker knowledge
    c. use of bonuses and pay incentives
    d. providing closer supervision and guidance

24. Procrastination, inaction, and indecision are most characteristic of the _____ style of career decision making.
    a. vigilant
    b. complacent
    c. defensive-avoidant
    d. hypervigilant

25. An I/O psychologist hears someone make such claims as "He was really stressed out, and because of that he was often angry" and can predict that the individual may be experiencing
    a. "road rage"
    b. "desk rage"
    c. "private rage"
    d. "postal rage"

26. Which of the following is a method to increase employees' well-being?
    a. open confrontation of problems
    b. adhered to structured schedules
    c. employee empowerment
    d. both A and C

27. Which view holds that with advanced technology, humans can solve any problem presented to them?
    a. ecological worldview
    b. traditional Western view
    c. psychological view
    d. historical view

28. Mrs. West uses multiple instructional approaches (lectures, group activities, and Internet discussion) in her classes to ensure each student has the opportunity to find an instructional method by which he/she can best learn the material. Mrs. West is utilizing the
    a. direct instruction
    b. open teaching
    c. Universal Design for Instruction
    d. flextime instruction

LANGUAGE DEVELOPMENT - Applied Psychology

Word roots

In Old French, *environ* meant "around" and was a combination of two words: *en* (in) and *viron* (a circuit). This combination evolved into English terms such as environment and environmental, which you will find used throughout this text.

How is psychology applied in business and industry?

Preview: The Towering Inferno (p. 662)

(662) ***The Towering Inferno***: the title of a well-known movie about a devastating fire in a high-rise building

Industrial-Organizational Psychology—Psychology at Work (pp. 662-666)

(662) ***better to wear out than to rust out***: it is better to be active and productive than to be idle

(663) ***simulator***: a machine that artificially duplicates the conditions one is likely to experience in performing a certain skill

(663) ***extracurricular activities***: activities at school other than academics

(663) ***socioeconomic status***: an overall ranking based on characteristics such as education and occupation; used to describe people's positions in society

(665) ***Who's Who***: a listing of brief biographical sketches of famous people in a particular field

Theories of Management—What Works at Work? (pp. 666-670)

(666) ***assembly line***: an arrangement of machines, equipment, and workers in which work passes from operation to operation in a direct line until the product is assembled (put together)

(666) ***goaded***: urged into action

(666) ***quotas***: outcomes that must be reached

(666) ***like well-oiled machines***: efficiently operating like a well-maintained machine

(666) ***autonomy***: self-directed freedom

(666) ***meshed***: combined

(666) ***sabotage***: destruction of an employer's property or the hindering (slowing down) of manufacturing by discontented workers

(666) ***feedback***: evaluation; corrective information

(667) ***absenteeism skyrockets***: the number of people staying home from work increases rapidly

(667) ***intrinsically***: internal

(668) ***bend hours***: allow flexibility in work schedules

(670) ***scratched the surface:*** examined in a superficial, quick manner

What have psychologists learned about the effects of our physical and social environments?

Environmental Psychology—Life in the Big City (pp. 670-678)

(671) ***saving a place***: keeping a place available for someone who comes at a later time

(672) ***vandalism***: willful or malicious destruction of public or private property

(672) *graffiti*: writings or drawings made on some public surface

(672) *sustainable population*: the population the earth can maintain or hold given a finite set of resources

(672) *teeming*: filled to overflowing

(672) *demographers*: those who study the statistical characteristics of human populations

(673) *rampant*: widespread

(673) *fending off*: keeping away; repelling

(673) *callousness*: feeling no sympathy for others

(674) *blunting*: lowering

(674) *Carl Sagan*: well-known scientist who popularized astronomy and other areas of science through books and television programs

(677) *truancy*: purposely missing or "skipping" school

(678) *wanted to be alone*: Greta Garbo, a famous Swedish film star, was known for valuing her privacy; in her accented English, "want" sounded like "vahnt" in her well-known line, "I want to be alone"

How has psychology improved education?

Educational Psychology—An Instructive Topic (pp. 679-680)

(679) *bribery*: using money or favors to influence another's actions

(679) *video arcade*: an amusement center containing video games

(679) *breaking in*: orienting and getting accustomed to a new work situation

(680) *podcast*: broadcasting a lecture to other schools to reduce the teacher's travel from school to school on daily basis

(680) *blogs*: an individual's personal activities, opinions, and comments that are posted on the Internet so that others can read them (an Internet diary)

What does psychology reveal about juries and court verdicts?

Psychology and the Law—Judging Juries (pp. 680-682)

(680) *arbitration*: hearing of a case by an appointed person

(680) *bail*: money given in order to obtain a prisoner's release from jail

(680) *parole*: a conditional release of a prisoner

(680) *forensic*: used in legal arguments or courts of law

(680) *white-collar crime*: non-violent crimes, such as income tax evasion, fraud, etc., committed primarily by persons in professional occupations

(680) *mock*: pretend; simulated

(681) *swindling*: cheating

(681) *slips out*: given out by mistake

(681) *quirks*: traits someone has that set him/her apart from other people

(682) *acquitted*: found not guilty of a crime

(682) *net effect*: final result

(682) *cadets*: trainees

Can psychology enhance athletic performance?

Sports Psychology—The Athletic Mind (pp. 682-685)

(683) *"homegrown"*: coaching methods that coaches created themselves

(683) *umpires*: officials in baseball who oversee the game and make decisions during the course of play

(683) *balls*: in baseball, a pitch to the batter that is too high, too low, or too far from the batter

(683) *strikes*: in baseball, a ball pitched to the proper area that the batter misses or hits far to the side of the playing area

(683) *home plate*: in baseball, the place where the batter stands to bat and where a runner must return in order to score a run (point)

(684) *facilitate*: make easier

(684) *choking*: making a mistake at a crucial moment

What can be done to improve communication at work?

Psychology in Action: Improving Communication at Work (pp. 686-688)

(686) *muddled*: unclear; confused

(686) *give me a hand*: help me

(686) *kinda*: kind of

(686) *trendy*: fashionable

(686) *buzz words*: important-sounding, usually technical words often of little meaning and used chiefly to impress others

(686) *jargon*: technical language of a special activity or group

(686) *lingo*: special vocabulary of a particular field of interest

(687) ***servile***: submissive

(687) ***stilted***: artificial, stiff, or unnatural

(687) ***dispute***: disagreement

(687) ***digressing***: talking about subjects not related to the current topic

Solutions

RECITE AND REVIEW

How is psychology applied in business and industry?

1. practical problems
2. counseling
3. industrial
4. sports
5. work
6. relations
7. jobs; job
8. competent
9. biographical
10. personal; bias
11. tests; computerized
12. evaluations; work
13. group

Theories of Management—What Works at Work? Pages 666-670

1. X; Y
2. X; Y
3. Y; management
4. teams
5. quality
6. productivity
7. Theory Y
8. career
9. culture
10. anger; stresses; unfairly
11. Healthy; confrontation; empowerment

What have psychologists learned about the effects of our physical and social environments?

1. settings; social
2. territorial
3. crowding
4. abnormal
5. crowding
6. crowding
7. damage ; generations
8. depleting; unhealthy; air
9. Western; humans; unlimited; ecological; interdependent
10. rewards; goal
11. environmental
12. buildings; buildings; behavioral

How has psychology improved education?

1. learn; instruct
2. learner; response
3. lecture; discussion
4. instructional

What does psychology reveal about juries and court verdicts?

1. legal
2. simulated; objective
3. selection; personality

Can psychology enhance athletic performance?

1. participation
2. sports; skills
3. response
4. mental
5. Peak
6. adjust; attention
7. evaluate

What can be done to improve communication at work?

1. clearly

2. slang
3. names

4. speak
5. actively

6. message
7. understanding

CONNECTIONS

How is psychology applied in business and industry? Pages 662-670

1. A.
2. G.
3. D.
4. F.

5. C.
6. B.
7. J.
8. E.

9. I.
10. H.

What have psychologists learned about the effects of our physical and social environments? Pages 670-678

1. I.
2. E.
3. F.
4. C.

5. G.
6. A.
7. H.
8. B.

9. J.
10. D.

How has psychology improved education? What does psychology reveal about juries and court verdicts? Pages 679-682

1. B.
2. E.

3. D.
4. A.

5. C.

Can psychology enhance athletic performance? What can be done to improve communication at work? Pages 682-688

1. E.
2. C.
3. G.

4. B.
5. A.
6. F.

7. D.

CHECK YOUR MEMORY

How is psychology applied in business and industry? Pages 662-670

1. F
2. T
3. F
4. T
5. F
6. T

7. T
8. F
9. F
10. T
11. F
12. F

13. T
14. F
15. T
16. F
17. F
18. F

19. T	22. F	25. T
20. F	23. F	26. T
21. T	24. T	

What have psychologists learned about the effects of our physical and social environments? Pages 670-678

1. F	7. F	13. T
2. F	8. T	14. F
3. F	9. F	15. T
4. T	10. F	16. F
5. F	11. T	
6. T	12. T	

How has psychology improved education? Pages 679-680

1. T	3. T
2. T	4. F

What does psychology reveal about juries and court verdicts? Pages 680-682

1. T	3. F	5. F
2. F	4. F	

Can psychology enhance athletic performance? Pages 682-685

1. T	4. T	7. T
2. T	5. F	8. F
3. F	6. T	9. T

What can be done to improve communication at work? Pages 686-688

1. T	4. T	7. F
2. F	5. F	8. T
3. T	6. T	

FINAL SURVEY AND REVIEW

How is psychology applied in business and industry?

1. principles; research	5. Industrial-organizational	9. biodata
2. clinical; counseling	6. personnel	10. interview; halo
3. organizational	7. Personnel; analysis	11. vocational; aptitude
4. environment; education	8. critical	12. assessment center

13. basket; leaderless

Theories of Management—What Works at Work? Pages 666-670

1. scientific; human; relations
2. efficiency; psychological
3. participative; objectives
4. self-managed
5. quality; circles
6. satisfaction; morale
7. enrichment
8. vigilant
9. citizenship
10. Desk rage; job
11. Healthy; open; participation

What have psychologists learned about the effects of our physical and social environments?

1. Environmental; behavioral
2. markers
3. Over-population
4. crowding
5. density
6. attentional; overload
7. pollution; resources
8. activities; depleting; air
9. traditional Western; ecological worldview
10. monetary; commitment
11. assessment
12. Architectural

How has psychology improved education?

1. Educational
2. strategy; reinforcement; review
3. direct instruction; open; discussion
4. Universal

What does psychology reveal about juries and court verdicts?

1. law
2. mock
3. Demographic; authoritarian

Can psychology enhance athletic performance?

1. performance
2. task; analysis
3. Motor; chains
4. motor; programs
5. flow; mental
6. arousal; rehearse
7. strategies

What can be done to improve communication at work?

1. message
2. vocabulary; jargon
3. polite
4. expressive; nonverbal
5. listener; attention
6. purpose
7. evaluation

MASTERY TEST

What can be done to improve communication at work?

1. C, p. 679
2. B, p. 684
3. B, p. 662
4. A, p. 677
5. B, p. 666
6. D, pp. 680-681
7. D, p. 663
8. D, p. 678
9. B, p. 671

10. A, p. 684
11. C, p. 672
12. B, p. 664
13. C, pp. 679-680
14. A, p. 663
15. B, p. 673
16. C, p. 668
17. C, p. 664

18. A, p. 684
19. D, p. 666
20. B, p. 687
21. A, p. 666
22. D, p. 681
23. B, p. 669
24. C, p. 668
25. B, p. 669

26. D, p. 669
27. B, p. 675
28. C, p. 680

GLOSSARY INDEX

Since some of the terms and phrases are repeated in later chapters of the text, the terms and phrases are alphabetized for quick and easy access. Next to the terms are page numbers where the terms can be found in the text.

3-D movies (197):   a popular movie format in the 1950s where patrons wore special glasses to view specially-prepared movies; objects in the movies appeared to "pop out" to viewers

95-mile-an-hour beanballs (649):   baseball pitches aimed at the head of the person who is at bat

a catch in your breathing (266):   a short pause in breathing

a cheese fancier (177):   a person who likes to eat cheese

a dusty storehouse (297):   a storage area that is not often used

a flash of anger (59):   a sudden, quick burst of anger

a flash of brilliance (363):   an insightful moment

a large blowup "Bo-Bo the Clown" doll (288):   an inflatable life-sized plastic doll for children to play with

a mind like a sieve (297):   a very poor memory

a mind like a steel trap (297):   a very good memory

a quick trip to a casino would allow the person to retire for life (216):   if a person really had ESP, he or she could gamble and be sure of winning lots of money

a radio that isn't quite tuned in (172):   a radio that is not receiving a station clearly

a rash of (336):   a huge spreading or increasing of something

a wealth of information (32):   a large amount of information

aardvark (298):   a South African mammal that eats ants and termites

abducted (303):   kidnapped; taken against one's will

ablaze with activity (57):   extremely active

Aborigines (224):   original inhabitants of a region

About $30 an hour. (And going up.) (24):   You need to pay $30 more to visit a psychiatrist than if you visit a psychologist

absence makes the heart grow fonder (613):   a common saying meaning that if friends or lovers are separated they will grow fonder of each other

absenteeism skyrockets (667):   the number of people staying home from work increases rapidly

absent-minded (321):   having the tendency to be forgetful

accentuate (484):   make more obvious

accessories (646):   people who contribute as assistants in the committing of an offense

accosted (626):   spoken to in a challenging or aggressive way

acquitted (682):   found not guilty of a crime

acute chest pain (276):   sudden, sharp pain in the chest

acute stereoscopic vision (198):   outstanding depth perception

added an interesting wrinkle (418):   contributed something new

addicted (182):   unable to give up

adulterated (246):   mixed with other (often unknown) substances; made impure

aesthetic (463):   pleasing and nice to look at

affirmative action (632):   action that provides equal opportunity (in employment, college admissions, etc.) to members of all ethnic and social groups

agendas (436):   plans of things that need to be done

age-old questions (235):   questions that have been asked for a long time ago without clear answers

aghast (477):   horrified

agility (77):   the ability to move quickly and with coordination

agitated (694):   excited and upset

aimless schools (133):   schools that do not seem to have clear goals for its students

albeit (445):   although

albinism (87):   hereditary condition that causes a lack of pigment (color) in skin, hair, and eyes (eyes are pink)

alien (65; 180):   foreign; belonging elsewhere

all grown up with no place to go (133):   a reference to the fact that some young people may be being pushed too quickly through the adolescent stage of development

allegiance (637):   loyalty

allergies (174):   reactions such as sneezing, coughing, and itching caused by sensitivity to substances in the environment such as pollen or dust

alleviate (570):   reduce; lessen

allies (618):   friends

aloof (617):   reserved; distant

altruism (423):   concern for others

altruistic (651):   characterized by unselfish regard for the welfare of others

amassed (643):　gathered

ambidextrous (80):　able to use either the right or left hand equally well

ambiguities (427):　uncertainties

ambiguity (345; 590):　possibility of several interpretations

ambiguous(489):　able to be interpreted in more than one way

ambivalence(447):　uncertainty

ambivalent (616):　having both positive and negative feelings toward something

amenities (275):　things that provide material comfort

American Nazi Party (293):　racist political group opposed to minorities, especially Jews

amnesia (490):　temporary loss of memory

amplify (422):　to make big, enlarge

anabolic steroids (76):　any of a group of synthetic steroid hormones; sometimes used by athletes to temporarily increase muscle mass

analogies (358):　similarities

and the like (106):　other similar things

anecdotal evidence (42):　evidence that could explain a claim

anecdotes (43):　retelling of personal incidents or stories

anesthetized (88):　put into a state of sleep or altered consciousness with a drug

anglers (280):　men or women who fish

anguish (532):　distress; suffering; sorrow

animal magnetism (237):　a mysterious force that Mesmer claimed enabled him to hypnotize patients

animate (468):　to give life to

anonymous (577):　unidentified

antidotes (528):　remedies

antiquated (636):　old

anti-Semitism (641):　prejudice against Jews

anti-social (104):　contrary or hostile to the well-being of society

apathetic (502; 538):　showing little or no feeling or concern

aphrodisiac (250):　a substance that increases sexual performance or desire

appraise (503):　determine the severity of

arbitrary (384): based on individual preference or convenience

arbitrary (478): selected at random or without reason

arbitration (680): hearing of a case by an appointed person

are pushed (other articles are pushed in ads) (210): try very hard to sell

arrogance (462): too much pride and sense of self-importance

artificial lighting (169): indoor, rather than outdoor, lighting

asexuality (434): lack of sexual interest for both the same sex (homosexuality) and the opposite sex (heterosexuality)

assault (478): physical confrontation

assembly line (666): an arrangement of machines, equipment, and workers in which work passes from operation to operation in a direct line until the product is assembled (put together)

astute (468): observant

at the root of (105): the source or origin

atlas (61): map of the brain

atmosphere of growth (574): conditions that will allow the patient to improve

atrophy (551): wasting away; decreased in size

attest (42): to declare truthfully

attracts (265): draws something to it

attuned (156): responsive to

augment (311): to expand

autobiographical (305): historical events and records of one's life

autonomy (666): self-directed freedom

aversion (578): intense dislike

avid (310): passionate and enthusiastic

award custody (354): when parents divorce, a judge will decide with which parent the child or children shall live

awash (46): overflowing

B.B. King plays the blues (58) a famous musician known for his distinctive blues music

baby buggy (94): baby carriage

Baby I'm Stuck on You (95): a song title used by Coon to indicate extreme fondness

Bach (52): composer of classical music

back off (615):   become more reserved, less friendly

backfires (212):   a loud banging noise made by a vehicle due to improper combustion

bad spot (593):   difficult situation

(680): bail   money given in order to obtain a prisoner's release from jail

baited (with drugs) (282):   substances planted to see if the dogs can detect them

baited (645):   teased or taunted into action

balloon up (391):   to gain weight very rapidly

balls (683):   in baseball, a pitch to the batter that is too high, too low, or too far from the batter

bar (238):   prevent

bark (76):   outer layer

Barney and Friends, Sesame Street, and Mr. Roger's Neighborhood (651):   popular educational programs for children

barred (358):   prevented

bartending (336):   serving drinks at a bar

bask in the glow (462):   enjoy the good feelings

bassoon (262):   a musical instrument

bat an eyelash (542):   show a response

bathing (402):   soaking up

battle of the bulge (394):   efforts to control overeating and obesity

battle of the sexes (431):   implies fighting for superiority between men and women

be thrown off (the polygraph may be thrown off) (413):   give inaccurate readings

bedevil (497):   to torment, create great distress

been there (595):   have had similar experiences

begets (650):   causes or produces

being of light (148):   when one is surrounded by a very bright light

belch (339):   burp

belittlement (490):   causing to seem little or less

bend hours (668):   allow flexibility in work schedules

benign (231):   harmless

bereaved (489):   grieving

bereavement (524): state of grieving after the death of a loved one

Bermuda Triangle (45): an area of the ocean where some people claim that ships are mysteriously lost

berserk (581): crazy; derives from "berserker," a particularly fierce type of early Norse warrior

better safe than sorry (272): it's better to do everything possible to bring about a desired result than to fail

better to wear out than to rust out (662): it is better to be active and productive than to be idle

beyond the void (135): past the emptiness that exists in one's future

bias (46): slanted to include too many members of one group

bicker (615): to argue

bigotry (641): prejudice

Bill Cosby (336): a popular black comedian and situational comedy star

Bill Gates (122): the CEO of Microsoft computer company

billboard (419): a large panel displaying outdoor advertising

billow in (508): great waves (in this case, of smoke) flowing in

binges (245): unrestrained use of drugs

Bingo! (279): I won!; Bingo is a board game where the winner yells Bingo!

biocomputer (70): combination of biology and computing, in this case the brain

birdie (108): variation of the word bird, often used when talking to children

bird's eye view (198): seeing the world from the perspective of a high-flying bird

Birds of a feather flock together (191; 613): just as birds of one type tend to stay together, so do people or things with similar characteristics group together

bitch (212): a derogatory term for a woman

blackouts (251): periods of loss of consciousness or memory

blazing hot (13): very hot (blazing suggests fire)

bleak (126; 559): lacking warm or cheerful qualities

blind alleys and lead balloons(505): blind alleys lead nowhere; balloons made of lead would not fly; therefore both are symbols of frustration

blinders (165): flaps on both sides of a horse's eyes to prevent it from seeing objects at its sides

blitz (634): intensive campaign

blob (52): a small lump of thick consistency

blogs (680): an individual's personal activities, opinions, and comments that are posted on the Internet so that others can read them (an Internet diary)

blooming and pruning(88):   changing the structure of the neural network

blossom (372; 479):   come forth; to develop

blotting out (233):   to get rid of

blown it (514):   failed

Blue Monday (410):   because Monday is the beginning of the work and school week, it is a "blue," or sad day

blue (514):   sad

blue-collar workers (40; 641):   workers in trades, industrial settings, and manual labor; refers to the blue work shirts many such workers wear on the job

blunted (513):   dulled and uninterested

blunting (674):   lowering

body maps (99):   representation of the body in the brain

boil down (16; 321; 334):   to reduce or narrow; to summarize

boisterous (42; 466):   being loud, wild, and disorderly in behavior

bombards (71):   to send without stopping

boom box (173):   large and loud radio; often carried

both camps (378):   groups on either side of the issue

bottled up (520):   kept inside

bottleneck (209):   the relatively narrow area of a bottle; used here to indicate a slowdown in information

bouncing off the walls (42):   acting very excitedly or wildly

boycott (657):   refusal to have dealings with a store or some other institution in order to express disapproval

brain (134):   very intelligent; "A" student

brainstorms (358):   sudden bright ideas

brainy (379):   slang term for smart

Branch Dravidian tragedy (637):   the self-destruction of the religious cult led by David Koresh in Waco, Texas in April, 1993

break out (139):   find a way to leave an uncomfortable or unpleasant situation

break the case (303):   solve the crime; find the criminals

breaking in (679):   orienting and getting accustomed to a new work situation

breathe fire (176):   suggestive of being sensitive to spicy food

breech birth (79):   the delivery of a baby rear end first, rather than head first

bribed (408):   paid to act a certain way

bribery (679):   using money or favors to influence another's actions

bridges to sexual satisfaction (454):   ways by which one can have sexual pleasure

brighter subjects (64):   more intelligent

brimming (12):   overflowing

bristles (170):   very fine fibers at the top of hair cells

broken record (627):   repetition of one phrase over and over

broken the ice (492):   concluded an introduction; became acquainted

bronchitis (497):   respiratory illness centered in the lungs

browsing (527):   looking over casually

brush with death (575):   a dangerous situation that could have been fatal

brushes with the law (488):   illegal actions

brussels sprouts (116):   one of the small edible heads on the stalks of plants closely related to the cabbage

brute (283):   mean, insensitive person

budding (324):   inexperienced

buffer (657):   protect

buffoons (25):   people who look foolish; clowns

bulldog tenacity (280):   bulldogs were bred to hold on to a bull's nose and not let go; therefore this means extreme stubbornness, refusal to give up

bullring (55):   an arena used for fighting bulls

bump the price up (624):   increase the price

bumper sticker (621):   a sticker that one puts on the back of any car or vehicle that has a short message on it

bungee jumping (182):   a sport requiring a person to jump off a point of great height with his/her legs tied to a strong elastic rope to prevent him/her from hitting the water or ground below as the rope pulls him/her back a few feet

burned the midnight oil (403):   stayed up late studying

butterflies (409):   feeling of nervousness

buzz words (686):   important-sounding, usually technical words often of little meaning and used chiefly to impress others

bystander apathy (16):   lack of interest or concern among witnesses to an accident or crime

cabin fever (561): extreme irritability and restlessness resulting from living in isolation or within a confined indoor area for a long period

cadets (682): trainees

callousness (673): feeling no sympathy for others

callused (47): skin that has become thick and hard

camouflaged (192): disguised, hidden

camphor (174): crystalline substance with a strong odor, generally derived from the wood of the camphor tree

carbonized (627): charred or burnt

careen (225): to sway from side to side as one flies quickly through the air

caregiver (87): a parent or significant other person who cares for a child

Carl Sagan (674): well-known scientist who popularized astronomy and other areas of science through books and television programs

Carnegie Hall (322): a famous New York City concert hall; it is a sign of success to be able to perform there

carried away (178): over-enthusiastic

carry-over (472): continuation

cataract (189): clouding of the lens of the eye

catching some rays (160): slang for sun-tanning; Coon is making a joke because in vision the eye actually does "catch" light rays

catharsis (591): getting rid of one's problems through the process of purging by releasing emotions

causation (32): the act that produces or causes an effect

cave dwellers (86): people who live in caves

censor (469): one who represses or forbids unacceptable notions or ideas

chafe (520): become irritated by

chameleon (417): lizard that can rapidly change skin color to blend in with the surroundings

chaotic (469; 550): confused; totally disorganized

charisma (459): special magnetic charm or appeal

charlatans (47): people who pretend to be experts of a profession

Charles Darwin (18): the scientist who proposed the theory of evolution

chasm (419): deep hole in the earth

chat rooms (443): sites on the Internet where individuals may type messages that will be seen by everyone in the "room" at that time

cheapskates (611): stingy, miserly people

check out their split ends (276): examine the ends of one's hair (especially girls); a sign of boredom

checkerboard (156): a board used for playing the popular games of checkers, chess, and backgammon

checking up on (562): investigating

Chernobyl (402): city in former U.S.S.R. where a nuclear power plant accident occurred, injuring and killing many people

child molestation (child molesting) (443): sexual abuse of children

childproof (90): removing items that a child might damage or destroy or that might be dangerous to the child

child-rearing (103): raising of children

choking up (409): fail to perform effectively because of fear

choking (684): making a mistake at a crucial moment

chronic (127): continuously occurring over a long period of time

circuit (320): a path

circumcised (336): having the foreskin of the penis removed

clammy (543): damp

clamors (470): the act of demanding

clashes (21): strong disagreements

clashing (166): not matching

claustrophobia (580): fear of small, closed-in spaces, such as closets

cleaned out (279): lost all of one's money

clear-cut (45): having a well-defined description

clench (258): close tightly

clerical work (364): work as a secretary, data clerk, or other similar jobs

cliques (134): circle or group held together by common interests or views

close to the vest (614): keeping it to one's self

close-minded (641): not willing to accept or try out new ideas

cloying (176): too rich or too sweet

clueless (449): lacking an understanding

coagulated (177):   thickened into a mass

coax (58):   to persuade gently

cobblestone street (200):   a street paved with round, flat stones

cobweb (173):   spider web

cohabitation (445):   living together as if married

coherent (67):   the pieces are in an organized and logical manner

coincidence (39):   two events happened to occur at the same time by chance

coined (237):   created

cold sweats (247):   chills caused by sweating due to anxiety, nervousness, or fear

collectivism (462):   philosophy that everyone works together for the good of the group; welfare of the group is more important than individual desires

collide (170):   to hit against something

color blindness (375):   the inability to distinguish colors; the world is seen in shades of grey

colossal (497):   huge

Columbia space shuttle disaster (620):   reference to the space shuttle accident that killed all the astronauts on board in February, 2003

come to grips (570):   understand and accept

come to terms with (147):   accept

coming to light (75):   being discovered

commands (202):   instructions one gives to a computer program

commitment (535):   sending someone involuntarily to a mental institution

compensate (208):   neutralize the effect of; counterbalance

compulsively (252):   uncontrollably

concentration camps (512):   places of imprisonment for soldiers and others during the Vietnam War and other wars

conception (14):   the moment when egg and sperm meet and a new being is created

condom (448):   thin sheath for the penis, usually made of latex, used for contraception and for the prevention of STDs

condones (446):   pardons or overlooks

confirm (33):   prove or verify

Confucian-steeped Korean culture (657): Korean culture is greatly influenced by the teachings of Confucius, a Chinese philosopher

congenital (129): existing at birth

conscientious (335): extremely careful and attentive to details

contorts (409): twisting of the face into unusual shapes

contraband (282): illegal items

contraceptives (449): devices or medicines to prevent pregnancy

convergence (608): come together; agree

convulsions (245): abnormal, violent, and involuntary contractions of the muscles

copulate (399): have sex

corollary (48): something that naturally accompanies or follows

corporal punishment (130): punishment, such as spanking, inflicted on the body, usually of a child

cosmic aura balancer (27): a guide who tries to help you balance unseen forces around the body

covert (578): hidden

covet (641): to wish for; to desire

cowboy (134): a person who dresses in traditional Western wear, listens to country music

coyote (395): wild canine that resembles a wolf or large dog

crack down (134): suddenly becoming very strict in order to control the child's behavior

cramming (312): studying a large amount of information in a short amount of time just before an examination

crank letter (552): irrational, eccentric letter

crash (after which they "crash") (245): hit a very low point

crash landings (196): used to describe landings of airplanes under emergency conditions; here referring to the falls that babies take when they are first learning to crawl and walk

Crayolas (123): Brand name for colorful "crayons" that children use for drawing

crews (135): similar to gangs, but with less connotation of bad behavior

criminal (134): a person who acts in antisocial ways

crochet (288): a type of needlework done with a small hook

cross-country skiing (297): snow skiing across large distances

crossroads (72): a place where two or more paths come together

crotchety (151): stubborn, bad-tempered

crude (157):   not sophisticated; simple

crystallized (318):   formed and hardened

culprit (193):   that which is causing something

cultivate (97):   to develop or build

cultivate (351):   to increase in size or number by tending to it

cultivate (381):   to encourage

curb (437; 499; 597):   to control and reduce

curtain falls (146):   life is coming to an end

cuts your hours (613):   reduces one's working schedule

cybershrinks (577):   online psychologists or counselors

cybertherapy (576):   psychology via computer

cynicism (487):   the belief that selfishness motivates human actions

cysts (246):   closed sacs developing abnormally in a structure of the body

dandy (437):   very good and fine

darted (497):   moved suddenly and quickly

Darwin (330):   Charles Darwin (1809-1882), the scientist who proposed the theory of evolution

Data of Star Trek (475):   a human robot character in the popular futuristic Star Trek television series

daunting (105; 322):   overwhelming, intimidating, or scary

daze (333):   state of confusion

dazzling speed (94):   great speed

deaden public sensitivity (317):   to reduce the public's concern

dead-end job (139):   a job offering no hopes of promotion or advancement

deadlock (620):   a situation where no one is willing to change his/her decision; therefore, the situation has come to a complete stop and is not moving forward

death can be an excellent yardstick for measuring (148):   death is used as an index to measure what is important

death penalty (632):   punishment for a crime where the sentence is death

debase (446):   to lower in value or dignity

decipher (115):   to translate or break down

decoys (96):   persons or an inanimate objects that have similar characteristics as other live objects that are used to trick live objects into believing the inanimate object is alive and friendly

deduced (18): inferred from reason

deductive reasoning (112): to reason from the general to the specific

defective (628): faulty; lacking in some essential ingredient

defer (358): put off; postpone

degrade (218): to break down

degrease your brain (249): to slow down your brain's activity; to make it sluggish or slow moving

dehydration (224): abnormal loss of body fluids

delirium (224): a state of mental confusion accompanied by delusions, hallucinations, and illusions

delve (331): to dig deep into something

demeaned (421): lowered a person's pride or self-respect

demeaning (606): degrading

demographers (672): those who study the statistical characteristics of human populations

denominations (696): religious groups

depletion (388): lessening or loss

deranged (364): insane

desensitize (290): to make less sensitive to something

designed culture (19): a culture that is created using positive reinforcements to produce wanted behaviors from individuals.

despicable (443): worthy of disgust or contempt

despondency (559): depression

detachment (502): state of being uninvolved, uninterested

deteriorate (252): become worse

detour (348): a longer way than the direct route or usual procedure

devil's advocate (620): one who argues in support of the less accepted or approved alternative

dewdrop (156): a very small drop (amount) of moisture found in the early morning resulting from overnight condensation of moisture in the air

dextrous (68): skillful with one's hands

diabolical (310): extremely difficult or fiendish

die in the box tests (216): the person being tested is asked to guess which number is showing on a die (singular of dice) that is hidden in a box

diffusion of responsibility (16):   responsibility for action is spread out and lessened; it is not clear who should act

digressing (687):   talking about subjects not related to the current topic

dilapidated (459):   falling apart

dire (575):   desperate; terrible

dirty old man (145):   stereotype of an old man pursing young women or girls for sexual purposes

disabling (57):   to be too painful for functioning

disc jockey (226):   an announcer for a radio show that plays popular music

discern (14):   understand

disconfirm (29):   prove not true in all cases

discord (89):   disagreement or argument between people

disinhibits (240):   takes away inhibitions or restraints on behavior

dismayed (599):   upset; alarmed

dismissal (145):   being ignored and not taken seriously

disparities (197):   differences

disperse (621):   spread apart

dispute (687):   disagreement

dissenter (620):   one who disagrees

distilled (590):   extracted or taken from

distorted (68):   twisted and bent out of its original shape

distorted (i.e., distorted perception) (587):   unclear; misinterpreted

distractibility (85):   ability to have one's attention drawn in different directions

distraught (126):   being upset and overwhelmed with sadness

dizzying speed (123):   with rapid, rotating speed

do a double take (210):   look, look away, and look back, stop and stare

doctored (203):   altered, changed

dodge (285):   avoid

dodging life's hard knocks (150):   avoiding life's more difficult and painful experiences

dog the heels (611):   pursue; harass; annoy

doggedly (280):   in a determined or persistent manner

dogmatic (641): a steadfast certainty of belief or opinion

dominoes (53): flat, rectangular blocks used as pieces in a game of the same name

doomsday group (632): a group who believes that the end of the world is coming soon

double latte (274): refers to a latte − a drink made with espresso and steamed milk -- made with 2 shots of espresso instead of 1

double whammy (524): being attacked by two things at once

down about school (591): unmotivated or depressed about school

down and out (558): weakened or incapable; depressed

down (514): in a low mood

drab (160): dull

drain off (650): to empty out or remove

drawbacks (284): undesirable effects

dreary (124): sad and gloomy

drew a blank (306): could not remember

dried out (252): stopped drinking

drills (112): repeatedly instructs and tests a person

drink in (156): experience

dripping faucet (209): water slowly coming from a faucet in drops

drive a hard bargain (625): make a good business deal, favorable to one's self

drooled (263): salivated

drop the bomb (233): to give bad news

drudgery (407): dull and fatiguing work

druggy (134): a person who uses drugs and is involved in the drug culture

dumped (i.e., my girlfriend dumped me) (585): abruptly broke a relationship with

dumped (298): removed

dunces (36): stupid, ignorant people

duress (135): forced compliance

dust begins to settle (434): after the debate has subsided

dysfunctional (652): not operating or not operating properly

Early ripe means later rot; the gifted tend to fizzle out as adults (371): a fruit or plant that matures earlier will rot earlier; in the same way, the misconception is that the gifted will mature early but later lose their special abilities

easy as A-B-C (585): easy as learning the alphabet

ebb and flow (76): decreasing and increasing

ebb and flow (i.e., of dream images) (255): the coming and going

ebb (441): to decline

eccentric (351): odd; strange

echolocation (225): using sounds to locate where objects are in the environment

eclectic (590): a combination of very different styles

eclipsed (347): reduced in importance or reputation

Ecstasy (243): relatively new, chemically-synthesized stimulant drug

Edison (330): Thomas Alva Edison (1847-1931), the American inventor who conceived the electric light, phonograph, and microphone

educated guesses (34): guesses based on the best information available

eerie (233): weird, strange

effeminate (433): displaying female characteristics of expressiveness and emotional behavior

egg carton (332): a box designed to hold one dozen eggs

eggheads (371): slang for intellectuals, or very intelligent people

egotistical (636): self-centered

Einstein (330): Albert Einstein (1879-1955), the physicist whose theories of relativity transformed physics and helped to create the atomic age

elaborate (322): to expand with details

Electra (472): character in a Greek tragedy who killed her mother

electrocute (621): to kill by electric shock

elite (406): finest, best

eluded (323): escaped from

emanate (183): to come from or produce

embedded (168): enclosed in

embeds (179): pushes into

embody (338): to represent something

embrace (472): believes in; holds to be true

eminent (406): prominent, famous

empathy (422): the ability to share in another's thoughts and emotions

empirical answers (138): solutions to problems based on the use of good data and solution strategies

empirical (538): based on careful observation or experience

empower (105): to give one power or the right to perform or carry out activities

emulate (406): to model your actions after someone you admire

emulating (657): imitating

encyclopedia (304): a work in several volumes that contains information on all branches of knowledge

endearment (449): affection

engulfed (148): swallowed up or wrapped up

enigma (555): puzzle

entrance into life (123): the idea that life begins when the child starts elementary school, around 6 years old

epidural block (185): anesthesia given to prevent feeling in the lower part of the body

erotic (650): materials tending to arouse sexual desire

errant (637): misbehaving, not following orders

erred (619): made a mistake

escalating (637): increasing

escapades (230): adventures

Eskimo (647): native people of northern Canada, Greenland, Alaska, and eastern Siberia

ESP (47): extra sensory perception; knowledge outside what could be learned through the senses

ether (174): colorless, highly flammable liquid with an aromatic odor

euphoria (61; 224): a sense of well being; feeling happy and good all over

euthanasia (632): mercy killing or assisted suicide for persons with terminal illness

exact map (124): a set of rules to follow

exaltation (480): great happiness

exasperatingly selfish (111): to be overly selfish

excels (467): is good at; performs well at

executive (470): the one in charge

exert (621): force

exhibitionism (537):   sexual stimulation through the exposure of one's genitalia to others to obtain shock

exhibitionist (256):   a person who displays himself or herself indecently in public

exonerated (218):   to be cleared of blame

exploit (405):   to use to one's own advantage

expressed (84):   shown

extracurricular activities (663):   activities at school other than academics

fabled town of Lake Woebegone (657):   the hypothetical town described by host Garrison Keeler on National Public Radio (NPR)

facet (479; 533):   an area or component

facilitate (684):   make easier

fake each other out (654):   fool each other by showing false emotion

fake (487):   to deliberately answer in a misleading manner

faked the whole thing (159):   made it all up

fall short (292):   fail to reach your goal

fallacy (564):   false belief

familiarity breeds contempt (613):   a common saying meaning that the more one knows about a person, the less one likes that person

family barge (636):   the family car, typically considered old, large, inefficient (and probably ugly)

fanatic (280):   enthusiast

fared (483):   worked out; succeeded

farfetched (314):   unbelievable

fascism (641):   tendency toward strong autocratic or dictatorial control

fastball (53):   a type of pitch thrown very fast by the pitcher at a baseball game

feat (281):   accomplishment

feedback (666):   evaluation; corrective information

feel for (654):   care about

feelers (578):   antennas

fending off (673):   keeping away; repelling

fetishism (537):   erotic fixation on an object or bodily part

feverishly (148):   intensely, very fast

fidgeting (443):   moving around restlessly or nervously

fight or flight (59):   a point at which a person or other animal decides to face danger or flee from it

fissuring (556):   divisions among the lobes of the brain

fixing the "hydraulics" of erectile problems (451):   trying to find solutions to the problem of increasing blood flow and pressure to the penis

flaccid (442):   not erect; limp

flamboyant (546):   elaborate or colorful behavior; showy

flash cards (133):   cards presented one at a time to children to teach them to read, do math, improve spelling, etc.

flashbacks (581):   remembered images of events from the past

flawed (352):   containing defects or errors

fleeting (52; 298):   passing quickly; not lasting

flood of relief (184):   the letting go of worry

flotation chamber (224):   an enclosed box where a person can be isolated from most sensory inputs; the person literally "floats" in saline-saturated water and is cut off from sounds, smells, and other sensations as much as possible

flunk (606):   fail

flurry (298; 379):   a quick movement

flustered (627):   confused; agitated

flying by the seat of your pants (177):   operating an airplane without the use of instruments; in general, doing a task without really knowing what one is doing

folklore (613):   traditional customs, stories, or sayings of a people

folksy (628):   old-fashioned; out of date

fondling (443):   caressing, touching

foolproof (79):   absolute; true

foraged (175):   searched for

foreboding (561):   feeling that something harmful or bad is going to happen

forecast (16):   to predict

foreclosure (516):   the claim of ownership of a property such as a home when no payment has been made over time

foremothers (20):   women who preceded our present time

forensic (680):   used in legal arguments or courts of law

foreshadowed (369):   having shown or predicted an incident before it occurs

forfeit (293):   give up, lose

forge (380):   form, bring into being

forging (135):   creating

forlorn (97):   unhappy and miserable

forsake (656):   give up or abandon

forte (471):   originally a musical term meaning loud or strong, it is also used to mean strength or one's specialty

fortitude (624):   courage; strength

foul-mouthed (39):   using obscene, crude, and socially unacceptable language

foxy (198):   clever, sly

frazzled (13):   tired out; close to losing control and falling apart

free spirit (636):   independent

free-for-all (645):   brawl or fight

freeze up (147):   become unable to express one's thoughts or feelings

frenzied cities (330):   fast-paced cities

frenzy (280):   intense activity

Freud believed that mental life is like an iceberg (20):   the unknown of the unconscious mind is hidden below consciousness like the large part of a submerged iceberg is below the surface of the water

Freud would have had a field day (512):   would have been pleased with all of the possibilities

Freudian slips (20):   While the mind is thinking about the obvious, the tongue speaks about hidden, unrevealed thoughts

frivolous (345):   not important enough or worthy of receiving attention

frugal (636):   avoiding unnecessary purchases; thrifty

full circle in the cycle of life (149):   from birth to death

full flowering of (109):   full development of

furiously (276):   wildly

fusion (334):   a blending of jazz, rock, Latin, and improvisation to form a modern, smooth type of jazz

futile (350; 507):   useless

futile (575):   hopeless

futility (147):   uselessness

Galileo(330): Galileo Galilei (1564-1642), the Italian astronomer and physicist who pioneered the use of the scientific experimental method and developed the first refracting telescope

Gallantly (66): heroically

gambling with their lives (448): putting their life at risk

game of chance (691): gambling

gamma rays (156): very short wavelength rays emitted by radioactive substances

gangsta rapper (86): someone who performs the type of music known as "gangsta rap"

gas-guzzler (636): not fuel efficient

Gatorade (398): a drink that is taken especially after exercise to help restore minerals lost through perspiration

gauge (199; 480): measure

gauntlet of modern life (140): the difficulties one encounters in living in the present time

gay (439): homosexual

gelatin-like (179): soft and very pliable substance

gemstones (72): mineral or petrified material that can be cut and polished for jewelry

genius (363): an exceptionally intelligent person

genocide (644): the systematic, planned destruction of an entire race or political or social group

gestural (338): using motions of the hands or body as a means of expression

get a shot (266): get an injection

get blown out of proportion (527): become exaggerated in importance

get the large half of a wishbone (272): refers to the practice in which two people pull on opposite sides of a chicken or turkey breastbone; the person who has the larger piece when the bone breaks is considered to be the one who will get what he or she wished for

getcha (107): get you

gimme (339): give me

give me a hand (686): help me

gizmos and doohickeys (330): names for machines or tools often used when the true name is unknown or not remembered

glandular activity (18): activity results from glands that make up the endocrine system

gleaned from (480): gathered information from

go belly-up (511): stop working

go for it (470):   go after what you want; do it

go up in smoke (87):   disappear

goad (476; 666):   something that urges or stimulates into action

goatee (26):   a beard that has been trimmed down to a point on the chin

goggles (195):   large glasses or lenses

golden era (235):   period of great happiness, prosperity, and achievement

goldsmith (350):   a craftsman who works with gold

good vibrations (170):   the title of a well-known pop music song; implies feeling good

gorge (396):   eat to excess

gossip (592):   to share personal information with someone about other people

got caught on (356):   got stuck on a problem

gotcha (107):   got you

gouging (540):   forcing out with the thumb

gourmet (175):   a person very knowledgeable about good food and drink

grab bag (275):   a bag that is filled with various small prizes that a child may reach in and pick a prize that he/she wants as a reward for being good

gradients (200):   gradual changes or variations

graffiti (672):   writings or drawings made on some public surface

grandparent boom (141):   a sudden surge in the number of people who are grandparents

grandstand catches (60):   in baseball, to catch the ball so as to impress the fans

grappling (562):   struggling and trying to cope

G-rated (289):   General audience; something anyone can watch

green and miserable with motion sickness (180):   feeling nauseated; sick to the stomach

groggy (402):   sleepy

grooms (270):   cleans, licks itself

grossed out (597):   disgusted

grossly obese (482):   extremely overweight

grossly (205):   to a very large extent

grotesque (203):   bizarre, differing very much from what is normal

Ground Zero (504):   the place where the twin towers of the World Trade Center stood

grown-ups (115): adults

grubbies (610): old, unattractive clothes

grunge rock (334): type of alternative rock music characterized by more distortion and slower tempos; it often incorporates elements of punk rock and heavy metal

gulf (481): a space or an opening

gullible (14; 434): believe everything you hear

gun control (632): attempts to legislate the possession of guns

guru (14): personal religious teacher and spiritual guide

gut responses (267): emotional responses, made without thinking

gut wrenching (650): emotionally difficult

gut-level response (482): arising from one's innermost self, instinctual

hacker (134): one who is very interested in computers

had some rough spots (616): having been in difficult situations

half-hearted effort (611): not trying as hard as one could or should

half-truth (73): something that appears to be totally true but is not completely so

Halloween (416): celebrated on October 31; children wear masks and costumes and go to neighbors' houses asking for candy

hallucinations (226): imaginary perception of objects that do not exist in reality

halo (614): in art, a circle of light around the head of a person that indicates holiness, goodness, or virtuousness; in psychology, the tendency to rate a person too high or too low on the basis of a single trait

ham (brings out the "ham" in many people) (240): actor; a person who overacts

Hamlet (306): a play written by William Shakespeare

Hang out a shingle (27): start up a business by hanging up a sign

hang-up (471): problem; barrier

haphazard (28): not planned; random

haphazardly (271; 283): marked by lack of plan, order, or direction

harbors embers of mental brilliance that intense practice could fan into full flame (373): we each may have unrealized potential that could be turned into major ability if we worked at it

hard-of-hearing (173): partially or totally deaf

hard-wired (94): coded into our genes

harebrained scheme (348): foolish idea

has it in for me (592):   is against me; doesn't like me

hassling (591):   annoying, bothering

haven (455):   a safe place

head banging (129):   a self-injurious behavior often done by children with autism; the child repeatedly bangs his or her head against a wall or other solid object

head cheese (180):   sausage made from the head, feet, and sometimes tongue and heart of a pig

Heads, and the subject is in the experimental group, tails, it's in the control group (36):   the person is placed in one group or the other according to which side of a coin lands facing up (in other words, completely according to chance)

heads (691):   the side of a coin with the face on it

heart arrhythmias (246):   irregular heartbeat

heated debate (363):   intense discussion and sometimes disagreement

Heaven's Gate (637):   cult based on the idea that extraterrestrial beings would take the group members away in a UFO if they left their bodies behind (committed suicide); this event was to take place at the time of the appearance of the Hale-Bopp comet in 1997, at which time the members committed group suicide

heaving (two meanings) (180):   moving rapidly up and down; vomiting

heavy (If you are an aging rock star, you will no doubt call everything "heavy," man.) (206):   slang for "meaningful" or "significant"

heavy metal (334):   energetic and highly amplified rock music with a hard beat

heft (17):   to get the feel of, to lift something up

heinous (555):   evil; horrible

hemmed in (44):   held back from doing something

hemophilia (87):   a condition that characterizes excessive bleeding due to inadequate coagulation of the blood

hemophiliacs (448):   those who have a blood disease characterized by delayed clotting of the blood and resulting tendency to bleed easily

hide in the closet (266):   avoid being found

high points (333):   the most interesting parts of a game or event

high-strung (42):   nervous; easily excited

highway hypnotism (224):   refers to the fact that drivers on long distance trips sometimes lose concentration due to the sameness of the road and scenery

hilarious (230):   very amusing or funny

Hillary Clinton (122):   New York Senator and wife of former American President Bill Clinton

hip-hop (334):   a style of music and dance that derives from inner-city street culture; rap music is part of hip-hop

hip-hop type (460):   a type that derives from inner-city street culture; it includes rap music and a style of dress and dance

histrionic (534):   very emotional; displaying emotion to gain attention

hit like a thunderbolt (66):   hit very fast and deadly

hit rock bottom (253):   reached the lowest point personally and emotionally

hitchhike (506):   to travel from place to place by getting free rides from motorists

hitchhiker (198):   a person who asks for rides from passing cars or trucks

hits (214):   correct answers

hitting below the belt (454):   being unfair and hurtful

HIV (87):   human immunodeficiency virus; precursor to AIDS

hives (517):   an allergic disorder that causes the skin to itch and break out in bumps

hobbled (432):   to make movement difficult

hocked gem (299):   a gem that has been pawned or traded in

Hockey cards (114):   cards that show famous hockey players that many children use to trade for the cards they want

holdover (198):   something that continues to exist from previous times

home base (97):   a baseball reference and a place of safety and refuge

home plate (683):   in baseball, the place where the batter stands to bat and where a runner must return in order to score a run (point)

homegrown (683):   coaching methods that coaches created themselves

Homo sapiens (647):   human beings

hooch (546):   building where members of the military live; barracks

hooting and whooping (459):   yelling with pleasure and excitement

hoots of laughter (166):   loud laughter

Hopi of Northern Arizona (464):   a Native American tribe found primarily in the American southwest

hot water bottles (185):   soft plastic bottles filled with water and put on injured parts of the body to relieve pain

hothousing (112):   a botanical term meaning to force plants into early blooming, and used here to mean to push children too fast, too early

hotshot (462):   a person who displays great skills and abilities

hourglass (343):   an instrument for measuring time consisting of a glass container having two sections, one above the other; sand, water, or mercury runs from the upper section to the lower in one hour

human potential (587):   belief that humans have the potential to be fully alive and functioning at the highest level possible

humankind (15):   all human beings considered as a whole

hunch (29; 241):   guess

hung over (36):   feeling sick (headache, stomachache) because of drinking too much alcohol the day before

hung up (343):   delayed, detained by

hunger pangs (390):   extreme feeling of hunger

hurdles (190):   difficulties, problems, barriers

hyper (43):   excessively active

hyperactive (16; 536):   excessively active; always moving about and cannot sit still

hyperventilation (224):   excessive rate of respiration (breathing)

hypnosis (61):   an altered state of consciousness in which a person responds easily to suggestions

hypnotic susceptibility (691):   one's ability to be hypnotized

hypothetical (304):   assumed as an example

I can't handle it (550):   inability to cope with life's difficulties

I must be a total zero (585):   I must be worthless

IBM (300):   International Business Machines, a very large U.S.-based computer company

ice packs (185):   wraps containing ice to put on injured parts of the body to relieve pain

icing on your study cake (323):   being easy to review

icons (202):   small images on a computer screen used to represent functions or programs

If the doors of perception were cleansed, man would see everything as it is, infinite (220):   to see without judgment leads to an accurate view of the surrounding world

if you've seen one tree, you've seen them all (219):   the tendency to use a single example to generalize to all objects in a category

iguana (230):   large tropical American lizard

illicit (245):   illegal

illusion (199):   a misleading image presented to vision

illustrious (110):   well known for extraordinary achievement in academia

immobilized (233):   incapable of movement

immunize (attempts to "immunize" youths) (500):   give them information that will keep them safe, just as immunizations are given to keep people from getting sick

imp (326):   a playful and naughty being

impart (199):   to show

impede (505):   slow; make difficult

implications (42):   possible results

impossible dream (140):   a goal in life that is very unlikely to be attained

impotence (573):   inability to perform sexually

impromptu (609):   unplanned; unrehearsed

in droves (610):   in large numbers

in the blink of an eye (268):   this phrase has 2 meanings: in the future we can detect dementia very easily and quickly and the test can be done with the blinking of one eye.

in the eye of the beholder (389):   according to each person; each person will measure the value in their own way

in the long run (497):   eventually

in the zone (52):   peaking in performance in a particular athletic skill

in your corner (620):   on your side; supportive of you

incapacitated (262; 532):   incapable of functioning normally

incentives (389; 583):   motivating factors

incestuous (473):   having to do with sexual relations between two people who are closely related

incompatible (283):   not in accord with each other; not suitable for use together

incongruity (210):   not conforming to the expected pattern, inconsistent

incubation (350):   period during which ideas are developed

incubation (i.e., infection…don't appear for 10 years) (448):   period between the infection of an individual and the appearance of symptoms of disease

incubator (96):   a machine in which eggs (e.g., chickens and ducks) are kept at a controlled temperature to facilitate hatching

incursion (336):   a hostile entrance into a territory

indoctrinating (637):   intense teaching and instruction intended to convert a person's basic beliefs

inductive reasoning (112):   to reason from the specific to the general

industrial settings (582):   factories

inept (129):   unable to perform well in certain situations; not competent

inert substances (37):   substances that have no active properties to affect behavior

inert (91):   does not have the ability to respond

infallible (217; 637):   without mistakes

infatuated (211):   in love

inferences (609):   guesses

inferred (460):   resulted from, deduced from observation

infidelity (617):   unfaithfulness

infirm (142):   weak due to health problems

inflammatory claim (383):   a statement that intends to produce strong feelings

inflate (377):   artificially increase

inflated conclusion (390):   an exaggerated and incorrect conclusion

infusion machine (38):   a machine that allows doctors to inject saline and other solutions into a vein rather than multiple veins of their patients.

ingenious (419):   very clever

ingenuity (129):   a person's own ability and resourcefulness toward solving a problem

ingrained (203; 537):   innate, firmly fixed

ingredients (for psychosis) (558):   list of factors that contribute to psychosis

ingredients (406):   characteristics

inherently (479)   involved in the framework or essential character of something

initiation rites (182):   ritualistic procedures sometimes used to admit people to organizations such as fraternities or sororities

innate intelligence (368):   intelligence one is born with

innate (189):   inborn; a biologically inherited ability

innocence of vision (479):   experiencing and seeing the same object like it was seen for the first time

insights (256):   self-knowledge

instant replay (333):   used in televised sports to repeat a play that has just taken place

institutions (374): secure, hospital-like settings for persons with profound mental retardation or very severe mental illness

integrates (189): blends together

integrity (600): honesty

intercepted (577): read or found out by others

interdependence (103): when people view themselves as members of their group from which they receive their status and self-worth

interminable (579): never ending or continuous

interns (228): recent graduates of medical school (in this case) doing their first year of supervised practice; they tend to work long hours in hospital

interplay (91): to influence one another

intrepid (216): fearless

intricate (380): complicated

intricately shaped (175): complex and elaborately designed

intrinsically (667): internal

introverted (351): being wholly concerned with and interested in one's own mental life

intuitions (257): something known or sensed without evident rational thought

invading (61): taking over and doing harm

IQ (89; 697): a measure of intelligence

irony (67): statements in which the intended meaning is the opposite of the usual meaning

irony (232): a result that is different, or the opposite, from what is expected

island of brilliance. . . in a sea of retardation (363): displaying an extraordinary talent or skill while other mental capabilities are developmentally retarded

isolated (30): not connected to anything else

it is based on...patented gadgets (215): tricks done by magicians and by those who practice ESP on stage use devices that can be bought in magic supply stores, such as trick playing cards or dice

it takes a lot of cooks to spoil the broth (158): one cook wouldn't spoil the soup, but the changes introduced by a lot of cooks might be enough to spoil it

It's the hook that eventually snares the addict (244): the drug produces good feelings that the person wants to repeat taking it again and again. The repeated behavior causes the person to become an addict

itching to discover (29): having a strong desire to discover

it's not nice to fool Mother Nature (96):   it doesn't work well to go against natural animal instincts and development

J. K. Rowling (122):   the author of the Harry Potter series

Jamaican-accented (214):   a language accent that sounds like the person is from Jamaica

jargon (686):   technical language of a special activity or group

jarring (641):   disturbing

Jeffrey Dahmer (554):   convicted murderer, who drugged his victims, sexually molested them after death, and removed and ate their body parts, which he kept stored in a refrigerator

Jennifer Lopez (122):   an American singer and actress

jet lag (140; 402):   condition characterized by fatigue and irritability that occurs following long flights through several different time zones

jigsaw puzzle (646):   a puzzle consisting of small, irregularly cut pieces that are to be fitted together to form a picture

jingle (544):   short verse or song used repetitively with commercials to fix them in your memory

jock itch (444):   ringworm; or itching in the crotch area

jock (134):   athlete

jog (322):   trigger or revive

jogging (303):   to encourage remembering

John F. Kennedy (318):   President of the U.S. in the early '60s

John Glenn (122):   an American astronaut

joined the ranks of the homeless (595):   become homeless

joint (224):   marijuana cigarette

journals (30):   periodicals that present research and reviews in a specific subject area

juggler (179):   a performer who entertains by throwing and keeping a number of objects in the air at the same time

jumbled (182; 190):   mixed up; not organized

jumbo jet (209):   largest of jet aircraft

jump the gun (212):   start the race before the starting gun fires

junk food (292):   food with little nutritional value

just around the corner (543):   about to happen soon

kaleidoscope (156):   a constantly changing pattern or scene

karate chop (71):   hitting with the side of the hand

keen (27):   insightful

keep your bearings (459):   understand the text; keep your orientation

keyed-up (654):   prepared and ready to act

killer instinct (647):   innate desire to kill

kinda (686):   kind of

kinesthesis (180):   sensory information given by organs located in the muscles, tendons, and joints and stimulated by bodily movement

knockoffs (266):   imitations of famous-brand products

knuckle under (623):   submit

kosher (658):   following the rules specified by Jewish law (usually refers to eating and food preparation)

Ku Klux Klan (293):   a racist secret society in the U.S.; its members are opposed to minorities

labor of love (500):   a job or activity that one cares about greatly

labored (68):   with difficulty

laden (555):   full of

language dance (107):   the development of language through the interaction between the child and the caregivers

lapses (240):   interruptions

Las Vegas or a similar gambling mecca (279):   Las Vegas is a city where gambling is legal, so people who like to gamble (play for money) are attracted there; Mecca is a Moslem holy city to which Moslems make pilgrimages (a religious trip); therefore, a mecca is a place visited by many people

lax (607):   not strict

leaning on the horn (13):   blowing the horn in an automobile

leap to any conclusions (79):   make a decision before looking at all the facts

left out (77):   not invited; not included

left-brained (431):   preference for using the left hemisphere of the brain

legacy (648):   something that has come from the past; passed down from one's ancestors

legal cures (130):   using the law to solve social problems

legitimate (576):   certified

lesbians (439):   female homosexual persons

let off steam (126):   acting out normally unacceptable behavior by expending excess energy

lethal (499; 619):   deadly

lethargic (13; 238):   drowsy; lacking energy

lets you down (521):   disappoints you

Lewis Carroll (332):   A pseudonym for Charles Lutwidge Dodgson, the famous English author who wrote Alice in Wonderland and Through the Looking Glass

liability (217):   something that is to a person's disadvantage

liberalization (445):   the encouragement of individuals to have the maximum freedom to express their opinions and ideas

light years (156):   the distance light will travel in one year at 186,000 miles per second

like well-oiled machines (666):   efficiently operating like a well-maintained machine

linebacker (203):   in football, a defensive player positioned behind the linemen

lingo (686):   special vocabulary of a particular field of interest

link (577):   connection

literal (256):   actual, obvious; exact meaning

lithium chloride (395):   a liquid poison

lived richly (124):   having lived an active and productive life without regrets

loaded coin (697):   a coin that has the tendency to land only on one side (e.g., always landing on heads up)

loaded (611):   drunk

loafing (527):   resting; relaxing

loner (473):   one who avoids social contact with others

loophole in the statement (39):   the statement has a misleading logic (sound judgment based on inference)

lopsided (80; 203):   not symmetrical or balanced in shape

lucid (141; 258):   having a clear understanding and awareness

lull (443):   to slowly convince

lulled (637):   calmed

lumberjack (459):   logger; one who cuts trees for lumber

lunged (420):   rushed forward suddenly

lure (636):   to draw someone away from their normal path

lymph nodes (523):   rounded masses of lymph tissue (lymph is a fluid that bathes the tissues and contains white blood cells)

macho fantasy (436):   a fantasy contrived by men that depicts male sexual desires

macro (226):   large

Madame Curie (330):   Marie Curie (1867-1934), the French chemist who first isolated the radioactive element radium; she was the first person to win two Nobel prizes

madness (225):   archaic term for severe mental illness

Madonna (190):   famous blonde popular singer, considered by some people to resemble Marilyn Monroe

maggots (597):   fly larvae

major league pitchers (271):   the players on major baseball teams who have the position of pitcher

major league (53):   referring to the top baseball teams

major overhaul (571):   complete repair

make monkeys out of (339):   make fools of

make-or-break (497):   an event or activity that can determine success or failure in some aspect of one's life

making a scene (627):   exhibiting anger or improper behavior

maladaptive (128):   poorly adjusted

maladies (537):   illnesses

male chauvinist (634):   a person who believes men are superior to women and speaks and behaves accordingly

maligned (551):   to be criticized, smeared

marathons (404):   long-distance foot-races, usually of 26 miles

Mardi Gras (224):   a very large, crowded street party celebrated in New Orleans forty days before Easter

Marilyn Monroe (190):   famous blonde movie actress (1926-1962)

marine snail (320):   sea snail, as opposed to a land snail

marital discord (129):   tension and disagreement within a marriage

marksmanship (336):   the art of shooting

marred (150):   damaged

Mars Climate Orbiter (620)   signals from the orbiter probe were lost as it entered orbit around Mars; no signal has been detected since

Martha Graham (330):   (1893-1991), a well-known American dancer and choreographer

Martin Luther King Jr. (318):   an African-American political figure who advocated peace and racial equality

martyr (349):   great or constant sufferer

mask (134):   cover up

masochism (182):   taking pleasure in receiving pain

masquerading (80):   wearing a mask to cover and disguise one's face

mass media (500):   television, radio, newspapers

mastery (538):   ability, knowledge of an area

Maya Angelou (122):   author, poet, historian, musician, songwriter, actress, playwright, film director, and civil rights activist; wrote I Know Why the Caged Bird Sings and other works

measles (87):   a contagious viral disease characterized by red circular spots on the skin

Mechanistic (somewhat mechanistic view of human nature) (23):   can be explained by mechanical laws; no free will

meddling old woman (145):   stereotype of an older woman interfering in the affairs of others

medicine man (380):   healer and spiritual leader in Native American, Central and South American tribal groups; shaman

medium-priced meal (208):   an average cost for a meal

mellowing (138):   being made gentle and accepting by age or experience

melodramatic (522):   exaggerated; overly dramatic

meltdowns (620):   nuclear power accidents

melting pot (656):   all the ingredients (people in this case) are blended together, and individual identity is lost

memory-like or dream-like experiences (73):   experiences that are not real, but seem to be so

menagerie (100):   collection of wild animals kept for exhibition

mental giant (286):   extremely intelligent

mental scratch pad (298):   an area of the brain for writing and reading notes; it doesn't exist in a literal form, but is used here to represent working memory

mental territory (114):   ways of thinking, reasoning, and problem-solving

mentalists (47):   type of magician whose tricks involve knowing what people are thinking

meshed (666):   combined

meticulous (214):   very careful and precise; detail oriented

Michelangelo (330):   Michelangelo Buonarrotti (1475-1564), a famous Renaissance artist who created such famous works as the statue of David and the ceiling mural in the Sistine Chapel in Rome

Milestones (94; 122):   significant points in development

military inductees (369):   persons drafted or who enlisted in the armed forces

mime (338):   to imitate actions without using words

mimic (417):   copy

mimics (91):   people who copy the actions of others

mind reading (454):   attempting to know what another person is thinking without actually asking him or her

mired (431):   stuck

miscarriage (246):   failure to continue a pregnancy (loss of the fetus)

misery loves company (612):   a common saying meaning those in an unpleasant situation like to be with others in the same situation

misshapen (160):   deformed; not in the normal shape

mission (479):   purpose or goal

mnemonist (309):   a person who uses special techniques (mnemonics) to improve the memory

mock (680):   pretend; simulated

mod (134):   short for modern; one who is bold in dress, style, behavior

model (104):   the best example of

monogamous relationships (449):   intimate relationships with one partner only

Monopoly (112):   a popular board game in which players attempt to buy and control property and industries

monotonous (224):   unchanging

moon madness (47):   belief that a full moon causes certain people to commit crimes or act strangely

moral compass (137):   one's sense of right or wrong that guides behavior

moral high ground (644):   the superior moral position

mores (445):   moral attitudes

morphine (182):   an opium-like drug used against pain

mosh pit (224):   slang term for an area at a music concert where audience members dance aggressively, often slamming themselves into one another

motion sickness (180):   nausea, and sometimes vomiting, caused by the motion of a car, boat, or airplane

movie censor (334):   person who gives ratings to movies depending on their sexual content and amount of violence

Mozart (14; 330):   Wolfgang Amadeus Mozart (1756-1791), a famous Austrian composer and pianist

MTV (298):   a television station that plays music videos

mud to brew (34):   coffee to make

muddled (335; 686):   unclear; confused

mugging (650): attacking and robbing an unsuspecting person

multimillionaire (693): a person who has two or more millions of dollars

musky (174): having an odor like musk, a substance with a penetrating, long lasting odor obtained from the male musk deer and used in perfume

mustard packs (185): wraps containing powdered mustard that are put on injured parts of the body to relieve pain

mute (583): not speaking

mutism (552): inability to speak

myopia (251): nearsightedness

National Enquirer (46): a weekly tabloid newspaper that publishes wild, sensational stories that are often untrue

National Guard (634): a militia force recruited by each state in the U.S., equipped by the federal government, and called into active duty in the case of national or state emergencies

nature-nurture debate (84): the influence of heredity versus environment

navigate around the town (286): move from place to place in your town

Nein! Nein! Basta! Basta! Not! Dude! (108): ways of saying "no" in different languages. The word "Dude" is an American slang expression young people, mostly males, use with each other as a form of greeting or as a reference to each other

neon lamps (190): type of electric lighting characterized by bright colors that glow

nerds (371): slang, derogatory word for intellectual people

nervous tics (467): nervous habits or actions

net effect (682): final result

neurotic (351): emotionally unstable or troubled by anxiety

new arrival (98): the new child in the home

Newton (330): Sir Isaac Newton (1642-1727), the physicist and mathematician whose ideas created modern physics; he first described the Law of Gravity

nil (438): none

nitpicking (44): unjustified criticism

nit-picky (335): overly critical

No man is an island, entire of itself (605): "No man is an island, entire of itself" is a line from a well-known poem by the 16th-17th century English writer John Donne. It means that each person needs others, and each person's actions have an effect on others.

nomadic (506):   wandering; having no permanent home

nostalgic (149):   longing to relive the experience

notorious (624):   very well known

novices (346):   beginners; amateurs

nudist (334):   person who wears no clothes in groups and special places (nudist camps)

nuisance (45):   something that is annoying or troublesome

nutritionists (308):   those who specialize in the study of proper eating, diets, and the way food is used in the body

obesity (392):   extreme overweight

obnoxious (285):   very offensive or objectionable

obscured (217):   hidden

obsolescence (146):   uselessness; reference to being out of date

obstinate (474):   being stubborn

occult (45):   beyond the range of ordinary knowledge; mysterious

odds are (28):   it is likely

Oedipus (472):   character in a Greek tragedy who unknowingly married his mother and killed his father

off-color jokes (466):   improper or inappropriate jokes that can be offensive

off-line (235):   not of primary or conscious processing

offshoot (472):   development; derivation

ominously (612):   in a threatening or alarming way

on a higher plane (34):   on a more important level

on hold (472):   postponed; put off until a later time

on par (340):   on an equal level

on stage (134):   standing out, being deliberately different from other people

on the sly (419):   secretly

on the verge (565):   on the edge of danger

on top of the world (532):   great; wonderful

one more item on the menu (438):   masturbation is just one more way to have sexual pleasure

one-finger salute (497):   an impolite gesture with the middle finger used to indicate anger or disgust

ongoing symphony (61):   current activities of all parts of the brain performing together as a unit

online (443; 576): accessing and using the Internet

OOOh pobrecito (108): Spanish for "Oh, poor baby"

open-minded (14): able to accept new ideas

opposites attract (613): the belief that persons with opposite personalities, interests, values, etc. will be attracted to one another

Oprah Winfrey (122) an American actress

optimal (101): the best

optimal (265): maximum

orators those distinguished for their skill as public speakers

organic farmer (380): farmer who doesn't use chemical pesticides or fertilizers

orient (632): to make familiar

orphanage (377): a state-operated house where children without parents or relatives to take care of them live until they are adopted

Orthodox Jews (658): Jews who strictly apply the principles and regulations of the Torah and Talmud (Jewish sacred book and traditions) to modern living

Ouija boards (239): a game that involves one asking questions and with one's hands on a marker, moving around a board of letters to spell out answers

out-groups (641): minority groups

outlandish (351): very out of the ordinary, strange

outreach clinics (599): clinics usually set up in neighborhoods to make it easier for people to access health care

over the hill (142): old, past the prime of life

overhaul (384): to completely rework, redesign

overrides (66): takes control over

Ozzy Osbourne (352): a well-known rock star; recently the star of a popular television series along with his wife and two children

paint too grim a picture (132): describing a situation as holding little hope

panorama (12): wide-ranging view

pantomime (338): dramatic presentation that uses no words, only action and gestures

panty-girdle (110): a woman's elasticized underwear

Papua New Guinea (194): western Pacific nation that includes the eastern half of the island of New Guinea, north of Australia

paradoxical (233): something that seems contradictory yet may still be true

paranoia (253): belief that one is being watched, pursued, or persecuted

paranoid delusions (245): irrational beliefs that one is being persecuted; distrustfulness

parents who "ground" their teenage children (274): parents who punish teenagers by forbidding them to go out

parole (680): a conditional release of a prisoner

parrot back (129): repeat or echo back

party animals (608): people who thoroughly enjoy partying, often at the exclusion of other responsibilities

pass out at the door (you would probably pass out at the door) (180): you would faint because of the overpowering bad smell

passed out (189): became unconscious

passive (471): inactive and not showing feeling or interest

payoff (279): money won

PCBs (87; 374): polychlorinated biphenyls, often found in soil and are suspected cancer-causing agents

PCP ("angel dust") (556): a psychedelic drug that causes vivid mental imagery

Pearl Harbor attack (318): the Japanese attack on American ships in Pearl Harbor (Hawaii) on December 7, 1941 that led the U.S. to enter World War II

pea-sized (75): very small; the size of a pea

peek (61): look inside something, usually through a small opening

peekaboo (101): (peek-a-boo) a game to amuse a baby in which the caregiver repeatedly hides his or her face then reveals it again to the baby

penchant (289): habit, desire

pent-up (627): held in; unexpressed

people with two left feet (77): clumsy, uncoordinated people

perfectionists (548): people who must have and do everything "just right"

performance demands (451): perceptions by the male that he must perform sexually

perplexing (16): very hard to understand

persevere (372): persist in spite of opposition

persistent (280): stubborn, determined

perverts (443): those who engage in sexually deviant behavior

pessimistic (pessimism) (463): the tendency to emphasize the worst possible outcome

peyote (224):   a primitive drug derived from an American cactus

phenomenal (310):   outstanding

phobic (453):   reaction based on irrational fear

phony (562):   fake; false

pi (310):   in geometry, the ratio of the circumference of a circle to its diameter

pick-off moves (276):   an advanced play used by the pitcher in a baseball game to keep a runner from stealing (taking) a base

piecework (280):   paid per job completed

ping-pong (269):   table tennis

pipe-bombing (649):   using a type of homemade bomb for destructive purposes

pitfall (43; 353):   a hidden danger or difficulty

placebo (693):   a substance having no effect but given to a patient or subject of an experiment who supposes it to be a medicine

placid retreats (330):   calm, quiet places to go to get away from one's fast-paced life

plague the field (214):   to trouble

plague (233; 340; 462):   bother greatly

plaque (498):   fatty substances deposited in the inner layers of the arteries

playing catch with a Frisbee (57):   a game in which a round plastic disk (a Frisbee) is thrown back and forth between people

PlayStation Portable (267):   hand-held video game

plight of children (98):   the crisis condition of children

plot (436):   story

plumbing the depths…gone down the drain (his adult interest in plumbing the depths of the psyche might have gone down the drain) (126):   Coon is using a humorous metaphor to suggest that his adult interest in examining the psyche might have totally disappeared

plummets (140):   drops rapidly

podcast (680):   broadcasting a lecture to other schools to reduce the teacher's travel from school to school on daily bases

poker chips (275):   tokens used in a card game to take the place of money

police lineups (307):   a line of people arranged for inspection by the victim or witness of a crime to help identify the criminal

pop of a flashbulb (217):   sound the flash of a camera makes

porpoises (15): a black, blunt-nosed whale of the North Atlantic and Pacific Ocean

port (324): left side of a ship, boat, airplane, or space shuttle as one faces forward

posses (135): gangs, but not necessarily gangs who act in antisocial ways

possession by spirits (225): the belief that an evil spirit (such as the devil) or the spirit of a dead person can inhabit the body of a living being

postgraduate (25): training or education beyond the bachelor's degree

posttraumatic stress disorder (638): cognitive, emotional, behavioral, and physiological effects occurring after a trauma or tragedy in one's life

postulated (469): to have claimed without proof

pot (What's in the pot?) (253): marijuana

potency (442): ability to engage in sexual intercourse; somewhat archaic term

potent (253): powerful

potions (610): liquids

POW (637): prisoner of war

precocious (372): developed earlier than normal

predators (395): animals that hunt and kill for food

predispose (488): influence

prejudice (41): judgments made before contrary information can be gathered or learned

preludes (445): introductions, preparation

premise (253): something assumed or taken for granted

prep (134): one who dresses or behaves like a student at a preparatory school (neatly and classically)

primal feeling facilitator (27): a guide who tries to help you understand your most basic feelings

prime beef (336): top grade cattle meat ready for consumption

prime (308): activate, stimulate

primed (637): prepared

prized (482): valued; thought of as important

prizefight (650): boxing match for money

probe (17): examine in detail

procrastinate (316; 611): put off; do later rather than immediately

prodigies (406): highly talented people, especially children

prodigious (373): extraordinary

programmers (621):   people who develop computer software

prophetic (213):   predictive of the future

protect roadrunners from the Wile E. Coyote (395):   in a well-known children's cartoon television show, Wile E. Coyote attempts by trickery to capture and eat the Roadrunner (a type of desert bird that runs fast)

provisional (45):   until more information can be found

provocative (622):   tending to stimulate or excite interest

prowler (411):   a person moving about secretly, as in search of things to steal

prying (555):   looking for information; being nosy

pseudo (562):   false; pretended

psych jockeys (576):   radio psychologists; because music announcers on the radio are called "disc jockeys," Coon calls radio psychologists "psych jockeys"

psyched up (528):   psychologically ready; prepared

psychics (213):   people who claim to be sensitive to nonphysical or supernatural forces and influences

psychoanalysis is the "granddaddy" of more modern psychotherapies (572):   psychoanalysis is the first and oldest form of psychotherapy from which others are descended

psychological variables (695):   concepts in psychology, such as attitude, aggression, intelligence, etc. that can be measured according to some scale

Psychologists would drown in a sea of disconnected facts (30):   they would be very confused

psychoses (532):   basic mental derangements characterized by loss of contact with reality

pudgy (84):   short and plump

pulling the plug (651):   unplugging the TV from the outlet

pumped up (462):   made to feel good, strong, and competent

pumping iron (511):   lifting heavy weights in order to build muscle

punk music (334):   marked by extreme and often offensive expressions of social discontent

punk (212):   a derogatory term for a juvenile delinquent, a young person who has been in trouble with the law

punk (134):   one who dresses or behaves like a punk rocker (for example, with hair dyed purple or has numerous body piercings)

puns (257)   the humorous use of words in such a way as to suggest two or more meanings

puritanical (443):   extremely strict in morals; refers to the Puritans of the 16th and 17th centuries who favored extreme moral strictness

purported (213):   supposed; claimed

pushy (643): overly aggressive

put others on hold (209): temporarily ignore

put yourself down (597): criticize yourself harshly

put yourself in Steven's shoes (297): imagine you are Steven

puttering (527): moving or acting aimlessly or idly; engaging in trivial tasks

Putting the Brakes on Behavior (282): stopping behavior

queasy (183): feeling ill or sick to one's stomach

queer (212): a derogatory term for a homosexual

quell (285): to end or put a stop to

quirks (302; 681): traits someone has that set him/her apart from other people

quit cold turkey (248): stop smoking completely and suddenly instead of gradually

quotas (666): outcomes that must be reached

racial profiling (639): identified on the basis of racial characteristics

radical (18): changes of a sweeping or extreme nature

rampage (39): an uncontrollable aggressive act of violence

rampant (216; 612; 673): widespread

randomly (34): by chance; not according to any set plan

rap (334): characterized by lyrics that are spoken rather than sung

rapper (134): one interested in rap music

rapport (565; 589): a good relationship or closeness

rat chow (376): rat food

rave (224): all night dance parties for young people

raw data (693): original set of data from a survey, experiment, sample, etc.

real hit (266): very popular

realm (52): area of interest

real-world success (371): success in the world outside of the school environment; practical success

reared apart (467): raised in separate homes

rebirther (27): a guide who takes you through the birth experience again

rebound insomnia (232): inability to sleep after one has stopped taking sleeping pills

rebuffs (625): rejections; criticisms

rebuke (284; 478):   yelling at a person because one disapproves of her/his actions

recapturing (323):   bringing back

recipe for psychosis (558):   a description for generating psychosis

recluse (545):   hermit; one who prefers to be alone

recoil (410):   to pull back quickly in a reflexive move

recoup (691):   get an amount back equivalent to your losses

redneck (641):   derogatory term for a white, Southern or Western (Rocky Mountain states), rural, and working-class person

reductionistic (neutral, reductionistic, mechanistic view of human nature) (23):   reducing to the simplest terms

reenacts (586):   acts out something that occurred previously

reflective (380):   able to think in depth about something

regressions to more infantile behavior (126):   behaving like a child

rehashing old arguments (314):   going over the same points again and again

remnant (75; 388):   left-over; something that was once used to aid human survival, that is still with us, but is now unnecessary; remains

reprimands (282):   scolding; expressions of disapproval

resinous (253):   of leftover material

restrained (86):   held back from responding

retaliate (506):   to get revenge

retard (231):   to slow down something

revelation (225):   enlightenment, discovery of personal truth

rheumatoid arthritis (517):   disease characterized by pain, stiffness, and swelling of the joints

rich tapestry (41):   filled with luxurious and abundant diversity of color

richer language (109):   a complex language by which to communicate

riddle (12):   puzzling question

ridicule (620):   teasing someone or making them the object of laughter

riff (52):   a repeated phrase of music, usually supporting a solo improvisation

right hand not knowing what the left hand is doing! (66):   a confused state where a person or a group seems to hold two view points at once, and both sides are unaware of the other

right-brained (431):   preference for using the right hemisphere of the brain

right-hand man (or woman) (77):   the important person near one's side

rigid (637):   stiff and inflexible

ring a bell (Does the Name Pavlov Ring a Bell?) (263):   Is it familiar to you?

ring of truth (44):   sounds like it could be true

ripe old age (76):   living a long time until you are old

ripe targets (626):   the object (i.e., women) is set to be taken advantage of, attacked

risk-taking (102):   behaviors that have a potential for harm

rival (468):   be competitive with

road map (112):   a guide for getting from place to place

road map (122):   a guide to help you live a happier life

rock the boat (620):   disturb the situation; make changes

rocky road or garden path (122):   a rocky road symbolizes difficulties in life; a garden path means an easy and pleasant life

role-play (586):   pretend to be another

Rolfer (27):   a person who gives deep massage for therapy

Romanian orphanages (98):   desperately understaffed orphanages in the country of Romania where the children suffer from too little care and attention

room left over to spare (84):   extra capacity

rote (368):   memorization

rote (341):   use of memory, usually with little intelligence

rough-and-ready illustration (177):   quick and easy demonstration

rude awakening (639):   unpleasant realization

rule of thumb (270):   guideline; practical method

run amok (102; 358):   behave in a totally wild or undisciplined manner

runner's high (182):   an adrenaline surge that athletes often report that provides energy to continue competing

running in place (432):   running, but not getting anywhere

Russian roulette (449):   the practice of spinning the cylinder of a gun loaded with one bullet, pointing the gun at one's head, and pulling the trigger; here it means taking extreme risks with one's health

sabotage (422):   ruin future chances of accomplishing something

sabotage (i.e., by assembly line workers) (666):   destruction of an employer's property or the hindering (slowing down) of manufacturing by discontented workers

sage (234):   wise person

salsa (334):   popular music of Latin American origin combining rhythm and blues, jazz, and rock

samplers (605):   brief introductions

sanctioned massacres (623):   authorized slaying of large masses of people at one time

sanctions (620):   rules or laws

sanctuary (589):   a safe place

Santa Clause (111):   a mythical figure who delivers toys and other presents to children at Christmastime

sarcasm (67):   saying the opposite of one's true feelings for humor or insult

satirize (486):   to make fun of

saturate (350):   to fill up as much as possible

sauerkraut (180):   a salted, fermented cabbage dish from Germany

sauna (404):   a dry heat bath

saunters (280):   walks slowly

saving a place (671):   keeping a place available for someone who comes at a later time

sci-fi movies (61):   science fiction movies

scolding (273; 478):   expressing disapproval

Score one for those who favor heredity (85):   those people who favor heredity as the most important factor are correct in this case

scramble (292):   mix up, put out of order

scrapbook (314):   a blank book in which items such as newspaper articles or pictures are collected and kept

scrapes (126):   predicaments or difficult or embarrassing situations

scratched the surface (670):   examined in a superficial, quick manner

seasoned (404):   experienced

Seattle (246):   The capital city of the state of Washington; well-known for high consumption of coffee

sedatives (232):   drugs that calm nervousness or excitement

see through (492):   to understand beyond the surface level

see-saw back and forth (228):   going back and forth

seething (481):   boiling

self-defeating (584):   in opposition to one's self

self-talk (586): what people tell themselves

seminal (434): original and influential work

senile old fool (145): stereotype that an older person is forgetful, childlike, and foolish as a result of old age

senile (313): showing a loss of mental abilities as a result of old age

sensational (25): intended to produce a thrilling effect

sensitive (55): highly responsive to certain neurotransmitters

sensory deprivation (240): being cut off from information normally received through the five senses

septum (175): partition of tissue that separates the nostrils

serial marriages (126): a series of two or more marriages

sermon (498): lecture or talk by minister or priest

servile (687): submissive

settling down (138): a period of calmness and reflection

sexual mores (637): norms for sexual behaviors (e.g., when, with whom, where, and how to have sexual encounters)

sexual prop (436): a tool, such as sexy outfits that males and females wear, to enhance sexual arousal

shabby (622): run down; poorly kept

shades (170): sunglasses

shallow (614): not deep; not looking for deeper and meaningful explanations

shapes up (272): improves

sharp pangs of grief (148): feelings of intense sadness

sharp (160): in focus

sharp-edged humor (292): harsh, often sarcastic

sheepishly (166; 583): in an embarrassed or timid manner

shift work (402): working schedule that frequently changes, for example, from day to evening to night, then back to day

shifty eyes (417): indicating a tricky nature

shoot baskets (195): play basketball

shop 'til you drop (478): going shopping until one is exhausted and does not have the energy to move anymore

shop steward (139): a person who manages a shop

shortchange (372): cheat

shortchanges (i.e., it shortchanges problem-focused coping) (505): making it less effective

short-circuit (354): an event that reduces the effectiveness of something (thinking) because parts of the process involved were not completed

shortcuts (354): methods of doing something more directly and more quickly than usual

show off (273): try to attract attention by one's behavior

show-off (372): one who thinks that he or she knows all the answers

showered with gifts (471): being given lots of gifts

shrinks (24): a slang term for psychiatrists or head doctors

shuffling (233): to move the feet by sliding along without raising the feet

shut down (228): turn off; become inactive

siblings (376): brothers and sisters

side effects (452): unwanted consequences of taking medications

sidestep (285): to avoid or go around

siesta (228): nap

silence may be golden (285): the common saying "silence is golden" means that quiet moments are rare and should be enjoyed

silent killer (499): a deadly disease with little or no outward warning signs

similarities blaze brightly (468): more attention is paid to the similarities than to the differences

simulated (39): copied or of similar condition of the original

simulated (691): made up data

simulated (606): pretend; faked

simulator (663): a machine that artificially duplicates the conditions one is likely to experience in performing a certain skill

sink or swim (337): one either fails completely or succeeds in an attempt at doing something

sire (618): to be the father of

sizable effect(467): to have a considerable effect, or to influence greatly

sized up (484): evaluated; measured

skeptical (43; 326): critical, not believing that everything you read is true

sketches (462): samples of drawings

ski bum (484): a person who spends a great deal of time on the ski slopes

skinned (691): lose all your money

skydiving (399):   the sport of jumping from an airplane with a parachute

skydiving (195):   the sport of jumping out of an airplane with a parachute; here referring to the baby jumping off the table

slapstick (418):   type of comedy

Sleep Wars (232):   Coon is making reference to the popular science-fiction movie "Star Wars"

sleeping-pill junkies (232):   people who are addicted to sleeping pills

sleight of hand (203):   skill and dexterity used to trick the eye in stage magic

slips of the tongue (20):   The tongue speaks before the mind realizes all of the consequences

slips out (681):   given out by mistake

sloppiness (215):   showing a lack of care

slot machine (279; 582):   a device in a gambling casino into which a patron puts money and hopes to win a larger amount of money

slumping (417):   assume a drooping posture; bending over

slurs (644):   insults

smart aleck (372):   one who wants to be the center of attention

smog (200; 634):   a combination of smoke and fog; air pollution

smother love (125):   love that is so close and confining that the person being loved cannot "breathe"

snake oil (596):   in the past, traveling salesmen sold "tonics," or fake medicine, supposedly made from a variety of ingredients (such as snake oil) to cure illnesses

snap judgments (532):   hurried decisions

snapshots (206):   a picture at a particular point in time

snarling (420):   growling

snicker (263):   laugh in an unkind way

snuff (248):   powdered tobacco to be inhaled, chewed, or placed against the gums

soak up (91):   gather in information, similar to how a sponge gathers in water

sobriety test (177):   a test (such as making a person walk a straight line) to determine if someone has been excessively drinking alcohol

socialized medicine (634):   the provision of medical services for everyone in the country and paid for by the government through taxation

socioeconomic status (663):   an overall ranking based on characteristics such as education and occupation; used to describe people's positions in society

sodomized (447): forced to engage in anal sexual intercourse

soiling (126): having a bowel movement at night in bed or during the day in clothing, rather than using the bathroom as needed

solitary confinement (240): kept alone in a prison cell

someone you could easily push around (490): someone who is easily bullied or influenced by others

Sousa march (610): reference to the music of John Philip Sousa; marches are pieces of music with a strong beat suitable for marching

sowed some wild oats (445): engaged in sexual intercourse with casual partners

spare change (224): money that bystanders will give to street performers or beggars

sparing the rod (285): a Biblical phrase meaning to not punish

sparsely traveled (653): very little traffic

speed freak (245): a person addicted to stimulant drugs

spell disaster (226): lead to a disaster

spice of life (388): that which makes life exciting

spidery (52): composed of thin threads like a spider's web

spike (249): adding a mind-altering substance to someone's drink without his or her knowledge

spin-out (129): a child with autism may have an underreactive vestibular system in which he/she may perform certain behaviors such as spin him/herself around and around in circles to stimulate this system.

spiral (of aggression) (650): increasing in severity, frequency

spiteful (465): malicious, nasty

spleen (523): organ that destroys red blood cells, stores blood, and produces white blood cells

split-second (486): very fast

spoiling (100): implying that babies will turn out "bad" because of too much attention

spontaneously (436): arising from a natural feeling or momentary impulse

Sports Illustrated (615): a popular magazine devoted to sports

sprinters (401): runners who compete in short, fast races

spurred (172): to have increased motivation and interest to start something

spurts (280): brief periods of time

squalid (572): dirty; filthy

squirming (417): twisting about; moving around

stage fright (224; 409; 492): fear of appearing before crowds to perform, give a speech, etc.

stalled (13):   stopped, engine won't start

standoffish (643):   cold and reserved

Stanford University (365):   a highly-respected university in California

Star Wars series (199):   series of famous science fiction movies

starboard (324):   right side of a ship, boat, airplane, or space shuttle as one faces forward

starting blocks (212):   fixtures on the track where a runner places his or her feet prior to starting a race

starved for attention (282):   badly needing and looking for attention

starving to death (262):   so hungry you feel you will die

steep yourself (258):   immerse yourself; concentrate very hard

stigma (392; 562):   mark or sign of shame

still-young night (225):   early in the night

stilted (687):   artificial, stiff, or unnatural

stimulus (156):   something that causes an activity or response

stockade (100):   a place where prisoners are kept

stop intellectualizing (576):   stop analyzing the situation

stormy and troubled (616):   in reference to relationships, when a couple experiences stress, difficulties, and the threat of breaking up

stranded (16):   left without means to depart or leave

streamline (606):   simplify

strenuous (233):   vigorously active

strife (641):   clashes and conflict

strikes (683):   in baseball, a ball pitched to the proper area that the batter misses or hits far to the side of the playing area

stringently (45):   being narrowly and strictly defined

stroke of genius (348):   clever idea

stubby (84):   short, blunt, and thick like a stub

stuck on mental tasks (68):   unable to solve problems using thinking

stupor (226; 594):   a state of limited consciousness

stuporous (552):   mental apathy and dullness

stymied (346):   confused

sublimate (470):   to redirect an urge toward a more socially accepted activity

subliminal self-help tapes (159): audiotapes that are supposed to contain hidden messages that will influence a person subconsciously; played "below" the level of hearing

subliminal (46; 158): functioning below the level of awareness

submissive (478): allowing oneself to be governed by another

subsided (583): lessened

subsidize (255): to support financially; to fund

succumbed (637): to have yielded

sucker ("that sucker I saw yesterday...") (339): used as a general term to refer to a person or object (slang)

sugar buzz (42): overexcitement and nervous energy caused by eating foods or drinking beverages that contain large amounts of sugar

sugar highs (42): same as a sugar buzz (see above definition)

summercamp blues (97): slight sadness while away from home

superficial (124): lacking depth, commitment

superglue (97): a type of adhesive with extremely tight bonding

superstitions (272): beliefs or practices resulting from trust in magic or chance

surfer (134): one who dresses and acts like a person who spends time at the beach surfing

surrender to experience (219): have overconfidence in one's own experience

susceptibility (85; 237): inability to resist

suspend (358): postpone while waiting for further information

suspension bridge (419): a bridge, river, or canyon that has its roadway hanging from cables anchored on each side

sustainable population (672): the population the earth can maintain or hold given a finite set of resources

swarming (497): to hurriedly move as a group in one area

swastika (211): symbol used by Adolf Hitler in Nazi Germany, and so perceived as an anti-Semitic (anti-Jewish) symbol

swat (184): hit

swayed (220; 484): influenced

sweep him off to a weekend hideaway (48): take him away for a romantic weekend trip

sweeps down the axon (53): moves very fast down the axon

swift (379): quick thinking

swindling (681): cheating

switching station (72):   place where railroad cars are changed from one track to another; in this case, the meaning is that the thalamus is the area of the brain where information from the senses is routed to the correct part of the cortex

switching station (319):   refers to the station at a railroad where trains are switched from one track to another, as memory switches from long term to short term

synchronization (403):   happening at the same time

synthesize (37):   to combine into a single unit

syphilis (87):   a contagious disease transmitted by sexual intercourse or other intimate contact

taboos (345):   restrictions imposed by social custom

tacitly (445):   implied or indicated indirectly

tailgating (281):   very closely following a car

tailored (114):   carefully chosen and fit to certain information

tails (691):   the side of a coin opposite the face

tainted (395):   contaminated; having something bad added

take it easy (517):   relax

take the edge off (185):   decrease the pain

takes a toll or take their toll (453; 501):   have a negative effect

takes a break (280):   takes a rest from a job or task

taking stock (140):   assessing one's situation

talent will surface (406):   talent (inborn skill) will eventually become obvious

tallied (142):   added up

tampered with (31):   affected by

tampered (508):   interfered

tangible (275):   something that can be touched

tap (257):   gain access to

tapestry (605):   heavy, reversible textile that has designs or pictures woven into it

tattooing (184):   making designs on the body by inserting color under the skin or by producing scars {"producing scars" usually termed scarification; different from tattooing}

T-bone (505):   a beef steak

tear it up (72):   destroy

techno geek (460):   a person who spends much of his or her time with technical things such as computers

teeming (672): filled to overflowing

teetotaler (499): a person who drinks very little alcohol; an inexperienced drinker who gets drunk very quickly

telling (483): revealing; effective

telltale (66): something that serves to disclose information

terminal illness (135): an illness from which there is no hope of recovery

terminate (600): end; stop

testimonials (47): statements recommending a product or treatment

testy (365): irritable

That guy is really wacko. His porch lights are dimming. "Yeah, the butter's sliding off his waffle. I think he's ready to go postal (532): slang expressions for "crazy" and "insane" (which are themselves slang words for mental illness)

Thanksgiving turkey (280): the customary meal on the American holiday of Thanksgiving, celebrated in November

the Arapesh, the Senoi, and the Navajo (647): the Arapesh and Senoi are tribes in Malaysia; the Navajo refers to a Native American tribe

the benefit of the doubt (643): overlooking problems or deficits

the best of times, the worst of times (132): the opening line of the book, A Tale of Two Cities, and used here to reflect the ups and downs of adolescence

the Challenger space shuttle disaster (318): the spaceship that exploded shortly after take-off, killing everyone on board (January, 1986)

the Columbia space shuttle disaster (318): the spaceship that disintegrated while reentering the earth's atmosphere, killing everyone on board (February, 2003)

the devil and the deep blue sea; the frying pan and the fire (507-508): both are common sayings that mean one has to choose between two equally unpleasant choices

the die is cast (138): decisions made cannot now be changed, and one's fate is now set

the enforcer (503): a reference to a person who might use physical threat to collect a debt

the graying of America (141): a large proportion of Americans are reaching middle age, and their hair may be turning gray—a typical sign of aging

the infirm and demented to aerobic-dancing grandmothers (145): a comparison of the weak and the insane grandmothers to the healthy and active grandmothers

the jury is out (352): a judgment hasn't been made yet

the last straw (511): the final event in a series of difficulties

The lion and the lamb shall lie down together (226): according to the Bible, at the end of the world enemies will become friends, even in the animal world

the Mafia (552): organized crime group

the nightly roller coaster ride (228): a roller coaster is an amusement park ride that causes the rider to go up and then quickly down steep inclines; here referring to the fact that sleep is characterized by stages, from the lightest (stage one) to the deepest (stage four)

the pill (449): oral medication taken to prevent pregnancy

the presence of a police car brings about rapid reductions in driving speed...and, in Los Angeles, gun battles (281): refers to the fact that some drivers on the freeways in Los Angeles have fired weapons at other drivers

the straw that broke the camel's back (505): a common saying that means the last negative event in a series of negative events

The Towering Inferno (662): the title of a well-known movie about a devastating fire in a high-rise building

the womb to the tomb (84): from birth to death

there's more to it than meets the eye (165): the subject is more complex than it first seems to be

they swallow things easily (471): this statements has two references; individuals in the oral stage seek pleasure by swallowing things and these individuals have the tendency to believe anything told to them even if the information is false.

This, too, shall pass (106): A Biblical reference meaning "Do not worry, soon this trouble will be over also"

Those who live by their wit die with their wits (143): people who are healthy and maintain a stimulating environment throughout their life tend to retain their intellectual abilities in their 60s

thrash (230): to move or toss about

thread a needle (195): putting thread through the very small opening in a needle; the first step in sewing

Three-Mile Island (402): location of a U.S. nuclear power plant accident

threshold (395): a set point or amount; a dividing line

throw tantrums or throws a temper tantrum (273): yell, scream, or throw things in order to get what one wants

tied the knot (151): to have gotten married

Tiger Woods (122): an American professional golfer

tightwad (510): someone who is very careful about spending his/her money

tip the scales (565): have a deciding influence

to "buy" outrageous claims (45): to believe claims that are too extraordinary to be true

To be forewarned is to be forearmed (516): a common saying meaning that if one knows about a danger ahead of time, one can prepare against it

to break through the wall of silence (172): in this case, to hear sounds with the use of a hearing aid

to capture attention (209): to make one aware or take notice

to curb (130): to control, prevent

to make out (I was too far away to make out what he was eating) (31): to be able to see; distinguish

to pass the time (144): to do something simply because there is nothing else to do

to pitch in (…so no one feels required to pitch in.) (16): to get involved

to put it bluntly (217): to say plainly

to thine own self be true (151): a Biblical phrase meaning to honor oneself and to stay committed to one's set of values

to weave (303): to form and connect by moving side to side

tofu (52): soybean curd, often eaten as an alternative to meat

tokens (275): something that can be exchanged for desired goods or services

tomboys (431): girls who prefer the company and the activities of boys

tossed salad (656): all the ingredients (people in this case) are together but keep their original identity

touched off by (304): is reached and recalled

towered over (132): being much taller than another

toying with (276): playing with; fingering aimlessly

transcend (14): to rise above or go beyond the limits of

transpire (257): happen

transsexual (427): person who undergoes surgery to modify the sex organs to have them appear the same as those of the opposite sex

trapeze artist (91): a performer on the "trapeze," a bar suspended in the air by two ropes

trappings (648): signs and indications of

traumatic (317): very disturbing or upsetting

treat (280): something good to eat, like candy

tremors (246): uncontrollable shaking

trench coats (442): In a rare form of exhibitionism, exhibitionists may wear raincoats (trench coats) with no clothing under the coat

trendy (686): fashionable

tricky (588):   difficult

trivet (24):   a short-legged metal or ceramic plate for holding hot dishes at the table

trivial (100; 236; 313):   of very little importance

trophy wives (618):   wives chosen primarily for their physical attractiveness so men can "show them off"

truancy (128; 677):   purposely missing or "skipping" school

tuba (610):   large brass musical instrument that makes a deep sound

tug of gravity (179):   gravity pulling one down

tune (93):   adjust behavior according to each learned skill

tuned out (184):   ignored

tuned (204):   pay attention to

tune-up (288):   general adjustment of a car to improve performance

tuning fork (170):   a metal device that gives a fixed musical tone when it is struck with or against another object

tuning in and tuning out (180):   slang for paying attention (tuning in) and not paying attention (tuning out)

tuning the car's radio (209):   selecting a station on the radio

turbulent time (123):   a difficult, rough, and troublesome time

turmoil (617):   a confusing and unpredictable state or situation

turns cold and distant (273):   one ignores and does not talk to another person.

tutors (114):   people who serve as one-to-one instructors or guides to others

TV zombie effect (33):   watching too much television turns people into passive and uninterested students

tweeter (158):   loudspeaker for very high-pitched sounds

twisting your arm (257):   making you do something that you would rather not do

twitch (68):   move with a sudden motion

two-edged sword (384):   can be used in more than one way; can have both positive and negative results

tyrant (228):   absolute ruler

UFOs (45):   Unidentified Flying Objects. Typically refers to alien space craft visiting earth

umpires (683):   officials in baseball who oversee the game and make decisions during the course of play

unbiased (691):   not leaning one way or the other

under the gun (408):   working under intense pressure

undercurrent (21):   an underlying or hidden attitude; a hint

unduly (634):   being excessive, unjustifiable

unfolds (90):   develops

uninhibited (463):   not restrained by social norms; informal

universal (84):   found everywhere, among all cultures

unleashed a flood of (304):   having allowed an abundance of information to be released or come out all at once

unleashes tears and bottled-up feelings of despair (148):   letting go of feelings of hopelessness, often resulting in expressions of grief.

unleashes (314):   releases

unmanned (57):   without a human present to operate a jet

until even brighter beacons are flashed into the shadowy inner world of thought (62):   until newer and better techniques reveal more about the little-understood world of thought

unwittingly (478):   not intentionally

Upper Paleolithic (86):   late Stone Age (30,000 years ago), characterized by use of rough stone tools

uppers (244):   stimulant drugs

upshot (162):   result

uptight (526):   tense, nervous

urban areas (103):   the core or central areas of large cities

urban cowboys and Skol bandits (248):   urban cowboys are men who live in cities, but attempt to act like cowboys (here by using chewing tobacco); Skol is a popular brand of chewing tobacco

urological exam (436):   an inspection of the genital and urinary track of men

use it or lose it view (144):   a belief that if one does not continue to do things they have been accustomed to doing, they will lose the ability to do those activities

use it or lose it (438):   suggests that if one is sexually active, there is a tendency to remain sexually active; not being sexually active can lead to a loss of sexual desire

USN (300):   United States Navy

vacuum (170):   empty space

vague (44):   very general, not specific

Van Gogh (325):   Vincent Van Gogh (1853-1890), a well-known Dutch painter

vandalism (672):   willful or malicious destruction of public or private property

vaporize an attacker (278):   make the attacker disappear; destroy the attacker

vegetable (594):   a person whose brain only functions to the degree of keeping the body alive; he/she is not conscious and no longer has higher brain functions

vestigial (175):   bodily organs such as the appendix that have evolved to the point where they are no longer needed or used

veteran (255):   person with long experience

Vexing (311):   troublesome and problematic

vicarious (580):   to experience something through another person

vicariously (478):   experienced indirectly

vicious cycle (451):   in this case, the inability to sustain an erection leads to anxiety about having an erection, which in turn contributes to the inability to sustain an erection

Victorian era (444):   the time period when Queen Victoria reigned in England (1837-1901), characterized by excessive modesty regarding sexual matters

video arcade (679):   an amusement center containing video games

videoconferencing (576):   communication through a two-way set-up that involves video (through the use of television or computer monitors), audio (through speakerphones or computer speakers), and microphones

Vietnam Veterans Memorial (314):   a memorial in Washington, D.C. that consists of a black marble wall containing the names of all Americans who died in the Vietnam War

vigilant (71):   being alert and on the lookout for trouble

vista (388):   a view, scenery

vividly (598):   clearly

void (156):   empty space

voyeurism (539):   practice of seeking sexual stimulation by observing unsuspecting others who are unclothed or engaging in intercourse

vulnerability (558):   open to influence; easily hurt

wacky (330):   strange and unusual

wake-up calls (140):   events that produce an understanding and recognition of the truth and reality of the situation

walk under a ladder (272):   considered by some people to bring bad luck

wandering eye (202):   a condition in which an eye is constantly moving

wanted to be alone (678):   Greta Garbo, a famous Swedish film star, was known for valuing her privacy; in her accented English, "want" sounded like "vahnt" in her well-known line, "I want to be alone"

wanton (644):   without reason; unjustifiable

warehouses (595):　huge buildings that store merchandise not needed for immediate use; Coon is suggesting that mental hospitals were once used as a place to store patients that society did not want around

warping (240):　turning or twisting out of shape

warthog, dervish, gargoyle, aardvark (134):　words that Coon humorously included with his list of names that students were commonly called in high school; these names are legitimate words, but are probably not used to identify types of students

wary (547):　cautious

wave of activity (53):　the advance of a signal

wavering (595):　unreliable

weaned (232):　slowly removed from

weather adolescence (132):　get through the adolescent period of life

weekend passes (275):　permission to leave (in this case) the hospital for the weekend

wee-wee (108):　childish expression for needing to urinate

welter (151):　a massive collection

we're all in the same boat (645):　we are all in the same situation

wet (Washoe once "wet" on…) (339):　urinated

wet look (94):　reference to a style in which the hair appears to be damp; Coon is using the phrase humorously

What dis? (107):　What is this?

whatchamacallit (333):　what you may call it; used when the exact name for something cannot be remembered

what's right is right (77):　a stated position, usually moral, for which there is no dispute

wheel of fortune (Is intelligence determined by the genetic "wheel of fortune"…?) (363):　the wheel of fortune is a large wheel which is spun and prizes are won depending on where the wheel stops spinning; thus the author is referring to the theory that the genes inherited from one's parents determine one's intelligence

when your "spare tire" is well inflated (392):　when you have too much excess weight across your midsection

where to draw the line (533):　where to find the dividing point between two positions

whirlwind (124):　very rapid

white-collar crime (680):　non-violent crimes, such as income tax evasion, fraud, etc., committed primarily by persons in professional occupations

who you regard as "family" (15):　close non-related people who you consider as your relatives.

Who's Who (665):   a listing of brief biographical sketches of famous people in a particular field

wide-angle view (67):   an analogy to photography; the big picture; a broad, encompassing view

widget (194):   gadget, unnamed item considered as an example

wiggling (125):   a squirming motion allowing one to maneuver through small spaces

wine taster (173):   a person whose job it is to sample wines in order to judge their quality

wiped out (297):   erased; taken away

wired for action (57):   set up and ready to go

wired in (467):   unchangeable

wired (52):   refers to how the nervous system is put together and how it works

wishful thinking (581):   wanting something so much that one interprets reality in such a way as to support one's desires

wit (as one wit once observed) (252):   an intelligent and funny person

witchcraft (571):   use of sorcery or magic by a person (a witch) believed to have such power

with conviction (597):   with force

with joyful abandon (477):   in an unrestrained manner; free and careless

withdrawing (473):   removing oneself from social contact

wizards (571):   persons believed to be skilled in magic

wobbly crawl (93):   unsteady movement on hands and knees

wood-sawing (234):   snoring

word blindness (128):   being unable to make out words and therefore being unable to read

word salad (550):   the result of not following the proper use of grammar when speaking English; when one constructs sentences in a seemingly random manner.

World Series (306):   a series of baseball games played each fall to decide the professional championship of the U.S.

wrapped up (491):   too focused on oneself

wry (480):   ironically humorous

X-rated movies (133):   movies of such a nature (usually pornographic) that admission is denied to those under a specified age (usually 17)

X-rated (650):   labeled as having a high level of sexual content

yardstick (137):   an index for measurement

Ye Olde Double Standard (611): the old double standard; the idea that there is one set of rules to be applied to women, and a different set of rules for men

yielded (619): conformed

YMCA (300): Young Men's Christian Association, an international organization that promotes the spiritual, social, and physical welfare of young men

You can't teach an old dog new tricks (12): it is difficult for people (as well as dogs) to learn new ways of doing things

your temporal lobes would light up (68): your temporal lobes would begin to process the music from your MP3 player

You're an ass! (416): telling someone he or she is a stupid or disagreeable person (usually considered vulgar)

zaniest (459): silliest; exhibits odd and often comical behavior

zany (330): wild and crazy

zap flies (196): to kill flies

Zero. Zip. Nada (215): words meaning "no outcome"

zips along (53): moves along at a fast speed

zodiac (44): an imaginary belt in the nighttime sky that contains the apparent paths of the planets

zoo-keeper mother (101): mothers who have too many children to look after and have too much to do to be able to interact with each appropriately.

zooms in on (67): an analogy to photography; gets closer to a small portion of the picture